"In this outstanding volume, López-Claros, Dahl, and Groff document the existential challenges facing our global institutions, from environmental decline and the failure of existing international security mechanisms to mass population flows and the crisis of sovereignty and civil society engagement. The resulting landscape might seem hopeless and overwhelming, if not for the authors' innovative, wide-ranging, and thought-provoking recommendations for reshaping existing institutions to expand their relevance and effectiveness. Their ideas for updating our seven-decades-old structures include creating an international peace force, ratifying a United Nations Bill of Rights, reforming the UN Security Council and International Monetary Fund, establishing a civil society chamber, and beyond. Readers may not endorse every one of their suggestions, but they are invited into a fascinating game of 'what if?' and 'why not?' It is an invitation that should not be missed."

Ambassador Donald Steinberg, Board member, Center for Strategic and International Studies

"The current UN-based world system of governance, largely formulated in the mid-20th century after the Second World War, is not up to dealing satisfactorily with 21st-century problems. But it is what we have. The authors of this book suggest radical, even breathtaking, reforms to enable global governance to cope with current and prospective global problems, from keeping and enforcing peace, to inhibiting – if not preventing – financial crises, to protecting residents of all countries from governmental abuse, to mitigating and adapting to climate change. These are desirable objectives, not yet feasible in a world of nationalistic states devoted to narrow national sovereignty. But political leaders eventually die, and the authors take comfort that today's youth, tomorrow's leaders, are much more conscious of today's global problems. This book provides an illuminating and provoking starting point for expanding our institutional ability to solve them."

Richard N. Cooper, Maurits C. Boas Professor of International Economics, Harvard University

"López-Claros, Dahl, and Groff propose radical reforms to the charter that authorizes and rules the United Nations, and other methods of improving the current muddled state of global governance. Their case is persuasive. This book's trenchant analysis of what ails the running of the globe should be read by policymakers everywhere, and certainly by those many citizens who concern themselves with fostering a better and more functional world. Change comes slowly, but this book is a prodding catalyst."

Robert I. Rotberg, Harvard Kennedy School, author of On Governance

"The bold idealism championed by López-Claros, Dahl, and Groff is just what the planet needs, with not a moment to lose if we are to halt and reverse the trajectory of imminent disaster on which we have set ourselves. As a former Ambassador to the United Nations with first-hand experience on the UN Security Council, I applaud the vision laid out for transformational change grounded in past institutional experience."

Amanda Ellis, Executive Director Hawaii & Asia Pacific, Arizona State University, Julie Ann Wrigley Global Institute of Sustainability

GLOBAL GOVERNANCE AND THE EMERGENCE OF GLOBAL INSTITUTIONS FOR THE 21ST CENTURY

Is there any hope for those who despair at the state of the world and the powerlessness of governments to find a way forward? *Global Governance and the Emergence of Global Institutions for the 21st Century* provides ambitious but reasonable proposals to give our globalized world the institutions of international governance necessary to address effectively the catastrophic risks facing humanity that are beyond national control. The solution, the authors suggest, is to extend to the international level the same principles of sensible governance that exist in well-governed national systems: rule of law, legislation in the common interest, an executive branch to implement such legislation, and courts to enforce it. The best protection is unified collective action, based on shared values and respect for diversity, applying widely accepted international principles to advance universal human prosperity and well-being.

This title is also available as Open Access on Cambridge Core.

AUGUSTO LOPEZ-CLAROS is Executive Director of the Global Governance Forum. During 2017–19 he was Senior Fellow in the School of Foreign Service at Georgetown University. He is former Director of the Global Indicators Group at the World Bank and Chief Economist at the World Economic Forum. He is coauthor of *Equality for Women = Prosperity for All* (2018).

ARTHUR LYON DAHL is President of the International Environment Forum and a retired senior official of UN Environment. He is the author of *In Pursuit of Hope: A Guide for the Seeker* (2019), *The Eco Principle: Ecology and Economics in Symbiosis* (1996) and *Unless and Until: A Baha'i Focus on the Environment* (1990).

MAJA GROFF is an international lawyer based in The Hague, working on multilateral treaties, at international criminal tribunals and teaching at the Hague Academy of International Law. A graduate of Harvard, Oxford and McGill Universities, she has drafted international legal policy documents and published on private and public international law, human rights and global governance.

Global Governance and the Emergence of Global Institutions for the 21st Century

AUGUSTO LOPEZ-CLAROS

Global Governance Forum

ARTHUR LYON DAHL

International Environment Forum

MAJA GROFF

Global Governance Forum

CAMBRIDGE
UNIVERSITY PRESS

CAMBRIDGE
UNIVERSITY PRESS

University Printing House, Cambridge CB2 8BS, United Kingdom

One Liberty Plaza, 20th Floor, New York, NY 10006, USA

477 Williamstown Road, Port Melbourne, VIC 3207, Australia

314–321, 3rd Floor, Plot 3, Splendor Forum, Jasola District Centre, New Delhi – 110025, India

79 Anson Road, #06–04/06, Singapore 079906

Cambridge University Press is part of the University of Cambridge.

It furthers the University's mission by disseminating knowledge in the pursuit of education, learning, and research at the highest international levels of excellence.

www.cambridge.org
Information on this title: www.cambridge.org/9781108476966
DOI: 10.1017/9781108569293

First published 2020

A catalogue record for this publication is available from the British Library.

Library of Congress Cataloging-in-Publication Data
NAMES: Dahl, Arthur L., author. | Groff, Maja, author. | López-Claros, Augusto, author.
TITLE: Global governance and the emergence of global institutions for the 21st century /
Arthur L. Dahl, International Environmental Forum, Maja Groff, The Hague Conference,
Augusto Lopez-Claros, Georgetown University, Washington DC.
DESCRIPTION: United Kingdom ; New York, NY : Cambridge University Press, [2020] |
Includes bibliographical references and index.
IDENTIFIERS: LCCN 2019040768 (print) | LCCN 2019040769 (ebook) | ISBN 9781108476966 (hardback) |
ISBN 9781108701808 (paperback) | ISBN 9781108569293 (epub)
SUBJECTS: LCSH: International cooperation.
CLASSIFICATION: LCC JZ1308 .D34 2020 (print) | LCC JZ1308 (ebook) | DDC 341.7–dc23
LC record available at https://lccn.loc.gov/2019040768
LC ebook record available at https://lccn.loc.gov/2019040769

ISBN 978-1-108-47696-6 Hardback

Contents

Preface

The world today is facing unprecedented challenges of governance far beyond what the United Nations (UN), established 75 years ago, was designed to face. The grave effects of global climate change are already manifesting themselves, requiring rapid, far-reaching, and unprecedented changes in all aspects of society to arrest catastrophic and probably irreversible consequences. Science has uncovered the frightening and rapid collapse in global biodiversity, threatening ecosystems across the planet that maintain the correct functioning of the biosphere, essential to human life. But there is more; there are other global catastrophic risks. There is today a diminished faith in our political leaders and the institutions that underpin our systems of governance; public disillusionment with hyper-partisan politics and willingness to believe populist promises; disturbingly high levels of income inequality; still much too persistent and widespread human rights violations; and the spread of corruption, coinciding with the rise of autocratic leaders, often intent on awakening the voices of nationalisms which were so destructive during past centuries. The recent rejection by some nations of the benefits of multilaterism and international cooperation, which have been at the center of the postwar global order, has heightened the risks of fundamental instabilities that could precipitate a range of major crises, disregarding the lessons of the past.

The forces of globalization have been undermining traditional institutions of government – including the state itself – and creating alternative centers of power. New forms of knowledge and networking, of information flows and manipulation, of finance and commerce, of digitization and artificial intelligence, are accelerating rates of change, undermining the traditional roles of various institutions, forms of organization, inherited assumptions and cultural patterns no longer adapted to the requirements of an emerging world society catalyzed by science and technology. The pushback of fundamentalist and reactionary movements, inter-state attempts to destabilize competitors in a struggle for domination, and the increasing social fractures exploited for political ends are putting societies under strain and creating conditions for greater anarchy and chaos.

There are, however, also forces of integration and global progress at work, with positive examples of vibrant international civil society action, unprecedented cultural and scholarly exchange, economic innovation, technological solutions, and movements dedicated to human transformation and well-being; but they may not yet be sufficiently strong to overcome the current forces of dissolution and breakdown that are accelerating. To address the growing planetary climate crisis, the Intergovernmental Panel on Climate Change (IPCC), convened under the auspices of the UN, has warned that only a decade remains to contain the damage caused by present energy systems and land use. The UN, in its 2030 Agenda, has called for a fundamental transformation in society, a paradigm shift away from the present trajectory, but government response has been lukewarm, with little political will for the efforts that are necessary. Humanity seems to be in a state of collective denial.

Our world is like a bus packed with passengers hurtling along a winding mountain road, with several people fighting for the driver's seat and no one really in control. Across the economic, social, and environmental domains, there are increasing predictions of severe crises ahead, some of them possibly taking the world into uncharted territory, with possibly irreversible effects. The resulting fear and frustration are driving the rise of populist movements and the rejection of multilateralism, a turning inward when the need is to reach out to each other and collaborate in finding solutions to our problems.

The last time that there was a serious debate about the kind of global order that needed to be created to ensure sustainable and just international peace and security, and to create a basis for universal human prosperity, was when the United States entered World War II and President Roosevelt called for the creation of the United Nations in early 1942. In early discussions, proposals for the UN Charter imagined an international entity informed by sound federalist principles, including the creation of a legislative body with some powers to enact laws that would be binding on member states. But the need to ensure the support of the Soviet Union and US Senate approval of the UN Charter resulted in a considerably weakened and structurally flawed organization.

In the late 1950s, Grenville Clark and Louis Sohn, in their groundbreaking *World Peace through World Law*, offered a comprehensive range of proposals to address the built-in flaws of the UN system. But, while much admired in many policymaking circles, their ideas did not trigger the reforms they suggested. By then the world was in the midst of the Cold War and entered a decades-long process of historically unprecedented arms build-up by the major powers, with multiple conflicts across the planet, great losses in human life and delayed economic and social development as resources were diverted to this arms race. Sixty years later, it is becoming increasingly evident that our current UN-based order, already known in 1945 to be inadequate, cannot cope with an increasingly complex and interconnected world and does not yet possess the mechanisms that are vital to address a multitude of shared planetary problems.

We think that the time is ripe to reexamine the architecture of our current institutions of global governance, not as an academic exercise but to assist in catalyzing processes of change that lead to concrete progress. Failure to strengthen the international order now will increase the likelihood of societies around the world being overwhelmed by global crises with devastating worldwide consequences. The survivors may be forced to rebuild a global institutional framework after a third world war or nuclear exchange, the collapse of the global economy, a pandemic wiping out a significant part of the world's population, or extreme climate change which is already beginning to produce mass migrations, any of which would overwhelm existing institutions.

Each of us, from our different economic, legal, and environmental perspectives, our shared common values and decades of experience within the international system, has felt the need to make the intellectual effort to overcome the blockage of diminished expectations for global governance, and to map possible ways forward. This book is the result. Too many "realists" say that change is not possible, but the other reality is the awareness of the multiple crises ahead, if not already upsetting the planet's equilibrium, and of the human suffering that will inevitably result.

Our cautious optimism to engage in such discussions now, in the year of the 75th anniversary of the UN Charter, is grounded on several, mutually reinforcing factors.

First, the current system has few credible defenders who are persuasively arguing that the status quo is the optimal strategy, and that human society can just "muddle through" for the next several decades without meaningfully addressing some of the risks that cast a shadow over its collective future.

Second, the world is immeasurably more integrated today than half a century ago, and the costs of non-cooperation are also much higher. A war between global powers, in the age of nuclear weapons, would be unimaginably more catastrophic in its consequences than anything humanity has witnessed in the past. The 2008 financial crisis started in one country but rapidly spilled over and became global, deeply destabilizing, and costly.

Third, civil society and the business community are empowered today in a way that was not the case in the 1950s. Many major successful initiatives in the area of international cooperation in the past several decades – from the creation of the International Criminal Court to the Paris Agreement on Climate Change, to the Treaty on the Prohibition of Nuclear Weapons – could not have been undertaken without the involvement of stakeholders beyond government. These relatively new forces of transnational civil society are showing increasingly sophisticated and effective methods to catalyze and shape significant changes in the architecture of global governance.

Fourth, science and communications technologies and the spread of education have made it much easier to mobilize public opinion. There is much greater awareness, globally, of the problems facing the world and the risks that they carry. At the same time, the intellectual and professional classes in various fields, whether in international law, business, economics or the international civil service generally, are increasingly frustrated with institutions as they stand, creating much latent capacity for engagement in global governance reform. There is great potential for "bottom-up" and "top-down" synergies among communities of interest who are deeply concerned about global catastrophic risks and current institutional limitations.

We hope this book will start a discussion on the reforms that are necessary to enhance the effectiveness of the global institutional architecture in order to respond proactively to the risks that threaten the future of humanity. Of course, we do not have all the answers, but we want to show that reasonable answers are possible and that reforming global governance is not utopian, but a necessity for our survival. Rather than tinkering at the margins of the present UN system, we propose a comprehensive set of reforms that would correct its fundamental flaws, empowering institutions of global governance to address the multiple problems and catastrophic risks we face and enabling us all to respond constructively to reduce or eliminate them. We envision a system with justice at its core and an equitable sharing of responsibilities, a system that can put its high principles into action, building on its ethical foundations to achieve unprecedented progress in the development of global civilization.

The proposals that we submit here are put forward in a spirit of humility, as a contribution to the necessarily wide-ranging consultations on how to catalyze and to craft reforms that will allow us to build on our strengths – from the spread of knowledge and new technologies to the availability of wealth and resources, citizen engagement, the progressive empowerment of women, our inherent international cultural diversity, among others – to chart a better future. We invite all to join in an effort to stimulate creative thinking, to explore possible governance mechanisms, institutional reforms, and pathways forward toward a positive and secured collective future. The enormous difficulties of this undertaking and the challenging times ahead should be acknowledged, but every global citizen needs to be inspired by positive visions of the better future that is possible. The world urgently needs an ever-widening circle of those working for the institutional and social reforms necessary to transition to a sustainable, globalized yet diverse society.

Reshaping international governance is not ultimately solely about institutions, structures or even funding. It is about protecting all that we hold dear and ensuring a safe path for humanity during and beyond the 21st century. It is about leaving to our children and successive generations a better world than the one we were born into, one in which they find the conditions that will enable them to develop fully all their capacities, not one in which they will have to deal with the painful consequences of an unpredictable and deeply dysfunctional global order.

Acknowledgments

We are very much in debt to a number of colleagues who have provided us with feedback, insights, encouragement and support during various stages of this project. We would like to mention, in particular, Robert Ahdieh, Payam Akhavan, Anthony C. Arend, Gustaf Arrhenius, Louis Aucoin, Ludvig Beckman, Samantha Besson, Kit Bigelow, Andreas Bummel, Lidia Ceriani, Diana Chacon, Benedicte Vibe Christensen, Drew Christensen, Sean Cleary, Richard Cooper, Mary Darling, Clark Donnelly, Bani Dugal, Zachary Elkins, Amanda Ellis, Claudia Escobar, Natividad Fernandez Sola, Jose Maria Figueres, Marc Fleurbaey, Nancy Peterson Hill, Lise Howard, Maria Ivanova, Didier Jacobs, Sylvia Karlsson-Vinkhuyzen, Saeko Kawashima, Robert Klitgaard, Sanford Levinson, Amy Lillis, Maryann Love, Paulo Magalhaes, Cristina Manzano, Jessica Mathews, Bahia Mitchell, Joachim Monkelbaan, Eduardo Pascual, Richard Ponzio, Rod Rastan, Eduardo Rodriguez Veltze, Robert Rotberg, Daniel Runde, Mahmud Samandari, Natalie Samarasinghe, Steve Sarowitz, Donald Steinberg, Mirta Tapia de Lopez, Teresa Ter-Minassian, Christie S. Warren, Thomas G. Weiss, Christian Wenaweser, John Wilmot, Mark Wolf, Erol Yayboke and Guillermo Zoccali.

We are particularly grateful to Mats Andersson, Jennie Baner, Bjorn Franzon, Charlotte Petri Gornitzka, Christer Jacobson, Magnus Jiborn, Fredrik Karlsson, Sarah Molaiepour, Jens Orback, Johan Rockstrom, Kate Sullivan, Laszlo Szombatfalvy, Folke Tersman and their colleagues at Sweden's Global Challenges Foundation and the eminent members of the international Jury, who awarded us the New Shape Prize in 2018 for a proposal that contained the key ideas of this book and whose support and encouragement have made a critical difference in terms of our ability to turn those ideas into the more detailed proposals contained here. One of us is especially grateful to Joel Hellman, Dean of the Edmund A. Walsh School of Foreign Service at Georgetown University, for their hospitality during the entire period of this project. Georgetown has provided a nurturing environment for the research underpinning this work and Clare Ogden, Fellows Administrator, provided efficient assistance on multiple occasions.

Herman Bajwa, Manon Beury, Nahid Kalbasi, Dorine Llanta, Issac Liu, Yasmina Mata, Nima Nematollahi, John Miller and Allison Semands provided high-quality support as research assistants on many occasions over the past year and a half. We are grateful to John Berger and Chloe Quinn at Cambridge University Press, and Elizabeth Stone at Bourchier, for managing the various aspects of this project, from helping us turn our ideas into a book project, to copyediting of the final manuscript. Nancy Ackerman from AmadeaEditing provided expert additional editorial help. Any limitations and imperfections in the book, however, are the responsibility of the authors.

The views expressed in this book are the authors' own and do not necessarily reflect those of the organizations with which they are affiliated.

PART I

Background

1

The Challenges of the 21st Century

We have organizations for the preservation of almost everything in life that we want but no organization for the preservation of mankind. People seem to have decided that our collective will is too weak or flawed to rise to this occasion. They see the violence that has saturated human history and conclude that to practice violence is innate to our species. They find the perennial hope that peace can be brought to the earth once and for all a delusion of the well-meaning who have refused to face the "harsh realities" of international life – the realities of self-interest, fear, hatred, and aggression. They have concluded that these realities are eternal ones, and this conclusion defeats at the outset any hope of taking the actions necessary for survival.

Jonathan Schell, *The Fate of the Earth*[1]

INTRODUCTION

Most careful observers of our contemporary global landscape would have no difficulty in accepting the claim that we have entered a period in human evolution characterized by the "acceleration in the velocity of our history and the uncertainty of its trajectory."[2] The current age is one of expectations and hope as well as deepening contradictions, uncertainties and emerging risks. The forces of globalization have brought about the elimination of many physical and psychological barriers, precipitating a massive transfer of power and influence away from traditional centers (mainly governments), and in turn contributing to the empowerment of civil society and the decentralization of decision-making. They have facilitated increasing connectedness but also alienation, the concentration of wealth in the hands of a narrower circle, higher expectations of continued improvements in living

[1] Schell, Jonathan. 1982. *The Fate of the Earth*, London, Jonathan Cape, p. 185.
[2] Brzezinski, Zbigniew. 1993. *Out of Control: Global Turmoil on the Eve of the 21st Century*, New York, Macmillan, pp. ix–x.

3

standards and growing concerns about the sustainability of our development path. We have celebrated the dramatic improvement in various indicators of human welfare that has taken place in the past half-century, including remarkable progress in average life expectancy, a sustained drop in infant mortality and a rise in literacy, against the background of a sharp reduction in the incidence of extreme poverty[3]; but we have also awakened to the realization that the high economic growth rates that fueled these favorable trends have in parallel led the planet to run up against binding environmental constraints and often resulted in social alienation and widening inequality. As we were already warned decades ago, there are limits to growth,[4] and we are reaching them as predicted.[5] Our current trajectory cannot continue without a collapse in one form or another, and the past is not a good guide to the future.

Our present epoch seems to be increasingly characterized by fear of the future with growing insecurity, social fragmentation and polarization, and a lack of hope, even among the young who often face a more uncertain future than that of their parents. The economic system favors profits for the rich over employment for the masses, with many in the middle seeing decades without improvement, if not falling

[3]   Between 1950 and 2016, world gross domestic product (GDP) per capita expanded at an annual average rate of 2.1 percent and this expansion was associated with a remarkable evolution in three key indicators of human welfare. In the half-century between 1960 and 2016, infant mortality fell from 122 to 30 per 1,000 live births; average life expectancy at birth rose from 52 to 72 years, a 38 percent increase that has no known historical precedent; and adult illiteracy fell from 53 to 14 percent. Equally impressive was the sharp drop in the incidence of poverty: data from a World Bank study show that between 1990 and 2015 – a period that includes the globalization phase of the twentieth century – the number of poor people living on less than \$1.90 per day (the poverty line used for the definition of extreme poverty) fell from about 2 billion to slightly less than 740 million, a historical low. The reduction in extreme poverty, however, was largely accounted for by the very high economic growth rates in China and, to a lesser extent, in India. In areas suffering from fragility, conflict, and violence the poverty rate climbed to 36 percent in 2015, up from a low of 34.4 percent in 2011, and that rate will likely increase. In sub-Saharan Africa the number of extremely poor people actually rose from 276 million in 1990 to 413 million in 2015. Furthermore, using a less austere poverty line of \$3.20 per day, the number of poor in sub-Saharan Africa in 2015 was about 667 million. At this higher poverty line, the number of poor in the world is closer to 2 billion people, which is still an unacceptably high number.

[4]   Meadows, Donella H., Dennis L. Meadows, Jorgen Randers, and William W. Behrens III. 1972. *The Limits to Growth.* A Report for the Club of Rome's Project on the Predicament of Mankind, New York, Universe Books. The original report was updated in 1992 (Meadows, Donella H., Dennis L. Meadows and Jorgen Randers, 1992. *Beyond the Limits: Confronting Global Collapse, Envisioning a Sustainable Future,* White River Junction, VT, Chelsea Green) and again in 2004 (Meadows, Donella, Jorgen Randers and Dennis Meadows, 2004. *Limits to Growth: The 30-Year Update,* White River Junction, VT, Chelsea Green) only confirming the basic premise.

[5]   MacKenzie, Debora. 2012. "Doomsday Book." *New Scientist,* January 7, pp. 38–41, shows the original projections to be remarkably accurate.

backward, and half the world population still struggling to meet basic needs.[6] Poverty, exclusion and neglect present fundamental social challenges, with no easy solutions in sight. The world economy is running on increasing debt, threatening a return to the financial chaos of a decade earlier, but with governments' room for maneuver significantly reduced. The forces of disintegration are reflected in growing evidence of the failing institutions of governance, with often discredited leadership, widespread corruption, loss of public confidence, and the recent rise of populist, reactionary and autocratic movements rejecting multilateralism and diversity. Contributing to all this is a generalized loss of moral responsibility, higher ethics or values, even spirituality, able to fill the vacuum of any higher human purpose in a materialistic society.[7]

There are counterbalancing forces of integration, and many signs of progress, including at the global level in the United Nations (UN) and elsewhere, that need to be reinforced and extended if we are to avoid a collapse and make the necessary paradigm shift and fundamental transition to a more sustainable future as called for in the 2030 Agenda.[8] In a globalized economy and society, improved global governance must play an important role at this crucial moment when change is increasingly urgent for environmental, social and economic reasons.

It is not easy to set priorities among the many challenges of today, as all are interrelated. Their complexity calls for new approaches suitable for dynamic, integrated systems evolving through constant innovation in technologies, forms of communications, patterns of organization and institutional frameworks. The challenge for mechanisms of governance at all scales of human organization is to accompany and steer these processes to ensure the common good, setting limits that prevent their being captured by the already rich and powerful for their own benefit, and ultimately ensuring a just society that guarantees the well-being of every person on the planet.

---

[6] The World Bank's poverty database indicates that a full 48 percent of the world's population lives on less than US$5.50 per day, a sum that leaves such people vulnerable in the event of loss of a job or other such shocks. At best, people living below this poverty line struggle on a day-to-day basis to make ends meet.

[7] We are aware of studies such as Pinker's that show that, by some objective measures, life on the planet is better than ever, but this is not the perception of the general public, and current forces have the potential to reverse previous gains. Pinker, Steven. 2011. *The Better Angels of Our Nature: Why Violence Has Declined*, New York, Viking. See also his *Enlightenment Now: The Case for Reason, Science, Humanism and Progress*, 2018, New York, Viking.

[8] United Nations. 2015. *Transforming Our World: The 2030 Agenda for Sustainable Development.* Outcome Document of the Summit for the Adoption of the Post–2015 Development Agenda, New York, September 25–27, 2015. A/70/L.1. New York: United Nations. www.un.org/ga/search/view_doc.asp?symbol=A/70/L.1&Lang=E

Environmental Challenges

In the scientific community, the major areas of urgent concern have been climate change, biodiversity loss and pollution. To take just a few examples: global carbon dioxide emissions from fossil fuels have grown at an average annual rate of 2 percent since 1990 and hit record levels in 2018,[9] reflecting the continued growth of the global economy,[10] and a sharp rise in energy consumption in China, accompanied by the weakening of natural carbon sinks, such as forests and seas. Not surprisingly, large volumes of Arctic ice have melted and accelerated flow in Greenland glaciers and now in the Antarctic is contributing to rising sea levels.

Even when world economic growth came to a halt in 2009 because of the global financial crisis, these perturbing trends were not reversed, as the present scale of human activity was only marginally and temporarily affected, and world economic growth again took off shortly thereafter. In the absence of other measures aimed directly at reducing emissions, only a sustained, deep economic depression such as that witnessed during the 1929–1933 period, or some other major crisis, might have an impact on the pace of accumulation of carbon dioxide in the atmosphere. However, expecting an economic depression to help temporarily mitigate the challenges of global warming is hardly a commendable solution, involving severe social costs.

While economic growth and technological innovation have led to a massive increase in global wealth, this has resulted in serious degradation of the planet's natural resources, now accelerated by climate change, and is leading to emerging supply constraints. It is estimated, for instance, that by 2025 the number of people living in regions with absolute water scarcity will have risen to some 1.8 billion. Climate change, soil erosion, and overfishing are expected to reduce food production and are likely to put upward pressure on food prices in coming years. Climate change also is limiting energy options. The quantity of carbon in oil wells, gas fields and coal mines presently producing, not counting less conventional sources of fossil energy such as fracking and tar sands, is already about five times the remaining capacity of the atmosphere to absorb carbon without passing 2°C of global warming, meaning that we must leave 80 percent of existing fossil fuel reserves in the ground and stop developing new resources.[11] The latest science says we must not exceed 1.5°C and have only about 12 years to turn the corner in the energy transition to

---

[9] Evarts, Eric C. 2018. Report: Global CO2 emissions at record levels in 2018. *Green Car Reports*. www.greencarreports.com/news/1120348_report-global-co2-emissions-at-record-levels-in-2018.

[10] According to the International Monetary Fund's *World Economic Outlook*, average annual global economic growth between 1990 and 2018 was 3.6 percent. A slowdown in the aftermath of the 2008–2009 global financial crisis has since been reversed.

[11] McKibben, Bill. 2012. "Global Warming's Terrifying New Math." *Rolling Stone*, August 2, 2012. www.rollingstone.com/politics/news/global-warmings-terrifying-new-math-20120719.

renewable resources,[12] requiring unprecedented efforts at all levels. A recent study identifies the requirements decade by decade to phase out the use of fossil fuels and to make the transition to renewable sources of energy if the commitments made in the Paris Agreement in 2015 are to be met.[13] Yet there is no mechanism to push countries to abandon lucrative sources of revenue or companies to write off 80 percent of their assets, or to determine how to share the burden of such a fundamental transition in which there will be winners and losers.

Human impacts on the planet now exceed many natural processes, to the point that the modern era is increasingly being labeled as the Anthropocene. *Homo sapiens* has become an invasive species, degrading the environment and pushing beyond planetary boundaries.[14] Science is beginning to determine the survivability of human civilization at the planetary level. The more we degrade planetary carrying capacity now, the lower will be the standard of living in a sustainable world society, at least in the short term.[15]

These environmental challenges are at the interface of science and policy-making. As much as some decision-makers may want to deny it, there is an objective reality to environmental characteristics and processes that can be measured and monitored with the tools of science. Science can determine past and present impacts, and increasingly can predict and model future consequences. Action can be postponed, generally increasing the costs and negative consequences over time, but it cannot be avoided. Fortunately, new information technologies that make data and knowledge widely available also strengthen our ability to use that knowledge to improve decision-making at all levels if there is the political will to do so.

While much more needs to be done to refine and extend research on future trajectories for human society, the issues requiring governance at the global level are already defined. This in itself is one of the strongest justifications for global governance, since many of the environmental systems being impacted (climate, ozone layer, nitrogen and phosphorus cycles, etc.)[16] can only be managed through concerted action by all nations.

---

[12] IPCC. 2018. Global Warming of 1.5°C (SR15), Special Report. Summary for Policy Makers. Geneva, Intergovernmental Panel on Climate Change, October 2018. www.ipcc.ch/report/sr15/
   UN Environment. 2018. Emissions Gap Report 2018. Nairobi: United Nations Environment Programme. www.unenvironment.org/resources/emissions-gap-report-2018.

[13] Rockström, Johan, Owen Gaffney, Joeri Rogelj, Malte Meinshausen, Nebojsa Nakicenovic, and Hans Joachim Schellnhuber. 2017. "A Roadmap for Rapid Decarbonization." *Science* Vol. 355, No. 6331, pp. 1269–1271. DOI: 10.1126/science.aah3443.

[14] Rockström, Johan, et al. 2009. "A Safe Operating Space for Humanity." *Nature* Vol. 461, pp. 472–475, DOI:10.1038/461472a; Published online September 23, 2009. Updated in Steffen, Will, et al. 2015. "Planetary Boundaries: Guiding Human Development on a Changing Planet." *Science* Vol. 347, No. 6223. DOI: 10.1126/science.1259855.

[15] Meadows, Donella H., Dennis L. Meadows, and Jorgen Randers, 1992. *Beyond the Limits: Confronting Global Collapse, Envisioning a Sustainable Future*, White River Junction. VT, Chelsea Green.

[16] Steffen et al., "Planetary Boundaries."

Yet there is no global environmental authority. Policy in this area is currently done via ad hoc approaches involving elements of international cooperation, voluntary compliance, and large doses of hope. In the absence of a body having jurisdiction over the global environment with corresponding legal enforcement authority, the international community has, de facto, abdicated management of the world's environment to chance and the actions of a few well-meaning states. Even the 2015 Paris Agreement ratified by 185 countries pledging reductions in emissions,[17] if implemented in full, will not prevent a warming in excess of 1.5°C, the threshold recognized by climate scientists as necessary to avoid "potentially devastating consequences."[18]

Social Challenges

While environmental challenges represent the outer boundaries to a sustainable planetary society, there are also a number of inner social boundaries below which no just and equitable society with adequate wealth and resources should descend, with poverty as the most central issue. The failure of the present economic system to distribute its increasing wealth more equitably has led to growing inequality and the consequent social instability.

Alongside the pursuit of economic growth without regard to environmental and social costs, there are other forces at work that are already having a major impact on our system's institutional underpinnings which have been crucial to the progress achieved during the past half-century. Key among these are population growth and the corresponding pressures on resources. According to the *World Energy Outlook* published by the International Energy Agency, global energy demand is expected to grow by more than 25 percent by 2040,[19] reflecting the addition of some 1.7 billion people to the world's population and the corresponding need for housing, transportation, heating, illumination, food production, waste disposal, and the push for sustained increases in standards of living. Because many of the mothers who will bear these close to 2 billion children are already alive today, this expected increase in the world's population – barring some unexpected calamity – will materialize and will be largely concentrated in urban environments in developing countries.

Beyond the inevitable pressures on resources, rapid population growth in the poorest parts of the world in the next several decades will lead to growing imbalances

---

[17] While reporting to the UNFCCC is binding, the Nationally Determined Contributions (NDCs) are purely voluntary and determined by each government. https://unfccc.int/process/the-paris-agreement/nationally-determined-contributions/ndc-registry
[18] Stern, Nicholas and Samuel Fankhauser. 2016. "Climate Change, Development, Poverty and Economics," Grantham Research Institute on Climate Change and the Environment. The recent withdrawal of the United States from the Paris Agreement shows how fragile even the most balanced agreements can be to the whims of individual leaders.
[19] See www.iea.org, International Energy Agency, *World Energy Outlook 2018*, Executive Summary, p. 1.

and a broad range of challenges for governments, businesses, and civil society. For instance, in the Middle East and North Africa, high fertility rates and the highest rates of population growth in the world will put an enormous strain on labor markets. These countries already suffer from the highest rates of unemployment in the world. To simply prevent these rates from rising further, it will be necessary to create well over 100 million new jobs within the next decade and a half – an extremely tall order. The job creation needs of these countries are nothing new and were present already at the outset of this century; the failure to do so has led to major political and social instability in the region in recent years.[20]

Unemployment is in fact one of our most important social challenges, as it is a driver for exclusion and marginalization, with consequences including increasing crime, drug trafficking and use, juvenile delinquency, family breakdown, domestic violence, and migration in search of better opportunities. Meaningful employment is essential for human dignity and a place in the community, and work in a spirit of service to the community has important benefits including refining human character and empowering individuals to develop their human potential. No one should be deprived of the opportunity to work, and one purpose of good governance should be to guarantee this opportunity. Neither governments nor private actors have found a solution to this challenge at present. Some have proposed a guaranteed minimum income. While this could be an effective tool to alleviate poverty and provide a safety net for vulnerable groups, it does not address the problem of unemployment and the associated waste of resources. Work is necessary for individual and social health.

In sharp contrast to poor regions with rapid population growth, the populations of countries such as Italy, Japan, Russia and others in the industrial world will continue to shrink; a demographic trend which, in turn, will put huge pressure on public finances as states attempt to cope with growing numbers of pensioners and related social and health expenditures.

Many of today's social problems are the consequence of the globalization of finance and commerce, against the background of a refusal to accept social globalization, the free movement of people, as well as the global implementation of civil and human rights, among other things, in order to ensure a "humane" global governance.[21] Some countries have an excess of unemployed youth, while others lack young workers to support an aging population. Some countries lack the basic means to support their present or anticipated population, while others have large underpopulated areas and lack the people to develop their resources. Yet the idea that natural movements of populations could rebalance these disparities is politically

---

[20] On this point see Augusto López-Claros and Danielle Pletka. 2005. "Without Reforms, the Middle East Risks Revolution." *International Herald Tribune*, April 8.

[21] See, e.g., Falk, Richard. 2014. *(Re)Imagining Humane Global Governance*, Abingdon, UK and New York, Routledge.

anathema, in contrast to the nineteenth century when immigration built economies. Obviously, much must be done at the level of public education, trust in
institutions, just and equitable distribution of resources, and infrastructure development before such adjustments can become reasonable possibilities, but improvements to international governance can lay the foundation for the gradual
elimination of this inconsistency and associated imbalances.

The social challenges of globalization have also grown far beyond the capacity of
the present system. While human rights have long been a central concern of the
international community, violations of basic rights continue to be persistent and
widespread. Migration has become a new issue of planetary scale and is anticipated
to accelerate as climate change displaces increasing numbers in the years ahead.
The global community will face a mixing of populations for which it is presently
totally unprepared. Yet there is no international body charged with giving binding
legal effect to the noble principles enshrined in the Universal Declaration of
Human Rights and subsequent international human rights instruments building
on its principles, to hold states to account for these international obligations (see
Chapter 11).

Economic Challenges

In our globalized world, powerful demonstration effects are at work as everyone can
now see how the wealthy live. The spread of instant communication and the
Internet have led billions of people in China, India, Latin America, and other parts
of the developing world to aspire to lifestyles and patterns of consumption similar to
those prevailing in the advanced economies. Furthermore, these populations are
often unwilling to postpone such aspirations and increasingly expect their governments to deliver rising levels of prosperity, implicitly pushing for a more equitable
distribution of the world's resources. Yet between 1988 and 2008 over 60 percent of
the gains in global income were concentrated in the top 5 percent of the global
income distribution.[22]

Thus, a fundamental development question that we face today is how to reconcile
the legitimate aspirations of citizens in the developing world for the high economic
growth rates that in the post-war period led to such remarkable improvements in
global standards of living, with the challenges of a planet and an economic system
under severe stress as a result of the pressures put on it by that very economic
growth.[23] The only way to make resources available for the half of the world

---

[22] Milanovic, Branko. 2013. "Global Income Inequality: Historical Trends and Policy Implications for the Future." PowerPoint presentation at the World Bank.

[23] The destabilizing effect of thwarted economic aspirations is not only a problem affecting the
developing world. The quantitative historian/mathematical ecologist Peter Turchin predicted
some years ago a risk of political instability and impending crisis in Western Europe and the
USA peaking in 2020, driven by forces of economic inequality. The only way to avoid such a

population struggling to make ends meet will be for those in wealthy countries to reduce their own resource consumption and adopt simpler, more sustainable lifestyles supported by a circular economy to eliminate waste. Justice and sustainability both require that we re-think the consumer society on which the present economy is largely built, and that we sensibly address some of the short-term dislocations that this might entail, while ensuring development to meet the basic needs and ensure the security of the poor. Driving this transition and minimizing its negative effects will have to be a government responsibility, since there is bound to be significant inertia within the private sector.

Another challenge is the growing risk of a global financial collapse when the present debt bubble bursts. The global economy has no lender of last resort. There is no reliable, depoliticized mechanism to deal with financial crises. Whether a country receives or is refused an International Monetary Fund (IMF) bailout in the middle of a financial meltdown is a function not of a transparent set of internationally agreed rules, but rather of several other factors, including whether the IMF's largest shareholders consider the country to be a strategic ally worth supporting. There is also no effective international legal framework to ensure that global business enterprises are socially, environmentally and economically responsible.

Security Challenges

Unfortunately, environmental, social and economic challenges are not by any means the only sources of risk to humankind's global outlook. Noted political thinkers have periodically argued that major war between sovereign states may be on its way to obsolescence.[24] There has been a dramatic increase in recent decades in the price of war and "diminishing expectations of victory's benefits."[25] Close international interdependence and the emergence of an integrated global economy, the growing sophistication and destructive power of weapons systems (including nuclear weapons) have drastically expanded the scale of the losses in human lives and property associated with the kinds of conflict which, on two occasions, were witnessed in the 20th century. The global economy has never had higher levels of productive capacity, and average life expectancy is at an all-time high; hence the

crisis, Turchin argues, would be to reduce social inequality. Turchin, Peter. 2010. "Political Instability May Be a Contributor in the Coming Decade." *Nature* Vol. 463, p. 608. DOI:10.1038/463608a.

[24] More generally, scholars such as Steven Pinker and Peter Turchin have sought to demonstrate overview data of the trajectory of declining violence within our societies over the long term and increasing human capacities for large scale cooperation. See: Pinker, *The Better Angels*. Turchin, Peter. 2016. *Ultrasociety: How 10,000 Years of War Made Humans the Greatest Cooperators on Earth*. Chaplin, Connecticut, Beresta Books.

[25] See, for instance, Michael Mandelbaum's "Is Major War Obsolete?," *Survival*, Vol. 20, No. 4 Winter, 1998–1999, pp. 20–38.

potential costs of global war are also at an all-time high. Furthermore, the rewards of war among states – loot, land, glory, honor – which for many centuries propelled nations to war, have given way to populations in search of growing prosperity, social security and various forms of protection. Military conscription is on its way out in most countries and is no longer regarded as an obligation of citizenship; in many parts of the world, war is increasingly seen as a form of criminal enterprise. Yet there are ongoing military conflicts around the globe, with the highest level of refugees fleeing war since the end of World War II, and – at the time of writing of this book – a seeming resurgence in "great power" contests and threats of using weapons of mass destruction.

Nevertheless, a range of national governments, despite the clear restrictions on the international use of force set out in the United Nations Charter, have seemingly not given up their perceived right to wage war, or at least to prepare for the same;[26] there is a vast military industrial complex that underpins today's system of sovereign states, and arms races are again accelerating. Indeed, in the view of some experts a "sovereign state is a state that enjoys the right and the power to go to war in defense or pursuit of its interests" and these states are ready "to employ war as the final arbiter for settling the disputes that arise among them."[27] So, war in fact has not become obsolete; the calculus of war has shifted but the risks have not gone away.[28] According to the Arms Control Association, the world's nine nuclear powers have about 9,600 nuclear warheads in military service among them.[29] And there are several dozen nations with the capacity to build nuclear weapons. Nuclear

---

[26] There is a strong legal argument (including by influential US international legal scholar Louis Henkin) that the current United Nations Charter effectively outlawed "war": see also Chapter 10. This is apparent from the plain reading of the Charter and the collective security model it seeks to establish, but national cultures and political language have often not made adjustments to this new reality.

[27] Schell, *The Fate of the Earth*, pp. 186–187. The Chilean coat of arms states, unambiguously, "by reason or by force," suggesting the country's readiness to use force to defend national interests. One can assume that this is a general threat, issued to all potential adversaries, including the likes of the United States and China. Where reason does not achieve the desired ends, force will, regardless of the human cost.

[28] However, it should be noted that better, non-violent means to resolve inter-state conflict have already been established by the international community, and we argue in this book that they should be strengthened, consolidating the collective security system under the United Nations Charter, which includes or refers to a range of clear mechanisms and institutions for the peaceful settlement of inter-state disputes. Such institutions and principles have not yet effectively taken root as a foundation for international relations. This has certainly been because of geopolitical reasons, but also because there has been inadequate training and basic literacy on these means to ensure a comprehensive shift to a culture of peaceful international dispute resolution.

[29] Arms Control Association. 2018. *Nuclear Weapons: Who Has What at a Glance.* June 2018. www.armscontrol.org/factsheets/Nuclearweaponswhohaswhat [accessed January 13, 2019].

proliferation thus remains yet another example of global institutional failure.[30] The recent withdrawal of the United States from the Intermediate-Range Nuclear Forces Treaty is just the latest example of the systemic failure and precariousness of arms control agreements as currently constituted.

Recent prominent warnings, issuing from members of the US foreign policy establishment, among others, have underlined the grave danger the world still faces with the current approach to nuclear weapons and nuclear "security," for example.[31] In *Destined for War: Can America and China Escape Thucydides's Trap?* Graham Allison quotes the Greek historian's explanation that "it was the rise of Athens and the fear that this instilled in Sparta that made war inevitable" and notes that "when a rising power threatens to displace a ruling power, the resulting structural stress makes a violent clash the rule, not the exception."[32] In 12 of the 16 cases over the past five hundred years when a major rising power threatened to displace a ruling power the result was war; a sobering observation against the background of an escalating trade war between China and the US at the time of writing.

These risks are aggravated by the poor quality of political leadership in so many countries today, with narcissistic personalities and authoritarian instincts, and all the signs of leaders corrupted by power, disregarding reasoned advice and expert opinion, and often isolated from the realities around them.[33] It would be all too easy in such circumstances to stumble unwittingly into a war that could then not be controlled.

INADEQUACY OF EXISTING MECHANISMS

Faced with such a complex set of threats to human civilization, if not the survival of the human species, how do we find a way forward? A central element of a strategy aimed at generating a sustainable development path in the context of a peaceful world will have to be a significant new capacity to enforce international law, and the reform of legal institutions and current mechanisms of international cooperation, which have turned out to be largely inadequate to manage the global challenges that we face. While there has been considerable progress within the limitations of the present system, its fundamental failings have become increasingly evident. The process of globalization is unfolding in the absence of equivalent progress in the creation of an international institutional infrastructure that can support it and

---

[30] See, for instance, https://foreignpolicy.com/2018/10/31/trump-is-pushing-the-united-states-toward-nuclear-anarchy/

[31] See, for instance: Shultz, George P., William J. Perry, Henry A. Kissinger, and Sam Nunn. 2007. "A World Free of Nuclear Weapons." *Wall Street Journal*, January 4.

[32] Allison, Graham. 2017. *Destined for War: Can America and China Escape Thucydides's Trap?* New York, Houghton Mifflin Harcourt, pp. xiv–xv.

[33] For a case study of the risks run in confronting complex problems, serious risks and urgent societal needs when leadership is self-interested and inadequate see Lewis, Michael. 2018. *The Fifth Risk*, New York: W.W. Norton.

enhance its potential for good. Whether we focus our attention on climate change and the broad range of associated environmental calamities, nuclear proliferation, the workings of the world's financial system, or growing income disparities, the fact is that major planetary problems are being neglected because we do not have effective problem-solving mechanisms and institutions strong enough to deal with them. Or, put differently, a range of inherently global crises cannot be solved outside the framework of global collective action involving supranational cooperation and a fundamental rethinking of the meaning of "national interest."[34]

The reality is that existing institutions are incapable of rising to the challenges of a rapidly changing world because they were designed for another era. Indeed, the United Nations itself and the associated infrastructure of specialized agencies, which were created to attend to a variety of global problems, find themselves increasingly unable to respond to crises, sometimes because these agencies lack the appropriate jurisdiction or mandate to act, sometimes because they are inadequately endowed with resources, and often because, within the limits of existing conceptual frameworks, they simply do not know what to do.

The concept of the nation state is in deep crisis. At its core, the nation state is defined by a geographical border, with governments elected – at least in the context of democracy – to safeguard the interests of citizens, to improve the quality of available services, to manage scarce resources, and to promote a gradual rise in living standards. However, as made abundantly clear during the 2008–2009 global financial crisis, the economic system is now no longer confined to national borders but straddles them in a way that is gradually forcing governments to relinquish or share control in a growing number of areas. Indeed, one of the main lessons to emerge from the financial crisis, as noted by former EU Commissioner Peter Mandelson, is that "a global economy needs global economic governance."[35] The same can be said for the environment and a range of other matters.[36]

Alongside the stresses put on institutions by the accelerating pace of global change, publics everywhere are showing growing dissatisfaction with the inability of national politics and politicians to find solutions to a whole range of global problems. This trend is likely to intensify and has given rise to a "crisis of governance," the sense that nobody is in charge; that while we live in a fully integrated

---

[34] Recent literature has set out the concept of Global Public Goods (GPGs), shifting perspectives from narrow conceptions of national interest to a recognition of the imperative of collective action to provide key shared goods at the international level, which bear directly on national well-being. See, e.g., Kaul, I., I. Grunberg, and M.A. Stern, 1999. *Global Public Goods: International Cooperation in the 21st Century*, New York, Oxford University Press.

[35] Mandelson, Peter, 2008. "In Defence of Globalization," *The Guardian*, October 3.

[36] For various suggestions as to how to manage effectively various global commons and GPGs, see, e.g., Kaul, I., P. Conceição, K. Le Goulven, and R.U. Mendoza (eds.). 2003. *Providing Global Public Goods: Managing Globalization*, Oxford, Oxford University Press.

world, we do not have an institutional infrastructure that can respond to the multiple challenges that we face.[37]

Efforts in the United Nations and in International Law

Indeed, existing mechanisms to tackle global issues are woefully inadequate. The current practice of international law, including through treaties, conventions and other international agreements – very much at the core of how the international community has confronted global challenges in the past – have proven generally ineffective to address urgent problems. Becoming a party to these treaties is voluntary, and countries can usually withdraw when they wish. The international norms negotiated and set out in international treaties are, however, enormously valuable, often representing extraordinary efforts to achieve consensus on shared global values and legal principles; what is generally missing is effective implementation, monitoring, and enforcement of these international principles.

For example, the Kyoto Protocol to the UN Framework Convention on Climate Change was negotiated in 1997, but only entered into force in 2005. The United States, until 2008 the largest emitter of global warming gases in the world – now overtaken by China – never ratified the Protocol, and Canada withdrew in 2012. It was, therefore, a foregone conclusion that the goals it set for global emissions by 2012, already admittedly inadequate, would not be reached. The Kyoto Protocol was intended primarily to build trust between nations so that they would make the necessary efforts to address a global challenge, starting with those who primarily caused the problem, but several of the key players proved to be largely untrustworthy. Where enforcement mechanisms exist at all, monitoring and enforcement of such treaties is lax and painfully slow.

During the 1990s the United Nations took a lead role in organizing a series of major intergovernmental conferences, beginning with the Earth Summit in Rio de Janeiro in 1992.[38] This was followed by conferences on social and economic development (Copenhagen), women (Beijing), population (Cairo), human rights (Vienna), and so on. These conferences, however, while generally good for raising awareness of the underlying problems, have proven to be inadequate for concrete problem-solving. Long on declarations and in some cases deteriorating into circus-like chaos (e.g., the 2001 Durban conference on race), they have not shown

---

[37] See the excellent discussion of these issues provided by Rischard, J.F. 2002. *High Noon: 20 Global Problems and 20 Years to Solve Them*, New York, Basic Books. See also the Commission on Global Security, Justice and Governance. 2015. *Confronting the Crisis of Global Governance*, The Hague, the Netherlands, The Hague Institute for Global Justice and the Stimson Center.

[38] United Nations. 1992. *Agenda 21: Programme of Action for Sustainable Development*. United Nations Conference on Environment & Development, Rio de Janeiro, Brazil, June 3–14, New York, United Nations. https://sustainabledevelopment.un.org/content/documents/Agenda21.pdf

themselves to be reliable mechanisms for effective cooperation on the urgent problems confronting humanity. The Rio+20 UN Conference on Sustainable Development in 2012[39] was intended to reaffirm government commitments, to define a green economy that would alleviate poverty and work for sustainability, and to agree to new international institutional arrangements, but it only succeeded in making minor adjustments to existing institutions, and to propose a high-level political forum whose function is still being defined. It demonstrated once again that governments are incapable of addressing urgent global problems effectively within the present system.

However, Rio+20 did launch a wide consultative process of governments with inputs from civil society that led in 2015 to a UN General Assembly Summit approving the 2030 Agenda and its 17 Sustainable Development Goals (SDGs) and 169 targets.[40] This provides a useful framework to consider what mechanisms of governance, and at which levels, will be necessary to achieve the SDGs by 2030 and to continue beyond toward planetary sustainability. The goals and targets are aspirational and global, with each nation expected to determine its national contribution toward meeting the goals, and to measure its progress using national indicators adapted from those proposed by the UN Statistical Commission.[41]

Some multilateral agencies, including those associated with the United Nations system, have acquired a critically important role in recent decades. They are repositories of knowledge and expertise and, in some cases, have essentially taken over important functions in central areas of economic governance: for instance, international trade and the dispute settlement mechanism in the case of the World Trade Organization. However, they remain hampered in many other ways, including lack of access to adequate resources to finance their activities and the reluctance of many of the larger countries to cede national sovereignty in particular areas. In this respect, the European Union has, without doubt, gone further than any other country grouping in creating a supranational institutional infrastructure to support an ambitious process of economic and political integration (see Chapter 3).

---

[39] United Nations. 2012. *Report of the United Nations Conference on Sustainable Development,* Rio de Janeiro, Brazil, June 20–22. A/CONF.216/16. New York, United Nations. www.un.org/ga/search/view_doc.asp?symbol=A/CONF.216/16&Lang=E

[40] United Nations. 2015. *Transforming Our World: The 2030 Agenda for Sustainable Development.* Outcome document of the Summit for the adoption of the post-2015 Development Agenda, New York, September 25–27. A/70/L.1. New York, United Nations. www.un.org/ga/search/view_doc.asp?symbol=A/70/L.1&Lang=E

[41] However, the hold of national sovereignty on this process is demonstrated by the insistence of governments that only data provided or verified by their national statistical offices should be used, and UN agencies must not use data from remote sensing or other sources that has not been approved at the national level. While most national statistical services make an effort to be objective and free from political interference, this is sometimes not the case. A robust scientifically based international system of environmental data collection is therefore necessary to keep governments honest and to realize the SDGs successfully.

The G7 and G20

Yet another attempt at reinforcing existing mechanisms of international cooperation was the creation in the mid-1970s of the G7, a "club" made up of the world's seven largest economies. The motivation was to create a high-level body to discuss "major economic and political issues facing their domestic societies and the international community as a whole."[42] The G7 has been a good forum for open debate about global problems, but not a particularly effective problem-solving body. In the public imagination, its semi-annual meetings are largely perceived rather as excellent photo opportunities, not as brainstorming sessions focused on particular problems requiring urgent solutions. Unlike, for instance, the 1944 Bretton Woods Conference which lasted three weeks and resulted in the creation of a new world financial system, G7 meetings are actually intended to *preserve* the status quo.[43]

Its communiqués are negotiated by deputies ahead of the Summit itself and much time is spent in getting the wording of these declarations just right. In time, critics have pointed out some obvious deficiencies, the first being, of course, that by now, the G7 are no longer the world's seven largest economies. In 1999, recognizing that the global economy had evolved, a broader grouping was created – the G20 – but neither the Swiss nor the Dutch nor the Spanish were particularly happy to be excluded. Switzerland is one of the world's most competitive economies and its financial institutions manage a significant share of private wealth; the Netherlands is one of the most generous international donors, and, according to the Center for Global Development, one of the countries with the most development-friendly policies.[44] Spain is a country whose economy is more than twice that of Argentina (a member of the G20). One can also question whether such self-selected and rather arbitrary bodies of powerful countries should determine global policies.

Moreover, the G7 (and to a lesser extent the G20) remain, in fact, official and formalistic bodies focused on representatives from the executive branches of national governments. Their deliberations bring to the table heads of state and a small coterie of civil servants. There is no formal representation from the business community, nor do civil society representatives participate. Given the global nature of the problems we face and the increasingly shared perception that solutions to these will require broad-based collaboration across various stakeholder groups, these

---

[42] See: "40 Years of Summits: Addressing Global Challenges," https://issuu.com/g7g20/docs/40-years-of-summits.

[43] López-Claros, Augusto. 2004. "Sixty Years after Bretton Woods: Developing a Vision for the Future," http://augustolopezclaros.com/wp-content/uploads/2018/06/BrettonWoods_Rome Summary_Jul2004_A4.pdf?x28456.

[44] See the Center for Global Development's *Commitment to Development Index 2015*, where Denmark, Sweden, Norway, Finland, Netherlands, and France occupy, in that order, the top six ranks (www.cgdev.org).

groups suffer from a deficit in legitimacy.[45] They are not a fair representation of humanity and, as such, cannot be expected to make important, informed decisions on its behalf.

INCREASING INTERNATIONAL COOPERATION

Effective, credible mechanisms of international cooperation – which are perceived to be legitimate and capable of acting on behalf of the interests of humanity, rather than those of a particular set of countries – are absolutely essential if the world is to meet the challenge of striking the correct balance between concern for the environment and the policies that must underpin such concern and the need to ensure that the global economy develops in a way that it provides opportunities for all, particularly the poor and the disadvantaged, in a context of peace and security. It is our view that the existing intergovernmental system is not capable of achieving this level of cooperation; what is required is a more fundamental strengthening of the relationships between countries and peoples.

An examination of one specific aspect of the broader question of interdependence is useful. The world has been transformed during the last several decades by technological progress, which, in turn, has had a dramatic impact on the nature of economic and political phenomena and in the way nations relate to each other. Greater economic integration made possible by rapid developments in transport and communications in particular have made evident the need for greater international cooperation. Jean Monnet, the father of the European Union, observed perceptively that economic integration was forcing nations to accept voluntarily the same rules and the same institutions and that, as a result, their behavior toward each other was also changing. This, he said, was permanently modifying relations between nations and could be seen as part of the "process of civilization itself."[46]

Jürgen Habermas has recently offered similar commentary as to the nature of and the need for the essentially "civilizing process" underway in the development of

---

[45] The population of the G7 – 763 million – accounts in 2017 for about 10.3 percent of the world's population; that is, a small minority.

[46] The philosopher Bertrand Russell, who wrote much about the implications of interdependence, said that "[i]n the new world the kindly feelings toward others which religion has advocated will be not only a moral duty but an indispensable condition of survival. A human body could not long continue to live if the hands were in conflict with the feet and the stomach were at war with the liver. Human society as a whole is becoming in this respect more and more like a single human body and if we are to continue to exist, we shall have to acquire feelings directed toward the welfare of the whole in the same sort of way in which feelings of individual welfare concern the whole body and not only this or that portion of it. At any time, such a way of feeling would have been admirable, but now, for the first time in human history, it is becoming necessary if any human being is to be able to achieve anything of what he would wish to enjoy."

supranational law and institutions.[47] But greater interdependence has also created tensions arising out of the potential conflict between national sovereignty and efforts to solve common problems. Indeed, it is not inaccurate to say that at present most countries' commitment to integration and increased international cooperation coexists with a reluctance to confer some traditional aspects of sovereign prerogative to supranational institutions, stemming from a desire to safeguard (real or perceived) national interests. Therefore, one key question in the years immediately ahead is whether greater economic integration – fueled by further technological change, no longer under the control of any single sovereign state – will inevitably lead countries to seek yet more common ground across a range of areas traditionally considered as matters exclusively within the national domain. Will the ongoing abdication of some national sovereignty in the economic sphere also lead to similar processes of significantly increased international cooperation in the sphere of collective security and environmental governance, for example?

Globally, most people have come to recognize the need for the existence of a certain number of institutions at the *national* level to guarantee the effective working of society.[48] Everyone understands the need for a legislature to pass laws, for an executive branch to implement the law, and for a judicial branch to interpret the law and to pass judgment whenever differences of interpretation arise. Most would agree with the notion that a central bank and other financial institutions are needed to regulate different aspects of the economic life of a nation. Indeed, it is not inaccurate to say that a sign of general social progress is the extent to which such institutions in a particular nation have been allowed to develop and, in the process, managed to bring stability and a measure of prosperity to the life of a nation.[49]

Conversely, the *absence* of such institutional progress undermines the creative energies and the vitality of a nation and holds back its development. Indeed, when experts gather together to discuss the terrible plight of the most troubled parts of the developing world and to analyze the factors as to why the quality of life has stagnated to such an extent during the past several decades, a central topic of the debate is institutional failure and the reasons behind this failure. At the same time, it is also clear that national institutions and governments, in an increasingly interdependent

---

[47] Habermas, Jürgen. 2012. "The Crisis of the European Union in the Light of a Constitutionalization of International Law." *The European Journal of International Law* Vol. 23, No. 2, pp. 335–348, at pp. 337–338.

[48] For example, Adam Smith, considered the establishment and maintenance of an effective justice system a vital public good which represented one of three core "duties" of a national government; one could in a parallel fashion see that such a public good is imperative at the international level. Smith, Adam. 1937. *The Wealth of Nations* New York, The Modern Library, p. 767.

[49] Scholars Daron Acemoglu and James Robinson, in an influential thesis, have suggested that types of "inclusive" public institutions, supported by rule of law, have been fundamental for the development of successful, prosperous nation states. Acemoglu, Daron and Robinson, James A. 2013. *Why Nations Fail: The Origins of Power, Prosperity and Poverty*, London, Profile Books.

world, are less and less able to address key problems, many of which have acquired unavoidable international dimensions.

First, governments are increasingly unable to do the kinds of things that they used to be able to do in the past and that, in people's minds, came to be identified with the very essence of government. Richard Cooper, one of our most insightful international economists, states that "the increasing internationalization of the economy has led to an erosion of our government's capacity to do things the way it used to."[50] This, in turn, can and sometimes has led to a kind of paralysis on the part of governments, a sense that since the world has changed and it is no longer under their control – or at least they have less control over it than used to be case – the optimal policy response is to do nothing. Yet publics have vastly higher expectations about economic policy and are unlikely to be placated by their leaders telling them that there is very little that can be done because the effectiveness of traditional policies and instruments has been greatly reduced by processes outside of their control. The result is a profound sense of public dissatisfaction and/or apathy and a rise in populism that one can perceive in many countries.[51]

The failings of the present international institutional arrangements in the political sphere are even more obvious. From earlier crises in Rwanda, Yugoslavia and Sudan, to the myriad crises unfolding in the Middle East, one can see increasing evidences of the failure of the international community to address urgent and sometimes tragic problems because of the absence of international institutions charged with the power, jurisdiction and vision to act in instances or situations within nations that lie beyond their jurisdiction. When close to a million people in Rwanda are murdered within a brief span of time, and the images of the carnage are relayed to every corner of the world, there seems very little that the international community can do, other than wring its hands, express regret, and helplessly stand by lamenting its impotence. This is an eloquent indictment of the tragic shortcomings of the present international political system. It had been this kind of insight that led two Harvard intellectuals, Grenville Clark and Louis. B. Sohn, in the 1950s to write about the need for the establishment of institutions "on a world scale corresponding to those which have been found essential for the maintenance of law and order in local communities and nations."[52]

---

[50] Cooper, Richard N. 1988. "International Cooperation: Is It Desirable? Is It Likely?" address, International Monetary Fund Visitors' Center, Washington, DC.

[51] Cooper, in "International Cooperation," adds that "The United States occasionally responds to this erosion by lashing out and extending its jurisdiction to the rest of the world, leading to international friction. I see extraterritoriality, as it is called, as a natural, although not necessarily a desirable, response to the erosion of our capacity to control our own environment."

[52] Clark, G. and Sohn L.B. 1966. *World Peace through World Law: Two Alternative Plans*, Cambridge, MA, Harvard University Press, p. xi. Sohn was a Harvard law professor who attended and contributed to the San Francisco Conference establishing the United Nations and who also served as a counselor to the Legal Adviser of the US Department of State. Clark was a Wall Street lawyer and a remarkable public intellectual who collaborated closely with

A NEED FOR CONCRETE PROPOSALS

The above considerations lead to the following question: What is the most adequate response to the erosion of policy effectiveness? One obvious starting point is realizing that much of the ineffectiveness of government action (and the accompanying paralysis) stems from the fact that actions are being carried out by individual sovereign states, acting alone, in full use of their (rapidly diminishing) powers, whereas joint, coordinated actions, based upon clear and legitimate common goals, can restore (sometimes to a great extent) the utility of the previously ineffective policy. The realization is that, in an increasingly interdependent world, national institutions are less and less able to address problems that are fundamentally international in character. The implications that this realization carries for the exercise of political authority, are the motivating forces behind many of the present experiments in various parts of the world, which seek integrative processes and the building of supranational institutions to support and direct such processes. Chief among these experiments one must note the economic, political, and institutional developments in the context of the European Union.[53]

Albert Einstein – who together with Bertrand Russell and others gave a great deal of thought to the political requirements in the new climate created by the arrival of nuclear weapons – believed that one way to address the evident failings of the international institutional framework was to create a new breed of truly supranational organizations. In 1946, soon after the creation of the United Nations and very much aware of this organization's limitations, he wrote:

> The development of technology and of the implements of war has brought about something akin to a shrinking of our planet. Economic interlinking has made the destinies of nations interdependent to a degree far greater than in previous years.... The only hope for protection lies in the securing of peace in a supranational way.

several US presidents on a range of issues, including as an advisor to the Secretary of War during World War II. He spent the last 20 years of his life as a tireless promoter of world peace. He was elected to and served for many years on the Corporation, the body that governs Harvard University. According to the Harvard Square Library, a digital depository of historical materials: "Perhaps the most interesting thing about Clark was the quiet and unobtrusive manner in which he conducted his public activities. He was given the epithet 'statesman incognito,' because he was virtually unknown to the general public but known very well to a few thousand persons of large influence in national affairs. This was the way Clark wanted it. Caring nothing for publicity, he took pride in his role as an independent critic, free to suggest solutions whenever the need arose." "There was something about him, an independence of spirit, a dogged curiosity, a supreme indifference to ignorant criticism, that made him a unique member of the 'establishment.'" www.harvardsquarelibrary.org/biographies/grenville-clark/

[53] In an interesting op-ed piece entitled "Sovereignty vs. Suffering," Brian Urquhart, former UN Under-Secretary General for Special Political Affairs, observed that "many developments of our time challenge the validity of the principle of national sovereignty. Communications technology, pollution, radioactive debris, the flow of money, the power of religious or secular ideas, AIDS, the traffic in drugs and terrorism are only a few of the phenomena that pay scant attention to national borders or sovereignty," *New York Times*, April 17, 1991.

A world government must be created which is able to solve conflicts between nations by judicial decision. This government must be based on a clear-cut constitution which is approved by the governments and the nations and which gives it the sole disposition of offensive weapons. A person or a nation can be considered peace loving only if it is ready to cede its military force to the international authorities and to renounce every attempt or even the means of achieving its interests abroad by the use of force.[54]

Russell held similar views:

A much more desirable way of securing world peace would be by a voluntary agreement among nations to pool their armed forces and submit to an agreed international authority. This may seem, at present, a distant and Utopian prospect, but there are practical politicians who think otherwise. A World Authority, if it is to fulfill its function, must have a legislature and an executive and irresistible military power. All nations would have to agree to reduce national armed forces to the level necessary for internal police action. No nation should be allowed to retain nuclear weapons or any other means of wholesale destruction... In a world where separate nations were disarmed, the military forces of the World Authority would not need to be very large and would not constitute an onerous burden upon the various constituent nations.[55]

In the aftermath of the chaos and destruction unleashed by World War II, Einstein, Russell, Clark and others laid out an important argument in favor of the creation of an international authority, explaining that the time had passed when military conflicts and their associated damage could be reasonably contained. In the nuclear age, war had become unthinkable and its consequences universal. A conception of national sovereignty, which had always been understood to mean the right of a country to defend its interests by the use of force if necessary, but the exercise of which had assumed that conflicts would remain largely confined to given geographic areas, no longer served the interests of anyone.[56] On the contrary, thus understood, traditional or narrow conceptions of national sovereignty cast a dark shadow over the future of everyone. Hence the notion eventually emerged that lasting international peace will be feasible only in the context of the creation of effective global institutions based on the principle of collective security. Or, as put by Schell: "I would suggest that the ultimate requirements are in essence the two that I have mentioned: global disarmament, both nuclear and conventional, and the

---

[54] Einstein, Albert. 1956. *Out of My Later Years*, New York, Philosophical Library, p. 138.

[55] Russell, Bertrand. 1961. *Has Man a Future?*, London, Penguin, p. 121.

[56] In addition, legal scholars/political philosophers such as Hans Kelsen, have long criticized the primitive and self-contradictory nature of an international system based on ill-defined notions of sovereignty and sovereign self-help rather than on centralized juridical bodies and other institutions which are technically necessary for any system based on the rule of law. See e.g., Kelsen, Hans. 1942. *Law and Peace in International Relations*, Cambridge MA, Harvard University Press.

invention of political means by which the world can peacefully settle the means that throughout history it has settled by war."[57]

THE URGENCY OF ACTION

Given the compelling circumstances with which humanity is currently confronted, a substantial and carefully-thought-through reform effort is needed to enhance dramatically the basic architecture of our global governance system. Such a reform should be grounded in key ideas that have motivated those of past generations who have risen to the difficult challenge of providing practical leadership and vision in the international sphere. Indeed, the proposals described in this book in many respects build upon the worthwhile suggestions of clear-sighted thinkers who have come previously.[58]

Moreover, the suggested significant steps forward to enhance global governance are consciously "incremental" in the sense that they are grounded on fundamental points of law already agreed by states worldwide, and upon foundational principles "baked into" the DNA of the existing international order. An organic process of growth has occurred within the current United Nations and international governance institutions. This has included the building of levels of trust and an understanding of the practical importance of international cooperation, which would have been unimaginable in past decades; an enhanced architecture is now required to implement this learning and awareness.

The cost of inaction is high, and the inhibitions to action come rather from our own flawed thinking rather than a realistic estimation of human will and capacity. In the words of Jonathan Schell:

> Our present system and the institutions that make it up are the debris of history. They have become inimical to life... They constitute a noose around the neck of mankind, threatening to choke off the human future, but we can cut the noose and

---

[57] Schell, *The Fate of the Earth*, p. 227.
[58] Among the most significant proposals for UN reform are: Clark and Sohn. *World Peace through World Law: Two Alternative Plans*; Boutros Boutros-Ghali, *An Agenda for Peace: Preventive Diplomacy, Peacemaking and Peace-keeping*, Report of the Secretary General Pursuant to the Statement Adopted by the Summit Meeting of the Security Council on January 31, 1992, New York; *Partners for Peace: Strengthening Collective Security for the 21st Century*, New York, United Nations Association of the United States, 1992. Stassen, Harold. 1994. *United Nations, A Working Paper for Restructuring*, Lerner Publications Company, MN; US Commission on Global Governance, *Our Global Neighbourhood: Report of the Commission on Global Governance*, Oxford University Press, 1995; Schwartzberg, Joseph E. 2013. *Transforming the United Nations System: Designs for a Workable World*, United Nations University Press. www.brookings.edu/book/transforming-the-united-nations-system/; Falk, Richard. 2014. *(Re)Imagining Humane Global Governance*, Abingdon, UK and New York, Routledge; Commission on Global Security, Justice & Governance. 2015. *Confronting the Crisis of Global Governance*. Report of the Commission on Global Security, Justice & Governance, June 2015. The Hague, The Hague Institute for Global Justice and Washington, DC, The Stimson Center.

break free. To suppose otherwise would be to set up a false, fictitious fate, molded out of our own weaknesses and our own alterable decisions.[59]

The risk of the catastrophic collapse of the present system is not negligible. The rise of autocratic leaders, public disillusionment with partisan politics, and the general decline in the quality of leadership in government are all increasing the risks of fundamental instabilities that could precipitate major crises. If we do not act now to strengthen the international order, we may be forced to rebuild a global institutional framework after a major war, the collapse of the global financial system, a pandemic wiping out a significant part of the world's population, or extreme climate change producing famines and mass migrations, any of which would overwhelm existing institutions at the national and global levels (see Chapter 17). Planning to strengthen international governance should include both the possibility of rapid progress through acts of consultative will, and, if necessary, reconstruction once a major calamity has forced countries to see that there is no alternative, as previously occurred after World Wars I and II.

The set of proposals presented in this book explicitly builds upon current international structures put in place in 1944–1945 with the adoption of the UN Charter and the creation of the United Nations and its various specialized agencies. Despite its flaws, it would be politically unrealistic to follow a path that did not focus on the reform and the very substantial strengthening of the current UN system, which, remarkably, already involves the participation of virtually all nations of the world and has developed, over the last decades, a range of significant mechanisms of consultation and cooperation. Building upon and fundamentally improving existing structures seems the sensible way to proceed. Moreover, certain basic Charter features enshrined at the time of its adoption remain largely or wholly unimplemented or insufficiently utilized (e.g., Chapter VI on the Pacific Settlement of Disputes and Art. 43 related to collective security operations); focusing on the further realization of such Charter attributes has the benefit of consolidating upon existing points of universal agreement.

The UN was built upon progressively developed, precursor attempts to solve key issues of global governance, including core problems of international conflict/ interstate war (e.g., the 1899 and 1907 Hague Peace Conferences, The League of Nations, the 1928 Kellogg–Briand Pact or the General Treaty for Renunciation of War as an Instrument of National Policy). The Charter itself contains a formula for reform (Chapter XVIII), and informal mechanisms in practice without a Charter amendment have developed to enhance significantly or to extrapolate from its provisions (e.g., to enable peace-keeping operations). A general Charter review conference was anticipated to be held within ten years of its adoption, under Charter

---

[59] Schell, *The Fate of the Earth*, p. 219.

Art. 109(3), but was never held; the clear mechanism for general Charter review and reform is one important attribute that has remained largely unrealized.

A challenge in proposals to address our multiple current predicaments is striking the right balance between proposals that are so ambitious as to have negligible chances of being seriously considered and proposals that are seen as more "politically feasible." The latter involve tweaking at the edges of our current UN-based systems of governance, but that would fail to find meaningful solutions to urgent contemporary problems, and additional global risks that are now on the horizon. A further complicating factor is that what may not be politically feasible today may be so judged a few years later, particularly after a severe crisis, such as occurred with the founding of the EU and the current UN system in the aftermath of World War II.[60]

This proposal envisages a range of revisions to the UN Charter, which would provide the legal basis for enhanced mechanisms of international cooperation and global governance, supplemented by other reforms not requiring formal Charter amendment. Parts of this proposal build on the monumental work on Charter revision done by Clark and Sohn in the late 1950s and early 1960s,[61] which remains the most detailed and thorough despite many contributions since their time.[62] All these proposals need to be adapted to the needs of a drastically changed world, facing a much broader set of global challenges than those originally addressed at that time.

Our proposals seek to go to the heart of the flaws purposely built in to the UN Charter at its inception to ensure its acceptance by the great powers at the time, fresh from a perilous and horrifying international conflict. They needed to be reassured that the new organization represented no threat to their notions of absolute national sovereignty; notions that are now retarding the effective management of global risks. We challenge the assumptions behind this traditional thinking and seek to provide a framework for innovative new proposals, while suggesting practical ways forward. Changes of this magnitude cannot be planned in detail in advance, and no one knows what future events might, of necessity, create

---

[60] The creation of something like the European Union in 1938 would have been considered unthinkable. The European Coal and Steel Community, however, came into being in 1951, paving the way for the Treaty of Rome in 1957 and the developments that followed thereafter. Some would argue that the creation of the EU was made possible by the untold human suffering and economic collapse associated with World War II. The point here is that what is considered politically feasible at a moment in time is very much a function of one's vantage point. Or, as was once put by a Brazilian diplomat: "Unless we aim for the seemingly unattainable, we risk settling for mediocrity."

[61] See Clark and Sohn, *World Peace through World Law*, 1966.

[62] For an excellent overview of many of the most important contributions to the debate on the foundations of world order see the volumes edited by Richard Falk, Samuel S. Kim, Saul H. Mendlovitz and others. In particular, *Toward a Just World Order*, 1982; *International Law and a Just World Order*, 1985; and *The United Nations and a Just World Order*, 1991.

opportunities to move forward. We hope that this book will stimulate new thinking and learning as we pursue a path to effective global governance.

PROTECTING NATIONAL AUTONOMY

In fact, in a globalized world where many of the most cherished characteristics of national sovereignty in terms of security, economic management, social and cultural independence, and environmental protection have eroded – if not almost entirely escaped from – national control, national autonomy can best be protected by a new level of global governance. Arms races and threats of conflict, the economic crisis of 2008, increasing pressures from cross-border migrants and refugees, and climate change (among many other issues) demonstrate the contagion at the heart of global crises that can leave no nation untouched. International mechanisms to anticipate global risks, develop preventive measures where possible, increase resilience and reduce vulnerability, and – when necessary – assist with rescue and reconstruction, are the best insurance against impacts for which national sovereignty is no longer an adequate defense.

Just as the rule of law and social security at the national level are the best protection for the individual well-being of each citizen, similarly in today's global system will the national autonomy of each state best be served by strong mechanisms for the international rule of law, collective security, and environmental management. As the threats from unmanaged global crises increase, rapid investment in the construction of a reinforced framework for global collaboration and preventive action must be a priority for any enlightened leadership looking after the progress and prosperity of their nation.

OPPOSITION TO DEEP REFORMS AND AN EVOLVING INTERNATIONAL LANDSCAPE

Some opposition to the reforms such as those proposed in this book can be anticipated, in particular from vested interests and also from those with versions of national identity who lack an awareness or understanding of the urgent and often complex nature of our shared global challenges. The veto of the permanent members of the Security Council is also a fundamental flaw in the UN Charter that has long prevented the implementation of some of its more important provisions, including Charter revision. The 1945 Charter was termed by the Prime Minister of New Zealand during negotiations as a "series of . . . petrified platitudes," as it could only be amended with the consent of the great powers.[63]

---

[63] Meyer, Cord Jr. 1945. "A Serviceman Looks at the Peace." *The Atlantic Monthly*, Vol. 176, No. 3, p. 46.

This historic blockage might be addressed in several ways: by the possibility of creating a new organization to replace the United Nations, as the UN replaced the League of Nations, if the great majority of governments decide to adopt this path as a consequence of the UN's paralysis; and the unfortunate option to turn to proposals for significant reform after a catastrophic failure of the UN to prevent a third world war or some similar collapse of the global system with widespread suffering (see Chapter 21). There are also intermediate scenarios and incremental steps that we explore more generally throughout the book, as we suggest possible transition processes for the various reform proposals.

More generally, international policy-making processes and the maturation of aspects of global civil society campaigns and coordination mechanisms have made significant strides since the original framing of the Charter, particularly in the last 30 years or so (notably since the end of the Cold War), to overcome traditional resistances and blockages. Such changes open up a range of new opportunities and techniques to catalyze and sustain major international reform efforts. There are many lessons to be learned from dramatic achievements in modern international law that have come about as a result of global civil society coalitions joined with "middle power" states in what have been termed "smart coalitions." Indeed, such coalitions were noted as a significant and quite singular hopeful trend in the 2015 report *Confronting the Crisis of Global Governance*, co-chaired by former US Secretary of State Madeleine Albright and former Nigerian Foreign Minister and UN Under-Secretary General for Political Affairs Ibrahim Gambari.[64] The recent achievements of such smart coalitions include the International Criminal Court, the "Mine Ban Treaty," the UN Convention on the Rights of Persons with Disabilities, and the recently adopted Treaty on the Prohibition of Nuclear Weapons. Many of these projects seemed dramatically unrealistic at the outset and have defied (or side-stepped) geopolitical forces and the realities of superpower politics. A positive case can be made for how such techniques can be used for substantial but incremental aspects of the proposed UN reforms, short of the dramatic scenarios described in the preceding paragraph.

Moreover, this book more generally seeks to encourage a culture/paradigm shift (in fact exemplified by transnational civil society coalitions and their accomplishments) to a global governance model firmly anchored in global and human interest rather than in narrow – and often self-defeating – national interest (the proposed enhancement of the General Assembly and a possible advisory Civil Society Chamber are a clear institutionalization of this perspective; see Chapters 4–6). Such a shift is connected to our proposals for a transition to an international order genuinely based on the rule of law, including international human rights protections, support

---

[64] Commission on Global Security, Justice & Governance. 2015. *Confronting the Crisis of Global Governance*. Report of the Commission on Global Security, Justice & Governance, June, The Hague, The Hague Institute for Global Justice and Washington, DC, The Stimson Center.

for which we have copious authoritative statements of UN bodies and heads of state (see Chapters 10 and 11). We see the enhancement of the juridical aspect of the international governance system (following on prominent jurists/philosophers such as Hans Kelsen and Immanuel Kant) – and a public intellectual argument for the same – as a key to addressing the global human interest and the "vertical" dimension of geopolitical inequality (e.g., all states should be held to account before the International Court of Justice, individuals should have recourse to more effective remedies for human rights violations than those provided by the nonbinding complaint procedures). We argue that concepts of social contract, legitimate governmental authority and rule of law, that are firmly established at the national level in many countries, should dominate the international arena, discursively and actually, and a (global) public case should be made for adhering to these values (see Chapter 20). The inevitability of superpower or great power dominance should be contested; our collective focus should rather shift to the difficult – but crucial and achievable – work of institution-building and to establishing processes that can earn the trust of all and hold powerful actors to account.

We call for a renewed public intellectual conversation, focusing on ambitious and systemic changes to our current global governance architectures, breaking the ice of dialogues that have remained frozen for far too long. We hope that this book, at the very least, will serve as a conversation starter, seeking also to break the vicious circle of "benign neglect and low expectations" – to paraphrase former UN High Commissioner for Human Rights, Navi Pillay – which has indeed quite consistently plagued UN reform discourse in political circles. Our collective energies should be focused on reinvigorating bold proposals and reform pathways to enable the UN to move from being simply a platform to debate competing national interests, to become one promoting the common global interest on a range of urgent matters. We ignore such conversations at our own peril.

WHAT IS AHEAD

The book is organized as follows. Chapter 2 will present a historical overview of the concept of global governance. The idea of pooling aspects of national sovereignties as a way of establishing a stable framework for international peace, security, and prosperity has a distinguished lineage going back many centuries. It is useful to understand this history, not only to gain insights into the motivations of various proposals, but also the reasons for their success or lack of uptake at various junctures. The relevance of these lessons for the future is particularly important. The very ambitious proposals put forward by Clark and Sohn in the late 1950s, much admired in many circles at the time, did not go beyond generating an interesting debate among experts; the onset of the Cold War did much to stifle any meaningful action. We argue that much has changed in the last 60 years and that we no longer have the luxury of avoiding taking action on a number of fronts. In Chapter 3, we review the history of the gradual evolution of supranational institutions from the experience of the European Union; an interesting model to consider or draw from on the international plane. We then make specific proposals to enhance the collective security mechanisms of the Charter, as well as the legislative, executive/management and legal dimensions of the United Nations, as these constitute central institutional attributes for effective global governance. Chapters 4 and 5 will look in greater detail at some of our core proposals in respect of reforms of the UN General Assembly and will make the case for the creation of a Second Chamber attached to the General Assembly in the near term without the need for Charter amendment. Supporting advisory mechanisms to the legislative and policy-making processes, including a possible Civil Society Chamber, are proposed in Chapter 6.

Chapters 7 and 8 will discuss the replacement of the UN Security Council by a management-oriented Executive Council, and completing the collective security mechanism of the Charter through the creation of an International Peace Force. Chapter 9 will deal with the issue of disarmament as another essential dimension of collective security. Strengthening the international rule of law, ensuring the peaceful settlement of international disputes, the creation of an International Human Rights Tribunal and the need for a UN Bill of Rights will be the subject of Chapters 10 and 11. Chapter 12 will present some proposals for the creation of a new funding mechanism to finance the operations of a reformed UN system.

Our focus then shifts to the governance response to specific global threats to all nations and to human well-being. Chapter 13 will look at the UN specialized agencies, which we see as playing a growing and central role in managing and establishing the parameters for enhanced international cooperation in a number of areas. We then illustrate this with case studies in the economic, environmental and social areas, including the global economy, inequality, and the private sector in Chapter 14; financial governance through a reformed IMF in Chapter 15; global environmental governance for climate change and biosphere integrity in Chapter 16, and population and migration in Chapter 17. Chapters 18 and 19 address the cross-cutting and system-wide issues of confronting corruption and enhancing the power of education at the international level, while Chapter 20 offers some comments on the shared values and principles needed for significant global reform. Chapter 20 also offers an overview ("Operationalizing Key Attributes and Values of a New Global Governance System") of how a key set of the proposed substantial global governance reforms could be operationalized, in a values-based governance environment. We wrap up our proposals in Chapter 21 with scenarios of possible futures and proposed concrete steps forward in coming years, and the concluding Chapter 22, which addresses some of the roots of present failures in our current system, and the seeds of success building on a higher vision of shared human purpose and potential to assemble positive forces for global governance.

2

A History of Global Governance

It is the sense of Congress that it should be a fundamental objective of the foreign policy of the United States to support and strengthen the United Nations and to seek its development into a world federation open to all nations with definite and limited powers adequate to preserve peace and prevent aggression through the enactment, interpretation and enforcement of world law.

House Concurrent Resolution 64, 1949, with 111 co-sponsors

There are causes, but only a very few, for which it is worthwhile to fight; but whatever the cause, and however justifiable the war, war brings about such great evils that it is of immense importance to find ways short of war in which the things worth fighting for can be secured. I think it is worthwhile to fight to prevent England and America being conquered by the Nazis, but it would be far better if this end could be secured without war. For this, two things are necessary. First, the creation of an international government, possessing a monopoly of armed force, and guaranteeing freedom from aggression to every country; second, that wars (other than civil wars) are justified when, and only when, they are fought in defense of the international law established by the international authority. Wars will cease when, and only when, it becomes evident beyond reasonable doubt that in any war the aggressor will be defeated.

Bertrand Russell, "The Future of Pacifism"[1]

By the end of the 20th century, if not well before, humankind had come to accept the need for and the importance of various national institutions to secure political stability and economic prosperity. With some differences to reflect individual country histories and circumstances, most people today accept the need for a legislative body to enact laws, an executive to implement them and to run the government, a judiciary endowed with power to interpret the law when needed, a

---

[1] Russell, Bertrand. 1943–1944. "The Future of Pacifism." *The American Scholar*, Vol. 13, No. 1, pp. 9–10.

central bank to issue the currency and regulate the financial markets and safeguard financial stability, a police force to guarantee the safety of citizens, and so on. It is widely acknowledged that when such institutions are weak or do not function effectively, a country will not develop smoothly. Depending on the particular institutional shortcomings identified, countries may remain stuck in a poverty trap, may face political upheavals, civil strife, violence, and crime. Indeed, much of the practice of good governance today is concerned with strengthening the institutional underpinnings of society and buttressing the rule of law (see Chapter 20).

The notion that humanity might evolve to a stage where we would broaden our mental horizons and expand our loyalties to a wider circle is not a recent phenomenon. From the time of Jesus to the industrial revolution, life for most people has been tough and brutishly short. Economic historians have estimated that average economic growth over this period was virtually nonexistent; this meant that for a typical individual, there was very little change during their lifetime in the objective material circumstances surrounding daily life. Most people lived under what today we would characterize as an incredibly austere poverty line and famines were frequent, long and lethal. Disease and pandemics of various kinds kept population in check or, as in the case of the Black Death, reduced the population of Europe and parts of Asia by upwards of a hundred million people. Because there was virtually nothing to distribute, rulers were not in a position to grant benefits to some groups (e.g., the army) without taking away from others. This led to the proliferation of authoritarian regimes which, to survive, generally ruled with a combination of an iron hand and, where necessary, terror. This is not to say that the industrial revolution eliminated the incidence of poverty and violence, but the economic growth that it brought about did expand the range of opportunities for many people, some of whom could now pursue other interests beyond mere survival. This was surely a factor, for instance, in the development of our scientific and technological capacity.

EARLY VISIONS

It should not surprise us that, against the background of a limited and difficult material environment and rough social conditions, characterized by episodic phases of political instability and violence, there would be occasional calls for exploring alternative political arrangements or organizing human affairs in a way that was conducive to some semblance of the rule of law at the international level. In 1311 Dante Alighieri wrote a political tract under the title of *De Monarchia*,[2] which was translated into English and published in 1949 as *On World Government*. This is an extraordinary document, putting forward the notion of the unity of humanity, the role of the human mind as the epitome of perfection, the desirability of liberty under

---

[2] Alighieri, Dante. 2008. *On World Government*, translation by Herbert W. Schneider, New York, Griffon House Publications.

the rule of law, and the need for a supranational power, to resolve disputes between city or state governments. Dante wrote: "it is evident that mankind, too, is most free and easy to carry on its work when it enjoys the quiet and tranquility of peace. To achieve this state of universal well-being a single world government is necessary."[3]

In his paper "An Essay towards the Present and Future Peace of Europe" (1693), William Penn made the case for a federal European state to keep the peace. This state would govern relations between its members within a common legal framework, including a supranational parliament and respect for the sovereignty of members within their domestic territories.[4] Again, Penn's essay is an excellent example of the extent to which poverty and the prevalence of violence and war among states prompted leading thinkers to make proposals aimed at securing a more solid foundation for peace and prosperity. Twenty years later the French cleric Charles Castel de Saint-Pierre (1658–1743) in his "Plan for the Perpetual Peace in Europe" called for the creation of a European confederation. It was left to Jean-Jacques Rousseau, however, who was the recipient of Saint-Pierre's collected papers upon his death, to popularize his ideas and to quote from his writings in his own essay *A Project of Perpetual Peace* (1761), and to highlight that Saint-Pierre had indeed been eloquent in his condemnation of existing political arrangements in Europe, which he characterized as being laden with "perpetual dissensions, brigandage, usurpations, rebellions, wars and murders," which distracted peoples from more productive pursuits and had led him to call for the creation of *un gouvernement confédérative* where "all its members must be placed in such a mutual state of dependence that not one of them alone may be in a position to resist all of the others." This may well be one of the earliest calls for the establishment of a system of collective security.

Without doubt one of the most important experiments in international cooperation based on the rule of law were the initiatives taken in America in the 18th century, beginning with the Declaration of Independence in 1776, the Articles of Confederation ratified by the 13 states in 1781 and the subsequent adoption of the US Constitution of 1787. The motivation of the framers of the new constitutional order that emerged in the United States and as reflected, for instance, in the *Federalist Papers* written by Alexander Hamilton, James Madison and John Jay, is very much in keeping with the concerns raised by Enlightenment thinkers in Europe around the same time. A loose confederation of states was not likely to provide a basis for meaningful cooperation across state borders and to ensure the peace.

What was necessary was a supranational form of governance that established a legal framework with binding rules on the citizenry. Hamilton had often said that "if men were angels, no government would be necessary," that people must be brought

---

[3] Dante, *On World Government*, pp. 6–7.
[4] William Penn. 1910. *The Peace of Europe: The Fruits of Solitude and Other Writings*, New York, J.M. Dent and Sons.

under the "mild and salutary coercion" of the law, if they are to avoid the "destructive coercion of the sword." What emerged out of the Constitutional Convention in Philadelphia was a system that sought to balance the interests of states with the need to have a strong central government that would operate under the rule of law and with clearly identified limitations on its powers, to guard against the dangers of authoritarianism and the infringement of individual civil liberties.

Benjamin Franklin, who had spent nine years in Paris as America's first ambassador to the French Court wrote, soon after the Convention in 1787, the following to a friend back in France: "If the Constitution succeeds, I do not see why you might not in Europe carry the project of good Henry IV into execution, by forming a Federal Union and One Grand Republick of all its different States and Kingdoms by means of a like Convention, for we had many interests to reconcile."[5] Supporters of the idea of establishing a world federation have often pointed to the American experience as an example of the benefits of federalism under the rule of law. From an economic perspective, there is little doubt that creating an integrated single economic space, in time, provided many advantages to producers and consumers. The federal government was given powers to regulate interstate trade, to issue a single currency and regulate the financial system, to issue debt in an integrated market subject to the same rules, and to build a body of commercial law and other legislation that strengthened the cohesion of the internal market, protecting the US economy from the inefficiencies of varying and multiple local regulatory frameworks. By the early part of the 20th century the US was already emerging as the world's largest and most dynamic economy, something that in turn was reflected in growing political power.

Henry Kissinger regards Immanuel Kant as the most accomplished philosopher of the Enlightenment period and makes a persuasive case that much of his greatness is a reflection of his political philosophy and the vision that he offered for peace in Europe.[6]

Humanity, Kant reasoned, was characterized by a distinctive "unsocial sociability," the "tendency to come together in society, coupled however, with a continual resistance which constantly threatens to break this society up." The problem of order, particularly international order, was "the most difficult and the last to be solved by the human race." Men formed states to constrain their passions, but like individuals in the state of nature each state sought to preserve its absolute freedom, even at the cost of "a lawless state of savagery." But the "devastations, upheaval and even complete inner exhaustion of their powers" arising from interstate clashes

---

[5] Quoted in Joseph Preston Baratta. 2004. *The Politics of World Federation*, Vol. 1: *United Nations, UN Reform, Atomic Control*, Westport, CT, Praeger, p. 28. Baratta's impressive, well-documented and highly readable two-volume *The Politics of World Federation* has been a vital source for this chapter.

[6] Kissinger, Henry. 2014. *World Order*, New York, Penguin Press, p. 40.

would in time oblige men to contemplate an alternative. Humanity faced either the peace of "the vast graveyard of the human race or peace by reasoned design."[7]

Kant's proposal for this "peace by reasoned design" was a voluntary federation of nations relating to each other within a framework of respect for agreed rules of conduct, in which governments would act in the public interest in peaceful ways because the citizens would no longer wish to face the rigors and consequences of armed conflicts. Kant's "league of peace" would be a departure from the then prevailing order based on unenforceable treaties and alliances, which had resulted in centuries of instability and warfare, to one based on the rule of law (see Chapter 10). In time the system would evolve into a peaceful world order and "a perfect civil union of mankind."

Kant was under no illusions about the current state of human society in his time; he perfectly understood the tensions between conceptions of national sovereignty and the need to seek common ground with other states also intent on providing security and prosperity to their peoples. But rather than argue that these tensions would coexist forever, occasionally erupting into episodes of killing, savagery and destruction, he thought that humankind had the capacity to learn and to evolve into a more peaceful social order. Kant, unfortunately, was ahead of his time. It would take the nations of Europe another 160 years or so and upwards of 50 million dead before his vision of a united Europe would coalesce in the Treaty of Rome in 1957. It is difficult to take issue with Kissinger's admiration for Kant. Against the background of hundreds of years of hostilities, violence, and conflict, one cannot fault Kant for arguing that there was a better way to establish a more sensible political order in Europe, even though, in retrospect, it does seem that Europeans opted for a century and a half of graveyards before finally agreeing to "lay the foundations of an ever-closer union among the peoples of Europe" and to "ensure the economic and social progress of their countries by common action to eliminate the barriers which divide Europe (see Chapter 3)."[8]

THE LEAGUE OF NATIONS

There are important lessons to be learned from earlier failures and successes in attempts to create international institutions to bring peace to the world, as many of the same issues will face our own proposals set out in this book. It is therefore instructive to review the creation of the League of Nations in some detail.

This was the next substantial initiative aimed at laying the groundwork for the kind of political vision earlier put forward by the likes of Saint-Pierre, Rousseau, and Kant. It came against the background of World War I and the efforts by President Woodrow Wilson to create a permanent international organization made up of the

---

[7] Kissinger, *World Order*, p. 40.
[8] Preamble to the Treaty of Rome, 1957.

leading powers of the day, with the specific aim of preventing war. He sought to abandon a tradition of isolationism in favor of a more robust engagement with the world and, in particular, war-torn Europe. The United States had emerged as a global economic power, very much tied through bonds of industry, commerce, and finance with the rest of the world. Wilson argued for what he saw as an established American commitment to democracy and an aversion to the traditional European system of alliances; its ability to project its values upon other nations would be hampered by a policy of isolation and a continued aversion to what the Founding Fathers had called "foreign entanglements."

In a speech delivered to the US Senate on January 22, 1917, President Wilson said:

> The present war must first be ended; but we owe it to candor to say that, so far as our participation in guarantees of future peace is concerned, it makes a great deal of difference in what way and upon what terms it is ended. The treaties and agreements which bring it to an end must embody terms which will create a peace that is worth guaranteeing and preserving, a peace that will win the approval of mankind, not merely a peace that will serve the several interests and immediate aims of the nations engaged. The question upon which the whole future peace and policy of the world depends is this: is the present war a struggle for a just and secure peace, or only for a new balance of power? If it be only a struggle for a new balance of power, who will guarantee, who can guarantee, the stable equilibrium of the new arrangement? Only a tranquil Europe can be a stable Europe. There must be, not a balance of power, but a community of power; not organised rivalries, but an organised, common peace.

Kissinger notes that Wilson's concept of "community of power" would in time reemerge as the principle of "collective security." He adds that "the League of Nations ... would be founded on a moral principle, the universal opposition to military aggression as such, whatever its source, its target, or its proclaimed justification."[9] One cannot fail to be impressed with the streak of idealism that runs through Wilson's countless interventions in support of the establishment of the League. One senses the heavy burden of responsibility weighing on him because of the United States' participation in the war. In a speech in 1919 he noted: "My clients are the children; my clients are the next generation. They do not know what promises and bonds I undertook when I ordered the armies of the United States to the soil of France, but I know, and I intend to redeem my pledges to the children; they shall not be sent upon a similar errand."

Because the United States had had a long aversion to these "foreign entanglements" (in his Farewell address President George Washington had said "it is our true policy to steer clear of permanent alliance with any portion of the foreign world" and

---

[9] Kissinger, *World Order*, p. 262.

in his inaugural speech Thomas Jefferson had echoed similar concerns: "peace, commerce, and honest friendship with all nations – entangling alliances with none.") President Wilson had moved cautiously, concerned not to awaken similar sentiments among the US political establishment. In a speech in New York City on September 27, 1918, he stated:

> We still read Washington's immortal warning against "entangling alliances" with full comprehension and an answering purpose. But only special and limited alliances entangle; and we recognize and accept the duty of a new day in which we are permitted to hope for a general alliance which will avoid entanglements and clear the air of the world for common understandings and the maintenance of common rights.[10]

In reviewing the key elements of this story one must mention the role played by the League to Enforce Peace, a civil society organization with 300,000 members, which counted as supporters some of the leading figures in the American peace movement as well as academia and the business community.[11] We have come to think of nongovernmental organization as being essentially a late 20th century phenomenon, and partly a response to the inability of governments to address fundamental problems of concern to citizens everywhere. In this respect, by tapping into a deep yearning for peace by multitudes of people appalled by the killing and savagery of the Great War (over a four-and-a-half month period from July to November of 1916 well over a million British, French, and German soldiers perished in the bloodiest and most senseless Battle of the Somme), the League to Enforce Peace played an instrumental role in creating the conditions for the emergence of the League of Nations.

The League to Enforce Peace put forth four proposals. First, that the United States should create a League of Nations in which nonpolitical questions of international law should be submitted to a judicial tribunal. Second, members of the League should "jointly use their military force to prevent any one of their number from going to war" before submitting the question to the tribunal. Third, political questions should be submitted to a council of conciliation before members took up arms and went to war. And, last, that efforts be made through international conferences to codify international law, tapping into the precedents set by the tribunal. As envisaged, the League of Nations would force countries to go through a process of negotiation and peaceful conflict resolution before implementing the decision to go to war.

---

[10] Ambrosius, Lloyd E. 2002. "Wilson's League of Nations: Collective Security and National Independence," in *Wilsonianism: Woodrow Wilson and His Legacy in American Foreign Relations*, New York, Palgrave Macmillan, 51–64.

[11] The president of the League to Enforce Peace was former US President Taft, its chairman was Harvard University president Lawrence Lowell and President Wilson's Secretary of War, Newton Baker, was also an active member.

The aims of the League to Enforce Peace were modest from the outset and some historians have argued that these modest goals were an important factor in defining the ultimate scope and reach of the League of Nations when it was created; in particular, the League's emphasis on arbitration and the pledge to defend the territorial integrity and political independence of its members, a theme to which we return below in this section. In contrast with the UN Charter, which was drafted under the leadership of the US State Department, the drafting of the Covenant of the League of Nations began in mid-1917 and was carried out by an ad hoc committee that included President Wilson's trusted advisor Edward M. House and the famous journalist Walter Lippman.[12] Whereas the UN Charter was drafted at a time when the outcome of World War II was clear and was the result of deliberate negotiations involving representatives from the Soviet Union, China, and Great Britain as well as the United States, the Covenant was the result of a much more hurried process, under huge pressure from momentous political events playing out in the world at large, such as the Bolshevik revolution.

The final stages of the negotiation on the Covenant took place during the Paris Peace conference in 1919 bringing World War I to an end. But the Covenant discussions, which lasted a grand total of 10 days in February of that year were peripheral, with the main drafting by now being done by a multinational group of 19 commissioners which, on the American side, included President Wilson and Colonel House. Meetings took place mostly in the evenings, after the arduous sessions of the peace conference. In his accounting of the proceedings, Joseph Baratta notes that at one point, "House produced a plan that Wilson later rather hastily modified by eliminating the court of justice, casting aside at a stroke the object of years of internationalists' efforts, and adding military sanctions, in addition to economic sanctions, against states that resorted to war in defiance of an arbitral award or League recommendation."[13]

There are several Covenant articles worth highlighting including. Article 5 states "Except where otherwise expressly provided in this Covenant or by the terms of the present Treaty, decisions at any meeting of the Assembly or of the Council shall require the agreement of all the Members of the League represented at the meeting," effectively giving each member country veto power over any decisions of the Council, considerably weakening the League from its inception. Article 8 establishes a number of provisions for disarmament by stating that "members of the League recognise that the maintenance of peace requires the reduction of

---

[12] Lippman was one of the most eloquent advocates for strengthening the role of the United States in global affairs, far more ambitious than Wilson in his vision of a foreign policy that put the United States at the center of efforts to secure a lasting peace.

[13] Baratta, *The Politics of World Federation*, Vol. 1, p. 39.

national armaments to the lowest point consistent with national safety and the enforcement by common action of international obligations" and calls for plans for arms reductions by states to be reviewed by the Council at least every ten years. This was an important admission of the connection between war and the activities of the military industrial complex and must be regarded as a key innovation in the concept of international order, which the Covenant tried to bring into being.

Article 10, apparently the most important in Wilson's view and outlining a key new principle in international relations, states: "The Members of the League undertake to respect and preserve as against external aggression the territorial integrity and existing political independence of all Members of the League," an early attempt at formulating the elements of a system of collective security. President Wilson characterized Article 10 at a famous speech in Pueblo, Colorado, on September 25, 1919, as follows:

> Yet Article 10 strikes at the taproot of war. Article 10 is a statement that the very things that have always been sought in imperialistic wars are henceforth forgone by every ambitious nation in the world ... You will see that international law is revolutionized by putting morals into it. Article 10 says that no member of the league, and that includes all these nations that have done these things unjustly to China, shall impair the territorial integrity or the political independence of any other member of the league.

A number of the articles provided for peaceful settlement of disputes and arbitration and conciliation (e.g., Articles 12, 13, and 15). Wilson was an ardent believer in the notion that nations would not so easily go to war if they had an opportunity to consult and, in the presence of disinterested parties, outline the thrust of their grievances and dispassionately explore ways to resolve them in peaceful ways. At a speech in the University of Paris on December 21, 1918, he had said:

> My conception of the League of Nations is just this, that it shall operate as the organized moral force of men throughout the world, and that whenever or wherever wrong and aggression are planned or contemplated, this searching light of conscience will be turned upon them and men everywhere will ask, "What are the purposes that you hold in your heart against the fortunes of the world?" Just a little exposure will settle questions. If the Central powers had dared to discuss the purposes of this war for a single fortnight, it never would have happened, and if, as should be, they were forced to discuss it for a year, war would have been inconceivable.

In this respect, the "cooling off" periods embedded in the Covenant – lasting in some case up to nine months before war could be declared – were intended to avoid a repetition of the events of 1914, when the nations of Europe mindlessly stumbled upon the bloodiest and most violent war ever undertaken, largely because of the absence of mechanisms to consider the reasons for and the likely consequences of their actions.[14,15]

Nevertheless, the Covenant (Article 15) stated that failing arbitration/conciliation efforts the states reserved "to themselves the right to take such action as they shall consider necessary for the maintenance of right and justice," meaning states reserved for themselves the right to go to war to defend national interests. So, the League most definitely did not eliminate war as an instrument of national policy. It would not be until the Kellogg–Briand Pact of 1928 (also known as the General Treaty for Renunciation of War as an Instrument of National Policy) that a basis in international law would be established for the elimination of war between sovereign states (see Chapter 10). These provisions regrettably had little success in practice at the time, though the Pact was ultimately ratified by the vast majority of the nations of the world, including the major powers, and the provisions would find their way into the UN Charter in 1945.

The League, as conceived in the Covenant, had very weak enforcement mechanisms for violation of its articles and thus was not an effective mechanism to restrain some of its signatories from violating some of its key provisions, as happened with the Japanese invasion of Manchuria, Hitler's occupation of the Rhineland and Mussolini's incursions into Ethiopia. Unhappy with League resolutions, countries could simply opt to withdraw, as per Germany, Italy, Argentina, Brazil, and Chile, among several others.

Opposition to the League within the US Senate was, broadly, of two types. Senator William Borah had problems with the enforcement mechanisms embedded within the Covenant. In the absence of successful arbitration or conciliation, war would be inevitable and members would be called upon to adopt aggressive

[14] Wilson came back to this point often. In his speech in Pueblo, Colorado he asked: "Is the League an absolute guaranty against war?" No; I do not know any absolute guaranty against the errors of human judgment or the violence of human passion, but I tell you this: With a cooling space of nine months for human passion, not much of it will keep hot. I had a couple of friends who were in the habit of losing their tempers, and when they lost their tempers they were in the habit of using very unparliamentary language. Some of their friends induced them to make a promise that they never swear inside the town limits. When the impulse next came upon them, they took a streetcar to go out of town to swear, and by the time they got out of town they did not want to swear. They came back convinced that they were just what they were, a couple of unspeakable fools, and the habit of getting angry and of swearing suffered great inroads upon it by that experience. Now, illustrating the great by the small, that is true of the passions of nations. It is true of the passions of men however you combine them. Give them space to cool off. I ask you this: If this is not an absolute insurance against war, do you want no insurance at all? Do you want nothing? Do you want not only no probability that war will not recur, but the probability that it will recur? The arrangements of justice do not stand of themselves, my fellow citizens. The arrangements of this treaty are just, but they need the support of the combined power of the great nations of the world." https://umvod.wordpress.com/wilson-the-pueblo-speech-speech-text/

[15] See Clark, Christopher. 2012. *The Sleepwalkers: How Europe Went to War in 1914*, New York, HarperCollins.

measures against the offending party(ies), involving possible boycotts, blockades, and the like. For him the application of the principle of collective security would translate quickly into war, not peace, thereby negating the very purpose of the League. Additionally, it would undermine the United States' image as a peaceful, democratic nation firmly committed to liberty for all. He also thought that, in practice, the burden of actions under Article 10 would overwhelming fall on the United States, Great Britain, France, and Japan, its four more powerful members, something that would inevitably put the United States in the role of world police-man or, worse, dictator, damaging the "soul of democracy." While these objections were not without merit, his proposed solutions were perhaps somewhat impractical. He was of the view that a combination of world public opinion and voluntary compliance by countries with respect to the rulings of the League's Council would suffice.

Senator Henry Cabot Lodge, the majority leader and chairman of the Committee on Foreign Relations had a far more fundamental set of objections. He proposed 14 reservations to the Covenant, many of which could be characterized as "killer" in nature, essentially intended to strengthen US power within the League or exempt it from many of its obligations. The US would have no obligations under Article 10, such as the ability to command troops and ships without Congressional approval; it would reserve for itself the right to take sides in a future conflict between China and Japan, thereby rendering Council decisions in that event largely redundant; it would accept no monetary obligations to the League, meaning that the cost of running the League would have to be borne by other countries; it would make no meaningful commitments on disarmament under Article 8, reserving for itself the right for a military build-up in the event of threats to its security; it would accept no obligations to join other organizations created as a result of League initiatives, among others. Senator Lodge was willing to endorse the Covenant and accept US membership in the League subject to his 14 reservations; President Wilson took an uncompromising stance, unwilling to accept conditions which, in his view, would render the League weaker than it already was. Regrettably, the drafting and ratification of the Covenant turned quickly into a partisan political issue within the US, made worse by President Wilson suffering a massive stroke in October 1919. Weakened physically and in poor health, he was not able to take the leadership role that would have been necessary to ensure victory on the Senate floor. On March 19, 1920, the Covenant was voted down by a margin of seven votes.

One fascinating question that has been discussed and debated in the decades following the demise of the League and the onset of World War II is the counter-factual: would history have taken a difference course if the United States had been a member of the League? To take one of several potential examples, when the League in 1935 was considering sanctions against Italy for its actions in Ethiopia, one question that came up during Council deliberations was: Would the United States, one of the world's largest economies, honor such sanctions or would it otherwise seek to gain commercial advantage by undermining them? Would the presence of the United States in the League have prompted an early application of the Covenant's Article 19, in principle allowing revisions to the Treaty of Versailles which, it is commonly acknowledged, imposed onerous terms on Germany? Such revisions might have gone some way to allay German grievances which fueled the rise of Hitler and his revanchist aspirations.

We are of the view that it is unreasonable to claim that the League failed *because* the United States was not a party to it, rather than from its own structural weaknesses, such as the need for unanimity in its decisions through the power of the veto, or the absence of effective enforcement mechanisms for its decisions, to take two examples. The United States was very much part of the creation of the United Nations and adopted the UN Charter *without reservations*. Its participation, however, as noted earlier, has not prevented decades of war, civil strife, human rights violations, large-scale killing and pillaging, and the emergence of a host of other problems that threaten global security and prosperity. This is partly because, as we will argue later, many of the flaws embedded in the League's Covenant were transplanted to the UN Charter. A more likely interpretation is that the League, on the whole, failed because of the destructive power of lingering nationalism and militarism, deeply embedded in the national consciousness of its member countries; something that the League was too weak to reverse or cure on its own.[16] Indeed, it would take yet another global conflagration and countless deaths, destruction, and economic collapse before the European members of the League sobered up and saw fit to create the European Union, as a more effective antidote to centuries of misguided nationalism – humankind's primary "infantile disease," to paraphrase Albert Einstein.

The League's weaknesses notwithstanding, it did manage to generate considerable support and enthusiasm in various quarters. In Great Britain, membership in the League of Nations Union, yet another civil society organization created to promote the ideals of the League, reached 407,000 by 1931. Some of its leading members organized a Peace Ballot in 1934–1935 in which 11 million people voted for Great Britain to remain in the League and another 7 million people voted in support of the proposal that aggression should be confronted by international military force. These are extraordinary numbers, only a few percentage points lower, as a proportion of the population, of the share of people who voted during the Brexit referendum in June 2016; they reflect broad-based support for the vision of world order offered by its founders and partly embedded in the League's Covenant.

---

[16] A related question is whether the League was doomed to fail also because of colonialism and its related contradictions. The few League successes tended to involved conflicts between sovereign nations, where the parties had generally equal status before the Council, in a way that, for instance, Italy and Ethiopia did not.

A smaller but impressively influential organization established in Great Britain in 1932 was the New Commonwealth Society (NCS), with Winston Churchill as president. It had its own journal, many of its members were prolific writers and disseminators of internationalist ideals of cooperation. According to Baratta, the NCS urged the establishment within the League of a world equity tribunal "to settle political disputes beyond the capacity of the World Court and establishment of an international police force to enforce decisions of the League or equity tribunal."[17] Its proposals for the creation of an international police force found their way into Chapter VII of the UN Charter, whose Article 43.1 states: "All Members of the United Nations, in order to contribute to the maintenance of international peace and security, undertake to make available to the Security Council, on its call and in accordance with a special agreement or agreements, armed forces, assistance, and facilities, including rights of passage, necessary for the purpose of maintaining international peace and security."

The significance of the League – its ultimate failure aside – may well lie in the fact that it was a first attempt to pool national sovereignties together to deal with the problem of armed conflicts and aggression. It was a distinctive milestone, a tenuous first step in a long process intended to strengthen and improve the effectiveness of mechanisms of international cooperation.[18]

A FEDERAL UNION OF DEMOCRATIC STATES

The 1930s were a difficult period. The early part of the decade witnessed the full global ramifications of the Great Depression, including job losses without parallel in recent economic history. The rise of protectionism and economic nationalism exacerbated international tensions and, against the background of a struggling League, highlighted the weaknesses of existing arrangements to ensure peace and economic stability. Japanese aggression, the rise of German militarism under Hitler and the country's multiple territorial claims on other parts of Europe, the ineffectiveness of the League to deal with Mussolini's abuses in Ethiopia, all contributed to create a climate of pessimism in some circles but also led to a range of initiatives intended to deal in some way with these crises. Just as the League to Enforce Peace had played a central role in the United States in promoting the creation of the League of Nations, a similar civil society organization bearing the name of Federal

---

[17] Baratta, *The Politics of World Federation*, Vol. 1, p. 75.

[18] The absence of the United States notwithstanding, the League did have a few successes, particularly during the first decade following its creation. Three examples often cited are (1) a 1920 League arbitration of a dispute between Poland and Czechoslovakia over the coal-rich area of Teschen, which resulted in a stop to the fighting following a League decision for both countries to share the territory; (2) a Greek invasion of Bulgaria in 1925 which led to an appeal by Bulgaria to the League and a League request to Greece to withdraw its troops, which it accepted; (3) a territorial dispute between Finland and Sweden in 1921 over the Aaland Islands, with the League siding with Finland's claim and Swedish acceptance of the ruling.

Union was created in Great Britain in 1938 with the express purpose of promoting a federation of democratic states. Federal Union advocated a multistage process, to be initially focused on the unification of Europe, and followed by an Atlantic union that would include the United States and Canada and to evolve, in due course, into a world federal union.

One is impressed not only by the scope of its ambitions but also by the high caliber of the intellectuals and politicians it was able to attract as strong supporters, including Arnold Toynbee, Lionel Curtis, William Beveridge, Lionel Robbins, Clement Attlee (who would succeed Winston Churchill as Prime Minister in 1945) and Ernest Bevin, a future foreign minister. The organization grew quickly after Hitler's invasion of Poland in 1939 and played an instrumental role in Winston Churchill's offer to France to form a union with Great Britain in June 1940 (see below). According to Baratta, Federal Union's main argument was that:

> to secure the peace, humanity had to move beyond a league of sovereign states to a federation of states and peoples based on common *citizenship*, for the league principle was a proven failure; moreover, such a federation could not rely on mere sentiment against war but had to *organize power* superior to that of national states that so far had been established in history.[19]

WINSTON CHURCHILL'S PROPOSAL TO FRANCE TO CREATE AN ANGLO-FRENCH UNION

One of the more fascinating (and little known) episodes during the early part of World War II was the offer made by Winston Churchill to the French government to create an Anglo-French union. With the strong possibility of a German invasion of France on the horizon, French Prime Minister Paul Reynaud came to London to discuss avenues of collaboration to reinvigorate the war effort. A Supreme War Council had been set up in September of 1939 bringing together the top echelons of the British and French governments to coordinate and collaborate on various facets of the conduct of the war.

Similar machinery had been established for joint economic planning under the leadership of Jean Monnet as a result of which trade agreements were signed in early 1940 and an Anglo-French Industrial Council was formed to strengthen economic cooperation between both countries. Monnet saw these early efforts at economic and security cooperation between Great Britain and France as an opportunity to leverage greater cooperation on a Europe-wide basis. He was not alone in these efforts; he was joined by his deputy Rene Pleven (then working at the French embassy in London and who would later on become a French Prime Minister) and Sir Arthur Salter on the British side, both of whom felt that closer links between

---

[19] Baratta, *The Politics of World Federation*, Vol. 1, p. 75 (emphasis in original).

Great Britain and France would be an antidote to German militarism. Other officials on both sides saw these efforts aimed at fortifying Anglo-French links as extremely important from a strategic perspective; they would boost French morale at a time of mortal danger associated with Germany's early military successes, they could discourage Nazi designs on France, given the combined size of Anglo-French forces and economic power, and might also crystallize ideas for a new Europe and offer an alternative to several countries standing on the fence, at times lured by the power and ideologies of the Third Reich.

Reynaud and several of his ministers met in London as members of the Supreme War Council on March 28, 1940, and both governments issued a joint declaration pledging never to seek a separate armistice with the Germans[20] and their support for "an international order which will ensure the liberty of peoples, respect for law and the maintenance of peace in Europe."[21] The next several weeks witnessed the German invasion of the Netherlands and Belgium, the collapse of the Chamberlain government in Great Britain and the installation of Winston Churchill as the new prime minister heading a national coalition government, the evacuation of British (and some French and Belgian) troops from Dunkirk and Italy's declaration of war on France and Britain. A meeting of Churchill's War Cabinet on June 15 considered and approved a proposal drafted by Jean Monnet and others[22] to create a union of the United Kingdom and France. The Declaration of Union stated in part:

> The two Governments declare that France and Great Britain shall no longer be two nations, but one Franco-British Union. The Constitution of the Union will provide for joint organs of defence, foreign, financial and economic policies. Every citizen of France will enjoy immediately citizenship of Great Britain, every British subject will become a citizen of France…During the war there shall be a single War Cabinet, and all the forces of Britain and France, whether on land, sea or in the air, will be placed under its direction.[23]

De Gaulle (who was in London at the time) and Pleven read the French translation of the Declaration to Prime Minister Reynaud over the telephone who, in his memoirs would later say that "this sensational turn of events could only fill me

---

[20] The Declaration stated in part: "The Government of the French Republic and His Majesty's Government in the United Kingdom and Northern Ireland mutually undertake that during the present war they will neither negotiate nor conclude an armistice or treaty of peace except by mutual agreement."

[21] Shlaim, Avi. 1974. "Prelude to Downfall: The British Offer of Union to France, June 1940." *Journal of Contemporary History*, Vol. 9, No. 3, p. 32.

[22] Baratta, *The Politics of World Federation*, Vol. 1, p. 86, indicates that this group included Arthur Salter, Desmond Morton, Churchill's personal assistant, Rene Pleven, and Sir Robert Vansittart. It is also evident that their work drew from an earlier document prepared by Arnold Toynbee in February of 1940 titled: "Act for the Perpetual Association between the United Kingdom and France."

[23] The full text of The Declaration of Union is provided in Shlaim, "Prelude to Downfall," p. 50.

with joy since it was to give me a new argument for keeping France in the alliance."[24] In his own account of the war, Churchill admits that he was under no illusions about the difficulties of implementing the Union, but that he was encouraged by the enthusiasm of those around him (including of those on the French side who were representing Prime Minister Reynaud) and that "in this crisis we must not let ourselves be accused of lack of imagination."[25] Paul Reynaud took the Declaration to his Conseil Superieur but found himself in a minority. His Deputy Premier Camille Chautemps thought that the proposed union would turn France into a British province. Several members of the Council expected a British defeat within weeks and agreed with Marshall Petain who stated that the Union would, in practice, mean "fusion with a corpse." At least one member (Jean Ybarnegaray) thought that it would be better to be a Nazi province. Shlaim refers to statements made by de Gaulle and Charles Roux, the Secretary General of the French Foreign Ministry, which suggest "acute Anglophobe feelings" in the upper echelons of the French political establishment "in the wake of his country's military defeat."[26] By now, in any case, the focus of those around Reynaud was how to secure favorable terms in an armistice with Germany, something that was achieved several days later, signed by Hitler at Compiegne, in exactly the same railroad car used for the signing of Germany's surrender in 1918.

Historians are divided on the significance of the Declaration. Some have argued that the motivation for the Declaration was largely tactical;[27] it was a last-minute attempt to prop-up France's flagging determination to keep the fight and win the war rather than to quickly abdicate to Germany's military might. Shlaim persuasively argues that efforts to strengthen Anglo-French economic and security links at the outset of the war were genuine and enjoyed strong support on both sides but were initially seen in a medium-term context; part of a broader effort to redefine and deepen economic and political cooperation in Europe, using an Anglo-French Axis as the basis. They were not initially intended to result in a proposal envisaging "reciprocal rights of citizenship, a customs union, a single currency and the joint financing of post-war reconstruction, as well as a single War Cabinet and a unified supreme command."[28] Whereas Churchill had stated in no uncertain terms that Britain would never surrender and had galvanized public opinion in his country to support the war effort, Marshall Petain had made it clear to Churchill that turning Paris into rubble would not affect the ultimate outcome: French defeat at the hands of the superior German armies.[29]

---

[24] Shlaim, "Prelude to Downfall," p. 51
[25] Ibid, p. 49.
[26] Ibid, p. 57.
[27] Ibid.
[28] Ibid, p. 48.
[29] Ibid, p. 48.

Others, however, have taken a broader view, arguing that the Declaration was the main inspiration, after the war, for French initiatives to create the European Coal and Steel Community in 1951 and the more ambitious European Community in 1957, under the leadership of Jean Monnet (see Chapter 3). Churchill's private secretary Sir John Colville made it clear that although everyone understood the great difficulties to overcome to make the Union possible, there was also a view that "we had before us the bridge to a new world, the first elements of European or even World Federation."[30] The Declaration was significant in other ways as well. The consequences of French refusal were immediate and catastrophic. Prime Minister Reynaud, who only a few months before had committed his country not to sign a separate armistice with Germany resigned and Marshall Petain was installed at the head of a new government. Churchill's concerns that the French navy would be captured by the Nazis and used against Britain and others in the war effort led him to order its destruction which in turn led Petain to sever diplomatic relations with Great Britain, abolish the Constitution and set up an authoritarian regime with fascist overtones and at times keen to collaborate with the German occupiers.

Petain did not have a happy ending. He was tried for treason and sentenced to death in 1945; his sentence was commuted to life imprisonment. Paul Reynaud was arrested by the Petain administration, surrendered to German forces and was imprisoned until the end of the war but had a distinguished political career thereafter. In 1951 he wrote:

> I have continued to think that a Franco-British Union, as Churchill proposed it, could have served as the basis for the unification of all Europe. And I became more and more convinced, during my years of enforced reflection, that after the Allied victory, it would be necessary, in order to win the peace, to take up again the offer Churchill made to win the war.[31]

One can speculate as to what might have happened if Prime Minister Reynaud had, in fact, persuaded his Council to endorse the Declaration which, beyond the immediate objectives of creating a brand-new federal structure with common policies across the entire spectrum of government, was fundamentally intended to ensure France's presence in the alliance against Nazi Germany. One can surmise that France would have initially borne the brunt of German aggression and witnessed, as was feared, considerable destruction and fatalities and perhaps, in any case, ultimate military defeat. On the other hand, it is not clear what might have been the consequences for the prosecution of the war of stiff French military resistance and, one assumes in keeping with the contents of the Declaration, a much stronger level of British support and commitment to the survival of France, now a part of a Franco-British Union. Monnet admitted that "the whole business

---

[30] Baratta, *The Politics of World Federation*, Vol. 1, p. 91.
[31] Reynaud, Paul. 1951. *Unite or Perish: A Dynamic Program for a United Europe*, New York, Simon and Schuster, p. 6.

ended in failure, but think what it would have meant if the political offer of union had succeeded. There would have been no way of going back on it. The course of the war, the course of the world might have been different. We should have had the true beginnings of a Union of Europe."[32] Richard von Coudenhove-Kalergi made a persuasive case that the exiled governments of Poland, Czechoslovakia, Belgium, the Netherlands, Luxembourg and Norway "would certainly have acceded to an Anglo-French Union."[33]

How might the United States have reacted in the face of the destruction of France? Perhaps those members of the Council who did not support the Union were also aware that building up the institutions of a new federal structure in the middle of a war against a powerful aggressor, was a close to hopeless cause, difficult in any case under peacetime conditions but nearly impossible under the threat of German bombs and artillery. More important, whereas by 1940, as noted above, there was broad-based support in Great Britain for federal causes and other inter-nationalist initiatives – such as the 1934–1935 Peace Ballot – there were very few comparable experiences in France, where the notion of "common citizenship" might have appeared quaintly premature to most members of the public and the ruling elite. Federalist initiatives cannot flourish in a political vacuum; if citizens are to be asked to accept a vision of shared government and shared institutions, they need to be persuaded of the benefits and that these will outweigh the costs.

There is a final irony in the story of the Declaration of Union. After the war, France was very much a leader in the effort to secure a lasting basis for peace and prosperity through the creation of supranational institutions. The transformation of the European Community into the European Union in the 1990s would have been impossible without the strong partnership of Chancellor Kohl and President Mit-terrand. To this day, France remains largely committed to a vision of a stronger Europe and an ever-closer union as called for in the Treaty or Rome. Marine Le Pen's alternative vision for France within Europe – closed borders, protectionism, a rejection of ethnic and cultural diversity – was roundly defeated during the 2017 elections. It is Great Britain, a late entrant into the European Community in 1973, that remains much more conflicted about the vision implicit in a united Europe, as made abundantly clear during the past three years by the Brexit saga, not to say tragicomedy.

EARLY THINKING ON THE UNITED NATIONS

With the League in profound disrepair by the time Germany invaded Poland and with the entry of the United States into the war following the Japanese attacks on Pearl Harbor in December of 1941, efforts were set in motion for the creation of a

---

[32] Quoted in Shlaim, "Prelude to Downfall," p. 61.
[33] Shlaim, "Prelude to Downfall," p. 61.

new organization that might provide a more secure basis for peace and prosperity. The organization that emerged from these efforts at the San Francisco conference in 1945 was the United Nations, but the work program leading to this outcome had begun several years before and was the result of long and delicate negotiations.

Within three weeks of the United States entering the war, President Roosevelt set up an Advisory Committee on Post-War Foreign Policy under the direction of then Secretary of State Cordell Hull and Undersecretary Sumner Welles. The aim of the Committee and, in particular, its Permanent International Organization subcommittee, was to work on the design of an organization that would secure global peace and security while avoiding some of the weaknesses associated with the League of Nations. On January 1, 1942, the United States, Great Britain, the Soviet Union, and China plus 22 nations then involved in the war effort against the Axis powers set up an alliance in which members pledged to fight until victory, not to make a separate peace with the enemy, and to work for the establishment of a broad-based and effective system of international security as outlined in the August 14, 1941, Atlantic Charter. The name adopted for this alliance was the United Nations, suggested by President Roosevelt himself.[34] By 1945 it included 51 nation states as members. The establishment of the Committee – made up of senior State Department Officials, some leading academics and several civil society representatives – was no small act of imagination. In early 1942 the war effort was not going well for the United States and its allies; Japan had made major territorial gains in Asia and Germany had largely brought Europe, other than Great Britain, under its control and was intent on conquering Russia as well.

One of the Committee members has left an invaluable record of the proceedings from which it is possible to glean the evolving nature of the debate and thinking about the sort of organization that was to be created.[35] It is noteworthy that up to October 1943 much of the focus centered on the future establishment of some type of international entity founded on federalist principles, not unlike in conception to the model adopted by the United States during its Constitutional Convention in 1787. This would have implied the creation of a legislative body with substantial powers to enact laws that would be binding on member states. Because this legislature – even under a fairly narrow vision of the areas in which it would have

---

[34] This initiative is now referred to as the Declaration by United Nations; it was drafted at the White House on December 29, 1941, by President Roosevelt, Prime Minister Churchill, and aide Harry Hopkins. Short and to the point, it states: (1) Each Government pledges itself to employ its full resources, military or economic, against those members of the Tripartite Pact and its adherents with which such government is at war. (2) Each Government pledges itself to cooperate with the Governments signatory hereto and not to make a separate armistice or peace with the enemies. The foregoing declaration may be adhered to by other nations which are, or which may be, rendering material assistance and contributions in the struggle for victory over Hitlerism.

[35] According to Baratta, *The Politics of World Federation*, Vol. 1, p. 96, it was Harley A. Notter, author of Permanent International Organization Minutes 1, US National Archives.

jurisdiction – might be tempted to assume a broader mandate, there were discussions on a draft Bill of Rights to guarantee basic freedoms and protections for citizens, such as those identified by President Roosevelt in his 1941 State of the Union address, including freedom of speech and worship. Roosevelt pointed out that two other freedoms – from want and fear – implied the establishment of arrangements that would "secure to every nation a healthy peacetime life for its inhabitants – everywhere in the world" and also meant "a world-wide reduction of armaments to such a point and in such a thorough fashion that no nation will be in a position to commit an act of physical aggression against any neighbor – anywhere in the world." These concepts found their way into the final version of the UN Charter, which, in the case of freedom from want contains what is perhaps the first explicit commitment on the part of the international community to promote economic and social development.[36,37]

These broader, more ambitious visions for future international cooperation were confronted with a strong dose of reality in October 1943 at a conference in Moscow to discuss the vision of global order then being embedded in the draft UN Charter. The Soviet authorities were more concerned with the war effort. In particular, they were keen to obtain Allied support for the opening in 1944 of a second front, which might divert German military resources away from Russian territory. In reviewing the content of the discussions at this point one cannot avoid getting the sense that the Russians would not object to some form of collective security mechanism, provided it was based on great power (meaning the United States, Great Britain, the Soviet Union, and China) unanimity through the exercise of the veto. As long as the United Nations was founded on the principle of the sovereign prerogatives of certain privileged members (e.g. including the USSR) and was, thus, rendered into a largely harmless organization, the Soviets would not object.[38] For their part, within the Committee, there were growing concerns about avoiding the fate of the League

---

[36] Article 55a states: "the United Nations shall promote: a) higher standards of living, full employment, and conditions of economic and social progress and development."

[37] In his address President Roosevelt concluded that these four freedoms were "no vision of a distant millennium. It is a definite basis for a kind of world attainable in our own time and generation. That kind of world is the very antithesis of the so-called new order of tyranny which the dictators seek to create with the crash of a bomb," www.facinghistory.org/universal-declaration-human-rights/four-freedoms-speech.

[38] The Declaration of the Four Nations on General Security, dated October 30, states: "the governments of the United States of America, United Kingdom, the Soviet Union, and Nationalist China, in accordance with the declaration by the United Nations of January, 1942, and subsequent declarations, to continue hostilities against those Axis powers with which they respectively are at war until such powers have laid down their arms on the basis of unconditional surrender. They also recognize the necessity of establishing at the earliest practicable date a general international organization (the United Nations), based on the principle of the sovereign equality of all peace-loving states, and open to membership by all such states, large and small, for the maintenance of international peace and security," http://avalon.law.yale.edu/wwii/moscow.asp.

and ensuring that the UN Charter would ultimately secure Senate approval. Under-secretary Welles, a strong advocate of a more federalist vision for the United Nations, had left the State Department shortly before the Moscow conference and there was a shift in the focus of the discussion away from what might be *desirable* to what might be *politically feasible*, particularly in light of the presence of powerful strains of isolationist sentiments within the US Congress. In this respect, it is of some interest to highlight the content of Senate Resolution 192 dated October 14, 1943 – sponsored by Senator Thomas Connally of Texas – in which, by a vote of 85 to 5 "the Senate recognize the necessity of there being established at the earliest practicable date a general international organization, based on the principle of the sovereign equality of all peace-loving states."

Beyond these purely domestic political considerations, it is also clear that, against the background of an ongoing military conflict of global proportions, there would be scarce resources and time to promote, on a global scale, a vision of world order that might receive the endorsement of large segments of the public, to ensure an adequate degree of democratic legitimacy for the new body being created. Instead, to prevent creating an organization that would have the same flaws of the League of Nations, an effort was made to embed within the UN Charter clauses that would allow for the strengthening of mechanisms of international cooperation in the future, as circumstances evolved.

The UN Charter would give the veto power to the four great powers only, not to every member as had been the case with the League. The Charter would ultimately introduce strong language on the promotion of human rights, in a way that the League had not done. Once it was clear that the idea of a world legislature with binding powers on member states was premature, the proposal for attaching a Bill of Rights to the UN Charter was abandoned. Since the draft Bill of Rights had included the possibility of the right of petition by private citizens to the International Court of Justice, there was, apparently, some concern among the US authorities about what the implications of this might be against the background of widespread discrimination against African Americans and members of other minorities. The US civil rights movement would, after all, still be several years in the future.[39]

---

[39] It is generally agreed that the Dumbarton Oaks Proposals drawn up by the superpowers were a given, to be amended only by a substantial majority, and there was scant reference to human rights in the original draft proposals. According to UN specialist Ruth Russell (1958), the United States briefly considered including an international bill of rights, but, among other things, it could not find an acceptable way to enforce it in the international legal order and abandoned the idea. At the San Francisco conference, they suggested that the General Assembly study and recommend measures for promoting human rights, but the British and Soviet delegates balked at that proposal, the latter convinced that human rights and basic freedoms were not germane to the task of international security. Nevertheless, a range of delegations from other states in San Francisco suggested that the promotion of human rights should indeed be a tool to maintain international peace and security. Panama stated that the failure to resolve the pernicious economic, social and political consequences of World War I was a principal cause of the continued conflicts plaguing humanity to that date. Venezuela expressed the view that

The abandonment of the Bill of Rights notwithstanding, the final version of the Charter adopted in San Francisco did contain a number of provisions on human rights that were not insubstantial in their scope and character (see Chapter 11). The Preamble reaffirms "faith in fundamental human rights, in the dignity and worth of the human person, in the equal rights of men and women and of nations large and small." Article 55c endorses: "universal respect for, and observance of, human rights and fundamental freedoms for all without distinction as to race, sex, language, or religion." And Article 56 pledges all members "to take joint and separate action in co-operation with the Organisation for the achievement of the purposes set forth in Article 55." These undertakings would result in the adoption, in 1966, of the International Covenant on Civil and Political Rights and the International Covenant on Economic, Social and Cultural Rights, both of which significantly strengthened the legal underpinnings of the Charter's commitments to the defense of human rights.

A COMPROMISED UNITED NATIONS

Two other issues that were present in the deliberations around the design and scope of the United Nations concerned the voting mechanisms and the distribution of power within the organization. Some experts – most notably Grenville Clark – had argued for a system of weighted voting, with voting power linked to some objective criteria, such as population size, trade flows, levels of defense spending, and the like, to accommodate the huge disparities in the size and economic heft of the membership. This was not accepted and as is well known, in the end the General Assembly was established on the basis of the principle of one-country-one-vote. Weighted voting, however, was adopted at the Bretton Woods institutions – the International Monetary Fund and the International Bank for Reconstruction and Development – the two organizations that were created at the United Nations Monetary and Financial Conference held in July 1944 in Bretton Woods, New Hampshire.

since the principal object of the new World Organization would be to prevent rather than cure, addressing economic, social, cultural, educational, and health problems was paramount. Although other states suggested that the protection of individual human rights should be dealt with independently of issues of peace and security, with some expressing fears about "imposing" human rights and freedoms in individual countries or leading to expectations of the UN beyond what it could successfully accomplish, it was the Latin American nations that championed their inclusion in the Charter. Ultimately, the US delegation – urged on by the range of NGOs invited to the meeting – persuaded the British, Soviet and Chinese delegations to go along with the amendments that would include human rights promotion among the "purposes" of the UN and provide for a "Commission" to promote human rights under the Economic and Social Council (see Chapter 11).

Not unrelated to this, one concern with the establishment of a Security Council in which the five major powers (France was included as a permanent member of the Council in 1945) had veto power was the perception of the creation of an imperialistic organization in which the permanent members of the Council would, de facto, be running the world (see Chapter 7). To start with, the veto itself was perceived by many as undermining the democratic legitimacy of the organization; it was seen as a practice that could not be defended on the basis of any principle of just governance. Nonpermanent members of the Security Council accepted to be bound by the limitations of a two-thirds majority whereas the permanent members accepted no such constraints. More important – and with huge practical and political implications – some argued that a system was being created in which the organization would not be able to deal with problems and/or conflicts *between* the major powers or between a major power and a smaller country. Since, it was to be expected, many if not most major security problems in the future were likely to involve directly or indirectly one of the major powers (given their strategic importance, their economic size, their large geographic footprint in the case of the Soviet Union, China, the United States and, of course, the British Commonwealth) the United Nations, as conceived, would be largely useless to do what it was set out to do, namely,

> "To maintain international peace and security, and to that end: to take effective collective measures for the prevention and removal of threats to the peace, and for the suppression of acts of aggression or other breaches of the peace, and to bring about by peaceful means, and in conformity with the principles of justice and international law, adjustment or settlement of international disputes or situations which might lead to a breach of the peace." (Article 1.1)

The kinds of collective security interventions envisaged in Article 42 would inevitably be hamstrung by challenges of collective action and the national interests of those with permanent seats on the Security Council, as opposed to following an order based on international law and an impartial, principled approach to international intervention.

E.B. White, one of the most prolific contributors to *The New Yorker* magazine at the time, gave voice to these concerns thus:

> Sir Alexander Cadogan, head of the British group at the conference (Dumbarton Oaks), said that "the nations of the world should maintain, according to their capacities, sufficient forces available for joint action when necessary to prevent breaches of the peace." A good point. A good point but an old story. The peace of the world was breached when Fascism began to spread its crimes against society in the nineteen-twenties, but although there was at that time among the nations of the world plenty of force available to prevent the breach, there was no tendency toward joint action. Nor will there be any tendency toward joint action as long as the world is run on the principle of national sovereignty, by a system of agreements between

sovereign nations. There will never by any tendency toward joint action until it is too late. Therefore, the problem is not how to make force available for joint action but how to make world government available so that action won't have to be joint.[40]

These concerns were more than amply justified by the experience in the decades that followed the adoption of the UN Charter and the creation of the United Nations. In particular, the tens of millions of fatalities associated to more than 200 armed conflicts, with the predictable consequences for delayed economic and social development. As noted earlier, the Korean war in 1950 and Iraq's invasion of Kuwait in 1990 remain the sole examples of interventions supported by the collective security mechanisms put in place when the organization was created.

It is of some historical significance that during the deliberations in San Francisco (April to June 1945) leading to the adoption of the Charter, the Chinese representative, Dr. T.V. Soong, the foreign minister, stated on April 26: "We must not hesitate to delegate a part of our sovereignty to the new International Organization in the interests of collective security."[41] Several days later, on May 1, he made available to the press a statement in which he expressed his government's willingness to give up the unilateral veto in the Security Council provided the other veto-wielding countries did the same. He was not alone. Colombia joined Poland, Mexico, and eight other Latin American nations in expressing opposition to the veto. As a concession to Australia, which voiced similar concerns, the final version of the Charter included Article 109 allowing for the possibility that "a General Conference of the Members of the United Nations for the purpose of reviewing the present Charter may be held at a date and place to be fixed by a two-thirds vote of the members of the General Assembly and by a vote of any nine members of the Security Council." Such a conference has never been held.

A BROADER VISION FOR THE UNITED NATIONS

The above notwithstanding, there were strong strains of thought within the United States establishment arguing for a broader vision of world order that would go beyond an entrenched and regressive principle of national sovereignty called for by the Soviet Union and the likes of Senator Connally. Representative William Fulbright, for instance, had given a speech in New York in September of 1943 in which he hinted that rigid sovereignty may be largely illusory:

> The oft-repeated objection to any system of collective security, that we must never sacrifice our sovereignty, is, in my opinion, a very red herring. If sovereignty means anything, and resides anywhere, it means control over our own affairs and resides in the people ... They may delegate all, or any part of the power to manage their

---

[40] White, E.B. 1946. *The Wild Flag*, Boston, Houghton Mifflin, p. 26, published in *The New Yorker*, September 9, 1944.

[41] Quoted in China Institute of International Affairs, 1959. *China and the United Nations*, New York, Manhattan Publishing Group, p. 23; see also pp. 64, 139.

affairs to any agency they please. So far they have delegated part to their city government, part to the county, part to the State, and part to the Federal Govern-ment. Certainly it cannot be denied that twice within twenty-five years we have been forced, against our will, into wars which have seriously threatened our free existence. To this extent, the supreme control over our affairs, over our destiny, is at present imperfect. Therefore, if we can remedy this defect, by a delegation of limited power to an agency designed to prevent war, to establish law and order, in which we participate fully and equally with others, how can this be called a sacrifice, a giving up of anything?[42]

Grenville Clark, deeply disappointed with the outlines of what was being put together by the major powers during the Dumbarton Oaks conference, which he viewed as no more than an attempt to revive the League of Nations, and not particularly concerned about finding himself in a minority, proposed a set of general principles that should guide the establishment of any organization that would have the maintenance of peace and security as its principal mandate.[43] He argued that "to be *effective* in the maintenance of peace the 'general international organization' must have some *definite* and *substantial* powers to make decisions binding upon the member countries in matters of war and peace" (emphasis in the original). He thought that if member countries could not agree "upon well-defined powers of an effective nature that they are willing to yield, and upon the terms in respect of representation upon which these powers are to be granted, it seems clear that no world authority really adequate to maintain peace, will arise in our time."[44]

In respect of these powers Clark thought that a unicameral World Congress should be granted narrowly limited jurisdiction on matters pertaining to the main-tenance of peace and that these powers should be supplemented by the creation of a court with the "authority to make 'final and binding' adjudication of *all* unsettled disputes between member countries" (italics in the original). On all other issues concerning internal political, economic, and social aspects of governance, powers would be retained by individual member states. He proposed majority voting within this world legislature to guard against the "fatal defect" of the veto which the League had granted to its members. To ensure fairness, Clark put forward a detailed proposal for a system of weighted voting that, while giving effective control in the chamber to the four major powers (on account of their population and overall geopolitical importance),[45] it would still give a voice to all countries who wished to

---

[42] Quoted in Baratta, *The Politics of World Federation*, Vol. 1, p. 106.

[43] Clark, Grenville. 1944. "A New World Order: The American Lawyer's Role," *Indiana Law Journal*, July, pp. 289–300.

[44] Clark, "A New World Order," p. 292.

[45] The reason why in 1944 a population-weighted distribution of voting power would give effective control of the chamber to the four largest powers, was linked to the fact that the population of the British Commonwealth and Empire was 557 million and included not only the United Kingdom, but also India, Australia, New Zealand, Canada, and other territories, while the population of China at that time was 457 million. The addition of the United States and the

join; membership would be open to all since it was important for "the whole world to share fully and fairly in the maintenance of world order."[46] Clark added a sense of urgency to his proposals, aware of the unique opportunity provided by the war and the desire of the public to create a stable foundation for a permanent peace.

Clark followed this up with a full-page article in the October 15, 1944, edition of the *New York Times*, making a number of important additional points.[47] He observed that the proposed one-nation-one-vote principle then being discussed for the General Assembly was a not very carefully disguised attempt to make the Assembly wholly subordinate to the Security Council, to turn in fact the Assembly into a powerless body and to exclude it deliberately from discussions about war and aggression. Since the UN would be founded on the principle of "sovereign equality," giving each member in the Assembly an equal vote would satisfy the principle but would then end up sidelining the General Assembly, since it would not be acceptable for "Panama and Luxembourg (to) have an equal vote with the United States and the Soviet Union." Furthermore, the granting of the veto would mean that "any of the Big Five may, by its sole fiat, paralyze the whole world organization." The combination of a powerless Assembly and a Security Council hampered by the veto would "be a weak reed to support the peace of the world." He then proposed to give the Assembly adequate but narrowly defined powers to "matters directly and plainly concerned with the forestalling or suppression of aggression." The Security Council "would function under delegated powers from the Assembly and purely as its agent." Clark expressed concern that the drafting of the UN Charter might fall victim to the otherwise understandable "human tendency for the American participants to defend their handiwork" and argued that other countries should be allowed to join in in the deliberations leading to the final draft. Thinking about the future conference where the draft would be agreed and voted on he said that the big powers should take time to weigh in on all proposals and that country representatives to such a gathering should draw from a wider pool of talent, and not be limited to professional diplomats and military men. No doubt thinking about the Senate vote that, a quarter century earlier, had doomed United States participation in the League of Nations, he argued that the time had come for the United States to consider moving to a system where ratification of treaties would be determined by a majority vote in the US Congress. He regarded the requirement of a two-thirds majority in the Senate as "an anachronism which is not only unfair to ourselves but capable also of vast damage to the whole world." In his view, the treaty provision of

Soviet Union resulted in a total that was in excess of half of the world's population at that time, which was around 2.3 billion.

[46] Clark, "A New World Order," p. 298.

[47] This extraordinary document was published as a Letter to the Editor, occupying most of an entire page, under the heading: "Dumbarton Oaks Plans Held in Need of Modification. Viewed as Repeating Essential Errors of League of Nations and Offering No Assurance of International Security – Some Remedies Suggested." *The New York Times*, October 15, 1944.

the US Constitution "has already done deadly work in trimming down what might have come out of Dumbarton Oaks."

Clark would come back to the general principles outlined in "A New World Order" in *World Peace through World Law* in the late 1950s; he (and his co-author Louis Sohn) would focus instead on reforming the UN Charter that came out of the San Francisco conference. By the time Clark made some of these arguments in mid-1944, the consensus – at least among those participating in the Dumbarton Oaks conference that worked on the UN Charter during the period of August 21– October 9, 1944 – had moved on to a far more restrained vision of what would likely secure sufficient support from members. Those assembled at Dumbarton Oaks were simply not ready to contemplate the creation of an organization with binding enforcement powers over its member states, in which nationals would in some way become citizens of a larger global polity, in which a legislature would presumably have the authority to tax and promulgate other binding legislation, and in which an international security or police force would provide a measure of collective security. Cord Meyer, who was an important member of the US delegation to the San Francisco conference claims that the delegates at the conference had fairly narrow margins of freedom, not only because of the need to ensure US Senate ratification but also because the broad outlines of the United Nations had been agreed by Churchill, Roosevelt and Stalin during their meeting in Yalta in February of that year, where the post-war order was discussed and broadly agreed upon.[48]

While Clark may not have had official opinion behind him there were many others in the federalist movements who shared his concern that an essentially revived League based on the principle of sovereign equality and with a veto that would make the organization largely impotent to deal with crises, was all that we would have to show after the devastation of the war. The *New Yorker's* E.B. White put it very well when he wrote:

> The name of the new peace organization is to be the United Nations. It is a misnomer and will mislead the people. The name of the organization should be the League of Free and Independent Nations Pledged to Enforce Peace, or the Fifty Sovereign Nations of the World Solemnly Sworn to Prevent Each Other from Committing Aggression. These titles are clumsy, candid, and damning. They are exact, however. The phrase 'United Nations' is inexact, because it implies union, and there is no union suggested or contemplated in the world of Dumbarton Oaks. The nations of the world league will be united only as fifty marbles in a dish are united. Put your toe on the dish and the marbles will scatter, each to its own corner.[49]

---

[48] Meyer, Cord. 1945. "A Serviceman Looks at the Peace," *The Atlantic Monthly* Vol. 176, No. 3, September, pp. 43–48.

[49] White, E.B., *The Wild Flag*, p. 26, published in *The New Yorker*, October 21, 1944.

Cord Meyer's account in *The Atlantic Monthly* of what emerged from the San Francisco conference is of particular interest not only because of his role as a member of the US delegation but also because, as a wounded veteran of the war effort, perhaps more than most delegates, he was fully aware of the war's most immediate consequences. "It is the men in the front line who must kill and then discover on the still-warm body letters and pictures much like those they own themselves, the disturbing proof of a mutual humanity." Meyer thought that the fundamental problem in San Francisco was the unwillingness of the major powers to move to a world in which they might have to give up any of the attributes of sovereign power, in particular the freedom "from any interference by others in its internal affairs and equally free in its external affairs to make any decisions that it wishes."[50]

Given the large number of sovereign players, the growing degree of international interdependence and the increased destructive power of available weapons, such a system was not only unstable but would be characterized by chaos and anarchy. Peace, security, and prosperity within the United States were guaranteed by a law-based system in which powers of the states were circumscribed in some areas and subordinated to those of the federal government in others, and where there was an unshakable and legally based commitment to resolve conflicts in a peaceful way. At the international level, under the system created in San Francisco:

> any disagreement is a potential source of armed conflict, and each nation must rely, for the protection of its interests, on the amount of armed force it is able and willing to bring to bear in a given situation. We should frankly recognize this lawless condition as anarchy, where brute force is the price of survival. As long as it continues to exist, war is not only possible but inevitable ... . The cycle of increasingly destructive wars in which we are caught is the direct and inevitable result of the attempt to prolong the political system of absolute national independence under changing conditions that make it increasingly unworkable.[51]

Meyer was particularly harsh in his characterization of the veto power seized by the major powers for themselves. Among the consequences of the veto he noted that: (1) "a major power can violate every principle and purpose set forth in the Charter and yet remain a member of the Organization by the lawful use of the veto power expressly granted to it";[52] (2) amendments to the Charter required ratification by the five veto-wielding powers, a feature that gave them the power to permanently prevent any change or reform whatsoever; (3) if one of the Big Five was not a party to a dispute, it could "prevent even the investigation of the case by the Security Council." The veto power would also have consequences for the application of the provisions included in the Charter allowing the use of force in certain

---

[50] Meyer, *The Atlantic Monthly*, p. 44.
[51] Meyer, *The Atlantic Monthly*, pp. 44–45.
[52] Meyer, *The Atlantic Monthly*, p. 45.

circumstances. He cautioned against the "popular misconception" that the weaknesses embedded in the League of Nations Covenant in this area had somehow been addressed in the UN Charter. This was not the case. All that the Charter envisaged was an agreement by members to voluntarily make available to the Security Council a portion of their military forces when the Council saw fit to take military action. But the veto granted to the five major powers meant in practice that they would be exempt from such actions being taken against them or against any smaller state that they wished to protect.

He thought that such a system, exempting the major powers in its most fundamental provisions from the application of force in the interests of international peace and security, could not be characterized as being law-based in any meaningful sense of the word. Instead, it bordered "on hypocrisy or self-delusion" since the use of violence could be justified as police action only in a system in which the same rules applied to all participants in an even-handed way. He also noted the sharp limitations imposed on the International Court of Justice whose jurisdiction would be limited to "the interpretation of treaties, to fact-finding, and to the determination of reparations" but only in cases where both parties to the dispute agreed to give the court the ability to do so. Furthermore, the Charter made no provisions nor established a mechanism "through which the restless inhabitants of the colonial areas can find their way to political freedom."[53] Absent such machinery, the likely outcome would be bloody conflicts, a prediction fully borne out by events over the next several decades. In summary "the International Organization is, at present, as incapable of dealing with the probable causes of another war as a fire extinguisher is of quenching a forest fire."[54]

Meyer was sympathetic with the views voiced by New Zealand Prime Minister Fraser during the San Francisco conference who, speaking on behalf of smaller nations "upset the monotonous ritual of empty oratory and petty disagreement into which the Conference often subsided" by referring to the Charter as "a series of platitudes – and petrified platitudes at that."[55] Touching upon the same points raised by Clark the previous year on the watering down of the Charter to ensure US Senate approval, Meyer wrote that:

> the final price paid for Senate approval is an Organization that the United States can join and still retain intact every attribute of independence. The record of the hearings in the Senate Foreign Relations Committee are a tragi-comic commentary on what was achieved at San Francisco. To allay the fears of even the most unregenerate isolationist, every impotent inadequacy of the Charter was stressed as a positive assurance that in ratifying it we were committing ourselves to nothing.[56]

---

[53] Meyer, *The Atlantic Monthly*, p. 46.
[54] Meyer, *The Atlantic Monthly*, p. 47.
[55] Meyer, *The Atlantic Monthly*, p. 46.
[56] Meyer, *The Atlantic Monthly*, p. 47.

We have dwelt at length on the views of Clark and Meyer because they were both extremely well-connected observers of the process and the thinking that went into the design of the current UN Charter and associated UN institutions, and also because they were inordinately prescient in the identification of the consequences for international peace and security resulting from the weaknesses and flaws that were embedded in the organization, as the price for its creation.

Kissinger makes the argument that the transition from a world of alliances and balance of power practices to one of collective security was never expected to be an easy one. Part of the problem stems from the fact that alliances are concrete undertakings; countries make commitments in respect of particular interests which can be fulfilled. Collective security, on the other hand, "is a legal construct addressed to no specific contingency. It defines no particular obligations except joint action of some kind when the rules of peaceful international order are violated. In practice action must be negotiated from case to case."[57] He notes that in the post-UN Charter world there are only two cases of "successful" interventions based on the principle of collective security but that in both cases the UN endorsed intervention only after the United States had made it clear that in the absence of such endorsement it would act unilaterally; the United Nations thus merely ratified a decision already made unilaterally by the United States.[58] Such intervention was more an attempt at ex post control by the UN of the American intervention rather than the result of internal deliberations within the UN reflecting a moral commitment to the ideals of the UN Charter and the principles of justice embedded therein.

We do not share Kissinger's pessimism. The UN was and remains limited in its ability to take a leadership role in meaningfully addressing, for instance, Saddam Hussein's invasion of Kuwait in 1990 because it does not have an enforcement mechanism to give operational meaning to whatever moral outrage it may feel in the presence of grave violations of the Charter. With an International Peace Force at its disposal, the implementation of the principle of collective security would not be such an insurmountable undertaking. One cannot analyze such a principle in isolation of the circumstances in which the principle is being implemented or,

---

[57] Kissinger, *World Order*, p. 264.

[58] UN Security Council Resolution 83 adopted on June 27, 1950, found that North Korea's invasion of the Republic of Korea was a violation of the peace and demanded the withdrawal of North Korean forces and recommended that: "members of the United Nations furnish such assistance to the Republic of Korea as may be necessary to repel the armed attack and to restore international peace and security in the area." UN Security Council Resolution 678 was adopted on November 29, 1990, giving Iraq a January 15, 1991, deadline to withdraw its troops from Kuwait. The Security Council also gave the green light to states to use "all necessary means" to force Iraq out of Kuwait after the deadline. This Resolution provided the legal authorization for the Gulf War which followed, when Iraq failed to withdraw its troops by the deadline.

more to the point, not being implemented. We will come back to the issue of an International Peace Force in Chapter 8.

THE DRAFT OF A WORLD CONSTITUTION AND THE DUBLIN CONFERENCE

It is worthwhile to describe a fascinating initiative undertaken by the Committee to Frame a World Constitution, a group of (mainly) University of Chicago intellectuals who, dissatisfied with the UN Charter and against the background of the destruction in Hiroshima and Nagasaki, began meeting from November 1945 to July 1947 to discuss what a Federal Republic of the World might look like, whether following a global conflagration or in the absence of one. Its Preamble is a definite improvement over the UN Charter's. It says:

> The people of the earth having agreed that the advancement of man in spiritual excellence and physical welfare is the common goal of mankind; that universal peace is the prerequisite for the pursuit of that goal; that justice in turn is the prerequisite of peace, and peace and justice stand or fall together; that iniquity and war inseparably spring from the competitive anarchy of the national states; that therefore the age of nations must end, and the era of humanity begin; the governments of the nations have decided to order their separate sovereignties in one government of justice, to which they surrender their arms; and to establish, as they do establish, this Constitution as the Covenant and fundamental law of the Federal Republic of the World.

A section on declaration of duties and rights states that:

> it shall be the right of everyone everywhere to claim and maintain for himself and his fellowmen: release from the bondage of poverty and from the servitude and exploitation of labor, with rewards and security according to merit and needs;[59] freedom of peaceful assembly and of association, in any creed or party or craft, within the pluralistic unity and purpose of the World Republic; protection of individuals and groups against subjugation and tyrannical rule, racial or national, doctrinal or cultural, with safeguards for the self-determination of minorities and dissenters.

Perhaps the most interesting part of the World Constitution is the identification of powers that are attributed to this new world government. As will be remembered, Clark and Sohn's own revisions to the UN Charter were intended to strike a balance between the need to have appropriate powers, to ensure that the UN would be able to actually deliver peace and security on the one hand, and the need to retain

---

[59] It is interesting to speculate whether one implication of this right would be the right to a universal basic income, that would pull every global citizen above a suitably defined world poverty line (see Chapter 14).

responsibilities at the national level in those areas where it made sense to preserve a large measure of national control, to safeguard diversity and local preferences, on the other. The framers of the World Constitution endeavored to achieve the same middle ground sought by Clark and Sohn though, in the end, the granting of powers given to the world government is definitely more ambitious. In particular, jurisdiction is mainly extended to: the maintenance of peace and the enactment and promulgation of laws to that effect binding upon member states and individuals; the judgment and settlement of international disputes and the prohibition of interstate violence; the supervision and final adjudication on border disputes between member states or on the creation of new states; the administration of territories not yet ready for political independence; the organization and management of the federal armed forces; arms control, including the establishment of limitations on national armies; the establishment of whatever agencies may be necessary to promote economic and human development; the collecting of taxes and the preparation of a federal budget; the creation of a world central bank to issue money and regulate the financial sector;[60] the regulation of international trade; and the supervision and formulation of the legal basis for the movement of peoples across international borders.

The work of the Committee is significant not because it was taken up for debate at the higher echelons of government in the United States and other among major powers – it was not. By the end of the San Francisco conference, President Roosevelt, Winston Churchill, Joseph Stalin and many of their allies were largely satisfied with what had been brought into being, namely a weak-by-design organization that would not threaten in any significant way the unfettered sovereignty of its founding members. It was significant partly because of the intellectual heft and credibility of many of the Committee's members, but mainly because the hundreds of hours of open debate and consultation that took place over a period of 20 months forced these distinguished gentlemen to grapple with the whole range of issues and principles that underpin the creation of new mechanisms of global governance.[61]

The Committee was part of a much larger group of intellectuals mainly in the United States and Europe, who felt strongly that with the arrival of nuclear weapons, the context for warfare had changed in fundamental ways. In his contribution to the first appeal of the Emergency Committee of the Atomic Scientists, Albert Einstein

---

[60] Article 43 of the 47-article Constitution calls for the adoption of a universal auxiliary language, a federal currency and a universal system of measures.

[61] The Committee included Robert M. Hutchens, the Chancellor of the University of Chicago and Chairman of the Board of Editors of the Encyclopedia Britannica; Mortimer J. Adler, Professor of the Philosophy of Law and Associate Editor of the Great Books of the Western World; Stringfellow Barr, former President of St. John's College; Wilber G. Katz, Dean of the Law School, University of Chicago; Robert Redfield, Professor and Chairman of the Department of Anthropology, University of Chicago; G.A. Borgese, Professor of Humanities, University of Chicago, and others.

spoke for many when he said: "the unleashed power of the atom has changed everything save our modes of thinking, and thus we drift toward unparalleled catastrophe." In an editorial titled "Modern Man is Obsolete" in the *Saturday Review of Literature*, Norman Cousins, the editor, had lamented that "on August 6, 1945 a parachute containing a small object floated to earth over Japan [and] marked the violent death of one stage in man's history and the beginning of another" with humanity discovering the means for its destruction but not the means for its preservation and survival. Cousins was part of the 48 luminaries who participated in the Dublin conference organized by Grenville Clark in October 1945 "to explore how best to remedy the weaknesses of the United Nations Organization and to seek agreement upon and to formulate definite amendments to the Charter or other proposals to remedy these weaknesses."[62] Indeed, it is not unfair to say that the Dublin conference, which preceded the work of the Committee, was the main inspiration for the latter's work.

In her excellent biography of Grenville Clark, Nancy Peterson Hill notes that the Dublin conference was hosted by Clark and US Supreme Court Justice Owen Roberts and attracted a constellation of leading educators, attorneys, journalists and business leaders including Stringfellow Barr, Norman Cousins, Alan Cranston (a future US Senator from California), Cord Meyer (who had been present at the San Francisco conference as part of the US delegation and was later to be the first president of the United World Federalists), Kingsman Brewster (a future president of Yale University), and Clarence Streit (author of *Union Now – A Proposal for a Federal Union of the Leading Democracies*, an international best-seller published on the eve of World War II).[63]

Over a period of five days this eminent group met at the Dublin Inn in New Hampshire and consulted on how best to respond to the perceived inadequacies of the United Nations. An early point of contention at the conference was whether to advocate for, as had been done so compellingly by Clarence Streit, a union of the world's 15 leading democracies that would develop joint institutions and policies based on a common citizenship, and thus create a huge economic and military power, far exceeding that of the Axis powers, or to advocate a world order that would be all-inclusive and bring in the Soviet Union and other nondemocratic regimes. Clark was on the inclusive camp and, not without difficulty, he spearheaded the majority in this direction. The Declaration issued by the conference is of great historical interest, not only because it would find echo two years later in the work of the Committee that offered the draft World Constitution, but also because it would

---

[62] Quoted by Baratta, *The Politics of World Federation*, Vol. 1, from the invitation issued by Clark to the participants, p. 146.

[63] Peterson Hill, Nancy. 2014. *A Very Private Public Citizen – The Life of Grenville Clark*, Columbia, University of Missouri Press, MO.

establish an intellectual framework for the proposals made by Clark and Sohn in 1958 in *World Peace through World Law*.[64]

In its eight resolutions the Declaration of the 1945 Dublin Conference states:

1. That the implications of the atomic bomb are appalling; that upon the basis of evidence before this conference there is no presently known adequate defense against the bomb and that there is no time to lose in creating effective international institutions to prevent war by exclusive control of the bomb and other major weapons.
2. That the United Nations Charter, despite the hopes millions of people placed in it, is inadequate and behind the times as a means to promote peace and world order.
3. That in place of the present United Nations organization there must be substituted a World Federal Government with limited but definite and adequate powers to prevent war, including power to control the atomic bomb and other major weapons and to maintain world inspection and police force.
4. That a principal instrument of the World Federal Government must be a World Legislative Assembly, whose members shall be chosen on the principle of weighted representation, taking account of natural and industrial resources and other relevant factors as well as population.
5. That the World Federal Government should be responsible to the World Legislative Assembly.
6. That the Legislative Assembly should be empowered to enact laws within the scope of the limited powers conferred upon the World Federal Government, to establish adequate tribunals and to provide means to enforce the judgments of such tribunals.
7. That in order to make certain the constitutional capacity of the United States to join such a World Federal Government steps should be taken promptly to obtain a Constitutional Amendment definitely permitting such action.
8. That the American people should urge their government to promote the formation of the World Federal Government, after consultation with the

---

[64] Upon receiving the Grenville Clark Prize in 1981, George Kennan, America's foremost diplomat and historian, had this to say about *World Peace through World Law*: "To many of us, these ideas [of *World Peace through World Law* for a program of universal disarmament and for a system of world law to replace the chaotic and dangerous institution of unlimited national sovereignty] looked, at the time (1958), impractical, if not naïve. Today... the logic of them is more compelling. It is still too early, I fear, for their realization on a universal basis; but efforts to achieve the limitation of sovereignty in favor of a system of international law on a regional basis are another thing; and when men begin to come seriously to grips with this possibility, it is to the carefully thought out and profoundly humane ideas of Grenville Clark and Louis Sohn that they will turn for inspiration and guidance" (quoted in Baratta, *The Politics of World Federation*, Vol. 1, p. 24).

other members of the United Nations, either by proposing drastic amendments of the present United Nations Charter or by calling a new world Constitutional Convention.

As with the work of the Committee two years later, the Dublin Declaration had no major immediate effect on public opinion, with many seeing it as an act of disloyalty against the background of the recent founding of the United Nations. Others were either turned off or intimidated by its call for the creation of a world government, with the associated images of an Orwellian superstate controlling every aspect of planetary life, choosing to ignore the Declaration's clear statement that laws would be enacted within the scope of the limited powers conferred upon the government. The Declaration is significant because it was prescient in its anticipation of the problems which an ineffective United Nations would bring about over the ensuing decades. With the onset of the Cold War the world entered into an arms race and nuclear weapons continue to threaten humankind's future, except that we now have over 9,000 nuclear warheads in the hands of nine nuclear powers (and many others with aspirations to join the club), with enough destructive power to make the world uninhabitable. The United Nations was singularly ineffective in ensuring peace and security for its members and a vast range of other global problems emerged due to the absence of mechanisms for meaningful international cooperation. Were Clark alive today (two minutes before midnight, in the view of the Bulletin of the Atomic Scientists' Doomsday Clock) and were he to summon to Dublin some of the world's leading thinkers to explore solutions to our current global challenges, he might well wish to get started where he and his colleagues left off on October 16, 1945, the day the Declaration was issued.

So, the Committee to Frame a World Constitution's deliberations were part of a much larger effort taking place in various locations and led by various people, across both sides of the Atlantic. What was exceptional about it was its systematic character and the huge time commitment made to the project by its members. This is what was done in Philadelphia from May to September in 1787 during the Constitutional Convention that gave birth to the United States of America and one can imagine a similar future gathering aimed at confronting the growing recognition that our present order is lamentably defective and will need to be reformed to address our widening governance gap.

3

European Integration: Building Supranational Institutions

There is a remedy which . . . would in a few years make all Europe . . . free and . . . happy. It is to re-create the European family, or as much of it as we can, and to provide it with a structure under which it can dwell in peace, in safety and in freedom. We must build a kind of United States of Europe. In this way only will hundreds of millions of toilers be able to regain the simple joys and hopes which make life worth living. The process is simple. All that is needed is the resolve of hundreds of millions of men and women to do right instead of wrong and to gain as their reward blessing instead of cursing.

Our constant aim must be to build and fortify the United Nations Organisation. Under and within that world concept we must recreate the European family in a regional structure called, it may be, the United States of Europe, and the first practical step will be to form a Council of Europe. If at first all the States of Europe are not willing or able to join a union we must nevertheless proceed to assemble and combine those who will and who can. The salvation of the common people of every race and every land from war and servitude must be established on solid foundations, and must be created by the readiness of all men and women to die rather than to submit to tyranny.[1]

Winston Churchill

As moving beyond a UN system founded on traditional concepts of national sovereignty to a system with significantly strengthened supranational institutions is such a challenge, it is worth looking in some detail at the best recent example of such a process in the creation of the institutions of the European Union. While the nations of Europe may share many characteristics because of their proximity and historical, religious and cultural heritage, they also speak diverse languages, used and use different currencies, and had a long history of conflict and war to overcome.

---

[1] Winston Churchill, speech delivered at the University of Zurich, September 19, 1946. https://rm.coe.int/16806981f3; see also: https://europa.eu/european-union/sites/europaeu/files/docs/body/winston_churchill_en.pdf.

The lessons from the process of European integration can serve as one useful model for the greater challenges of building an enhanced institutional architecture at the global level.

It is generally accepted that World War II, with all the terrible destruction and economic upheavals it unleashed, provided the initial impetus to the European nations' desire for greater economic cooperation. Jean Monnet, the father of the European Community, once said that:

> Over the centuries, one after another each of the principal nations of Europe tried to dominate the others. Each believed in its own superiority, each acted for a time in the illusion that superiority could be affirmed and maintained by force. Each in turn was defeated and ended the conflict weaker than before. Attempts to escape this vicious circle by sole reliance on a balance of power failed repeatedly – because they were based on force and unrestricted national sovereignty. For national sovereignty to be effective, in an expanding world, it needs to be transferred to larger spheres, where it can be merged with the sovereignty of others who are subject to the same pressures. In this process, no one loses; on the contrary, all gain new strength.[2]

As one studies early attempts at various forms of economic cooperation in Europe, it becomes clear that the ultimate and most important goals were always political stability and unity. For example, the 1951 Treaty, signed by six governments, that created the European Coal and Steel Community (ECSC) set out "to substitute for age-old rivalries the merging of their essential interests; to create, by establishing an economic community, the basis for a broader and deeper community among peoples long divided by bloody conflicts, and lay the foundations for institutions which will give directions to a destiny henceforward shared."[3] The establishment of the ECSC was not seen as an end in itself but, rather, as a first step in a lengthy process that had the potential to lead toward greater economic and political integration. At about the time that the ECSC Treaty was signed, for example, France proposed the creation of a European defense community to bring the armed forces of Europe under the control of a federal authority. As this would have entailed the existence of a common foreign policy, a proposal was considered by the members to create a new community with powers in the areas of foreign affairs, defense, economic and social integration, and human rights. But the ensuing debate showed that there were significant differences among member states in the degree of

---

[2] Jean Monnet, quoted in Fontaine, Pascal, 1988. "Jean Monnet: A Grand Design for Europe," *Periodical 5*, Luxembourg: Office for Official Publications of the European Communities, pp. 30–31.

[3] *Treaties Establishing the European Communities*, Luxembourg, Office for Official Publications of the European Communities, 1987, pp. 23–32. The treaty establishing the European Coal and Steel Community was signed on April 18, 1951, by Belgium, France, West Germany, Italy, Luxembourg, and the Netherlands.

commitment to the principle of integration and in the extent to which each was willing to transfer authority in specific areas. The failure to establish a viable European defense community, however, convinced the ECSC countries that European integration would have to proceed with less ambitious objectives. To this end the foreign ministers of the ECSC countries appointed a committee – under the chairmanship of Paul-Henri Spaak, the Belgian foreign minister – to look into the issue of further integration. In mid-1956, the committee's proposals were approved and intergovernmental negotiations set in motion with the aim of establishing the European Atomic Energy Commission (EAEC) and the European Economic Community (EEC). The treaties of Rome establishing these two institutions were signed by the six founding members (Belgium, France, Italy, Luxembourg, the Netherlands, and West Germany) on March 25, 1957; together with the earlier ECSC Treaty they formed at the time the constitution of the European Communities.

Following the successful economic opening up of the late 1950s and early 1960s, which had greatly expanded European trade, by the early 1980s the prevailing feeling in Europe was that the enthusiasm had tapered off for fulfilling the objectives of the Treaty of Rome that had launched the EEC – which called for the creation of a common market, free of trade barriers, in which goods, services, labor, and capital would move without hindrance across national boundaries. Instead, Europe found itself in the midst of economic stagnation, witnessing the recovery of the American and Japanese economies, worried about the emergence of the newly industrialized countries of East Asia, and increasingly aware that the so-called Common Market was perhaps not that "common." While existing tariffs had been removed, they were sometimes replaced by hidden barriers: Germans would not allow imports of beer from other countries for "health reasons"; Italians would not allow imports of pasta because these were not done with the "right" kind of flour. The impetus for attempts at reinvigorating the process of economic integration during the second half of the 1980s, especially in the context of the now famous Europe 1992 program (see below), did not come from fears of renewed armed conflict. Rather, in an interesting innovation quite unlike anything we have seen in the history of the United Nations, it came from businesses and from entrepreneurs who realized that Europe could not be competitive with the United States, Japan and the newly industrialized countries if it did not put an end to economic divisions.

The fear of being left behind economically is what galvanized the European Community into action. The strategy eventually adopted by European leaders consisted of three main components. First, they would identify a comprehensive list of barriers that needed to be eliminated to create a wholly unified, efficiently integrated European market; in the end the list came to include some 300 items. Second, they would lay out a clear timetable to be followed to get those measures (or "directives" as they were called in European Community jargon) adopted by the end of 1992. Third, they would amend the Treaty of Rome to make it possible for the

300 directives to be adopted by "qualified majority voting" among ministers rather than by unanimity; this was the heart of the so-called Single European Act.[4]

Given the desire to act to stem further decline, why was this particular set of proposals appealing to European Community members? One can point to at least three factors. First, "Europe 1992" (as the program was eventually called) was perceived as a practical goal with clearly defined objectives and a magic date attached at the end as a powerful symbol. Second, an absence of priorities (which would favor one country's interests over another's) and an emphasis on practical ends was thought to be an advantage. Rather than focus, for example, on the political consequences of a common immigration policy, it was decided that it would be desirable to have a community with "no security controls at frontiers"; the two are equivalent but the latter was more politically palatable. Third, Europe 1992 was also perceived as a massive process of deregulation; the mood in Europe was ripe for this, given the increasing emphasis on market-oriented economic policies and the removal of rigidities and economic distortions. Many consider that if Monnet had been alive he would have approved of the entire project as being in harmony with his own thinking about economic and social progress. He once noted that:

> There will be no peace in Europe if states are reconstructed on the basis of national sovereignty, with all that that implies in terms of prestige politics and economic protectionism. The nations of Europe are too circumscribed to give their people the prosperity made possible and hence necessary by modern conditions. Prosperity and vital social progress will remain elusive until the nations of Europe form a federation or a "European entity" which will forge them into a single economic unit.[5]

Monnet may have been more of a diplomat than an academic economist, but it is evident that he instinctively understood the importance of creating a large unified economic space – a key driving force in the rise of the United States as a global economic power – for economic efficiency and prosperity.

MUTUAL RECOGNITION

A central feature of the Single European Act, eventually ratified by European parliaments in 1987, was the incorporation of a novel and singularly important

---

[4] "Qualified majority voting" refers to a voting system in which each country's voting power roughly reflects its economic size. The decision to eliminate a particular barrier could go forward if there were support for it from enough countries to constitute a majority in terms of the voting power, even if this meant, for example, that only five out of the twelve countries supported a particular decision. At the time that the Single European Act was ratified there were a total of 76 council votes distributed as follows: Britain, France, Italy, and West Germany – ten votes each; Spain – eight votes; Belgium, Greece, Holland, and Portugal – five votes each; Ireland and Denmark – three votes each; and Luxembourg – two votes.

[5] Monnet, quoted in Fontaine, *Jean Monnet*, pp. 20–21.

concept: *mutual recognition.* Throughout much of the 1970s the road to a common market was thought to lie in "harmonization." The European Community would pass norms on such things as taxes, banking licenses, insurance, public health standards, professional qualifications, and so on. These would need to be approved *unanimously* by the member states; then the barrier in question would be removed. Understandably, the process was extremely slow and frustrating, with community interests often sacrificed to national interests, and the principle of unanimity often abused. But in 1979 the European Court of Justice, one of the founding institutions of the Community, examined a case and established an important precedent.

The case involved a then-West German company that wanted to import a French liqueur but found it could not do so because the liqueur's alcohol content was lower than that required by German law. This resulted in a lawsuit, and the European Court of Justice eventually decided that West Germany was discriminating against foreign competitors and that it could not block the import of a product sold in France unless it could prove that the import should be banned on health, consumer protection, or similar grounds. This, of course, West Germany was unable to do.

The case turned out to have vast implications; it became the most effective weapon in demolishing previously hidden barriers to economic change. As a result of the gradual application of the principle of mutual recognition, which this case established, commercial banks in one country could establish themselves in all countries; insurance policies could be sold across borders; and a Spanish physician could go to Germany and claim recognition for his or her professional credentials, to name but a few examples.

BORDER CONTROLS

The entire Europe 1992 program was initially predicated on the notion of a Europe without frontiers, given public perceptions of these as powerful symbols of division separating sovereign states. The issue has several aspects. First, there was the aspect of customs posts themselves and their impact on trade flows. By the mid-1980s, the direct annual cost to firms of customs formalities for intra-European Community trade was thought to be in the tens of billions US dollars. There was, however, more to the elimination of customs controls than finding jobs for more than 50,000 customs officials who would no longer be needed in a frontier-free Europe. Customs posts have much to do with taxes: they protect a country's indirect taxes from relative tax advantages available in other countries; and, they allow governments to collect the value added tax (VAT) that is due to them. A sudden elimination of customs controls would result in large diversions of tax revenue as businesses and consumers made purchases across state borders to benefit from sometimes sharply different VAT rates. It had been established, for example, that in the United States sales tax differentials of up to 5 percentage points were possible between contiguous states before incentives were created for large cross-border purchases. In this area the

European Community Commission decided to work for greater tax harmonization. The idea was to narrow substantially differences in tax rates.[6]

But a Europe without frontiers also meant the elimination of passport controls, which in turn had implications for gun control, immigration laws, visas for non-European Community residents, and so on. The difficulties were numerous. Some countries had strict gun controls; others less so. Denmark has passport-free arrangements with Scandinavian countries; hence an airplane arriving in Madrid from Copenhagen, from the perspective of a Spanish immigration official, could have as many Norwegian as Danish citizens, thus requiring some degree of monitoring and control, since Norway is not a member.

Notwithstanding the technical difficulties, considerable progress was made once the Europe 1992 program was launched. Border controls were significantly streamlined in the late 1980s with the introduction of a Single Administration Document (SAD) that replaced more than 30 documents required by trucks crossing European Community frontiers. On January 1, 1993, the SAD itself was eliminated and replaced by a system that shifted tax control away from the borders to the producing firm. This was facilitated by a Council of Ministers' decision in 1991 significantly narrowing the range of variation for VAT rates. From the outset there was universal consensus that it would be extremely important for the European Community to succeed in this area. It would be difficult, indeed, to claim victory for the goal of a Europe without frontiers in the presence of continued border controls. One of the authors was working at that time as an economist in the Southern European division of the International Monetary Fund and remembers a highly symbolic meeting between the Prime Ministers of Spain and Portugal, Felipe Gonzalez and Anibal Cavaco Silva, at the Spanish–Portuguese border, to remove and permanently erase any physical indication of the existence of a border between both countries. An unthinkable gesture when both countries joined the United Nations in 1955; a highly popular move in the Europe that was emerging by the second half of the 1980s.

The single-market program involved many other elements and projects, dealing with such issues as the freedom of individuals and enterprises to move money across borders, including the right to open bank accounts in any other European Community member states; the right of individuals and enterprises to sell financial services across borders; the opening of public procurement to previously exempt sectors, and, more importantly, to firms in other member countries; measurements and quality control standards (e.g., so that light bulbs made in any European country

---

[6] For a few goods – cigarettes, alcoholic beverages, fuels – the issue is considerably more complicated. A liter of pure alcohol in Britain carried about US$30 in tax; in Greece the tax was about US$0.70. "Harmonization" was thus complicated by public health concerns; Britain's concerns were quite legitimate, as there was ample evidence supporting the thesis that lowering the price of alcoholic beverages had an immediate adverse impact on alcohol-related problems, including traffic fatalities, incidence of cirrhosis mortality, and so on.

could be used all over Europe, computers made compatible, etc.); air and road transport coordination, eliminating a number of existing restrictions; and so on.

A HISTORICAL PERSPECTIVE

The European Union's first 60 years may best be characterized as a series of achievements tempered by setbacks and innovations in the wake of stagnation. The member states' commitment to integration and increased cooperation has coexisted with a reluctance, stemming from a desire to safeguard national interests or identity, to transfer aspects of governmental authority to European Union institutions. The extent and the speed of progress has thus been largely determined by the relative strength of these two forces. Overly ambitious initiatives – like some that preceded the creation of the European Community – have been discouraged, and ways have been found to keep the pace of change attuned to domestic political realities. The unanimity rule adopted in 1966, which effectively gave members veto power over Community decisions on the grounds that they might wish to defend vital interests, is a good example of the latter force gaining the upper hand. In time it led to segmentation in the decision-making process, weakening the chances for consistency between different policies, and the ability to implement worthwhile pan-European policy goals generally.

In spite of the setbacks, the last several decades have been significant progress in a number of key areas. The European Monetary System succeeded at first in creating stability in exchange rates through a greater coordination of financial policies, and led subsequently to the creation of a monetary union, the establishment of the European Central Bank and the launch of the euro.[7] While the evolution of this institution has not been trouble free, with the system coming under heavy strains in the aftermath of the global financial crisis in 2008–2009, it has gained new members (19 as of early 2019) and practical experiences to date have resulted in a number of initiatives to strengthen its institutional underpinnings. One of the most significant developments in the history of the EU – and one that has had a profound influence upon the evolution of the Union – is the unanimous ratification in 1987 by the member states of the Single European Act, an amendment of the 1957 Treaty of Rome. In addition to providing for the completion of the single market by restricting the rights of members to veto decisions in many key areas, particularly those pertaining to the elimination of barriers to the free flow of goods, services, labor, and capital, the Single European Act provided for a significant streamlining of the decision-making process. It became the legal instrument that permitted the speedy implementation of the legislative agenda set out for the completion of the single

---

[7] Ungerer, H., J. Hauvonen, A. López-Claros, and T. Mayer. 1990. "The European Monetary System: Developments and Perspectives." *Occasional Paper No 73*, Washington, DC, International Monetary Fund.

market. The Act also brought under the jurisdiction of the Treaties new fields of concern – for example, the environment – and set up a permanent Secretariat for political cooperation on foreign policy matters. Furthermore, it recognized the competence of the Community in the area of monetary policy and enhanced the consultative rights of the European Parliament.

More recently, the Treaty of Lisbon, which entered into force on December 1, 2009, amending the 1993 Maastricht Treaty and the 1957 Treaty of Rome, introduced a number of major reforms, significantly expanding many functions of the European Union. In particular, it broadened the use of qualified majority voting to some 45 new policy areas in the Council of Ministers, it strengthened the powers and jurisdiction of the European Parliament, it created the posts of President of the European Council and a High Representative of the Union for Foreign Affairs and Security Policy, and made the EU's bill of rights, the Charter of Fundamental Rights, legally binding. It also gave countries the right to leave the EU – the now famous Article 50 being used by the United Kingdom to negotiate the terms of Brexit.

The above is not to suggest that EU developments and reforms have been smooth and linear. At times they have been shrouded in controversy and soul searching, such as that which took place following Ireland's initial rejection of the Lisbon Treaty in 2008. There were those who thought that the problem with the EU is that it is too diverse to expect that all member states will ratify any given treaty or wholeheartedly approve any given policy. It was pointed out that the United Kingdom and Denmark obtained a number of opt-outs out of the Maastricht Treaty, that the Schengen open-border area included Iceland, Norway and Switzerland, but excludes the United Kingdom, Ireland, Bulgaria and Romania, that the eurozone had at the time 18 members, not 28, that the Lisbon Treaty would partially exempt Britain and Poland from the Charter of Fundamental Rights, and so on. So, from this perspective, the way forward would be to accept a process of integration that allows for different speeds. All members must be democracies, there must be respect for human rights and countries must participate in the single market, but, beyond this, countries may choose which policies they are able to participate in, depending on their individual circumstances. Others argued that the Lisbon Treaty was a sideshow, distracting from key practical concerns of the Union.

A core problem connected with the seeming European malaise was likely that, notwithstanding the impressive achievements during the past several decades, its influence in the world was waning because it had failed to implement the sorts of reforms that would make it the most competitive economy in the world. All the hand-wringing about the Lisbon Treaty missed the point that the EU continued to be saddled with inefficient economic policies – the Common Agricultural Policy, obsolete regulatory regimes, a system of higher education which, long ago, abdicated leadership to the United States, among other things. From this perspective the focus should shift from Treaty negotiations to ensuring, for example, that EU members stopped spending more on declining industries than in research and development, and that the EU makes it easier to facilitate cross-border mergers to build world champions instead of capitulating to national interests. In other words, some would argue that the seemingly more glamorous work of treaties and constitutions should be downplayed, and priorities shifted to concrete and important work on the nuts and bolts of economic and institutional reforms.[8] Others would say that the problem with the EU is not that its citizens are confused – such as the Irish during the Lisbon Treaty debates – rather that they are cynical and the leadership is to be blamed because they themselves are cynical. EU policies do not comprehensively address citizen's concerns (and/or many citizens within EU countries remain unaware of the benefits of EU policies). "There is now a widespread impression across Europe – and especially among the young – that it is in danger of offering pseudo-democracy, remote bureaucratic government thinly disguised by a European parliament," is how one Oxford professor put it.[9] So, the problem is framed as one of political legitimacy and engagement. Some of these arguments (as well as several others put forth on the basis of false narratives) were embraced in the United Kingdom in 2016 by those pushing for Brexit, especially by older voters.

None of these observations is without merit; they all reflect the diversity of opinion that is to be expected in the context of mature democracies, where the business community, civil society organizations and the media are free to voice concerns and opinions, and to propose new policy priorities and initiatives. The business of bringing 28 nations to work effectively together, against the background of centuries of deeply engrained nationalisms and the defense of the "national interest" above everything else is a challenging undertaking. That the process sometimes encounters setbacks is fully to be expected. Few would deny, however, that viewed against the starting point of 1957 (or, perhaps more appropriately, the chaos and devastation of 1945), the progress has been immense and the EU remains by far the most comprehensive experiment in supranational economic and political integration, with potentially significant lessons for the rest of the world, including in respect of the establishment of international peace.[10] Moreover, a recent "Eurobarometer" survey has found the highest levels of support for the Union in 35 years, with two-thirds of Europeans believing that their nation has benefited from membership in the EU, and 60 percent considering EU membership a good thing.[11]

---

[8] Treaty negotiations, of course, are extremely important for laying the foundations for further economic and political integration, identity formation, institutional strengthening based on common values, and so on. At the same time, concrete and coherent economic policies must be implemented as essential complements.

[9] Siedentop, Larry, *Financial Times*, July 2, 2008.

[10] Half of the top 50 countries with the highest income per capita in the world are members of the European Union. The same is true for the top 20.

[11] See European Parliament, *Eurobarometer Survey Shows Highest Support for the EU in 35 years*, EU affairs, May 23, 2018. www.europarl.europa.eu/news/en/headlines/eu-affairs/20180522STO 04020/eurobarometer-survey-highest-support-for-the-eu-in-35-years.

ECONOMIC VERSUS "POLITICAL" UNION

If one begins with the idea that the ultimate aim of greater economic integration was always political stability and cohesion, it is well worth asking what are likely to be the further political transformations of an economically unified Europe. Will the mighty forces pushing nations in the direction of greater economic cooperation inevitably lead to yet greater degrees of political integration? Will there eventually be an entity which could be considered a United States of Europe, as envisioned by Churchill? Monnet believed passionately that the process of economic integration he had helped launch in the 1950s would lead to a United States of Europe. He did not know what form the government would take, but he thought that a united Europe would create a new political model for the world.

There are several lines of thinking on this subject. Some see greater economic integration as an ongoing process, as a stepping stone toward a European Federation, one in which countries would become member states, having further ceded aspects of national sovereignty to European federal institutions in important areas. Others view a united, more integrated regional economy as an end in itself, not necessarily involving a delegation of authority in other areas, particularly on issues traditionally considered most sensitive, such as common defense, aspects of foreign policy (e.g., relations with third countries, such as China), deeper cooperation on taxation issues, among other things.

Those in the first group argue that increasing economic unity will give way eventually to a single foreign policy, for example, as Europeans begin to speak with a single European voice on issues affecting the welfare of the world. Political unity is thus seen as a gradual and evolutionary, but largely inevitable, organic historical process. A noted European businessman captured the feeling when he observed in a US National Public Radio broadcast that "[t]he question of national sovereignty and its abdication to a greater body is something in the hands of the young. It will come through increasing trust and increasing travel, as the memories of the bitterness of the past, particularly the last 30 to 40 years, gradually fade away."

Such bitterness is to be replaced gradually by a growing European consciousness: The idea that there is no contradiction between being a good German or Italian and a good European. The evidence seems to suggest that this broadening of loyalties, what Bertrand Russell used to call "the expansion of one's mental universe," is rapidly taking root in Europe as survey after survey has consistently revealed strong popular support for the ideals that gave rise to the birth of the EU, if not always the bureaucratic forms that these ideals have given rise to. Others, however, show considerably less enthusiasm for a veritable "United States of Europe"; a long history of nationalism and conflict seems sometimes to weigh heavily on their minds.[12]

---

[12] Consider the following words from Mrs. Margaret Thatcher, former Prime Minister of Britain:

"Nations should trade more freely but not share national sovereignty with some European conglomerate or superstate administered from Brussels. Just look at the difficult language

It is important not to confuse "unity" with "uniformity." One must guard against the latter and would wish to preserve the diversity and distinctiveness of various cultures and national traditions – in the case of Europe as it manifests itself in different languages, customs, food, music, and other expressions of a given culture. Unity with diversity has been a fundamental goal of the European project, and has been a successfully implemented goal of other complex federated projects, such as those of Canada and Switzerland.[13] At the international level, the emergence of stronger global institutions should indeed embrace such a principle as a key value.[14] Moreover, obstacles commonly raised to closer federation, include, indeed, the "language problem" and the issue of "different stages of development" – it is not clear why these should be seen as insurmountable barriers. German and Portuguese businesspeople, for example, have meaningful interchanges all the time; they speak in English (the current de facto global commercial and diplomatic language). Preserving the diversity of language does not mean, for example, that one cannot learn additional, common languages to communicate across countries and cultures, as indeed, it is more and more commonplace in Europe to find youth speaking three or four European languages. Learning an additional common language is not a betrayal of one's cultural or national identity. On the contrary, to the extent that it allows one to learn about other peoples, their hopes, desires, fears, it will likely enhance understanding of one's own background.

Regarding the "different stages of development," these exist between countries and can be a challenge to deal with. This was evident, for instance, in recent years in the context of the euro crisis, as different approaches to fiscal policy – Germany's cautious management of its public accounts versus more "liberal," not to say unsustainable, tendencies in some Southern European members – put pressures on the EU's institutional architecture. But there is evidence that rather than leading to political fragmentation and disunion, they may have shown the advantages – actually, the need – for greater coordination.

---

problem. Just look at the different stages of development. It is not possible to have a United States of Europe. What is possible is that the 12 countries steadily work more closely together on things we do better together, so we can trade more closely together, and have fewer formalities across borders. But not to dissolve our own infinite variety, our own nationality, our own identity." Mrs. Thatcher expressed similar sentiments at her famous 1988 Bruges speech: https://www.margaretthatcher.org/document/107332

[13] Indeed, "United in diversity" is the motto of the European Union. "It first came into use in 2000. It signifies how Europeans have come together, in the form of the EU, to work for peace and prosperity, while at the same time being enriched by the continent's many different cultures, traditions and languages." https://europa.eu/european-union/about-eu/symbols/motto_en.

[14] "We may have different religions, different languages, different colored skin, but we all belong to one human race" is how UN Secretary General Kofi Annan put it. https://americasunofficialambassadors.wordpress.com/2013/08/04/.

On many occasions over the past several decades there have been sentiments that European integration might be slowed as a result of changes in the international political environment, including the process of German reunification, processes of economic and political transformation in eastern Europe and among the former members of the Soviet Union in the 1990s, the aftershocks of the 2008–2009 global financial crisis, the impact of migratory flows from troubled countries in the Middle East in the more recent past, and so on. These developments have generally been followed by a renewed commitment on the part of EU states to whatever aspect of the integration agenda is perceived to be under threat. So, to take an example, on February 7, 1992, the 12 member states signed the Maastricht Treaty on the European Union, which called for the introduction of a common European currency by 1999 and significantly expanded the power and spheres of influence of European institutions. It also gave legal meaning to the concept of union citizenship and associated civil rights. The Treaty entered into force on November 1, 1993, following ratification by the member states.[15] These initiatives were considerably strengthened in the period 2004–2007 with the entry of 12 additional countries into the European Union, thereby bringing membership in the Union to a total of 28 countries (with a combined population of 512 million) and thus creating the largest trading bloc in the world.[16]

IMPLICATIONS FOR THE FUTURE

The present processes of European integration have a significance that transcends their immediate stated objectives. Beyond the eminently technical and occasionally dry nature of the issues underlying these processes, the European countries may find in the end not just increased material prosperity but something far more enduring – the forging of a shared identity and a durable peace among European nations.[17] Three things may be said in this respect.

First, a case can be made that the tragic experiences of the 20th century may have led to fundamental changes in European consciousness; in particular the willingness of its citizens to permanently set aside warfare as a way to settle differences and

---

[15] As noted by Klaus-Dieter Borchardt, a senior European Community official: "The introduction of Union citizenship created a direct link between European integration and the people it is meant to serve. Union citizenship confers concrete civil rights. As Union citizens, nationals of the member states can move freely throughout the union and settle wherever they wish. They have the right to vote and stand as candidates in municipal elections in the member state where they reside. This has major implications. Indeed some member states had to amend their constitutions to make it possible" (*European Integration: The Origins and Growth of the European Union* [Luxembourg: Office of Official Publications of the European Communities, 1995] 64).

[16] Croatia became the 28th member of the EU on July 1, 2013.

[17] See, e.g., Fry, who uses the EU as one of his examples of a stable "peace system," evidencing what he posits are the common cross-cultural requirements for the establishment of such a system. Fry, Douglas P. 2012. "Life without War." *Science*, Vol. 336, p. 879.

resolve conflicts. It is a triumph not just for the citizens of France and Germany but for all of humankind to state with certainty, despite a long history of conflict and bloodshed, that the two countries will never again be at war with each other – as a consequence, in large measure, of over 60 years of economic integration.[18] It says that, in the long run, reasoned cooperation will prevail, signifying a maturity of vision and in statecraft. We can only hope that such maturity and vision will be seen in leadership at the international level.

Second, in the coming together of previously warring nations, one can see a reaffirmation of the universality of certain human values. Two frequent arguments put forward by those opposed to the creation of supranational institutions as a way of addressing the complexities of an increasingly interdependent world are that the world is, in fact, too large and too diverse to be united. The first observation has been made largely irrelevant by the swift progress in the fields of transport and communications, which in the last decades have brought human beings much closer to each other, if not always in spirit, at least physically – a process that has also forced increasingly more of the planet's population to reexamine many long-held prejudices (although there is still a great deal of work to do in this respect). But, more important, in the post-World War II period more than in any previous era, human beings have begun to find that there is much more that unites them than separates them. Skins may have different shades, different languages may be spoken, and worship may take different forms, but the majority of humankind desires a peaceful world, economic well-being and security, social justice, and a stable environment.[19] The recognition of this sharing of aspirations and values by increasingly greater numbers of people holds great promise for our future and may well be the driving force of further processes of globalization, the occasional setbacks notwithstanding (see Chapter 20 for a discussion of shared global values).[20]

---

[18] This point was forcefully made by German Chancellor Merkel and French President Macron during the Paris Peace Forum held in November of 2018 to commemorate the 100th anniversary of the end of World War I, holding hands together, in front of the graves of some of the 17 million soldiers and civilians who perished in that conflict.

[19] See, for instance, the evidence presented by Schwartz, S.H. 2012. "An Overview of the Schwartz Theory of Basic Values." *Online Readings in Psychology and Culture*, Vol. 2, No. 1. https://doi.org/10.9707/2307-0919.1116. Schwartz identifies ten basic personal values that are recognized across cultures and explains their origins. He argues that values form a circular structure that is culturally universal and presents findings from 82 countries that suggest that although individuals from different cultures may "reveal substantial differences in the value priorities," the average value priorities of most societal groups exhibit a similar hierarchical order.

[20] Yes, there has been a rising tide of nationalism in some corners of the world and resurgent autocracies in the likes of Russia, Turkey and Venezuela, but the latest Economic Intelligence Unit's Democracy Index 2018, shows that 68.3 percent of the world's countries can be classified as nonauthoritarian, only slightly lower than the 69.5 percent registered in 2008. Freedom House's Freedom in the World Index shows broadly similar results: in 2018, 75 percent of the 195 countries included in the index were either free or partly free. In 2008, 78 percent of the 193 countries assessed were free or partly free.

Third, in some sense, to the extent that the present European experiment has already succeeded, and may move toward further integration in the future, one of the more important implications for the rest of the world may not necessarily be the increased benefits resulting from the recognition of common economic interests, but rather the model it exhibits for the setting up of a yet more secure supranational institutional basis for a lasting peace. What started out in 1957 as a seemingly unambitious project to reduce barriers to trade among six trading nations may, in retrospect, come to be regarded as a significant step toward laying the foundations – and modeling the possible processes – of also establishing a durable international peace. The slow, sometimes frustrating, but steady process of consultation, of finding common ground, of giving and taking, may have enhanced the sensitivity of European leaders to broader concerns. The European Council, the heads of state of Europe, has been meeting two to three times a year since 1975.[21] Is it a surprise that, ever so slowly and tentatively, they would have come up with some truly constructive initiatives, such as that embodied in the successful Europe 1992 program? Similarly, at the international level, much dialogue has already occurred, and the international community would do well to forge stronger common institutions with progressively enhanced decision-making capacities (as we suggest in this book), and to focus its energy on forging workable common policies to address the pressing, multiple global challenges we face.

---

[21] A long-standing problem with the European Community was the absence of real authority. Monnet thought that, unless the Heads of State were brought into the decision-making process, progress would be slow. Hence in 1973 he pushed for the creation of the European Council, which is made up of Heads of State of the member countries. In time, through its regular two or three meetings a year, the Council has had an enormous impact on decision-making. The combination of majority voting, growing popular support for EU institutions in general (which, of course, is a key issue from the perspective of politically conscious statemen and stateswomen) has greatly accelerated the development of the EU. In the 18-month period from early 1988 to mid-1989, 150 decisions were taken, the equivalent of an entire decade of work in earlier times.

PART II

Reforming the Central Institutions of the United Nations

4

The General Assembly: Reforms to Strengthen Its Effectiveness

The General Assembly ... Proclaims this Universal Declaration of Human Rights as a common standard of achievement for all peoples and all nations, to the end that every individual and every organ of society, keeping this Declaration constantly in mind, shall strive by teaching and education to promote respect for these rights and freedoms and by progressive measures, national and international, to secure their universal and effective recognition and observance, both among the peoples of Member States themselves and among the peoples of territories under their jurisdiction.[1]

We reaffirm that democracy is a universal value based on the freely expressed will of people to determine their own political, economic, social and cultural systems and their full participation in all aspects of their lives.[2]

This chapter presents an overview of the evolution of the United Nations General Assembly, its most important achievements and remaining weaknesses, and relevance. It argues that the UN Charter should be amended to allow the introduction of a system of weighted voting, to better reflect the relative significance and influence of its 193 members. A particular proposal will be presented, updating the work done by Schwartzberg.[3] We discuss its merits and limitations and propose that a gradual system of direct election of Assembly members be introduced. By way of example, we also present the UN Charter's Articles 9–11 on General Assembly composition, functions and powers and how these Articles could be amended to reflect the new system of weighted voting and the enhanced powers that are envisaged for the Assembly under a revised Charter.

---

[1] 217 (III). International Bill of Human Rights, 183rd plenary meeting, December 10, 1948.
[2] UN General Assembly. 2005. 2005 World Summit Outcome. Resolution A/RES/60/1 adopted September 16. New York, United Nations, paragraph 135. www.un.org/ga/search/view_doc.asp?symbol=A/RES/60/1 paragraph 135.
[3] Schwartzberg, Joseph E. 2013. *Transforming the United Nations System: Designs for a Workable World*. Tokyo, United Nations University Press.

KEY ACHIEVEMENTS AND WEAKNESSES

It is possible to have a lively debate about how representative the UNGA is, including the reasons why the founders of the United Nations embedded in the Charter the principle of one-country-one-vote for the General Assembly (Article 18 (1)); indeed, in Chapter 2 we presented the likely most plausible explanation, reflecting the rather uneven distribution of political power at the time and the desire of the Big Four to ensure a UN that would not challenge their national prerogatives. Article 18(2) identifies a number of questions on which decisions of the General Assembly are to be made by a two-thirds majority of the members present and voting, including "recommendations with respect to the maintenance of international peace and security, the election of the non-permanent members of the Security Council, the election of the members of the Economic and Social Council, the admission of new Members to the United Nations, the suspension of the rights and privileges of membership, the expulsion of Members" and, of course, questions relating to the budget.

Other Articles of Chapter IV of the Charter on the General Assembly envisage a dual role; it shall be a body for high-level deliberation, but it will also have administrative oversight of the UN system. We are sympathetic to the views put forward by Grenville Clark – discussed in Chapter 2 – that the Big Four saw the one-country-one-vote system under Article 18(1) as a natural manifestation of the principle of "sovereign equality" of its members and an attempt to create a body that would play a mainly advisory role to the Security Council, which would be the locus of real power within the organization. As noted in Chapter 2, the one-country-one-vote principle undermined at the outset the credibility of the General Assembly and may have been a deliberate attempt to weaken it with respect to the Security Council.

In the early stages of the United Nations – certainly during the first decade and possibly through the late 1950s – the one-country-one-vote principle did not prevent the emergence of a working majority led by the United States and many of its allies in Europe and Latin America, which easily accounted for more than half of the UN membership. This in turn, resulted in the Soviet Union feeling isolated within the General Assembly and exercising its power through repeated use of the veto in the Security Council. During the first ten years of the United Nations, the Soviet Union exercised its veto no less than 80 times, the vast majority of instances used to reject applications for membership from a large number of countries. In sharp contrast, the United States did not exercise its first veto until 1970, a full 25 years after the creation of the UN.[4] Article 4 of the Charter establishes the criteria for membership, which, in essence requires countries to be "peace-loving states" that accept the obligations

---

[4] Of the 119 vetoes exercised between 1946 and 1970, the Soviet Union accounted for 108 or 91 percent of all vetoes cast. During the first 50 years of the United Nations there were a total of 285 vetoes in the Security Council of which, the Soviet Union (Russia after 1992) and the United States accounted for 211, or 74 percent of the total.

that it contains and makes membership conditional upon recommendation of the Security Council. It is clear that in these earlier periods the Soviet Union and the other members of the Council had very different understandings of the meaning of Article 4. Thus, Spain's application for membership did not succeed until 1955 because of its earlier collaboration with the Axis powers during World War II. Indeed, only ten new members were admitted during the UN's first ten years because of the Soviet veto.[5]

The first big push for expanded membership came in 1955 when 16 new states were accepted into the organization, with a second wave of new entrants taking place in 1960–1961 when 22 new countries became members, reflecting a quickening in the pace of decolonization. In time, as United Nations membership expanded beyond its original 51 founding nations, the organization was gradually transformed into a body dominated by economically small and (often) politically less influential states. Thus, an Assembly that already in 1945 did not reflect in a meaningful way the economic size, population and influence of its members saw the problem greatly accentuated as its membership expanded in the following decades, particularly in the developing world. For instance, membership of African countries rose from four in 1945 to 42 in 1969 and 55 today or from 5.9 percent of the membership to 28.5 percent today. Of course, along the way, the United Nations became truly universal, with its current 193 members accounting for over 99 percent of world gross national product (GNP) and this has been a remarkable (and welcome) development in its own right.

The first decade of the United Nations did see some important achievements reflecting the prevailing distribution of power and the working majority led by the United States. The first session of the General Assembly took place in London on January 10, 1946, and it dealt with the issue of nuclear weapons. The UN Charter is silent on the issue of nuclear weapons because the San Francisco Conference where the Charter was adopted was concluded six weeks before the explosions in Hiroshima and Nagasaki. Against the background of the fearsome destructions caused by these bombs there was an intense debate in policymaking circles, in the academic community, and in the pages of the international press about what the advent of

---

[5]   In this respect, it is interesting to quote from a statement made by the United States delegation on the Soviet Union's vetoing practices: "The Soviet Union's practice of vetoing applicants, who qualify for membership according to its own admission, unless its private candidates are admitted at the same time, makes it all the more essential, in our view, that other Members observe scrupulously adherence to the law of the Charter . . . . When a permanent member of the Security Council seeks to use its veto powers to coerce its fellow members into a violation of the Charter, they should resist it just as vigorously as they would resist any other form of coercion. The thwarting of the majority will by such methods cannot, we think, be called a deadlock; it is a hold-up" (quoted in Marin-Bosch, Miguel. 1998. *Votes in the UN General Assembly*, The Hague: Kluwer Law International, p. 28.) This is a good example of the kind of abuse of power which many of the delegates to the 1945 San Francisco Conference warned against in discussing the existence of the veto.

nuclear weapons would mean for the newly created organization: in particular, in light of its stated desire "to save succeeding generations from the scourge of war" and the explicit identification in Article 26 of the Security Council's responsibilities to formulate plans "for the establishment of a system for the regulation of armaments" (see Chapter 9).

Perhaps appropriately, the General Assembly's first resolution dealt with the problems raised by the discovery of atomic energy and established the Atomic Energy Commission, whose terms of reference include making proposals for the "control of atomic energy to the extent necessary to ensure its use only for peaceful purposes," and "for the elimination from national armaments of atomic weapons and of all other major weapons adoptable to mass destruction." In 1947, the Security Council established the Commission for Conventional Armaments to deliver proposals in the area of armaments reduction and delimitation of armed forces more generally. The Commission had limited success. By 1949 the Soviet Union had succeeded in obtaining nuclear weapons of its own and the Cold War entered an intense phase, which saw over the next several decades a substantial accumulation of conventional and nuclear armaments. These developments notwithstanding, the General Assembly did try to strengthen the role of the UN in the negotiation of disarmament agreements. One important achievement was active engagement in the setting up of various fora addressing global disarmament issues, as of the 1950s and early 1960s, including the UN Disarmament Commission (UNDC) and what would eventually become the Conference on Disarmament (CD) in Geneva established in 1978. The precursor body to the CD was initially made up of ten and then 18 members; it had grown to 61 members by 1996 and to 65 members by 2018. The CD in time became the principal venue for the negotiation of various disarmament treaties, including the 1963 Partial Test Ban Treaty, the 1968 Nuclear Non-Proliferation Treaty (NPT), the 1972 Biological Weapons Convention, the 1992 Chemical Weapons Conventions (CWC), and the 1996 Comprehensive Test Ban Treaty, among others (see also Chapter 9).

As a result of these, according to Marin-Bosch "Today over 180 nations are committed, in legally binding, multilateral instruments such as the NPT or in nuclear weapon-free regional treaties, to refrain from acquiring nuclear weapons. And that is very significant."[6] A more recent and potentially very important initiative is the Treaty on the Prohibition of Nuclear Weapons adopted by 122 nations on July 7, 2017, which prohibits the development, testing, production, stockpiling, transfer, use, or threat of use of nuclear weapons. This initiative was launched with a General Assembly Resolution issued in December 2016 and the Treaty was negotiated with impressive speed in the three-week period leading up to its signing. None of the nuclear weapons states signed it, nor did NATO members approve it, but the Treaty

---

[6]   Marin-Bosch, *Votes in the UN General Assembly*, p. 67.

is an eloquent reaffirmation of the idea that the use or threat of use of nuclear weapons has no moral justification whatsoever.

The various arms limitation initiatives cited above spearheaded by the General Assembly have had other positive collateral implications. For instance, in 1967, the nations of Latin America and the Caribbean signed the Treaty of Tlateloleco, in which they committed themselves not to acquire nuclear weapons and secured a legally binding pledge from the nuclear weapon states (NWS) not to use nuclear weapons against them, thereby creating a nuclear-free zone in the region. This in turn, encouraged the signing of similar treaties for other regions of the world including the 1985 Treaty of Rarotonga (South Pacific), the 1995 Treaty of Bangkok (South East Asia), and the 1996 Treaty of Pelindaba (Africa). These treaties are not particularly well known but are significant nevertheless, and the countries that have signed them have, thus far, fulfilled their commitments and therefore, contributed to slowing down nuclear proliferation. Of particular significance in this regard was the 1968 NPT (which entered into force in 1970), which established a clear-cut distinction between non-nuclear weapon states (NNWS) and the then five acknowledged nuclear weapon states. In 1995 when the NPTs signatories met to review their nuclear weapons commitments, the NNWS parties decided to permanently and unconditionally opt out of building nuclear weapons. This sharply highlighted the gap with respect to the NWS that remain unwilling to give up their nuclear weapons. At the time China, France, Russia, the United Kingdom, and the United States pledged to move toward nuclear disarmament.

In parallel to these efforts, there was also an attempt within the UN system to delineate more clearly the legal underpinnings of the use of nuclear weapons. For instance, in 1993, the World Health Organization, and then the UN General Assembly, sought an advisory opinion from the International Court of Justice on the legality of the use of such weapons, given the widespread and damaging health and environmental effects, so eloquently laid out in Jonathan Schell's 1982 monumental *The Fate of the Earth*, which also addressed the moral dimension of the use of nuclear weapons. In its advisory opinion of July 8, 1996, the International Court of Justice concluded that "the threat or use of nuclear weapons would generally be contrary to the [applicable] rules of international law," and reminded states that "[t]here exists an obligation to pursue in good faith and bring to a conclusion negotiations leading to nuclear disarmament in all its aspects under strict and effective international control" (in particular under the terms of the widely ratified NPT).[7] These initiatives may have contributed to the five NWS feeling increasingly isolated within the UN on questions of nuclear disarmament. By the 1980s the United States and the Soviet Union had opted for conducting disarmament

---

[7] International Court of Justice. 1996. Legality of the Threat or Use of Nuclear Weapons, Advisory Opinion of July 8, 1996. I.C.J Reports 1996, pp. 226–267. The Hague, International Court of Justice. www.icj-cij.org/files/case-related/95/095-19960708-ADV-01-00-EN.pdf.

negotiations outside of the UN framework; for instance, the SALT-I and SALT-II treaties were the results of bilateral negotiations between the two superpowers and did not involve any of the established UN mechanisms. Article VI of the NPT imposes an obligation on its signatories not only to conduct negotiations on nuclear disarmament but actually to conclude such negotiations at some point in the not too distant future.[8]

A second example: In 1948, the General Assembly issued Resolution 217 (III), International Bill of Human Rights, which contained the Universal Declaration of Human Rights. As we have noted earlier, whereas the League's Covenants had been largely silent on issues of human rights, the UN Charter explicitly embedded a range of human rights provisions, such as that contained in Article 55 (c). The Charter calls upon the United Nations to promote "universal respect for, and observance of human rights and fundamental freedoms for all without distinction as to race, sex, language, or religion." The 1948 Resolution was endorsed by 48 of the then 58 member states. The significance of this Resolution cannot be overstated. It contributed to a major strengthening of the legal framework underpinning the observance of human rights at the global level and led to the negotiation of a wide range of international instruments addressing multiple dimensions of the human rights agenda, including on the status of refugees, genocide, the rights of women, slavery, torture, and several others. It led also to the 1966 adoption by the General Assembly of the International Covenant on Civil and Political Rights, and the International Covenants on Economic, Social and Cultural Rights (see also Chapter 11).

While the General Assembly's promotion of human rights is, without doubt, one of the most important areas of achievement, the Assembly also played a critical role in the process of decolonization. The UN Charter recognized explicitly the principle of the self-determination of peoples (Article 1(2)) and it was left to the General Assembly to identify territories that were non-self-governing or trust territories under League of Nations mandate. In this respect, the General Assembly had, as early as 1946, identified 74 non-self-governing territories (mainly colonies) belonging to the following UN member states: Australia, Belgium, Denmark, France, Netherlands, New Zealand, the United Kingdom, and the United States. Spanish and Portuguese colonies were added to this list in 1960. The challenge for the General Assembly was how to encourage the implementation of the principle of self-determination against the background of, at times, strong resistance from some members to even recognize that such territories were indeed colonies. For instance, for many years Spain and Portugal argued that territories under their control were

---

[8] Indeed, Article VI states "Each of the Parties to the Treaty undertakes to pursue negotiations in good faith on effective measures relating to cessation of the nuclear arms race at an early date and to nuclear disarmament, and on a treaty on general and complete disarmament under strict and effective international control."

"overseas provinces" (e.g., Angola, Sao Tome) and that as such they were subject to the protections embedded in Article 2(7), where the Charter proscribes the UN from "interven[ing] in matters which are essentially within the domestic jurisdiction of any state." A similar case was made by France in respect of Algeria and some of its other colonies.

It is beyond the scope of this chapter to go into a detailed description of the role played by the General Assembly in the process of decolonization, but suffice it to say that various General Assembly Resolutions, many of them pressing colonial powers to establish clear timetables for the granting of independence to their dependent territories, and firmly restating the legitimacy of peoples' aspirations for independence, did much to strengthen the credibility of various grassroots political movements aimed at securing independence in various corners of the world. This resulted in a rapid increase in UN membership; by 1969, the United Nations had 126 members with the vast majority of the new entrants being former colonies, particularly in Africa.

The various General Assembly declarations touching upon the theme of human rights and its subsequent efforts to assist in the codification of the associated international law are a very good example of a larger body of work where the Assembly has sought to codify a series of norms pertaining to the behavior of states. The list of norms developed on various themes is long and includes a broad range of subjects, such as the peaceful uses of outer space, the environment and management of the global commons, the Law of the Sea, terrorism, peaceful coexistence of religions and cultures, the elimination of violence against women, elaborations on the importance of peaceful international dispute resolution, the essential elements of democracy, among a vast range of other progressive and humanitarian issues. While some of these initiatives have foundered in terms of implementation because of the absence of adequate enforcement mechanisms and/or the unwillingness of states sometimes to take seriously their commitments to resolutions that they themselves have supported through their representatives in the General Assembly, one must nevertheless recognize that the Assembly has played a useful catalytic role in helping to identify important core principles to guide the behavior of states, akin to the development of much needed Codes of Conduct.

In parallel to these important resolutions addressing issues of global concern, there were also attempts during the first decade to improve the working of the UN against the background of the distortions introduced by the repeated exercise of the veto by the Soviet Union. In this regard, Resolution 377 (V), also known as the "Uniting for Peace" Resolution, attempted to empower the General Assembly with the ability to act when the Security Council's decision-making machinery had come to a standstill because of the exercise of the veto (in this case, that of the Soviet Union) and there were major issues of peace and security at play. In other words, the General Assembly made an explicit attempt to enter into the power vacuum created by a Security Council that was paralyzed. In particular, the Resolution resolves that if the Security Council, because of lack of unanimity of the permanent members, fails to exercise its primary responsibilities for the maintenance of international peace and security in any case where there appears to be a threat to the peace, breach of the peace, or act of aggression, the General Assembly shall consider the matter immediately with a view to making appropriate recommendations to Members for collective measures, including in the case of a breach of the peace or act of aggression, the use of armed force when necessary, to maintain or restore international peace and security.[9]

Additionally, the UN Charter contains as a primary objective the furtherance of the economic and social development of peoples. The Preamble refers to "the promotion of the economic and social advancement of all peoples" as an important objective of the international community. The General Assembly's record in this area is, in our estimation, considerably more mixed than its achievements in the area of human rights. The Economic and Social Council (ECOSOC) was intended to play the central role in the implementation of these objectives and strengthened the link between the United Nations and its specialized agencies. ECOSOC's beginnings were relatively auspicious, leading to the creation in 1947 of the General Agreement on Tariffs and Trade (GATT). This set in motion several global rounds of trade liberalization, which contributed to a significant expansion of international trade and to a boost in economic growth for the global economy. The last of these, the Uruguay Round, eventually led in 1995 to the establishment of the World Trade Organization (WTO).

There seems to be general agreement, however, that by the turn of the century ECOSOC's role in the area of social and economic development was much diminished. Several factors appear to have contributed to this. First, many of the specialized agencies began operating with a considerable degree of independence. For instance, the International Monetary Fund (IMF) and the World Bank (created in 1944 at the United Nations Monetary and Financial Conference in Bretton Woods, New Hampshire) were founded with governing structures based on weighted voting, enabling the larger UN members to influence issues of economic development through their participation in the Boards of these organizations, leading to what became known, sometimes disparagingly, as the "Washington Consensus." The fact that both the IMF and the World Bank had complete financial autonomy sharply weakened the link with the United Nations and thus with ECOSOC. By the onset of the global financial crisis in 2008, the World Bank and particularly the IMF had decades of experience in crisis management, and in the promotion of policies intended to tackle poverty and to encourage better economic management. Not surprisingly, both organizations played a major role

---

[9] Rauschning, D., K. Wiesbrock, and M. Lailach, 1997. *Key Resolutions of the United Nations General Assembly 1946–1996*, Cambridge, Cambridge University Press, p. 79.

in addressing the impact of the crisis, with ECOSOC very much on the sidelines, both conceptually and operationally.

The second factor for the loss of ground by ECOSOC in the economic development space was the emergence of a large number of UN conferences convened by the General Assembly and with the extensive participation of civil society organizations on a range of global issues including population (1994), the environment (1992, 2012), social issues (1995), women (1995), and human rights (1993), which shifted the locus of debate beyond ECOSOC itself. ECOSOC credibility and legitimacy and its ability to occupy a significant position in the economic and development space may have been undermined by the fact that, like the General Assembly, it operates on the basis of a one-country-one-vote system. This in practice has meant that small developing countries had an outsize influence, prompting the larger members to channel their concerns through the WB and the IMF where they had in practice much greater influence. The presence of a large contingent of small developing countries representing a significant proportion of the world's population in the General Assembly did also at times lead to polarization over the priorities of economic development between those defending global economic interests and those calling for more social and economic justice. An example of this are the debates that took place leading to General Assembly Resolutions on the "New International Economic Order," which never took off in any operationally meaningful way, and it is probably accurate to say were largely ignored by the leaderships of the IMF and the World Bank. Not surprisingly, with the empowerment of smaller states within the General Assembly, the principle of sovereign equality has become deeply entrenched.

An interesting indicator of this phenomenon is provided by the assessed contribution to the budget of the lowest-income UN members, which was set at 0.04 percent in 1946 but had been reduced to 0.001 percent by the 1990s, or 40 times less. Furthermore, Switzerland's contribution to the budget (1.151 percent) exceeds the cumulative contributions of the 120 countries with the smallest assessed shares. Indeed, the cumulative contribution of the 129 members with the lowest assessed shares, which is the minimum number of countries required for a two-thirds majority, is 1.633 percent. This is only slightly higher than the contribution of Turkey (1.371 percent) and lower than the contribution of Spain, the country with the next highest contribution (2.146 percent). A body organized on the basis of a principle that equates the voting power of China with a population of close to 1.4 billion people with that of Nauru having a population of about 13,000 (or over 106,000 times less) was fated to be less effective, and this distortion manifested itself in a number of ways. First and foremost, given the powers granted to the Assembly by the Charter over budgetary matters, is the perverse way that budget discussions, practices, and procedures evolved over time (discussed in detail in Chapter 12).

Another factor in the marginalization of the General Assembly stems from the nonbinding nature of Assembly resolutions, which by 2018 exceeded 18,000; the vast majority of them with no tangible operational repercussions on the ground. It is thus difficult to disagree with statements such as

> [a]lthough the Security Council regained prominence after 1990 as a forum for managing international conflict, the General Assembly's inability to break with its mind-numbing routine of debating and adopting resolutions (often multiple resolutions) on the same long list of topics contributes greatly to its continued obscurity. . . . Today it is overshadowed even within the UN not only by the more active Security Council but also by the series of UN global conferences and summits on particular issues.[10]

MOVING TO A SYSTEM OF WEIGHTED VOTING

Amending the UN Charter to introduce a system of weighted voting has been the subject of extensive discussions over the years. It figured prominently in Clark and Sohn's *World Peace through World Law*, where they presented detailed proposals on how to distribute the voting power among its members, and has been the subject of extensive research since then. We present a proposal in this chapter and comment on the challenges of devising a sensible system of representation. The motivation is not purely to create a voting structure that more closely resembles what currently exists at the World Bank and the International Monetary Fund, which have operated on the basis of weighted voting since 1944 and, therefore, more clearly represented members' economic and political power. It is actually principally about empowering the General Assembly to discharge more effectively the responsibilities given to it by Article 10 under the Charter, which grant it fairly wide discretion to discuss and make recommendations on a wide array of issues. Although Article 12 specifically gives the Security Council jurisdiction over interstate disputes and matters of international peace and security, the General Assembly can play, and has at times played, a role on such issues, particularly when the Security Council has been blocked or unable to act because of the exercise of the veto. (See for instance, the discussion above on the "Uniting for Peace" General Assembly Resolution and the factors that prompted it.) In such instances, an Assembly with a voice that more fairly represented the relative size of its members could speak with a greater measure of credibility that has generally been lacking under the one-country-one-vote system. In time, a reconstituted Assembly could be given the power to issue resolutions that are binding on its members and carry the force of international law. Expanding the powers of the General Assembly by turning it into a budding world legislature – the global equivalent of the European Parliament, with a more narrowly defined set of prerogatives and substantive jurisdiction – will never happen unless countries feel

---

[10] See M.J. Peterson's contribution on the General Assembly (Chapter 5), to *The Oxford Handbook on the United Nations* (2007), p. 106.

that there is broad correspondence between the size of the country and its voting power. But the issue goes well beyond redressing what has been perceived as a quaint (not to say unfair, given that the major powers in 1945 actually wanted it this way) system of representation. In fact, it overwhelmingly has to do with creating a body to occupy at least part of the space in the power vacuum that exists today to deal with urgent global problems for which we do not have the problem-solving mechanisms and institutions to address them.

In the paragraphs that follow we will present several options for a system of weighted voting. We agree with Schwartzberg that such a system should be based on a set of valid principles and objective criteria, applied to all members in an even-handed way. It should also be flexible enough to allow for evolution over time, to reflect changes in the data underpinning the indicators. It goes without saying that it should deliver a set of weights that is perceived by members as being realistic and fair.

A MODIFIED SCHWARTZBERG PROPOSAL

Schwartzberg has put forward a proposal that uses three variables to arrive at a set of weights for membership in the General Assembly.[11] Each of these variables tries to capture some key principle, seen to be central to the creation of an equitable system of weighted voting. In particular, population size, to reflect each member's accumulated demographic history and the idea that countries with larger populations represent a larger cross-section of humanity. The size of the member's economy is a second variable, on the grounds that it is the driving factor determining the size of each country's absolute contribution to the United Nations' budget. While, as noted in Chapter 12 presenting a new funding mechanism, each country contributes a fixed share of their gross national income (GNI), their financial contributions differ markedly and clearly larger countries have a correspondingly larger impact on UN operations. Schwartzberg chooses to label this second variable "contributions to the UN budget" but this is a purely semantic distinction, since these contributions are exclusively dependent on a member's GNI. The third variable is intended to capture the "legal/sovereign equality of nations principle, according to which all nations are counted equally." All factors are weighted equally and are calculated, respectively, as percentages of the total population of all 193 members, their share of world GNI and their current voting power in the General Assembly, meaning that each country is allocated a 0.5181 percent share (e.g., 1/193). We will discuss this latter principle later in this section and examine its ramifications. Table 4.1 presents the results of applying this methodology, with updated data for all the variables but with an important modification. We believe this modification is justified on methodological grounds, and also to allay potential concerns on the part of many countries,

---

[11] Schwartzberg, *Transforming the United Nations System: Designs for a Workable World.*

TABLE 4.1 *Updated General Assembly voting shares under a modified Schwartzberg proposal*

					Scenarios	
Country	Assessed share[1]	Population[2] in %: P	GDP share[3] in %: C	Membership share[4] in %: M	I: W share[5] in %	II: W share[6] in %
Top 20 contributors						
USA	22.000	4.350	19.981	0.5181	8.283	8.956
China	12.005	18.515	16.947	0.5181	11.993	10.346
Japan	8.564	1.693	5.238	0.5181	2.483	3.592
Germany	6.090	1.104	3.990	0.5181	1.871	2.571
United Kingdom	4.567	0.882	2.817	0.5181	1.406	1.989
France	4.427	0.896	2.765	0.5181	1.393	1.947
Italy	3.307	0.809	2.142	0.5181	1.156	1.545
Brazil	2.948	2.795	2.588	0.5181	1.967	2.087
Canada	2.734	0.490	1.748	0.5181	0.919	1.247
Russian Federation	2.405	1.930	2.592	0.5181	1.680	1.618
Republic of Korea	2.267	0.329	1.775	0.5181	0.993	1.157
Australia	2.210	0.687	1.331	0.5181	0.726	1.019
Spain	2.146	0.622	1.534	0.5181	0.891	1.095
Turkey	1.371	1.078	1.406	0.5181	1.001	0.989
Netherlands	1.356	0.229	0.889	0.5181	0.545	0.701
Mexico	1.292	1.725	1.704	0.5181	1.316	1.178
Saudi Arabia	1.172	0.440	1.137	0.5181	0.698	0.710
Switzerland	1.151	0.113	0.636	0.5181	0.423	0.594
Argentina	0.915	0.591	0.769	0.5181	0.626	0.675
Sweden	0.906	0.134	0.545	0.5181	0.399	0.520
Other countries						
India	0.834	17.885	5.404	0.5181	7.936	6.412
Poland	0.802	0.507	0.778	0.5181	0.601	0.609

Indonesia	0.543	3.526	1.932	0.5181	1.992	1.529
Iran	0.398	1.084	0.929	0.5181	0.844	0.667
South Africa	0.272	0.757	0.525	0.5181	0.600	0.516
Nigeria	0.250	2.549	0.683	0.5181	1.250	1.106
Egypt	0.186	1.303	0.627	0.5181	0.816	0.669
Pakistan	0.115	2.631	0.614	0.5181	1.254	1.088
Lesotho	0.001	0.030	0.004	0.5181	0.184	0.183
Liberia	0.001	0.063	0.004	0.5181	0.195	0.194

1. Assessed budget contributions for the period 2019–2021 as determined by the General Assembly.

2. P is each country's population share in the total population of all 193 UN members, 2017.

3. C is calculated as the weighted average of a country's GDP share at market prices and GDP at PPP, for all 193 UN members, using 2017 numbers.

4. M is current voting power in the General Assembly (1/193), in percent.

5. W = (P+C+M)/3.

6. Based on 2019–2021 assessed budget shares.

particularly in the developing world, that the formula is not biased against them by the choice of metric used to assess economic size. Whereas Schwartzberg uses GNI at market prices, we use the weighted average (with equal weights) of gross domestic product (GDP) at market prices and GDP at purchasing power parity (PPP) rates.[12]

In particular, we use the International Monetary Fund's World Economic Outlook database for both GDP metrics for 2017, as opposed to 2009 in the Schwartzberg proposal. Two scenarios are presented in the Table 4.1. In Scenario I, the size of the economy variable is set as a percentage of each country's share in world GDP, as calculated per the above method. So, for China for instance, this is set at 16.947 percent. In Scenario II, the size of the economy variable is captured by the actual assessed contribution rates established by the General Assembly for the period 2019–2021. This scenario is useful for comparison purposes, in the event that members did not accept to have contribution rates equal to the same fixed proportion of their GDP (as in Scenario I) and the current ad hoc arrangements prevailed which, as noted in Chapter 12, involve measures of GNI and a multiplicity of other factors, such as the burden of external debt, and so on. The table presents data for 30 countries; the top 20 contributors, which account for 83.83 percent of the total assessed budget (and a larger share if one were to include voluntary contributions) and several others deemed to be of interest, including a few small members for comparison purposes. In Scenario I, which embodies a new funding mechanism for the budget, the ten largest voting shares in the General Assembly are held by China (11.993 percent), the United States (8.283), India (7.936), Japan (2.483), Indonesia (1.992), Brazil (1.967), Germany (1.871), Russia (1.680), the United Kingdom (1.406), and France (1.393). Small countries such as Kiribati, Lesotho, and Liberia, all of

---

[12] GNI figures are generally quite close to GDP and include income which the country derives from its investments abroad. Thus, for instance, if a Japanese citizen owns a business in Germany and receives income from this source in the form of dividends, this is counted in GNI for Japan, whereas it is not in GDP. The rather more important change is to introduce two different measures of GDP in calculating the GDP share. The issue here is the appropriate way to compare incomes of individuals living in countries with different currencies. One possible approach has been to convert national incomes into dollars at the market exchange rate. However, one can make a strong case that what matters in comparing whether someone is rich or poor is not how many dollars that person can buy in the foreign exchange market, but rather what standard of living that income can support in the country where the person lives. For instance, in India in 2017 the average person's annual income in rupees converted into US dollars at the market exchange rate was equal to $1,976. However, because the cost of living in India (food, housing, transportation, health services, a whole range of other nontradable goods) is much lower than in the United States, the same number of rupees was equivalent to an American income of about $7,194, still low by international standards but over three times the level suggested by a simple conversion via the market exchange rate. Using PPP exchange rates rather than market exchange rates has the effect of boosting poor countries' income and thus narrowing the gap with respect to the rich countries. By using a weighted average of both GDP measures, we strike a balance between both metrics. Incidentally, this is the way the IMF calculates its quota shares for member countries.

which at present enjoy the lowest assessed contribution rate to the budget of 0.001 percent, have voting shares of 0.173, 0.184 and 0.195 percent, respectively. Table A1 in the Annex presents the voting shares under Scenario I for all 193 UN members. The results in Scenario II show somewhat smaller voting shares for China, India, Indonesia, and Russia and somewhat bigger shares for the United States, Japan, Germany, Brazil, the United Kingdom, and France. The voting power of the smallest countries is virtually unchanged, given their very small contributions to the budget.

It is interesting to note that in Scenario I the voting shares of Russia, the United Kingdom, and France, the three veto-wielding members of the Security Council other than China and the United States, are the 8th, 9th, and 10th largest in the General Assembly and are all under 2 percent.[13] Perhaps few things express more eloquently the irrationality of the veto power in 2018 than these numbers. A credible mechanism to allocate voting power in the General Assembly on the basis of sensible principles may run up against a perceived diminished stature in the world of these three countries in particular, with respect to the positions occupied in 1945 at the San Francisco Conference. In 2017, for example, Russia's GDP was roughly equivalent to the size of Spanish GDP, which itself is less than 8 percent of the size of the US economy. Of course, the solution to this problem is not to confer the power of the veto to India, Japan, Indonesia, Brazil, and Germany, but to do away with the veto altogether, as we argue in Chapter 7 on the creation of the Executive Council. The voting privileges within the Security Council remain an unreasonable anachronism.

The merits of the above proposal notwithstanding, it is not wholly exempt from criticisms. An argument can be made that it introduces incentives whereby UN members gain voting power by boosting economic and population growth above the global average. If governments are intent on the pursuit of high-quality economic growth that might be mirrored in a sustainable environment and improved income distribution metrics, as opposed to simply higher GDP, or stabilizing or even slowing down population growth, their voting power in the General Assembly could be eroded over time. We feel these concerns are legitimate and would thus consider the updated Schwartzberg proposals presented above as a major improvement over the one-country-one-vote system, but as a transitional arrangement, pending the arrival of better economic metrics, which more intelligently capture measures of human welfare and sustainability.

Furthermore, the above arguments notwithstanding, it is also possible to have some misgivings about the third factor in the Schwartzberg proposal, based on the "sovereign equality of nations" principle which attributes a one-third weight to each country's voting share in today's General Assembly based on the practice of

---

[13] Scenario II delivers results that are broadly similar, with all three countries' shares just under 2 percent.

one-country-one-vote. At a purely methodological level, the effect of introducing this third factor is to increase the voting shares of the smaller countries and reduce the voting shares of the larger ones. Viewed as a political and transitional factor, introduced to entice the smaller countries to vote for an amendment to the UN Charter that would move the General Assembly to a system of weighted voting, it could make good sense. It would signal to members that voting shares in the General Assembly are not purely based on relative size factors – such as population and the size of the economy as embedded in the GNI/GDP – but include an additional factor that confers some value to the concept of nationhood and the importance of diversity, regardless of the size.

One could also argue that such proposal could be sold to member countries as delivering a system that builds upon the existing one-country-one-vote structure, in operation since 1945 and that would be part of a comprehensive set of reforms that would deliver multiple other benefits to members, including the smaller countries, as noted elsewhere in this volume (e.g., the introduction of a more genuine international rule of law and a system of collective security that would allow a redirection of budgetary resources to more productive ends).

But it is also possible to argue the opposite case. The one-country-one-vote principle could be considered undemocratic, although it has at times given a stronger voice to diverse states and peoples who might not normally be heard or considered influential, arguably to the benefit of the whole organization. However, its application (coupled with the veto power in the Security Council) has turned the United Nations into a less effective organization and the General Assembly, in particular, into a body given too often to political posturing and to the issuing of resolutions that carry the weight of nonbinding recommendations. They do not yet have adequate international democratic legitimacy, as they give the citizens of large countries such as China and India a tiny fraction of the voice given to the citizens of microstates. One could also argue that, other things being equal, it would discourage countries from granting independence to territories with ethnically distinct populations, or from political union as they would lose out voting share. Czechoslovakia doubled its General Assembly voting power when it split into Slovakia and the Czech Republic in 1993.

Embedding – even with a one-third share – the one-country-one-vote practice into a new system of weighted voting might also have other undesirable long-term implications. In the US senate, the state of Wyoming (with a population of slightly more than half a million) has the same number of senators (2) as the state of California, with more than 39 million people. When the US Senate votes to approve an international treaty, for instance, as it did in 1945 when it approved the UN Charter, the weight given to a citizen of Wyoming is 70 times larger than that given to a citizen of California. So, the principle of even-handedness of treatment or the application of the same criteria to all members is considerably strained in this version of the Schwartzberg proposal.

One key argument put forth by those who think that significant reforms are needed at the United Nations is that, in an interdependent world in which the meaning of national borders is being eroded through the forces of globalization, we need to strengthen our mechanisms for international cooperation. We need to join forces and work across national boundaries to address major global problems that take scant notice of notions of nationhood and sovereignty. To address the challenges of climate change, for instance, we need to think and act like world citizens, not in the traditional ways that put the national interest above everything else and which, it must be said, have been largely responsible for our failure to take meaningful actions to mitigate its impacts.

The challenge, in designing a proposal for weighted voting in the General Assembly, is one of balance. The principle of "sovereign equality" has in this context generally been damaging to the United Nations' credibility. One can argue that individual humans – regardless of their nationality or other distinguishing feature such as ethnic origin, gender and so on – should be regarded as equal in terms of their rights and responsibilities, and that we should develop global governance systems that are based on the principle of equality of opportunity, the fundamental principle of the inalienable dignity of the individual human person, and the essential unity of the human race. However, a demographic measure, by itself, could give the most populous countries a de facto power of veto over major decisions of the General Assembly that require a two-thirds majority.

Using a measure of the weight of the economy such as the share in world GDP can seem logical in terms of relative contributions to the UN budget (who pays the bills calls the tune), but it could also be argued that giving the rich and powerful a bigger voice than the poor because they have more money is fundamentally unjust.

The sovereign equality principle (based in part on the principle of self-determination of peoples), while it may seem antidemocratic, acknowledges that the great diversity of nations in size, culture, forms of governance, and experience within the global system needs to be reflected in, and contribute to, global deliberative processes, to enrich them in a way that purely quantitative representation cannot. Minority perspectives can shed additional light on issues that might not at first be apparent to the majority, and decision-making can be strengthened as a result.[14] Our proposal aims at a just balance between these different perspectives.

---

[14] For this reason, and for other reasons of adequate representation and equity among peoples, we would suggest that in any new representative body constituted, special attention be given to ensuring that the voices of indigenous persons around the world are adequately represented and heard, building on the work already done at the UN Permanent Forum on Indigenous Issues.

AN UPDATED CLARK AND SOHN PROPOSAL

In *World Peace through World Law* (1966) Clark and Sohn made a strong case for the introduction of a system of weighted voting in the General Assembly. Clark, in particular, as we saw in Chapter 2, had played an active part in the debates leading to the creation of the United Nations and advocated for a stronger role for the General Assembly, seeing it as the seed of a global legislature with powers in a narrowly defined set of areas, mainly to do with peace and security questions. In framing their proposals and suggesting a particular set of voting shares they faced a number of challenges that are no longer present today. In 1960 there were 99 United Nations members that had joined the organization as fully independent states, but there were close to 100 million people living in non-self-governing and trust territories that, in their view, should also be represented. They also would have faced onerous data collection problems, both as regards coverage across countries and in terms of the quality of the sparse information available, for instance on internationally comparable measures of national income, particularly for developing countries. In setting the criteria for determining voting shares they considered a number of variables but felt that "the introduction of any such other factors would raise so many complications and involve such uncertain and invidious distinctions that is it wiser to hold to the less elaborate formula herein proposed,"[15] which was to link voting shares to population but in a way that created population groupings (e.g., the four largest nations, the next eight largest nations, the next twenty largest nations, and so on) and allocated the same voting share to all countries within each one of these groupings. They did this in a way that allocated proportionally fewer shares to the most populous states, an early application of the principle of digressive proportionality. In their discussion of voting shares Clark and Sohn laid out some principles to guide the determination of voting shares, including that every nation should be entitled to some representation no matter how small, that there should be a reasonable upper limit on the voting share of the most populous countries and that no factors other than population should be considered. Additionally, it was important to have a General Assembly that would not be very large and unwieldy. So, in their proposed allocation, the four states with the highest populations – China, India, the Soviet Union, and the United States – each would be entitled to 30 representatives in a Chamber comprising 568 members, equivalent to a 5.282 percent voting share each. Clark and Sohn's application of the principle of digressive proportionality meant that the 12 largest nations with a 1960 population of 2,186 million people would be allocated 240 representatives, while the remaining 87 nations with a population of 891 million would be entitled to 311 representatives. Clark and Sohn spent considerably more time discussing how representatives to this body would be chosen, what would be the length of service and the relevant areas of legislative authority.

---

[15] Clark and Sohn, *World Peace through Law*, p. xxi.

TABLE 4.2 *Updated General Assembly voting shares under modified Schwartzberg proposal and updated Clark proposal*

Country	Modified Schwartzberg proposal[1]	Updated Clark proposal[2]
Top 20 contributors		
United States of America	8.283	5.277
China	11.993	5.277
Japan	2.483	1.319
Germany	1.871	1.319
United Kingdom	1.406	0.660
France	1.393	0.660
Italy	1.156	0.660
Brazil	1.967	2.639
Canada	0.919	0.528
Russian Federation	1.680	1.319
Republic of Korea	0.993	0.660
Australia	0.726	0.528
Spain	0.891	0.660
Turkey	1.001	1.319
Netherlands	0.545	0.396
Mexico	1.316	1.319
Saudi Arabia	0.698	0.528
Switzerland	0.423	0.264
Argentina	0.626	0.660
Sweden	0.399	0.396
Other countries		
India	7.936	5.277
Poland	0.601	0.528
Indonesia	1.992	2.639
Iran	0.844	1.319
South Africa	0.600	0.660
Nigeria	1.250	2.639
Egypt	0.816	1.319
Pakistan	1.254	2.639
Lesotho	0.184	0.264
Liberia	0.195	0.264

1. From Table 4.1.
2. Allocates voting shares in relation to population using thresholds set at 300, 160, 70, 40, 20, 10, and 1 million people.

Table 4.2 presents an updated Clark and Sohn proposal for the current 193 members that reflects the spirit of their original allocation. It is possible to generate variants of this proposal that distribute voting shares in a way that is somewhat more generous with countries with high populations.

In light of the above discussion and mindful of the various limitations identified for each of the two proposals, we would like to side with the modified updated

Schwartzberg proposal. On balance, we think this is the one that better captures the multiple factors that must be considered in coming up with a system of weighted voting in the General Assembly that is fair and transparent, striking a broadly acceptable balance between giving larger countries greater voice, while ensuring that smaller nations maintain an adequate level of representation. Although both proposals – Schwartzberg's and Clark and Sohn's – are a major improvement over the current system, it is, of course, possible to imagine alternative methodologies to come up with a set of country weights. One should, in any case, see these proposals as transitional arrangements, and as more sensible options to the current one-country-one-vote system, but likely to evolve in time as better data become available.

The Box at the end of this chapter presents Articles 9, 10 and 11 of the current UN Charter on the General Assembly composition, functions and powers. By way of illustration we also present amended versions of the same Articles to be consistent with the updated system of weighted voting proposed here and the enhanced functions and powers of the General Assembly, in light of other proposals made in subsequent chapters. These proposals and revisions concern only the peace and security functions in the UN Charter. A new but similar article will be needed to define the legislative functions and powers of the General Assembly concerning the management of the global environment.

SELECTION OF MEMBERS

We propose a substantial revision of the powers, composition and method of voting of the General Assembly, as initially laid out in the revised Articles 9–22 of the UN Charter. In the first instance, the General Assembly would be given some powers to legislate with direct effect on member states, mainly in the areas of security, maintenance of peace and management of the global environment, with other issues (e.g., surveillance of global financial policies) remaining under the purview of the relevant specialized UN agencies and other international bodies. The General Assembly would take on further legislative powers in progressive steps subject to review of such powers every five years by its members. Powers delegated to the General Assembly would be explicitly laid out and enumerated in the revised Charter which would also contain – in a revised Article 2 on Purposes and Principles – clarity as to what powers would remain vested with member states to protect national autonomy and would not be delegated to the Assembly, following, for example, the EU model of subsidiarity (and proportionality), and/or a clarification of the proper division of powers as seen in systems characterized by federal forms of government. The General Assembly would retain its considerable powers of non-binding recommendation in any areas deemed to have an impact on the welfare of the world's people.

In respect of the manner of selection of the Assembly's representatives we propose the gradual introduction of full popular vote, in three separate stages. In the first stage – lasting eight years or two four-year terms of the General Assembly – representatives would be chosen by their respective national legislatures or, in their absence, according to procedures within other duly constituted governance structures. In the second stage, at least half of the deputies would be chosen by popular vote within a given country; this stage would also last eight years. Finally, in the third stage all deputies would be chosen by popular national vote. Such elections would have to be certified by an impartial international elections board, according to international standards of free and fair elections, before the representative could be confirmed for service in the Assembly. While it may seem a stretch that all countries of the world would be expected to eventually elect their international representatives by popular vote, it has been noted that, in parallel with the wide array of statements emanating from UN bodies affirming the importance of democracy (see those mentioned in Chapter 5, below), as of the 1990s on the international plane, an emerging global "consensus" has been observed that democratic societies might be the "sole feasible social structure."[16] As regards voting procedures within the General Assembly, decisions would be made by a majority of representatives present and voting, with particularly sensitive issues requiring potentially larger majorities and including, in some cases, at least two-thirds of the representatives of the 19 most populous nations.

Current UN Charter

Chapter IV   *The General Assembly Composition*

Article 9
1.   The General Assembly shall consist of all the Members of the United Nations.
2.   Each Member shall have not more than five representatives in the General Assembly.

Functions and Powers

Article 10
The General Assembly may discuss any questions or any matters within the scope of the present Charter or relating to the powers and functions of any organs provided for

---

[16]   See, e.g., Wouters, J., Bart De Meester, and C. Ryngaert. 2004. *Democracy and International Law*, Leuven, Leuven Interdisciplinary Research Group on International Agreements and Development (LIRGIAD), p. 4. Richard Falk has wryly observed that despite widespread zeal for and agreement on democratic processes among western nations in particular, there has been "surprisingly little spill over with respect to world politics," with "most liberal democracies [...] quite comfortable with the lack of popular participation, transparency, accountability, even the rule of law, when it [comes] to the procedures and decisions of international institutions." The current proposals seek to assist in remedying this dissonance. Falk, Richard. 2014. *(Re)Imagining Humane Global Governance*. Abingdon, UK and New York, USA, Routledge, p. 125.

in the present Charter, and, except as provided in Article 12, may make recommendations to the Members of the United Nations or to the Security Council or to both on any such questions or matters.

Article 11
1. The General Assembly may consider the general principles of cooperation in the maintenance of international peace and security, including the principles governing disarmament and the regulation of armaments, and may make recommendations with regard to such principles to the Members or to the Security Council or to both.
2. The General Assembly may discuss any questions relating to the maintenance of international peace and security brought before it by any Member of the United Nations, or by the Security Council, or by a state which is not a Member of the United Nations in accordance with Article 35, paragraph 2, and, except as provided in Article 12, may make recommendations with regard to any such questions to the state or states concerned or to the Security Council or to both. Any such question on which action is necessary shall be referred to the Security Council by the General Assembly either before or after discussion.
3. The General Assembly may call the attention of the Security Council to situations which are likely to endanger international peace and security.
4. The powers of the General Assembly set forth in this Article shall not limit the general scope of Article 10.

Revised Articles 9, 10, and 11[17]

Chapter IV   *The General Assembly Composition*

Article 9
1. The General Assembly shall consist of Representatives from all the member nations.[18]
2. The number of representatives in the General Assembly shall be directly proportional to each member nation's voting share. The voting share shall be determined as the arithmetic average of each member's world population share, world GDP share, and a membership share which shall be equal for all members.
3. The apportionment of Representatives pursuant to the foregoing formula shall be made by the General Assembly upon the basis of world censuses and GDP estimates as compiled and published in the World Bank's World Development

---

[17] For a fuller discussion of these revisions, please see Clark and Sohn, *World Peace through World Law*, 1966, pp. 20–40. The revised language for these articles provided here, updates the work done and published by Clark and Sohn then.

[18] In deference to the large number of people still living under colonial arrangements in the early 1960s, Clark and Sohn suggested adding "and from the non-self-governing and trust territories under their administration." To the extent that there are still some people – however few – living in such non-self-governing territories at the time the Charter is amended it will be important to ensure that they have adequate representation.

Indicators. The first census shall be taken within ten years after the coming into force of this revised Charter and subsequent censuses shall be taken in every tenth year thereafter, in such manner as the Assembly shall direct. The Assembly shall make a reapportionment of the Representatives within two years after each such census.

4. Until the first apportionment of Representatives shall be made by the General Assembly upon the basis of the first world census, the apportionment of Representatives in the Assembly shall be based on the latest and most authoritative figures compiled by the United Nations Population Division.

5. Representatives shall be chosen for terms of four years, such terms to begin at noon on the Third Tuesday of September in every fourth year.

6. For the first two terms after the coming into force of this revised Charter, the Representatives from each member nation shall be chosen by its national legislature, or, in the absence of such a body, by the government through a process of consultation to ensure broad representation, except to the extent that such legislature may prescribe the election of the representatives by popular vote. For the next two terms, not less than half of the representatives from each member nation shall be elected by popular vote and the remainder shall be chosen by its national legislature, unless such legislature shall prescribe that all or part of such remainder shall also be elected by popular vote; provided that any member nation entitled to only one Representative during this two-term period may choose its Representative either through its national legislature or by popular vote as such legislature shall determine. Beginning with the fifth term, all the Representatives of each member nation shall be elected by popular vote. The General Assembly may, however, by a two-thirds vote of all the Representatives in the Assembly, whether or not present or voting, postpone for not more than four years the coming into effect of the requirement that not less than half of the Representatives shall be elected by popular vote; and the Assembly may also by a like majority postpone for not more than four years the requirement that all the Representatives shall be elected by popular vote. In all elections by popular vote held under this paragraph, all persons shall be entitled to vote who are qualified to vote for the members of the most numerous branch of the national legislatures of the respective nations, with the results being subject to international electoral certification.

7. Any vacancy among the Representatives of any member nation shall be filled in such manner as the national legislature of such member nation may determine. A Representative chosen to fill a vacancy shall hold office for the remainder of the term of his predecessor.

8. The Representatives shall receive reasonable compensation, to be fixed by the General Assembly and to be paid out of the funds of the United Nations.

9. There will be a limitation of three four-year terms on the length of service of Representatives.

Functions and Powers

Article 10
The General Assembly shall have the power:

a. to enact legislation binding upon member nations and all the peoples thereof, within the definite fields and in accordance with the strictly limited authority hereinafter delegated;
b. to deal with disputes, situations, threats to the peace, breaches of the peace, acts of aggression and matters relating to management of the planetary environment, as hereinafter provided;
c. to make nonbinding recommendations to the member nations, as hereinafter provided;
d. to elect the members of other organs of the United Nations, as hereinafter provided;
e. to discuss, and to direct and control the policies and actions of the other organs and agencies of the United Nations, with the exception of the International Court of Justice; and
f. to discuss any questions or any matters within the scope of this revised Charter.

Article 11
1. The General Assembly shall have the primary responsibility for the maintenance of international peace and security, and for ensuring compliance with this revised Charter and the laws and regulations enacted thereunder.
2. To this end the General Assembly shall have the following legislative powers:
    a. to enact such laws and regulations as are authorized by Annex I of this revised Charter relating to universal, enforceable and comprehensive national disarmament, including the control of nuclear energy and the use of outer space;
    b. to enact such laws and regulations as are authorized by Annex II of this revised Charter relating to the military forces necessary for the enforcement of universal and comprehensive national disarmament, for the prevention and removal of threats to the peace, for the suppression of acts of aggression and other breaches of the peace, and for ensuring compliance with this revised Charter and the laws and regulations enacted thereunder;
    c. to enact appropriate laws defining the conditions and establishing the general rules for the application of the measures provided for in Chapter VII;
    d. to enact appropriate laws, as needed, establishing what acts or omissions of individuals or private organizations within the following categories shall be deemed offenses against the United Nations: (1) acts or omissions of government officials of any nation which either themselves constitute or directly cause a threat of force, or the actual use of force by one nation against any other nation, except that no use of force in self-defense under the circumstances defined in Article 51 of this revised Charter shall be made such an offense; (2) acts or omissions of any government official or any other

individual or any private organization which either themselves constitute or directly cause a serious violation of Annex I of this revised Charter or of any law or regulation enacted thereunder; (3) acts or omissions causing damage to the property of the United Nations or injuring any person in the service of the United Nations while engaged in the performance of official duties or on account of the performance of such duties; and (4) acts or omissions of any individual in the service of any organ or agency of the United Nations, including the United Nations International Peace Force, which in the judgment of the General Assembly are seriously detrimental to the purposes of the United Nations;

e. to enact appropriate laws:
   (1) prescribing the penalties for such offense as are defined by the General Assembly pursuant to the foregoing subparagraph (d);
   (2) providing for the apprehension of individuals accused of offenses which the Assembly has defined as sufficiently serious to require apprehension, such apprehension to be by the United Nations civil police provided for in Annex III or by national authorities pursuant to arrangements with the United Nations or by the joint action of both;
   (3) establishing procedures for the trial of such individuals in the courts administered by the United Nations, provided for in Annex III; and
   (4) providing adequate means for the enforcement of penalties.

3. No such law shall, however, relieve an individual from responsibility for any punishable offense by reason of the fact that such individual acted as head of state or as a member of a nation's government. Nor shall any such laws relieve an individual from responsibility for any such offense on the ground that he has acted pursuant to an order of his government or of a superior, if, in the circumstances at the time, it was reasonably possible for him to refuse compliance with that order.

4. The member nations agree to accept and carry out the laws and regulations enacted by the General Assembly under paragraph 2 of this Article, and the decisions of the Assembly made under this revised Charter including the Annexes; provided, however, that any member nation shall have the right to contest the validity of any such law, regulation or decision by appeal to the International Court of Justice. Pending the judgment of the Court upon any such appeal, the contested law, regulation, or decision shall nevertheless be carried out, unless the Assembly or the Court shall make an order permitting noncompliance, in whole or in part, during the Court's consideration of the appeal.

5. As soon as possible after the coming into force of this revised Charter, the Executive Council shall negotiate with any state that may not have become a member of the United Nations an agreement by which such state will agree to observe all the prohibitions and requirements of the disarmament plan contained in Annex I of this revised Charter, and to accept and carry out all the laws, regulations, and decisions made thereunder, and by which the United Nations

will recognize the right of any such state and of its citizens to all the protection and remedies guaranteed by this revised Charter to member nations and their citizens with respect to the enforcement of Annex I and the laws, regulations, and decisions made thereunder. If a state refuses to make such an agreement, the Executive Council shall inform the General Assembly, which shall decide upon measures to be taken to ensure the carrying out of the disarmament plan in the territory of such state.

5

A World Parliamentary Assembly: A Catalyst for Change

The assembly's very existence would also help promote the peaceful resolution of inter-national conflicts. Because elected delegates would represent individuals and society instead of states, they would not have to vote along national lines. Coalitions would likely form on other bases, such as world-view, political orientation, and interests. Compromises among such competing but nonmilitarized coalitions might eventually undermine reliance on the current war system, in which international decisions are still made by heavily armed nations that are poised to destroy one another. In due course, international relations might more closely resemble policymaking within the most democratic societies in the world.[1]

Richard Falk and Andrew Strauss

The United Nations is not a world government, but it is our primary forum to discuss issues and risks of global significance in an increasingly interdependent world. Whether it is perceived as being imbued with a strong dose of democratic legitimacy matters a great deal for its effectiveness, credibility, and ability to become a problem-solving organization. For all of these reasons, and for those expressed below, we suggest the establishment of a significantly reformed General Assembly as explained in Chapter 4. Until such significant reforms are realized, in this chapter we also sketch out the possibility of an interim "World Parliamentary Assembly" that could serve as an advisory body to the General Assembly, acting as a type of "second chamber," and greatly enhancing the legitimacy of the UN as a global decision-maker as soon as possible.

This is particularly important because the United Nations General Assembly itself on a number of occasions has expressed its unambiguous support for democratic forms of governance for its members. For instance, General Assembly Resolution 44/146 (1989) on

---

[1] Falk, Richard and Andrew Strauss. 2001. "Toward Global Parliament." *Foreign Affairs*, January/February. https://ssrn.com/abstract=1130417

Enhancing the effectiveness of the principle of periodic and genuine elections [stressed] its conviction that periodic and genuine elections are a necessary and indispensable element of sustained efforts to protect the rights and interests of the governed and that, as a matter of practical experience, the right of everyone to take part in the government of his or her country is a crucial factor in the effective enjoyment by all of a wide range of other human rights and fundamental freedoms, embracing political, economic, social and cultural rights.[2]

And General Assembly Resolution 55/2 (2000), one of the more substantive resolutions issued in recent decades, also known as the United Nations Millennium Declaration, states: "We consider certain fundamental values to be essential to international relations in the twenty-first century." These include: freedom, equality, solidarity, tolerance, respect for nature, and that "democratic and participatory governance based on the will of the people best assures these rights."[3] Clearly the United Nations voice in these important matters would carry considerably more weight if it were seen itself as being imbued by adequate levels of democratic legitimacy.

The idea of establishing a second chamber at the United Nations has existed since the organization's inception. Grenville Clark and Louis Sohn wrestled with the issue as they worked on *World Peace through World Law* in the 1950s. While not actually recommending the creation of a bicameral UN, they stated: "We hold no dogmatic views on this difficult subject, the essential point being that there must be some radical, yet equitable, change in the present system of representation in the General Assembly as a basis for conferring upon the Assembly certain essential, although carefully limited, powers of legislation which it does not now possess."[4] The idea is certainly older than the UN; the founders of the League of Nations for a time considered adding a people's assembly as part of the League's initial organizational structure.

One key motivation was to enhance the democratic character of the UN by establishing a firmer linkage between the organization and the peoples it was meant to serve. The preamble to the UN Charter starts with "We the peoples" and highlights our determination to "save succeeding generations from the scourge of war" and to achieve other noble ends. But, in time, the General Assembly, which comes closest among the UN's existing agencies to representing the will of the people, falls far short of this. The men and women who serve on the General Assembly are diplomats representing the executive branches of their respective governments and there is generally no meaningful, direct linkage between them

---

[2] UN General Assembly. 1989, "Enhancing the Effectiveness of the Principle of Periodic and Genuine Elections," Resolution 44/146, para. 2. www.un.org/documents/ga/res/44/a44r146.htm.

[3] UN General Assembly. 2000. "United Nations Millennium Declaration," General Assembly Resolution 55/2. New York: United Nations. para. 6. www.un.org/millennium/declaration/ares552e.htm

[4] Ibid., p. xxi.

and the people they are supposed to represent. In fact, in many countries, there is no linkage between the governments themselves and the people they rule over because they are not working democracies. In his open letter to the General Assembly of October 1947 Albert Einstein stated:

> the method of representation at the United Nations should be considerably modi-fied. The present method of selection by government appointment does not leave any real freedom to the appointee. Furthermore, selection by governments cannot give the peoples of the world the feeling of being fairly and proportionately represented. The moral authority of the United Nations would be considerably enhanced if the delegates were elected directly by the people. Were they respon-sible to an electorate, they would have much more freedom to follow their consciences. Thus we could hope for more statesmen and fewer diplomats.[5]

In time, rather than bring a measure of democratic legitimacy to the General Assembly by providing for the direct election of its members – an innovation that would require amendments to the UN Charter, as outlined in Chapter 4 – proposals emerged that put forward the creation of a second chamber, a World Parliamentary Assembly (WPA), complementary to the General Assembly, which would continue to be the main locus of government-to-government interactions. The WPA would help bridge the democratic legitimacy gap that arises when an organization, through its actions (e.g., the drafting of Conventions, decisions to intervene or not on behalf of the international community in various conflicts, the actions of its various specialized agencies and related organizations) can affect in tangible ways people's welfare, but those affected by these decisions have little input in how they are formulated, arrived at, and implemented, thereby creating a disconnection between citizens and the United Nations.

In Chapter 4 on the General Assembly we argued in favor of giving the General Assembly greater powers to legislate in a narrow set of areas, to empower it to actually begin to deliver on the main aspirations embedded in the UN Charter. We think that this idea would gain greater acceptance and better outcomes would be ensured if the UN moved, as quickly as possible, to establish interim mechanisms that also represent peoples more directly, not just governments and/or states. Gov-ernments' main interest at the UN to date, by and large (either consciously or through the power of inertia), is the preservation of a system overly reliant on a too-narrow conception of the sovereign state. With the possible exception of the member states of the European Union, they are mainly motivated by the belief that "a nation-state cannot be subjected to, or made accountable for the decisions of any authority beyond itself."[6] This may have been a convenient ideological foundation

[5] Einstein, Albert. 1947. "To the General Assembly of the United Nations., para. 10. http://lotoisdumonde.fr/initiatives/FSMAN/Einstein-UN-letter-1947-oct.pdf.

[6] Heinrich, Dieter. 2010. *The Case for a United Nations Parliamentary Assembly*, Berlin, Committee for a Democratic U.N., p. 9.

for the UN for the major powers in 1945 but it has increasingly turned into an absurdity – close to 200 sovereign states operating in an interdependent world increasingly in need of a global rule of law, but bound by a chaotic patchwork of different, at times contradictory, sets of rules.

Representing the interests of the global citizenry, a new WPA, advising the current UN General Assembly, could bring in a fresh global perspective on the broad array of unresolved problems that we currently confront. It would be in a stronger position to promote higher levels of international cooperation because its members would be called upon to see such problems through the lens of humanity's better interests rather than narrow national considerations. The WPA also could be a much more effective catalyst for advancing the process of reform and transformation at the United Nations itself because, as we shall explain below, its members would have a much looser linkage with their respective governments and their specific national – as opposed to global – priorities. In the 2010 version of his original paper making the case for the establishment of a United Nations Parliamentary Assembly, Heinrich notes that such a body could also play a role in reinforcing democratic tendencies in many corners of the world and foster "a new planetarian ethos by symbolizing the idea of the world as one community."[7]

SETTING UP A WORLD PARLIAMENTARY ASSEMBLY

Article 22 of the UN Charter states: "The General Assembly may establish such subsidiary organs as it deems necessary for the performance of its functions."[8] It is likely that the creation of a WPA would be seen in the spirit of the "important questions" identified in Article 18 of the Charter, which require a two-thirds majority of those members present and voting for approval, but would not require the approval of the permanent members of the Security Council. So, building public and governmental support for a General Assembly resolution putting in motion the establishment of a WPA would be the first step in what would likely be a multi-stakeholder process, involving wide consultations. However, this process will not start from zero. The creation of a WPA has already received strong endorsements from a number of major organizations and bodies. In 1993 the Canadian House of Commons Standing Committee on External Affairs and International Trade recommended that "Canada support the development of a United Nations Parliamentary Assembly."[9] In 2005, with the support of the Committee for a Democratic UN – now known as Democracy without Borders – 108 Swiss Parliamentarians sent an

---

7   Ibid., p.12.
8   For an excellent overview of the full range of issues pertaining to the setting up of a WPA, see Leinen, Jo and Andreas Bummel. 2018. *A World Parliament: Governance and Democracy in the 21st Century*, Berlin, Democracy without Borders.
9   8th Report of the Standing Committee on External Affairs and International Trade, House of Commons, Parliament of Canada, Spring 1993, chaired by Hon. Jon Bosley, 1993.

open letter to UN Secretary General Kofi Annan calling for the establishment of a WPA.[10] That same year the Congress of the Liberal International followed suit by calling "on the member states of the United Nations to enter into deliberations on the establishment of a Parliamentary Assembly at the United Nations."[11]

Also in June 2005 (and again in July 2018) the European Parliament issued a resolution that called for "the establishment of a United Nations Parliamentary Assembly (UNPA) within the UN system, which would increase the democratic profile and internal democratic process of the organisation and allow world civil society to be directly associated in the decision-making process," also stating that "the Parliamentary Assembly should be vested with genuine rights of information, participation and control, and should be able to adopt recommendations directed at the UN General Assembly."[12] These declarations were given further stimulus in 2007 with the establishment of the International Campaign for a United Nations Parliamentary Assembly, an umbrella organization that, as of 2018, has brought together over 150 civil society groups and 1540 parliamentarians from 123 countries. It defines itself as:

> a global network of parliamentarians, non-governmental organizations, scholars, and dedicated citizens that advocates democratic representation of the world's citizens at the United Nations. A United Nations Parliamentary Assembly, UNPA, for the first time would give elected citizen representatives, not only states, a direct and influential role in global policy.[13]

The World Federation of United Nations Associations issued a resolution at their World Congress on October 21, 2018, stating that it "supports steps towards the creation of a United Nations Parliamentary Assembly" and that the UN "must address the democratic deficit within global decision-making processes" if it is to be successful "in the pursuit of creating a better world for all and ensuring that no one is left behind."[14] A similar resolution was issued in May of 2016 by the Pan-African Parliament.[15]

---

[10] Establishment of a Parliamentary Assembly at the UN, Committee for a Democratic United Nations, February 8, 2005: https://en.unpacampaign.org/about/declarations/unpa-appeal/en/.

[11] Strengthening citizens representation on international level through an UN Parliamentary Assembly, Resolution adopted by the 53rd Congress of the Liberal International on May 14, 2005, in Sofia.

[12] www.europarl.europa.eu/sides/getDoc.do?type=TA&language=EN&reference=P6-TA-2005-0237. The 2018 resolution was arguably even stronger than that of 2005, requesting that the EU's governments call for "the establishment of a United Nations Parliamentary Assembly" and to support a "UN 2020 summit" that would consider "comprehensive reform measures for a renewal and strengthening of the United Nations."

[13] https://en.unpacampaign.org/

[14] https://en.unpacampaign.org/11200/world-congress-of-united-nations-associations-calls-for-a-un-parliamentary-assembly/.

[15] https://en.unpacampaign.org/7629/pan-african-parliament-calls-on-african-union-to-support-the-creation-of-a-un-parliamentary-assembly/.

Despite these initiatives and prominent statements, it is reasonable to assume that there will be some opposition. The obstacles are likely to be of at least two kinds. First, there may well be resistance within some of the member states of the UN, for whom institutional inertia is a defining characteristic. This might be particularly the case for some of the larger states, including those with veto power in the Security Council, which might hesitate to introduce institutional innovations that could upset internal power relationships or that might introduce a degree of unpredictability – or simply change – in the management of UN affairs. For that reason, it will likely be necessary to approach this project in a multistaged way. In the first instance, the WPA would, as described above, be set up as a consultative body, with the power to make recommendations on issues of international concern but with no effective political power; an adjunct institution to the General Assembly with responsibilities that would be difficult to perceive as a threat to the established political order. Learning from past experience, it would be useful to continue to support the building of a civil society coalition that would make the case for the establishment of such a body and would seek to obtain the support of sympathetic governments to play a catalytic role within the General Assembly, building a critical mass of support. In this regard, governments such as that of Canada and the European Parliament could be potentially important allies.

There is, moreover, a useful model to guide the future evolution of the WPA. The European Parliamentary Assembly was established by the six founding members of the European Economic Community (EEC) (Belgium, France, Germany, Italy, Luxembourg, and the Netherlands) and met for the first time on March 19, 1958. It initially had 142 members drawn from the parliaments of the EEC's six members, with the Assembly subsequently changing its name to the "European Parliament" in March 1962. In the early years, members of the European Parliament served in a dual national and European capacity, but at a Summit Conference in Paris in December 1974 the decision was taken to move to direct election of members by universal suffrage, with the first such election taking place in June 1979. With the accession of Denmark, Ireland, and the United Kingdom in 1974, the number of members of the European Parliament (MEPs) was increased to 198. Successive enlargements took place with the accession of Greece in 1981, Spain and Portugal in 1986, and other countries in later years. The Treaty of Lisbon in 2009 capped the number of MEPs at 751.

More important, however, than these membership enlargements, reflecting the growth of the EU from 6 to 28 members over the past several decades, has been the expansion of its powers. The Treaty of Luxembourg significantly expanded the powers of the Parliament in budgetary matters in April of 1970, to coincide with a shift in the sources of funding of the EEC, from member state contributions to its own resources. The 1987 Single European Act made accession and association treaties for prospective new members subject to parliamentary approval. The Maastricht Treaty in 1992 expanded the powers of Parliament by making the membership of the Commission subject to parliamentary approval, de facto giving it control over the EU's executive functions. These powers were further expanded with the Treaty of Amsterdam in 1997, which devolved to the European Parliament certain powers from national governments to other areas such as legislation on immigration, adopting European legislation in certain areas of civil and criminal law, and foreign and security policy. The Treaties of Nice (2001) and Lisbon (2009) saw further expansion of the Parliament's powers, with the latter adding some 45 areas where the Parliament would essentially share a codecision role with the Council of Ministers.

From its humble beginnings as a parliamentary assembly in 1958, the European Parliament has moved over the past decades to the center of decision-making on issues of concern to the European Union and has attained a large measure of democratic legitimacy. Interestingly, its members are not grouped by nationality but by broadly shared political persuasions or beliefs, suggesting that shared ideas and values are now considered more important that political geography. A European Parliament model, with stages of incremental and progressive development (e.g., by initially establishing a parliamentary advisory body at the UN under Article 22 of the Charter), however, is not the only proposal on the table for the setting up of a WPA at the UN. Some have suggested an amendment to the UN Charter under Article 109 to establish a more robust legislative body in the first instance (see Chapter 4) which, however, requires the approval of two thirds of the UN's members and the assent of all permanent members of the Security Council, a high barrier to clear.[16]

Launching a WPA under the power given to the General Assembly under Article 22 to establish subsidiary organs may be a more promising approach than seeking an amendment to the Charter. Indeed, the case can be made that getting 129 members of the General Assembly to support a WPA resolution would not be an insurmountable obstacle since there is, in general, broad awareness that, as currently constituted, the United Nations is no longer "fit for purpose" and there is a need to narrow the governance gap associated with our collective inability to confront serious global problems. If anything, this sense that our current global order is in need of significant repair might well intensify in coming years, under the onslaught of a multitude of unresolved global problems.

A possibly more promising and speedier approach than persuading 129 members of the General Assembly to launch a WPA could be through a standalone treaty

---

[16] Article 109 states: "1. A General Conference of the Members of the United Nations for the purpose of reviewing the present Charter may be held at a date and place to be fixed by a two-thirds vote of the members of the General Assembly and by a vote of any nine members of the Security Council. Each Member of the United Nations shall have one vote in the conference. 2. Any alteration of the present Charter recommended by a two-thirds vote of the conference shall take effect when ratified in accordance with their respective constitutional processes by two thirds of the Members of the United Nations including all the permanent members of the Security Council."

which might get the WPA off the ground with the participation of some 30 members, representing a broad spectrum of the UN's membership. This could set a process in place for the subsequent ratification by other members. A similar procedure was followed, of course, for the creation of some of the UN's leading and/or long-standing organizations, such as the World Health Organization (WHO) and the International Labor Organization (ILO).

In any event, as the above discussion makes clear, there are multiple paths to the establishment of a WPA. Another possibility would be to follow the model used in the negotiations of the Land Mines Treaty; a "single negotiating text method" could be adopted for the creation of the WPA, with first discussions taking place outside UN structures. Initial efforts to establish the WPA in this scenario could include consultations between like-minded, sympathetic stakeholders and could be enabled by the support of a core group of supportive states. While desirable, it would not be essential to have the consent of all or even the majority of nations to get this institution off the ground. Any state could join this initiative and it is expected that citizens would urge their governments to support the WPA. In time, as the WPA gained democratic legitimacy, it could be integrated into the international constitutional order, attached as an advisory body to the General Assembly, consistent, as noted earlier, with Article 22 of the UN Charter that empowers the Assembly to create "subsidiary organs."

It is not unreasonable to expect that WPA members, given their closer links to national parliaments and their constituents, might then see themselves less bound to national interests and priorities. Diverse coalitions might then emerge and the WPA's very existence would contribute to finding creative solutions to global problems. The power, ingenuity and efficacy of coordinated transnational civil society movements, including "smart coalitions" with like-minded states, have proven themselves in the recent remarkable successes of, for example, the creation of the International Criminal Court (ICC) and the Land Mines Treaty (see Chapter 21 for more information on transnational civil society coalitions and "citizen diplomacy").

A second kind of objection or obstacle to the establishment of a WPA, as discussed in Chapter 4 in relation to a significantly reformed General Assembly, would likely stem from a potential lack of agreement on the basic architecture of such an organ. Who would be its members? What would be the criteria for representation in a community of member nations ranging in population size from China and India to Palau and Nauru? How would one address the issue of the nondemocratic nature of many of the members of the UN? Would countries' participation in the WPA be based on the principle of one-person-one-vote or some other principle that could be applied consistently across all members? Might democratic nations object to the participation of nondemocratic/authoritarian regimes in an institution that would have as a key primary purpose to bring to the UN a measure of democratic legitimacy?

These are central questions, but they are amenable to sensible proposals and solutions that will be useful in planning the broader UN reform. Obviously, the design of the WPA's architecture would have to employ a consultative process and involve a broad cross-section of humanity. A high-level panel, or expert group, within or external to the UN could be set up to review existing answers to the above questions and to suggest, as needed, alternative avenues. In the pages that follow we put forward two alternative proposals, one that builds on the work done in this area by Dieter Heinrich[17] and Joseph Schwartzberg[18] and another which was originally proposed by Richard Falk and Andrew Strauss.[19] These proposals are distinctive from those set out in Chapter 4, as they are relevant for an Assembly at first constituted by members appointed or chosen from members of national parliaments or similar bodies.

A MODIFIED HEINRICH/SCHWARTZBERG WPA

Heinrich and Schwartzberg envisage a WPA made up of members appointed by or chosen from members of national parliaments of UN member states, a proposal very much in the spirit of the formation of the European Parliament. Neither is opposed to the direct election of members, but both consider it as being premature; a complex undertaking for which, given the diversity of the UN membership and the different political regimes currently in existence, the international community is not yet ready for. It is, of course, a desirable goal for the future, a natural conclusion to an evolutionary process that would have several intermediate stages. As a start, national parliamentarians as members of the WPA would certainly bridge in a clear way part of the democratic deficit at the UN. They would in general be more representative of the populations of their respective countries than unelected government bureaucrats and/or diplomats serving their countries at the United Nations. As they would generally do in their home countries, members of the WPA would see themselves as representing their countries' citizens and could play the role of advocates for the United Nations in their home countries. Their participation in the WPA should also broadly reflect the distribution of political power in the national parliament across the different political parties and persuasions (e.g., right, left, green, etc.). Furthermore, we would strongly favor the introduction of some gender quota system, to ensure sufficient gender diversity in the WPA. At the

---

[17] Heinrich, Dieter. 2003. "Extension of Democracy to the Global Level," in Saul H. Medlovitz and Barbara Walker (eds.), *A Reader on Second Assembly & Parliamentary Proposals*, New Jersey, Center for UN Reform Education, pp. 68–73; Heinrich, *The Case for a United Nations Parliamentary Assembly*.

[18] Schwartzberg, Joseph E. 2013. "A Credible Human Rights System," in *Transforming the United Nations System: Designs for a Workable World*, Tokyo and New York, United Nations University Press.

[19] Falk, Richard and Andrew Strauss. 2001. "Toward Global Parliament," *Foreign Affairs*, Vol. 80, No. 1, January/February, New York, pp. 212–220.

moment, according to data compiled by the Interparliamentary Union, on average the share of women in parliaments worldwide in 2019 stands at slightly more than 23 percent. There is credible evidence from a range of studies about the benefits of higher participation of women in village councils, national parliaments, corporate boards in publicly listed companies, and other such decision-making bodies; introducing approximately a 40 percent quota for women in the WPA, therefore, would be highly desirable.[20,21]

There would be no obligation for countries to participate in the WPA; member country governments could opt out if they wished. Countries could also be given the option to choose distinguished citizens (e.g., former members of national parliaments, retired judges, eminent citizens at large) as WPA members if they felt that the double burden of serving in the national parliament and the WPA might represent an excessive claim on their time, particularly if, as could be expected, the WPA would be available for business and deliberations during a not insignificant portion of the calendar year. By the same token, countries that felt they had the institutional machinery in place for the direct and credible election of WPA members from the outset could not reasonably be prevented from opting to do so, in a voluntary fashion. The activities of the WPA would be funded from the UN budget and the cost of its operations is not initially expected to be onerous. In any event, as we discuss in Chapter 12 on a new funding mechanism for the UN, there would be adequate resources available to finance these activities under the 0.1% of gross national income (GNI) annual funding target we are recommending.

Members could serve for four-year terms, subject to a two-term limit. We think that this would be desirable to avoid the emergence of a professional political class for which long tenures in office can sometimes contribute to a shift in incentives and motivations, with remaining in office at times overriding all other considerations. Deliberative bodies can also benefit from infusions of fresh blood, new perspectives and the energy of younger (and maybe more idealistic) new generations of leaders. One would hope also that the WPA would be good training in the workings of democracy, and this could be an invaluable experience for members from countries with limited, imperfect, or nonexistent traditions of consultative democracy. We also think that there is merit in the idea that WPA members should be provided with legal protections, in particular against possible retaliation from their home governments for taking positions that they might perceive in the global

---

[20] As we will see below, under a variety of schemes under consideration for the apportionment of WPA members from the UN membership, many countries will have no more than one representative. In such cases, governments will have to commit to give women in their respective constituencies the opportunity to be chosen by ensuring, for instance, that there are enough women in the lists of eligible candidates drawn from each parliament.

[21] On the empirical evidence about the benefits of improving women's political empowerment, see López-Claros, Augusto and Bahiyyih Nakhjavani. 2018. *Equality for Women = Prosperity for All: The Disastrous Crisis of Gender Inequality*, New York, St. Martin's Press.

public interest, but which governments might judge as counter to established national priorities and/or policies, as determined by the government then in power.

One early challenge in the setting up of the WPA would be how to manage the participation of nondemocratic and/or authoritarian regimes. Painful tradeoffs are likely. On the one hand, since the WPA is brought into being to imbue the UN with a greater degree of democratic legitimacy, one would favor processes for the election of its members that would exemplify the very principles of accountability, transparency, consultation, and rule of law that underpin accepted norms of good governance (as discussed in Chapter 20 on the principles and values underpinning global governance reforms). On the other, one would wish a WPA that was truly universal in its representation of the human family and this would mean, inevitably, including those parts of the world where citizens, often through no fault of their own, are ruled by autocratic regimes and governments that either do not believe in the periodic legitimization of rule through the ballot box and/or would not wish to put themselves through that test. How to guard against, for instance, China ensuring that all of its (likely several dozen) members to the WPA would be card-carrying members of the Communist Party?

There may be no easy solution to this particular quandary in this first stage of the WPA, where its role will be largely advisory. Laurenti regards the existence of nondemocratic states as being an insurmountable obstacle to the creation of a WPA, because the presence of representatives from these countries (e.g., Belarus, China, Cuba, North Korea, Sudan, Syria, Venezuela, many countries in the Arab world, and a significant number in sub-Saharan Africa) would undermine the WPA's desirable democratic character.[22] We do not wish to minimize the importance of this concern. However, the existence of authoritarian regimes did not prevent the creation of the UN itself and the General Assembly's membership is made up of fully democratic states, some that are flawed in their democratic character, and many others that are characterized by various shades of authoritarianism.

That is, unfortunately, the state of democracy in the world today. Close to 32 percent of the countries included in *The Economist*'s Democracy Index 2018 are authoritarian regimes of some form or other.[23] But, as noted earlier, their presence in the General Assembly has not prevented that body from endorsing democratic and participatory forms of governance as the most desirable option for

---

[22] Laurenti, Jeffrey. 2003. "An Idea Whose Time Has Not Come," in Saul H. Medlovitz and Barbara Walker (eds.), *A Reader on Second Assembly & Parliamentary Proposals*, New Jersey, Center for UN Reform Education, pp. 119–129.

[23] According to The Economist's Democracy Index 2018, of the 167 countries covered in the index, 20 are full democracies, 55 are flawed democracies, 39 are hybrid regimes, and 53 are fully authoritarian. The index brings together five key elements of democracy that capture the electoral process and pluralism, the functioning of government, political participation, political culture, and civil liberties. So, a total of 114 countries are nonauthoritarian, equivalent to 68.3 percent of the total.

its members. Thus, rather than wait for the time when all members will be democratic (possibly a very long time), we would favor an approach that was broadly inclusive, and that as long as the majority of the WPA's members were democratic, the Assembly could still function effectively and be a catalyst for change. Laurenti also raises questions, with the possibility of the appearance of this new global institution, about the willingness of citizens to tolerate the stresses that would be placed upon them by the existence of a global "mandatory regime" that would be "dominated by people unlike themselves," by "aliens" as he calls those of a different nationality.[24] We will come back to this issue in the last section of this chapter. Suffice it to say now that, in the early stages, there is very little in our vision of a WPA that is "mandatory" in nature; its role would initially be largely advisory, like the European Parliamentary Assembly set up in 1958.

One possible compromise, for instance, might be for the General Assembly resolution establishing the WPA to set out a list of minimum qualifications that would need to be fulfilled to be accepted into membership. If, for instance, one possible criterion for membership would be that there be no pending legal cases against the member for financial improprieties, 40 percent of the members of the Brazilian legislature would be automatically disqualified. More generally, rather than establishing criteria that would aim for the lowest common denominator, one would wish to encourage the selection of members that were recognized objectively for their integrity and a distinguished life of public service. In this respect, one option worthy of serious consideration would be to ask national parliaments (or similar bodies, where parliaments do not exist) to elect their WPA members by secret ballot, to free voting members from the usual sectarian/partisan, or other pressures that so often stand in the way of electing the most capable and worthy candidates.[25] In any case, given the current state of democracy in the world, it is to be expected that the WPA would have a clear democratic majority among its members.

DISTRIBUTION OF WPA MEMBERSHIP

A central issue to resolve is the determination of country membership in the WPA. The principle of one-person-one-vote, at this stage in human history at least, likely poses insurmountable practical challenges. China's population overwhelms that of most other countries; this would result in highly skewed membership in favor of China, a nondemocratic UN member. Understandably, there might be strong opposition to the creation of a body intended to boost the democratic legitimacy

---

[24] Laurenti, "An Idea Whose Time Has *Not* Come."

[25] Such a process could be certified at the international level (with the help of impartial election observers seconded to the national level at the time of election), before representatives could take their seats within the WPA.

TABLE 5.1 *UN member state representation in a WPA: Modified Schwartzberg/ Heinrich proposal*

Seats per nation [1]	Number of nations	%	Number of seats	%	Population in millions	%	Average population per seat
1	107	55.4	107	18.9	441.08	5.9	4.1
2–3	58	30.1	127	22.4	1422.41	19.0	11.2
4–9	20	10.4	112	19.8	1745.90	23.3	15.6
10–20	5	2.6	58	10.2	827.26	11.0	14.3
21–69	3	1.6	163	28.7	3051.29	40.7	18.7
Total	193	100.0	567	100.0	7487.94	100.0	13.2

1 Seats per nation determined by relative population and GDP shares, as well as UN membership factor as described in text.

of the United Nations being dominated in its membership by a country with a very limited tradition of democracy. For this reason, Schwartzberg, for instance, goes back to the criteria that he proposed for determining voting power in the General Assembly, consisting of three elements: population share (P), relative contributions to the UN budget (C), which, as noted earlier, is a proxy for the share of the country in world GNI, and a membership factor (M) which is simply 1/193 percent, to represent a country's current voting power in the General Assembly under the one-country-one-vote system. The arithmetic average of these three shares $(P + C + M)/3 = W$ determines a country's relative weight or share in the WPA membership.

The total number of seats in the WPA for country j, S_j, will then be determined by the ratio of W_j to D, where D is defined as the weight for the smallest member. Thus, to take the example of China, $W_j = 11.993$, as derived in Table 4.1. For the 193 members of the United Nations, D = 0.173. So S_j for China would be 11.993/ 0.173, which rounded to the nearest integer translates into 69 members in the WPA. For Bangladesh $W_j = 1.015$ from which one can derive that, rounded to the nearest integer, the country would have six WPA members. Table 5.1 below presents a summary of the data, using population and GDP figures for 2017. The WPA would thus have a total of 567 members, with the United States (48), India (46), and Japan (14) having the second, third and fourth largest representations. A total of 107 countries would have one representative each. While these countries account for 5.9 percent of the world's population, they would nevertheless account for 18.9 percent of the total number of seats in the WPA. This reflects the bias toward small countries which the Schwartzberg proposal builds in deliberately through the introduction of the "UN membership" factor in the determination of the membership weights. Three countries, China, the United States, and India, accounting for 41 percent of the world's population, would have a total of 163 representatives, or

TABLE 5.2 *UN member state representation in a WPA: Seat distribution as per Penrose population*[1]

Seats per nation	Number of nations	%	Number of seats	%	Population in millions	%	Average population per seat
1	53	27.5	53	6.7	36.81	0.5	0.7
2–3	65	33.7	162	20.4	444.39	5.9	2.7
4–9	60	31.1	344	43.2	2126.18	28.4	6.2
10–20	13	6.7	163	20.5	2154.98	28.8	13.2
21–37	2	1.0	74	9.3	2725.58	36.4	36.8
Total	193	100.0	796	100.0	7487.94	100.0	9.4

1 Penrose population is defined as the square root of a country's population in millions.

28.7 percent of the total. Each of the deputies representing countries small enough to have only one WPA member, would represent an average of 4.1 million people, whereas one of the Chinese representatives would represent some 20 million people.

The above method could be in operation for four parliamentary terms, lasting a total of 16 years. It is expected that during this period the WPA would gain in legitimacy having joined in or influenced numerous General Assembly resolutions, having taken up for debate and made recommendations on a broad range of matters of international concern, including those issues that straddle national borders, such as climate change, human rights, poverty, income distribution, gender equality, rule of law and the like, and having mobilized public opinion in support of the goal of strengthened international cooperation. As the profile of the WPA expanded, a case could be made to move to a system that determined membership in the body solely on the basis of population, but in a nonlinear way, relying on the principle of degressive proportionality, meaning that smaller states would be entitled to more seats than would be called for under a system that allocated places strictly in proportion to their population. One such option would be the so-called Penrose method which assigns seats in relation to the square root of the country's population, rounded to the nearest million, subject to the proviso that all countries will be entitled to at least one member. Table 5.2 shows that two countries, China and India, accounting for close to 37 percent of the world's population, would have a total of 74 members, or slightly over 9 percent of the membership, each of whom would represent some 37 million people. The Penrose method therefore has the effect of reducing further the share allocated to the most populous states, as reflected in the larger number of people represented by each WPA member.

We have presented the above two scenarios to underline that there is a range of possibilities for the determination of membership shares in the WPA. The issue is partly technical and partly political. The European Union does not use a fixed formula to determine the relative representations of national deputies in its parliament; country shares are periodically negotiated and some nontangible factors may enter into the consultations, affecting the ultimate outcome. While it will be necessary to come up with a membership mechanism that will be perceived as reasonably objective, fair-minded, and enhancing the credibility of the WPA before the public, a considerably more important set of issues will be those concerned with the functions of the WPA, its role within the UN system, its relation to the General Assembly, and the role it would play in strengthening support at the global level for the United Nations.

Schwartzberg envisages an ultimate transition for the WPA where membership in it would be completely delinked from the nationality of its members. Abstracting from national borders, one would divide the world into a sufficiently large number of electoral districts and elect members for the WPA in each district, broadly in conformity with the principle of one-person-one-vote. We do not believe that this approach would be feasible in anything like a reasonable time frame as it would likely skew the membership of the WPA toward the more populous states and thus would be resisted by many member states. Even in the European Parliament, already operating under a system of broad degressive proportionality, the criterion for membership is still based on the nationality of candidates. What is likely to happen in the EU – and could thus be a harbinger for the future as regards the whole world – is that with increased intra-EU migratory flows, there will be shifts in the composition of national populations over time with, for instance, a significant proportion of the population of Spain, say, being of non-Spanish origin, mainly from other EU states. Made eligible to vote and to be voted for, one could imagine a situation where Spain's WPA contingent could have a significant number of non-Spanish members. Something like this, of course, has already happened within national territories; there is no impediment whatsoever for a member of the Spanish parliament representing, say, Madrid, to be a former resident of Barcelona or Bilbao. As of now, the only requirement is that he/she be a Spanish citizen. In keeping with this analogy, one would say that in that distant future, the only requirement for membership in the WPA would be that the person be a world citizen.

One important question to settle over the longer term is whether the WPA would retain indefinitely its role as an advisory body, with the locus of political power remaining firmly in place with the General Assembly, whose members would, as noted earlier, be ultimately elected by popular vote. And, if the answer to this question is no, suggesting in time a more political role for the WPA, how would these powers relate to those already granted, in a revised Charter, to the General Assembly? We do not think that this difficult issue needs to be decided now. There is considerable merit to the idea of introducing within the UN the institutional infrastructure for an advisory mechanism, as soon as possible, that more fully reflects the aspirations and priorities of the people, not just nation states as is the case with the General Assembly today. If the UN Charter amendments that would make it possible to introduce a system of weighted voting in the General Assembly are a longer-term goal, then the coming into being, in a much shorter time horizon, of a WPA with extensive advisory powers is an initiative worth pursuing on its own merits. Whether to grant the WPA powers that transcend the merely advisory is a decision that can be taken *after* the General Assembly is in operation as a budding world legislature, with narrowly defined powers in the areas of peace and security and management of the global environmental commons, under a system of weighted representation. What is clear, however, is that a WPA in operation would be an excellent preparatory step for the eventual emergence of a General Assembly with legislative powers.[26]

---

[26] See Bummel, Andreas. 2019. *The Case for a UN Parliamentary Assembly and the Inter-Parliamentary Union*, Berlin, Democracy without Borders. Bummel examines the relationship between the Interparliamentary Union (IPU), an umbrella organization of 178 parliaments established in 1889, and the WPA. He argues, convincingly, that the functions, powers and organizational characteristics of both bodies are complementary and that even if the WPA quickly came into being, there would always be a need for the nurturing of relationships and exchange of ideas and mutual encouragement across parliaments of the world which the IPU has successfully fostered over its 130 years of existence.

6

Advisory Mechanisms to Support Global Policymaking

Science and technology, as part of their contribution to economic and social development, must be applied to the identification, avoidance and control of environmental risks and the solution of environmental problems and for the common good of mankind.

Stockholm Declaration 1972, Principle 18[1]

We must ... base our analysis in credible data and evidence, enhancing data capacity, availability, disaggregation, literacy and sharing.

UN 2014[2]

On an institutional level, a global entity with a strong scientific advisory capacity is needed to streamline reporting and decision-making processes, including the voices of non-state actors. It must coherently link environmental issues to social and economic priorities, for none of these can advance in isolation.

Bahá'í International Community, 2008[3]

The legislative function in the reformed United Nations, whether solely in the General Assembly or also with a World Parliamentary Assembly (WPA), will need a number of supporting advisory mechanisms if it is to exercise its broad responsibilities effectively in the global interest (e.g., for specialized scientific, technical, and other expertise). A strong civil society voice including nongovernmental

---

[1] United Nations. 1972. *Report of the United Nations Conference on the Human Environment,* held at Stockholm, June 5–16, 1972. A/CONF.48/14. New York, United Nations. Stockholm Declaration, Principle 18.

[2] United Nations. 2014. *The Road to Dignity by 2030: Ending Poverty, Transforming All Lives and Protecting the Planet,* Synthesis Report of the Secretary-General on the Post-2015 Agenda. Document A/69/700, December 4, 2014. New York, United Nations. www.un.org/ga/search/view_doc.asp?symbol=A/69/700&Lang=E.

[3] Bahá'í International Community. 2008. *Eradicating Poverty: Moving Forward as One.* http://bic.org/statements-and-reports/bic-statements/08-0214.htm.

organizations (NGOs) has been shown to contribute constructively to global policy-making. A broad scientific advisory process is also needed to provide authoritative reports on the state of the planet and to prepare reports on emerging or problematic technologies that may require global legislative action. An Office of Ethical Assessment could alert legislators to the ethical implications of issues under consideration.

A CHAMBER OF CIVIL SOCIETY

Richard Falk and Andrew Strauss published an insightful article titled "Toward World Parliament" in the journal *Foreign Affairs* in which they made the case for the creation of a second chamber, deriving its authority directly from organized global citizenry, within the UN and supporting the UN General Assembly.[4] The post–Cold War period has witnessed what Jessica Mathews called "a novel redistribution of power among states, markets, and civil society. National governments are not simply losing autonomy in a globalized economy. They are sharing powers – including political, social, and security roles at the core of sovereignty – with businesses, with international organizations, and with a multitude of citizens groups, known as NGOs."[5] The Commission on Global Governance, co-Chaired by former U.S. Secretary of State Madeleine Albright and former Nigerian Foreign Minister and UN Under-Secretary-General for Political Affairs Ibrahim Gambari, also called for the facilitation of practical contributions by elements of civil society within a reformed UN system.[6] The proposal for a Civil Society Chamber or permanent Forum would formalize the May 2000 UN Millennium NGO Forum where Secretary General Kofi Annan invited 1,350 individuals representing a broad spectrum of civil society organizations to consult on critical global problems and to present recommendations to the Millennium Summit of Heads of State, the largest such gathering ever.

The members of this Chamber would not represent their respective states but would rather serve as advocates of particular issues of global concern that transcend national borders, from the environment and management of the global commons, to human rights, to world peace and security, gender equality, and the global fight against corruption, to name only a few. NGOs could be accredited for membership using an enhanced version of current UN accreditation procedures under

---

4   Falk, Richard and Andrew Strauss. 2001. "Toward World Parliament," *Foreign Affairs*, Vol. 80, No. 1, January/February.
5   Mathews, Jessica T. 1997. "Power Shift." *Foreign Affairs* Vol. 76, No. 1, pp. 50–66. Three excellent examples of effective coalitions of like-minded states and nonstate actors aimed at precipitating reforms over the past several decades involved the International Campaign to Ban Landmines, the Coalition for the International Criminal Court and the adoption of Responsibility to Protect doctrine as a global norm. Civil society groups also played a central role in the establishment of the Extractive Industries Transparency Initiative among very many other initiatives.
6   Commission on Global Governance. 1995. *Our Global Neighbourhood: Report of the Commission on Global Governance.* Oxford, Oxford University Press, Chapter 4.

ECOSOC and other UN bodies/initiatives. Falk and Strauss did not provide specific proposals on how to go about electing the members of this Chamber and how membership would be distributed across thematic areas. But there are currently some 5,000 NGOs with consultative status at ECOSOC and it should not be an insurmountable problem to come up with criteria that might allow choices to be made to elect some 700–800 members to cover a representative spectrum of issues of global concern. For the 2000 NGO Forum the UN invited two groups of NGO representatives: Those from organizations with consultative status with ECOSOC, and those accredited to thematic UN conferences during the 1990s. However, NGO representatives to the Chamber could also be selected by alternative criteria, including possibly by a representative, independent international expert appointment committee, and/or some form of popular vote where such elections could take place freely, without government interference, while also ensuring broad thematic representation.

Such an initiative could begin as a Forum, meeting regularly, and would recognize that solutions to some of our most critical problems require multistakeholder engagement. Over time, it could facilitate the emergence of a Chamber of Civil Society which would also play a central advisory role with respect to the General Assembly.

ADDRESSING GLOBAL CATASTROPHIC RISKS

The ultimate goal of this dimension of UN reform will be to arrive at an effective decision-making capacity to address global challenges, able to enforce binding policies and legislation necessary to control and hopefully avert them. Such reforms will need sufficient legitimacy to be able to build wide public support for the Chamber's proposals and decisions, which will need to place the global interest above the particular interests of powerful governments, businesses, and economic actors which may resist such changes in the collective public interest. While it will take time to reach this stage of maturity in global governance, much can be done to prepare the foundations for an effective legislative process.

A Chamber of Civil Society would be one arena for creative and constructive debate to build consensus across a wide range of stakeholders. A number of additional supporting mechanisms will be necessary to support this process, many of which can be created without waiting for reformed mechanisms to be fully in place, and which could even hasten the process. The preparation of reforms and other initiatives in the area of international cooperation requires steps of investigation, exploration of alternatives, consultation with stakeholders, and the preparation of documents capturing the emerging consensus, before it is debated in a decision-making setting. Even when binding understandings are not yet possible, the precise definition of problems and risks can help to push voluntary action by governments and other actors. Advisory bodies would be made up of individuals chosen primarily on the basis of professional credentials and a credible track record of expertise. They could initially mainly focus their efforts and attention on a small set of pressing global catastrophic risks, including climate change and the whole range of issues associated with the deterioration of the environment, nuclear proliferation, and the peace and security challenges this raises, as well as the broader set of economic development problems stemming from poverty and worsening trends in income distribution.

There is an excellent precedent for such an approach in the Intergovernmental Panel on Climate Change (IPCC), created in 1988 by the United Nations Environment Programme (UNEP) and the World Meteorological Organization (WMO) to prepare an agreed scientific basis for actions to address climate change. Its early reports helped to provide the impetus for the adoption of the UN Framework Convention on Climate Change (UNFCCC) signed at the Rio Earth Summit in 1992, and subsequent reports built the momentum for the adoption of the Paris Agreement in 2015. Its experts are nominated by all the world's governments but participate in their independent capacities as experts. They review all the relevant scientific literature, assess it through open peer-reviewed processes, and their summary conclusions are reviewed and endorsed by all member governments, seeking to ensure that their conclusions represent the consensus on the best science available, as illustrated by their most recent special report.[7]

In the scientific domain beyond the most urgent, global catastrophic risks, the General Assembly would also need a number of general supporting advisory mechanisms to provide additional specialized scientific, technical, and other expertise. For example, a broad scientific advisory process would be required to provide authoritative reports on the state of the planet, building on more specific advisory bodies such as the existing IPCC, and the comparable Intergovernmental Science-Policy Platform on Biodiversity and Ecosystem Services (IPBES). For climate change, for example, it will be necessary to determine the planetary limits for greenhouse gas concentrations as the basis for negotiations on the allocations for each country to respect those limits, as only objective science can provide a sufficient basis for the difficult sharing of responsibilities to return within those limits. Similar scientific assessment processes will be needed for other global risks, such as global pollution risks from chemicals and nuclear radiation, the management of plastics and other persistent wastes, the need to remain within other planetary environmental boundaries such as for biogeochemical cycles, and the management and equitable distribution of the planet's natural resources and sources of energy. Global dimensions of land use, freshwater supplies, the atmosphere and the oceans will eventually need to be covered. This will require groups of experts of the greatest knowledge and confidence, similar to those making up the IPCC, in all the relevant

---

7   IPCC. 2018. *Global Warming of 1.5°C* (SR15), Special Report. Summary for Policy Makers. Geneva, Intergovernmental Panel on Climate Change, October. www.ipcc.ch/report/sr15/.

domains, to ensure that decisions are taken and revised as necessary based on the best information available. Such groups could be established for each global domain or risk identified.

A similar advisory process for the risks of new technologies in an Office of Technology Assessment will be needed to prepare reports on emerging or problematic technologies that may require global legislative action, such as geoengineering,[8] genetic modifications and new creations, nanotechnologies, access to and security of information and communications technologies, the damaging manipulation of public opinion, and uses of artificial intelligence, among others. The combination of information technologies and biotechnologies with artificial intelligence risks marginalizing masses of people and making their jobs irrelevant, while collecting more information about entire populations, making them passive consumers easily manipulated and controlled. The whole process of governance could be transformed, undermining democracies and fostering dictatorships by making extreme centralization possible; yet the development of these technologies is largely in the private sector beyond any regulation or control.[9] Proper assessment of the risks would support the necessary global legislation to regulate the handling and ownership of data and ensure that technological developments support rather than undermine the common interest.

Even social and economic challenges can present global risks that need to be assessed objectively, far from partisan or ideological considerations, such as the impacts of and solutions to extreme economic inequalities (Chapter 14), or the protection of and assistance to migrants and displaced persons whose numbers will increase dramatically if climate change and resource destruction are not brought rapidly under control (Chapter 17). The inequalities that continue to drive excessive rates of population growth beyond what resources can support need to be addressed so that the human population can be brought naturally back into balance with the carrying capacity of the planet. Authoritative reports on these issues could help to build concerted global action to reduce the risks.

An ethical advisory process in an Office of Ethical Assessment would also be useful to remind decision-makers of the fundamental values and ethical principles accepted by all governments in the various international resolutions, statements, and authoritative reports, and to provide insights on the ethical implications of issues under consideration, such as impacts on the overall security situation, broadly defined, on human rights and on future generations.

---

[8] This gap in governance has recently been highlighted by the Brookings Institution for geoengineering and gene drive technologies in West, Darrell M. and Jack Karsten. 2017. *Solutions for Global Science Issues Require New Forms of Governance.* Brookings Institution blog, May 4. www.brookings.edu/blog/techtank/2017/05/04/solutions-for-global-science-issues-require-new-forms-of-governance.

[9] Harari, Yuval Noah. 2018. "Why Technology Favors Tyranny." *The Atlantic*, October. www.theatlantic.com/magazine/archive/2018/10/yuval-noah-harari-technology-tyranny/568330/.

One cannot overestimate the impact that a global consultative process operating on the basis of scientific evidence and driven by considerations of the public global interest (rather than allegiance to narrower priorities, which is often the subtext to discussions motivated by national sovereignty) would have in changing the current dynamic of large-scale inertia on the part of governments to rise to confront the critical problems that we face. A WPA and/or Chamber of Civil Society would establish a direct connection between the UN system and the global citizenry, which at the moment either does not exist or is too weak to make a reliable difference. Having a larger measure of democratic legitimacy, its deliberations and recommendations would be imbued with a degree of credibility and urgency that existing organs such as the Security Council and the General Assembly have lacked, at great cost to global welfare and our collective future. This could thus become a powerful catalyst for actual change across the global governance system.

ENHANCING UN LEGISLATIVE CAPACITY TO CONSOLIDATE GLOBAL SOLIDARITY AND COMMUNITY

In his persuasive case for the establishment of a WPA, Dieter Heinrich sees this body as a powerful catalyst to enhance the quality of the debate about the nature of international cooperation and the extent to which our current global order still serves the interests of humanity. An excessively state-centric ideology, which dominated the debates that took place in the period leading to the founding of the United Nations and that have dragged on since 1945, is not only inherently anarchic but is no longer a reliable basis to confront and to manage the problems that assail the world. In his view, the fundamental question that we need to ask is: Is the world a community of peoples or a collection of sovereign states? And is the only way to serve effectively the interests of citizens – and national communities themselves – in an increasingly interdependent world exclusively through the actions of national governments? The answer to this question is clearly no; this has been reflected in the growing recognition that there are global interests that transcend national borders, and that governments are increasingly impotent to deal with a range of problems that straddle national borders. The state-centric predilections that have underpinned our global order in recent decades can be seen as anti-democratic as they fail to recognize that, ultimately, sovereignty vests in the people – in this case, the global citizenry – rather than in the states that properly should be vehicles of the public trust, committed also to solving international problems.

On the occasion of the 2000 Annual Meetings of the World Bank and the IMF in Prague, Vaclav Havel, the then president of the Czech Republic and one of Europe's most enlightened political leaders, said that the time had come "to address another restructuring, concerning the system of values on which contemporary civilization rests." In practice this would mean adopting a system of values that is consistent with the emergence of a rapidly integrating and interdependent community of nations. Havel's vision of humanity desperately in need of a new concept of global order finds resonance in the writings of anthropologists, for many of whom the notion of "the psychic unity of mankind" is nothing new. George Murdock claimed that "all peoples now living or of whom we possess substantial historical records, irrespective of differences in geography and physique, are essentially alike in their basic psychological equipment and mechanism, and the cultural differences between them reflect only the differential responses of essentially similar organisms to unlike stimuli or conditions."[10] And Craig Venter, one of the scientists who led the effort to map the human genome, declared that "there is only one race – the human race,"and that if one asks what percentage of our genes is reflected in our external appearance, the basis by which we talk about race, the answer seems to be in the range of 0.01 percent.[11]

It may yet be many years before the generality of humankind becomes conscious of the *scientific* basis of its "oneness," but it is not too early to cultivate the values of shared human identity. We need to develop broader loyalties that correspond to our newly acquired psychic unity. For the benefits of globalization to be fully realized, we need to acquire a sense of solidarity that extends to the whole human family, not just the members of our own particular tribe. Many philosophies and faith traditions have principles that will support the development of this vision. Pope Francis has written: "There has been a growing conviction that our planet is a homeland and that humanity is one people living in a common home ... . Interdependence obliges us to think of *one world with a common plan* [original emphasis]."[12] A central principle of the Bahá'í Faith is that "the earth is but one country and mankind its citizens."[13] The English mathematician and philosopher Bertrand Russell spoke of the need to "expand our mental universe" to match the increasingly global vision provided by scientific advancement and discovery. He said that our sense of collective well-being would have to extend to the whole of humanity as it was evident that human society was increasingly behaving as a single organic entity. These observations, made well over half a century ago, are self-evident in the age of globalization. Strengthened supporting mechanisms such as a WPA and a Civil Society Chamber would be a powerful symbol that national borders are, when it comes to our shared global challenges and shared human identity, contingent, that they have contributed to overemphasizing ultimately superficial and artificial distinctions, and that "world citizenship" may in fact be a legitimate and meaningful concept, reflecting a gradually emerging set of broadly shared values. The

---

[10] Murdock, George. 1965. *Culture and Society.* University of Pittsburg Press.
[11] Angier, Natalie. 2000. "DNA Research Shows Race Is Only Skin Deep." *The International Herald Tribune*, August 24.
[12] Pope Francis. 2015. *Laudato Si': On Care for Our Common Home*, §164.
[13] Bahá'u'lláh. 1990. *Gleanings from the Writings of Bahá'u'lláh.* US Bahá'í Publishing Trust, p. 346.

establishment of these broader solidarities, incarnated in novel international bodies with greatly enhanced effectiveness as described, would be a signal step not only in imbuing the United Nations with a healthier dose of democratic legitimacy than it currently has, but it would also strengthen the architecture of global governance to tangibly improve the lives of all the peoples of the world.

7

UN Executive Council: Beyond an Outdated Paradigm

The proposition, incredible as it may seem, is that any one of the Big Five may, by its sole fiat, paralyze the whole world organization.

Grenville Clark, 1944[1]

Perhaps the greatest weakness in the present UN Charter – with respect to its essential function to maintain peace and security in the world – is the Security Council as currently configured, and in particular the right of veto maintained by the five permanent members, the "P5" (China, France, Russia, the United Kingdom, and the United States).[2] The Security Council is the only UN organ whose decisions are legally binding on all member states, and which can authorize military action and other invasive measures to enforce its decisions.[3] Yet it is unfairly constituted, and its essential legitimacy is increasingly called into question. Moreover, the type of geopolitical "power politics" that have often been channeled through the Security Council (incarnated in the very notion of a "P5" group of military/economic powers) is a troubling anachronism. Rather, international solidarity and intensive *cooperation* among states with disproportionate economic and other resources – such as China and the US – are crucially needed to confront our global challenges.[4]

Older and outdated definitions of sovereignty assert the right to make war to defend "national interests" or to extend power or territory by force. The UN Charter

---

[1] Clark, Grenville. 1944. "Dumbarton Oaks Plans Held in Need of Modification: Viewed as Repeating Essential Errors of League of Nations and Offering No Assurance of International Security – some Remedies Suggested." *New York Times*, October 15.

[2] For further historical background see Chapter 2.

[3] Art. 2(7) of the Charter notes that the application of enforcement measures determined by the Security Council under Chapter VII are not subject to the general rule of UN nonintervention in "matters which are essentially within the domestic jurisdiction" of states.

[4] See, e.g., Rubin, Robert. 2019. "Why the World Needs America and China to Get Along." *The New York Times*, January 2.

consciously sought to put an end to these aspects of state behavior. However, the five victors at the end of World War II (and in particular the core "Big Three") insisted on maintaining a type of "absolute" national sovereignty over the new global body with their veto power, inserting a fatal flaw into UN implementation of the concept of collective security, and throughout Charter architecture.

Subsequent rivalries and ideological differences between the permanent members have frequently paralyzed Security Council action when this was deemed to be in the interest of one or more of the P5.[5] The desire to maintain hegemony, to protect or further self-interest, to destabilize others, to avoid criticism or accountability, have all prevented action for collective security or on other important matters, allowing too many conflicts to flourish and undermining the international rule of law. Fifth High Commissioner for Human Rights Navi Pillay has noted of the Security Council that: "[s]hort-term geopolitical considerations and national interest, narrowly defined, have repeatedly taken precedence over intolerable human suffering and grave breaches of – and long-term threats to – international peace and security," noting crises in Afghanistan, Central African Republic, Democratic Republic of Congo, Iraq, Libya, Mali, Gaza, Somalia, South Sudan, and Sudan, as illustrating the international community's systemic failure to prevent conflict. Speaking directly to the Security Council, Pillay noted: "I firmly believe that greater responsiveness by this council would have saved hundreds of thousands of lives."[6]

The blockage has extended to denying the Security Council (and hence the UN as a whole) effective means to enforce its decisions through adequate international forces ready to respond rapidly to defuse a crisis or to keep the peace. Agreements under Article 43 of the Charter, where all members of the UN were meant to make available to the Security Council armed forces, assistance, facilities and other support to ensure the even-handed maintenance of international peace and security, were never completed: it was the responsibility of the Security Council to lead and facilitate the negotiation of these agreements "as soon as possible." Hence, "one of the most important innovations of the UN Charter, as compared to the Covenant of the League," remains unrealized.[7]

---

[5] See, e.g., the summary provided at: Council on Foreign Relations. 2018. *The UN Security Council.* www.cfr.org/backgrounder/un-security-council

[6] "UN Human Rights Chief Rebukes Security Council." *Al Jazeera America*, August 21, 2014. http://alj.am/1msfyFF.

[7] See Chapter 8, proposing the establishment of a UN International Peace Force to remedy this situation. The Security Council was also responsible for drafting a plan for the regulation of armaments under Article 26, which was not actualized (see Chapter 9). Nico Kirsch, "Ch. VII: Action with Respect to Threats to the Peace, Breaches of the Peace, and Acts of Aggression, Article 43," in Simma, Bruno, Daniel-Erasmus Khan, Georg Nolte, Andreas Paulus, and Nikolai Wessendorf (eds.). 2012. *The Charter of the United Nations: A Commentary*, Oxford Commentaries on International Law series, 3rd ed., 2 vols. Oxford, Oxford University Press, Vol. II, p. 1356.

As described in discussion of the General Assembly (see Chapter 4), the veto has often been used and misused throughout the history of the UN. For a time in the 1990s it looked as though the permanent members might begin a new pattern of focused collaboration and voluntarily restrain their use of the veto as a first step forward.[8] There have also been recent initiatives to request the P5 to voluntarily abstain from using their veto power in the context of addressing situations of mass atrocity; a proposal that has been supported by one of the P5 veto-bearing members, France.[9] UN observers have recently noted, however, that China, Russia, and the United States have shown signs of renewed efforts at geopolitical dominance, with commentators speculating as to a new "Cold War" and/or a possible "Thucydides Trap" (between China and the US),[10] with these countries again beginning to use their veto more frequently, to advance individual agendas or to counter each other.[11] There is no sign of this attitude changing in the immediate future.[12] Indeed, a recent Security Council resolution on Syria, calling for a 30-day ceasefire, was ignored with impunity even by members who voted for it, discrediting the Council further.[13]

Any amendments or alterations to the Charter under Articles 108 or Article 109 require ratification by all the permanent members of the Security Council, ensuring that they can block the removal of their right of veto as well as improvements to the UN Charter architecture itself. This ensures that the P5 may regularly give primacy to perceived national interests over the most essential collective

---

[8] Katirai, Foad. 2001. *Global Governance and the Lesser Peace*, Oxford, George Ronald.

[9] Prominent civil society groups have also been very active on this issue. For example, at an event involving the governments of France and Mexico, as well as Amnesty International, Human Rights Watch, the World Federalist Movement, and the Global Centre for the Responsibility to Protect, Dr. Simon Adams delivered the following joint statement: "[I]t is an unfortunate reality that the veto has sometimes been used, not to defend against 'the scourge of war,' or to 'reaffirm faith in fundamental human rights,' but to shield perpetrators of mass atrocities from accountability. In one of the most tragic examples from our times, on four occasions since October 2011 the veto has been exercised by Russia and China to protect the government of the Syrian Arab Republic from resolutions meant to address crimes against humanity and war crimes committed against the Syrian people." *Remarks at Ministerial Side-Event: Regulating the Veto in the Event of Mass Atrocities*, September 25, 2014, New York, United Nations Headquarters. www.globalr2p.org/publications/337.

[10] See, e.g., Allison, Graham. 2017. "The Thucydides Trap: When One Great Power Threatens to Displace Another, War Is Almost Always the Result – but It Doesn't Have to Be." *Foreign Policy*, June 9.

[11] China has historically used its veto the least of the P5, but its veto use has risen markedly in recent years. See: Council on Foreign Relations. 2018. *The UN Security Council*. www.cfr.org/backgrounder/un-security-council.

[12] Wouters, Jan and Tom Ruys. 2005. *Security Council Reform: A Veto for a New Century*. Working Paper No. 78, June. Leuven, Institute for International Law, K.U. Leuven, www.law.kuleuven.be/iir/nl/onderzoek/working-papers/WP78e.pdf.

[13] Security Council resolution 2401 of 24 February 2018 called for a nationwide ceasefire in Syria for 30 days starting from February 24, with little effect on fighting.

responsibilities owed to the United Nations and to the international community generally.

The special status of the permanent, veto-bearing members of the Security Council in fact is in tension with the principle of "sovereign equality" of states as equal subjects of international law, bearing rights and responsibilities, as set out in Article 2(1) of the Charter. This notion was an important and largely novel concept introduced with the establishment of the UN, transcending classical notions of sovereignty founded on unfettered and relative (military) power among states, coexisting or colliding in an essentially anarchic environment. This apparent contradiction within the Charter's own terms, with the unique position accorded to the P5, has been justified by some on the basis that "states bearing the greatest institutional responsibility should also have the greatest say in critical disputes," as they undertake exceptional responsibilities in service of the whole international community.[14] Unfortunately, the ideal of impartial service to the international community by a unified P5, in accordance with the purposes and principles of the Charter, has been upheld all too infrequently; the inherent contradiction within the UN system represented by this privileged status has led to an eroded legitimacy and faith in the collective mechanisms established by the Charter, and in the UN itself.

Related to the issue of the legitimacy of the current permanent members of the Security Council are the criteria that have been or might be applied to determine which "special" nations should be part of this narrow group, as shown in the lengthy debates around the potential expansion of the Security Council and its permanent members that have occurred since 1945. The "Big Three" victors of World War II initially formed the nucleus of permanent members, after which an invitation was extended to China (as one of the envisioned "Four Policemen") and then additionally to France, in a process showing the largely negotiated/ad hoc nature of the Council's original composition. The precursor League of Nations Council, while consisting of representatives of the Principal Allied and Associated Powers emerging from World War I (France, the UK, Italy, and Japan), allowed for the addition of permanent members according to shifting political circumstances on the international landscape. It would be helpful if such contingent or impressionistic criteria, based on historical events[15] or notions of perceived shifts of sovereign power and influence, were to be replaced with more modern and objective standards of

---

[14] Franck, Tom. 1990. *The Power and Legitimacy among Nations*. Oxford, Oxford University Press, p. 177. More realistically, it seemed simply the only way to entice and to keep such states at the table at the time of Charter adoption.

[15] While it is of course of historical importance that the victors/allies of WWII ushered in the UN system, it is telling that the "enemy states" clauses in the Charter are now regarded as obsolete, with suggestions that they should be deleted from the text. According to the Charter, all members of the UN must be "peace-loving" states and must commit fully to the goals and rules of the organization, by virtue of ratifying the Charter (see Art. 4).

membership (see the proposals below). This evolution would move the international community further beyond an era characterized by fluctuating alliances and anarchic state competition, consonant with a rule-based international order and with the significant enhancements of UN machinery such as those suggested in this book. The goal should be to ensure a principles-based international architecture with checks and balances and strong international institutions to protect against abuses of power by *any* actor. Brute force has been discredited as a basis of influence or claims to special international privileges,[16] and this norm should be clearly reflected in international institutions.

The origins of this critical flaw in the Security Council have been discussed in detail in the historical Chapter 2 of this book. Only such a weakness at the heart of the system would allow for US Senate approval and satisfy the exigencies of Stalin, whose endorsements of the Charter were essential. However, the vocal opposition to such a configuration was clear among the majority of states at negotiations in San Francisco, and states only agreed to the arrangement based on the inclusion of Article 109(3), which promised a general Charter review conference within ten years of its adoption.[17] Such a general review conference has, of course, never been held. Three quarters of a century later, it is irresponsible to allow such a central flaw to persist in any system of global governance, in particular given the legislative history of this compromise. If it is left as it is, the international community runs a risk – particularly given current trends – of enabling a further regression in international power politics to a more primitive time, giving tacit acquiescence to an outdated paradigm that undermines the rules-based international order that we are meant to be building.

THE SECURITY COUNCIL AT PRESENT

Under the UN Charter as it stands, the enumerated functions and powers of the Security Council are:

- to maintain international peace and security in accordance with the principles and purposes of the United Nations;
- to investigate any dispute or situation that might lead to international friction;

---

[16] See Article 2(4) of the Charter on the prohibition of the threat or use of force; a fundament of the contemporary international legal order.

[17] Witschel notes that "the significance of Art. 109 has been more in the political-psychological sphere, as it was a major factor in overcoming the resistance of many small and medium-sized States to the 'Yalta formula' stating the right to veto in San Francisco. The prospect of a review conference in the foreseeable future, when the cards would be reshuffled, gave them consolation and hope." Georg Witschel, "Ch. XVIII Amendments, Article 108," in Simma et al. *The Charter of the United Nations*, p. 2234.

- to recommend methods of adjusting such disputes or the terms of settlement;
- to formulate plans for the establishment of a system to regulate armaments;
- to determine the existence of a threat to the peace or act of aggression and to recommend what action should be taken;
- to call on members to apply economic sanctions and other measures not involving the use of force to prevent or stop aggression;
- to take military action against an aggressor;
- to recommend the admission of new members;
- to exercise the trusteeship functions of the United Nations in "strategic areas";
- to recommend to the General Assembly the appointment of the Secretary General and, together with the Assembly, to elect the Judges of the International Court of Justice.[18]

It is precisely in these areas of proactively maintaining peace and security, resolving disputes, regulating armaments, applying sanctions and taking military action if necessary, that the UN system has so frequently failed to take action when needed, as crises today around the world illustrate only too well.[19] We will elaborate on these issues in the Chapter 8, where we discuss the extent to which the UN has succeeded (or not) in fulfilling its peace and security mandate.

PAST PROPOSALS FOR SECURITY COUNCIL REFORM

Everyone, it seems, except those most interested, have acknowledged this fatal flaw in the UN Charter. The configuration of the UN Security Council and its permanent members has been a frequent subject of reform efforts within the organization since 1945, with more recommendations for Council reform than any other UN body.[20] As the Security Council is a significant central power in the UN, states outside the permanent members have been struggling for many years to acquire similar prerogatives, preferably with permanent seats and possibly with a veto, to acknowledge their importance as contributors to the UN budget or as the most powerful states in their region. This fight for power and prestige, seemingly far from

---

[18] United Nations Security Council. (n.d.). www.un.org/en/sc/about/functions.shtml (accessed July 30, 2018).
[19] Council on Foreign Relations. 2018. *The UN Security Council.* www.cfr.org/backgrounder/un-security-council
[20] Schwartzberg, Joseph E. 2013. *Transforming the United Nations System: Designs for a Workable World,* Tokyo, United Nations University Press. www.brookings.edu/book/transforming-the-united-nations-system/

a motivation to create an effective body for the UN's most important and sensitive function, is fueled by the injustice in the present unbalanced membership.[21]

Calls for reform have been raised, for example, in the General Assembly citing Article 2(5) of the Charter, where all members of the UN are obligated to give the organization "every assistance in any action it takes in accordance with the [...] Charter," with states noting that "the effectiveness, credibility and legitimacy of the work of the Security Council will be enhanced by its improved representative character, its better ability to discharge its primary responsibility and to carry out its duties on behalf of all members," citing the "special responsibility" of the P5 to further the principles of the UN.[22] The General Assembly has similarly expressed frustration with deadlock in the Security Council and its inaction in fulfilling international responsibilities in specific situations, for example, in its 1950 "Uniting for Peace" resolution (see Chapter 4) . In this resolution it took the unprecedented step of suggesting that the GA make "appropriate recommendations to Members for collective measures, including ... the use of armed force," due to lack of unanimity of the permanent members of the Council and thus their failure to act in response to the situation on the Korean Peninsula.[23]

The most significant reflection on the issue of Security Council reform within the UN began in 1993, when the General Assembly established an Open-Ended Working Group on the Question of Equitable Representation on and Increase in the Membership of the Security Council. After a lack of progress, the UN Secretary General appointed the High-level Panel on Threats, Challenges and Change in 2003, which proposed two possible reform options in 2004. Various groups of states, pushing their own agendas, have also made proposals, but their conflicting priorities have always prevented consensus on changes and led to the repeated failure of reform efforts.[24] For example, a group of African countries (representing the African Union) advocated for two permanent seats with the veto (just like Europe) and consistently refused any compromise, including in 2005 and 2013.[25] It has been observed that "[e]ver since the Great Powers gave birth to the United Nations, the

---

[21] Security Council membership expanded in 1965 from 11 to 15 members. Since then membership in the UN has risen from 117 to 193 countries, leading to a substantial drop in the proportional presence in the Council of nonpermanent members, thus further undermining its representative legitimacy.

[22] UNGA "Draft Resolution Introduced by Afghanistan, Belgium, Bhutan, Brazil, Czech Republic, Denmark, Fiji, France, Georgia, Germany, Greece, Haiti, Honduras, Iceland, India, Japan, Kiribati, Latvia, Maldives, Nauru, Palau, Paraguay, Poland, Portugal, Solomon Islands, Tuvalu and Ukraine," July 6, 2005, UN Doc A/59/L.64. See also UGA "Draft Resolution," January 5, 2006, UN Doc A/60/L.46.

[23] UNGA Res 377 (V), November 3, 1950. UN Doc A/RES/377(V).

[24] Swart, Lydia and Jonas von Freiesleben J. 2013. *Security Council Reform from 1945 to September 2013*, New York, Center for UN Reform Education. http://centerforunreform.org/?q=node/604.

[25] Ibid. The original request of the Africa Group was two seats with veto (p. 4) and the G4 (Brazil, India, Japan and Germany) resolution in 2005 also included seats with veto (p. 7). The Africa Group has continued to insist on the veto through 2013 (p. 45).

veto debate has been extremely emotionally charged. Often the debates have resembled those of a squabbling couple, with both parties – the P5 and other UN Member States – presenting their views and not giving much attention to the validity of the other's arguments."[26] Between regional rivalries, political disputes, inflexible positions, and the preference of the five permanent members for the status quo, none of these proposals have gone anywhere, leaving five states with blocking power over the whole UN system. A new paradigm, with a principles-based approach, is needed in order to break the impasse, and to ensure an effective UN executive body.

Among the more recent proposals emanating from an academic, Schwartzberg has devoted substantial attention to reforming the Security Council.[27] His carefully reasoned proposals focus on a revised Council membership comprising representatives from 12 regions, in which each regional representative casts an objective, mathematically determined weighted vote. He carefully composes regions by both geographic and political/cultural interests, seeking both demographic and economic balance, aiming to increase the attractiveness of his proposals to most, if not all countries, to overcome their resistance to change. He aims to see delegates more democratically elected, with a greater focus on meritocracy and legitimacy.

He also proposes to circumscribe and even phase out the veto, while acknowledging the difficulty in doing so. For example, in a transition period over the first five years, two negative votes by permanent members would be required for a veto, then three for the next five years, and four for the last five years. Another suggestion would be to narrow the range of issues subject to a veto, also progressing over time. This could start by prohibiting the use of a veto when a permanent member is a principal party to any issue, extending then to egregious human rights violations including genocide and ethnic cleansing (following on recent similar proposals), the use of inspection teams and monitors, the application of economic sanctions, and finally, authorization of armed intervention in an area of actual or impending military conflict.

The resistance to change by permanent members of the Security Council with a veto will likely continue to be a stumbling block to the proposals made here, which is why we discuss as a possible alternative the replacement of the UN Charter with a new Charter for a successor organization, by a process escaping from the veto and the paralysis it has engendered (see Chapter 21). While it might be difficult to ignore all the present permanent members in implementing such a change, moving forward without one or two in the short term might be sufficient to bring them to the table. A severe crisis might also catalyze an acknowledgment that the advantages of a legitimate, representative and functional UN executive body outweigh those of

---

[26] Wouters, Jan and Tom Ruys. 2005. *Security Council Reform: A Veto for a New Century.* Working Paper No. 78. Leuven, Institute for International Law, K.U. Leuven, p. 34. www .law.kuleuven.be/iir/nl/onderzoek/working-papers/WP78e.pdf.

[27] Schwartzberg, *Transforming the United Nations System.*

current anachronistic privileges, which breeds deadlock and dissatisfaction within the international community.

Another argument for fundamental reform of the Security Council provisions of the UN Charter relates to the overall systemic reform proposals set forth in this book, which seek to adapt the UN institutions to the challenges of the 21st century. The permanent need for a Security Council as the central authority in the UN system assumes that nations will always want to make war, and that the most important role of global governance will always be to prevent war between nations. The other mechanisms proposed in this book seek to create the conditions necessary for effective governance, with binding legislation that is commonly accepted, a judiciary able to resolve differences and impose its decisions on disputing parties, and an executive with sufficient force at its disposal to employ proportionate coercive measures against a recalcitrant government. With these measures in place the threat of interstate war will gradually fade even further, to be replaced by a new wave of positive efforts to build a prosperous, cooperative international order. The notion of a Security Council as currently incarnated should become as obsolete as the Trusteeship Council is now, although its functions will likely need to be retained for a transitional period. We therefore suggest that a renewed UN system do away with the Security Council in its name and current form and implement a set of adjusted executive functions, eliminating the concept of permanent members and the veto at the same time.

SUCCESSOR ORGAN: UN EXECUTIVE COUNCIL

Our proposed Charter reform would replace the Security Council with an Executive Council composed of 24 members. As the General Assembly would itself be reformed to become a more balanced and representative body of all the governments and peoples of the world, it would become the main seat of power in the reformed UN. The Executive Council, in a range of matters, would operate in cooperation with and under the jurisdiction of the General Assembly, and its main focus would be shifted to implementation, management and effective operation of the United Nations, with collective security implementation as only one of a range of executive functions.

The composition and organization of the Executive Council would reflect the principles used in determining the national composition and representation of the reformed General Assembly (see Chapter 4). This means that each country's voting power in the Executive Council would be determined as the arithmetic average of three factors: its share in total world population, its share in world gross domestic product (GDP) and a membership share that is the same for all countries, set at 1/193 percent. Membership in the Executive Council would therefore be of two types: the United States, China, India, the European Union and Russia each would be allotted one seat. The other 19 seats would be allocated to the other

161 members, clustered regionally and consulting among themselves on an on-going basis in relation to the matters before the Executive Council. Each seat would have the same weighted voting power as its governments have in the reformed General Assembly. So, for instance, drawing from the data in Table 4.1 in Chapter 4 and Annex Table 1, the United States would have a voting power of 8.283 percent, China's would be 11.993 percent, Russia's would be 1.680 percent and the European Union's would be set at 14.374 percent. These weights would be revised every ten years, to reflect changes in world population and a country's relative GDP share, as noted in the revised Article 9(3) presented in Chapter 4.[28] All governments would therefore have a voice in the Executive Council.[29]

Other proposals for representation on the UN's apex executive body have been put forward for consideration, such as the elaborate representation by regions proposed by Schwartzberg for the Security Council, as described above.[30] An election of Council members by the General Assembly was also proposed by Clark and Sohn at a time when the UN was much smaller, with the three most populous states being continuing members and eight of the next 16 largest nations represented in rotations of four years.[31] The remaining 13 members would be chosen by the Assembly from the other member nations, also in 4-year rotations. Whatever the formula chosen for a re-constituted UN Executive Council, careful thought should be given to ensure depoliticization, fairness and functionality.

The paralyzing veto of the five permanent members of the Security Council should be eliminated.[32] Instead, decisions of the Executive Council on important

---

[28] We are not uncomfortable with the wide disparity in voting shares between Russia and the EU in the single-chair constituency. First, increasingly, on a variety of issues, EU members are speaking with a single voice on foreign policy matters. Indeed, the Lisbon Treaty provided for a foreign minister for the EU and that role has been filled for the past decade. Second, Russia having a single chair is largely a symbolic move, in recognition of its erstwhile status as a member of the P5. In our proposals, Russia's voting power is, as noted above, 1.680 percent, or roughly 8.5 times less than that of the European Union.

[29] A hypothetical example of how voting would take place within the Executive Council will be useful. Let's assume, for argument's sake, that Argentina, Bolivia, Chile, Paraguay, Peru and Uruguay, the Southern Cone constituency, are allocated one of the 24 chairs. The voting power of this chair would be equal to the sum of the voting power of all 6 members, as determined in Chapter 4 and shown in Annex Table 1. They would rotate among themselves which country sits at the table representing the group and would have to work out internally how they vote as a group. These rotations could be for two-year periods. In the event of disagreements among the six on a particular issue, the representatives seated at the time on behalf of the six would have the final word. As noted elsewhere, the World Bank and the IMF were established under a scheme of weighted voting and decision-making has generally worked well under a system that allocates voting power differentially across the membership. (For further discussion see Chapter 15.)

[30] Schwartzberg, *Transforming the United Nations System*.

[31] Clark and Sohn, p. xxi.

[32] Grenville Clark had noted in 1944 that the "combination of a nearly impotent Assembly, on the one hand, and, on the other, a Council that is hamstrung, or at best hampered, by the right of any one of the Big Five to veto sanctions must be a weak reed to support the peace of the world." Clark, "Dumbarton Oaks Plans Held in Need of Modification."

matters as defined in an amended second paragraph to Article 27 of the UN Charter, would be by a two-thirds majority of the voting power of all members, possibly including a majority of the eight members of the Council with the highest populations, and a majority of the 16 other members of the Council. For normal business, decisions would be taken by consensus or by majority vote, as necessary. Subject to its ultimate responsibility to the General Assembly, the Executive Council, as the executive arm of the new United Nations, would have broad authority to monitor, supervise and direct various aspects of the work program in the areas of security, conflict prevention and management of the global environment in particular, as well as other areas of priority identified by the General Assembly. The Secretary General could serve as the chair of the Executive Council, to provide coherence and continuity within the UN system, and to link to the UN Secretariat.

The Executive Council could take over certain specific current functions of the Security Council, such as recommending the admission of new members (as appropriate) and recommending to the General Assembly the appointment of the Secretary General. Its primary function, however, would be general organizational oversight and ensuring good governance, transparency, efficiency and coherence of an effective new UN system, including through administrative and other system-wide reforms. As one of its first tasks, it could conduct an executive review of the present multiplication of specialized agencies and convention secretariats, and propose consolidation or coordination, where necessary, while ensuring continuity in functions.

A related specific issue for the Executive Council could be to review (in consultation with relevant UN specialized agencies and other bodies) and, where appropriate, consolidate or replace the many different intergovernmental meetings, governing councils, conferences of the parties, and commissions that have proliferated across the intergovernmental system.[33] The latter has led, among other things, to the same governments sometimes taking incoherent and even contradictory decisions in different bodies with equal standing. There is clearly a place for regional debate, and a need for technical intergovernmental expertise and guidance in specific areas, but, where possible, the form and mandate of these intergovernmental mechanisms should be rationalized, along with the legislation that underlies them. Based on such reviews, the Executive Council could also recommend any necessary legislative changes to the General Assembly in its narrowly defined areas of responsibility for international security and the environment, aiming for coherent/consolidated global legislation to replace present ad hoc measures, international conventions and other multilateral

---

[33] For example, the Basel, Stockholm, Rotterdam, and Minamata Conventions all deal with international risks from chemicals and hazardous wastes. It would be logical to replace them with a single legislative text on international chemical management that could be extended to other hazardous chemicals as needed.

agreements.[34] Some functions of intergovernmental debate and decision-making in these areas could be folded into the General Assembly's own responsibility, and others continued in well-defined contexts through subsidiary bodies and mechanisms. Particularly small and developing states are disadvantaged with the requirement to be represented at so many meetings and would benefit greatly from systemic reforms to the present intergovernmental machinery.

As the Executive Council will focus on management of the UN System and the implementation of programs and policies as determined by the legislative branch, a transition should be organized to transfer the Security Council's primary functions for peace and security to the General Assembly. The reformed General Assembly as a legislative body may be too cumbersome, especially at the outset, to respond rapidly in a crisis,[35] and even the Executive Council may not initially be well adapted to this role, requiring strong subsidiary, supporting bodies building on those already existing under the current Security Council and within the UN Secretariat.

The usual channel of governments bringing issues of peace and security to the Security Council has too often been framed by political or ideological biases that make consensus difficult. To improve management and the capacity for neutral response, initial review of security issues by the Executive Council could be supplemented by a smaller, expert-centered body (at arm's length from political actors), within which no party to a conflict would have a decision-making role, in order to preserve its neutrality and to be able to make swift and transparent recommendations for rapid intervention for collective security or humanitarian protection in nascent conflicts before they get out of hand — just as police intervene to prevent or stop illegal acts within nations and communities. Such a body could

---

[34] The initial GA areas of responsibility for international security and the environment already provide ample scope for consolidation, with over 500 multilateral environmental agreements. Success in this area could create sufficient trust to extend the GA mandate to other areas.

[35] Under the current Charter, the General Assembly has subordinated yet complementary responsibility (see Arts. 11 and 12) with the Security Council for the maintenance of international peace and security (however, see, e.g., above on the proactive General Assembly Uniting for Peace Resolution when it considered that the Security Council was not fulfilling its primary responsibility). The historical use of the "war powers," allotted by the US Constitution to Congress, but in practice in the modern era often wielded by the executive, may be an interesting case study in exploring a suitable model to employ at the international level for collective security action or other urgent measures for the maintenance of peace and security. The American Founders were keen to ensure civilian oversight of military powers, and mistrustful of standing armies, executive control over the military, and concentration of this power in any one branch of government. As then-Congressman Abraham Lincoln wrote in 1848, "Kings had always been involving and impoverishing their people in wars, pretending generally, if not always, that the good of the people was the object. This, our [Constitutional] Convention understood to be the most oppressive of all Kingly oppressions and they resolved to so frame the Constitution that no one man should hold the power of bringing this oppression upon us." Abraham Lincoln to William H. Herndon, February 15, 1848, *Collected Works of Abraham Lincoln*, Vol. 1. http://quod.lib.umich.edu/l/lincoln/lincoln1/1:458.1?rgn=div2;view= fulltext.

have at its disposal powers to recommend or oblige a range of means of conflict resolution according to particular circumstances, from regional engagement/cooperation, investigation and trust-building, through binding judicial resolution or arbitration, to sanctions and enforcement by collective use of force.[36] This could be in addition to active supervision of the enforcement of decisions of the Executive Council, including those ensuring the enforcement of rulings of the International Court of Justice or other conflict-resolution bodies.

This could, for example, be the role of a new, consolidated Office for Peace and Security within the Secretariat with independent powers of investigation and reporting to ensure that the Executive Council has access to the best neutral information concerning any dispute. It would operate under the overall supervision of the Executive Council, and within the context of any additional legislation for this purpose adopted by the General Assembly. It could include restructured peace-keeping and peace-building functions as well as investigative and observer capacities and could manage the International Peace Force discussed in Chapter 8, with another branch of the Secretariat allotted the specific responsibility to formulate plans for the establishment of a system to regulate armaments (see Chapter 9).

In reassessing the current Security Council's peace and security function, as defined under the present UN Charter, consideration could be given to creating a number of specialized offices for security to advise the Executive Council beyond the Office for Peace and Security. These offices would address other priority global responsibilities of the renewed United Nations: one for environmental security[37] and the other for social justice and security, including mass human rights violations, where intervention within or between states, according to strict criteria, may be required in the global common interest.[38] Although there may be overlap in these issue areas in practice and in specific situations, the three areas require quite

---

[36] The use of force in the collective interest, or other interventions and international measures/missions, should be subject to clearer protocols based on technical and well-established criteria and principles, as already exist under international law, or to be further elaborated. Moreover, such offices and functions should be grounded in research-based and cross-disciplinary expertise to ensure the greatest efficacy of international operations. See, for example, the critique and analysis of the success of peacekeeping operations to date offered in: Autesserre, Séverine. 2019. "The Crisis of Peacekeeping: Why the UN Can't End Wars." *Foreign Affairs*, January/February.

[37] Elliott, Lorraine. 2002. *Expanding the Mandate of the UN Security Council to Account for Environmental Issues*. UN University Position Paper. http://archive.unu.edu/inter-linkages/docs/IEG/Elliot.pdf. Issues that might be considered could include an environmental accident with significant transboundary impacts (Chernobyl, Fukushima) or chemicals discovered to represent major threats to human health or biodiversity (endocrine disrupters, neonicotinoids).

[38] Subedi has recently argued for the elevation of the current UN Human Rights Council to a principal organ of the UN with powers to refer matters, inter alia, to the Security Council and the International Criminal Court, also entrusting it with "powers to take some measures not involving the use of force to ensure compliance" (see: Subedi, Surya P. 2017. *The Effectiveness of the UN Human Rights System: Reform and the Judicialisation of Human Rights*, London and New York, Taylor & Francis, pp. 247–248).

different knowledge bases and technical responsibilities, and could each provide the action arm for a major global component of the UN, at least during a transitional period while interstate conflicts, cross-boundary impacts, and recalcitrant actors continue to contribute to international crises. Each would be able to either make authoritative recommendations, and/or to take certain binding decisions with relevant means of enforcement, subject to review as necessary by the Executive Council in consultation with the General Assembly. The possibility to submit a dispute to binding arbitration/adjudication, or to appeal to the International Court of Justice on legal questions, would be assured, but would not be suspensive in cases of urgency. It would be anticipated that the level of international conflicts would gradually decline under the new international system, rendering the security function progressively less necessary.

Well-known history (see Chapter 2) highlights the concerns already expressed at the time of the creation of the UN, by Grenville Clark and by many other influential political actors and commentators, that the concept of the Security Council as it currently stands was fundamentally flawed from the outset, only embraced in order to protect the prerogatives of the great powers, but leaving the organization itself hamstrung. The troubled history of unaddressed conflict, unimplemented provisions of the UN Charter under Security Council responsibility, and international deadlock on a range of humanitarian crises since the founding of the United Nations is a warning to correct this flaw and to create a more rational, coherent international executive body.

8

Completing the Collective Security Mechanism of the Charter: Establishing an International Peace Force

Here, then, is the problem which we present to you, stark and dreadful and inescapable: Shall we put an end to the human race; or shall mankind renounce war?... The abolition of war will demand distasteful limitations of national sovereignty. But what perhaps impedes understanding of the situation more than anything else is that the term "mankind" feels vague and abstract. People scarcely realize in imagination that the danger is to themselves and their children and their grandchildren, and not only to a dimly apprehended humanity. They can scarcely bring themselves to grasp that they, individually, and those whom they love are in imminent danger of perishing agonizingly ... We appeal as human beings to human beings: Remember your humanity, and forget the rest. If you can do so, the way lies open to a new Paradise; if you cannot, there lies before you the risk of universal death ... There lies before us, if we choose, continual progress in happiness, knowledge, and wisdom. Shall we, instead, choose death, because we cannot forget our quarrels? ... We invite this Congress, and through it the scientists of the world and the general public, to subscribe to the following resolution: "In view of the fact that in any future world war nuclear weapons will certainly be employed, and that such weapons threaten the continued existence of mankind, we urge the governments of the world to realize, and to acknowledge publicly, that their purpose cannot be furthered by a world war, and we urge them, consequently, to find peaceful means for the settlement of all matters of dispute between them.

The Bertrand Russell–Albert Einstein Manifesto, July 9, 1955.[1]

In this chapter we begin by highlighting the fact that proposals for the creation of an international security or peace force were actively discussed around the time of the establishment of the League of Nations and were taken up again in the period leading to the creation of the United Nations. We note that the UN Charter contains core, explicit undertakings in the area of peaceful settlement of international disputes (see Chapter 10) and what is now referred to as "peace enforcement," and then describe the various instruments that were developed over time as

---

[1] www.atomicheritage.org/key-documents/russell-einstein-manifesto.

the UN sought to give operational meaning to the peace and security principles embedded in the Charter. In this respect, we analyze the experience with peace-keeping operations and some of the lessons that can be drawn from their mixed success. We then analyze the extent to which there has been a fairly dramatic erosion in the effectiveness of the uses of warfare and violence to achieve particular national strategic objectives and argue that the current system of global security is absurdly costly in relation to the meager security benefits it confers. We then present a proposal – based on the work done by Grenville Clark and Louis Sohn in the 1950s/1960s – for the creation of an International Peace Force, to be established in parallel to a process of comprehensive international arms control (Chapter 9), and ensuring adequately strengthened mechanisms for the peaceful settlement of disputes(Chapter 10). Our proposal includes a discussion of a number of operational issues that emerge when considering the establishment of such a Force, many of them based on an assessment of several decades of experience with peacekeeping.

EARLY ATTEMPTS

The creation of an international military force to empower the League of Nations to secure the peace was actively discussed in the period leading up to the adoption of the League's Covenant. A draft of the Covenant drawn up by former French Prime Minister Leon Bourgeois specified in considerable detail the military sanctions that would be applied against countries that disturbed the peace.[2] The Bourgeois Committee called for the creation of an international force or, as a second option, the setting up of a force made up of national contingents to be at the service of the League. A permanent international staff would provide for the organization and training of the force or coordinate the training of the national contingents and would be responsible for implementing whatever military action was ultimately endorsed by the League. Furthermore, the staff would also be given responsibility for monitoring the armaments of League members and the extent to which these were consistent with the Covenant's disarmament provisions; it was understood that in this they would act with equanimity and independence.

According to F.P. Walters influential segments of public opinion in France "refused to believe that the League could ensure the world's peace unless it possessed at least the rudiments of military power."[3] Although other countries

---

[2] According to the Nobel Prize Foundation Leon Bourgeois (1851–1925) was "a man of prodigious capabilities and diversified interests" who can be regarded as the "spiritual father" of the League of Nations. During a most distinguished life of public service spanning several decades he served as French Minister of Justice, Minister of Foreign Affairs, Minister of Public Works, Prime Minister, head of the French delegation to the 1899 Hague Peace Conference, President of the Chamber of Deputies, French representative to the League of Nations Commission chaired by President Woodrow Wilson, President of the French Senate and first president of the Council of the League of Nations. www.nobelprize.org/prizes/peace/1920/bourgeois/biographical/.

[3] Walters, F.P. 1965. *A History of the League of Nations*, Oxford, Oxford University Press, p. 62.

supported the Bourgeois proposal, they were not willing to take an uncompromising stance on the issue, given adamant opposition on the part of the British and American delegations. President Wilson, in particular, had argued that public opinion in America would not accept foreign inspections of the American military establishment, a point shared by the British representative, Lord Robert Cecil. In the end, the idea was abandoned, not because in and of itself it lacked merit, but mainly because the strongest advocates of the League felt that domestic political considerations would not allow for this more ambitious vision of the League's role in the maintenance of international peace. Bourgeois' ideas, however, were not set aside entirely. Not only was he awarded the 1920 Nobel Peace prize for his ardent support of the League, but, at the 1932 Disarmament Conference held in Geneva the French Minister for War, Andre Tardieu, proposed that all major weapons systems of all member countries be set aside and used only under a League mandate and that an international police force be placed under the jurisdiction of the Council of the League of Nations, in a regime that would also involve compulsory arbitration and a more robust sanctions regime.

The French proposal, often associated with French Prime Minister Edouard Herriot, elicited a warm response from Albert Einstein, who on November 18, 1932, issued a statement in which he made a number of compelling points: "I am convinced that Herriot's plan represents an important step forward with regard to how, in the future, international disputes should be settled. I also consider Herriot's plan to be preferable to other proposals that have been made." He then went on to say that in the search for solutions the framing of the question to be addressed was essential. Rather than asking "under what conditions are armaments permissible and how wars should be fought" he argued that the starting point must be whether nations were "prepared to submit all international disputes to the judgement of an arbitration authority," which had been established by the consent of all parties seeking to establish security guarantees. He thought that:

> the renunciation of unlimited sovereignty by individual nations is the indispensable prerequisite to a solution of the problem. It is the great achievement of Herriot, or rather France, that they have announced their willingness, in principle, for such a renunciation. I also agree with Herriot's proposal that the only military force that should be permitted to have truly effective weapons is a police force which would be subject to the authority of international organs and would be stationed throughout the world.

He then went on to identify two ways in which the Herriot proposals could be improved. First, he thought that "the police formations should not be composed of national troop units which are dependent on their own governments. Such a force, to function effectively under the jurisdiction of a supranational authority, must be – both men and officers – international in composition." Second, in respect of the French call to train militias he indicated that:

the militia system implies that the entire population will be trained in military concepts. It further implies that youth will be educated in a spirit which is at once obsolete and fateful. What would the more advanced nations say if they were confronted with the request that every citizen must serve as a policeman for a certain period of his life? To raise the question is to answer it. These objections should not appear to detract from my belief that Herriot's proposals must be gratefully welcomed as a courageous and significant step in the right direction.[4]

The Bourgeois proposals, progenitors of the subsequent Herriot plan, had been put forward at a time when the outlines of the Covenant were still being formulated and thus could, at least in theory, be considered to have some viability. The French proposals in 1932 had little likelihood of being accepted as they would have involved a rewriting of the Covenant, something that the major powers were unwilling to contemplate. Furthermore, in putting forward these proposals and reviving the idea of an international police force, the French may have been partly motivated by their growing concerns about German militarism and the need, as they saw it, to continue to keep Germany tied to the stringent Versailles Treaty restrictions. Germany in fact soon left the League in 1933 and embarked upon a process of rapid military build-up.

In his comprehensive account of the League's history Walters does point to the one and only – remarkably successful – international force assembled by the League in late 1934, to monitor and supervise the holding of a plebiscite in the Saar territory; a basin that had been part of Germany but had become a League mandate after the end of World War I. A contingent of some 3,300 troops made up of British, Italian, Swedish, and Dutch soldiers reached the Saar in December of 1934. Walters notes that:

> From that moment all fear of disorder was at an end. The mere presence of the troops was all that was needed, and they were never called upon to use their arms. The relations between the different contingents were excellent throughout. Relations with the Saarlanders were also good: the local Nazi leaders tried at first to organize a boycott, describing the Force as a new army of occupation and ordering their followers to avoid all fraternization. But their efforts were a total failure. The troops enjoyed a popularity which they well deserved.[5]

The next instance of an active debate on the possible creation of an international security force was in the period leading up to the adoption of the UN Charter in 1945. We have already discussed in Chapter 2 how a bolder vision of the United Nations considered before the October 1943 Moscow conference had to quickly adjust to the requirements of the Soviet Union under Stalin and, increasingly, to perceptions of what, in due course, would be acceptable to the US Senate, whose ratification was essential to ensure the participation of the United States in the United Nations. Three individuals that made important contributions to this debate during this period and in

[4]   Nathan, Otto and Heinz Norden. 1960. *Einstein on Peace*, New York, Avenel Books, pp. 205–206.
[5]   Walters, *A History*, p. 593.

the years immediately following the establishment of the United Nations were Granville Clark, Albert Einstein, and Bertrand Russell. In a way that was not the case during the discussions around the League's Covenant, the draft UN Charter generated a great deal more informed debate, from individuals who were not necessarily aligned with particular governments, but were sympathetic to the efforts of President Roosevelt and his team to bring into being an international organization to secure the peace. The motivations varied, but very much at their center was the feeling that, with the arrival of nuclear weapons, the context for warfare had changed in a fundamental way. Nations had gone to war in decades and centuries past, or had threatened to do so, assured that the costs could be maintained within acceptable levels due to the implicit constraints imposed by the state of prevailing weapons technologies.

In his discussion of the rise and fall of the "war system," Schell gives several fascinating (and not so well-known) examples of the inexorable logic of warfare in the pre-nuclear age. In 1898, France and Britain were, for several weeks "at the edge of war over a fetid swampland, which neither country valued," a worthless piece of land in a remote area of Sudan called Fashoda. "The disparity between the puniness of the prize and the immensity of the war being risked in Europe disturbed even the most pugnacious imperialists" observes Schell.[6] Since Fashoda, like Egypt, was on the road to India and India was the heart of the British Empire, the war logic dictated that it must be defended at all costs. In the end, though war orders were sent to the English fleet in the Mediterranean, conflict was averted at the last minute because the French backed down.[7]

A second example pertains to a Franco-Russian alliance negotiated in 1894 which envisaged all-out war against Germany in the event of an attack but did not specify what the aims of such a war would be. Clausewitz had taught that absolute war always needed to be subordinated to the strategic requirements of policy, but the treaty underpinning this particular alliance put forward the idea of war as an end in itself. This is how Schell puts it: "And when General Raoul Mouton de Boisdeffre, the principal architect of the treaty on the French side, was asked what Frances's intentions regarding Germany would be after a victory, he replied, 'Let us begin by beating them; after that it will be easy.'[8] Regarding the war's aim, Kennan concluded: 'There is no evidence, in fact, that it had ever been discussed between the two governments.'"

Within a few weeks after the bombing of Hiroshima and Nagasaki, in an interview given to a United Press reporter on September 14, 1945, Einstein had expressed the view that "as long as sovereign states continue to have separate armaments and armaments secrets, new world wars will be inevitable."[9] A few weeks later

---

[6] Schell, Jonathan. 2003. *The Unconquerable World: Power, Nonviolence, and the Will of the People*, New York, Metropolitan Books, p. 40.

[7] Ibid., p. 40.

[8] Ibid., p. 42

[9] Nathan and Norden, *Einstein on Peace*, p. 336.

Russell – who, over the years, maintained an active correspondence with Einstein – rose in the House of Lords on November 28 and said:

> We do not want to look at this thing simply from the point of view of the next few years; we want to look at it from the point of view of the future of mankind. The question is a simple one: Is it possible for a scientific society to continue to exist, or must such a society inevitably bring itself to destruction? It is a simple question: but a very vital one. I do not think it is possible to exaggerate the gravity of the possibilities of evil that lie in the utilization of atomic energy. As I go about the streets and see St. Paul's, the British Museum, the Houses of Parliament, and the other monuments of our civilization, in my mind's eye I see a nightmare vision of those buildings as heaps of rubble with corpses all round them. That is a thing we have got to face, not only in our own country and cities, but throughout the civilized world.[10]

As noted earlier in this book, with his typical mathematician's logic, Russell, in an article for *The American Scholar* in 1943/44 had written: "Wars will cease when, and only when, it becomes evident beyond reasonable doubt that in any war the aggressor will be defeated."[11] Meaning that with an international security force effectively having a monopoly on the use of military power, no nation would use force against another nation because it would not have the means to confront a multinational response. Moreover, beyond responding to such a threat, many nations have increasingly internalized the values and principles of peaceful coexistence and the norm of international nonuse of force with the advent of the 1945 Charter (see Chapter 10); such an internalized value should continue to be consolidated in the future, making violations of international law in this respect an even more deeply held taboo.

Einstein expanded upon his earlier interview in a radio address on May 29, 1946, by stating:

> The development of technology and military weapons has resulted in what amounts to a shrinking of our planet. Economic intercourse between countries has made the nations of the world more dependent upon one another than ever before. The offensive weapons now available leave no spot on earth secure from sudden, total annihilation. Our only hope for survival lies in the creation of a world government capable of resolving conflicts among nations by judicial verdict. Such decisions must be based upon a precisely worded constitution which is approved by all governments. The world government alone may have offensive arms at its disposal. No person or nation can be regarded as pacifist unless they agree that all military power should be concentrated in the hands of a supranational authority, and unless they renounce force as a means of safeguarding their interests against other nations. Political developments, in this first year since the end of the Second World War, have

---

[10] Quoted in *The Fate of the Earth*, by Jonathan Schell, p. 183.
[11] Russell, Bertrand. 1943. "The Future of Pacifism," *The American Scholar* Vol. 13, No. 1, pp. 7–13. Published by The Phi Beta Kappa Society. www.jstor.org/stable/41204635.

clearly brought us no closer to the attainment of these goals. The present Charter of the United Nations does not provide either for the legal institutions or the military forces which would be necessary to bring real international security into being. Nor does it take into account the actual balance of power in the world today.[12]

He then went on to suggest that the United States and Russia as the main victorious war powers could, by themselves, create the legal framework that would ensure universal military security.

Clark was no less active. As the main adviser to US Secretary of War Henry Stimson, Clark had been involved in most important decisions on the conduct of the war and had seen up close the dire consequences – human, economic, political – of global warfare. In the summer of 1944, when it became increasingly clear that the Allies would emerge victorious, Clark, who had spent several years in Washington as an unpaid public servant, staying with his wife at a suite at the St. Regis hotel, decided to return to law practice in New York and was told by Stimson: "Grenny, go home and try to figure out a way to stop the next war and all future wars."[13] Clark's A *Plan for Peace*, published in 1950 contains a first set of fairly detailed proposals for the creation of a Peace Force attached to the United Nations;[14] we will say more on this later in this chapter.

THE UN CHARTER AND THE PEACEFUL SETTLEMENT OF DISPUTES

The United Nations came into being against the background of over 60 million casualties, the destruction of significant portions of countries' physical infrastructure, and the associated economic collapse. It is not surprising therefore that the Charter refers in high-minded language to the determination of the international community to "save succeeding generations from the scourge of war," lays out various principles for the peaceful coexistence of its members and calls for the strengthening of existing mechanisms of cooperation "to maintain international peace and security." Article 1 of the Charter, in particular, specifically refers to the UN taking:

> effective collective measures for the prevention and removal of threats to the peace, and for the suppression of acts of aggression or other breaches of the peace, and to bring about by peaceful means, and in conformity with the principles of justice and international law, adjustment or settlement of international disputes or situations which might lead to breaches of the peace.

The principles that are to guide United Nations actions in this area are spelled out in Chapters VI and VII of the Charter on the Pacific Settlement of Disputes (Articles 33–38) and Action with Respect to Threats to the Peace, Breaches of the Peace, and

---

[12] Nathan and Norden, *Einstein on Peace*, pp. 379–380.
[13] Nancy Peterson Hill. 2014. A *Very Private Public Citizen: The Life of Grenville Clark*, Columbia, University of Missouri Press, p. 153.
[14] Clark, Grenville. 1950. A *Plan for Peace*, New York, Harper & Brothers Publishers.

Acts of Aggression (Articles 39–51), respectively. The Articles embedded in Chapters VI and VII are an attempt to establish a foundation of legal and moral legitimacy to enable a range of UN actions intended to protect the peace. In the paragraphs that follow we will review briefly what mechanisms emerged, in practice and over time, to operationalize some of the noble sentiments contained in the Charter in this area, so central to what the UN was set out to achieve.

The peaceful settlement of disputes (Chapter VI) was seen as an essential element of avoiding armed conflicts (see also Chapter 10). However, at the insistence of the Big Four during the drafting stage of the UN Charter, Article 2(3) narrowed the scope of dispute settlement to *international* cross-border disputes, with internal disputes falling within the sovereignty of states.[15] This was done to protect state prerogatives as most governments were unwilling, in 1945, to have an international organization interfering in internal disputes. Initially, this sharply curtailed the sphere of action of the UN, given that the overwhelming majority of conflicts in recent decades have been of an internal nature.[16] And it also added an additional layer of complexity to potential UN responses given the nature of such internal conflicts, with the fighting often taking place between militias, armed civilians and guerrillas with ill-defined front lines and with civilians often being the victims of the brunt of the violence. These internal conflicts also proved to be destructive of state institutions in a way that traditional interstate conflicts with well-defined frontlines were not.

Article 33 of the Charter identifies the various mechanisms that are to be used by the parties to a dispute seeking to peacefully settle their differences. Article 51, however, allows for the interim use of countermeasures and a narrow but inherent right of self-defense by states, with an obligation to report such cases immediately to the Security Council so that it may take the necessary measures to secure international peace and security, in line with its authority and responsibility. In time, the United Nations developed a range of instruments aimed at resolving conflicts between and within states entailing aspects of preventive diplomacy, peacekeeping, disarmament, sanctions, and the like. It also sought to define and operationalize some of these instruments in a formal way, typically in the context of General Assembly resolutions. For instance, members could enter into *negotiations* to address various types of

---

[15] UN Charter Article 2(4) states that all members shall refrain from the threat or use of force, which effectively may be interpreted to involve a ban on coercion and the use of force. GA resolution 2625 (XXV) of 1970 ("Declaration on Principles of International Law Concerning Friendly Relations and Cooperation Among States in Accordance with the Charter of the United Nations") was a first attempt to define the content of "peaceful settlement of disputes," which was the subject of more detailed elaboration in a subsequent GA declaration in 1988, which broadened the interpretation of the scope of Article 2, which deals only with existing disputes.

[16] This remains the case today. For instance, the Stockholm International Peace Research Institute's 2017 Yearbook notes that "of the 49 active conflicts in 2016, 2 were fought between states (India-Pakistan and Eritrea-Ethiopia) and the other 47 were fought within states and over government (22), territory (24) or both (1)." See, SIPRI Yearbook 2017: Armaments, Disarmament and International Security, Stockholm, Sweden.

conflict – political, social, legal and so on. Negotiations are limited to the states concerned, which are empowered to "shape its outcome to deliver a mutually agreed settlement."[7] For their success, negotiations assume the willingness of states to compromise, but may imply the imposition of solutions on the weaker party. Thus, to take an example, a negotiation between China and the Philippines on the status of various small islands in the South China Sea might not lead to results satisfactory to the latter party, given the lopsided nature of both parties' relative strengths.

In an *inquiry* or process of *fact finding*, the parties may initiate a commission of inquiry to establish the facts of the case, but the recommendations would not usually be legally binding. *Mediation* generally involves the good offices of a third party to assist in finding a resolution and to prevent escalation. It is seen as perhaps the oldest and most often used method for peaceful settlement and was enshrined in The Hague Conventions on the topic of 1899 and 1907. *Conciliation* is a combination of fact finding and mediation to propose a mutually acceptable solution to parties in dispute. Conciliation proposals are not binding, but parties may accept them unilaterally or through agreement; many international treaties contain provisions for the referral to disputes to compulsory conciliation. GA resolution 50/50[18] of 1995 establishes the UN framework for conciliation. *Arbitration*, first set out in The Hague Conventions of 1899 and 1907, employs settlement by arbitrators of the parties' choice, in a manner intended to be consistent with prevailing legal standards. Parties agree to abide by the outcome, which is binding. Arbitration has been used in territorial disputes or, for example, when parties may differ in their interpretations of bilateral or certain multilateral treaties. *International tribunals* refer mainly to the International Court of Justice (ICJ) and the range of other international courts and tribunals, most of which have been established since the adoption of the Charter. The decisions of the ICJ are final and cannot by appealed.[19] International tribunals, which have proliferated in the modern era, are used, for example, to clarify or settle interpretation and application of treaties, border disputes among states, matters related to the Law of the Sea, the international use of force, the application of cross-border investment agreements, and individual liability for war crimes, among other things.[20]

---

[17] Mani, Rama. 2007. "Peaceful Settlement of Disputes and Conflict Prevention," in Thomas G. Weiss and Sam Daws (eds.), *The Oxford Handbook on the United Nations*, New York, Oxford University Press, pp. 300–322, at p. 304.

[18] The resolution is known as "United Nations Model Rules for the Conciliation of Disputes Between States." It was adopted at the 87th plenary meeting of the GA, on December 11, 1995. The full text can be found in Rauschning, Dietrich, Katja Wiesbrock, and Martin Lailach. 1997. *Key Resolutions of the United Nations General Assembly 1946–1996*. Cambridge, Cambridge University Press, pp. 23–26.

[19] See Article 60 in the statute of the ICJ, with, however, an application for revision allowed under Article 61 if new decisive facts become known.

[20] The ICJ remains the highest-level organ for the settlement of disputes, and while its decisions are binding they apply only in cases where states have voluntarily submitted the cases for consideration, even though they are party to the Court's Statute by virtue of being a member of

The Charter encourages the involvement of *regional agencies* in the settlement of disputes under its Article 52. Such regional bodies may include the Arab League, the Association of Southeast Asian Nations (ASEAN), the Organization of American States (OAS), the African Union (AU), the Council of Europe, the Organization for Security and Co-operation in Europe (OSCE), the European Union (EU), as well as others. An important challenge in the effective operation of regional mechanisms has been how to harmonize their work with that of the United Nations itself. However, when regional efforts fail, the situation may be referred to the Security Council, where the most vital question then becomes whether the dispute threatens international peace, thus falling within the Security Council's mandate.

DEVELOPMENT OF THE CONCEPT OF A STANDING FORCE

Article 43(1) of the UN Charter states: "All Members of the United Nations, in order to contribute to the maintenance of international peace and security, undertake to make available to the Security Council, on its call and in accordance with a special agreement or agreements, armed forces, assistance, and facilities, including rights of passage, necessary for the purpose of maintaining international peace and security." Article 43 was considered, by the drafters in San Francisco, to be absolutely fundamental to the new centralized collective security mechanism of the Charter. However, remarkably, these Chapter VII provisions were never implemented and thus, the Security Council had not actually had, armed forces at its disposal even though Article 24(1) establishes that the Security Council bears "primary responsibility for the maintenance of international peace and security" when parties are unable or unwilling to settle their disputes peacefully, or other situations arise. Faced with a host of conflicts and destabilizing situations in various parts of the world, a number of initiatives have emerged from within the UN to bridge the gap between its peace and security mandate and the absence of appropriate instruments to carry it out.

For instance, in 1948 Secretary General Trygve Lie proposed the creation of a "UN Guard Force" of up to 5,000 soldiers to be recruited internationally, mainly to assist in the administration of truces, protecting the transparency of plebiscites and other duties of a limited nature, not unlike those of a constabulary nonparamilitary force. Lie made it clear that his proposal was not intended as a substitute for the armed forces that were to be made available to the Security Council "as soon as possible" under Article 43, but still encountered strong opposition from the Soviet

the UN. While a minority opinion may have previously regarded the ICJ as irrelevant or as a "toothless bulldog" because, among other things, the majority of UN members have not agreed to submit to its general compulsory jurisdiction, there has been remarkable modern use of the Court and there is evidence that in those cases where the Court has issued decisions, compliance by the affected parties has been relatively high (Mani, "Peaceful Settlement of Disputes and Conflict Prevention," p. 311 and see Chapter 10).

Union representatives, who did not feel comfortable with an even minimalist interpretation of the commitments made in that Article. Although Lie went out of his way to emphasize that it would not be a striking force, that it would be at the disposal of the Security Council and the General Assembly, and that it would be largely used in the administration of plebiscites and in the supervision of truce terms, he was forced to water down his proposal to an 800-person UN Guard. According to Roberts, even the United States, the United Kingdom, and France had expressed reservations about the scale of such a force, with the US representative stating that, "[w]e are inclined to think that the original proposal was somewhat too ambitious, and that it did encroach somewhat on the military theme."[21] This stands in sharp contrast to the initial thinking within the US government in discussions leading to the ratification of the UN Charter when, according to Urquhart, "the United States estimate of the forces it would supply under Article 43, which was by far the largest, included twenty divisions – over 300,000 troops – a very large naval force, 1,250 bombers and 2,250 fighters."[22] This swift change in attitude seems to have been precipitated by the onset of the Cold War and Soviet demands that all the great powers make equal contributions, irrespective of their relative size.

Lie, however, was persistent and he took advantage of the outbreak of the Korean War in June of 1950, the UN's authorization for a US-led force to repel North Korea's attack and the General Assembly's call in its Uniting for Peace resolution alluded to previously (see Chapter 4) – which called on its members to keep forces trained, organized and equipped for UN service[23] – to propose the creation of a UN Legion made up of volunteers. But, by 1954 Lie's successor, Dag Hammarskjold, withdrew such proposals from further consideration and the issue itself retreated as the patterns of the Cold War became entrenched and significantly intensified.

Dag Hammarskjold sought to make a distinction between "quiet diplomacy," consisting mainly of the involvement of the Secretary General in bringing together the parties in conflict, and "preventive diplomacy" which consisted in developing and nurturing the infrastructure for peacekeeping operations. Article 98 of the Charter had granted the Secretary General the right to "perform such other functions as are entrusted to him" by the various UN organs and Hammarskjold was proactive in projecting the role of the UN as peacekeeper in a number of instances,

---

[21] Roberts, Adam. 2008. "Proposals for UN Standing Forces: A Critical History," in Vaughan Lowe, Adam Roberts, Jennifer Welsh, and Dominik Zaum (eds.), *The United Nations Security Council and War: The Evolution of Thought and Practice Since 1945*, New York, Oxford University Press, p. 102.

[22] Urquhart, Brian. 1993. "For a UN Volunteer Military Force," *New York Review of Books*, June 10, p. 3.

[23] The language of the resolution states: "*Recommends* to the States Members of the United Nations that each Member maintain within its national armed forces elements so trained, organized and equipped that they could promptly be made available, in accordance with its constitutional processes, for service as a United Nations unit or units..."

such as during the 1956 Suez Canal crisis and in the early 1960s in the Congo, not always with the full support of the membership.

After 1956 peacekeeping forces and the infrastructure around them developed gradually through the introduction of so-called standby arrangements, which Roberts defines as "national contingents which were made available for particular UN operations through specific agreements with the troop-providing governments."[24] The debate about replacing these with a standing force took place largely in the academic community, with proposals such as that put forth by the Carnegie Endowment for International Peace in 1957,[25] and the more substantive and ambitious work done by Clark and Sohn in 1958 and in the following years.

The end of the Cold War prompted a more active approach to peace enforcement and conflict management and prevention by the UN. In particular, it boosted in a major way the role of the Security Council in this area and led to a sharp increase in the number of peacekeeping missions mandated by the Council. With the collapse of tightly centralized control in countries such as the Soviet Union and Yugoslavia, festering, long-repressed conflicts – often with an ethnic or religious underpinning – suddenly came to the fore, which was reflected in a much larger number of peacekeeping operations deployed. For instance, while in early 1988 there were ten such operations in place involving about 9,600 military personnel, by the end of 1994 there were 34 operations employing 73,400 troops. (As was noted in Chapter 12 on funding the United Nations, spending on peacekeeping operations rose from under $30 million in 1971 to close to $9 billion in 2017.) Furthermore, the Security Council has broadened the scope of its attention beyond conflict prevention and management to include humanitarian issues, monitoring human rights abuses, terrorism, democratization, the promotion of gender equality, the building up of court systems, and so on. The General Assembly's role has become more muted in contrast to the pre-end-of-the-Cold War era where it at times occupied the space created by Security Council gridlock, brought about by the frequent use of the veto.[26] Article 99 gives a role to the Secretary General in the area of the maintenance of international peace and security, and various secretary generals over time have taken an activist role in this area, often serving as mediators in a range of conflicts or coming forward with various initiatives that would enhance the peace promotion mandate of the UN.[27] Examples include important roles played by secretary generals in conflicts in the Middle East, Southern Africa, the Iran–Iraq

[24] Roberts, "Proposals for UN Standing Forces: A Critical History," pp. 103–104.

[25] Frye, William R. 1957. *A United Nations Peace Force*, New York, Oceana Publishers.

[26] In this respect, GA resolution 377(V) (Uniting for Peace) makes specific reference to the consequences to the lack of unanimity of the permanent members of the Security Council and the role that the General Assembly is expected to play to ensure collective measures aimed at restoring the peace and "the use of armed force when necessary to maintain or restore international peace and security."

[27] The role of the Secretary General under Art. 99 is actually considered to be an example of "reform of the Charter through practice," where the Secretary General performs his role ex

war, Soviet involvement in Afghanistan in the 1980s, and Namibian independence, to name a few.

An Agenda for Peace 1992 was an early attempt to give new life to the United Nations' role in this area, with Secretary General Boutros Boutros-Ghali putting forth a range of proposals, including a possible return to the spirit and the letter of Article 43. While admitting at the outset that readily available armed forces on call "may perhaps never be sufficiently large or well enough equipped to deal with a threat from a major army equipped with sophisticated weapons . . . they would be useful, however, in meeting any threat posed by a military force of lesser order,"[28] the Secretary General put forth the idea of creating "peace enforcement units" to support the work of peacekeepers in maintaining ceasefires. Their mandate would be clearly defined and would be made up of troops who had volunteered for such service.

Brian Urquhart, a former Under-Secretary General of the UN published an influential piece in the *New York Review of Books* in 1993 in which he argued that the time had come to revive Trygve Lie's 1948 idea. The problem with the Security Council was now less the abuse of the veto by the major powers and more its inability to carry through on its decisions, with this flaw having tragic real-life consequences on the ground, such as in Rwanda and Bosnia. With reference to Bosnia in particular, he argued that "a determined UN peace enforcement force, deployed before the situation had become desperate, and authorized to retaliate, might have provided the basis for a more effective international effort."[29] Urquhart identified flaws in the UN's peacekeeping arrangements that have largely remained unchanged in the 25 years since he made his case, provoking spirited debate. Key among existing flaws is the unwillingness of governments to put their troops in harm's way for conflicts perceived to take place in distant lands that could at times be both violent and open-ended. Because peacekeeping forces not only report to the UN command but also to their own country's military commands, the authorities at home have a built-in bias not to intervene, in the interests of minimizing casualties, among other reasons. Over time, this has resulted in massive tragedies, such as Srebrenica in 1995 when, as noted by Autesserre, "the Dutch commander of a peacekeeping battalion, outnumbered and outgunned, had his soldiers stand by as Serbian forces rounded up and killed some 8,000 Muslim men and boys."[30]

But this was not the only problem. Peacekeeping forces are often poorly trained and equipped. They are put together in response to the emergence of conflicts and often, as in Rwanda, arrive too late to make a difference. A standing force of volunteers would address the problem of training by providing this on an ongoing

officio, of his own volition, without necessarily bringing the matter to the attention of the Security Council.

[28] Quoted in Roberts, "Proposals for UN Standing Forces: A Critical History," p. 106.

[29] Ibid., p. 3

[30] Autesserre, Severine. 2019. "The Crisis of Peacekeeping: Why the UN Can't End Wars," *Foreign Affairs*, January/February 2019, pp. 101–116.

basis; hence the use of the equivalent term "rapid reaction" to highlight a state of readiness that is not to be found in forces that are put together in calls to members by the Security Council, which then has to await for offers of help from interested parties. In this respect, by strengthening the ability to prevent conflicts, such forces could help minimize the terrible human and social costs (not to mention economic and financial inefficiencies) of late interventions. The volunteer nature of enhanced arrangements, likewise, could be expected to deflect the possible political ramifications associated with contingents that are drafted by their respective governments into peacekeeping roles. As we shall see below, these issues are all addressed in the proposals we put forward for an International Peace Force.

Perhaps no other failed UN intervention highlighted the weaknesses of current approaches to peacekeeping than the events in Rwanda in 1994 when, over a period of slightly more than four months 800,000 people were killed. This large-scale genocide of primarily Tutsis was at a time when, in the consensus of experts and subsequent inquiries made to assess what had gone wrong, a modest-sized international force could have prevented much of the killing.[31,32]

Upon taking office in early 1997, Secretary General Annan placed conflict prevention at the top of the UN agenda and spoke of shifting the United Nations from a "culture of reaction to a culture of prevention," stating that "one of the principal aims of preventive action should be to address the deep-rooted socio-economic, cultural, environmental, institutional, and other structural causes that often underlie the immediate political symptoms of conflicts."[33] Peaceful settlement was thus seen as being closely linked to conflict prevention, with the latter also aiming to address the deeper causes of conflict – poverty, inequality, corruption, lack of opportunity, human rights violations, to name a few (see discussion of addressing these issues more systemically at the global level in Chapters 13–18). Therefore, conflict prevention at UN missions and by bilateral and multilateral actors should

---

[31] See, for instance, *Report of the Independent Inquiry into the Actions of the United Nations during the 1994 Genocide in Rwanda*, UN document S/1999/1257, December 16, 1999.

[32] Walter, Barbara F., Lise M. Howard, and V. Page Fortna, 2019. "The Extraordinary Relationship between Peacekeeping and Peace," unpublished manuscript. Walter, Howard and Fortna argue that peacekeeping failures like Somalia, Rwanda and Bosnia aside, the more recent experience with these operations has been more positive, including in Namibia, Cambodia, Mozambique, Sierra Leone, Ivory Coast, Guatemala, and several others. In particular, they write that "using different datasets and statistical models, leveraging different time periods, and measuring peacekeeping in somewhat different ways, dozens of researchers at different universities, with diverse funding streams and different agendas, have all found that peacekeeping has a large, positive, and statistically significant effect on reducing violence of all sorts" (p. 1) and that "less peacekeeping will not make the world safer" but will only "facilitate more violence" (p. 4). In Howard, Lise M. 2019. "Five Myths about Peacekeeping," *Washington Post*, July 14, p. B2, the author suggests that at least part of the disappointment with UN peacekeeping operations may stem from unreasonable expectations placed upon them, given the constraints against which they typically operate. She sensibly argues that "peacekeeping is a tool of conflict management, not conflict resolution" (p. B2).

[33] Mani, "Peaceful Settlement of Disputes and Conflict Prevention," p. 311.

address the interconnections and the tensions between security and economic and social development.

In July 2006 Annan further widened the scope of conflict prevention by referring to "systematic prevention," taken to mean "measures to address global risks of conflict that transcend particular states."[34] The Rwandan Genocide played a catalytic role in these discussions and in the negotiation of the Rome Statute for the International Criminal Court (ICC), which entered into force in 2002, allowing for the prosecution of war criminals; its explicit intention to battle against impunity for grave international crimes was expected to play an additional role in deterring conflict and abuse (see Chapter 10).

Efforts since the end of the Cold War to operationalize the UN's conflict prevention mandate have not been free of controversy. Some have argued that because preventive diplomacy could involve the use of force, the Security Council should focus its efforts on funding UN peacekeeping and enforcement rather than the less well-defined issue of conflict prevention. Very often states come to the Security Council after the crisis has erupted and the opportunity for prevention is long gone. Some countries see prevention as a justification for intervention; furthermore, developing countries saw a trade-off between a peace and security focus and, in a world of constrained resources, a lack of focus on social and economic development needs. And finally, it was not always clear what "conflict prevention" meant in practice and this has complicated countries' involvement. In his Supplement to *An Agenda for Peace*, issued in 1995 on the occasion of the Fiftieth Anniversary of the United Nations, Secretary General Boutros-Ghali noted that "when in May 1994 the Security Council decided to expand the United Nations Assistance Mission for Rwanda (UNAMIR), not one of the 19 Governments that at that time had undertaken to have troops on stand-by agreed to contribute."[35] Indeed, this situation was repeated when, in the aftermath of the genocide, the Secretary General issued appeals to 60 governments for troops for a peacekeeping force to protect 1.2 million Rwandan refugees in camps in Zaire and he received a total of zero responses, again underscoring the fatal flaw associated with the absence of a permanent standing force.

PEACE ENFORCEMENT: FURTHER CONSIDERATIONS

There are significant differences in the types of UN operations that have emerged in the context of the application of the principles contained in Chapter VII of the Charter. One issue that has emerged is the asymmetric nature of peace enforcement

---

[34] Annan, Kofi, 2006. Progress Report of Armed Conflict, A/60/891, UN General Assembly. New York.

[35] See Boutros-Ghali, Boutros. 1997. *An Agenda for Peace 1995*. New York: United Nations Publications, p. 18.

operations under this chapter, which in recent decades have involved mainly events in poorer, developing countries as the main threats addressed by the peace and security mandate of the United Nations. This asymmetry is not unlike that which exists in International Monetary Fund operations, with the Fund having considerable leverage in shaping national domestic policies for those countries (generally in the developing world) that borrow from it, and the organization having little influence in helping reverse unsustainable policies in countries that are systematically important and that may pose threats to the global economy (see Chapter 15). A prime example of this is the 2008–2009 global financial crisis, which eloquently revealed the inability of the IMF to coerce some of its largest shareholders into adopting regulatory regimes for their financial sectors that might be consistent with global financial stability.

Peace enforcement operations have generally been delegated to governments or groups of countries working as part of a coalition, with such operations a way in which the Security Council seeks to impose its will via military or economic actions. These operations may involve the protection of supplies in war-torn areas, ensuring freedom of movement, or securing agreements against various parties that may be seeking to undermine the peace. The Security Council has sought to use a combination of economic and military power with the relative importance of each depending on individual country circumstances. The first Chapter VII operation took place in Korea in 1950 and was only made possible by the absence of the Soviet Union from the Security Council at the time. Article 47 of the UN Charter calls for the establishment of a Military Staff Committee to "advise and assist the Security Council on all questions relating to the Security Council's military requirements for the maintenance of international peace and security, the employment and command of forces placed at its disposal, the regulation of armaments, and possible disarmament." This initiative fell victim to the onset of the Cold War in the late 1940s and the Committee has never played the role foreseen in the Charter and, thus, Chapter VII operations remained dormant for several decades.

The next Chapter VII interventions came in 1991 with the invasion of Kuwait by Saddam Hussain's Iraq and authorization in 2001 for the establishment of an International Security Assistance Force (ISAF) in Afghanistan. Peace enforcement operations have not been free of controversy, with many critics stating that the distinction between pacification and militarism has been blurred over time. Such critics point, for instance, to the fact that until relatively recently (up to the time of the failed Somalia intervention in the early 1990s) the US military itself did not unambiguously identify the differences between "war," peace enforcement, and peacekeeping. In any case, none of the above interventions involved the United Nations at the operational level but were largely based on US political leadership and military deployment, with no UN input to speak of. This may have reflected an established tradition that saw UN soldiers ("The Blue Berets") as an element of peaceful diplomacy with strict controls on the use of fire, typically limited to cases of self-defense. One further limitation or drawback of interventions led by a country or group of countries – in the absence of a UN force under the jurisdiction of the Security Council – is that an impression can be created that the operations are mainly serving the strategic interests of the country or countries contributing troops and equipment, rather than the interests of the international community as reflected in the will of the United Nations. This, in turn, may contribute to undermine the legitimacy of the intervention. This particular problem would, of course, be addressed in the context of a UN International Peace Force where the command and control would be wholly under UN auspices; we will say more on this in the sections below.

The 1960 Congo mission was the first where UN peacekeepers were allowed to enter into military action but found themselves poorly prepared. This early intervention experience succeeded in eroding the consensus for peacekeeping, with states henceforward seeking short mandates to be renewed only if not vetoed by the Security Council. In other instances, peacekeepers (e.g., Cambodia, 1992–1993) relied on the consent of the government and were required to withdraw even in the face of limited opposition.

The failures in Somalia, Yugoslavia, and Rwanda in the first half of the 1990s, in turn, greatly undermined the credibility of traditional peacekeeping. A permanent tension emerged between the objective of peacekeeping and peace enforcement despite UN efforts to update existing mandates, as was the case in Somalia. At times Security Council resolutions could not be implemented because of the lack of adequate ground force capability to either put a stop to the conflict or to protect safe areas. An example of this tension was French President Chirac's proposal to retake Srebrenica, which was opposed by the British who argued that the UN force had no mandate to go to war. Or the position taken by the United States, the United Kingdom, and France that prevented the Security Council from rescuing Tutsis during the Rwandan genocide and the associated denials that genocide was in fact even taking place. Indeed, in the case of France, critics have pointed to the fact that the country supported the Hutus on account of strong historical, political, and economic links, largely turning a blind eye to the killing. A third example of a failed, ineffective UN operation concerns Darfur, where the UN and the African Union "decided that respecting Sudanese sovereignty was more important than conducting a military response capable of protecting the civilian population."[36]

UN action to secure the peace has been obliged to operate against the background of the constraints imposed by narrow interpretations of Article 2(7) of the Charter, which states that "nothing contained in the present Charter shall authorize the United Nations to intervene in matters which are essentially within the domestic jurisdiction of any state." Given that, as noted earlier, most conflicts over the past half a century have largely been *internal* in nature, the end result has often been an approach to peacekeeping and peace enforcement that is overly timid and, hence,

---

[36] Pugh, Michael. 2007. "Peace Enforcement," in Thomas G. Weiss and Sam Daws (eds.), *The Oxford Handbook on the United Nations*. New York, Oxford University Press, pp. 370–387.

ineffective. States in the middle of a conflict have often been reluctant to accept UN involvement, reflecting the primacy of national sovereignty over security and/or humanitarian considerations, and the the organization has itself contributed to the creation of a culture that embodies the belief that "the United Nations cannot impose its preventive and peace-making services on Member States who do not want them."[37] These attitudes, in turn, led to the emergence of a set of overly limited "principles" of peacekeeping which included such concepts as the consent of the parties, neutrality, and the nonuse of force except in cases of self-defense. The idea that the UN should remain neutral between warring parties without a mandate to stop the aggressor and impose a cessation of hostilities flow from a design flaw in the UN Charter, reinforced by the Big Four's desire not to grant the UN any concrete and effective (as opposed to theoretical, "on paper") responsibility to actually deliver on the peace and security ideals of its Charter. As we will see below, in our proposals for the creation of a United Nations International Peace Force, there is an urgent need to move to a system of genuine collective security and conflict prevention, where the primary aim of the United Nations is to secure the peace and protect citizens from the effects of violence in an impartial manner, as opposed to entrenching a too-narrow view of state sovereignty, to the detriment of all.

In many cases of UN intervention a key question has often been: Can peace enforcers challenge the sovereign right of domestic authorities to do as they please, which may often involve persecutions, killing, and other forms of massive human rights violations? Can humanitarian motives in fact be grounds for international enforcement action? The Somalian failure very much brought humanitarian justification into the center of the debate on the nature of UN peace enforcement. Secretary General Boutros-Ghali made the argument that in chaotic domestic environments characterized by massive abuses, the need for humanitarian interventions should take precedence over concerns about state sovereignty. Later on, Secretary General Annan made a case for a redefinition of state sovereignty that was consistent with the rights of individuals to peace and security. This thinking underpinned the justification used by NATO for its intervention in Yugoslavia in 1999, with peace enforcement for the protection of populations leading to the development of the concept of the "responsibility to protect" ("R2P"), reflected in the 2005 World Summit Outcome Document of global leaders.

The remarkable high-level acceptance of the R2P doctrine was preceded by the 2001 International Commission on Intervention and State Sovereignty (ICISS), established by the Canadian government, with Gareth Evans, former Foreign Minister of Australia, and Algerian diplomat Mohamed Sahnoun, serving as cochairs.[38] In a nutshell, the commission report recommended "three pillars" to

---

[37] Boutros-Ghali, Supplement to *An Agenda for Peace*, p. 13.
[38] See summary discussion in Buitelaar, Tom and Richard Ponzio. 2018. "Mobilizing Smart Coalitions and Negotiating Global Governance Reform," in William Durch, Joris Larik, and

the R2P doctrine, with principled collective military action employed only as a last resort. The ICISS underlined, first, the primary responsibility of every state to protect its own populations from atrocity crimes (e.g., genocide, war crimes, ethnic cleansing, and crimes against humanity), in accordance with their national and international obligations, with a second, parallel responsibility of the international community to encourage and support states in fulfilling their responsibilities. Only when a state is manifestly failing to protect its population should the international community take collective action, first employing appropriate diplomatic, political, humanitarian means, and then, if necessary, military means, in accordance with the Charter. The R2P norm has been the object of very substantial civil society engagement and support, with a convened International Coalition for the Responsibility to Protect (ICRtoP).[39] The doctrine has informed multiple resolutions of the Security Council and other UN organs since its adoption by the World Summit in 2005.[40]

One challenge faced by the UN in Chapter VII operations has been, as noted above, the generally low level of enthusiasm by UN states to participate in enforcement operations. Many states seem to be of two minds as regards their collective responsibilities under Chapter VII as UN members and their propensities to zealously safeguard notions of domestic sovereignty regardless of circumstance. In *An Agenda for Peace* in 1992 the Secretary General recommended that under Article 40 of the Charter the Security Council consider using peace enforcement units in clearly defined circumstances, but the veto-wielding members showed little interest. Recourse to regional organizations has also not produced the desired results because these have generally been poorly equipped in operational military capacity for multilateral roles. A related problem pertains to the difficulties faced by parties involved in a military intervention in maintaining adequate levels of impartiality. Michael Pugh argues that "the concept of peace enforcement remains an extremely underdeveloped area of military doctrine – even though it is perhaps most needed."[41]

THE INTERNATIONAL EVOLUTION OF WAR AND VIOLENCE:
A STORY OF DIMINISHING RETURNS

At the same time and in parallel to these incomplete and rather erratic efforts at the United Nations to give reliable operational meaning to Chapter VII Charter commitments, there have been significant changes in our understanding of the use of

---

(eds.), *Just Security in an Ungoverned World*. Oxford, Oxford University Press, pp. 463–487; 465–467.

[39] See www.responsibilitytoprotect.org/.

[40] See for example the list provided by the Global Centre for the Responsibility to Protect, January 22, 2018, *UN Security Council Resolutions and Presidential Statements Referencing R2P*. www.globalr2p.org/resources/335.

[41] Pugh, *Peace Enforcement*, p. 384.

violence to achieve political ends. One need not be naïve about the future of warfare to understand the constraints that have emerged in recent decades on the use of violence as a result of developments in technology and the process of economic integration. International warfare in centuries past was characterized by great disparities of power, with conquering nations enjoying a superior technological advantage, which could be used to overwhelming effect. Hernan Cortes subjugated the vast Aztec civilization with a grand total of 500 men, 10 bronze cannons and 12 muskets. A similar story can be told about Francisco Pizarro and his band of adventurers and religious fanatics in respect of Atahualpa and the battle in Cajamarca where fewer than two hundred Spanish soldiers, with horses and some firearms, overcame an army of 80,000 Incas.[42] Whether we refer to the arrival of Robert Clive in India, the opium wars in China, Commodore Perry's sailing into Japanese waters to compel the Japanese to trade with the rest of the world, or the excesses of African colonization, military might in centuries past was extremely effective in delivering (ill-gotten) economic and political power, in subjugating other peoples, and empowering and enriching those that had the technological advantage.

---

[42] Jared Diamond argues that "the biggest population shift of modern times has been the colonization of the New World by Europeans, and the resulting conquest, numerical reduction, or complete disappearance of most groups of Native Americans." He goes on to describe the weapons technology that gave the numerically inferior Spanish forces the advantage – the guns and steel – and allowed them to subjugate populations that vastly outnumbered them, citing as an example one key encounter between the all-powerful Inca emperor Atahualpa and Spanish conquistador Francisco Pizarro, which took place in the Peruvian town of Cajamarca, on November 16, 1532. Atahualpa was an absolute ruler to his people, the incarnation of a Sun god and universally revered, while Pizarro led, in Diamond's words, "a ragtag group of 168 Spanish soldiers ... in unfamiliar terrain." When the Spanish first happened on the emperor's encampment at Cajamarca, they were terrified by the sheer quantity of Inca troops, who according to one eye witness numbered 80,000 and filled an entire plain. Communicating through interpreters, Atahualpa invited Pizarro to a meeting where he promised he would not be harmed. When presented with a ceremonial copy of the Bible, however, the emperor at first did not understand how to open the book, then took the Spanish Friar's attempts to help him as an insult. Once the book was opened, he did not understand the language and inscriptions within, and finally threw it to the ground in anger. The Friar took this as a sign that the emperor did not submit to God's authority and gave his blessing for Pizarro to attack. This Pizarro did at once, giving orders to his soldiers to fire guns into Atahualpa's startled assemblage, and sounding the trumpets to call down his hidden cavalry. The emperor himself, who was taken prisoner and later executed by Pizarro, conceded that the Spanish killed 7,000 of his men that day, without suffering a single casualty of their own. Despite their miniscule numbers, the superior weaponry and steel armor of the Conquistadors, as well as the presence of mounted troops – a phenomenon unknown to Native Americans – gave them an advantage that proved sufficient to overcome and scatter a much larger army. This same pattern of a clash between cultures, compounded by technological advantages, would repeat itself across the New World in years to come, resulting in the subjugation and decimation of its native populations. Diamond, Jared. 1997. *Guns, Germs, and Steel, the Faith of Human Societies*, New York, W.W. Norton & Company.

But that period is long gone and what has emerged is a rapid and irreversible erosion in the ability of military power to deliver the spoils of the past. The arrival of nuclear weapons and the spread of democratic forms of governance, plus a greater recognition by people everywhere of what the anthropologist Robert Murdock calls "the psychic unity of mankind," the sense that the differences between various cultures and nations – which have frequently figured prominently as justifications for war – are sometimes artificial and often skin-deep, have contributed to shift in a dramatic way the trade-off between the utility of violence and the costs of violence.[43] And thus, we have a growing list of examples of some of the most powerful states in the world – often endowed with nuclear weapons and the ability, at least in theory, to totally obliterate their adversaries, having to face military humiliations. Schell points to nuclear-armed Britain failing to achieve any of its strategic objectives in the Suez crisis of 1956 against Egypt; France was not able to retain control of Algeria during its war of independence; the United States and the Soviet Union failed utterly in Vietnam and Afghanistan, respectively, and China had its own unsuccessful border disputes with Vietnam in 1979 and the ensuing years.[44] The presence of the Soviet Union and China in this list suggests that one cannot appeal to the argument that there is something inherently decent in democratic regimes that makes the use of nuclear weapons to achieve strategic objectives an impossibility.[45] The issue here is that the world has come around to agree with President Truman, who once remarked that "starting a nuclear war is totally unthinkable for rational men" and that it will never make any sense to shed the blood of millions for some marginal, perceived strategic advantage.

While it has always been ethically unacceptable (and is now seen as such by many populations around the world), the use of violence as an instrument to promote the national interest has also thus been undermined by the very sharp increase in the costs – economic, human, political – of its use. This, of course, is not to say that the world is protected from the delusions of the powerful. It does not mean that World War III will be forever averted. We have not yet devised a system of governance that permanently protects citizens against the dangers of mentally unstable or irrational leaders (which, by and large, are still overwhelmingly men) from rising to power and misusing that power, too often linking military demonstration with types of national "honor" or prestige. But, the calculus of war has shifted and has shown that the utility of violence as a tool to achieve national ends is a pale

---

[43] Which is not to suggest that there will not continue to be sectarian conflicts in various corners of the world, including those with geopolitical overtones.

[44] Schell, *The Unconquerable World, Power, Nonviolence, and the Will of the People*, p. 360.

[45] While India and Pakistan have been later entrants to the nuclear club, we would argue that similar arguments apply to them as well. South Asia is one of the more densely populated areas in the world. It is difficult to imagine the death toll following an exchange of nuclear weapons between both countries.

shadow of what it was in the pre-nuclear days. Nuclear mass extermination was never and is hardly ever likely to be an attractive political option.

In 2002 the United States released its National Security Strategy. Formulated in post–September 11 days of 2001, it postulated an extremely muscular view of the country's role in the world, one in which the United States – in the words of the US president – "has, and intends to keep, military strengths beyond challenge, thereby making the destabilizing arms races of other eras pointless, and limiting rivalries to trade and other pursuits of peace," but also one in which US "forces will be strong enough to dissuade potential adversaries from pursuing a military build-up in hopes of surpassing, or equaling, the power of the United States." The experience, in practice, however, has been enormously more complicated, and costly. American interventions in Iraq and Afghanistan have been extremely expensive. According to the Watson Institute for International and Public Affairs at Brown University, through the 2017 fiscal year the Departments of Defense, Homeland Security, and Veteran Affairs had spent about $4.3 trillion on the wars in Iraq, Afghanistan, Pakistan and Syria since 9/11.

A large share of this consisted of so-called Overseas Contingency Operations, which are subject to special appropriations and the bulk of which were accounted for by the first two of the countries listed above. This sum – equivalent to some 23 percent of GDP in 2017 dollars – is expected to be augmented by at least another trillion dollars (5.4 percent of GDP) in respect of future health and other benefits expenditures for US veterans. Given the ubiquitous presence of budget deficits in the United States over the past many years (18 years of consecutive budget deficits since 2001 and projected deficits for the foreseeable future), much of the military spending has been associated with a remarkable rise in public indebtedness. It is thus necessary to factor into the costs of Iraq and Afghanistan the burden on the budget of additional interest payments on the public debt, which could easily add another 15 percent of GDP. But these numbers, dire as they are, only capture accounting costs, not opportunity costs and productivity losses. How many net additional million jobs could have been created by redirecting some of the monies allocated to the war effort to investments in healthcare, infrastructure, clean energy, education, and other productivity-enhancing areas?[46] Would a trillion dollars make a difference in the fight against cancer or the mental illnesses that afflict a growing share of the US population? The questions are too painful to raise.

The above is not to suggest that all the above military spending was an entirely wasted effort. The goal of dislodging the Taliban from power in Afghanistan and, for instance, thereby helping release its 11 million women and girls from the restrictions imposed on them by the mental obscurantism of its men, had considerable support

---

[46] These costs vastly exceed the projections made in the pre-war period which, in the case of Iraq, had put an upper bound of about two hundred billion dollars. Also excluded here are expenses borne by other countries, such as the United Kingdom.

in the countries that eventually joined in the war effort. The point is rather to highlight that, almost 20 years later, there is no certainty that, in the absence of further deployment of financial resources to maintain a military presence there, the Taliban would not, in fact, stage a comeback taking us, full circle, back to the beginning of the war, with little to show that would even closely match the scale of the financial effort, to say nothing of the cost in lives.[47]

Which brings us back to Schell's principal insights in *The Unconquerable World*: the utility of violence has dramatically declined in recent decades as a tool for the promotion of the national self-interest and:

> violence, always a mark of human failure and a bringer of sorrow, has now also become dysfunctional as a political instrument. Increasingly, it destroys the ends for which it is employed, killing the user as well as the victim. It has become the path to hell on earth and the end of the earth. This is the lesson of the Somme and Verdun, of Auschwitz and Bergen-Belsen, of Vorkuta and Kolyma; and it is the lesson, beyond a shadow of a doubt, of Hiroshima and Nagasaki.[48]

Our current system of governance and our efforts to provide peace and security at reasonable cost fail utterly (see Chapter 9). On the whole, it is a massive waste of public resources because it does not achieve even some of the most elementary strategic objectives established at the outset of the hostilities. And, in the nuclear age (with also a range of other weapons of mass destruction existing or on the cusp of development), it holds the seeds of our potential collective destruction.

The Institute for Economics and Peace, an independent nonpartisan think-tank, estimates that the total economic impact of violence in 2017 was in the order of $14.8 trillion, equivalent to 18.5 percent of world GDP or $1,988 per annum per person. Direct costs associated with violence include accounting losses linked to government spending on the military, judicial systems, healthcare, and police. Indirect costs capture losses resulting from violence perpetrated in the course of the year and would include such items as productivity losses resulting from injuries, foregone economic output resulting from premature fatalities associated with murder, as well as reduced economic growth because of prolonged war or conflict. The report analyses three broad categories of costs: security services and prevention-oriented costs; armed conflict related costs; and costs resulting from interpersonal violence.[49] The two largest contributors to the costs of containing global violence are military expenditures – accounting for 37 percent of the total cost – and internal security expenditures, which mainly capture preventive actions linked to police, judicial and

---

[47] For a compelling, insightful discussion of these issues and the growing gap between the cost of US defense and the benefits delivered see Mathews, Jessica T. 2019. "America's Indefensible Defense Budget," *The New York Review of Books*, July 18, pp. 23–24.

[48] Schell, *The Unconquerable World*, p. 7.

[49] See also Chapter 11 on the linkages researchers have found between in particular women's personal security and peaceful foreign policy orientations of various nations.

prison system spending and account for 27 percent of the total. It then follows that the total economic impact of violence is approximately 105 times more than annual Official Development Assistance and exceeds the total net outflow of global foreign direct investment by a factor of eight. It also exceeds by a factor of about 350, total annual lending commitments made by the World Bank. The individual country costs range from over 50 to 70 percent of GDP in countries such as Syria, Iraq, and Afghanistan, to less than 3 percent of GDP in Japan, Switzerland, Austria, Iceland, Canada, and Denmark. Clearly, the establishment and implementation of an effective "International Peace Force," to centralize and contain global security spending, could have vast security and economic ramifications, releasing substantial resources to promote economic and social development and shared prosperity.

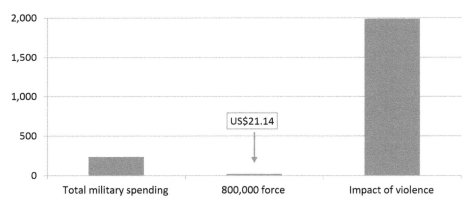

FIGURE 8.1 Military spending under an international Peace Force (US$ per person per year)

THE ESTABLISHMENT OF AN INTERNATIONAL PEACE FORCE

Our proposal envisages the creation of an International Peace Force, deriving its ultimate authority from the reformed General Assembly via the Executive Council. As noted earlier, "Security Forces" to be in a state of readiness and available to the UN Security Council for Chapter VII action were envisioned in the Charter through the negotiation of agreements "as soon as possible," as stipulated in Article 43(3); these agreements were never concluded. Clear terms for the establishment of a new standing force or forces, with parameters of readiness and operation, would at last implement a mechanism envisioned in the current Charter system.

The existence of such a Force does not preclude the presence of national forces necessary to maintain order within national territories, but it does make available to the United Nations effective means for "the prevention and removal of threats to the peace, for the suppression of acts of aggression or other breaches of the peace, and for ensuring compliance with the revised Charter and the laws and regulations enacted thereunder."[50] This Force would consist of two components, a Standing Force and a Peace Force Reserve, both composed of volunteers. The Standing Force would be a full-time force of professionals numbering between 600,000 and 1,200,000 as determined by the General Assembly. Under plausible assumptions about salary costs for soldiers, support personnel and weapons systems for an internationally recruited force consisting of 800,000 soldiers, the cost would be roughly US$150 billion per year, or about US$21 per person on the planet per year, compared to US$234 in the current system (see Chart).[51]

To establish the legal basis for the creation of an International Peace Force a number of amendments to UN Charter Chapters VI and VII articles would be necessary. Grenville Clark and Louis Sohn in *World Peace through World Law* proposed several revisions to the Charter to make this possible. Our discussion here does not provide by any means as comprehensive a treatment of the underlying issues as that undertaken by Clark and Sohn, albeit at a different time in international history. Our intent here is twofold: first, to highlight some (but not all) of the key changes to the Charter that would be necessary to empower the UN in the area of peace enforcement; and, second, to identify some of the more practical considerations that would need to be borne in mind in respect of the creation of such a Peace Force and to make it operational.[52]

One major limitation of the present Charter, in terms of establishing a genuine peace and security system, is the absence of enforcement mechanisms and clear procedural requirements for the international obligation of all states to settle their disputes peacefully, and the lack of compulsory jurisdiction of the ICJ (see Chapter 10 on strengthening the international rule of law). Regardless of how intensely a particular dispute endangers the peace of the world, there is no provision in the Charter or the Statute of the International Court of Justice, which would practically oblige the parties, on a universal basis, to submit to peaceful settlement, including a

---

[50] See Clark and Sohn. 1966. *World Peace through World Law*, p. 321.

[51] It is beyond the scope of this chapter to examine in detail the resource implications of moving to a system of collective security by the establishment of an International Peace Force. Neither is the point of reference here the "total economic impact of violence," as a proxy for the expenditure that would be displaced by creation on an International Peace Force. Rather, the point of reference is total annual military spending. We accept that it will be necessary to examine the services that such a force would provide and compare these to the current cost of providing those services by the 193 countries member of the UN, a figure quickly approaching US$2 trillion in 2019. The US$150 billion figure assumes that about one-third of this would go toward funding the pay and benefits of the Standing Force. The annual cost of UN peacekeeping operations today is about US$8–9 billion, with total military spending in 2018 equivalent to about $1.8 trillion, or 200 times higher than the cost of total peacekeeping.

[52] The full range of issues that must be addressed in consultations leading up to the establishment of the Peace Force will be taken up in the future, building upon the seminal work done by Clark and Sohn. For now, and in the paragraphs that follow, we briefly address these two sets of issues.

judicial determination. As proposed in Chapter 10, a key revision to the Charter would establish the compulsory jurisdiction of the ICJ and would require all member nations, as appropriate, to submit international disputes that were amenable to solution through the application of legal principles to a final and binding decision by the ICJ.[53] Article 94 of the current Charter on the enforcement of decisions of the ICJ should also be strengthened to clarify that, for example, diplomatic and economic sanctions would be available under a revised Article 41 but also, as a last resort, military sanctions through the International Peace Force under a revised Article 42. The combination of the legal authority granted to the General Assembly or the Executive Council if authorized by the Assembly to direct the:

> submission of legal questions for final adjudication by the International Court of Justice, together with provisions for the enforcement of the Court's judgements, would definitely establish the principle of compulsory jurisdiction in respect of all legal issues substantially affecting international peace, and would constitute a great step forward in the acceptance of the rule of law between nations.[54]

It is useful to present here, by way of illustration, the UN Charter's version of Article 42 and what this Article might look like in a revised Charter that granted the General Assembly the authority for military interventions to secure the peace:

Article 42 – UN Charter: Should the Security Council consider that measures provided for in Article 41 would be inadequate or have proved to be inadequate, it may take such action by air, sea, or land forces as may be necessary to maintain or restore international peace and security. Such action may include demonstrations, blockade, and other operations by air, sea, or land forces of Members of the United Nations.[55]

Article 42 – Revised UN Charter: 1. Should the General Assembly, or the Executive Council if authorized by the Assembly, consider that measures provided for in Article 41 would be inadequate or have proved to be inadequate, it shall direct such action by air, sea, or land elements of the International Peace Force as may be necessary to maintain or restore international peace and security or to ensure compliance with this Charter and the laws and regulations enacted thereunder. Such action may include demonstrations, blockade, and other operations; but any such action shall be taken pursuant to the procedures and subject to the limitations contained in the terms of reference of the International Peace Force. 2. In cases in

---

[53] Clark and Sohn included such provisions in an expanded version of the Charter's Article 36.

[54] Clark and Sohn, *World Peace through World Law*, p. 101.

[55] Article 41 pertains to the use of sanctions and reads: "The Security Council may decide what measures not involving the use of armed force are to be employed to give effect to its decisions, and it may call upon the Members of the United Nations to apply such measures. These may include complete or partial interruption of economic relations and of rail, sea, air, postal, telegraphic, radio, and other means of communication, and the severance of diplomatic relations."

which the United Nations has directed action by the International Peace Force, all the member Nations shall, within the limitations and pursuant to the procedures governing its deployment, make available to the United Nations such assistance and facilities, including rights of passage, as the United Nations may call for.

The significance of this revision – which is largely drawn from Clark and Sohn – is obvious. The United Nations would no longer depend on the willingness of its members to contribute military forces but would have its own Peace Force, ready to be deployed by the General Assembly (or the Executive Council if authorized by the Assembly, consistent with the provisions for qualified majorities specified for important decisions – see Chapter 7) to restore international peace. The revised Article makes reference to an Annex (to be an integral part of the Charter), which lays out the procedures and other arrangements that have a bearing on how the Peace Force can be utilized and under what limitations and parameters. The revised Article changes the wording of the original from "may take such action" to "shall direct such action" with a view to strengthening the authority of the General Assembly in the area of military sanctions. Or, as noted by Clark and Sohn, "the conception is that, if the Assembly (or the Council) has reached a decision that measures short of armed force are or would be inadequate, it should be *required* to employ the United Nations Peace Force, since otherwise the United Nations would have to confess impotence to maintain peace."[56] This revised Article 42 would need to be read in conjunction with a revised Article 11 on the General Assembly's new functions and powers.

Furthermore, Article 43, which has turned out to be a highly inadequate provision to ensure a functional collective security system, relying, as it does on voluntary agreements between nations to make available to the UN military forces, could be amended in conjunction with the Annex on Peace Force arrangements, so that the United Nations would have adequate means even in extreme emergencies, subject to appropriate safeguards, to maintain or restore peace and to enforce compliance with respect to the revised Charter. This could be done by allowing the maximum limits on the sizes of the standing component and the Peace Force Reserve to be exceeded for a limited period of time.

Beyond the amendments to the Charter that would be necessary to provide the legal basis for UN military actions to secure the peace, it will be necessary as well to lay out the various practical issues that would underpin the establishment and the operations of the Peace Force. The nonexhaustive list in the following box, includes various provisions for the operation of this force, as a starting point for further elaboration. In this list we have drawn from Clark and Sohn's work, who gave a great deal of thought to such operational concerns which they perceived as important at the time of their writing.

---

[56] Clark and Sohn, *World Peace through World Law*, p. 117.

BOX: The International Peace Force: Selected Operational Considerations

Objectives

1   In the recruitment and organization of the International Peace Force, the objective will be to create and maintain a highly trained professional force such that it is fully capable of safeguarding international peace.
2   The International Peace Force will never be employed to achieve objectives inconsistent with the Purposes and Principles of the (revised) Charter.

Recruitment and Staffing (Personnel)

3   The members of the International Peace Force and its civilian employees, together with their dependents, will be entitled to all the privileges and immunities provided to UN personnel.
4   The Executive Council will appoint the first members of the Military Staff Committee. The terms of office of these initial members will begin on the same day and expire, as designated by the Council at the time of their appointment, one at the end of one year, one at the end of two years, one at the end of three years, one at the end of four years and one at the end of five years from that date. Later appointments will be for equal term lengths – to be determined from time to time by the Council, but never to exceed five years.[57]
5   The Military Staff Committee will prepare for the recruitment and training of both components and will organize the necessary administrative staff.
6   International Peace Force members will be recruited wholly by voluntary enlistment. The General Assembly will have no power to enact a compulsory draft law; and no nation may apply any sort of compulsion to require enlistment in the Peace Force, except under the exceptional circumstances described in Article 43 of the (revised) Charter and subject to the limitations in paragraph 35 below.
7   The members will be selected through international recruitment under the supervision of the Military Staff Committee based on their competence, integrity and devotion to the purposes of the United Nations, and will receive training on the high purpose of their mission and the ethical principles that should guide all their actions. With the exception of commanders at all levels, they must not be more than 35 years old at the time of initial enlistment.
8   The members will declare loyalty to the United Nations in a form prescribed by the General Assembly. They will be restricted from seeking or receiving instructions from any government or authority external to the United Nations. They will refrain from any conduct that might reflect poorly on their position as members of the Peace Force.

---

[57] The issue of whether it would be desirable to strictly limit terms of office to five years could be subject to further discussion. The virtues of lengthy experience have to be seen against the likely desire for diversity in membership.

9 The term of service of members of the standing component of the Peace Force will be between four and eight years, determined by the General Assembly.[58]

10 The term of service of Reserve members will be between six and ten years, also determined by the General Assembly. They will receive basic training for between four and eight months during the first three years of their term, and again during the remainder of their term, as determined by the Assembly in consultation with the Military Staff Committee.

11 The Force's officers will be selected, trained, promoted, and retired with a view to create a peerless officer corps. Opportunities for promotion to officer positions will be provided to highly qualified men and women from the rank and file.

12 The members of both components of the Peace Force will be recruited on as wide a geographical basis as possible, subject, except in extreme emergency (see paragraph 36), to the following limitations:

   a. The number of nationals of any nation serving at any one time in either component of the Peace Force cannot exceed 5 percent of the total enlistment of that component.

   b. The number of nationals of any nation serving at any one time in any of the three main branches of either component (land, sea and air) cannot exceed 5 percent of the total enlistment of that branch.

   c. The number of nationals of any nation serving at any one time in the officer corps of one of the three main branches of either component cannot exceed 5 percent of the officer corps for that branch.[59]

13. Units of the Peace Force will be composed to the greatest possible extent of different nationalities. No unit exceeding one hundred in number can be composed of nationals of a single nation.

14. The Peace Force will, to the extent authorized by the General Assembly, employ civilian personnel for the services and functions that do not need to be performed by military personnel; civilian personnel will not be deemed members of the Peace Force.

15 After being honorably discharged from the standing component of the Peace Force following at least two full enlistment periods, a member and their dependents will be entitled to choose the nation in which they wish to live, and they will be entitled to acquire the nationality of that nation if they are not already nationals.

---

[58] As noted above, there is clearly a tradeoff between the benefits of experience associated with long tenures in the Force and the advantages of rotation, diversity and giving opportunities to other young people to serve and then to take the skills gained and apply them in other areas of human endeavor; various approaches to this and other issues merit additional discussion.

[59] In the early stages of formation of the IPF, linguistic and doctrinal diversity is likely to pose a substantial challenge. For this reason, it may be necessary for recruits to be initially subjected to language training in English, the likely common language of the Force.

Administration

16. The General Assembly will adopt the basic laws necessary to provide for the organization, administration, recruitment, training, equipment, and deployment of the Peace Force's Standing and Reserve components.

17. The General Assembly will have authority to amend and enact the basic laws and regulations referenced in paragraph 16, and those deemed necessary for the organization, administration, recruitment, discipline, training, equipment, and deployment of the Peace Force.

18. If the General Assembly determines that the economic measures provided for in Article 41 of the (revised) Charter are inadequate or have proved to be inadequate to maintain or restore international peace or to ensure compliance with the (revised) Charter, and that the Peace Force has not reached sufficient strength to deal with the situation, the Assembly will direct such action by part or all of the national forces which have been designated in paragraph 35 as it deems necessary. This action will be taken within the limitations established in paragraphs 27–32.

19. The General Assembly will have authority to enact the laws and regulations deemed necessary for the strategic direction, command, organization, administration, and deployment of the national forces designated in paragraph 34 when action by any such national forces has been directed pursuant to paragraph 18.

20. The Military Staff Committee will have direct control of the Peace Force. The Executive Council may issue instructions to the Committee as it deems fit.

21. The expenses of the Peace Force and of the United Nations Military Supply and Research Agency (see paragraph 24) will be borne by the United Nations. The General Assembly will determine the compensation and allowances of the Military Staff Committee. After receiving a report from the Committee and the recommendations of the Executive Council, the General Assembly will determine the pay and allowances of the personnel of the Peace Force. The annual budget of the Peace Force will be prepared by the Committee, subject to the approval of the Executive Council. The annual budget of the Military Supply and Research Agency will be prepared by the Agency's management, subject to the approval of the Executive Council. Both budgets must be submitted to the General Assembly for consideration and approval.

Logistics

22. The standing component of the International Peace Force will be stationed at military bases of the United Nations, which will be spread around the world to enable prompt action in cases approved by the General Assembly, or the Executive Council if authorized by the Assembly. In order to ensure adequate regional distribution, the world will be divided by the Assembly into between 11 and 20 regions. Between 5 and 10 percent of the total strength of the standing component will be stationed at bases located in each of these regions, except when the Peace Force is taking action to maintain or restore international peace or to ensure compliance with the laws and regulations of the (revised) Charter.

23. The military bases of the United Nations will be obtained from or with the assistance of the nations in the relevant region. The bases will be acquired on long-term leases, by agreement and, as needed, by compensation.

Weaponry[60]

24. The International Peace Force will not possess or use any nuclear, biological, chemical, or other weapons of mass destruction.[61] The Peace Force will acquire its initial arms and equipment (including airplanes and naval vessels) through transfers from national military forces during the disarmament period specified in the (revised) Charter. Any further arms and equipment will be produced by the United Nations in its own production facilities. These facilities will be administered by the United Nations Military Supply and Research Agency and will be established by General Assembly legislation. The facilities will be initially equipped with machines, appliances, and tools discarded during the disarmament period. Further needs will be manufactured by the United Nations in its own plants – also administered by the Military Supply and Research Agency. The requirement that the production of arms, equipment, and machines be confined to the production facilities of the United Nations will not apply if the General Assembly declares an extreme emergency (see paragraph 36).

25. The United Nations Military Supply and Research Agency will, to the extent authorized and provided for by the General Assembly, engage in research related to the development of new military weapons, the improvement of existing weapons, and methods of defense against the possible illegal use of weapons of mass destruction and other weapons or modes of attack of concern.

26. The stocks of arms and equipment will be located on the United Nations' military bases. The facilities of the United Nations Military Supply and Research Agency will be located either on these bases or in areas leased by the United Nations for the purpose. The stocks and facilities will be geographically distributed to minimize the risk that any nation or group of nations might gain a military advantage by seizing the stocks or facilities situated in a particular region; between five and ten percent of the total amount of the stocks and of the total productive capacity of the facilities will be concentrated in each of the regions referenced in paragraph 22.

Action Protocol

27. Plans for possible action by the Peace Force to maintain or restore international peace or to ensure compliance with the (revised) Charter will be made by the Executive Council with the assistance of the Military Staff Committee.

---

[60] This section on weaponry should be read in conjunction with Chapter 9 addressing disarmament.

[61] While it would be inappropriate for the Peace Force to itself acquire and use weapons of mass destruction or other weapons considered to violate international humanitarian law, it should have the capacity to destroy such weapon systems, and to prevent their manufacture and use.

28. When action by the Peace Force has been directed by the General Assembly, or the Executive Council, the Military Staff Committee will be responsible for the final preparation and execution of such plans, subject to the general control of the Executive Council.

29. No action by the Peace Force will be permitted without prior authorization by the General Assembly, or the Executive Council. This provision does not prevent the Peace Force from taking necessary measures of self-defense in case of an armed attack on its bases, ships, or airplanes, or on its personnel stationed outside its bases.[62]

30. Any action by the Peace Force will be limited to operations strictly necessary to maintain or restore international peace or to ensure compliance with the (revised) Charter. The Peace Force will always avoid any unnecessary destruction of life or property and act in compliance with international humanitarian law. If in the case of a large-scale violation – which cannot be dealt with by more limited means – it is determined absolutely essential to destroy or damage an inhabited area, the inhabitants will be given sufficient warning so that they may evacuate in time. Whenever possible, and in particular when action is being taken to prevent rather than suppress a breach of the peace or a violation of the Charter, any use of force will be preceded by naval or air demonstrations, accompanied by a warning that further measures will be taken if the breach or violation does not cease. When a violation consists of the operation of prohibited or unlicensed installations, establishments, or facilities, the action of the Peace Force will be confined to occupation unless the destruction of such installations, establishments, or facilities is absolutely essential to prevent a continuation of the illegal operation.

31. When taking action, the Peace Force will be entitled to pass freely through the territory of any nation and to obtain from any nation assistance with respect to temporary bases, supplies, and transport as is needed. The General Assembly will enact laws regulating the extent of such assistance and the payment of fair compensation.

32. Upon the termination of any action by the Peace Force, it will be withdrawn as soon as possible to its bases.

33. The United Nations will have exclusive criminal and disciplinary jurisdiction with respect to the members of the Peace Force, its civilian employees, and their dependents in any area that the United Nations has leased for the use of the Peace Force. The General Assembly will enact laws specifying the penalties for offenses and providing for the apprehension, trial, and punishment of the accused. If the accused is found outside the area where the offense was committed, the authorities of the nation in which the person is found will assist in their apprehension and return to the area.[63]

---

[62] See Chapter 9 on disarmament.

[63] In this respect, this provision builds on the experience being accumulated in the context of the work of the International Criminal Court and other international criminal tribunals.

Member Obligations

34 During the transition period toward the establishment of the Peace Force and in coordination with the process of disarmament, each member nation will make available to the United Nations one tenth of its military forces. During this period, one fourth of the combined forces will be maintained in a state of immediate readiness for military action under the direction of the United Nations.

35 If the General Assembly declares the existence of a grave emergency, it will call all or part of the International Peace Force Reserve to active duty according to the following limitations: (i) If the call to active duty is for less than all of the Peace Force Reserve, members of the Reserve will be called in proportion to the number of nationals of the respective nations enrolled in the Reserve; (ii) The period of active duty required under any call must not exceed the period of the emergency, and no member of the Reserve will be obliged to serve after the expiration of the term of service for which they originally enrolled (see paragraph 9).

36 If the General Assembly has declared the existence of a grave emergency and if at that time the authorized strength of the standing component of the Peace Force is below its constitutional limit of 1,200,000 or the authorized strength of the Peace Force Reserve is below its constitutional limit of 2,400,000, the Assembly may increase the authorized strength of the Standing Force to 1,200,000 or of the Reserve to 2,400,000, or of both to these limits.[64] The Assembly may authorize these increases whether or not it has called to active duty part or all of the Reserve. The Assembly may call upon the member nations to assist in the recruitment of either or both components.

37 If the General Assembly has declared the existence of an extreme emergency and has directed an increase of the strength of the Peace Force beyond the maximum combined strength of 3,600,000 for both components (see paragraph 36), the Assembly may direct the member nations to cooperate in obtaining the needed additional personnel.

Quite aside from providing for security and promoting peace in various parts of the world, the creation of an International Peace Force, firmly anchored in the notion that force may at times be necessary to deliver justice and the rule of law, would

---

[64] The authorized limit on the number of troops envisaged here is slightly higher than 6 percent of the total number of active military personnel in the world in 2018. We are aware that it is the quality of personnel and equipment, the strategic doctrine, force configuration, and the ability to deploy an integrated force, fit for purpose in each assignment, that determines the efficacy of existing armed forces. Furthermore, these limits need to be seen in conjunction with the disarmament process, which, as noted in Chapter 9, is an integral component of the setting up of an International Peace Force. Nevertheless, the issue of the precise size of the standing force will need to be the subject of further study, beyond the scope of this book.

address one of the main flaws of our current UN system, namely, the absence of a reliable international mechanism to enforce certain decisions made by the Security Council in service of international peace and security, and to generally ensure compliance with Charter obligations and international law. An additional Charter amendment would enshrine the "Responsibility to Protect" ("R2P") doctrine for collective security action to protect minority groups and others threatened by mass atrocity or genocide, subject to further elaborated objective criteria, careful procedural control, and the oversight of independent experts. An oversight body could generally set protocols for, make recommendations in relation to, and monitor the implementation of actions of the International Peace Force and its collective security action (including in relation to the R2P doctrine).[65]

Subject to the safeguards identified above, and additional safeguards, as deemed necessary, the International Peace Force could be a vital instrument to enhance the credibility of the United Nations to prevent conflicts and maintain peace and security in the world. An equally important implication of bringing it into being would be the creation of a genuine mechanism of collective security, which would significantly reduce the pressure on countries to maintain extensive and expensive military establishments. Military expenditures are categorized by the IMF as "unproductive expenditures" – often large in relation to countries' unmet needs and with little beneficial collateral repercussions in terms of productivity and economic efficiency. Reductions in military spending at the national level could be reallocated to other ends, including education, public health, infrastructure, and other productivity-enhancing areas, thereby giving rise to a real "peace dividend."[66] During the transition, special attention would need to be paid to the reallocation of military, human, and economic resources to peaceful purposes, as discussed in Chapter 9.

CHALLENGES IN IMPLEMENTATION

There is no doubt that the proposals contained in this chapter are bold and ambitious in a way that Secretary General Trygve Lie's own ideas for setting up a small UN Guard Force in 1948 were not, even though they were so characterized by the major powers at the time, intent on reneging from their Article 43 commitments,

---

[65] Such independent/expert-based oversight should substantially assist in remedying the criticisms of past military interventions by the Security Council in general, and those thus far undertaken with a justification of the responsibility to protect doctrine (e.g., that they are politicized, unevenly deployed, focused on surreptitious "regime change," etc.). See, e.g., discussion in Buitelaar and Ponzio, "Mobilizing Smart Coalitions and Negotiating Global Governance Reform."

[66] In this respect, it is not unrealistic to think that more countries might also wish to follow in the footsteps of Costa Rica, which more than 50 years ago abolished its military, without any adverse repercussions for its security. A national police force has been more than effective in keeping the domestic peace, dealing with local crime, violations of traffic laws, and the like.

against the backdrop of the Cold War. There is no question that there would be major practical challenges in operationalizing a Peace Force of the size envisaged. Indeed, the contents of the Box above are intended to highlight the range of issues that arise in identifying various aspects of the operations of the Force, from recruitment and staffing, to training, financing, logistics, weaponry, action protocols, and the like. However, the very mixed picture that emerges from examining the results of more than half a century of UN peacekeeping operations and international military action underscores the difficulties in interventions intended to enforce the terms of the Charter and international law, prevent the outbreak of conflict, genocide, civil wars, to protect civilians, and to support humanitarian relief efforts. Such examination points convincingly to the United Nation's failure since its inception to provide for reliable and even-handed peace and security for the peoples of the world as called for in the Charter, and which have resulted in approximately 41 million deaths in wars and conflicts between 1945 and 2000.[67]

We think that in the absence of a large, properly trained and equipped Force, with sufficient legal authority to act on behalf of the international community through the United Nations, we will continue to bear the human and financial cost of our flawed international security arrangements. The proposals presented here address most of the arguments that have been put forward to explain the weaknesses of current peacekeeping and peace enforcement operations. These range from the inability of the United Nations to secure troop commitments within a time frame that would actually make a difference on the ground, to the issue of securing forces that would be appropriately trained and equipped, to the important question of allocating the responsibility for such operations (and the risks they entail) to the United Nations, not the national politicians who make the commitment to subject their national troops to potential hazards in far-off lands. We think that a large force as proposed would be a powerful deterrent to the use of violence to settle disputes; this is the lesson from 800,000 deaths in Rwanda and multiple millions elsewhere through the years.[68]

The concerns expressed at various times throughout the UN's history about the consequences of strengthening the organization's military mandate and associating

---

[67] Leitenberg, Michael. 2006. "Deaths and Wars in Conflicts in the 20th Century," Cornell University, Peace Studies Program, Occasional Paper 29. See detailed country-by-country estimates for the period 1945–2000 in Table 2, beginning on page 73.

[68] There is an interesting historical analogue here worth remembering from recent Polish economic history and its transition to a market economy in the early part of the 1990s. Faced with huge pressures on the exchange rate of the local currency, the zloty, the authorities negotiated the disbursement of a US\$6 billion "Stabilization Fund" with the IMF. The idea was to signal to markets that the monetary authorities had a huge war chest to defeat speculators and other market players who sought to profit from the devaluation of the currency. In the context of other supportive policies, the strategy worked brilliantly. The currency remained stable and the Stabilization Fund was never actually used. Its mere presence was a sufficiently powerful deterrent to dissuade financial speculators.

its operations more overtly with the use of military force are understandable, but, in our view, they largely miss the point. Appropriate safeguards and checks and balances in the establishment and employment of such a force to prevent its misuse, can and should be developed and put into practice. We would like to see the further "depoliticization" of the use of force at the international level, and a delinking of bloated military activity from forms of national identity and international prestige, which are anachronistic – and, of course, dangerous – in modern circumstances. Every state should rather seek the prestige of upholding and supporting the international rule of law, and the establishment of secure cooperation systems, based on clear international values and norms and strong institutions with robust checks and balances.

International peace operations and intervention should be a matter of primarily technical, not political, concern.[69] Currently, we pay a heavy price in human lives and suffer the loss of truly astounding financial resources by having a weak United Nations, hampered by inadequate resources and unable to act on a timely basis to prevent the sort of violence we have seen over the past decades. It seems wholly irresponsible and illogical to limit the UN's use of occasional force in the pursuit of peace and justice, while standing by helplessly as mass killing gets underway in Rwanda, Bosnia, Congo, Syria, and countless other places. The proposals presented in this chapter are intended to move beyond this moral swamp in which we have lived since 1945 and which has been so costly to the millions who have perished because of our failure to give the United Nations the instruments it needs to carry out its peace and security mandate.

---

[69] On this subject, see Chapter 10, and in particular Louis Henkin's analysis of the 1945 Charter and its nonuse of the terminology "war" (as an obsolete and dangerous cultural product), replacing it with technical terms related to breaches of international peace, collective security action, etc. Henkin, Louis. 1991. *Law and War after the Cold War* Vol. 15, No. 2, Maryland Journal of International Law, p. 147. http://digitalcommons.law.umaryland.edu/mjil/vol15/iss2/2.

9

Toward Systemic Disarmament: Resetting Global Priorities

The global arms trade, and its accompanying glut of military spending, continues to represent the single most significant perversion of worldwide priorities known today ... It buttresses wars, criminal activity and ethnic violence; destabilises emerging democracies; inflates military budgets to the detriment of health care, education and basic infrastructure; and exaggerates global relationships of inequality and underdevelopment. Without massive and coordinated action, militarism will continue to be a scourge on our hopes for a more peaceful and just 21st century.[1]

Oscar Arias, Former President of Costa Rica, Nobel Peace Laureate

If we are serious about nuclear disarmament – the minimum technical requirement for real safety from extinction – then we must accept conventional disarmament as well, and this means disarmament not just of nuclear powers, but of all powers, for the present nuclear powers are hardly likely to throw away their conventional arms while non-nuclear powers hold on to theirs. But if we accept both nuclear and conventional disarmament, then we are speaking of revolutionizing the politics of the earth. The goals of the political revolution are defined by those of the nuclear revolution. We must lay down our arms, relinquish sovereignty, and found a political system for the peaceful settlement of international disputes.[2]

Jonathan Schell

Introduction

Part of a fundamental global transition to the peaceful settlement of international disputes, to a full collective security model replacing the unilateral use of force,

---

[1] As quoted in de Zayas, Alfred-Maurice. 2014. *Report of the Independent Expert on the Promotion of a Democratic and Equitable International Order*, July, p. 3.
[2] Schell, Jonathan. 1982. *The Fate of the Earth*, London, Jonathan Cape, p. 226.

and to an international order based on a genuine rule by law, is to design and implement a clear, ambitious and systemic program – the "massive and coordinated action" referred to by Arias, above – of international arms control and disarmament.

The UN Human Rights Council has, for example, affirmed that an equitable and democratic international order requires, among other things, the realization of the "right of all peoples to peace," stating that:

> all States should promote the establishment, maintenance and strengthening of international peace and security and, to that end, should do their utmost to achieve general and complete disarmament under effective international control, as well as to ensure that the resources released by effective disarmament measures are used for comprehensive development, in particular that of the developing countries.[3]

In this chapter, as well as providing framing background perspectives relevant to tackling the very fundamental international problem of systemic disarmament, we sketch the outline of and starting points for robust new proposals, which would include UN Charter amendment, for the essential restructuring of global practices in relation to the current "glut of military spending." There have been, indeed, recent calls for the reform or revitalization of Article 26 of the UN Charter, which allotted to the Security Council a responsibility to develop comprehensive and concrete plans for a system for the global regulation of armaments.

In summary, in parallel with the creation of the International Peace Force (IPF), a new, consolidated and empowered Standing Committee on Disarmament should be established to develop, implement, and monitor a binding yet staged global disarmament process, to reduce national armaments to levels needed for self-defense only. During a preparatory period, an inventory of armaments would be undertaken, sites/facilities identified or constructed for their neutralization and decommissioning under UN monitoring and coordination, and the necessary budget and financial allocations organized. This would be followed by a phase of disarmament proper, which would be managed to be simultaneous and proportional among the greater powers in particular. Special attention would be given to nuclear arms and the long-term storage of the resulting wastes at neutral sites, as well as to new and emerging forms of weaponry such as programs for cyberwarfare. Unprecedented intensive global monitoring and verification would be needed to ensure that no arms are hidden or developed for later use.

Such an approach, indeed, forms part of the core of ensuring a stable and operable international collective security system (where the IPF is an effective

---

[3]   United Nations Human Rights Council, Resolution 25/15, March 27, 2014, paras 10 and 17.

"global policeman" rather than the "Big Four," as envisioned at the end of World War II), and adhesion to such a system should be a condition for acceptance of any state by the international community as a "peace-loving nation."[4] Such systematic global arms control has long formed one of the core aspirations of the international community (see the following section), and is made ever more urgent given current destabilizing forces, some of which are described in this chapter. The disruptive and unpredictable forces seen today, including in relation to technological developments, make a fragmented and piecemeal approach to arms control and disarmament – which the international community has adopted to date – wholly untenable.

Background

Comprehensive and controlled disarmament among the community of nations has been an aspiration of the international legal project since its very early years. The first Hague Peace Conference of 1899 convened by Nicholas II, Tsar of Russia, had as a main agenda item military and arms limitation among the then great powers (particularly focused in Europe at that time). British Lord Salisbury, in a speech to the London Guild Hall in 1887 reportedly urged Nicholas II's predecessor, Tsar Alexander III, to convene a major power disarmament conference, in the name of collective social progress.[5] Pragmatically, it was understood that the unsustainably expensive and destabilizing arms races in Europe (e.g., with a *Triple Alliance* of Austria-Hungary, Germany and Italy evolving in opposition to the *Entente* of France and Russia), were prohibitive in cost and risky to all those involved. World War I of course, would bear out these concerns, with the first and second (1907) Hague Peace Conferences proving themselves a failure on the core disarmament issues.

In terms of wasteful and destabilizing expenditures today implicated in the global arms trade, recent numbers are truly staggering. The Stockholm Peace Research Institute estimates world military expenditure in 2017 to have reached more than $1.7 trillion ($1,739 billion), representing "the highest level since the end of the Cold War, equivalent to 2.2 per cent of global gross domestic product (GDP) or $230 per person."[6] According to the IMF, military expenditures are "unproductive" in relation to countries' unmet needs and do not benefit productivity and economic

---

[4] Membership in the UN is open only to "peace-loving" nations under Article 4(1) of the Charter. As noted by Albert Einstein: "[a] person or nation can be considered peace loving only if it is ready to cede its military force to the international authorities and to renounce every attempt or even the means of achieving its interests abroad by the use of force." Albert Einstein. 1956. *Out of My Later Years*, New York, Philosophical Library, p. 138.

[5] Eyffinger, Arthur. 2011. *T.M.C. Asser [1838–1913]: Founder of The Hague Tradition*, The Hague, T.M.C. Asser Press, p. 46.

[6] Stockholm International Peace Research Institute (SIPRI). 2018. *SIPRI Yearbook 2018*. Stockholm, p. 6.

efficiency. The trade-offs or "opportunity costs" of countries' spending on military versus more productive social expenditures for the national – and international – economy, such as education, health and child care, are dramatic.[7]

The classical "security dilemma" of individual states or alliances explains the danger and the seeming inevitability of intensifying, tit-for-tat arms races, as described by security scholar Christopher Browning:

> The idea of the security dilemma suggests that in conditions of international anarchy, where states are ultimately dependent upon themselves for survival, states are necessarily prone to suspicion and worst-case scenarios. The security dilemma is characterized by a situation whereby a state fearful for its security, begins arming itself. Although for the state in question armament may be a purely defensive measure, this may appear unclear to other states who may interpret it as threatening, even despite – or perhaps precisely because – of proclamations otherwise. Indeed, armaments procured for defence can usually also be deployed offensively. Fearful that their own security is being undermined these states may respond in kind, in turn legitimizing the first state's concerns but requiring a further response later on. In this way a spiral of insecurity can develop, with war looming in the background as an ever-present possibility.[8]

Article 2(4) of the UN Charter prohibits the "threat or use of force" of member nations in their international relations, and the excessive or nontransparent build-up of armaments can present serious problems in this respect. As noted by Browning, it can be difficult to distinguish between the defensive and offensive nature of armaments acquired by a given nation. The International Court of Justice has explored, for example, in an Advisory Opinion on the *Legality of the Threat or Use of Nuclear Weapons*, whether a nation possessing nuclear weapons could be considered to be in violation of Article 2(4) of the Charter, by posing a threat of use of force and violating requirements of necessity and proportionality in the deployment of weapons under international law, even if anticipated to be used defensively.[9]

In relation to the overall global system today and the precarity of shifting global power dynamics – in particular but not only in relation to the US–China configuration – various authors have raised the alarm as to the care and focus currently required to navigate these new power constellations, to ensure that war

---

[7] Ke-young Chu, Sanjeev Gupta, Benedict Clements, Daniel Hewitt, Sergio Lugaresi, Jerald Schiff, Ludger Schuknecht, and Gerd Schwartz. 1995. *Unproductive Public Expenditures: A Pragmatic Approach to Policy Analysis*, Pamphlet Series, No. 48. Washington, DC, Fiscal Affairs Department, IMF, p. 1. www.imf.org/external/pubs/ft/pam/pam48/pam4801.htm.

[8] Browning, Christopher S. 2013. *International Security: A Very Short Introduction*, Oxford, Oxford University Press, p. 20.

[9] [1996] ICJ Rep 246f, para 48 et seq.

("cold" or "hot") is not inevitable.[10] One report notes the contemporary shifting "geostrategic relationships" where bipolar (Cold War) or unipolar (post–Cold War) models are no longer helpful, noting that while "it is clear change is under way, it is not clear what the outcome will be."[11] Given current dilemmas, it is urgent to devise effective, systemic solutions in order to halt spirals of insecurity and arms races, and to put in place a coherent, transparent, thorough and well-designed *global* security regime for the control and limitation of armaments, as was envisioned in the specific provisions on arms control and disarmament in the current UN Charter (see next section).

Key framing provisions of the 1945 UN Charter were in fact intended to lay the groundwork for a general international enabling environment to build sustainable trust among nations, in order to transcend traditional interstate security dilemmas and maximalist military competition. For example, the goal of the Charter is to create conditions necessary for the respect of international law (Preamble) and the peaceful settlement of international disputes under Chapter VI (to resolve, for example, territorial disputes, which have been a major cause of interstate wars; see Chapter 10), in order to transcend anarchic international conditions, which are the basis of "realist" thinking on the inevitability of war. The Charter requires that all members of the United Nations be "peace-loving" as a condition of membership (Art. 4(1)), should "live together in peace with one another as good neighbours" (Preamble), should "develop friendly relations" (Art. 1(2)), and must fulfill "in good faith the obligations assumed" under the instrument (Art. 2(2)).

All of these provisions, alongside the Charter articles relating to collective security,[12] undergird the contemporary international striving to move beyond anarchic conditions and irrational cultures of unhealthy military competition and opaque mistrust that drove the senseless wars of the past. These are the fundamental tenets of the modern international order that still must be made fully incarnate in state practice and institutions, and in practical, newly ambitious commitments in the sphere of arms control.

The UN Charter Provisions on Disarmament/Arms Control

The UN Charter gives both the Security Council (Article 26)[13] and the General Assembly (Article 11(1)) specific mandates in the sphere of arms control and

---

[10] See, for example: Allison, Graham. 2017. *The Thucydides Trap: When One Great Power Threatens to Displace Another, War Is Almost Always the Result – But It Doesn't Have to Be.* Foreign Policy, June 9.

[11] *SIPRI Yearbook 2018*, p. 1.

[12] The Charter stipulates that "armed force shall not be used, save in the common interest" (Preamble), and prohibits members from the threat or use of force (Art. 2(4)), with narrow exceptions: Security Council action for the purpose of international peace and security (Art. 42), and a narrow right to self-defense (Art. 51), only if an armed attack occurs, and only until the Security Council has taken measures necessary.

[13] Article 47 of the Charter stipulates that the Military Staff Committee advise and assist the Security Council on its work on "the regulation of armaments, and possible disarmament."

disarmament, clearly recognizing that these projects are integral to international peace and security, and also have a diversionary effect on the "world's human and economic resources" (see also discussion in Chapter 4 on GA engagement in disarmament issues).

The Security Council was tasked with the responsibility of formulating, with the assistance of the Military Staff Committee, "plans to be submitted to the Members of the United Nations for the establishment of a system for the regulation of armaments." Needless to say, no such plan was developed. Military competition – ironically – between key members of the Security Council intervened. Despite efforts in the later 1940s to begin to attempt to draft such plans, lack of unity among the permanent members of the Security Council, by 1952, essentially arrested these efforts, which have not been revived in a serious way since that time.

The General Assembly was tasked, in parallel, with the power to "consider the general principles of co-operation in the maintenance of international peace and security, including the principles governing disarmament and the regulation of armaments, and may make recommendations with regard to such principles to the Members or to the Security Council or both." Again, while there have been many excellent and aspirational statements issued by the General Assembly (and admirable piecemeal/incremental progress on disarmament which may be linked to a General Assembly initiative; see Box in this chapter), no significant comprehensive progress as anticipated by the Charter has yet been effected. One independent expert, calling the urgent need to reduce military expenditures worldwide an "endemic" barrier to development, has noted:

> The United Nations has adopted countless resolutions reflecting that understanding shared by think tanks and civil society alike. Nevertheless, in spite of accurate diagnoses, there has been little progress in redirecting military expenditures toward peaceful industries. Indeed, one of the challenges faced by the present mandate is precisely how to transform the ethically obvious into the politically feasible. [Continued examination is required of] this vast issue as a component of the overall strategy to overcome obstacles to the establishment of a just international order.[14]

Recent Developments in Arms Control

Against this backdrop, there have, however been some notable, positive recent developments in the disarmament field. For example, in relation to efforts to promote the nonproliferation of nuclear weapons, the Treaty on the Prohibition of Nuclear Weapons (TPNW; see Box) was adopted in 2017, as the first binding international treaty comprehensively prohibiting nuclear weapons. Talks had been

---

[14] de Zayas, *Report of the Independent Expert*, p. 6. https://wilpf.org/wp-content/uploads/2014/09/report-De-Zayas.pdf.

opened on the negotiation of this treaty in 2016 (mandated by a General Assembly resolution), impelled by the frustration of many states with the lack of progress of nuclear weapons states to make progress on nuclear disarmament in conformity with their obligations under the 1968 Treaty on the Non-Proliferation of Nuclear Weapons (NPT; see Box below). Commentators note the significance of the adoption of the TPNW as follows: "[t]he humanitarian initiative and attendant effort by a large group of non-nuclear-armed states and civil society actors to institute a global ban on nuclear weapons constitutes a process of collective resistance to entrenched power structures that perpetuate the existence of nuclear weapons."[15] The TPNW, adopted by 122 states (excluding the nuclear weapons states and their allies), is expected to have a normative and longer-term impact on the development of international law and the further stigmatization of nuclear weapons. Additionally, the broad-based civil society and non-nuclear weapon state efforts to convene negotiations and adopt the TPNW may have catalyzed a greater sense of urgency in various areas of global disarmament.[16] For example, there has been some recent movement on a number of topics at the Geneva-based Conference on Disarmament, the only standing international forum for negotiating arms control and disarmament agreements, with a new initiative to break through the gridlock that had left it, since 2009, unable to adopt a work program. The UN Secretary General has also released, in May 2018, a 73-page "non-paper," *Securing our Common Future: An Agenda for Disarmament*, outlining possible strategies on a wide range of current international disarmament issues, including an analysis of the deteriorating international security environment, addressing weapons of mass destruction, chemical, biological, outer space and new types of destabilizing strategic weapons, as well as conventional weapons, and challenges posed by new technologies, AI and cyberspace.[17]

However, against this backdrop of the apparent "coalition of the many" desiring to move forward proactively in global arms control, there have been worrying developments in particular on the bilateral plane. The United States has announced that it may withdraw from the Treaty on the Elimination of Intermediate-Range Nuclear Forces Treaty (INF Treaty) with Russia, a Soviet–US agreement from 1987, which facilitated the elimination of thousands of Soviet missiles based in Europe and paved the way for the end of the Cold War. Also, neither Russia nor the US have committed to extending the New START (the 2010 Treaty on Measures for the Further Reduction and Limitation of Strategic Offensive Arms), limiting strategic

[15] Ritchie, Nick and Kjølv Egeland. 2018. "The Diplomacy of Resistance: Power, Hegemony and Nuclear Disarmament." *Global Change, Peace & Security*, Vol. 30, No. 2, pp. 121–141.

[16] Hamel-Green, Michael. 2018. "The Nuclear Ban Treaty and 2018 Disarmament Forums: An Initial Impact Assessment." *Journal for Peace and Nuclear Disarmament*, DOI:10.1080/25751654.2018.1516493.

[17] Office for Disarmament Affairs. 2018. *Securing Our Common Future: An Agenda for Disarmament*, New York, United Nations.

nuclear forces, before its 2021 expiration, nor negotiate additional reductions under the regime. Since the US has withdrawn from the 2015 Joint Comprehensive Plan of Action (JCPOA) for Iran to limit its nuclear program, Iran hesitates to implement the arrangement (as of mid-2019), while the other partners to the agreement, the EU, France, Germany, the UK, China, and Russia, continue to honor the agreement. The US has also, subsequent to its 2018 "nuclear posture review," begun to manufacture new, low-yield nuclear warheads for Trident missiles, prompting some to suggest that this more flexible weaponry could lower the threshold for the instigation of a nuclear conflict.[18]

The current deterioration of the significant post–Cold War achievements in bilateral disarmament among the two involved "great powers" (which helped to make the world a safer place) has prompted Mikhail Gorbachev to write a *New York Times* opinion piece entitled *A New Nuclear Arms Race Has Begun*, citing the demise of the INF as the "latest victim in the militarization of world affairs." He issues the following warning to contemporary leadership's seeming compulsion to repeat old mistakes:

> Yet I am convinced that those who hope to benefit from a global free-for-all are deeply mistaken. There will be no winner in a war of all against all – particularly if it ends in a nuclear war. And that is a possibility that cannot be ruled out. An unrelenting arms race, international tensions, hostility and universal mistrust will only increase the risk.[19]

Currently, it does seem that, with an increasingly unstable international security environment where regression to previous patterns is a substantial risk, sober minds are turning their attention to the real, practical need for the international nonproliferation of a wide range of weapons types, existing or yet to be invented, with worrying new weapons technologies on the horizon. Uniquely ambitious comprehensive plans "for the establishment of a system for the regulation of armaments," that were to be the responsibility of the Security Council under the Charter, should be undertaken, taking advantage of the expertise and technical skill acquired in the field of arms control since the advent of the Charter (see Box). As with the adoption of the TPNW in 2017, a broader and more decentralized collective leadership is currently needed to push ahead on this topic. Early efforts by such bodies as the Commission on Conventional Armaments (CCA), established in 1947 as a subsidiary organ to the Security Council (upon recommendation of the General Assembly) and disbanded in 1952, could serve as an inspiration and starting point for modern efforts. For example, working papers and reports of the CCA began to analyze what it considered to be essential elements of an international system of

---

[18] See Borger, Julian. 2019. "US Nuclear Weapons: First Low-Yield Warheads Roll off the Production Line." *The Guardian*, January 29.

[19] Gorbachev, Mikhail. 2018. "A New Nuclear Arms Race Has Begun." *New York Times*, October, 25.

verification and control of armaments, and also the delineation of the range of basic challenges inherent to the regulation of armaments. New perspectives on "human security" can frame contemporary initiatives, alongside a consolidation and rationalization of the presently fragmented and outdated multilateral efforts developed since the Cold War, that are not fit for present needs and potentials.[20]

The Challenge

The challenge presented by ambitious and comprehensive global disarmament regimes – unlike anything the world has seen to date in this field – is a significant one, as systemic change in the global acquisition and use of arms would also represent a paradigm shift in social organization and a range of traditional cultural assumptions. A fundamental attribute of national sovereignty, before the era of the Charter's legal regime and precursor instruments, has been conceived to include the right to wage war on other nations in the defense or advancement of national interests, in a presumed anarchic environment. Apart from some indigenous societies, warfare has been part of human experience since before recorded history; and recorded history is largely the history of wars.[21] There is a certain "path dependency" in considering war and mass armed conflict to be inevitable.

Furthermore, war, or national war-readiness, as a demonstration of the ultimate use of force and display of power can play to the (mostly masculine) ego,[22] inflating the self-worth of autocrats and powerful elites, and even corrupting democratically elected leaders. The pride and glory that can be associated with military parades show this only too well. The instruments of war find their extension in militarized dictatorships, police states and repressive regimes, where the institutions of government are turned to the benefit of those in power rather than to the welfare of the population. Such governments, within a global intergovernmental system, will themselves become obstacles to the functioning of that system in general, and to

---

[20] See, e.g., the perspectives presented in: Borrie, John, 2008. "Tackling Disarmament Challenges," in Williams, Jody, Stephen D. Goose, and Mary Wareham (eds.), *Banning Landmines: Disarmament, Diplomacy, and Human Security*. Lanham, MD, Rowman & Littlefield, pp. 263–280.

[21] Keeley, Lawrence H. 1996. *War before Civilization: The Myth of the Peaceful Savage*. Oxford, Oxford University Press; Turchin, Peter. 2006. *War and Peace and War: The Rise and Fall of Empires*, New York, Plume Books (Penguin).

[22] Indeed, a landmark Security Council Resolution 1325 recognized "the important role of women in the prevention and resolution of conflicts, peace negotiations, peace-building, peacekeeping, humanitarian response and in post-conflict reconstruction and stresses the importance of their equal participation and full involvement in all efforts for the maintenance and promotion of peace and security [...] urg[ing] all actors to increase the participation of women and incorporate gender perspectives in all United Nations peace and security efforts" (see description at www.un.org/womenwatch/osagi/wps/). UN Security Council, *Security Council Resolution 1325 (2000) [On Women and Peace and Security]*, October 31, S/RES/ 1325 (2000). www.refworld.org/docid/3b00f4672e.html.

disarmament in particular, as genuine arms control may threaten the basis of their authority and facilitate their exit from power. An external enemy is important for some governments, and even for the identities which have been cultivated within certain nations.[23] However, such predispositions and historical tendencies only support the argument for strong international initiatives and mechanisms to hold national leaderships to account (for example under international criminal law or in relation to a new international anti-corruption court; see Chapters 10 and 18), to facilitate trust among peoples and nations, as well as intercultural knowledge, and to further shared international norms (see Chapter 20), including democratic and participatory governments at the national level, within a framing "culture of peace."[24]

Ending traditional security dilemmas and achieving disarmament are therefore also a human and social challenge, requiring changing minds and hearts, including, importantly, in leadership – and in the public conception of what leadership entails. Outdated political concepts of power as domination, and the control of substantial armies and navies and the power of life and death as instruments of that domination, have attracted certain personality types to leadership positions, often with the ends justifying any means. History is full of such examples. Where such people are in power today, they will cling to outdated notions of national sovereignty as a defense of their association with power. More mature concepts of leadership as service to one's country and its people (see Chapters 19 and 20), and as responsible, constructive and rational actors on the international stage, will be needed to engage governments in ambitious proposals for the reform of our current international system. More prominent leadership from the representatives of "middle powers," who may be more committed to and better understand the rational basis for a strengthened international system, are badly needed. Generally, reforms in many national government structures, changes in education, and broad civil society engagement are all necessary to move forward effectively and to reduce the number of countries which may feel threatened by global governance reforms (e.g., which suffer from insufficient democratization or legitimacy of leadership), and the international community must re-double its efforts to assist such countries.

Abolition of War

All this implies that a precondition for successful disarmament will be a general consensus among governments and in public opinion that, as war is prohibited as an anachronistic and unnecessary human institution (one can already see clear signs of

---

[23] It is noted that: "[m]ultiple studies suggest that identifying threatening enemies is often central to crystallizing a sense of purpose, community, and identity. As such, the enemy may even be something to be cherished and cultivated." Browning, *International Security*, p. 22.

[24] For example, further reinforcing and disseminating UNESCO's admirable range of "culture of peace" initiatives (e.g., see description of a range of initiatives on programming for building a culture of peace and non-violence at https://en.unesco.org/themes/building-peace-programmes).

this consensus; see Chapter 10), the means for its waging should be eliminated, with global armaments strictly controlled and subject to monitoring, in conformity with Charter norms. Credible alternatives to settle disputes must be available, and processes established to punish violators of key international norms and to bring recalcitrant governments into line. This chapter outlines some approaches that may be necessary to enable this transition and to reap the benefits of a global peace economy. For generations, many have hoped for a world without war, especially after suffering through one. We are convinced that, in the 21st century, this is now a realistic possibility for the following reasons.

First, with modern technology, the nature of warfare and its capacity for destruction have fundamentally changed. Yes, there were times in the past when a city was besieged and overwhelmed, its men and boys slaughtered and its women raped and taken into slavery, but the scale was different. War as combat only between large armies of soldiers or fleets of warships is largely a thing of the past. The distinction between military combatants and civilians has increasingly disappeared. Weakening "the enemy" means firebombing or laying waste to whole cities, targeting hospitals and schools, and driving out entire populations. Some attempts have been made to outlaw chemical and biological weapons, and antipersonnel mines that go on killing long after the end of a conflict, with moderate success. However, with the development of nuclear weapons with the capacity to vaporize whole cities, contaminate the atmosphere and trigger a nuclear winter wiping out most of the human race, war has given us the potential and the risk of collective suicide. The fact that the nuclear powers still contemplate war with these weapons and prepare for it defies logic and underlines the fundamental flaws in national governance as presently practiced.[25] Even those who believed that nuclear weapons "were essential to maintaining international security during the Cold War" based on the doctrine of deterrence, have argued that they now pose immense dangers to global society.[26]

---

[25] Recent reporting has tracked a worrying trend in this respect: "Speaking to reporters last week, former [US] defence secretary William Perry, an arms control advocate, said he was less worried about the number of nuclear warheads left in the world than by the return of cold war talk about such weapons being 'usable' ... 'The belief that there might be tactical advantage using nuclear weapons – which I haven't heard that being openly discussed in the United States or in Russia for a good many years – is happening now in those countries which I think is extremely distressing,' Perry said. 'That's a very dangerous belief'" (Borger, "US Nuclear Weapons").

[26] See, for example: Shultz, George P., William J. Perry, Henry A. Kissinger, and Sam Nunn. 2007. "A World Free of Nuclear Weapons." *Wall Street Journal*, January 4. They note that: "Nuclear weapons today present tremendous dangers, but also an historic opportunity. US leadership will be required to take the world to the next stage – to a solid consensus for reversing reliance on nuclear weapons globally as a vital contribution to preventing their proliferation into potentially dangerous hands, and ultimately ending them as a threat to the world." Others, such as UK Commander Robert Green (Royal Navy, Retired), have argued for the unsoundness of the doctrine of nuclear deterrence generally, advocating more "credible, effective, and responsible" alternatives. Green, Robert. 2010. *Security without Deterrence*, Christchurch, New Zealand, Astron Media.

Second, recent technological transformations are changing the nature of warfare in fundamental ways. The latest technologies of autonomous weapons guided by artificial intelligence are further shifting the strategic balance from deterrence to attack, as they make possible the simultaneous destruction of all or most of an adversary's retaliatory capacity.[27] The capacity of computers to process masses of data and to explore options allows them to make decisions almost instantaneously with no human intervention, empathy or ethical values. It may seem logical to program autonomous weapons for particular missions, but it would be impossible to model or control the simultaneous deployment of thousands of such weapons by both sides in a conflict. Such a war would rapidly spiral beyond any human control. As a result, the risk of war, intentional or accidental, is again increasing, in particular given the current unpredictable shifting of the geopolitical tectonic plates.

Third, war is no longer restricted to conflict between nation states or civil wars within a state. Many other actors are now involved, including terrorist organizations, fanatical religious movements, extremist groups situated on the far reaches of the political spectrum, and (transnational) organized criminal syndicates, all of which may be ready to kill and destroy without discrimination to reach their ends. Achieving peace no longer just means settling a dispute between countries, but must involve wider circles of participants and address many more causal factors.[28]

Fourth, technology has not only created new armaments, but also new capacities to organize for collective good, to communicate and understand multiple perspectives, to search for common solutions, to build wide public understanding and support, and thus to create trustworthy institutions to resolve disputes peacefully and to create and maintain peace. Technology has also given us the means for unprecedented, highly reliable monitoring and oversight for new, internationally-agreed arms control measures.

Finally, for those who believe that we have always made war and shall continue to do so, we can provide the contrary example of various systems evolving to maturity, as for example, noted in studies of aggregate data in relation to the decline in violence generally across societies.[29] We should be now striving to reach a point of social maturity at a planetary scale of organization, beyond irrational systems based on ad hoc violence and contested domination, which, indeed are dangerously anachronistic given current interdependence and the global challenges we are facing. One important part of this is to leave warfare behind and to create more rational, civilized forms of dispute prevention and settlement (see Chapter 10). Modern scholars have exposed the constructed nature of international relations

[27] Payne, Kenneth. 2018. AI, warbot. *New Scientist*, Vol. 239, No. 3195, pp. 41–43. September 15.
[28] See, for example, Part V of the recent UN Secretary General's document, "Strengthening Partnerships for Disarmament." Office for Disarmament Affairs, *Securing Our Common Future*, pp. 61–72.
[29] See, e.g., Pinker, Steven. 2011. *The Better Angels of Our Nature: Why Violence Has Declined*, New York, Viking. See also the cross-disciplinary research discussed in Chapter 10.

cultures marked by mistrust, secrecy and fear, and "competitive strategic mindsets," noting that "alarmist zero-sum thinking is not inevitable, but a self-fulfilling outcome of the tendency of political and military elites to unthinkingly accept realist worldviews" which consider conflict as inevitable.[30] With accelerating, looming environmental crises on the horizon, the only realist worldview today requires devising new "win-win" intensively comparative and collaborative problem-solving strategies at the international level.

Self-Defense

The maintenance of military forces is often justified as necessary for self-defense. In a world where governments cannot be trusted and aggression has been frequent, this is understandable given the anarchic global system without adequate governance mechanisms. At present, there exists under international law (e.g., the UN Charter and precedent-setting international decisions and analysis) a relatively well-defined concept of national self-defense and when it is legitimate and legal in response to an attack or imminent threat by another state or nonstate actor. However, there is no universally binding international rule of law or enforcement, where assessments of actions said to be made in self-defense can be regularly made by a supervising judiciary. Likewise, the current Security Council and its permanent members have latitude, when convenient, not to take preventive action, or to ignore belligerent activities which would cause a threat to a state, or would go beyond the more established definitions of self-defense under international law. A reformed international judicial system with compulsory jurisdiction, including over the international crime of aggression (e.g., universal jurisdiction of the International Court of Justice and the International Criminal Court; see Chapter 10) will largely cure any ambiguity in a definition of self-defense, an ambiguity which indeed may be deployed cynically – or in an over-broad way – by various actors.

Under the current UN Charter, states are entitled to defend themselves until such time as the collective security mechanism of the Charter takes effect (see Article 51). A future amended Charter should include a similar sensible provision, although with the collective security responsibilities shouldered by the UN IPF (see Chapter 8). During a transition period of staged international disarmament (see below), care will be needed to ascertain, based on objective/non-political peace and security expertise, the current, interim and future "self-defense" needs of states given the new paradigm of enhanced collective security. Ultimately, the national possession of armaments should be determined by a new standard of the need for "internal security" rather than for "self-defense," as a genuine system of international collective security takes root and its institutions mature.

---

[30] Browning, *International Security*, pp. 21–22.

Past Multilateral Disarmament Measures and Proposals

One would think that the suffering from World War II would push the nations most involved into intense efforts at disarmament to prevent future wars, as stipulated by the Charter. Unfortunately, for the military establishments of the victorious countries, the reverse was the case. Particularly between the United States and the USSR in the decades following World War II, disarmament proposals were repeatedly exchanged in the knowledge that they would be refused by the other side. If one side unexpectedly accepted a proposal from the other, it was rapidly withdrawn. The bilateral agreements adopted not infrequently served to authorize continued weapons development and it has been observed that disarmament proposals were generally made in bad faith to placate the public and other states.[31] This refusal of the major military powers to cooperate in reductions in armaments contrary to their strategic goal of wide spheres of influence continued for many years, with, however, the very important breakthroughs achieved in the late 1980s between the US and the USSR (beginning with the INF Treaty in 1987 signed by Reagan and Gorbachev). As noted above, these achievements are currently under serious threat.

It is in this context that intergovernmental efforts at disarmament, mostly within the framework of the United Nations, need to be evaluated. The Box below, "A short history of multilateral disarmament measures and proposals," based largely on UN sources, highlights the great efforts that have gone into multilateral disarmament agreements. Very regularly, however, the states with the most – or the most destructive – armaments have refused to cooperate fully, and disarmament efforts remain piecemeal, fragmented and prone to slow or obstructed progress.

Box A short history of multilateral disarmament measures and proposals[32]

After the chaos of World War I, the 1925 Geneva Protocol prohibited the use of asphyxiating, poisonous, or other gases (as well as biological weapons) in warfare, but little further progress was made on international disarmament until after World War II. The United Nations General Assembly, in its first resolution adopted January 24, 1946, established a United Nations Atomic Energy Commission and set forth the goal of eliminating all weapons "adaptable to mass destruction."

The 1963 Partial Test Ban Treaty aimed to end nuclear weapons testing in the atmosphere, underwater, and in outer space, but allowed it to continue underground.

One of the most successful agreements is the Treaty on the Non-Proliferation of Nuclear Weapons (NPT) which opened for signature in 1968 and entered into force

---

[31] Leitenberg, Milton. 1977. Disarmament and arms control since 1945. *Cross Currents*, Vol. 27, No. 2 (Summer), pp. 130–139. www.jstor.org/stable/24458313.

[32] Gillis, Melissa. 2017. *Disarmament: A Basic Guide*, Fourth ed., New York, United Nations Office for Disarmament Affairs.

in 1970. It may have discouraged some states from developing nuclear weapons, with a few obvious exceptions. On May 11, 1995, the Treaty was extended indefinitely. A total of 191 parties have joined, including the five originally recognized nuclear weapon states. Article VI of the Treaty requires all states parties to negotiate in good faith on effective measures related to the cessation of the nuclear arms race and to nuclear disarmament, as well as on a treaty on general and complete disarmament under strict and effective international control. In 1996, the International Court of Justice issued a unanimous advisory opinion ruling that Article VI of the NPT required nuclear weapon states parties to the Treaty "to bring to a conclusion, negotiations leading to nuclear disarmament." Four years later, at the 2000 NPT Review Conference, nuclear weapon states agreed to an unequivocal undertaking "to accomplish the total elimination of their nuclear arsenals." At the 2010 NPT Review Conference, a large number of states supported the idea of beginning work toward a comprehensive nuclear weapons convention. The Conference, however, was unable to reach agreement to pursue negotiations. The 2015 NPT Review Conference was unable to adopt a final document. Despite relative success in non-proliferation, the Treaty has failed to achieve nuclear disarmament.

The Convention on the Prohibition of the Development, Production and Stockpiling of Bacteriological (Biological) and Toxin Weapons and on Their Destruction, the Biological Weapons Convention (BWC), a new instrument to supplement the 1925 Geneva Protocol, was opened for signature in 1972 and entered into force in 1975. The BWC has no implementing body and no means of monitoring implementation or verifying compliance.

At the first special session of the General Assembly devoted to disarmament (1978), member states recognized that the "continued arms race" was a "growing threat to international peace and security" and declared that the build-up of arms "threatens to stall efforts at reaching the goals of development" (General Assembly resolution S-10/2).

The Convention on Prohibitions or Restrictions on the Use of Certain Conventional Weapons Which May Be Deemed to Be Excessively Injurious or to Have Indiscriminate Effects (more commonly called the Convention on Certain Conventional Weapons (CCW) and also known as the Inhumane Weapons Convention) entered into force in 1983. The CCW bans or restricts the use of specific types of weapons considered to cause unnecessary or unjustifiable suffering to combatants or to affect civilians indiscriminately. It has 125 states parties. The specific weapons targeted are described in protocols, which can be added as new risks are identified. They are the Protocol on Non-Detectable Fragments (Protocol I) with 118 states parties, the Protocol on Prohibitions or Restrictions on the Use of Mines, Booby-Traps and Other Devices as amended (Amended Protocol II) with 104 states parties, which is the sole legally binding instrument that explicitly covers improvised explosive devices; the Protocol on Prohibitions or Restrictions on the Use of Incendiary Weapons (Protocol III) with 115 states parties; the Protocol on Blinding Laser Weapons (Protocol IV) with 108 states parties; and the Protocol on Explosive Remnants of War (Protocol V) with 93 states parties.

In 1987 the United Nations Conference on Disarmament and Development was held without any significant effect.

The Convention on the Prohibition of the Development, Production, Stockpiling and Use of Chemical Weapons and on Their Destruction, the Chemical Weapons Convention, was opened for signature in 1993 and entered into force in 1997. The Convention bans the development, production, stockpiling and use of chemical weapons. It requires states parties to destroy all stocks of chemical weapons within 10 years of its entry into force, and has been ratified by 193 states. To ensure compliance with the Convention, the Organization for the Prohibition of Chemical Weapons (OPCW) was established to carry out verification activities.

In December 1993, the United Nations General Assembly adopted by consensus a resolution calling for the negotiation of a verifiable treaty banning the production of fissile materials for nuclear weapons. The Conference on Disarmament (CD), which has been mandated to negotiate the Treaty, has long been considered to be the sole multilateral negotiating forum for disarmament treaties. The CD, however, has failed since 1998 to agree to commence negotiations or formal discussions on any topic. In 2009, the CD adopted a program of work for the first time in more than a decade, but was unable to implement it and remained deadlocked through 2016.

The Comprehensive Nuclear-Test-Ban Treaty, which bans all nuclear-related test explosions, opened for signature in September 1996 but has not yet entered into force.

The Convention on the Prohibition of the Use, Stockpiling, Production and Transfer of Anti-Personnel Mines and on Their Destruction, also known as the Anti-Personnel Mine Ban Convention or the Ottawa Convention, was developed through what has become known as the Ottawa Process, a partnership between civil society, governments, and the United Nations. It was adopted in Oslo, Norway, on September 18, 1997, and opened for signature in Ottawa, Canada, on December 3, 1997, with 122 governments signing the Convention at that time. It entered into force in March 1999 and has 162 states parties.

Small arms in global circulation are estimated to total at least 875 million. The trade in small arms has not been well regulated and is the least transparent of all weapons systems. More than 80 percent of the ammunition trade seems to remain outside of reliable export data. In 2001, two UN instruments on small arms control were agreed upon. Under the Convention against Transnational Organized Crime, countries adopted a Firearms Protocol. On the broader topic of small arms and light weapons, countries agreed on a program of action focusing on preventing the illicit trade in such weaponry. This politically binding instrument encourages all UN member states to adopt measures at the national, regional and global levels to prevent, combat and eradicate the illicit trade in these weapons.

Currently, there are no multilateral treaties that deal with missiles and their proliferation, and discussions about missiles in all their aspects at the United Nations have, thus far, resulted in no concrete policy recommendations. The two existing instruments are the Missile Technology Control Regime established in 1987 with 35 participating states, and the 2002 International Code of Conduct against Ballistic

Missile Proliferation (also called The Hague Code of Conduct or HCOC) which has 134 subscribing states.

The Convention on Cluster Munitions, which outlaws the use, development, stockpiling, production, acquisition, retention and transfer of nearly all cluster munitions is the result of what has become known as the Oslo Process, the collaboration among governments, the United Nations, the International Committee of the Red Cross and other civil society groups to address the problem of cluster munitions. The Convention was negotiated and adopted at the Dublin Diplomatic Conference on May 30, 2008, and was opened for signature in December 2008, when it was signed by 108 states. It entered into force August 1, 2010. As of August 2017, 108 states had signed the Convention, of which 102 are states parties.

Until recently, there was no global set of rules governing the trade in conventional weapons. While a variety of national and regional control measures on arms transfers existed, they were too often lax or unenforced. In April 2013, the General Assembly approved the Arms Trade Treaty (ATT), the first-ever global treaty to establish common international standards to guide governments in deciding whether or not to authorize arms transfers. The ATT promotes cooperation, transparency, and responsible action by states in the international trade in conventional arms. The Treaty, which entered into force on December 24, 2014, regulates the international trade in almost all categories of conventional weapons – from small arms to battle tanks, combat aircraft and warships. Ammunition, as well as parts and components, are also covered. By August 2017, the ATT had 92 states parties.

Annually, Improvised Explosive Device (IED) attacks kill and injure more people than do attacks with any other type of weapon except firearms. The UN General Assembly passed a resolution (71/72) in 2016 urging, among other things, that states develop national policies to counter IEDs and take appropriate measures to strengthen the management of national ammunition stockpiles to prevent the diversion of materials for making IEDs to illicit markets and illegal and unauthorized groups.

In 2016, the United Nations convened an Open-ended Working Group (OEWG) taking forward multilateral nuclear disarmament negotiations. Subsequently, based on the recommendation of the OEWG, the General Assembly on December 23, 2016, adopted resolution 71/258, "Taking forward multilateral nuclear disarmament negotiations," in which it decided to convene a United Nations conference to negotiate a legally binding instrument to prohibit nuclear weapons. Subsequently, on July 7, 2017, the Treaty on the Prohibition of Nuclear Weapons, the first multilateral, legally binding instrument for nuclear disarmament to have been negotiated in 20 years, was adopted. The Treaty prohibits a range of nuclear weapon-related activities, such as undertaking to develop, test, produce, manufacture, acquire, possess, or stockpile nuclear weapons or other nuclear explosive devices, as well as the use or threat of use of these weapons. However, the 122 countries that have adopted it do not include the countries with nuclear weapons or their allies in NATO, for instance.

After all of these efforts, where are we today? Global military spending is currently higher than at any time since the end of the Cold War (upwards of $1.7 trillion or 2.2

percent of global GDP). As of 2017, there were approximately 3,750 nuclear weapons deployed and ready for use globally. About 2,000 of these are reportedly kept on high alert, ready to be launched within minutes. In total, there are an estimated 14,465 nuclear warheads (operational, spares, active and inactive storage and intact warheads scheduled for dismantlement), enough to destroy civilization many times over and destroy most life on earth.[33]

The costs related to nuclear weapons (to research, develop, build, maintain, dismantle, and clean up after them) are considerable. The United States spends about $30 billion per year just to maintain its stocks.[34] The United States Congressional Budget Office estimates that the total cost to modernize the country's nuclear forces will be more than $1.2 trillion over the next 30 years (this amounts to $4.6 million per hour for 30 years.) And the United States Department of Energy reports that weapons activities have resulted in the production of more than 104 million cubic meters of radioactive waste.

Notwithstanding the critical, but seemingly momentary, progress associated with the close of the Cold War between the then two world superpowers, the major powers, and other states with military ambitions (also in regional contexts), have generally not signed or become parties to agreements that may limit their military capacity, and many other states have not respected them at one time or another. As a rule, there are significantly inadequate or non-existent international verification and enforcement mechanisms. What has also substantially been lacking, in addition to good faith commitments to the positive mutual goals of disarmament, is trust between states, as the Charter sought to establish. As noted, "security dilemmas" have strong psychological components.[35] What good is an agreement if you do not expect your competitors to respect it, and cheating is assumed to be the rule rather than the exception within a culture of cynical, low expectations? The progress made has been based on the good will of a majority of states, but not the most militarily endowed, who are often jockeying for relative power and influence.

DISARMAMENT IN TODAY'S WORLD: TOWARD SYSTEMIC ARMS CONTROL AND DISARMAMENT

Disarmament is necessarily a complex and expensive process in itself, even apart from the destruction and recycling of arms and military equipment. It involves

---

[33] *SIPRI Yearbook 2018*, pp. 6 and 10; Stockholm International Peace Research Institute (SIPRI). 2017. Military Expenditure Database. www.sipri.org/databases/milex.

[34] Nuclear Threat Initiative. 2013. US Nuclear Weapons Spending Compared to Other Government Programs, October. www.nti.org/media/pdfs/US_nuclear_weapons_spending.pdf?_=1380927217.

[35] The Charter requires members of the UN to fulfill "in good faith" obligations assumed under the instrument (Art. 2(2)) and, as explained above, sought to create an enabling environment for states to live side by side in peace as good neighbors.

major industries and, not infrequently, an important part of national economies in countries with a significant military-industrial complex or arms sector. Local communities may be dependent on the spinoffs from the military presence. For millions of people, the military, as currently constituted, may be their profession and life, and millions of others are employed in the arms and related industries. Much research and technological development is funded for military ends and defense. Eliminating or repurposing such infrastructure may add up to some short or medium-term economic losses and a difficult transition for such economies. Disarmament is not just organizing the destruction of arms, but transforming a not insignificant part of society in some countries.[36]

It is not that the military is an essential part of any government or economy. Costa Rica abolished its army in 1949 to prevent further military coups d'état and has remained peaceful when many of its armed neighbors suffer from chronic violence. It has devoted its resources to more constructive uses and stands out as a model for its region. Why has no other state copied its example?[37]

As mentioned, disarmament cannot be undertaken if there is not already in place, or well on the way to being established, a binding alternative to war for dispute settlement and a legitimate international force sufficient to ensure collective security (see Chapters 8 and 10). The various processes of strengthening the international system need to be combined and carefully coordinated during a period of transition. Disarmament also needs to be integrated into a larger process of reallocation of national resources, redesign of certain aspects of the economy, and retraining of people. Funding will be necessary to provide both for the disarmament process itself, and for the alternatives to take the place of the military effort. Otherwise transformation may be resisted and the process blocked.

Proposals to Enable Modern Comprehensive Disarmament

At the international level, disarmament will only work to the extent that states feel that they are able to trust the process and objectively verify commitments; thus building trust through a range of the measures recommended here will be a necessary precondition and accompaniment to the disarmament process. "Confidence-building measures" are a necessary and common part of modern disarmament practice and should be employed systematically at the international level.[38] Each stage will

---

[36] However, it should be noted that many jobs are always being lost or redesigned as technologies change and industries evolve. Given the high level of expenditure for military purposes, there are ample funds available to finance economic transitions linked to de-militarization.

[37] A range of other sovereign states, however, do not have militaries or standing armies, many of which have long-standing agreements for defense with former occupying countries (for example, Monaco and France, and a range of small island states), usually not undergoing a process of demilitarization as was undertaken in Costa Rica.

[38] See, e.g., Meek, Sarah. 2005. "Confidence-Building Measures as Tools for Disarmament and Development." *African Security Studies*, Vol. 14, No. 1, pp. 129–132; and, Tulliu, Steve and

need to be carefully defined and balanced, and binding in application. Full transparency and regular monitoring and inspection will be necessary to assure governments that there is no evasion of obligations, and all governments are held to objective standards. As noted in Chapter 8, a UN IPF is envisaged to be established in parallel to the process of disarmament, not only so it can, in extreme cases, intervene if any country tries to destabilize the disarmament process to its own advantage, but also to deal with other conflicts and to significantly strengthen the UN's ability to fulfill its peace and security mandate.

A binding yet staged approach should be applied to the disarmament of all states for a reduction of armaments to those that are strictly necessary for self-defense,[39] an obligation that can be deduced from the language and intent of the current UN Charter (i.e., under which international use of force is strictly limited to self-defense or duly authorized collective security action). A revised Charter would make this norm clearer and binding on all states, with the corollary duty for states to disarm to appropriate levels within a certain timeframe. A special Standing Committee on Disarmament would implement and monitor this obligation. It could consist of 24 members representing all UN members. Following the proposal for member-ship in the Executive Council (see Chapter 7), five members (US, China, EU, Russia, and India) would get a single seat each and the remaining 161 members would be grouped in 19 clusters defined by geographical proximity and, to the extent possible, roughly equivalent voting power. Voting power for each of the 24 members would be identical to that in the General Assembly. Its first task would be to commission a transparent and arms-length scientific analysis by independent experts, without political interference, to determine the self-defense needs of each country, taking into account the existence of the new IPF. It has been noted that a key problem with multilateral disarmament processes to date is the extent to which they rely on consensus negotiations (in which parties try to maximize what they think to be in their own interests, to the detriment of a collective solution) without adequate mechanisms to ensure overall fairness in outcomes.[40] After the determin-ation of appropriate limits, a staged approach of disarmament to required levels would then proceed, with a preparatory period[41] and then a 10-year (or more) phase of disarmament proper (for most countries, depending on the weapons and equip-ment in need of decommissioning), all proceeding within the context of a thorough

Thomas Schmalerger, 2003. *Coming to Terms with Security: A Lexicon for Arms Control, Disarmament and Confidence-Building*, Geneva, United Nations, UNIDIR/2003/22.

[39] To be gradually transitioned, over time, to a new standard of their need for "internal security" rather than for "self-defense."

[40] See Borrie, "Tackling Disarmament Challenges," pp. 270–273.

[41] These preparatory measures could, for example, include extensive regional training and the strengthening of regional peace and security mechanisms, as well as those at the international level. See proposals, e.g., in "The Global Action to Prevent War Project." 2008. *Preventing Armed Violence and Ending War: Program Statement 2008–2010*. www.globalactionpw.org/wp/wp-content/uploads/program-statement-2008.pdf.)

monitoring and inspection system by independent experts empowered by the Standing Committee.[42] The latest techniques of remote sensing and monitoring/ intelligence-gathering should make it possible to ensure that disarmament is proceeding to completion and that no attempt is made to hide or dissemble arms for later use.

Disarmament, particularly of the "great powers," would have to follow a path of simultaneous execution by all nations, with every nation disarming proportionately. The work of the Standing Committee could consolidate, extend and incorporate, as appropriate, the United Nations Office for Disarmament Affairs, the Conference on Disarmament and other UN bodies or treaties linked to disarmament issues (e.g., the range of arms and weapons related treaties, the International Atomic Energy Agency – IAEA and other relevant bodies).[43] It should build on the acquired expertise and norms already agreed upon, while taking into account the new binding obligations of states under the revised Charter and binding commitments in existing instruments.

Nuclear weapons would be universally banned as immoral weapons of mass destruction, as required by the 2017 Treaty on the Prohibition of Nuclear Weapons, recently adopted by the majority of the world's states. However, as the countries with the most nuclear weapons have been opposed to the Treaty to date, it will take confidence building, delicate diplomacy and firm disarmament commitments set out in modern security regimes to bring all such countries to the table. Biological and chemical weapons have already been outlawed by treaty, but enforcement is difficult since they are so easily manufactured and used; enhanced mechanisms will have to be employed. New and emerging forms of weaponry and warfare, including autonomous weapons, military artificial intelligence systems, nanomaterials,[44] and cyberwarfare, would have to be anticipated and included. No state should remain with any means at its disposal that would allow it to force its will on other states. In exchange, its rights and security would be guaranteed by the system of collective security, with obligatory alternative peaceful means of dispute settlement.

Such a fundamental shift in a conception of the classical attributes of national sovereignty represented by the military will involve a paradigm shift that is difficult for some. The most difficult cases may be authoritarian governments for whom fear (linked with militarization and types of violence), both internal and external, is a key instrument with which they are able to maintain power. A number of such

---

[42] There have previously been similar detailed proposals for staged disarmament. See for example Johnson, Robert. 1982. "Toward a Dependable Peace: A proposal for an Appropriate Security System," in Falk, Richard, Samuel S. Kim, and Saul H. Mendlovitz (eds.) *Toward a Just World Order*, Vol. 1. Boulder, CO, Westview Press, ch. 18, pp. 271–283.

[43] Gillis, Disarmament and arms control; and the recent Office for Disarmament Affairs *Agenda for Disarmament* provide comprehensive overviews of the current UN and associated initiatives relevant to disarmament.

[44] Nanomaterials have potential for better armor and invisible camouflage, powerful explosives and miniature nuclear arms, and chemical weapons, among others.

governments have acquired, or sought to acquire, nuclear arms as the ultimate deterrent against any attempt to overthrow them from within or without. The military may be the principal instrument through which their power is exercised, when it is not the military itself that pulls the strings of government; such governments may see disarmament as prejudicial to their own power. The international community will need a strategy of positive incentives and stepped sanctions, or other coercive measures, if all other attempts to reason with such governments fail. Poor or dysfunctional national governance, in this domain as in all the other areas of the transition, will be a significant obstacle that may slow the application of comprehensive disarmament proposals.

Technical and Financial Challenges

Clark and Sohn considered in detail the main changes that would be needed in the UN Charter for effective disarmament, including a technical annex on the mechanics of disarmament that would be an inseparable part of the Charter.[45]

As mentioned above, the level of and specifics applied to the disarmament of individual states, and a common collective standard for such disarmament, in the light of the new capacities and collective security responsibilities of the IPF, will have to be determined by an independent expert body, which would devote significant study and technical expertise to determining these standards, as well as to standards for the crucial ongoing verification and inspection criteria. Importantly, such an international expert body will have to be insulated from political, entrenched bureaucratic military and other pressures (e.g., those of the business sector presently engaged in the lucrative manufacture of weapons), in order to ensure that its determinations and proposals are truly independent and impartially based on *technical* expertise. The financing of the transition from a system based primarily on national defense to a genuine international collective security system could also be addressed by such an international expert group, making fair and realistic assessments of the amounts of international funding needed for countries and the international community to transition, and at what points national governments, for example, could start transferring (very substantial, in some cases) national defense expenditures to investments in collective security.

Disarmament is a technically difficult and expensive process. Most military equipment has no other more productive uses, and is too specialized to be modified, and so must be disarmed, dismantled, and recycled. In any case, equipment that could easily be reconverted for military purposes should not be retained. Munitions in particular were never designed to be dismantled, and the explosives within them can become unstable over time. Dumping in the sea was practiced after the two

---

[45] Clark, G. and L.B. Sohn. 1966. *World Peace through World Law: Two Alternative Plans*, Cambridge, MA: Harvard University Press, pp. 203–280.

world wars, and created major problems later, so this is not an option. Nerve gases and biological weapons present special challenges requiring highly specialized facilities and precautions to neutralize them.

The military has usually been exempted from environmental regulations; many military facilities and arms factories are highly polluted and will require expensive clean-up. Firing ranges may be contaminated with duds and unexploded munitions. Returning such spaces to civilian uses will be a long and expensive process for which budgeting will have to be arranged.

Nuclear disarmament is a special case because of the dangerousness and toxicity of radioactive materials. The nuclear arms race has created an enormous burden that will inevitably weigh on future generations, producing large quantities of highly radioactive substances, which must be kept isolated from all contact with living things for many thousands of years, while ensuring that there is no risk of contamination over such a long period. The challenge in neutralizing the damaged Fukushima power plant is one example, as is the looming cost of dismantling the many nuclear power plants coming to the end of their useful lives. Adding the much greater quantity of radioactive isotopes from nuclear weapons and the facilities to manufacture them will make the problem much larger, especially since countries are still struggling to find safe places to store radioactive wastes. The risk of accidents is never zero.

It will be necessary to decide whether dismantling arms and storing the resulting wastes would benefit from economies of scale, suggesting the need for centralized facilities under United Nations control, or alternatively the risk of transporting such materials is too great and disarmament should take place close to the present locations of the arms. According to the "polluter pays principle," the countries that manufactured or purchased the arms should pay for their elimination, but there may be cases where the burden would be more than a country could bear and some sharing of costs would be justified.

Since the financial costs of disarmament will be very high, military budgets should first be diverted to finance the disarmament process and the return of industrial capacity, facilities, and personnel to civilian uses. The peace dividend will not be immediate but will only emerge over time as the disarmament process advances.

Another challenge will be the resistance of the arms industry and defense contractors that have long benefited from the present situation and will shrink dramatically, if not disappear, with substantial, effective disarmament. To the extent that their technologies have other peaceful uses, they should be assisted to diversify in that direction. Another short-term transitional option would be to use them to destroy existing stocks of arms and munitions, military vehicles, aircraft, and naval vessels. It will be important in the long term that no country retains the capacity to manufacture arms and rearm itself rapidly. As noted in Chapter 8, arms production for the IPF would be controlled, monitored, or directed by the United Nations and distributed so that no country could seize significant capacity and turn it to its own uses.

Accompanying Measures

While disarmament would be a specific responsibility under the revised UN Charter, it will have many larger implications that cannot be ignored. A major part of the world economy, and its allocation of financial, industrial, and human capital, is devoted to the arms industry and related supply chains, not to mention the number of people presently employed in the armed services of states. People fight for their jobs, and those who are armed professionally, especially, must be offered alternatives before they will willingly give up their present occupations. As arms factories are closed or transformed, those employed need to be offered equivalent or better options. The disarmament process should be accompanied by a major retooling of the economy toward constructive ends, such as improvements in infrastructure, the transition to renewable energy sources, environmental restoration, resettlement of displaced populations, and other major needs.[46] In this respect, the global 2030 Agenda and Sustainable Development Goals offer an excellent blueprint to guide reinvestment and retooling of economies worldwide.

As military forces are demobilized or remobilized to work on global common challenges, they should be moved immediately into alternative occupations, with appropriate retraining, making use of existing skills whenever possible.[47] For some, skills from air forces and navies may be directly transferable to their civilian

---

[46] It is not inconceivable that over the longer term the transition to an economy with a smaller military industrial complex might actually be a job-creating process, with new industries emerging that would be more wealth-creating than weapons manufacturing. The experience of the Soviet Union in this respect is illustrative. With the end of the Cold War the Soviet military industrial complex collapsed and, in the short term, this led to massive dislocations and a sharp contraction of output and employment. By 1999, however, the Russian economy had entered a robust period of expansion, including the emergence of thousands of new firms in the industrial, services and agricultural sectors. This transition in Russia was disorderly and chaotic and is certainly no model for the rest of the world. The social costs, in particular, were made worse by misguided policies in a number of areas but, without question, the transition in the end was beneficial for the country, as highlighted by a substantial increase in income per capita measured in dollars.

[47] For example, one recent proposal is to redirect military capacities and personnel to regional Peace Engineering Corps to assist with civilian infrastructure projects in support of the Sustainable Development Goals and humanitarian assistance. (Sky, Jasper. 2018. Repurpose the Military Initiative (RMI): A call to re-allocate 15% of military troops and spending to building civilian infrastructure where it's needed most. November 12, 2018. https://medium .com/@jaspersky/repurpose-the-military-initiative-rmi-a-call-to-re-allocate-15-of-military-troops-and-spending-7cb0bf846ea9). While it did not involve a transition out of the military industries, the experience of Spain in the first half of the 1980s is relevant here. Faced with overcapacity in steel, ship-building, textiles, and other sectors and with little prospects for a sustained recovery, the Spanish government implemented a program of industrial reconversion. It involved the shutting down of many of these industries – which had been a great burden on the budget – and the retraining of tens of thousands of workers to enable them to transition into other more promising sectors, as well as adequate compensation for those workers near the age of retirement. From the mid-1980s onwards Spain had one of the best performing economies in Europe. For further details see López-Claros, Augusto. 1987. *The Search for*

equivalents, and others will readily find a place in the security, emergency, and medical services. Leadership experience should also be easily incorporated into public institutions and the private sector. Since military personnel have always been paid from public funds, without the military contributing to the more productive economy, it should even be possible for the public funding to continue for a reasonable transition, so that financial security can be guaranteed to the personnel and their families. Similarly, communities that have benefited from the presence of military installations will need assistance in adapting their local economies, unless alternative uses for the facilities can be found immediately.

THE CURRENT CROSS-ROADS AND OVERCOMING POLITICAL OBSTACLES

As noted by Gorbachev, the risks we now face together with respect to renewed – and, in some corners, relatively new (e.g., with increased military spending in parts of Asia)[48] – arms races are deeply troubling. The 2018 non-paper on disarmament of the UN Secretary General, in its wide-ranging scope and urgency in tone, indeed reflects this reality.[49] At the same time, we are facing an unprecedented planetary climate change and environmental crisis which has no parallel in human history.[50] Both the current trends with respect to renewed and new/pending weapons development, and climate change and global environmental degradation suffer from fundamentally incomplete, inadequate and ineffective international governance regimes.[51] To confront the climate crisis, we badly need immediate and coordinated global investment in green technology, a proper green infrastructure to transition to

Efficiency in the Adjustment Process: Spain in the 1980s, Occasional Paper 57, Washington DC, International Monetary Fund.

[48] The *SIPRI Yearbook 2018*, p. 6 reports that: "Military expenditure in East Asia continued to rise, for the 23rd year in succession, and was up by 4.1 per cent compared with 2016."

[49] The report notes: "We are living in dangerous times. Protracted conflicts are causing unspeakable human suffering. Armed groups are proliferating, equipped with a vast array of weapons. Global military spending and competition in arms are increasing, and the tensions of the cold war have returned to a world that has grown more complex. In today's multipolar environment, the mechanisms for contact and dialogue that once helped to defuse tensions between two super-powers have eroded and lost their relevance. . . .This new reality demands that disarmament and non-proliferation are put at the centre of the work of the United Nations." Office for Disarmament Affairs, *Securing Our Common Future*, p. vii.

[50] We are told that we currently have a 12 year window to act. See: IPCC. 2018. Global Warming of 1.5°C (SR15), Special Report. Summary for Policy Makers. Geneva: Intergovernmental Panel on Climate Change, October 2018. www.ipcc.ch/report/sr15/. UN Environment. 2018. Emissions Gap Report 2018. Nairobi: United Nations Environment Programme. www.unenvironment.org/resources/emissions-gap-report-2018.

[51] The 2015 Paris Agreement, negotiated within the UN Framework Convention to address climate change, while admirable in aims and intentions, has no reliable enforcement mechanisms to ensure that targets with respect to global warming will be met.

a global *negative* carbon economy, as well as other mass investments for mitigation and adaptation to changing planetary conditions; all of this requires unparalleled international cooperation rather than a shockingly wasteful, distracting and destabilizing military contest. Indeed, it not only appears that major powers are again irresistibly being drawn into a suicide embrace with respect to weapons of mass destruction, but also in relation to the unabated and accelerating climate and global environmental crisis.[52] We are truly at a global cross-roads.

The problem of global systemic and comprehensive disarmament must be faced squarely, with new ambitious plans, if we are going to be serious about sustainable international security, and the freeing of requisite resources and energies for urgent needs.

On the positive side, since World War II, we have seen significant advances in arms control and disarmament science and techniques, with a great deal of knowledge and expertise acquired at the international, national and regional levels.[53] Also, as noted above, we have seen a proliferation of worthy attempts at international arms control/disarmament (however piecemeal and incomplete), which could form the basis of and be consolidated into new, genuinely comprehensive, binding and universal plans for the international community.[54] Additionally, there are the recent notable and encouraging successes of transnational civil society efforts and "smart coalitions" (of civil society groups working with "like-minded states"), which have achieved important progress in arms control, including the 1997 Mine Ban Treaty, and the 2017 TPNW on nuclear weapons, among others. It remains to be seen whether the normative "soft power" of civil society actors and coalitions of countries considered to be middle powers might be more willing to take substantial action toward the "ethically obvious," stepping into an enhanced leadership role for the benefit of the entire international system. As Gorbachev notes, "[f]aced with this dire threat to peace, we are not helpless. We must not resign, we must not surrender."[55] Another voice of moral authority, Pope Francis, has recently warned, at an interreligious cooperation event among Christians and Muslims, that the future of the human race is in peril unless religions resist "the logic of armed power ... the arming of borders, the raising of walls .... There is no alternative: we will either

---

[52] E.g., with the US and other states threatening to pull out of the Paris Agreement, and/or blocking consensus on key reports of implementing measures for the agreement.

[53] See, for example, the comprehensive knowledge presented in guides such as that developed by the United Nations Institute for Disarmament (UNIDIR), among many other resources, in Tulliu and Schmalerger. 2003. *Coming to Terms with Security: A Lexicon for Arms Control, Disarmament and Confidence-Building.*

[54] The 2018 UN Secretary General's document, *Securing Our Common Future: An Agenda for Disarmament*, seeks to present a comprehensive plan, albeit with the frame of existing UN institutions and the current UN Charter.

[55] Gorbachev, "New nuclear arms race."

build the future together or there will not be a future."[56] A serious plan for comprehensive international disarmament represents not only an ethical shift from the false and seemingly inexorable "logic of armed power," but would represent, if well-designed and implemented, a transition to more stable and practical international security, alongside the freeing up of substantial financial and human resources. Moreover, the Charter has laid the foundation and shown the way; it is up to us to complete its system.

[56] "Pope in UAE: Reject Wars in Yemen, Syria, Iraq and Libya." *Al Jazeera*, February 4, 2019. The article notes that, "At the end of the interfaith meeting, Francis and Sheikh Ahmed al-Tayeb – the grand imam of Egypt's Al-Azhar, the highest seat of learning in Sunni Islam – signed a joint statement on 'human fraternity' and their hopes for world peace . . . . They then laid the cornerstones for a new church and mosque to be built side-by-side in the UAE capital, Abu Dhabi." www.aljazeera.com/news/2019/02/pope-uae-reject-wars-yemen-syria-iraq-libya-190204155801553.html.

10

Strengthening the International Rule of Law

Law is, essentially, an order for the promotion of peace. Its purpose is to assure the peaceful living together of a group of individuals in such a way that they settle their inevitable conflicts in a peaceful manner; that is, without the use of force, in conformity with an order valid for all. This order is the law.[1]

Hans Kelsen

In a very real sense, the world no longer has a choice between force and law. If civilization is to survive, it must choose the rule of law.[2]

Dwight Eisenhower

INTERNATIONAL LEGAL INSTITUTIONS: A JOB HALF-DONE

The realization of the mandatory and systematic peaceful settlement of international disputes, the *practical* transition to binding adjudication at the international level, and the strengthening of key international legal institutions on a macro scale in service of the same, has, with some exceptions, received vastly inadequate attention in international policy circles and in academia. Yet, as Kelsen notes above, such a concrete transition would be the hallmark of a shift from primitive sociological conditions marked by precarious and unpredictable violence, to a rational system based upon sound international norms, facilitating a global durable peace and accompanying prosperity which could be associated with such a peace.

It would seem obvious that the transition from an essentially "war-lord" system at the international level – or a version of *Pax Romana* based on the most recent ascendant international hegemon – with war or the threat of war employed as a

---

[1] Kelsen, Hans. 1942. *Law and Peace in International Relations*, Cambridge, MA, Harvard University Press, p. 1.
[2] Larson, Arthur. 1969. *Eisenhower: The President Nobody Knew*, London, Frewin, p. 119.

means to resolve disputes or to further political goals (to paraphrase von Clausewitz), is a significantly inferior approach to international conflicts than would be a viable, effective rule-based international dispute resolution system. War has always been expensive, unpredictable, callous to suffering and wasteful of lives. This is even more the case given the stakes in contemporary times with modern warfare, as noted above by Eisenhower in 1958, and with intensifying salience resulting from recent developments in cyber warfare and "killer robots," not to mention ongoing nuclear and other threats (see Chapter 9). Moreover, in the current shifting global and regional power contests and the possibility of renewed arms races, it would seem to be in the enlightened self-interest of the vast majority of states to work for a truly rule-based international system with obligatory peaceful dispute settlement and more enforceable international law.

Every country in the world has something resembling a legal system, to varying degrees of efficacy, and is accustomed to the idea of judicial dispute resolution; the imposition of an international rule of law should be no great leap of imagination for any nation. Certainly, multiple UN statements and declarations (see below) testify to a consensus on the merit and centrality of the international rule of law for a viable global order. It is also hard to imagine any international system which could be deemed to be humane or civilized, by any definition, that is not based on the rule of law and duly constituted, legitimate international legal institutions.

The notion of "peace through law" is a key precept embedded at the heart of the modern international order, clearly conceived within the context of a variety of interdependent provisions of the current UN Charter. As the first enumerated purpose of the UN, the Charter sketches its system for the centralized monopoly on the use of force, to be employed only in the collective interest (within UN machinery and according to the principles established), and with the "adjustment or settlement of international disputes or situations which might lead to a breach of the peace [to be resolved] in conformity with the principles of justice and international law" (Article 1(1)). This purpose is interdependent with the setting up of a comprehensive system for the regulation of armaments under Article 26 of the Charter (see Chapter 9). As Louis Henkin convincingly argues, the Charter was in fact meant to outlaw war, noting that the terminology of "war" is only used once in the Charter's preamble as the "scourge" wished to be prevented. Instead the Charter uses new technical language in the context of the collective security system it establishes, including "threats to the peace," "breach of the peace," "acts of aggression," and "threat or use of force." Henkin notes that with the Charter, "international law sought to eliminate the word "war," the legal status of war, the institution of war, and the concept of war."[3]

---

[3] Henkin, Louis. 2005. "Symposium, War and Terrorism: Law or Metaphor." *Santa Clara Law Review*, Vol. 45, No. 4, p. 819. http://digitalcommons.law.scu.edu/lawreview/vol45/iss4/2.

More generally and relatedly, the Charter in its preamble, sets out a key goal of the UN to "establish conditions under which justice and respect for the obligations arising from treaties and other sources of international law can be maintained." More particularly, it encourages and establishes the means for "the progressive development of international law and its codification" (Article 13(1)(a)). The International Law Commission was created by the UN General Assembly in 1947 under Article 13(1)(a) and has undertaken a long series of significant studies in relation to its mandate. As a foundational instrument for a reformed international order, the Charter sketches a rather clear path for the progressive maturation of an international legal order, hopeful that the international community will do its homework.

Yet, despite these fundamental goals embedded in the 1945 Charter and in earlier international governance initiatives meant to establish systems for sustainable peace, today we can still meaningfully ask the question as to "[w]hy are scholars and decision-makers so focused on war and not peace more broadly?"[4] Part of the answer is that the conditions necessary for peace (both "positive" and "negative," with the latter being the mere absence of armed conflict and the former involving further integrative cooperation and other salutary features) may be less "observable," because they are more diffuse and involve more interactions and complex institutional interrelationships than do more discrete and event-based battles or wars, however devastating such conflicts may be.

Designing and ensuring a sustainable peace requires the strengthening of multiple parts of the international system, and in particular, we argue, properly implementing an international rule of law and Chapter VI of the Charter, which has also been seriously neglected. A key, indispensable part of the international system – alongside effective collective security institutions/norms and meaningful arms control/disarmament – are strong international legal institutions (see also Chapters 10 and 18, proposing an International Human Rights Tribunal and an International Anti-Corruption Court).

After some notes on the historical process of the establishment of the war prohibition in international law and notions of "peace through law," as well as dovetailing perspectives from modern peace research, this chapter turns to several international norms or institutions which, essentially, remain incomplete and inadequate, including Charter Chapter VI, the International Court of Justice (ICJ) and the International Criminal Court (ICC). It also briefly explores the establishment of an international judicial training institute and a possible office of an international attorney general (as proposed in the 1950s/1960s by Clark and Sohn), as further ways to strengthen the basic international legal infrastructure. Such efforts to make the international legal system more viable are interdependent with the ability to

---

[4]   Goertz, Gary, Paul F. Diehl, and Alexandru Balas. 2016. *The Puzzle of Peace: The Evolution of Peace in the International System*, Oxford, Oxford University Press, p. 3.

move toward a legitimate and effective (rule-based) collective security mechanism (see Chapter 8), and the potential for meaningful, substantial international disarmament, cutting off perennial arms races (see Chapter 9). Such efforts are particularly urgent given contemporary vicissitudes in international power configurations or aspirations.

FROM KANT TO HABERMAS: IN SEARCH OF A BROADER PERSPECTIVE

War is mischief upon the largest scale.[5]

- Jeremy Bentham

Philosophers and thinkers since at least Diogenes and Dante (see Chapter 2) have set forth a vision of some sort of globally shared *civitas* or rationally organized international order, well before Clark and Sohn and those thinkers proximate to the drafting and adoption of the 1945 UN Charter; the latter can indeed be seen as a testament of the soundness of the ideas of earlier philosophers. One should recall this intellectual history with respect to the centrality of the notion of international law and legal order in many of these visions.

It is not always well known that British philosopher Jeremy Bentham, credited, in fact, with coining the term "international,"[6] set forth a *Plan for an Universal and Perpetual Peace* in the late 1780s. It proposed "a plan of general and permanent pacification for all Europe" through binding treaties, with military reductions, the renunciation of colonies and "a Common Court of Judicature" to settle disputes between nations.[7] Immanuel Kant's 1795 essay on *Perpetual Peace* is more widely known,[8] where he sketches various models of unions of states, formed in service of international peace, and the preliminary requirements to create such a union (e.g., a prohibition on the use of force to interfere with the governments of another nation or annexation of another state's territory, certain laws of war including prohibiting the use of assassins, prohibition of secret reservations to peace treaties where future war is contemplated, the gradual abolition of standing armies, etc.). He also proposes three other conditions he deems as necessary foundations for a deeper, permanent peace among nations, most famously including the republican constitutional nature

---

[5] Bentham, Jeremy. 1789. *The Principles of International Law*, Essays 3 and 4: Of War, Considered in Respect of Its Causes and Consequences and A Plan for Universal and Perpetual Peace, London, Sweet and Maxwell (reprinted 1927).

[6] Crimmins, James E. 2018. "Jeremy Bentham." *The Stanford Encyclopedia of Philosophy* (Summer), Edward N. Zalta (ed.) https://plato.stanford.edu/archives/sum2018/entries/bentham/.

[7] Bentham, *Principles of International Law*.

[8] See also Chapter 2 for additional discussion of Kant's influence on global governance history. Kant, Immanuel (trans. and with introduction and notes by M. Campbell Smith). 1795. *Perpetual Peace: A Philosophical Essay*, London, George Allen & Unwin Ltd.

of their internal governments (as well as entering into a federation of free states and practicing a law of universal hospitality). He describes what he views as the realistic evolution of such a union of states as follows:

> For states, in their relation to one another, there can be, according to reason, no other way of advancing from that lawless condition which unceasing war implies, than by giving up their savage lawless freedom, just as individual men have done, and yielding to the coercion of public laws. Thus they can form a State of nations (*civitas gentium*), one, too, which will be ever increasing and would finally embrace all the peoples of the earth. States, however, in accordance with their understanding of the law of nations, by no means desire this, and therefore reject *in hypothesi* what is correct *in thesi*. Hence, instead of the positive idea of a world-republic, if all is not to be lost, only the negative substitute for it, a federation averting war, maintaining its ground and ever extending over the world may stop the current of this tendency to war and shrinking from the control of law.[9]

Aspects of Kant's vision of a weaker union of states as described has to some extent come true in the "negative" interstate peace generally felt to be established by the United Nations, now embracing essentially all countries of the earth. In terms of the further evolution of the international system, as Kant believed the idea of a genuine and more integrated "perpetual peace" of nations to be a moral and rational ideal (with moral/rational capacities inherent to the human subject), he affirmed its practicality: "[n]ature guarantees the coming of perpetual peace, through the natural course of human propensities; not indeed with sufficient certainty to enable us to prophesy the future of this ideal theoretically, but yet clearly enough for practical purposes."[10]

While the European Enlightenment saw a flurry of "perpetual peace" plans, the intellectual thread has continued, albeit usually not at center stage in international politics, which has tended to be dominated by international relations theorists and what have been called realist thinkers. Austrian jurist and legal philosopher Hans Kelsen wrote a number of works on the international legal system – as it then was and/or how it could or should be – before and around the time of the adoption of the 1945 UN Charter. Like any good jurist, but with a very singular confidence and broadness of view, Kelsen seems to clearly wish to see the international legal system built as a *legal system* parallel to what we find in functional national systems, advocating for the "slow and steady perfection of the international legal order."[11]

Writing *Peace Through Law* in 1944 just before the adoption of the Charter and seeking to learn from the frailties of the League of Nations arrangement, Kelsen was

---

[9]   Ibid., p. 136.
[10] Ibid., p. 157.
[11] Kelsen, Hans. 1944. *Peace through Law*. Chapel Hill, The University of North Carolina Press, p. ix.

adamant that strengthening international law was fundamental to preventing new world wars.[12] He advocated for the holding of individuals to account for war crimes and the *mandatory* settlement of disputes between states at an international court. Conflicts between states should be handled as legal matters, with international court(s) also empowered to develop the law over time, as has occurred in national systems. Kelsen viewed the establishment of mandatory international juridical mechanisms as less controversial than establishing, for example, an international legislature and executive, and more fundamental to the prevention of war and to the creation of a stable international order.

In our time, Jürgen Habermas has taken up the torch, recently criticizing policy-makers, within Europe (given certain events occurring at the time of his writing) and beyond, for what he diagnoses as a "[p]anic-stricken incrementalism betray[ing] the lack of a broader perspective" of the civilizational process of global society within which we find ourselves:

> The enduring *political* fragmentation in the world and in Europe is in contradiction with the systemic integration of a multicultural world society and is blocking progress in the process of legally civilizing violence between states and societies.[13]

He sees the need for

> a convincing new narrative from the perspective of a constitutionalization of international law that follows Kant in pointing far beyond the *status quo* to a future cosmopolitan rule of law: the European Union can be understood as an important step on the path toward a politically constituted world society.[14] (See Chapter 3.)

Indeed, at the international level, we now have functioning supranational legal institutions, such as the Court of Justice of the European Union and the European Court of Human Rights (among other important regional courts), which may point the way for further developments at the international level. Moreover, we have a great deal more technocratic and formal expertise developed in relation to the international administration of justice, with a by now very significant developed body of international law (based on International Law Commission work, decisions of the ICJ, the work of various other UN agencies, other treaty regimes, etc.) yet we seem to have far less self-confidence and assurance than thinkers such as Bentham, Kant, and Kelsen – or merely understanding – of the path on which we are on. Technically we are much better equipped to realize these compelling "civilizational" visions, embracing and reflecting the diversity of the whole of humanity.

---

[12] Ibid. See also, Kelsen, Hans. 1935. *The Legal Process and International Order*, London, Constable & Co.; and Hans. *Law and Peace in International Relations*.

[13] Habermas, J. 2012. "The Crisis of the European Union in the Light of a Constitutionalization of International Law." *The European Journal of International Law*, Vol. 23, No. 2, pp. 335–348, p. 340.

[14] Ibid.

THE THREAD OF HISTORY: EARLY EFFORTS AT
PEACE THROUGH LAW

In order to understand where we currently stand in terms of the evolution of an international legal system, it is also useful to recall parts of the history of the collective thinking, incorporated into early treaty law, which eventually lead to the ideas enshrined in the 1945 Charter. Proposals for a rational, rule-based international order to ensure "durable" peace have, as briefly described, an impressive pedigree of support from major philosophers, and also, a history of vigorous popular transnational civil society advocates who have been active from very early stages of interstate dialogue on international governance and on building a viable international "peace system."[15] As just one remarkable and illustrative example, women's organizations composed of thousands of individuals from 18 countries sent written and telegram messages to sister organizations around the world as well as to the governments of major powers convened by Tsar Nicholas II at the 1899 First Hague Peace Conference. Just one of these extraordinary messages reads as follows:

> We, the women of the United States, extend to the women of Germany sympathetic and affectionate greetings. We feel profoundly grateful that the women of the world have been aroused to the need of international relationship through their desire to support the initiative made by His Majesty the Czar of Russia in behalf of gradual disarmament.
>
> We of the United States regard gradual disarmament, the object of which the Conference at the Hague is convened, as the first step in a perhaps long but straight path which humanity is destined to walk, and which leads undeniably to the goal of universal peace maintained by universal obedience to the decisions of a permanent Court of Arbitration.[16]

As reflected in this telegram, the hope was that international, interstate arbitration – that is, neutral, third-party dispute resolution – along with "gradual disarmament," would be the vehicle to finally put an end to war. Such early "norm entrepreneurs"[17] included what we would now call "grassroots" civil society advocates, but also international officials, civil servants, and prominent diplomats, both active and retired. For example, recent scholarship has shed further light on the importance

---

[15] Fry, Douglas P. 2012. "Life without War." *Science*, Vol. 336, No. 6083, pp. 879–884.

[16] Sewall, May Wright. 1900. "Telegram Sent to Lenore Selena in Support of the International Demonstration of Women for the Peace Conference" in *The International Demonstration of Women for the Peace-Conference of May 15th 1899* edited by Lenore Selena. Munich, August Schupp, p. 70. Gratitude is owed to Professor Hope May and Ms. Taylor Ackerman for bringing greater attention to these valuable materials on early transnational civil society activity for international peace.

[17] Finnemore, Martha and Kathryn Sikkink. 1998. "International Norm Dynamics and Political Change." *International Organization*, Vol. 52, No. 4, pp. 887–917.

of the "Kellogg–Briand Pact" of 1928,[18] so-named for its conceivers, US Secretary of State Frank Kellogg and French Foreign Minister Aristide Briand.[19] The treaty, also known as the Paris Peace Pact, "condemn[ed] recourse to war for the solution of international controversies," and obliged the contracting parties to "renounce it as an instrument of national policy in their relations with one another" (Article 1). States joining the treaty, which included the US, France, Germany, Japan, the USSR, the UK, China, India, and others (for a total of more than 63 states world-wide and virtually all members of the League of Nations) agreed "that the settlement or solution of all disputes or conflicts of whatever nature or of whatever origin they may be, which may arise among them, shall never be sought except by pacific means" (Article 2).

The Pact has traditionally been assumed to be a failure as it did not succeed in preventing, obviously, the slaughter which was World War II. However, Oona Hathaway and Scott Shapiro have recently contested this view of the Pact, and rather position it as a watershed moment in laying the necessary normative ground-work for subsequent developments:

> The Peace Pact was naïve – but not for the reason most think. Outlawing war did work. If anything, it worked too well .... By outlawing war, states renounced the principal means they had for resolving their disputes. They demolished the existing system, which had allowed states to right wrongs with force, but they failed to replace it with a new system. This was in part because there already was an institution – the League of Nations – that seemed poised to resolved disputes. But the League of Nations was built on Old World Order principles. It, too relied on war and the threat of war to right wrongs and enforce the rules. In a world in which war was outlawed, however, the League's enforcement mechanism was grounded in a power that states were reluctant to wield.[20]

Hathaway and Shapiro note that while the "Pact repealed the core principle of the Old World Order" it "did not replace it with a new set of institutions," which would include, for example, a viable collective security mechanism and sufficiently strong peaceful international dispute settlement mechanisms (such as those we are sug-gesting in this book, building on the first efforts of the 1945 Charter). In the wake of the carnage of World War II and the failure of the League and related endeavors (including the Paris Peace Pact), the 1945 UN Charter constituted the next very significant advance in establishing and fleshing out crucial new international norms, with, also, an attempt to establish and pave the way for new institutions and mechanisms to support these norms. The Charter indeed could be seen to be

---

[18] *General Treaty for Renunciation of War as an Instrument of National Policy*, signed at Paris, August 27, 1928.

[19] Hathaway, Oona Anne and Scott Shapiro. 2017. *The Internationalists: How a Radical Plan to Outlaw War Remade the World*, New York, Simon & Schuster.

[20] Ibid., pp. xvi–xvii.

another quantum leap forward in establishing the binding obligation of peaceful settlement of international disputes and has been dramatically successful in many respects in greatly reducing the incidence of interstate war since 1945 (e.g., see the range of studies cited in Goertz et al.)[21] What is probably critical to realize at this juncture in history, is that the institutions, procedures, and basic knowledge of the need for a strong collective security system and peaceful international dispute resolution among national decision-makers, in practice, still remains dangerously weak; we are still in the middle of an important institution-building phase (and a phase of understanding the basic logic of the system meant to be established in 1945), as we take forward the "civilizational process" mentioned by Habermas.

MODERN PEACE RESEARCH

Contemporary peace research affirms that important international norms, gaining progressively widespread traction, do matter, as do supranational institutions, which provide opportunities for nonviolent international dispute resolution. In the "first systemic and comprehensive data set on international peace," Goertz et al. sketch how a normative "tipping point" was reached with the "hugely influential" norms on territorial integrity promulgated in the UN Charter and in the post-1945 era.[22] It has been shown empirically that boundary and territorial disputes are a prime cause of interstate conflict or "war," and Goertz et al. show, based on their comprehensive analysis, how the new international norms and the increasing range of international conflict management mechanisms available, including mediation and adjudication, have indeed led to the remarkable post–World War II "long peace" marked by a very significant statistical decline in interstate war.[23]

Hathaway and Shapiro likewise note the dramatic transition with respect to territorial annexation, pointing to an even earlier demarcation of a new international norm "taking hold" from the time of the Kellogg–Briand Pact:

> The New World Order is not simply the law. States actually obey it. There have been breaches, of course – for example, Russian president Vladimir Putin's brazen annexation of the Crimea in 2014. But the disparity between the world before and after the Peace Pact is extraordinary. Russia's seizure of Crimea is the first significant territorial seizure of its kind in decades ... in the century before 1928, states seized territory equal to eleven Crimeas a year on average ... the likelihood that a state will suffer a conquest has fallen from *once in a lifetime to once or twice a millennium* [emphasis in original].[24]

---

[21] Goertz et al., *The Puzzle of Peace*, p. 2.
[22] Ibid., pp. 4 and 7–8.
[23] Ibid., pp. 13 and 17–18.
[24] Hathaway and Shapiro, *The Internationalists*, pp. xvii–xviii.

Goertz et al. note the declining utility of the use of force as a means to tackle modern conflict, confronting "realist" assumptions head on that the use of force is generally the preferable or the common "go to" option.[25] In fact, furthering this observation, Azar Gat notes that "[a] map of the world's 'zones of war' strikingly reveals the correlation, and suggests the causal relationship, between modernization and peace."[26] He suggests the reason "is that the violent option for fulfilling human desires has become much less promising than the peaceful option of competitive cooperation … [and] [f]urthermore, the more affluent and satiated the society and the more lavishly people's most pressing needs are met."[27]

However, at the same time Gat warns that

> much of humanity is still going through the process of modernization, and is affected by its pacifying aspects, while struggling to catch up and charting various cultural and national paths, some of which are and may remain illiberal and undemocratic… [while at the same time] some parts of the world have so far failed in their efforts to modernize, yet experience many of the frustrations and discontents of that process.[28]

Such an observation puts in relief the crucial nature of other aspects and purposes of the United Nations (e.g., related to social and economic development), and the international system more generally in facilitating the delivery of sound, participatory governance and a measure of shared prosperity at the national level. Establishing international institutions on a firmer democratic footing (see Chapters 4 to 6 on enhancements to the General Assembly as it currently stands), improving global anticorruption and human rights oversight (see Chapters 11 and 18), and ensuring economic and environmental sustainability (see Chapters 13–16) are all vital initiatives in this respect.

UNITED NATIONS WORK ON THE INTERNATIONAL RULE OF LAW

The unanimously adopted 2015 Sustainable Development Goals exemplify a recent strong example of the international community's embrace of the central goal and importance of establishing and strengthening the "rule of law" at the international and national levels, across issue areas. In particular, Goal 16 is to "[p]romote peaceful and inclusive societies for sustainable development, provide access to justice and build effective, accountable and inclusive institutions at all levels," with

---

[25] Goertz et al., *The Puzzle of Peace*, p. 152.
[26] Gat, Azar. 2017. *The Causes of War and the Spread of Peace: But Will War Rebound?* Oxford, Oxford University Press, p. 245.
[27] Ibid., p. 250.
[28] Ibid., p. 251.

a specific target to "[p]romote the rule of law at the national and international levels and ensure equal access to justice for all."[29]

As mentioned, the UN Charter sought to establish, in 1945, the fundaments of an international order based on the rule of law. Building significantly on this foundation, within the last 20–25 years especially, a host of official international statements issued by various UN bodies and UN members collectively have reiterated an international commitment to the "rule of law" as a key principle in establishing a workable global order, as well as in addressing a range of specific issues of concern. The intensification of references to the rule of law as a governing principle at the global level was likely facilitated by a post–Cold War environment marked by fewer "ideological tensions" and far greater consensus for the governance model of "democratic polity founded on the rule of law," as reflected in the work of the United Nations (see, e.g., the bold 1996 report, *An Agenda for Democratization*, submitted by UN Secretary General Boutros Boutros-Ghali to the General Assembly).[30]

The UN General Assembly first notably considered the 'the rule of law' in connection with its 1993 Vienna World Conference on Human Rights, which convened representatives of 171 states, with some 7,000 participants overall, to chart out a new international human rights agenda.[31] The Office of the High Commissioner of Human Rights was subsequently established, with the Third Committee of the General Assembly also adopting annual resolutions on "strengthening the rule of law" from 1993 until 2002, reaffirming that "the rule of law is an essential factor in the protection of human rights, as stressed in the [Universal] Declaration [of Human Rights], and should continue to attract the attention of the international community."[32] Recent statements of the Human Rights Council have noted that "human rights, democracy and the rule of law are interdependent and mutually reinforcing," referring to work of the Secretary General to "address[...] the ways and means of developing further the linkages between the rule of law and the three main pillars of the United Nations: peace and security, human rights and development."[33]

[29] United Nations General Assembly. 2015. *Transforming Our World: The 2030 Agenda for Sustainable Development*, September 25, UN Doc. A/RES/70/1.

[30] Wouters, J., Bart De Meester, and C. Ryngaert. 2004. *Democracy and International Law*, Leuven, Leuven Interdisciplinary Research Group on International Agreements and Development (LIRGIAD), p. 4.

[31] United Nations. 2016. *The Rule of Law in the UN's Intergovernmental Work*. www.un.org/ruleoflaw/what-is-the-rule-of-law/the-rule-of-law-in-un-work/.

[32] United Nations General Assembly. 2002. *Strengthening the Rule of Law*, February 27, 2003, UN Doc. A/RES/57/221.

[33] United Nations General Assembly. 2015. *Human Rights, Democracy and the Rule of Law*. Resolution adopted by the Human Rights Council, March 23, UN Doc. A/HRC/28/L.24, p. 2; citing the UN Secretary General in United Nations General Assembly. 2014. *Strengthening and Coordinating United Nations Rule of Law Activities*. Report of the Secretary General, July 24, 2014, UN Doc. A/69/181.

The UN World Summit in 2005, and the resulting World Summit Outcome document, adopted unanimously by all world leaders convened, was another prominent occasion where the "rule of law" was highlighted as a key area of shared commitment.[34] The Outcome document delineates four areas of priority needing investment in order to "create a more peaceful, prosperous and democratic world": (1) development; (2) peace and collective security; (3) human rights and the rule of law; and (4) strengthening the UN.[35] The world leaders noted that "good governance and the rule of law at the national and international levels are essential for sustained economic growth, sustainable development and the eradication of poverty and hunger."[36] A section of the Outcome document devoted to the rule of law reiterated UN members' commitment to "an international order based on the rule of law and international law" and recognized the need for "universal adherence to and implementation of the rule of law at both the national and international levels."[37]

Following the World Summit, "The Rule of Law at the National and International Levels" was added to the agenda of the Sixth Committee (Legal) of the General Assembly, with a series of Assembly resolutions on that theme from 2006 to 2016, as well as annual reports on "Strengthening and coordinating United Nations rule of law activities" produced by the Secretary General.[38] A 2012 High Level Meeting on the Rule of Law was held upon the opening of the 67th Session of the General Assembly, where member states made over 400 pledges to advance rule of law concretely at the national and international levels, and, in their Declaration, among other things, "reaffirm[ed] that human rights, the rule of law and democracy are interlinked and mutually reinforcing and that they belong to the universal and indivisible core values and principles of the United Nations."[39]

The above is a sample of some of the notable highlights in recent UN rule of law "discourse," which stretches across a range of bodies and thematic areas, including also, for example, such issues as counterterrorism, transitional justice, gender equality, international development and sustainability, among other matters. The Security Council first introduced "rule of law" language into resolutions in 1996, and has engaged with this concept in a number of ways, including, for example, with the establishment of the special criminal tribunals for Rwanda and the former Yugoslavia, making referrals to the ICC, and passing resolutions in relation to rule of law as a key component in post-conflict peace-building situations.

---

[34] United Nations General Assembly. 2005. *2005 World Summit Outcome*, October 24, UN Doc. A/RES/60/1.

[35] Ibid., p. 3.

[36] Ibid., principle no. 11, p. 2.

[37] Ibid., p. 29.

[38] The reports and other key documents are available at www.un.org/ruleoflaw/key-documents/.

[39] UN General Assembly. 2012. *Declaration of the High-Level Meeting of the General Assembly on the Rule of Law at the National and International Levels: resolution/adopted by the General Assembly*, November 30, A/RES/67/1, p. 2.

THE NEED FOR AN INTERNATIONAL CULTURAL SHIFT

The legitimacy and soundness of the rule of law as the basis for the conduct of international affairs has been clearly recognized in authoritative "top down" international statements, endorsed by global political leaders representing virtually all of humanity, as well as in the incisive prescriptions of major thinkers, civil society advocates and far-sighted diplomats. If there is going to be further concrete progress on this topic and the political will to push through major reforms, there will likely also have to be the further cultivation of the necessary cultural conditions responding, for example, to the sociological/anthropological observation that "[t]he rule of law presupposes the coming together of commitment to common values (which are marked, at the level of custom, by the presence of spontaneous and collective sanctions such as moral disapproval) and of the existence of explicit rules and sanctions and normalized procedures."[40] Fortunately, however, we already see such trends in the cultural embrace of key international legal rules, as noted by Hathaway and Shapiro, and Goertz et al., above (see also, for example, the work of Harold Koh and others analyzing why many states might generally obey international law most of the time, despite the absence of vigorous enforcement).[41]

Education, therefore remains of supreme importance, certainly of the general public, who may be too easily manipulated by misinformation about more remote international institutions,[42] but also of the intelligentsia and "elites" of various nations.[43] Foreign service, diplomatic, and military personnel and leadership at all levels, too frequently still remain within exclusively military security or geopolitical perspectives in their approaches to international affairs and national security, and often do not have adequate knowledge of the primacy, practical operation, and fundamental purposes of international dispute resolution institutions. There is still insufficient training, at global, regional and national levels, of international diplomats in the peaceful settlement of international disputes and collective security as core aims of the post-1945 world order. Policymakers around the world should better understand the basic logic of why judicial dispute resolution is (far) superior to a "solution" by use or threat of force, for rational, ethical and very compelling financial and practical reasons. The international community is wont to complain

---

[40] Bourdieu, P. 1987. "The Force of Law: Toward a Sociology of the Juridical Field." *The Hastings Law Journal*, Vol. 38 (July), pp. 805–853.

[41] Koh, Harold Hongju. 1997. "Why Do Nations Obey International Law?" *Faculty Scholarship Series*. 2101. https://digitalcommons.law.yale.edu/fss_papers/2101).

[42] See Chapter 19. Education of the global public about enhanced international institutions is vitally important, in order that populations around the world understand their rationale and basic workings

[43] See, e.g., May, with a view on the requirement of elite buy-in to establish rule of law systems/culture. May, C. 2014. "The Rule of Law as the Grundnorm of the New Constitutionalism," in S. Gill and A.C, Cutler (eds.) *New Constitutionalism and World Order*, Cambridge, Cambridge University Press, pp. 63–75.

of the costs of various international tribunals (for example, international criminal tribunals); but these institutions, if invested in to be significantly more effective, are much cheaper than renewed arms races and "preventative" military expenditures (which, in fact, often have the opposite effect and destabilize relationships or situations in classic "security dilemma" scenarios; see Chapter 9).

Additionally, anthropologists have more recently weighed in in terms of analyzing the social conditions necessary for a durable peace among groups of administrative or "territorial sub-units," which would include, for example, states at the international level. Douglas Fry, in *Science*, has set forth a theory where he identifies at least six characteristics of "peace systems" among disparate groups of nations or other human communities.[44] The characteristics include: an overarching social identity; interconnections among subgroups; interdependence; nonwarring values; symbolism and ceremonies that reinforce peace; and, superordinate institutions for conflict management. Fry's examples of such systems include the Upper Xingu River basin tribes of Brazil, the Iroquois Confederacy of upper New York State, and the European Union (see Chapter 3 on the latter). Federated states, of course, are also a genre of a stable "peace system," likely possessing of the requisite characteristics identified by Fry. The international community at present has very substantial interdependence, and perhaps increasing interconnections among subgroups (in particular within various regions), but remains greatly lacking in the other characteristics identified by Fry, including adequate superordinate institutions for conflict management.

AN "UTTERLY UNSATISFACTORY STATE OF AFFAIRS": SUGGESTIONS FOR INSTITUTIONAL ENHANCEMENTS

In comparison with domestic legal systems, notes the great modern Italian jurist, Antonio Cassese, "the position of the international community appears totally rudimentary" in relation to promoting compliance with law and the preventing or settlement of international disputes in a compulsory and binding fashion.[45] With some exceptions, the international legal system has not yet matured into what might be considered a true rule of law system, and further vital steps should be taken toward remedying what Cassese has termed an "utterly unsatisfactory state of affairs."[46] Indeed, since the adoption of the 1945 UN Charter, types of mandatory and binding dispute settlement systems have developed in relation to various specific

---

[44] Fry, *Life without War*.
[45] Cassese, Antonio. 2005. *International Law (Second ed.)*, Oxford, Oxford University Press, pp. 278–279.
[46] Ibid., pp. 283–284, referring specifically to the situation under the Charter's current terms where "States are mandated to try to settle their differences by means other than force," but this "stringent obligation is accompanied by complete freedom of choice as to the means of settlement."

topics (such as in trade and the international regulation of the law of the sea), which show the international community's readiness to engage in such binding settlement, and present models that could be drawn upon for reform in other areas.

This section suggests overview perspectives on what we deem as necessary and fundamental enhancement of Chapter VI of the current UN Charter on the peaceful settlement of disputes, including, in particular, the strengthening of the ICJ. We also discuss the ICC as a key institution in the modern international order, the requirement of greatly enhanced international judicial training as a corollary to enhanced institutions, and a possible eventual office of UN Attorney General.

Obligations under Chapter VI of the Charter of the United Nations

Given the key place that the peaceful settlement of disputes was meant to play in the modern international order, Chapter VI on the Pacific Settlement of Disputes, which has not been implemented within the international system to the extent anticipated in 1945, is a notably unrealized attribute of the Charter. As discussed in Chapter 8 on the establishment of an International Peace Force – and as described above, in relation to the evolution of an international system away from the arbitrary and unpredictable use of force – peaceful settlement of disputes among states is a core principle that is also linked to viable collective security, prohibitions on the unilateral use of force, and disarmament; the latter become very difficult to realize without it. Perhaps because of historical biases toward notions of military security (and the mainstream assumption that states will always seek to jockey for "hard power"; contradicted by scholars such as Gat and others), Chapter VI remains largely an afterthought, both in academic and policy circles.

Article 2(3) of the Charter sets out the obligation of all UN members to "settle their international disputes by peaceful means in such a manner that international peace and security, and justice, are not endangered." Article 33(1) subsequently sets out a nonexhaustive "menu" of ways states may settle their dispute if it is likely to endanger the maintenance of international peace and security: "negotiation, enquiry, mediation, conciliation, arbitration, judicial settlement, resort to regional agencies or arrangements, or other peaceful means of their own choice" (see discussion in Chapter 8). Article 33(2) empowers the Security Council to "call upon" the parties to settle their disputes by such means when it deems it necessary in the interests of international peace and security, with other Articles under Chapter VI also giving the Security Council powers of recommendation in relation to conflicting parties or situations. However, unlike Chapter VII action by the Security Council, the consensus is that such suggestions of the Security Council are not binding on members. It is reported that John Foster Dulles, while serving as the US Secretary of State in the 1950s under President Eisenhower, had considered reforms to strengthen the pacific settlement of disputes as a priority topic in Charter revision, among several other matters, in the scope of a general Charter review conference that was meant to be held within 10 years of its adoption (he eventually abandoned hope of such a conference due to the Soviet position at the time, among other concerns).[47]

In relation to what has been accomplished under this Chapter since 1945, Tomuschat notes that "[a]ll observers agree that the SC [Security Council] has achieved only modest results in implementing Article 33(2) and more generally within the entire framework of Chapter VI," commenting that "[a]pparently, the institutional pressures exerted upon the parties to a dispute in accordance with Chapter VI are somewhat lacking in persuasive impact."[48] Also, if one accepts theories of leading by example, it is telling that currently only one permanent member of the Security Council has accepted compulsory jurisdiction of the ICJ (see the following section on the ICJ).

It seems clear that, due to the importance of this norm, Chapter VI should be transformed into a series of hard obligations, with binding procedures for the peaceful settlement of international disputes between parties, before collective security action or other coercive measures are contemplated. A revised Charter Chapter on the peaceful settlement of disputes could include clear procedures in relation to the sequencing and timing of the range of dispute resolution mechanisms currently listed in Article 33(1) ("negotiation, enquiry, mediation, conciliation, arbitration, judicial settlement, resort to regional agencies or arrangements"), striking a balance between some flexible choice as to method and an obligation to engage in peaceful resolution in a timely manner.

There now exist a range of models, for example that of the World Trade Organization (WTO), from which such an improvement could take inspiration. The WTO, currently with 164 state members, employs an innovative, multilayered dispute resolution procedure adopted in 1994, which involves first notification and consultation to find mutually satisfactory solutions, followed by employment of good offices or conciliation by the WTO. If this is not successful, a grievance can be escalated to a complaint to a panel of independent experts, which issues both interim and final reports, with opportunity for further comment and consultation in relation to these reports. A party may subsequently appeal to an appellate body (with monitoring of compliance with its report, and the possibility of countermeasures by the aggrieved party), with a final "appeal" to binding arbitration as the last level of dispute resolution.[49]

---

[47] See Scott, Shirley. 2005. *The Failure of the UN to Hold a Charter Review Conference in the 1950's: The Future in the Past?* ANZLH E-Journal, p. 76.

[48] Tomuschat, Christian. 2012. "Ch. VI Pacific Settlement of Disputes, Article 33," in Bruno Simma, Daniel-Erasmus Khan, Georg Nolte, Andreas Paulus, and Nikolai Wessendorf (eds.) *The Charter of the United Nations: A Commentary*, Oxford Commentaries on International Law series, Third ed., 2 Vols., Oxford, Oxford University Press, Vol. I, pp. 1069–1085, at p. 1085.

[49] See the description in Cassese, *International Law*, pp. 289–291. Other prominent legal scholars have suggested that the international community could generalize and follow the UN Convention on the Law of the Sea (UNCLOS) dispute resolution formula, another modern international dispute resolution system that has been deemed relatively successful.

To facilitate the efficacy of such mechanisms, additional standing bodies or panels of independent experts, such as within the frame of a new global "Mediation and Conciliation Commission," could also be created, whose recommendations would not be binding, except with the consent of the parties. Clark and Sohn in *World Peace Through World Law* suggested a "World Conciliation Tribunal" and a "World Equity Tribunal," with the former performing independent investigation of situations to seek to bring the nations concerned to agreement, and the latter possessing the authority to recommend a solution to a given dispute (while taking care to respect the determination of any crucial legal matters by the ICJ). Such bodies, which could remain complementary to similar bodies at the regional level, were considered to be necessary to ensure conflict prevention and general international or regional stability, and/or to put an end to long-standing and festering conflicts that impede cooperation and further economic and social development. Disputes could be referred to such bodies by the General Assembly or Executive Council, as required, before a conflict or potential conflict has ripened into a destabilizing situation.

In relation to the norms established in Charter Chapter VI, there has been by now widespread (albeit uneven) recourse to and acceptance of peaceful, third-party dispute resolution (primarily, but not exclusively, on a voluntary basis), across a range of important areas, with a truly impressive increase in use of supranational tribunals and other conflict resolution bodies.[50] Such state practice signals a general acceptance, at the "cultural" level, of these mechanisms, and a maturity of the international system, which can be further consolidated and firmly institutionalized. It is very costly if this main Charter mechanism lags far behind contemporary dispute resolution practice, especially as these provisions are meant to deal with very fundamental issues of international peace and security.

The International Court of Justice

Within the Charter's Article 33 list of enumerated methods, which states may employ to fulfill their obligations for the peaceful resolution of their disputes, is "judicial settlement." Again, at the domestic level, every legal system would be endowed with a system of judicial settlement of disputes, central to its operation, ensuring that duly constituted laws are applied and enforced.[51]

The preeminent judicial body created at the time of Charter adoption is found under its Article 92, establishing the International Court of Justice (ICJ) to serve as "the principal judicial organ of the United Nations," tasked with resolving interstate

---

[50] See, e.g., trends noted in Goertz et al. *The Puzzle of Peace.*
[51] Of course, alternative dispute resolution mechanisms such as mediation and arbitration also exist at the national level, but operate in a manner complementary to judicial settlement, and are done "in the shadow of the law" and with the supervision or assistance of the courts, for example in relation to the enforcement of agreements or awards.

disputes. The ICJ functions in accordance with the statute of the court that is annexed to the Charter. Because the ICJ and its statute are incorporated into the Charter, like various other aspects of the Charter, it has remained largely "frozen in time." Although there have been many suggestions for (usually modest) ICJ reform throughout its life, emanating from a variety of sources,[52] reform achievements have been largely confined to "practice directions" and fleshing out supplementary procedural rules relevant to the court's operation. International dispute resolution at more recent international institutions and under other important multilateral regimes (for example, as mentioned above, under the WTO or the UN Convention on the Law of the Sea (UNCLOS), or at various international criminal law tribunals) has, in the modern era, by now outpaced the ICJ in sophistication of design, functional architecture and rules of procedure and evidence. With the proliferation of international laws and intensifying interdependence among countries, which inevitably gives rise to disputes and legal matters to be clarified, a substantial update of the principal judicial organ of the United Nations is by now long overdue.

All members of the United Nations are *ipso facto* parties to the Statute of the ICJ under Article 93 of the Charter, which however, does not grant the court automatic jurisdiction over the parties to a given dispute. The ICJ may take jurisdiction over a case upon the agreement of the parties in relation to a specific dispute, based on a compromissory clause in an individual treaty to which a state is a party, based on what may be deemed to be acquiescence in a given situation, or upon special declarations accepting the compulsory jurisdiction of the court under Article 36(2) of its statute. Currently, states accepting the general compulsory jurisdiction of the court number 73 of the 193 members of the United Nations.[53] That is, less than 40 percent of the UN membership, and including only one of the permanent members of the Security Council, the United Kingdom. Moreover, states making declarations to accept the general compulsory jurisdiction of the court under Article

---

[52] E.g., see those summarized as a result of the work of the International Law Association (ILA) Study Group on UN Reform in: Yee, Sienho. 2009. "Notes on the International Court of Justice (Part 2): Reform Proposals Regarding the International Court of Justice – A Preliminary Report for the international Law Association Study Group on United Nations Reform." *Chinese Journal of International Law*, Vol. 8, No. 1, pp. 181–189.

[53] According to the ICJ website, at the time of writing, the following states have made declarations accepting the compulsory jurisdiction of the court: Australia, Austria, Barbados, Belgium, Botswana, Bulgaria, Cambodia, Cameroon, Canada, Costa Rica, Cote d'Ivoire, Cyprus, Democratic Republic of the Congo, Denmark, Djibouti, Dominican Republic, Dominica, Commonwealth of, Egypt, Equatorial Guinea, Estonia, Finland, Gambia, Georgia, Germany, Greece, Guinea-Bissau, Guinea, Republic of, Haiti, Honduras, Hungary, India, Ireland, Italy, Japan, Kenya, Lesotho, Liberia, Liechtenstein, Lithuania, Luxembourg, Madagascar, Malawi, Malta, Marshall Islands, Mauritius, Mexico, Netherlands, New Zealand, Nicaragua, Nigeria, Norway, Pakistan, Panama, Paraguay, Peru, Philippines, Poland, Portugal, Romania, Senegal, Slovakia, Somalia, Spain, Sudan, Suriname, Swaziland, Sweden, Switzerland, Timor-Leste, Togo, Uganda, United Kingdom of Great Britain and Northern Ireland, and Uruguay (see www.icj-cij.org/en/declarations).

36(2) may also declare certain "carve outs" or exceptions to such compulsory jurisdiction of the court, making its jurisdictional mandate sometimes look like a Swiss cheese of obligations.[54] Such a state of affairs seriously undermines the court's ability to be a true upholder and enforcer of international law.

With respect to the deficits of the ICJ and the international legal system to function as something akin to a "rule of law" system, Judge Rosalyn Higgins, former president of the ICJ, in addition to noting the curtailment of the court's ability to adjudicate based on the requirement of state consent and incomplete enforcement mechanisms, also notes that the executive of the United Nations, the Security Council (which is not itself representative of the UN membership as a whole) is not subject to judicial review. Furthermore, there is a lack of clear hierarchy in the application of international law due to the range of modern international courts and tribunals (e.g., without the ICJ or another tribunal clearly serving as a designated apex "Supreme Court").[55]

Despite these challenges, the ICJ has increasingly been made use of by states, with a noted increase in cases it hears, in particular beginning after the Cold War. At the time of writing, there were 17 cases pending before the Court, and six contentious cases already concluded in 2018. A great range of diverse countries, for example, from Asia, Africa, Latin America, and the Middle East – from all regions of the world – have sought recourse at the court, particularly in recent years. Multiple cases, currently and in past years since the court was established (more than 20 concluded and nine pending), concern territorial and boundary delimitation issues, which, as noted, are, historically, an empirically determined prime cause of interstate war.

Moreover, current cases pending on the ICJ's docket testify to the court being sought as an arbiter within complex or potentially volatile geopolitical conflicts which may pose a risk to regional or international security, and which have proven in whole or in part immune to diplomatic negotiation or solution. Such cases currently include, for example: Application of the International Convention on the Elimination of All Forms of Racial Discrimination (Qatar v. United Arab Emirates); Alleged violations of the 1955 Treaty of Amity, Economic Relations, and Consular Rights (Islamic Republic of Iran v. United States of America); Relocation of the United States Embassy to Jerusalem (Palestine v. United States of America). The Marshall Islands, in a series of applications to the ICJ concluded in 2016, on "Obligations concerning Negotiations relating to Cessation of the Nuclear Arms Race and to Nuclear Disarmament," sought to hold the nuclear weapons states of the United Kingdom, India, and Pakistan to account under their

---

[54] For example, Australia carves out, among other things, certain maritime delimitation issues, Canada, among other things, certain fisheries matters, and India, among other things, disputes relating to situations of hostilities, armed conflicts, self-defense, etc. Ibid.

[55] Higgins, R. 2007. "The Rule of Law: Some Skeptical Thoughts. Lecture at the British Institute for International and Comparative Law." Annual Grotius Lecture, London, October 16.

international obligations. While these latter cases were narrowly dismissed on a conclusion that "no legal dispute" was found (not uncontroversially), and did not proceed to an evaluation on the merits of the complaints, it shows the potential of even the smallest states to seek justice in the international arena before the court.

A redrafted Chapter XIV should give the ICJ general, compulsory jurisdiction under a revised UN Charter, with the General Assembly or Executive Council (replacing the current Security Council), in a binding fashion, also enabled to submit particular international disputes directly to the ICJ, if extrajudicial dispute resolution processes such as mediation or conciliation have proven unsuccessful or inappropriate. The jurisdiction of the ICJ over international legal disputes would thus be mandatory for all UN members, overturning the current voluntary approach of the court which requires states' agreement. The ICJ would henceforth have compulsory jurisdiction over all substantive matters pertaining to the interpretation and/or enforcement of international law, thus covering the matters outlined in Article 36(1) and (2) of the Court's statute, and other matters deemed appropriate within the revised Charter system (for example, judicial review of executive action), including the interpretation and application of a UN Bill of Rights (see Chapter 11) and a revised Charter itself.

Reforms are also needed of both the statute and procedural rules of the ICJ, in order to make it more modern, fair, and effective.[56] To protect the Court's independence and impartiality, the tenure of the 15 ICJ judges could be limited to one 9-year or 12-year term and the practice of appointing judges from the Security Council's "P5" nations, as well as ad hoc judges from the states party to litigation, would cease.[57] The judges of the reformed ICJ could be elected through strengthened procedures to ensure impartiality and the highest levels of competence; for example, by the General Assembly from candidate lists provided by the International Law Commission (giving due regard to global/regional distribution), after seeking recommendations from members of the highest courts of justice of member states, associations of international lawyers, and prominent legal academics. Other reforms could enhance the Court's advisory functions (expanding those bodies able to request an advisory opinion); powers to collect evidence and compel

---

[56] See, for example, the range of reforms proposed by Sir Geoffrey Palmer, who served as Attorney General, Deputy Prime Minister and Prime Minister of New Zealand, as well as a Judge ad hoc before the ICJ. Palmer, Geoffrey. 1998. "International Law and the Reform of the International Court of Justice," in A. Anghie and G. Sturgess (eds.) *Legal Visions of the 21st Century: Essays in Honour of Judge Christopher Weeramantry*. Alphen aan den Rijn, Kluwer Law International, pp. 579–600.

[57] Under the statute of the ICJ, "judges of the nationality of each of the parties" retain a "right to sit in the case before the Court" (Article 31(1)). Practice has shown that in the great majority of cases, these judges appear to side consistently with the party to the dispute with which they share a nationality. See, e.g., the analysis of Posner, Eric A. and Miguel de Figueiredo. 2005. "Is the International Court of Justice Biased?" *Journal of Legal Studies*, Vol. 34, June. www .ericposner.com/Is%20the%20International%20Court%20of%20Justice%20Biased.pdf.

testimony; supervise and oblige compliance with provisional or interim orders and final decisions; grant access to additional interested parties beyond states to intervene, submit amicus briefs or to be granted standing in certain contexts; and generally increase the resources of the Court and support for its judiciary. This would include the capacity to employ additional court-management and legal staff having expertise in the diverse, specialized areas of international law which are more frequently coming before the court. Enforcement of the judgments of the ICJ would also be supported by the Executive Council, in consultation with the General Assembly, through enforcement supervision and dialogue, sanctions or other measures deemed necessary to ensure compliance. As the international court system is enhanced, the hierarchies and interactions of the various international courts and tribunals and main organs of the United Nations (e.g., in relation to judicial review of executive action or international legislation passed) will also have to be thought through and coherently mapped.

One important model to explore (and/or improve upon) in the reform of the ICJ is the supranational Court of Justice of the European Union (CJEU), with its evolved architecture and functions (for example, the ability to issue binding preliminary rulings and the possibility of infringement procedures, among other things). Before the CJEU, not only states, but also organs of the European Union and individuals can be admitted as parties in certain circumstances. Such a wider granting of standing, subject to certain thresholds and criteria, as well as other capacities that the CJEU has acquired over time to be a more genuine interpreter and enforcer of European law, should be considered for a renewed ICJ, given the very crucial issues which are addressed by modern international law (e.g., biodiversity and climate among a range of other crucial issues). Efforts should be made to ensure that the ICJ may systematically activate actual implementation and enforcement of international law at the national level.

The International Criminal Court

Among the most dramatic achievements in the updating and enhancement of the international legal architecture in the post-1945 Charter world was the adoption of the constituting Rome Statute in 1998, and the commencement of operations of the International Criminal Court (ICC) some four years later, with its seat in the Hague, Netherlands. The then UN Secretary General Kofi Annan recognized the Statute of the ICC as a "gift of hope for future generations."[58] Certainly, since opening its doors, the Court has, in the public imagination, often become synonymous with a tribunal of last resort for civilian populations around the world seeking redress for ills

---

[58] United Nations, July 20, 1998, *Secretary General Says Establishment of International Criminal Court Is Gift of Hope to Future Generations*, Press Release SG/SM/6643 L/2891. www.un.org/press/en/1998/19980720.sgsm6643.html).

committed by unchecked powerful actors. The Court receives a regular surfeit of communications from civil society actors and others, complaining of general human rights abuses and other malfeasance outside its remit, and it has been argued, for example, that generalized governmental corruption (see Chapter 18) and a crime of "ecocide" should be added to the types of issues it may prosecute, among other matters. However, under its statute, the ICC currently has a mandate to prosecute individuals for the serious international crimes of genocide, crimes against humanity, war crimes, and the crime of aggression, although, as noted, many have called for a wider mandate that could include other well-established international crimes.[59] Prosecution of the notorious international crimes currently included in the Rome Statute might be considered to uphold the most basic tenets of an international civilization, with, in particular "war crimes," forming one of the oldest areas of international law found within the corpus of international humanitarian law (the source of those offenses considered to be "war crimes"), dating from at least the first Geneva Convention of 1864.

Such an "international penal tribunal" was also foreseen in the Genocide Convention of 1948,[60] adopted in the same year as the Universal Declaration of Human Rights. The modern foundations for the establishment of such a permanent international court are usually traced to the Nuremberg and Tokyo Trials of 1945–1948 in the wake of World War II, which were in turn preceded by unsuccessful attempts to prosecute leading figures responsible for World War I.[61] The idea received a further substantial boost when the Security Council took the unique and unprecedented step of establishing two ad hoc, supranational tribunals in the light of the global moral outrage felt in response to the brutal conflicts and humanitarian massacres witnessed in Rwanda and the former Yugoslavia:[62] In 1993, the International Criminal Tribunal for the Former Yugoslavia (ICTY), and in 1994, the International Criminal Tribunal for Rwanda (ICTR). Other ad hoc tribunals, specific to certain situations, have followed since (for example, the Special Court for Sierra Leone (SCSL), the Extraordinary Chambers in the Courts of Cambodia (ECCC), the Special Tribunal for Lebanon (STL), the Special Panels for Serious Crimes in East Timor (SPSC), the State Court of Bosnia Herzegovina (Court of BiH), the Kosovo Specialist Chambers and Specialist Prosecutor's Office (KSC), etc.).

---

[59] The model of the 1994 International Law Commission draft Statute, in fact, included a much wider range of international crimes that linked subject matter jurisdiction to the relevant treaty that states had signed up to, for example, those addressing terrorism, drug trafficking and piracy.

[60] *Convention on the Prevention and Punishment of the Crime of Genocide,* Article VI.

[61] The "grave breaches" as a category of war crimes included in the 1949 Geneva Conventions also placed a duty on contracting states to criminalize these crimes, to search out, punish or extradite perpetrators, and to prevent and suppress the commission of these crimes.

[62] Many would argue that this was a "fig leaf" response, due to the inability of the UN Security Council to agree on and adopt more robust measures to intervene to halt the carnage at the time (see Chapters 7 and 8).

Rather than focusing on discrete or regional conflicts in an ad hoc manner, the ICC is designed to be a permanent fixture in the international order, open to all states of the world to join. In order for the ICC to take jurisdiction and prosecute a given case, the territorial and nationality principle applies as a general rule:[63] Either the state on whose territory the crime in question has taken place or the state whose nationality the alleged perpetrator possesses must be contracting parties to the Rome Statute.[64] Furthermore, the ICC will only act if national proceedings in relation to a given case do not take place, based on the principle of "complementarity" which gives a priority to domestic proceedings. Only if national authorities are inactive or otherwise "unable" or "unwilling" to genuinely investigate or prosecute a particular case will the ICC step in. ICC proceedings can be triggered by three mechanisms; (1) upon referrals by states party to the Rome Statute; (2) by the UN Security Council, in which case the Court's jurisdiction is potentially universal; or (3) on the independent initiative of the Prosecutor, subject to judicial authorization. The range of ICC investigations since the establishment of the court have been triggered by all three of these means, with the UN Security Council referring two situations concerning nonparty states, in Darfur, Sudan,[65] and Libya, to the ICC.

The ICC has managed, to date, to issue 45 public indictments and to secure eight convictions (including four contempt of court convictions) and two acquittals, while several cases have been terminated (due to death of the suspect, insufficiency of evidence, or a transfer of the case to the national level), with upwards of 15 suspects remaining at large. This latter statistic illustrates, among other things, the difficulty often found in bringing indictees into custody, in particular if they are highly ranked political figures or powerful warlords. Reflecting its universal mandate, the ICC Office of the Prosecutor, at the timer of writing, had "preliminary examinations" open in connection with situations in countries as disparate as Afghanistan, Bangladesh/Myanmar, Colombia, Iraq/UK, Palestine, Nigeria, and The Philippines, among others. It had moved to the investigation phase in 11 additional situations, including in relation to situations in Georgia (South Ossetia), and a range of African nations, the majority of which were self-referrals to the court by the individual states or by the UN Security Council.

---

[63] If it is the UN Security Council that refers the situation, however, these limitations do not apply.

[64] Or have otherwise accepted the jurisdiction of the Court under Article 12(3); a state which is not a party to the Rome Statute may, "by declaration lodged with the Registrar, accept the exercise of jurisdiction by the Court with respect to the crime in question."

[65] This referral led to the issuance of arrest warrants for Sudanese President Omar al-Bashir in 2009 and 2010 for crimes against humanity, war crimes and genocide in Darfur. This was the first head of state wanted by the ICC, and also the court's first genocide charge. The UN Security Council, although referring the situation to the ICC, has subsequently not ensured al-Bashir's arrest.

The ICC weathered significant active opposition, in particular by the US, in its early years in terms of its potential jurisdiction over nonparty nationals,[66] as well as more recent campaigns again by the US, and led by some governments affiliated with ICC suspects, such as in Sudan and Kenya, accusing it of neocolonial bias. Recent criticisms have also plagued the court in relation to the length of proceedings, and low numbers of convictions to date; however, these issues are not unknown "growing pains" witnessed in other novel international legal institutions (for example, those confronting the ICTY and ICTR after they first opened their doors; see, e.g., those described by Prosecutor Carla Del Ponte[67]). The court has also faced a range of other exogenous challenges that have negatively affected cases, such as witness tampering, and lack of cooperation by states, leading to noncompliance findings under its statute. However, as Human Rights Watch has recently noted, and, as seen by the list of situations currently being examined – the court is unfortunately needed now more than ever as human rights crises marked by international crimes continue to proliferate;[68] ways must be found to strengthen the court and make it more effective, so that it can better achieve its far-reaching mandate.

The ICC and its Rome Statute, remarkably, have attracted no less than 122 of the 193 UN member states, located in every region of the world, which have voluntarily accepted the court's jurisdiction. One of the main and oft-heard criticisms of the court, however, is that it lacks true international universality, with key international or regional powers such as China, India, Iran, Israel, Russia, Turkey, and the US remaining outside of the ICC's membership.[69] Moreover, because of veto-wielding at the UN Security Council, other situations that might warrant referral to the ICC can currently be thwarted at the UN (for example, efforts to have the Syria situation referred to the ICC have been vetoed by some permanent members of the Security Council (see Chapter 7). Article 16 of the Rome Statute in fact also empowers the Security Council to seek a suspension of an ICC investigation or prosecution.

Therefore, a revised UN Charter should make acceptance of the jurisdiction of the ICC mandatory for all member states of the UN, with the Executive Council (with General Assembly authorization) also referring situations to the ICC, as

---

[66] Bosco, David. 2014. *Rough Justice: The International Criminal Court in a World of Power Politics*, Oxford, Oxford University Press.

[67] Del Ponte, Carla (in collaboration with Chuck Sudetic). 2009. *Madame Prosecutor: Confrontation with Humanity's Worst Criminals and the Culture of Impunity*, New York, Other Press.

[68] See, e.g., Human Rights Watch, December 8, 2018, *Human Rights Watch Statement for the General Debate of the International Criminal Court's Seventeenth Assembly of States Parties.* www.hrw.org/news/2018/12/08/human-rights-watch-statement-general-debate-international-criminal-courts).

[69] However, because of its territorial jurisdiction, several ICC situations have involved allegations against nationals of nonstate parties accused of committing crimes on the territory of ICC state parties (Russian nationals in Georgia or Ukraine, US nationals in Afghanistan, or Israelis in Palestine, etc.).

necessary and without the threat of the use of a veto power.[70] The revised Charter should universally and explicitly oblige member states to fully cooperate with ICC investigations, assist in the execution of its arrest warrants and comply with its decisions, with clear mechanisms for UN remedies and sanctions in response to ICC findings of noncompliance. Outside of UN Charter review and incorporation of the Court as an integral part of Charter obligations owed by all states within the international community, there is much that could be done in terms of interim measures, whether by the strengthening of the Rome Statute through amendment, or within the current Rome Statute framework. For example, this could include protocols in relation to expected or obliged state cooperation with investigations, apprehension of indictees and enforcement of decisions (e.g., the suggestion by former ICTY Prosecutor Carla del Ponte for a small, independent unit under or in cooperation with the Office of the Prosecutor to quickly apprehend and arrest indictees[71]). Adequate and reliable funding, also given the expanded case load of the Court remains also a perennial issue at the Assembly of States Parties.

More generally, in terms of its place in the overall international legal and governance system, the ICC, in the subject matter it covers, charts a transitional pathway toward a rule-based international order where the use of and threat of mass armed force ceases to play a dominant role in the conduct of internal and international affairs. As "great or regional powers" who wish to retain their "military flexibility" (or other nations who are concerned about possible scrutiny in relation to systemic domestic human rights violations; see Chapter 11) have to date avoided commitment to the Rome Statute, yet wider acceptance of the Court would signal a readiness of the international community to hold itself to account for the most basic standards of conduct. It would also likely signal that the international community has made significant steps toward a true collective security regime beyond balance of power politics, genuine progress on systemic disarmament, and the evolution of the Security Council as described in Chapter 7, where no state is to be considered to be "above the law" (see Chapters 7, 8 and 9). It has been noted that India, for example, has expressed its reservations about the role of the UN Security Council (e.g., its investigation/prosecution deferral powers under Article 16), which, from the perspective of that country, is too strong and not representative. Here, the criticism of the ICC may be enmeshed with the well-known criticism of the no longer representative composition of the Security Council.

---

[70] On this issue a current campaign, in fact, seeks to establish the possibility for a UN General Assembly vote for an ICJ advisory opinion on the legality of the exercise of UN Security Council vetoes over ICC referrals, promoted by the Open Society Justice Initiative (OSJI) and several states.

[71] See, e.g., "Del Ponte calls for snatch squad," *BBC News*, March 21, 2002. http://news.bbc.co.uk/2/ hi/europe/1884953.stm). Del Ponte called for a special squad of plainclothes agents, rather than uniformed soldiers, that should be sent to search for a fugitive at the time, Bosnian Serb leader, Radovan Karadzic, after two NATO raids seeking to capture him in Bosnia had failed.

Institute(s) for International Judicial Training

With strengthened international judicial bodies and mechanisms, there will be a heightened need for a skilled and well-trained international judiciary, to lend legitimacy to and confidence in its genuine impartiality and detachment from national or regional political concerns, and a sound understanding of international norms. Currently, there are persistent challenges at various international tribunals; for instance, international criminal tribunals, in relation to the interaction of various legal traditions and judicial approaches to procedural law, among other issues (e.g., with respect to divergences in civil and common law traditions, to highlight one example). There is a pressing need as well to ensure training that fully imprints upon international judges the nature of their international ethical duties and requirements of independence, and more dialogue, formation and education on court management and the conduct of international proceedings.

We propose the establishment of a modern and well-resourced international judicial training institute, possibly in cooperation with or under the auspices of the Hague Academy of International Law. The Institute could undertake and facilitate important, intensive international, national and regional capacity-building and training activities regarding international law – not only in relation to the functioning of the ICJ and the peaceful settlement of disputes, but also, for example, regarding the responsibility of national courts to conduct effective and genuine national proceedings under the ICC Rome Statute, and concerning international human rights norms, when the latter become subject to binding review. Depending on the domestic system for judicial formation, such an institute could take national nominees (to be confirmed subsequently by an international expert body), upon their completion of national judicial training or appointments. International training of a fixed term could be a prerequisite before sitting on any core international tribunal.

Office of the United Nations Attorney General

Many mature legal systems have established a general office of the Attorney General, at the national level, sometimes overlapping with the cabinet level position of a minister of justice, with oversight and system-wide functions related to the maintenance and improvement of the rule of law system of that jurisdiction. In civil law systems, such a posting or similar function (or parts of functions) might be found in the office of the "public prosecutor general" or "advocate general."

Clark and Sohn suggested the establishment of a post of UN Attorney General, to support a strengthened United Nations, in particular to help with enforcement of new laws and regulations under the revised Charter that they suggested, including violations of law under the comprehensive disarmament plan that they set forth.[72] Their centralized posting for Attorney General was to be complemented by a civil police force (which could carry out inspections and investigations), and by regional attorneys general, assisting regional courts in relevant prosecutions with respect to the international norms that they established concerning disarmament, and more broadly.

If the maintenance and integrity of a true international legal system is a key, refreshed and renewed goal of the international community, within a modern, 21st century institutional architecture, the establishment of Attorney General functions and institutional resources could be an important consideration. The (albeit limited) independent prosecutorial functions established already within the ICC, at the macro scale, are an extraordinary step forward in this respect, lighting the way for such offices at the international level, with new institutionalized and independent actors surveying the facts and law for matters in the global public interest, among other functions.

Appointed by the Executive Council and confirmed by the General Assembly, a new office of Attorney General of the UN system could perform functions similar to those provided nationally; for example, to be guardian of the rule of law; to serve as independent legal advisor to executive and legislative bodies on the constitutionality and legality of proposed action or legislation; to advise regarding types of international litigation pursued before various international courts in the global public interest; and to ensure proper administration of justice – including independence of the judiciary – across the international system.

CONCLUSION

It would be nice to see the international community get "back to basics" with respect to the building up of an appropriate, modern infrastructure for a significantly strengthened international rule of law and the peaceful settlement of international disputes, as mandated by the 1945 Charter, but insufficiently followed through; we are currently both blessed and plagued by institutions that are only half-built. It seems that it would be a highly productive investment to fortify and enhance key international legal institutions and explicit state obligations in this respect, given the enormous potential benefits to be gained by the international community. As a value and as a principle, the international rule of law and the peaceful settlement of disputes has been widely and repeatedly affirmed at the highest levels of international governance. Since 1945, work of the International Law Commission, case law of the ICJ, proliferation of international treaties, norms established within the frame of other international organizations or emanating from various UN organs,

---

[72] Clark, Grenville and Louis B Sohn. 1966. *World Peace through World Law: Two Alternative Plans*, Third ed. Cambridge, MA, Harvard University Press, p. 336.

the academic writing on a wide variety of areas by "highly qualified publicists" from various nations, etc., form and provide an extraordinary resource and an important body of work as a basis for the next evolutionary steps to be taken in the international legal system. Moreover, today there are viable models seen in the European Union and elsewhere that can significantly assist in charting the way forward.

As the second decade of the 21st century draws to a close, we seem to be living in a time where – to draw upon Francis Fukuyama's pronouncement – history appears to be restarting, with deeply uncertain and shifting global power configurations and doubt as to whether the so-named "liberal international order" established after World War II will survive. Middle power democracies have begun to band together and are being encouraged to take a global leadership role, in the interests of a stable, rule-based international order.[73] German Foreign Minister Heiko Maas, for example, recently proposed to a Japanese audience in Tokyo, "If we pool our strengths . . . we can become something like 'rule shapers,' who design and drive an international order that the world urgently needs."[74] Basic to any rule-based order are effective, systematic mechanisms for the implementation and enforcement of rules, with properly endowed, legitimate institutions to interpret and uphold those rules; strengthening key institutions for peaceful dispute settlement and to further the international rule of law should be central to the agenda of all those interested in a sustained international peace.

---

[73] Daalder, Ivo H. and James M. Lindsay. 2018. "The Committee to Save the World Order: America's Allies Must Step Up as American Steps Down." *Foreign Affairs*, November/ December.

[74] Ibid.

11

Human Rights for the Twenty-first Century

Whereas it is essential, if man is not to be compelled to have recourse, as a last resort, to rebellion against tyranny and oppression, that human rights should be protected by the rule of law,
Whereas it is essential to promote the development of friendly relations between nations

Universal Declaration of Human Rights (UDHR)

If there is one key to the entire question of war, it is *justice*. A fair world would be a far less conflicted one. Inequality and injustice are ripe causes of social unrest within a society; they have analogues in the international sphere which are heady prompts for conflict.[1]

A.C. Grayling

HUMAN RIGHTS AND GLOBAL GOVERNANCE

Set against the backdrop of the shocking and widespread atrocities committed during World War II, those negotiating the Charter in San Francisco settled on the inclusion of the language of "fundamental human rights" and "human rights and fundamental freedoms," interwoven into important provisions throughout the document.[2] This included mandates for the UN General Assembly and the Economic and Social Council (ECOSOC) to pursue studies and to conduct broader work on the theme. And, importantly, echoing the quotes at the beginning of this

---

[1] Grayling, A.C. 2017. *War: An Enquiry*, New Haven, CT, and London, Yale University Press, p. 234.
[2] This inclusion, building on the very passing reference to human rights in the Dumbarton Oaks Proposals, came after some debate among negotiating states (including a range of Latin American states and the Philippines arguing for stronger human rights provisions) and consultation with civil society representatives, advising in particular the US delegation. See, e.g., Burgers, Jan Herman. 1992. "The Road to San Francisco: The Revival of the Human Rights Idea in the Twentieth Century." *Human Rights Quarterly*, Vol. 14, No. 4, p. 476.

chapter, the new Charter intimately linked the promotion of universal respect for human rights to the "creation of conditions of stability and well-being which are necessary for peaceful and friendly relations among nations," and placed them under one of the several core "Purposes" of the United Nations: "[t]o achieve international co-operation ... in promoting and encouraging respect for human rights and for fundamental freedoms for all without distinction as to race, sex, language or religion."[3] ECOSOC was given the responsibility to form "commissions in economic and social fields and for the promotion of human rights."[4] It promptly convened a Commission on Human Rights in 1946, chaired by Eleanor Roosevelt, which pursued the successful work on the 1948 Universal Declaration on Human Rights (UDHR), laying strong foundations for the modern international human rights landscape we know today. John Foster Dulles, US Secretary of State in the 1950s, who had been engaged in Charter negotiations, called the Human Rights Commission the "soul" of the Charter.[5]

The Charter itself could be considered to be, among many other things, a watershed international human rights treaty, establishing clear and universal commitments for all states that choose to ratify the instrument – which today includes virtually every nation in the world.[6] This should be heartening to realize, as it serves as a basis for substantial further work that is badly needed to strengthen the current international human rights system. The Charter's preamble, moreover, *"reaffirm[s]* faith in fundamental human rights, in the dignity and worth of the human person, in the equal rights of men and women" (emphasis added), seemingly embracing a natural law or preexisting inherent basis for the rights to which it refers, as did prominent precursor national constitutional documents, such as the French and American declarations of the late eighteenth century. On the international plane, the 1919 League of Nations Covenant only included references to several specific human rights concerns, such as labor conditions, treatment of minorities ("native inhabitants") and traffic in women and children.[7]

Regardless of how one might label the moment of Charter adoption along a trajectory of the international human rights "project," it is clear from its text that the promotion of and respect for fundamental human rights, due to the frequency with which it is mentioned, is a central "system characteristic" of the new international order established out of the debris of World War II. Very importantly, according to

---

[3] Articles 55(c) and 1(3) of the UN Charter, respectively.

[4] Article 68 of the UN Charter.

[5] Quoted in Boyle, Kevin. 2009. "The United Nations Human Rights Council: Origins, Antecedents, and Prospects," in Kevin Boyle (ed.), *New Institutions for Human Rights Protection*, Oxford, Oxford University Press, pp. 11–47, 21.

[6] Subedi argues that, pursuant to the relevant provisions of the Charter, the UN has "an obligation to promote, protect and fulfil the rights of the people worldwide." Subedi, Surya P. 2017. *The Effectiveness of the UN Human Rights System: Reform and the Judicialisation of Human Rights*, London and New York, Taylor & Francis, p. 222.

[7] See Article 23 of the Covenant of the League of Nations.

the Charter's own plain wording, such respect was considered necessary to assure a sustainable international peace. From our vantage point, it would be hard to argue that respect for universal human rights would not continue to be a fundamental system characteristic of an updated, modern international order, as was already clear in 1945. The difference today, however, is that we would expect significantly greater intensification, sophistication and progression of these commitments by the international community. Contemporary notions of "good governance" also commonly include indices of accountability, respect for human rights and rule of law, among other things (see Chapter 20 for discussion on this theme).[8] Integrating the notion of human rights into a modality of good governance also implicitly answers the question "for whom" the governance is meant – indicating a governance system that is sincerely meant to promote the interests of and protect the generality of the population. We indeed argue in this book that the international community should strive toward such a goal of competent and values-based global governance, aiming to deliver a level of governance excellence, rather than acquiescing to the lowest common dominator and/or significantly flawed international institutions, which has too often been the case.

It is also difficult to envision a significantly strengthened UN and global governance system without also establishing in parallel a much strengthened international human rights architecture beyond what exists today. As with tackling the issue of corruption at the international level in a meaningful way (see Chapter 18), a shift to more widespread and regularized respect for fundamental human rights at the international level goes to the heart of governance functions across a wide range of issue areas, and speaks to a crucial dimension of the quality of governance itself, at all levels. It would seem necessary to put the range of enhanced international cooperation mechanisms suggested in this book, such as a true collective security facility (e.g., an International Peace Force), enhanced international legislative capacity, the updating of the Security Council to an Executive Council, etc., into the context of much firmer observance of and commitment to international human rights standards, so that these institutions and mechanisms would be subject to and function within an environment marked by shared international goals and values (see Chapter 20). If the international community is to draw substantially closer together in unprecedented collaboration at the global level, it will have to *reaffirm* a still greater commitment to the fundamental shared values embedded in core human rights, building a much more effective supporting international architecture for this goal. The current system within the UN for the implementation and "enforcement" of human rights commitments is still largely "political and

---

[8] See, e.g., discussion in Sano, Hans-Otto. 2007. "Is Governance a Global Public Good?" in Erik André Andersen and Birgit Lindsnaes (eds.),*Towards New Global Strategies: Public Goods and Human Rights*, Leiden, Martinus Nijhoff, pp. 217–236.

diplomatic rather than judicial,"[9] much to its detriment. This deficiency is no longer tenable and should be remedied. We discuss the pathways for such fundamental strengthening later in this chapter, after dealing with some broader background issues relevant to international human rights policy.

CASCADING EFFECTS: THE IMPORTANCE OF HUMAN RIGHTS FOR ONE AND ALL

As with the issue of corruption, spillover effects across borders are seen when there is widespread disrespect for fundamental human rights in another nation.[10] This is made clear in the Charter and the UDHR, with the link expressed between respect for human rights and conditions of international stability and peaceful relations among nations, with the "resort to rebellion" referenced in the UDHR when rights are not protected by rule of law. If we look at the individual rights enshrined in the "International Bill of Human Rights" (commonly understood to include the UDHR, the International Covenant on Economic, Social and Cultural Rights (ICESCR) and the International Covenant on Civil and Political Rights (ICCPR)), it can readily be seen how – in addition to embodying a basic social contract notion of "good governance" between leadership and the general population of a given country – there are a range of obvious (and by now well-documented) cascade effects resulting from the respect of fundamental human rights. Respect for rights helps to ensure wider governance integrity and broader social benefits across a given national system, and increasingly also across the international system, due to the extreme forms of interdependence brought by globalization.

To take just a few examples, the right to freedom of opinion and expression (as enshrined in Article 19 of the ICCPR), bearing on journalistic and civil society freedom and safety, is crucially important to protect against government and private sector corruption and abuses of power, to uphold the rule of law and to assist in ensuring the accountability of public leaders to governance quality standards, among other things. With current levels of transnational commercial and business activity, for example in the multinational enterprise (MNE) sector, populations (and regulators) need to stay informed about the nature of business activity abroad, including in relation to any connections with human rights abuses or corrupt government actors (for example, relevant to standards set by the OECD Guidelines for MNEs).[11] Reliable and thorough information provided by a robust civil space and critical press across the world is crucial to set local and international governance priorities, to ensure responsible business operations and to hold to account

---

[9] Subedi, *The Effectiveness of the UN Human Rights System*, p. 222.
[10] See Chapter 18, which also notes the common linkage between corrupt government actors and systemic human rights abuses, which, however, is not highlighted frequently enough in policy circles.
[11] www.oecd.org/corporate/mne/.

powerful actors who may be undermining the public good, at the national and international levels.

Internationally enshrined standards of gender equality, which have been called "a cardinal principle of the human rights ideology," are "essential for authentic democracy, for political development, for economic development, for population control, and for the preservation of the human environment."[12] Indeed, the World Bank has affirmed that women's empowerment is a key to unlocking economic growth potential, and there is a clear link between the education of girls and access to family planning in addressing climate change, among other issues.[13] On the peace and security front, women's personal security at the national level has been found to be correlated with international security: "[n]ew research … suggests that intimate partner violence may be a predictor of other forms of mass violence, conflict, and state insecurity."[14] There are also security implications of distorted sex ratios in China, for instance, linked to sex-selection abortion.[15] The protection of very fundamental human rights, as enshrined in existing international human rights instruments, is crucial for solving many of the global crises we confront today.

Recent events and scholarship have shown that serious systemic social problems and large-scale instability have been correlated with the lack of certain human rights protections – making the Charter and the UDHR, indeed, seem prescient. It has been widely observed that the aspirations of citizens for greater general freedoms, economic opportunity and respect for human rights led to the 2011 "Arab Spring" and brought serious and at times bloody instability to many countries.[16] Restrictions on religious freedom have been correlated with greater social instability.[17] The absence of quality education and meaningful economic opportunities can be linked to the erosion or malfunction of democratic forms of government, and the rise of

---

[12] Henkin, Louis. 1994. "Preface," in Louis Henkin and John Lawrence Hargrove (eds.), *Human Rights: An Agenda for the Next Century*. Studies in Transnational Legal Policy, No. 26, the American Society of International Law, Washington, DC, p. xv.

[13] For example, see the ranked solutions to arrest climate change offered by Paul Hawken's Drawdown Project: www.drawdown.org/solutions.

[14] Sieff, Michelle. 2017. "Violence against Women and International Security: Why Assault by Intimate Partners Deserves Greater Focus." *Foreign Affairs* (Snapshot), November 28, 2017.

[15] López-Claros, Augusto, and Bahiyyih Nakhjavani. 2018. *The Disastrous Global Crisis of Gender Inequality: Equality for Women = Prosperity for All*, New York, St. Martin's Press, pp. 33–34.

[16] See the discussion in Freedman and Houghton, for example, on the lack of treatment of various human rights situations related to the Arab Spring at the Human Rights Council. Freedman, Rosa, and Ruth Houghton. 2017. "Two Steps Forward, One Step Back: Politicisation of the Human Rights Council." *Human Rights Law Review*, Vol. 17, No. 4, pp. 753–769.

[17] Pew Research Center: Pew Forum on Religion and Public Life (2012, September). *Rising tide of restrictions on religion*, http://assets.pewresearch.org/wp-content/uploads/sites/11/2012/09/RisingTi deofRestrictions-fullreport.pdf; and Pew Research Center: Pew Forum on Religion and Public Life (February 26, 2016). *Latest Trends in Religious Restrictions and Hostilities*, http://assets .pewresearch.org/wp-content/uploads/sites/11/2015/02/Restrictions2015_fullReport.pdf.

forms of extremism or terrorism.[18] Extremes in economic inequality, linked also to lack of an adequate social safety net, basic social services and adequate employment, lead to an underperforming economy generally, in addition to other societally deleterious effects (see also the discussion on economic inequality in Chapter 14).[19] The absence of sufficient social security, accessible quality education and health care blocks upward mobility, opportunity and entrepreneurial creativity within a society.[20]

Given such correlations and connections, human rights should, as much as possible, be depoliticized and viewed instead through the lens of social stability, building capacities for rule-based governance, and forward planning for sustainable social and economic well-being, across diverse societies.

That this process of depoliticization has already been occurring in the international governance sphere is evidenced by the Sustainable Development Goals (SDGs) and the UN 2030 Agenda, which were adopted unanimously by governments worldwide. The range of goals and targets are linked with broad policy/governance aims, with various human rights strongly embedded in the goals and targets. To name just a few examples, Goal 4, "Ensure inclusive and equitable quality education and promote lifelong learning opportunities for all," is a contemporary iteration of ICESCR Article 13. Goal 5, "Achieve gender equality and empower all women and girls," of course supports a basic principle affirmed in the Charter, the UDHR, the ICCPR, the ICESCR and CEDAW (Convention on the Elimination of all Forms of Discrimination Against Women, among other instruments. Goal 16, "Promote peaceful and inclusive societies for sustainable development, provide access to justice for all and build effective, accountable and inclusive institutions at all levels," contains targets related to the combatting of human trafficking, violence and abuse of children, among a range of other concerns, reflecting a number of priority issues in the modern international human rights arena.

The SDGs, indeed, reflect a broader trend in UN policy thinking, where the well-being of the human person is becoming more clearly the focal point and prime beneficiary of governance efforts. A pivotal moment in this evolution occurred when a United Nations Development Program (UNDP) report introduced into the official international discourse the new concept of "human security," calling for an urgent

---

[18] Mertus, Julie A. 2005. *The United Nations and Human Rights: A Guide for a New Era*, Global Institutions Series, Abingdon, Routledge, p. 2.

[19] In the US context, Joseph Stiglitz has thoroughly treated this issue, noting the effects of serious inequality on macroeconomic and financial well-being, and on the rule of law and democracy itself. Stiglitz., Joseph. 2012. *The Price of Inequality*, New York and London, W. W. Norton & Company.

[20] Sweden, for example, has one of the highest social mobility rates in the world, with European countries generally proving more socially mobile than the United States. See Surowiecki, James. 2014. "The Mobility Myth." *The New Yorker*, March 3. www.newyorker.com/magazine/2014/03/03/the-mobility-myth.

paradigm shift in the meaning of security away from: "an exclusive stress on territorial security to a much greater stress on people's security," and "[f]rom security through armaments to security through sustainable human development."[21] Pakistani economist Mahbub ul Haq, who has been credited with introducing the concept, noted that "[w]e need to fashion a new concept of human security that is reflected in the lives of our people, not the weapons of our country."[22] The theme of human security was further advanced at the UN under Secretary-General Kofi Annan and his successors, and has been taken up by, among many others, civil society advocates and Nobel Peace Prize laureates such as Jody Williams.[23]

Indeed, beyond the traditional – and highly distracting – struggles for power among jealous sovereigns, these developments can help us start to understand what it now means "to live in a postimperial global society" and how we may find "common cause with the human beings with whom we share this fragile planet."[24] Notions of human security and, more generally, the placing of a human rights agenda at the forefront, across a range of governance concerns, again, answers the question, "for whom is (global) governance"? Human rights norms, alongside norms of constitutionalism, transparency, fairness and the rule of law (including for the meaningful protection of human rights), may be a key to understanding and designing a viable "post-imperial" world.

CULTIVATING A GLOBAL CIVIC ETHIC AND THE MORAL CASE FOR SIGNIFICANT HUMAN RIGHTS REFORM

The 1995 Commission on Global Governance called for "the broad acceptance of a global civic ethic to guide action within the global neighbourhood" and "courageous leadership infused with that ethic at all levels of society." The Commission added that "without a global ethic, the frictions and tensions of living in the global neighbourhood will multiply; without leadership, even the best-designed institutions and strategies will fail."[25]

Indeed, in tandem with an awareness of the more abstract governmental/governance benefits – at the national, regional and international levels – of a stronger, more functional and impartial international human rights system, there is a need for an ethical commitment at the level of culture. This is necessary to build the social

[21] UNDP. 1994. *Human Development Report*, New York, Oxford University Press, p. 24.
[22] Quoted in: Williams, Jody. 2008. "New Approaches in a Changing World: The Human Security Agenda," in J. Williams, S.D. Goose, and M. Wareham (eds.), Banning Landmines: Disarmament, Citizen Diplomacy, and Human Security. Lanham, MD: Rowman and Littlefield, pp. 281–297, p. 281.
[23] Ibid.
[24] Ignatieff, Michael. 2017. *The Ordinary Virtues: Moral Order in a Divided World*, Cambridge, MA, and London, Harvard University Press, p. 30.
[25] Commission on Global Governance. 1995. *Our Global Neighbourhood: Report of the Commission on Global Governance*, Oxford, Oxford University Press, p. 47.

momentum toward intuitive and second-nature responses – across all facets of global society, including but not limited to governments – that put the respect for human rights as a core concern and felt obligation, across our varied societies.[26]

Eleanor Roosevelt herself famously commented on the extent of the permeation of values throughout a given society that would be necessary in order to truly realize the goals of the UDHR:

> Where, after all, do universal human rights begin? In small places, close to home— so close and so small that they cannot be seen on any maps of the world. Yet they are the world of the individual person; the neighborhood he lives in; the school or college he attends; the factory, farm, or office where he works. Such are the places where every man, woman, and child seeks equal justice, equal opportunity, equal dignity without discrimination. Unless these rights have meaning there, they have little meaning anywhere. Without concerted citizen action to uphold them close to home, we shall look in vain for progress in the larger world.[27]

Such a vision does not simply leave the issue of application and implementation of human rights in the hands of government officials or judges, but re-grounds the "international human rights project" also in the intentions and actions of all people, regardless of what role we play in society.[28] The UDHR, in fact, under its provisions on education, affirms the necessity of general education, in all nations, in further-ance of respect for human rights, as well as of the key international values enshrined in the Charter:

> Education shall be directed to the full development of the human personality and to the strengthening of respect for human rights and fundamental freedoms. It shall promote understanding, tolerance, and friendship among all nations, racial or religious groups, and shall further the activities of the United Nations for the maintenance of peace. (Article 26(2))

Clearly, there has been little systematic follow-through by various governments on this UDHR obligation, which in fact, one can affirm with reasonable confidence, has been greatly overlooked in the designing of national curricula since 1948. The importance of such basic education on human rights should not be disregarded and

---

[26] See, e.g., an examination of the concept of "global civics" – the rights and responsibilities or ethical obligations we might assume, given our global interdependence, drawing from contri-butions with scholars and policy-makers in Chile, China, Egypt, India, Ireland, Turkey, the United Kingdom, Spain, South Africa, Bulgaria, Russia and the United States, in: Altinay, Hakan (ed.). 2011. *Global Civics: Responsibilities and Rights in an Interdependent World*, Washington, DC, Brookings Institution Press.

[27] Quoted in Church Peace Union. 1958. "In Your Hands: A Guide for Community Action on the 10th Anniversary of the Universal Declaration of Human Rights," New York.

[28] SDGs and the 2030 Agenda, indeed, take such an approach, underlining the necessity of the comprehensive action and engagement of all stakeholders, including private actors and individuals, for the realization of the SDGs.

should form part of all future efforts to secure a more viable international order (see Chapter 19, Education for Transformation).

Regardless of the gap in general public and professional education on human rights, the modern proliferation of civil society groups around the world speaks to the internalization of the international human rights mandate as a lived ethic of many people – and as a necessary instrument of survival for various communities. It is a validation of the universality, soundness and importance of international human rights norms, felt by citizens across the world at the grassroots level. For example, the number of nongovernmental organizations (NGOs) globally with ECOSOC consultative status (only ECOSOC-accredited NGOs can in turn apply to participate in the UN Human Rights Council's sessions as Observers) currently stands at 5,163 across all fields, with 24,000 entries included in a wider global civil society database sponsored by the UN Department of Economic and Social Affairs (DESA); a simple search on an independent NGO aggregator/volunteer connection search engine puts the number of civil society organizations dealing with human rights topics around the world at 3,508, which undoubtedly is an incomplete number.[29]

But beyond pockets of activists and dedicated professionals working in the human rights advocacy field in various countries, there may be a question of why other citizens and professionals should care about the international human rights project, in particular when one may have a relative place of privilege in a jurisdiction with established protections for various rights. Why should relatively privileged actors (including, e.g., businesses) care about something as abstract as improving the international institutional architecture for the protection of human rights? Why now, in a seemingly cynical world where the aspirations of the Charter or the UDHR may seem quaint in comparison with contemporary economic and technocratic globalized pursuits that have largely made amoral bargains or engaged in various trade-offs on human rights issues for balance of power, geopolitical stability or trade concerns?

There are the ethical imperatives that arise from simply knowing about the various types of human rights abuses that are occurring around the world. We are an information- and media-rich international society, with by now well-developed human rights reporting and monitoring mechanisms, both (inter)governmental and private; for example, well-supported international organizations such as Human Rights Watch and Amnesty International (both created post-1945), which have unprecedented reporting and citizen engagement capacity. At the time of writing, we need only look at the daily news to see the range of dramatic and ongoing human rights crises around the world, across regions, including in Yemen, Myanmar, Syria and Venezuela, to name a few. Moreover, recent reports by the UN Special Rapporteur on extreme poverty and human rights in relation to the United States

---

[29] See: ECOSOC and UN DESA databases, https://esango.un.org/civilsociety/, and the search engine of Idealist, www.idealist.org, respectively.

and the United Kingdom, underlining the gravity of these issues for both countries, have highlighted the relevance of UN human rights oversight to every country, even those with the greatest wealth and well-developed legal systems. As Michael Ignatieff has commented, "[i]n a globalized world, we do not have the luxury of moral closure."[30] We cannot say in the contemporary, almost instantaneous, information environment that "we did not know." Against this informational backdrop, there are new opportunities to assert collective and community values at the international level, to lift our standards and build credible new institutions.

As an international community we currently run serious moral risks, as well as very basic coherence and consistency risks, if we leave the international human rights system as it is, continuing, in practice, to largely take at face value the national and international statements of governments who officially claim to support human rights values. The international community to date has implemented a very strong system of financial and economic globalization, but has yet to move further toward what Richard Falk has labeled a "just new constitutionalism" or a "humane global governance" where international human rights, democratic and rule of law values are effectively implemented and upheld.[31] Neutrality in the face of the current system can reasonably be seen as a form of appeasement, and support for staying at the current weak level of international oversight and implementation of human rights may be considered a form of mere "therapeutic governance."[32] Amartya Sen notes that because we do not have an organization with the responsibility to actually deliver to people the noble principles of the UDHR, human rights as currently practiced are merely "heart-warming sentiments."[33] Exerting continued pressure, working hard to secure adequate funding and advocating systematically for more rational, technically sound, impartial international implementation mechanisms within the human rights architecture seems a small price to pay for those in a position to undertake such advocacy.

In addition to basic ethical imperatives, there are also arguments for significantly strengthening the international human rights infrastructure based on enlightened self-interest of all states and populations. Our collective inaction at least tacitly condones harm to others and facilitates various types of harm that will inevitably

---

[30] Ignatieff, *The Ordinary Virtues*, p. 23.

[31] Falk, R. 2014. "New Constitutionalism and Geopolitics: Notes on Legality and Legitimacy and Prospects for a Just New Constitutionalism," in S. Gill and A.C. Cutler (eds.), *New Constitutionalism and World Order*, Cambridge, Cambridge University Press, pp. 295–312.

[32] Sarah Nouwen uses this phrase in the context of lack of Security Council enforcement action, but it applies equally to the absence of human rights enforcement mechanisms: "For the Security Council, international criminal tribunals are instruments of therapeutic governance, providing an acceptable compromise between despicable apathy and authorisation of military interventions that UN members are unwilling or unable to carry out: if not peace, then justice." Nouwen, S. 2012. "Justifying Justice," in J. Crawford and M. Koskenniemi (eds.), *The Cambridge Companion to International Law*, Cambridge, Cambridge University Press, pp. 327–351, p. 343.

[33] Sen, Amartya. 1999. *Development as Freedom*, Oxford, Oxford University Press, p. 228.

come to all nations. As noted, the cross-border and cascade effects of systemic human rights abuses are very real, no matter where they may take place.

One dramatic example is the current "Refugee Crisis" in Europe (so-named by institutions of the European Union)[34] and the more general global displacement crisis, where in recent years more than 65 million people have been forcibly displaced from their homes – more people than in any period since World War II. The 1951 Refugee Convention, currently with 146 parties, indeed anticipates an uneven landscape in upholding human rights across the world, defining a refugee as:

> A person who owing to a well-founded fear of being persecuted for reasons of race, religion, nationality, membership of a particular social group or political opinion, is outside the country of his nationality and is unable or, owing to such fear, is unwilling to avail himself of the protection of that country; or who, not having a nationality and being outside the country of his former habitual residence as a result of such events, is unable or, owing to such fear, is unwilling to return to it.[35]

Leaving aside the general social and economic benefits that can flow from cross-border migration (e.g., benefits for economies with an aging population, the relaxation of labor market constraints, reductions in the cost of living; for a fuller discussion see Chapters 14 and 17), there are challenges – real and perceived – to welcoming and caring for such volumes of displaced persons who are looking for refuge under the 1951 Convention, or searching for fundamental economic and social well-being.[36] There is also the deep suffering of those forced to flee their home countries because of war, persecution, or economic hardship. Given the sheer volume of persons currently displaced for a variety of reasons (which will only grow in the foreseeable future given the effects of climate change), the diverse countries welcoming refugees should have a very strong interest in ensuring better human rights protections abroad, including with respect to social and economic rights, both in the direct interest of displaced persons, and also in the national interest if domestic resources are being overstretched. Various nations are having to deal with the governance weaknesses and insufficiencies of foreign states in the protection of human rights, and governments – often those with more functional systems – must often absorb challenges and costs related to these problems. It would seem logical that there would be a dramatic collective interest in ensuring much stronger global compliance with international human rights norms, certainly investing in international mechanisms that *should* be significantly advanced since 1951, with the intention of "working the 1951 Convention out of a job."

---

[34] See: https://ec.europa.eu/echo/refugee-crisis.

[35] Article 1(A)(2) of the Refugee Convention, as amended by the 1967 Protocol. UN General Assembly, Convention Relating to the Status of Refugees, July 28, 1951, United Nations, Treaty Series, Vol. 189, p. 137.

[36] See Chapters 13–17 in this book which share perspectives on addressing international economic governance issues, and other global risks that may drive mass migration, which is crucial to ensuring a workable world.

There are other striking examples that are touching the lives and affecting the basic stability – social, economic and otherwise – of citizens in nations where it was thought that standards of human rights and constitutional democracy were well established. Current cross-border meddling through social media and cyberattacks, for example, in the elections of democratic nations, a sort of cross-border infection of autocratic or democratically weak foreign systems where human rights abuses may be widespread, may pose an existential threat to those countries in which citizens have secured hard-won human rights protections over centuries. It is now clearer than ever that the protection of the rights of all, at the international level, is a safeguard, an insurance policy, for the well-being of all.

In such a landscape, moral closure is indeed a luxury. The various predicaments in which we currently find ourselves invite the "analysis of virtues at work in an unjust, dangerous, and uncertain world, a study of how people reproduce virtue – and moral order – in arduous circumstances";[37] our shared human rights values, affirmed widely and repeatedly at the international level, serve as a solid foundation for the international moral order in dangerous and uncertain times. As one author notes: "[e]specially today, when an imbalance of power prevails, strong international human rights institutions are needed," and "only the states that are disciplined to follow international human rights precepts will have the moral authority to lead."[38]

ON THE UNIVERSALITY OF HUMAN RIGHTS

No doubt repressive, illegitimate regimes will continue to invoke cultural relativism and state "sovereignty" to support their resistance to effective human rights enforcement. Overcoming that resistance is a standing item on the human rights agenda at the turn of the century and beyond.[39]

– Louis Henkin

A range of authors have very capably refuted the assertion that international human rights norms are an imposition of Western morality or philosophy. For example, the debate initiated in the 1990s by several governments asserting that international human rights norms contradict "Asian values" and are a Eurocentric imposition has been prominently tackled by Amartya Sen.[40] As Sen and others have noted, types of authoritarianism are not "especially Asian in any significant sense," and while the West may have "skeletons in its cupboards" and may be no stranger to hypocrisy on the topic of human rights (like other regions), this is not an excuse to compromise

---

[37] Ignatieff, *The Ordinary Virtues*, p. 30.
[38] Mertus, *The United Nations and Human Rights*, pp. 164–165.
[39] Henkin, "Preface," p. ix.
[40] Sen, Amartya. 1997. *Human Rights and Asian Values*, Sixteenth Annual Morgenthau Memorial Lecture on Ethics and Foreign Policy, May 25, Carnegie Council. www.carnegie council.org/publications/archive/morgenthau/254.

the rights of Asians. The case for rights, according to Sen, "turns ultimately on their basic importance and on their instrumental role," in Asia and elsewhere.[41] He also notes the various strands of philosophical thought in Asian social and intellectual history that assert the values of tolerance and respect for individual freedom; the grand dichotomy between Western civilization and "Asian values," "African cultures," etc., is a false one, Sen asserts, and moreover is unhelpful and distracting to an understanding of the actual cultural and historical complexity of our global society.[42]

Indeed, Chinese academic and Vice-Chair of the Human Rights Commission Peng Chun Chang played an influential role in the drafting of the UDHR. Along with other diverse members of the Commission (e.g., notably, from Lebanon, the Philippines and Chile), he very consciously wished to make the Universal Declaration relevant to all of humanity across philosophical traditions. Chang, for example, regularly drew on the thought of Confucius and Mencius in formulating his contributions and was reportedly helpful in finding compromise language across traditions at particularly difficult points in the discussions.[43] Charles Habib Malik from Lebanon likewise drew from his Greek Orthodox Christian background in his advocacy for and contributions to the development of the UDHR. Another expert from the Middle East, M. Cherif Bassiouni, has more recently deployed Islamic teachings for the development of clear international norms and binding accountability regimes for egregious international crimes such as genocide and crimes against humanity, in service of the development of modern international criminal law – affirming that Shari'a and Islamic law are not incompatible with contemporary international human rights law and international humanitarian law norms.[44]

Also in more recent times, philosophical concepts from diverse cultural traditions have achieved prominence in important national developments and beyond, also gaining international currency. For example, the moral philosophy of "Ubuntu," as interpreted by former Archbishop Desmond Tutu, was closely associated with the South African Truth and Reconciliation Commission (TRC). After having chaired the TRC, Tutu described Ubuntu in the following words: "It is not 'I think therefore I am.' It says rather: 'I am human because I belong.' I participate, I share."[45] The

---

[41] Ibid., p. 30.
[42] For a treatment of the "culture question" in relation to the universal rights of women, see López-Claros and Nakhjavani, *Equality for Women = Prosperity for All: The Disastrous Global Crisis*.
[43] See, e.g., the anecdotes relayed in: Humphrey, John P. 1984. *Human Rights and the United Nations: A Great Adventure*, Dobbs Ferry, NY, Transnational Publishers, p. 23.
[44] See, e.g., Bassiouni, M. 2013. "Islamic International Law and International Humanitarian Law," in M. Bassiouni (ed.), *The Shari'a and Islamic Criminal Justice in Time of War and Peace*, Cambridge, Cambridge University Press, pp. 150–248.
[45] Tutu, Desmond. 1999. *No Future without Forgiveness*, London, Sydney, Auckland and Johannesburg, Rider.

concept of Ubuntu, as employed by Tutu, speaks to Roosevelt's conviction that human rights form a part of concrete community commitments and processes.

Subsequent to the 2015 Paris Agreement addressing the existential planetary threat of climate change, the application of local and traditional techniques of community-building and decision-making have resulted in the Talanoa Dialogue, which blends substantive and "process/procedural" values (e.g., norms of participation and communication). The Dialogue is described as follows:

> Talanoa is a traditional word used in Fiji and across the Pacific to reflect a process of inclusive, participatory and transparent dialogue. The purpose of Talanoa is to share stories, build empathy and to make wise decisions for the collective good. The process of Talanoa involves the sharing of ideas, skills and experience through storytelling.
>
> During the process, participants build trust and advance knowledge through empathy and understanding. Blaming others and making critical observations are inconsistent with building mutual trust and respect, and therefore inconsistent with the Talanoa concept. Talanoa fosters stability and inclusiveness in dialogue, by creating a safe space that embraces mutual respect for a platform for decision making for a greater good.[46]

Among the world's major religious traditions, multiple interfaith declarations and statements, involving leaders of the various traditions, have affirmed the shared ethical core of all religions. An interfaith declaration entitled "Towards a Global Ethic," drafted at the 1993 Parliament of the World's Religions in Chicago by an assembly of religious and spiritual leaders from essentially every major world religion and spiritual movement, states:

> We affirm that a common set of core values is found in the teachings of the religions, and that these form the basis of a global ethic ... There already exist ancient guidelines for human behaviour which are found in the teachings of the religions of the world and which are the condition for a sustainable world order.[47]

These examples show that the diversity of cultural, religious and philosophical traditions need not be a barrier to the application of human rights and can indeed be a source of richness and a supplement to – and, indeed, a strong validation of – what has been agreed in official international documents. Moreover, there are a host of non-religious bases, including a purely legal positivist basis (e.g., international human rights have been agreed at the highest levels of political representation of national governments), as well as those offered by modern philosophers such as John Rawls, with his "original position" doctrine, that provide an ethical or social basis for

---

[46] United Nations. 2018. United Nations Framework Convention on Climate Change (UNFCCC), *Talanoa Dialogue Platform*. https://unfccc.int/topics/2018-talanoa-dialogue-platform.

[47] "Towards a Global Ethic," drafted at the 1993 Parliament of the World's Religions in Chicago, IL. https://parliamentofreligions.org/parliament/global-ethic/about-global-ethic.

the universal application of human rights. More generally, the capacity for empathy and the instinct for justice have been found to be indigenous to all of us: psychologists have found the human capacity for empathy and reactions to injustice to be universal. Our shared psychological nature "shape[s] the human response to justice and love – as well as to injustice, cruelty, trauma and violence."[48]

However, while *good faith*, principled adaption and cultural contexting of international human rights norms is positive, it must not preclude the clear delineation of "red lines" as to what should be considered, for example, as "harmful traditional practices" across various cultures.[49] For instance, practices such as female genital mutilation, son preference and female infanticide, early and forced marriage and so on have been found by international expert groups to violate international human rights, as they are harmful and undermine the dignity and well-being of certain group members, and should be stopped. Such principled and good faith dialogues are a part of group learning across every society, as we evolve cultures that better enable humans to flourish.

International actors, including the media, also need to become more knowledgeable about the seeds of doubt and confusion that may be sown by those threatened by the assertion of new systems that seek to protect human rights and vulnerable persons, as has been seen, for example, with the International Criminal Court and the public relations campaigns related to some of the indictees (see Chapter 10). There should be a more sophisticated diagnosis of the "cultural" argument and the concerns raised about imperialism. For example, an analysis as to whether such arguments: a) are a distraction or deflection from accountability, deployed by a certain group or individual within a society that benefits from *not* having a right or rights upheld; or b) indeed do raise an issue of genuine cultural tension or a relevant historical (or current) experience of imperialism or the imposition of double-standards that should be addressed;[50] or c) manifest a combination of both of these forces.

Beyond sensitivity to and genuine incorporation of cultural and civilizational diversity – which, as Sen notes, is simply a reality of our international society – Henkin has delivered a scathing rebuke to cultural relativist arguments:

---

[48] Penn, Michael, Maja Groff, and Naseem Koroush. 2019. "Cultivating Our Common Humanity: Reflections on Freedom of Thought, Conscience, and Religion," in *The Cambridge Handbook of Psychology and Human Rights*, Cambridge, Cambridge University Press.

[49] See, e.g., United Nations, Department of Economic and Social Affairs, Division for the Advancement of Women and United Nations Economic Commission for Africa, *Good Practices in Legislation on "Harmful Practices" against Women: Report of the Expert Group Meeting*, May 26–29, 2009.

[50] Paupp has generally highlighted the necessity of further "regionalization and intercivilizational dialogue" in the global human rights project, as well as a reorientation of international law to put the human rights to peace, security and development at the forefront, in furtherance of the (largely overlooked) legitimate aims and needs of the Global South. Paupp, Terrence E. 2014. *Redefining Human Rights in the Struggle for Peace and Development*, New York, Cambridge University Press, p. 82.

"Cultural relativism" will doubtless continue to be a battle cry into the next century. That may reflect the fact that, despite a half-century of the human rights movement, governments not yet committed to constitutionalism at home remain reluctant to be monitored and judged, and are particularly sensitive to international embarrassment.

. . .

The political representatives of all mankind have repeatedly committed themselves to the human rights idea and to its expression in the Universal Declaration of Human Rights. No political or cultural representative has purported to justify slavery, torture, or unfair trial as culturally legitimate. If in some few, isolated respects cultural hangovers run afoul of contemporary international standards – forms of slavery, female genital mutilation, amputation as punishment – the international community has declared them no longer acceptable and has demanded their termination as the price of living in international society in the 20th/21st centuries. That was the lesson the world unanimously taught to successive regimes in the Republic of South Africa when they sought to maintain systemic racial discrimination (apartheid).[51]

THE "UNFINISHED TASK"

Upon the adoption of the UDHR in 1948, while taking the opportunity to commemorate and embrace the extraordinary achievement of the completion of the Declaration, Eleanor Roosevelt called on the international community to, "at the same time, rededicate ourselves to the unfinished task which lies before us."[52] She described this work as including the completion of the international covenant on human rights (the two binding instruments that were ultimately adopted in 1966, forming part of the "International Bill of Human Rights") and *"measures of implementation* of human rights" (emphasis added). Unfortunately, such measures for the implementation of international human rights continue to fall far short of what is needed for something approaching a functional global system.

The disjunction between the very wide range of sound and widely accepted human rights norms and their meaningful implementation was described in the following way in the mid-1990s: "[d]espite the divisions of the Cold War, the international system developed fine human rights standards; it has not done well in achieving respect for those standards. All states have committed themselves to respect human rights standards, but they have not been prepared to see them implemented or enforced, to accept communal scrutiny of the condition of human

---

[51] Henkin, "Preface," pp. viii–ix; López-Claros and Nakhjavani note that in the human rights versus culture debate the same states that often insist on being "let alone" in relation to the gender issue, "[w]hen it comes to matters of military and economic aid, for example, there has been little or no such demand for independence" (*Equality for Women = Prosperity for All*, p. 146).

[52] See, e.g., discussion of Eleanor Roosevelt and the adoption of the UDHR in: Klug, F. 2015. *A Magna Carta for All Humanity: Homing in on Human Rights*, London, Routledge.

rights in their own countries, to scrutinize others, to establish monitoring bodies, or to welcome and respond to non-governmental monitoring."[53] Henkin goes on to note that this latter deficit in implementation and enforcement is "the major human rights task facing the international system." We agree with this assessment.

Contemporary critiques continue to echo this basic concern, with commentators calling for the gap between enforcement mechanisms and the existence of substantive rights to be closed,[54] and critics noting that the current system is based on a belief in something "that no longer exists … that enforcement would always be a matter of state discretion."[55] The relative impotence of international society to hold specific states to account that Henkin noted still essentially holds true today: "[i]nternational human rights are rights within national societies and the obligation to respect and ensure rights must fall on every society in the first instance. The international community can only observe, cajole, shame and otherwise induce governments and societies to respect and ensure those rights."[56] Observing, cajoling and shaming, although better than no scrutiny, has its limitations as an enforcement technique. It has also been noted that in recent decades a disproportionate amount of international attention has been focused on "mass atrocity crimes" (e.g., genocide, crimes against humanity, war crimes) with too little attention paid to the "continuous atrocities" of all-to-common systemic human rights abuses across societies;[57] such a diversion of attention "masks the harder questions" of how a stronger, more effective general international human rights system might be effectuated.

It is true that in recent decades greater numbers of states have joined the nine core international human rights treaties (with some correlation noted between becoming party to a given treaty and improvements in human rights standards in a given jurisdiction),[58] and a range of new individual complaint mechanisms, although optional, have been put in place under the various treaties or their protocols.[59] But the decisions issued under these individual complaint mechanisms are not binding on governments, and there is not much that the committees can do to

---

[53] Henkin, "Preface," p. xvii.
[54] See, e.g., Paupp, *Redefining Human Rights*, p. 96.
[55] Mertus, *The United Nations and Human Rights*, p. 162.
[56] Henkin, "Preface," p. xvii.
[57] Alston, Philip. 2014. "Against a World Court for Human Rights." *Ethics & International Affairs*, Vol. 28, No. 2, pp. 197–212.
[58] For example, World Bank research shows that within five years of countries accepting the obligations of CEDAW, there is a significant drop in the number of legal discriminations against women embedded in the laws of such countries. See Hallward-Driemeier, M., T. Hasan, and A. Rusu. 2013. "Women's Legal Rights over 50 Years: Progress, Stagnation or Regression?" Policy Research Working Paper No. 6616. See also Iqbal, Sarah. 2015. *Women, Business, and the law 2016: Getting to Equal (English)*, Washington, DC, World Bank Group.
[59] Pillay, N. 2012. "Strengthening the United Nations Human Rights Treaty Body System. A Report by the United Nations High Commissioner for Human Rights," United Nations Human Rights Office of the High Commissioner, p. 17. www2.ohchr.org/english/bodies/HRTD/docs/HCReportTBStrengthening.pdf.

ensure compliance, beyond applying their moral authority. Although it is highly praiseworthy that these procedures have been developed, they are piecemeal and still do not represent effective outcomes for the individuals around the world who have had their most fundamental rights violated – nor are they a sufficient deterrent for states to not repeat problematic behaviors.

In a 2012 report, then UN High Commissioner for Human Rights Navi Pillay outlined chronic problems of state engagement with the treaty bodies, noting, for example, that only 16 percent of states parties to human rights treaties were reporting on time, in line with their obligations.[60] Even more symptomatically, Pillay has observed that "even though human rights is one of the UN's three pillars, it remains so poorly funded, receiving only around 3% of the overall UN budget."[61] In a rebuke of the general and long-term neglect by the international community of the whole international human rights system, she has noted that:

> by resigning ourselves to the "inevitability" of noncompliance and inadequate resources, the system was left to suffer a long history of benign neglect to the point where, today, it stands on the verge of drowning in its growing workload, even when leaving aside the shocking fact that on average 23 per cent of States parties to one treaty have never engaged in the review procedure of that treaty.[62]

Zeid Ra'ad Al Hussein, Pillay's successor and the sixth United Nations High Commissioner for Human Rights (serving 2014–2018), has been even more pointed in his critique of the lack of global progress made on human rights, citing decades of "mediocre leadership," and noting that:

> too many summits and conferences held between states are tortured affairs that lack profundity but are full of jargon and tiresome clichés that are, in a word, meaning-less. What is absent is a sincere will to work together, though all will claim—again, under the lights and on camera—that they are wholly committed to doing so ... [T]he international community has been too weak ... to privilege human lives, human dignity, tolerance—and ultimately, global security—over the price of hydrocarbons and the signing of defence contracts.[63]

Echoing the warnings and admonitions contained in the UN Charter and the UDHR, Al Hussein calls for new thinking on human rights, marked by a sense of urgency, linking deteriorating human rights situations with fractures in various societies that set up dangerous "trip wires" for greater conflicts in the international system:

---

[60] Ibid., p. 9.

[61] The Global Justice Monitor. 2014. "Interview with Navi Pillay: 'Africa Has Benefited Most from the ICC.'" *Journal of the Coalition for the International Criminal Court*, Vol. 46, pp. 18–19.

[62] Pillay, "Strengthening the United Nations Human Rights Treaty Body System," p. 94.

[63] Al Hussein, Zeid Ra'ad. "Open Voices Grassroots Leaders Provide the Best Hope to a Troubled World," *The Economist*, August 30, 2018.

A fracture within society is often shorthand for human suffering or the existence of burning grievances. Before conflicts begin, suffering stems from three types of human rights violations. One is the denial of fundamental freedoms, such as of opinion, expression and peaceful assembly, creating a situation where life and fear of the state become inseparable. A second is the deprivation of basic services, such as legal and social protections or rights to education and healthcare, which often only confirms the hold of political elites over others. And third, feeding the first two, discrimination, structural and deep, propped up by racism, chauvinism and bigotry.[64]

Again, it seems artificial and naïve to think that thwarted human rights aspirations abroad would somehow not have cross-border and unpredictable global knock-on effects.

REFORM PROPOSALS: STRENGTHENING EXISTING MECHANISMS

As an integral part of establishing strong cultures that instinctively further human rights norms, and various forms of human rights leadership across sectors, strong national and international institutions are an imperative, as "good institutions, when supported by citizens of virtue, can stop the elites' downward spiral into predatory self-dealing."[65] International institutions that are strong, aspiring to standards of legitimacy, transparency and excellence, should be a clear aim in the contemporary international order; aspirations should rise far above Pillay's warning of resignation to a seeming inevitability of scarce resources and noncompliance. That institutions are worth investing in fits with the "institutional turn" in current development economics:[66] robust, inclusive, modern and rules-based institutions, including at the international level, create the conditions necessary for social and economic prosperity.[67]

Within the UN system, there have been progressive waves of limited reforms to the international human rights architecture, notably in 1993, with the creation of the Office of the High Commissioner for Human Rights (OHCHR), and in 2006, with the transition from the Commission on Human Rights (CHR), overseen by ECO-SOC, to the Human Rights Council (HRC), elected by the General Assembly. However, the HRC is still plagued by a range of issues that previously beset the CHR, namely, but not limited to, issues of legitimacy, independence, impartiality and election of Council members.[68] Despite the transition toward the regularized

---

[64] Ibid.

[65] Ignatieff, *The Ordinary Virtues*, p. 30.

[66] Ibid., p. 29.

[67] See, e.g., the hypotheses on state "success" set forth in: Acemoglu, Daron and James A. Robinson. 2013. *Why Nations Fail: The Origins of Power, Prosperity, and Poverty*, London, Profile Books.

[68] See recent discussion in Freedman and Houghton, "Two Steps Forward, One Step Back."

"Universal Periodic Review" (UPR) system (the periodic review of the human rights records of all UN member states, also established in 2006), and efforts to ensure greater system coherence, the challenges and inefficiencies in the current institutional arrangements and capacities are many and are well documented. These include, for example: lack of implementation mechanisms; noncompliance of states with decisions regarding individual complaints; failure of states to fulfil reporting duties (on time, if at all); inadequate resources and chronic under-resourcing; backlogs of reports and communications and overloading of the treaty bodies; the system's reliance on unpaid experts and on experts who may not have sufficient background to make quasi-judicial determinations on compliance; inadequate attention given to the independence of some human rights experts; insufficient support for and from the office of the UN High Commissioner for Human Rights; and complexity of and intransigent fragmentation within the system.[69] It has been noted that the current system may be "effective in promoting human rights, but not in protecting them."[70] Moreover, on the issue of legitimacy and credibility, it would be progress if the international human rights system could in the first instance aim to have adequate checks and balances on independence of oversight bodies and those comprising them so that headlines such as the following would be a thing of the past: "Same old scam: The UN Human Rights Council's lousy election."[71]

A range of authors have made worthwhile suggestions to improve the current system, based around the HRC and the existing treaty bodies, which, however, fall short of further key structural changes. These include, for example: strengthening the reporting procedure through improved report preparation and interaction between treaty bodies and states parties/other stakeholders; seeking a binding nature for findings of treaty bodies as well as better follow-up procedures and the strengthening of individual communications; strengthening the role of civil society in operations and procedures; and enhancing the Special Procedures of the HRC, and so on.[72]

---

[69] See, e.g., Broecker, Christen. 2014. "The Reform of the United Nations' Human Rights Treaty Bodies," *American Society of International Law*, Vol. 18, No. 16, www.asil.org/insights/volume/18/issue/16/reform-united-nations%E2%80%99-human-rights-treaty-bodies; Lhotsky, Jan. 2016. "The UN Mechanisms for Human Rights Protection: Strengthening Treaty Bodies in Light of a Proposal to Create a World Court of Human Rights," *Journal of Eurasian Law*, Vol. 9, No. 1, pp. 109–122; Abashidze, Aslan. 2016. "The Process of Strengthening the Human Rights Treaty Body System," *Journal of Eurasian Law*, Vol. 9, No. 1, pp. 1–13; Bassiouni, M. Cherif and William A. Schabas (eds.), 2011. *New Challenges for the UN Human Rights Machinery: What Future for the UN Treaty Body System and the Human Rights Council Procedures?* Cambridge, Antwerp and Portland, OR, Intersentia.

[70] Subedi, *The Effectiveness of the UN Human Rights System*, p. 222.

[71] *The Economist*, October 17, 2018.

[72] See, e.g., the range of reforms suggested in: Cherif and Schabas. *New Challenges for the UN Human Rights Machinery.*

More substantial suggestions for various structural reforms have been proposed by others, in particular "for determining the make-up of a credible HRC."[73] Schwartzberg has suggested, for example, that to ensure efficiency, the number of HRC members should be further reduced from 47 to 36; in addition to seats reserved for representatives of 12 specified regions (reflecting "current global realities"), a substantial number of seats should be filled by a slate of *at large* members (decoupled from national political pressures) to encourage truly competitive elections of high-quality candidates; to preserve freedom of speech and independence of judgment, HRC members must be guaranteed legal immunity for any acts taken in the performance of their HRC duties (and, if necessary, asylum); membership should have gender balance; and the special status of indigenous peoples should be recognized through the reservation of two HRC seats for their designated representatives. Subedi has likewise made recommendations to reform and "empower" the HRC, suggesting ways to credibly depoliticize the composition of the Council and suggesting the possibility of elevating its status yet further within the current UN Charter system, giving it a range of new powers to refer situations to existing bodies with enforcement powers such as the Security Council and the International Criminal Court.[74]

Suggestions such as these would no doubt significantly improve the credibility, efficacy and legitimacy of the current international human rights system, and should be implemented. Additionally, if we are seeking to craft a genuine international legal system, with a more authentic system of rule by law (for all the reasons set out in Chapter 10), there is the need to move also, in parallel, to court-based international legal mechanisms and judicial oversight of states' human rights obligations.

REFORM PROPOSALS: INTERNATIONAL HUMAN RIGHTS TRIBUNAL

As has been shown by well-established regional human rights courts – African, Inter-American and European – supranational judicial oversight of national human rights obligations can now be said to be relatively widespread and "popular" at the international level. Regional human rights commissions or committees in Asia and the Middle East/North Africa (e.g., under the auspices of the Association of Southeast Asian Nations (ASEAN) and the League of Arab States) have also been established within the last decade, laying the normative and institutional

[73] Schwartzberg, Joseph E. 2013. "A Credible Human Rights System," in Joseph E. Schwartzberg (ed.), *Transforming the United Nations System: Designs for a Workable World*, Tokyo and New York, United Nations University Press, pp. 110–128.

[74] Subedi also argues for referral power to a new International Court of Human Rights, a proposal that we would support. Subedi, *The Effectiveness of the UN Human Rights System*, pp. 247–255.

groundwork for further development and future individual complaint mechanisms and/or judicial oversight in these regions as well.

The existing regional human rights courts – in particular the longer-standing courts in Europe and the Americas – have already demonstrated the capacity of supranational courts to play a strong role in developing the respective regional human rights systems, within the frame of binding regional human rights treaties. The courts have seen progressively increasing caseloads (indeed, showing the strong "demand" side for human rights relief), and a significant role in clarifying the law, contributing to its progressive development. Such jurisprudence is important for any eventual international human rights court, which should be sensitive to regional and cultural diversity and conditions, and more generally to the progressive development and organic evolution of international human rights law within the frame of evolving societies across the world, driven by the facts of specific cases that come before tribunals.

We propose that an International Human Rights Tribunal should be established, and there are indeed a range of particular benefits to be gained through the establishment of a court-based oversight system for states' human rights obligations.[75] Prime among the arguments for such oversight is that the normal definition of a "rule of law" system includes the opportunity for the meaningful enforcement of established legal norms; legal norms established at the international level that are considered to be binding should therefore also be enforceable at the international level. There is a risk that the international human rights obligations will not be deemed credible or – indeed – binding, if there is not such a system whereby courts can issue impartial and enforceable decisions, with international oversight of this enforcement. One can certainly see this "risk" realized in the current state of affairs, judging from the human rights reports issued by a range of actors, both within and external to the UN, on various states' behaviors.[76]

The unique nature of judicial oversight would be another important benefit gained from an additional international layer to the global human rights "system." The independence and impartiality of judges, if well established and safeguarded,[77] has the potential to diffuse politicized situations at the national, regional and international levels, without reliance on a "name and shame" system where, for example, individual states may risk rupture of economic or diplomatic relations if

---

[75] See, e.g., those set out by Bilder and Subedi. Bilder also sketches various potential drawbacks. Subedi, *The Effectiveness of the UN Human Rights System*; Bilder, Richard B. 1994. "Possibilities for Development of New International Judicial Mechanisms," in Louis Henkin and John Lawrence Hargrove (eds.), *Human Rights: An Agenda for the Next Century*. Studies in Transnational Legal Policy, No. 26, the American Society of International Law, Washington, DC, pp. 317–346.

[76] Subedi, *The Effectiveness of the UN Human Rights System*.

[77] This is why, for example, we are proposing additional, enhanced "rule of law" institutions at the international level, including an international judicial training institute and a system-wide office of Attorney General; see Chapter 10.

they criticize another state's human rights abuses too vigorously.[78] Certain situations bearing on human rights violations, which may have implications for international peace and security, can also be objectively assessed, according to neutral principles of law, forming a basis for further collective action or support of the international community and/or allowing national political actors to "save face" by yielding to the decision of an impartial tribunal in a situation that might otherwise be politically sensitive.[79]

More generally, courts should have unique abilities and skills to determine facts and apply the law in human rights cases, devising appropriate remedies for any violations found, and playing a crucial role in leveling the playing field among actors who may have immensely different levels of power. One criticism of the existing international human rights individual complaints mechanisms is in fact the need for greater "judicial" expertise to be deployed in such mechanisms to address individual cases.

Finally, one of the primary complaints about the current international landscape with respect to international human rights norms is the persistent hypocrisy of state actors, and the gap between rhetoric and action, as noted by Commissioner Al Hussein. A clear and effective way for governments to demonstrate *actual* commitment to international human rights standards would be to subject themselves to international judicial oversight of human rights obligations. This is perhaps one of the strongest arguments for the establishment of international juridical mechanisms. International law has been criticized as perennially vacillating between postures of "apology and utopia,"[80] with high "utopian" moral ideas espoused by state actors, which serve, however, primarily or often as manipulative facades for what government actors perceive to be "state interest" or power. A commitment to a well-designed and adequately funded international human rights court would be a substantial step toward overcoming this vicious circle and moving to an international order genuinely based on "human security."

At the international level, the establishment of an international human rights court has been mooted for a number of years, with some proposals being more prominent than others, and none yet gaining significant practical traction. Proposals date from early in the postwar era, with Australia calling for the creation of a stand-alone international human rights court in 1947, and the United Kingdom at the same time making a counter-proposal that the International Court of Justice (ICJ) be mandated to give advisory opinions on human rights; the idea of an International

---

[78] Part of the justification of shifting to the HRC was to usher in a new era of dialogue and cooperation, beyond "name and shame" techniques. Freedman and Houghton, "Two Steps Forward, One Step Back," p. 756.

[79] Bilder, "Possibilities for Development," pp. 326–328.

[80] See, for example, Koskenniemi, M. 1990. "The Politics of International Law," *European Journal of International Law*, Vol. 1, pp. 4–32, p. 8.

Human Rights Tribunal was subsequently raised in international fora in the later 1960s and in 1993 at the Vienna World Conference on Human Rights.[81]

A high-profile proposal was put forth by the Swiss government in 2011 that a permanent, specialized World Court of Human Rights (WCHR) be created, generally based upon, but also improving, the current model of the European Court of Human Rights (ECtHR). Such an independent court would be established by way of treaty and would be "competent to decide in a final and binding manner on complaints of human rights violations committed by state and non-state actors alike and provide adequate reparation to victims."[82] This ambitious proposal drew the backing of a high-level "Panel on Human Dignity" that included former UN High Commissioner for Human Rights Mary Robinson; Theodor Meron, who served at the International Criminal Tribunal for the former Yugoslavia as president for multiple terms; independent experts from the UN Human Rights Council; and well-known human rights activists from, among other places, Austria, Brazil, Egypt, Finland, Pakistan, South Africa and Thailand. It also attracted the attention of various international organizations and scholars.

Despite the support for such a court from a broad range of influential actors, the 2011 proposal was seen by some at the time as too ambitious and too expensive. It was criticized, for example, for a number of the novel features suggested in the proposed blueprint of the court,[83] and more generally based on concerns about its complexity, the challenges of cultural diversity and the "distraction" from other projects or investments, in particular given an increased unwillingness among states to invest in "large-scale" international human rights initiatives.[84]

The issue of complexity of the international treaty-based human rights system, with potentially overlapping obligations among treaties, is a well-known problem, and exists whether or not an international court is established; rather, the establishment of such a body would provide an important opportunity for the consolidation

---

[81] Subedi, *The Effectiveness of the UN Human Rights System*, p. 239.

[82] *Protecting Dignity: An Agenda for Human Rights*, 2011 Report, Conclusions and Recommendations, p. 40. www.udhr60.ch/.

[83] Such as the fact-finding powers of the proposed court, the expansion of the range of situations in which recourse to the court might be had, the ability of the court to impose strong interim measures; much expanded advisory opinion powers on human rights treaties given to the ICJ, and the fact that all judgments would be final and binding. Alston, "Against a World Court for Human Rights."

[84] Ibid., p. 202. Alston notes that the ECtHR at the time involved a bill of US$90 million per annum, with no fact-finding, as was proposed by the international court, and covering "only" 800 million persons – that is, one-ninth of the global population. However, compared with annual global military spending (US$1.7 trillion), the potential costs of an international court seem modest if it were in fact to assist systemically with compliance with international human rights norms. Alston also correctly notes that "justiciability" of rights (e.g., making them subject to legal action before a judge) at the international level should not always or necessarily be positioned "over all other means by which to uphold human rights," including in relation to structurally embedded and "complex and contested problems." It is only one of a range of important tools or techniques for ensuring the promotion of and respect for human rights.

and clarification of various existing human rights norms and how they may inter-act.[85] Similarly, the issue of international cultural and legal diversity – another issue of complexity – as Sen has noted, is intrinsic to the nature of our rich and varied global society, and affects all areas of international law and international cooper-ation. The allocation of resources is an international policy choice and there is no reason that multiple, ambitious human rights investments cannot be undertaken in parallel. Remarkably, much has been accomplished in the international arena already in relation to human rights, in particular with respect to normative founda-tions and increased monitoring, despite dramatically meagre resources.

Further dialogue among experts and serious conversations should recommence in earnest as to the optimal design for an international human rights court, fit for modern circumstances and not compromising on impartiality and efficacy. Con-cerns such as those raised in relation to the 2011 proposal should be taken into account in further discussions as to how a future court should be engineered. Prime among these may be ensuring an independent and well-trained international judi-ciary, if they are to issue binding decisions (see Chapter 10, which proposes an international judicial institute), and the possible cultivation of staged or incremental implementation pathways for the realization of such an international court, while at the same time substantially increasing investment, at the global level, in human rights capacity-building and technical training for relevant system actors, including in relation to issues of cultural sensitivity and diversity.[86]

It is feasible to design an international human rights system that supports the oft-repeated "universality" of international obligations, while still respecting regional and national diversity, as well as the diversity of legal systems and traditions through-out the world; these issues are not beyond the reach of the potential techniques and approaches of an international judiciary that is properly equipped.[87] Moreover, mechanisms of "complementarity" or "subsidiarity" with national and regional courts or systems, and possible filtering through existing or enhanced regional human rights mechanisms, should be explored so as to empower national and

---

[85] Subedi, *The Effectiveness of the UN Human Rights System*, pp. 243–244.

[86] However, calls for capacity-building support from the international community should not be used as a smoke screen or an excuse for not complying with human rights norms at a national level when there is capacity but a lack of political will. See discussion in Freedman and Houghton, "Two Steps Forward, One Step Back." However, one could reasonably conceive of a phase-in/managed preparation period, with capacity-building and external reviewers, in the lead-up to a country becoming subject to an international human rights court.

[87] Intercultural challenges of global human rights adjudication should be kept in mind, but the growing sophistication, in particular among younger scholars who often possess intercultural versatility from a young age, with capacities to mediate between various political and cultural landscapes, should not be underestimated. At the moment there is an excess of international talent, of younger scholars and professionals in particular, who wish to work full time on international human rights issues; they are in need of credible new international tools and institutions where they may channel their commitment, energy and talent.

regional actors as much as possible, while still mapping out relevant hierarchies among courts.[88]

WAYS FORWARD: A NEW ERA FOR INTERNATIONAL HUMAN RIGHTS

As Barrett notes, "[w]hen the world succeeds in supplying global public goods, people everywhere benefit. Our international institutions, however, are clumsily suited to this task [as] they lack the coercive powers that every state uses to supply national public goods."[89] The delivery of a social and economic environment in which human rights are respected and upheld, as a key international "public good," has the official backing of virtually all governments in the world. Yet effective and neutral implementation and enforcement powers to meaningfully deliver such a good have yet to be fully built and this represents a fundamental flaw in the global order. Despite the progress made since 1948, including impressive advancements in the realm of norm creation and consolidation,[90] we still have a highly imperfect system that allows ongoing abuses on a massive scale.

Influential actors are raising the alarm regarding what they see as an urgent crisis in systemic human rights violations in various parts of the world, which may trigger broader (and additional) international conflagrations or system breakdown; meanwhile there are stunningly ambitious recent proposals for robust new international machinery, backed by prominent legal, human rights and other experts. It is clear from a governance and a cogent international policy perspective, for all the reasons sketched above, that we must fundamentally revamp existing institutions and move to a new era of global human rights implementation. If this important work is not carried forward, it is mistaken to think that any of us will remain immune to the effects of a world where systemic human rights abuses are allowed to flourish.

It is clear that it is time to establish an International Human Rights Tribunal, to give credibility to the international system. Membership in such a court should be made a requirement of UN membership under a revised UN Charter, which should set forth an updated human rights vision, the foundations for which were laid in

---

[88] For example, exploring what might be drawn from the ICC principle of "complementarity" in relation to regional or national human rights courts, or some adjusted EU notion of "subsidiarity," and/or following the ECtHR model to establish a court of "final appeal" after domestic remedies have been exhausted, while still applying a "margin of appreciation" to account for national diversity.

[89] Barrett, Scott. 2007. *Why Cooperate? The Incentive to Supply Global Public Goods*, Oxford, Oxford University Press, p. 190.

[90] This normative progress is clearly evident if one surveys the broad range of human rights instruments negotiated by the international community to date: United Nations Treaty Collection, Chapter IV: Human Rights. https://treaties.un.org/pages/Treaties.aspx?id=4&subid=A&lang=en.

1945.[91] Regardless of the specificities of various individual proposals for the final design of an International Human Rights Tribunal – the 2011 proposal for an international human rights court, or those of scholars or practitioners such as Subedi, Trechsel and others – these proposals should receive careful scrutiny, comparison and further development or amendment, taking into account the range of implementation pathways that have been followed in the incremental strengthening of regional human rights systems (e.g., with respect to the ECtHR).[92] More nuanced arguments and engineering of the various proposals and suggested configurations would be helpful, as well as the exploration of phases of development. In parallel, there should be substantial reform of the existing HRC and treaty body mechanisms, which would then be followed by the (staged) establishment of judicial mechanisms for the meaningful oversight of international human rights obligations.

One of the repeated arguments against a strengthened international human rights architecture, including an international court, involves funding concerns. Funding is a systemic issue in relation to a whole range of fundamental international institutional initiatives, and it is an issue for which the international community must find solutions, of which there are many (see Chapter 12). Moreover, well-thought-out consolidation and rationalization in the current human rights "system," with its overlapping functions and duplication, will also allow for economies at the national and international levels. But generally speaking, international legal institutions, such as those at the national level, require investment, and indeed, they should be properly resourced in order to fulfil their very elemental mandates to produce minimal conditions for a functional society. Human rights are supposed to be a part of fundamental citizen entitlements, and also one of the three main pillars of the UN. As noted by Navi Pillay, human rights are currently accorded a truly paltry proportion of the UN budget – about 3.7 percent, according to recent reporting.[93] This budgetary allocation alone is a testament to the neglect of the issue of human rights by the international community on the issue, despite clear and urgent

---

[91] Such a tribunal could also be established through a stand-alone treaty in advance of Charter revision; see Chapter 21, discussing various implementation pathways for the reform proposals contained in this book. Human rights compliance should also be tied systemically to economic incentives, development and other aid in an enhanced international order.

[92] Trechsel, Stefan. 2004. "A World Court for Human Rights?" *Northwestern Journal of International Human Rights*, Vol. 1, No. 1, pp. 1–18; Subedi, *The Effectiveness of the UN Human Rights System.*

[93] The latest information on the OHCHR website at the time of writing, under "Funding and Budget," states: "And yet, the regular budget only allocates a tiny percentage of the resources to human rights that are extended to the other two pillars. With approximately half of all regular budget resources directed to these three pillars, human rights receives less than eight per cent of those resources. The approved regular budget appropriation for the Office in 2018–2019 is US$201.6 million, just 3.7 per cent of the total UN regular budget." UN Office of the High Commissioner for Human Rights, "OHCHR's Funding and Budget." www.ohchr.org/en/aboutus/pages/fundingbudget.aspx.

widespread demand for forward movement; human rights are too important and too essential, by definition, to be the subject of such neglect.

The Need for an International Bill of Rights

Finally, with respect to limitations to and safeguards on enhanced UN powers under a potentially revised UN Charter with enhanced institutions (see Chapter 21), people around the world will want to be reassured that basic individual rights will not be violated in the process of the exercise of the UN's strengthened mandate as an international organization. The accountability of both individual states and of international governance bodies with respect to human rights must be strengthened. Following on the proposals of Clark and Sohn, a new Bill of Rights (annexed to a revised Charter) prescribing limits to UN action should be drafted to include fundamental human rights protections. The list developed by Clark and Sohn, for example, includes: the right to a fair trial for persons accused of violating provisions in the revised Charter or subsequent regulations and laws emanating therefrom; protections against excessive bail, cruel or unusual punishment, and unreasonable searches and seizures; prohibition of the death penalty; protections for freedom of conscience or religion, freedom of speech, the press and expression in various forms; and freedom of association and assembly. More recent models, such as the Charter of Fundamental Rights of the European Union (the provisions of which are primarily addressed to EU institutions and to national authorities when they are implementing EU law), could also be studied and drawn from to ascertain the appropriate modern protections at the international level. Application and interpretation of the Bill of Rights could be the responsibility of a new, specialized chamber of the ICJ.

12

A New United Nations Funding Mechanism

The General Assembly would adopt the annual United Nations budget covering all its activities, and would determine the amounts to be supplied by the taxpayers of each member Nation for that budget. These amounts would be allotted on the basis of each member Nation's estimated proportion of the estimated gross world product in that year subject to a uniform "per capita deduction" of not less than fifty or more than ninety per cent of the estimated average per capita product of the ten member Nations having the lowest per capita national products, as determined by the Assembly. A further provision would limit the amount to be supplied by the people of any member Nation in any one year to a sum not exceeding two and one half per cent of that nation's estimated national product.[1]

Grenville Clark

This chapter addresses the question of the funding the operations of the United Nations. It reviews the early history of UN funding and the systems that emerged as a result of the constraints that the UN Charter imposed on its members, with specific reference to the responsibilities given to the General Assembly on budgetary issues under the one country–one vote system. We also review the current structure of the UN budget, as regards both sources and uses of funds, based on the most recent data available, for the year 2016. The main focus of the chapter is on various funding mechanisms that have been put forth in the course of the history of the UN and beyond. These include Grenville Clark and Louis Sohn's proposals contained in *World Peace through World Law*; an examination of the advantages of the model currently used in the European Union, which itself evolved over time into a system of reliable, independent funding; a discussion of the merits of a Tobin-like tax on financial transactions as a way to fund not only UN operations but also other development needs; and a system that would allocate resources to the UN as a fixed proportion of each member's gross national income (GNI), without the multiple

---

[1] Grenville Clark, in Clark, Grenville and Louis B. Sohn. 1966. *World Peace through World Law: Two Alternative Plans*. Cambridge, MA, Harvard University Press, pp. xxxviii–xxxix.

exemptions and carve-outs that are in place in today's convoluted system of revenue generation.

EARLY HISTORY

Article 17 of the UN Charter indicates that "the General Assembly shall consider and approve the budget of the Organization. The expenses of the Organization shall be borne by the Members as apportioned by the General Assembly." The Charter does not provide guidance on the criteria that should be used to ensure fair burden-sharing across its members and, being mainly a statement of principles, it certainly does not comment on whether the UN should have a consolidated budget for all of its activities – as governments tend to have under the International Monetary Fund (IMF) concept of "general government" – or whether it should have several budgets for different areas of work, such as peacekeeping, general administration and so on.

Not surprisingly, what has happened is that a body of practices has evolved over time that has resulted in the emergence of a so-called regular budget which funds the UN Secretariat and its multiple activities, a peace-keeping budget, and a budget that finances the activities of its specialized agencies. These budgets are financed by assessed contributions from members. In addition, there is a separate budget that is funded by voluntary earmarked contributions from some of its wealthier members in support of particular agencies, projects and programs. Article 18 of the Charter states that budgetary issues are one of the "important questions" on which a two-thirds majority of the membership in the General Assembly will be required to make decisions. Article 19 of the Charter envisages the removal of voting rights in the General Assembly for countries which are more than two years in arrears in their contributions, though exceptions can be made when the cause of the arrears is "beyond the control of the Member." The General Assembly determines and updates from time to time a matrix of compulsory assessments for countries, establishing the share of the assessed budget that will be paid by each member.

The General Assembly has developed various formulas to determine individual member assessments based on the principle of "capacity to pay." A Committee on Contributions was established in 1946 that put forward a formula weighing "relative national incomes, temporary dislocations of national economies and increases in capacity to pay arising out of the war, availability of foreign exchange and relative per-capita national incomes."[2] On the basis of this formula, the United States was assessed a share of 39.89 percent in the early years but, under American pressure and some opposition from countries such as Canada and Great Britain, a ceiling on US

---

[2] Quoted from the *Yearbook of the United Nations, 1946–47*, New York, UN Department of Public Information, p. 217, in Laurenti, Jeffrey. 2007. "Financing," in Thomas G. Weiss and Sam Daws (eds.), *The Oxford Handbook on the United Nations*, Oxford, Oxford University Press, pp. 675–701, at p. 678.

contributions was agreed and implemented in several stages;[3] by 1974, the US assessed share had fallen to 25 percent and to 22 percent by 2005, where it has remained since. The incorporation of Italy in 1955, Japan in 1956 and, especially, Germany in 1973 greatly facilitated the reductions in the US contribution. Over time the General Assembly opted for a system to determine country contribution shares that many regarded as unduly complicated, using estimates of gross national product (GNP)/GNI per capita, levels of external indebtedness, with discounts given to low-income countries, offset by assessing higher contributions to wealthier members, and floors and ceilings negotiated from time to time on an ad hoc basis. A minimum contribution floor of 0.04 percent of the total budget was set at the outset of the organization's foundation, when the UN had 51 members. As low-income countries joined the United Nations in the next several decades, this floor was reduced on several occasions and it now stands at 0.001 percent and is paid by countries such as Bhutan, the Central African Republic, Eritrea, the Gambia, Dominica, Lesotho, Liberia, Sierra Leone, Togo and others.

China has recently overtaken Japan as the second-largest contributor at 12.005 percent, and Japan (8.564 percent) and Germany (6.090 percent) are the third- and fourth-largest contributors, respectively.[4] For many decades the USSR was the second-largest contributor (14.97 percent in 1964) but, with the collapse of the Soviet Union in 1991 and the resulting prolonged economic crisis during much of the 1990s, Russia's assessed share fell precipitously. By the early 2000s it would have been set at 0.466 percent, including a low-income developing country discount. Finding it perhaps difficult to reconcile this low contribution rate with its great-power status in the Security Council, the Russian authorities actually asked to make a higher contribution, set at 1.1 percent by 2000. It is 2.405 percent today. The top five contributors today account for 53.23 percent of the assessed budget (higher than the 50.85 percent during the 2016–2018 budget cycle), and the top 20 for 83.33 percent, meaning that the other 173 countries account for the remaining 16.67 percent. The five veto-wielding members of the Security Council accounted for 71.09 percent of the budget in 1946, but their share has come down to 45.40 percent in the assessments to be applied in the 2019–2021 term. The General Assembly has operated on the basis of the one country–one vote principle since its inception, which, understandably, has created tensions from time to time given its authority over budgetary matters. Switzerland's contribution (1.151 percent) exceeds the cumulative contributions of the 120 countries with the smallest assessed shares, a list that

---

[3] These countries argued that an artificial reduction in the assessed contribution of the United States would violate the principle of capacity to pay and shift the burden of the budget to other high-income countries, which would end up paying a higher share than justified by the size of their economies and other factors then in use to determine contribution rates.

[4] These are the assessed rates for the period 2019–2021. For the period 2016–2018, Japan was the second-largest contributor.

begins with the Dominican Republic, Lebanon, Bulgaria, Bahrain, Cyprus, Estonia, Panama, all the way down to Tuvalu and Vanuatu.

POLITICAL TENSIONS FROM THE ONE COUNTRY–ONE VOTE RULE

Since the Charter established a two-thirds General Assembly majority threshold to approve matters pertaining to the budget, and since the voting share of the two-thirds of the membership with the smallest assessed shares adds up to only 1.633 percent (a number only slightly higher than the contribution of Turkey), this created a situation where, de facto, on budgetary matters, the "tail" was often indeed "wagging the dog," in a big way. The imbalance stemming from the one country–one vote principle – which could have been easily anticipated in 1945 – has led to occasional calls from some of the larger contributors to introduce a system of weighted voting in the General Assembly on budgetary matters. As such proposals have not received the support of the smaller members constituting a solid majority in the Assembly, it has instead contributed to enhancing the de facto leverage of countries such as the United States, its largest contributor. It is outside the scope of this chapter to discuss the difficult relationship the United States has had with the United Nations on budgetary matters over the decades. Jeffrey Laurenti provides an excellent overview in his contribution to the *Oxford Handbook on the United Nations*.[5] US contributions have often been in arrears and fallen captive to internal domestic politics, and have resulted in the imposition of multiple demands and conditions over the years that have included, for instance, the introduction of a nominal zero-growth budget over a period of several years – which did much to undermine the effectiveness of various UN programs and initiatives – staff reductions, and the extraction of promises from the United Nations that it would not create a "UN standing army" nor debate, discuss or consider "international taxes." Since 1987, at the urging of the United States, the budget has been approved "by consensus."[6]

---

[5] See Laurenti, "Financing," pp. 675–701.

[6] It is instructive to quote Laurenti in this respect: "American nonpayment brought the UN to the brink of insolvency. Its reserve and capital accounts were drained to pay current expenses, and peacekeeping operations limped along as the regular budget borrowed from peacekeeping accounts, postponing reimbursements to troop-contributing countries till the promised US payments would arrive. By 1987, member states reached agreement on a budgetary package that reduced UN staffing, cut and froze overall spending, and established a new process for budgetary decision-making based on *consensus* – like the old League of Nations. The new process gave Washington more budgetary leverage, though not the weighted voting it had sought. Washington made only desultory payments on the arrears it wracked up [*sic*] in that two-year crisis. Indeed, the number of conditions it attached to its dues payments only multiplied. The Congress reduced its payments for its imputed share of the costs for the UN's office on Palestinian rights, a cause that was anathema in 1980s Washington; it attached withholding provisions to force the organization to create an independent inspector-general's office and to expel a coalition of gay and lesbian groups from UN-recognized nongovernmental status; it prohibited the US from approving any new peacekeeping mission in the Security

BUDGETARY MANAGEMENT

Unpaid contributions have greatly complicated budgetary management at the UN. Countries have built up arrears to the budget in some cases because they do not regard obligations to the UN as legally binding or, in any case, to exceed in importance whatever other claims there may be on their budgets at home, or because, as in the case of the United States and the Soviet Union, they were unhappy with particular policies or practices and wanted to use their contributions as leverage to prompt change. To take an example, in the 1960s the Soviet Union accumulated more than two years of arrears because of dissatisfaction with peace-keeping operations in the Congo. Faced with the possibility of the application of Article 19 and the removal of voting rights, the Soviet authorities threatened to pull out of the United Nations. Such threats were considered credible given that the Soviet Union had already pulled out from membership at the World Bank and the IMF, organizations they would rejoin in 1992 as 15 separate republics, with Russia inheriting the veto in the Security Council. These threats resulted in a compromise that led to the delinking of the peacekeeping budget from the regular budget. One, possibly unintended, effect of this was that, in time, countries tended to see their contributions to the regular budget as being of higher priority than those to peacekeeping operations, which then resulted in the accumulation of large arrears in assessed contributions for peacekeeping; by 2007 more than 85 percent of the latter budget was in arrears.

In the early years, peacekeeping operations were small and funded from the United Nations regular budget. After the Suez Canal crisis in 1956, peacekeeping was funded from a separate budget on the basis of assessed contributions, but under a system than that applied to the regular budget. This reflected in part the very nature of peacekeeping, with needs often arising in an unpredictable fashion, but also the fact that low-income countries often felt that the cost of such operations should be largely borne by the wealthier members. Thus, in 1973, against the background of two Arab–Israeli wars and growing demands for peacekeeping oper-ations, a system was put in place that created several categories of countries depending on the level of income per capita. Category D countries, all low-income and located mainly in sub-Saharan Africa, were granted a 90 percent discount with respect to their assessed contribution rates for the regular budget. Therefore, a country with an assessed rate of 0.015 percent for the regular budget would be expected to pay an additional 0.0015 percent to the peacekeeping budget. Other developing countries were classified as Category C and given an 80 percent dis-count. Thus, a country with an assessed rate of 0.75 percent would be assessed for an

Council until congressional leaders had had two weeks' notice to scrutinize the proposal. When a shift in party control catapulted UN foes into the chairmanship of key congressional committees in early 1995, the Congress simply refused to appropriate funds for major peace-keeping operations, and US arrears quintupled in just two years" (ibid., p. 689).

additional 0.15 percent as their contribution to peacekeeping. Category B countries, made up of high-income countries not members of the Security Council, would be expected to pay the same rate as applied to the regular budget (i.e., zero discount), and Category A countries consisting of the P-5 were expected to make up the shortfall.

Although this system was initially adopted on an interim basis for a one-year period, in practice it was renewed annually and remained in place until 2000, when a new compromise was arrived at that increased the number of country groupings to six and sharply reduced the discount applying to Category C countries, from 80 percent to 7.5 percent. In any case, in either system the burden of peacekeeping fell disproportionally on the United States, the United Kingdom and France, given the low assessed contributions of Russia and China which, in the latter case, by 1995 was 0.720 percent. This compromise notwithstanding, the United States imposed, unilaterally, a ceiling of 25 percent on its assessed contribution for peace-keeping. Laurenti sums up convincingly the UN's main problem in this area: "The refusal by the largest member states to pay assessed contributions whose level or purpose displeases them has become a recurrent feature of funding politics at the UN. The consequent fragility of its financial base is one of the UN's fundamental weaknesses."[7]

TABLE 12.1. *Total revenue of the UN system by UN agency and by financing instrument, 2016*

Agency	US$ millions				
	Assessed contribution	Voluntary untied	Voluntary earmarked	Other fees	Total 2016
UN Secretariat	2,549	0	2,063	535	5,147
UN Peacekeeping	8,282	0	392	52	8,726
Specialized agencies	3,142	5,060	24,230	3,028	35,463
Of which:					
FAO	487	0	770	39	1,296
WHO	468	113	1,726	57	2,364
IAEA	371	0	252	9	632
UNICEF	0	1,186	3,571	126	4,884
Total	13,973	5,060	26,685	3,615	49,336

Source: *Financing the UN Development System: Opening Doors*, New York, Dag Hammarskjold Foundation, United Nations MPTF Office, United Nations Development Program (UNDP). September 2018.

---

[7] Ibid., p. 687.

TABLE 12.2. *Assessed contributions to the UN system by UN agency, 1975–2016*

Organization	1975	1980	1985	1990	1995	2000	2005	2010	2015	2016
UN Secretariat	268	510	618	888	1,135	1,089	1,828	2,167	2,771	2,549
Specialized agencies	401	816	1,071	1,411	1,871	2,048	2,446	3,207	3,247	3,142
Of which:										
FAO	54	139	211	278	311	322	377	507	497	487
WHO	119	214	260	307	408	421	429	473	467	468
IAEA	32	81	95	155	203	217	278	392	377	371
UNESCO	89	152	187	182	224	272	305	377	341	323
Total	669	1,326	1,689	2,299	3,006	3,137	4,274	5,374	6,018	5,691

Source: *Financing the UN Development System: Opening Doors*, New York, Dag Hammarskjold Foundation, United Nations MPTF Office, United Nations Development Program (UNDP). September 2018.

TABLE 12.3. *Voluntary earmarked funding to the UN system by UN agency, 2005–2016*

Agency	2005	2010	2013	2014	2015	2016
UN Secretariat	848	1,361	1,440	2,321	2,094	2,063
Specialized agencies	14,325	18,906	22,255	23,957	23,112	24,230
Of which:						
WFP	2,963	3,845	4,095	4,943	4,469	5,108
UNDP	3,609	4,311	3,897	3,809	3,726	4,122
WHO	1,117	1,442	1,929	1,970	1,857	1,726
UNICEF	1,921	2,718	3,588	3,843	3,836	3,571
Total	15,196	20,300	23,725	26,423	25,401	26,685

Source: *Financing the UN Development System: Opening Doors*, New York, Dag Hammarskjold Foundation, United Nations MPTF Office, United Nations Development Program (UNDP). September 2018.

TABLE 12.4. *Total expenditure by UN agency, 2005–2016*

Agency	2005	2010	2013	2014	2015	2016
UN Secretariat	2,659	3,953	4,310	5,145	5,613	5,713
UN Peacekeeping[a]	5,148	7,616	7,273	7,863	8,759	8,876
Specialized agencies	18,340	28,866	30,863	33,360	33,688	34,176
Of which:						
FAO	771	1,415	1,380	1,246	1,219	1,202
IAEA	443	585	606	581	570	550
UNICEF	2,191	3,631	4,082	4,540	5,077	5,427
WHO	1,541	2,078	2,261	2,317	2,738	2,471
Total expenditures	20,999	40,435	42,446	46,368	48,060	48,765

[a] Figure for 2005 is not available; figure shown corresponds to 2007
Source: *Financing the UN Development System: Opening Doors*, New York, Dag Hammarskjold Foundation, United Nations MPTF Office, United Nations Development Program (UNDP). September 2018.

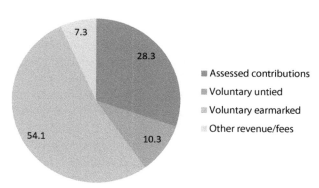

FIGURE 12.1. Total revenue of UN system by financing instrument, 2016.

It is useful to look at the level and the structure of funding of the UN in 2016, the latest year for which a fairly complete data set is available. We will also comment briefly on the evolution over time of some of the main revenue sources. There are several features worth highlighting.

- Assessed contributions to the UN budget in 2016 amounted to US$13,973 million, of which US$8,282 million was for peacekeeping (59.3 percent of the total), with US$2,549 million allocated to the UN Secretariat's so-called regular budget and US$3,142 million to the specialized agencies. The share of the peacekeeping budget in 1971 was a mere 6.1 percent of the total and had risen to 17.4 percent by 1991. There is some irony in the fact that the amounts allocated to peacekeeping operations rose most rapidly after 1991, with the end of the Cold War, a period that was expected to deliver the so-called peace dividend. It is noteworthy that even at US$8.3 billion in 2016, the peacekeeping budget amounts to about 0.5 percent of total world military spending.
- A total of US$5,691 million was allocated to the UN Secretariat and its 20 specialized agencies. The four largest recipients among these were the Food and Agriculture Organization (FAO), the World Health Organization (WHO), the International Atomic Energy Agency (IAEA) and UNESCO. By 1971 the regular budget accounted for about 40 percent of the assessed budget. This share had fallen to 18.2 percent by 2016.
- The share of the regular budget in the total budget (including voluntary earmarked contributions) has been on a downward trend, reaching 10.4 percent by 2016.
- The share of the assessed budget going to specialized agencies such as WHO, FAO and others fell from 54 percent in 1971 to 22.5 percent by 2016.
- The regular budget has remained small, growing from a very tiny base at the outset of the creation of the UN when the annual budget was less than US$20 million, at an average annual rate of about 2 percent in real terms. On a per capita basis, the regular budget is equivalent to about US$0.38 per year for every person on the planet.
- Of the US$26,685 million in voluntary earmarked contributions made by donors in 2016, US$24,230 was allocated to specialized agencies, with the rest going mainly to the UN Secretariat, with some small amounts allocated to peacekeeping. The largest recipients of earmarked contributions were the World Food Programme (WFP), the United Nations Development Programme (UNDP), WHO and UNICEF.
- Table 12.5 shows data on per capita assessed contributions corresponding to the 2015 budget, which recorded US$14,519 million in revenues. The 15 largest contributors to the UN budget on a per capita basis are

Monaco, Liechtenstein, Norway, Switzerland, Luxembourg, Qatar, Denmark, Australia, Sweden, Tuvalu, San Marino, Netherlands, Finland, Austria, and Canada. The five veto-wielding members of the Security Council occupy the following positions: France (22), the United States (26), the United Kingdom (27), Russia (57), and China (93). India is in 147th place. In per capita dollar terms these contributions range from US$23–38 in the case of Monaco, Liechtenstein, and Norway, to US$0.08 in the case of India, to about US$0.01 (one cent or less) in the case of the Democratic Republic of the Congo, Somalia and Bangladesh, the three lowest contributors. The United States' per capita contribution is US$9.88, while its national per capita defense expenditure for the 2018 fiscal year was US$2,050. That is, defense expenditures are 207 times larger than UN contributions on a per capita basis.[8]

- The EU, which has a GDP that is broadly comparable to that of the United States, contributes 29.3 percent of the assessed budget, compared with 22.0 percent for the United States.

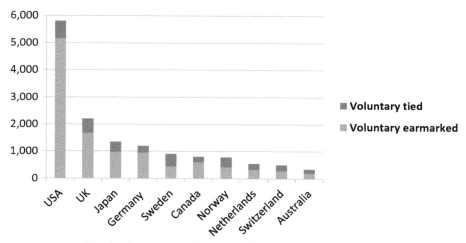

FIGURE 12.2. Total voluntary contributions of top ten countries, US$m, 2015.

Perhaps the most interesting feature of the data is the extent to which, by 2015, total voluntary contributions dwarfed contributions to the regular budget, by a factor of nearly 11, and even exceeded by a significant margin total amounts budgeted to specialized agencies, peacekeeping and the regular budget combined. Voluntary earmarked contributions tend to be lopsided, with four countries – the United States, the United Kingdom, Japan and Germany – accounting for about 42 percent of the total and the European Union accounting for about a third. The General

---

[8] If one uses defense expenditures for fiscal year 2020, this ratio rises from 207 to 218.

Assembly, which discusses, recommends and approves the assessed part of the budget, has little say on the uses of voluntary contributions, which tend to reflect individual donor country economic, political and developmental priorities. Donor countries have bypassed the General Assembly and use the United Nations infrastructure as a conduit to leverage the impact of their bilateral aid programs. In this way, they may use the UN label, while maintaining for themselves full discretion over how to spend these contributions. Some critics of voluntary funding, including Haji Iqbal,[9] point out that the UN Charter makes no provisions for such funding; it assumes that all UN expenditures will be based on assessed contributions paid by members and the General Assembly will retain authority over the levels and associated priorities of such funding. Indeed, from this perspective, voluntary contributions can be seen as having a wobbly legal foundation. One could argue that a rigid interpretation of the UN Charter on this point and, in particular, the application of the one country–one vote principle and the lopsided distribution of contributions across members would have long ago starved the UN budget of needed funds.

TABLE 12.5. *Per capita contribution of top 15 countries to UN budget[a]*

Country	Per capita contribution to UN budget, in USD	Rank
Monaco	37.71	1
Liechtenstein	26.98	2
Norway	23.47	3
Switzerland	19.88	4
Luxembourg	16.13	5
Qatar	14.92	6
Denmark	14.86	7
Australia	13.91	8
Sweden	13.89	9
Tuvalu	13.20	10
San Marino	13.07	11
Netherlands	12.63	12
Finland	12.07	13
Austria	11.96	14
Canada	11.71	15
France	10.92	22
United States	9.88	26
United Kingdom	9.87	27
Russian Federation	3.13	57
China	0.83	93
India	0.08	147

[a] For assessed contributions (i.e., excluding voluntary contributions) but also includes all permanent members of Security Council and India

[9] Haji, Iqbal. 1997. "The 'Problem' of Voluntary Funding," *UN Chronicle*, Vol. 34, no. 4, p.75, New York, United Nations.

Faced with the option of boosting contributions to the regular budget in order to match growing needs within a rapidly interdependent community of nations grappling with an expanding list of global challenges, but having little say on the use of such resources within the General Assembly, donor countries opened up a new avenue of funding over which they would have the control that they lacked within the regular budget. Thus, voluntary contributions were a natural response to the fiction that we live in a world in which Dominica, with its 0.001 percent contribution, should have an equal say over the disposition of resources as Japan, with a contribution 8,564 times larger. Nevertheless, one perhaps unintended consequence of the large volume of voluntary contributions with respect to assessed funding is that the majority of United Nations staff do not, in fact, ultimately work for the organization that pays their salaries. Rather, they work for the donor countries that provide the funding for the many programs to which these funds are earmarked. Likewise, while many people may think that the organization is run with a US$49 billion annual budget, the reality is much more modest; assessed contributions to the UN Secretariat budget in 2016 amounted to slightly more than US$2.5 billion.

PROPOSALS FOR UNITED NATIONS FUNDING

This situation has led many to argue that a strengthened UN system, with a broader set of responsibilities and strengthened and expanded institutions would need a reliable source of funding, free of the inconsistencies, opaque practices, arbitrariness and contradictions that have emerged through several decades of practice. It would also need to be delinked entirely from the kinds of domestic political considerations that have sometimes intruded upon budget debates and have held the UN's activities hostage to the demagoguery or bias of local politicians, the occasional emergence of isolationist tendencies in some member countries and so on. In light of the need for new, coherent solutions to funding a UN adequate for twenty-first century challenges we will put forth four proposals and examine their respective merits and potential problems. We feel strongly that any one of them would be superior to the current non-system.

A FIXED PROPORTION OF GNI

Under this proposal based on work by Schwartzberg,[10] the United Nations would simply assess member contributions at a fixed percent of their respective GNIs. Total world GNI at market prices in 2017 was US$79.8 trillion. A 0.1 percent of GNI contribution to the UN budget would generate US$79.8 billion, a sizable sum to start with. The main advantage of this system is simplicity and transparency. Every country would be assessed at the same rate; the criterion for burden-sharing is crystal

---

[10] Schwartzberg, Joseph E. 2013. *Transforming the United Nations System: Designs for a Workable World*, Tokyo, United Nations University Press.

clear. Contributions are linked to economic size – as in the current system – but without the need for carve-outs, exceptions, floors and ceilings, discounts and the need to develop "formulas" of questionable integrity and credibility. There is also no need to develop a separate UN tax collection machinery, which has been noted as a potential problem in other proposals put forward in the past to address the problem of UN funding. One potential criticism of this proposal is that the tax rate is not progressive; the same rate applies to all countries, regardless of the level of income. We feel that this feature is not a problem in the same way that flat taxes on personal income can sometimes be. First, there is nothing to prevent the UN from ensuring that most of the benefits of its activities and expenditures are, in any case, allocated to its lower-income members. This is, of course, already happening in the current system, particularly in the case of the spending channeled through its specialized agencies and programs. Therefore, the absence of progressivity in the tax rate assessed on contributions is more than offset by the presence of a large measure of progressivity in the allocation of benefits to lower-income countries.

Second, even at 0.1 percent of GNI the assessed tax rate is low. Countries typically spend an average of 2 percent of GNI on their militaries – 20 times more than their proposed contributions to the UN budget. To the extent that, at 0.1 percent of GNI, the UN would be empowered to do a great deal more in terms of the delivery of enhanced security to its members (see Chapter 8, as strengthening the rule of law and the other measures enhance the members' security significantly), this new system could make great economic sense, in terms of the benefits it would deliver. At present, there are a large number of countries for which their assessed contributions amount to less than five cents per person per year, amounts that are strikingly low and that have likely contributed to a culture of lack of ownership of the United Nations by many of its members. Furthermore, it would have another important advantage. Instead of empowering segments of public opinion – for instance in the United States, which have generally made much of the fact that their country contributes, say, 22 percent of the UN's assessed budget – now the narrative would simply shift to observing that all countries are assessed at the same (low) rate, thus ending the argument.

In any proposal for new funding mechanisms for the UN we need to move to a more representative system of weighted voting in the General Assembly, such as already exists at the World Bank and the IMF. It is not reasonable to expect the United States, China, Japan and Germany, the four largest contributors, accounting for 28 percent of the world's population, to account for 2 percent of votes in the General Assembly (e.g., as four out of 193 members). This imbalance has been a primary factor explaining the emergence of the distortions and inefficient practices and all-around chaos that today characterize UN finances. With the reformed model, at just 0.1 percent of GNI, contributions today would exceed the UN budget, generating resources that could, for example, be put in an escrow account "to enable the United Nations to respond expeditiously to unanticipated peacekeeping emergencies and major natural disasters.'"[11] Better yet, such excess resources could be invested, as Norway has done so successfully with its Petroleum Stabilization Fund. Moreover, since climate change shocks are expected to affect all members, one can imagine situations in the future where all members may have the right to draw on such resources in an emergency, as is the case, for instance, with many of the IMF's funding facilities. In the 1970s, even the United Kingdom and Italy gained access to the Fund's standby arrangements.

Furthermore, with a system of weighted voting in the General Assembly – meaning a more sensible system of incentives for members – one can imagine a gradual return to the vision that was originally laid out in the UN Charter, one in which expenditures would truly be subject to General Assembly oversight and scrutiny and voluntary contributions would not play the disproportionately large role that they play today. A final advantage of this system is that it would reposition the United Nations and, in particular, the Economic and Social Council (ECO-SOC), to play a more vital role in questions of economic and social development, as envisaged in the Charter.[12] The existing funding arrangements have done much to sideline the United Nations from vital debates that have taken place in recent decades, for instance, in terms of the response to the global financial crisis in 2008, with other groupings – the G-20 – playing a more prominent role but, obviously, facing legitimacy issues of its own because of the absence of voice for the other 173 members. We will call this the Schwartzberg proposal, in honor of its chief proponent.

THE CLARK–SOHN PROPOSAL

In *World Peace through World Law*, Clark and Sohn put forward a proposal of their own that merits examination. Because they envisage a considerably strengthened United Nations and anticipate a General Assembly operating under a system of weighted voting, they propose revisions to Article 17 which, for instance, "would greatly broaden the control of the General Assembly over the activities of all the specialized agencies, not only by requiring that the separate budgets of these agencies be approved by the Assembly, but also by making the general budget of the United Nations the main source of their funds."[13] Clark and Sohn's proposal assumes that each nation would contribute a fixed percentage of its GNP to the United Nations and does not specify what the domestic sources for those revenues would be. These contributions are an obligation of membership and there would be

---

[11] Schwartzberg, *Transforming the United Nations System: Designs for a Workable World*, p. 217. www.brookings.edu/book/transforming-the-united-nations-system/.

[12] No fewer than 11 articles of the UN Charter (Articles 62–72) are dedicated to identifying the powers and functions of ECOSOC. The founding members obviously envisaged that it would play a vital role in economic and social development debates and programs.

[13] Clark and Sohn, *World Peace through World Law*, p. 54.

no need for the United Nations to develop a tax collection machinery, beyond that already existing in member countries. They do, however, have very detailed proposals on the distribution of the burden across members, given a particular budget. It is an interesting exercise to see how the burden would change in their proposals, with respect to the assessments in force for the period 2016–2018. We will do this by describing their proposal first and then by updating their calculations using population and GDP figures for 2016.

For each nation's GNP, Clark and Sohn propose making a so-called per capita deduction that "would be equal to an amount arrived at by multiplying the estimated population of such nation by a sum fixed from time to time by the General Assembly, which sum shall be not less than fifty or more than ninety percent of the estimated average per capita product of the people of the ten member Nations having the lowest per capita national product."[14] The resulting amount would be the "adjusted national product" and the calculated shares of the budget attributed to each nation would be determined by the ratio between this concept and the sum of all "adjusted national products" for all member nations. They provide a useful illustration using notional GNP and population figures for two countries in 1980 (see pp. 351–352 in *World Peace through World Law*). We have done these calculations for just over a dozen countries, and Table 12.6 compares the assessments in use by the United Nations during 2016–2018 with those that would emerge from the Clark and Sohn proposal using updated figures.[15]

As can be seen, the main impact of their method is to substantially raise the assessed contribution of China, to do so marginally for the United States – both of which would now account for 40.2 percent of the budget, compared with 29.9 percent today – reduce the contributions of countries such as Japan, Germany, Norway, Sweden, and the United Kingdom, increase the contributions of countries such as India and Nigeria, and virtually eliminate the contributions of countries with the lowest income per capita. Malawi's assessed contribution, for instance, would drop from 0.002 percent today, to 0.000052 percent in the Clark–Sohn proposal. The ratio of the contribution rate of the United States to that of Malawi would rise from 11,000 today to 487,731 under their proposal.

We understand the motivation of Clark and Sohn in introducing something like a "low-income discount" for assessed contributions to the United Nations budget. They made these proposals in the late 1950s, when the incidence of extreme poverty was much higher than it is today and when living conditions, more generally, were appalling in much of the developing world. Average life expectancy in 1960 was 52 years, compared with 72 today, and infant mortality was, likewise, extremely high by

---

[14] Ibid., p. 350.

[15] The list of ten countries with the lowest income per capita in the world in 2017 (ordered from highest to lowest) includes Sierra Leone, Somalia, Democratic Republic of the Congo, Madagascar, Niger, Mozambique, Central African Republic, Malawi, Burundi, and South Sudan.

TABLE 12.6. *The Clark–Sohn proposal (in percent)*

UN member	Current assessment[a]	Adjusted assessment
Bangladesh	0.010	0.248
Brazil	3.823	2.379
China	7.921	14.820
France	4.859	3.350
Germany	6.389	4.729
India	0.737	2.578
Japan	9.680	6.706
Malawi	0.002	0.000052
Nigeria	0.209	0.481
Norway	0.849	0.505
Sweden	0.956	0.695
Russia	3.088	1.699
United Kingdom	4.463	3.572
United States	22.000	25.362
World	100.000	100.000
Memo items:		
Average income per capita for 10 poorest countries (US$)	418.1	

[a] Current assessments correspond to the 2016–2018 period

today's standards. Indeed, the current financing system already has some of this flavor, with low-income countries contributing considerably less than their indicative GNI share and high-income countries contributing correspondingly more. We favor a system that would impose a more equitable burden across the United Nations membership. There is much to be gained from developing countries seeing that they have a stake in a reformed United Nations and that they are contributing a fair share to an organization that, in any event, will, at least as regards its priorities in the area of economic and social development, be very focused on low-income countries, from support for fragile or post-conflict states, assistance in conflict prevention, various other types of national capacity-building and, more generally, dealing with the challenges of still very high levels of extreme poverty, illiteracy and malnutrition.

THE EU MODEL

Another option is to introduce a funding mechanism similar to that currently operating in the EU, where each country's payment is divided into three parts: a fixed percentage of GNI, customs duties collected on behalf of the EU (known as "traditional own resources") and a percentage of VAT income, all of which member states collect and allocate automatically to the EU budget. The EU has not developed a separate revenue collection machinery, with the collection of taxes left as a responsibility of individual states. This system has served the EU extremely well. It has provided a reliable source of funding that is independent of domestic political considerations. Member countries do not get to withhold contributions whenever they disagree with the orientation of particular policies (on which, in any case, they get to vote under a system of proportional voting), or when other domestic priorities emerge. The system provides a level of automaticity in funding that has eliminated discretion at the level of individual member states.

Consequently, the EU is able to frame budgets in a medium-term perspective – it approves a budget at six-year intervals – and can plan accordingly. As regards the tax base, for those countries without VAT (a minority of states), one possibility would be to allocate a share of indirect taxes on goods and services collected in each member country. The percentage of such taxes to be allocated to the UN budget could be pitched to achieve the desired end in terms of the volume of total contributions. For those few countries without well-developed systems of indirect taxation, one could use an alternative tax base, such as a share of taxes on corporate profits, assessed at levels that would achieve proportional burden-sharing across countries. One advantage of this proposal is its automaticity. Having agreed to pass on to the United Nations a share of VAT or indirect taxes, funding would not be subject to members' whims and discretion. As long as the United Nations was discharging its responsibilities as called for in the Charter and under the general supervision and oversight of the General Assembly, funding would flow regularly, empowering the organization to frame its activities in a medium-term framework, free of the uncertainties and vagaries of the current system.

A TOBIN-LIKE TAX

Another possibility is the tax proposed by James Tobin on spot currency transactions or its successor, a tax on financial transactions. Tobin made his initial proposals in the immediate aftermath of the collapse of the Bretton Woods system of fixed exchange rates in 1971, and its primary motivation was less to generate tax revenue and more to dampen the speculation that was contributing to heightened exchange rate volatility in foreign exchange markets, delinked from broader economic fundamentals, and placing a particularly heavy burden on producers and consumers of traded goods. Tobin's proposals have generated considerable debate, controversy and confusion over the years. It is worthwhile, therefore, to briefly summarize his thinking, particularly as it evolved over the 25 years following his Janeway Lectures at Princeton University in 1972 when the proposal was first made. By the mid-1990s, and against the background of multiple financial crises in various parts of the world, Tobin expressed particular concern about speculative attacks against countries that were undergoing some financial turmoil and were forced to increase interest rates sharply to defend their currencies, with deleterious effects on economic activity and employment.

Since he was skeptical that the world would quickly move to the full coordination of monetary and fiscal policies and the introduction of a common currency, he opted for throwing "some sand in the well-greased wheels" of international money markets.[16] Tobin lamented the exchange rate volatility that had emerged in the wake of the collapse of the fixed exchange rate regime in the early 1970s and noted that "in these markets, as in other markets for financial instruments, speculation on future prices is the dominating preoccupation of the participants ... In the absence of any consensus on fundamentals, the markets are dominated—like those for gold, rare paintings, and—yes, often equities—by traders in the game of guessing what other traders are going to think."[17] While he recognized that financial markets often imposed a degree of discipline on countries' monetary and fiscal policies, he thought that the punishment delivered by speculation often far exceeded the policy mistakes or misalignments brought about by the authorities, as had been the case in Mexico in 1994, and as would become clear during the 1997 Asian financial crises and other emerging market crises precipitated in its wake.

Tobin's essential point was to "penalize short-horizon round trips" in foreign currency transactions while not affecting in any significant way the incentives for trade in commodities and longer-term capital investments. He thought that a tax administered with some flexibility would be a better instrument to combat runaway speculation than bureaucratic controls and/or burdensome financial regulations. In his 1996 contribution to *The Tobin Tax – Coping with Financial Volatility*, he observed that 80 percent of foreign exchange transactions involved round trips of seven days or less, with the majority of these being of *one-day duration*.[18] By 1995, daily foreign exchange trading amounted to US\$1.3 trillion, or US\$312 trillion on an annual basis, dwarfing trade in equities and nearly 67 times larger than the total value of annual world exports.

Tobin commented that part of the opposition to the tax proposal was philosophical: it was "rejected on the same general grounds that incline economists to dismiss out of hand any interferences with market competition, including, of course, tariffs and other barriers to international trade in goods and services."[19] The belief that expectations of economic actors are rational and that financial markets are efficient and that ultimately "financial markets know best" is widespread among market participants, even though, Tobin argued, it was not clear to him that trade in financial assets and trade in goods and services were one and the same thing, subject to the same insights from economic theory that had long been in favor of free trade.

---

[16] See Tobin's "A Proposal for International Monetary Reform," his presidential address at the 1978 conference of the Eastern Economic Association, *Eastern Economic Journal*, Vol. 4, No. 3/4, pp. 153–159.

[17] Ibid., pp. 157 and 158.

[18] See his prologue in Mahbub ul Haq, Inge Kaul, and Isabelle Grunberg (eds.), *The Tobin Tax – Coping with Financial Volatility*, Oxford, Oxford University Press, 1996, pp. lx–xviii.

[19] Ibid.

By the time of the global financial crisis in 2008, James Tobin was no longer with us, but one can safely assume that he may have agreed with another Nobel laureate, Robert Shiller, and his statement that our "economies, left to their own devices, without the balancing of governments, are essentially unstable."[20] Such a tax, it was also argued, would also damage liquidity in currency markets, drive these markets to tax-free havens if it were not a universal tax, and so on.

John Maynard Keynes had already advocated a general financial transaction tax in 1936 to discourage the emergence of a class of speculators whose activities would be primarily motivated by the search for short-term profit linked to asset price changes and which, in his view, would needlessly add to market volatility. Keynes had warned that "it makes a vast difference to an investment market whether or not they (meaning serious investors who purchase investments on best long-term expectations of value) predominate in their influence over the game-players."[21] Tobin returned to and elaborated on his original proposal in 1978 in his presidential address to the Eastern Economic Association. He said:

> It would be an internationally agreed uniform tax, administered by each government over its own jurisdiction. Britain, for example, would be responsible for taxing all inter-currency transactions in Eurocurrency banks and brokers located in London, even when sterling was not involved. The tax would apply to all purchases of financial instruments denominated in another currency—from currency and coin to equity securities. It would have to apply, I think, to all payments in one currency for goods, services, and real assets sold by a resident of another currency area. I don't intend to add even a small barrier to trade. But I see offhand no other way to prevent financial transactions disguised as trade … Doubtless there would be difficulties of administration and enforcement. Doubtless there would be ingenious patterns of evasion. But since these will not be costless either, the main purpose of the plan will not be lost.[22]

Supporters of the so-called Tobin tax have noted that with more than US$5 trillion traded daily on the currency markets by 2016, a 0.05 percent tax could generate some US$2.5 billion per day in revenue (about US$600 billion on an annual basis), which could then be directed to multiple ends, from climate change

[20] Shiller, Robert. 2009. "A Failure to Control the Animal Spirits," *Financial Times*, March 9.
[21] Keynes, John Maynard. 1973. *The Collected Writings of John Maynard Keynes*, Volume VII: *The General Theory of Employment, Interest and Money*, London, Macmillan Press, p. 156. Noting that "when Wall Street is active, at least a half of the purchases or sales of investments are entered upon with an intention on the part of the speculator to reverse them the *same* day," Keynes observed that "the high brokerage charges and the heavy transfer tax payable to the Exchequer, which attend dealings on the London Stock Exchange, sufficiently diminish the liquidity of the market to rule out a large proportion of the transaction characteristic of Wall Street. The introduction of a substantial government transfer tax on all transactions might prove the most serviceable reform available, with a view to mitigating the predominance of speculation over enterprise in the United States" (p. 160).
[22] Ibid., pp 158–159.

mitigation and adaptation to worthy projects aimed at poverty alleviation, inclusive economic growth, global public goods and so on. Indeed, one could make the argument that the case for the tax has become stronger in the wake of the 2008–2009 global financial crisis. As a result of the multiple government interventions to mitigate the impact of the crisis, levels of public indebtedness in rich countries – the providers of the bulk of development aid – are sky high, higher, in fact, than at any time since the end of World War II, and this has sharply curtailed their appetite for substantially boosting development aid. Tobin, using the figures for trade volumes in foreign exchange for 1995 (US$1.3 trillion per day), thought that the revenue collected would be less because the introduction of the tax would dampen the volumes traded, particularly for trades with a very short horizon for which even a small tax, on an annualized basis, applied to multiple transactions would raise transaction costs significantly. He also noted that the lion's share of trading in the foreign exchange market took place among financial intermediaries, and were not customer–bank transactions, as were those supporting international trade in goods, for instance, or linked in some fashion to some real economic activity.

The Tobin tax proposals have generated a lively debate in policy-making circles and the academic community. Some have argued that a tax levied on currency transactions could, through creative financial engineering, be evaded. Moreover, not all foreign exchange purchases have a speculative dimension. There is a difference, it is argued, between hedging and speculation. Hedging is intended to protect the investor against unpredictable price changes; it is a way to limit price risk and can be seen as a form of insurance. Speculation, on the other hand, has the investor assuming greater risk in the expectation of a higher profit linked to price volatility and is, thus, no different than gambling. To avoid being fooled by the emergence of financial instruments that would disguise a foreign currency transaction (on which a tax would be due) in a different product (to which the tax would not apply), it might be better to shift the original Tobin tax idea, some argue, to a generalized transaction tax that would be broad enough to capture a wide spectrum of financial instruments.

In other words, one would wish to create a tax that would sharply limit the incentives for substitution across financial instruments or jurisdictions. Such a tax would have added benefits with respect to the original Tobin proposals. It could, in principle, generate more revenue, it would not disadvantage one type of financial transaction (i.e., foreign exchange trading) vis-à-vis others, and by discouraging speculation, it might actually steer financial resources to other more productive, value-creating ends, with a higher social return. Obviously, the level of the tax would be important. There is ample evidence from tax regimes across the developed and developing world that tax rates that are too high can unleash all sorts of perverse incentives (e.g., growth in the informal economy, tax evasion) that ultimately have totally counterproductive effects. On the one hand, according to the World Bank, countries in sub-Saharan Africa have the highest total tax rates in the world and also the narrowest tax bases and lowest levels of revenue collection.[23] On the other hand, the United Kingdom assesses a Stamp Duty on transactions on shares and securities without, it would appear, having hindered the growth of a robust financial sector. The Netherlands, France, Japan, Korea and other countries have introduced similar taxes as well.

There is also an interesting debate on the issue of how the tax would be collected. Here, the debate has evolved over the past several decades because of advances in technology and the concentration of financial transactions in a relatively small number of markets. Brazil introduced in 1993 a tax on bank transactions to widespread skepticism that the tax would actually work from a tax administration point of view, with many arguing that evasion would sabotage the effectiveness of the tax. However, digital technologies empowered the tax authorities and the tax proved to be fairly evasion-proof. Indeed, more generally, the arrival of online tax payments has reached even low-income countries by now and authorities are far more adept today at plugging revenue leakages that, in the past, were also associated with a high incidence of corruption. London, New York and Tokyo account for close to 60 percent of all foreign exchange trading; seven financial centers account for more than 80 percent of all transactions and, increasingly, transactions are cleared and settled in a centralized fashion, greatly facilitating tax collection. Tobin thought that the problem of tax evasion – which applies to all taxes and is hardly ever used as an excuse not to assess a particular tax – could be addressed in a number of ways. First, he thought that the tax could be collected by the countries themselves, and that developing countries in particular could be allowed to keep a significant share of the amounts collected to fund national development needs.

Second, tapping into a new revenue stream, countries could opt to lower other taxes, to reduce deficits, to ensure a more sustainable debt-servicing profile or to redress the effects of revenue losses linked to the globalized nature of the economy, with production and plant capacity much more mobile than had been the case at the turn of the twentieth century. This could create positive incentives for countries to voluntarily agree to the introduction of the tax. Given the international nature of the tax, he thought that the IMF's Articles of Agreement could be amended to make the introduction of the tax an obligation of Fund membership.[24] This would imply that IMF members would not have access to its various financing windows and other benefits if they opted not to introduce the tax. Since a large share of foreign exchange transactions are concentrated in a relatively small number of markets, some general agreement among a handful of financial centers would most likely suffice to capture a large share of the revenue.

---

[23] See, e.g., any recent issue of the Bank's *Doing Business* report.
[24] Amendments to the IMF's Articles of Agreement set a high bar; they require 85 percent of the voting power of the membership.

A clearly important issue pertains to the impact of a financial transactions tax on the economy. Would it reduce employment, not just in the financial sector but in other sectors of the economy that play a supporting role to finance, and by how much? Would it reduce liquidity in the markets? Would it lead to cross-border arbitrage as other jurisdictions (i.e., tax havens) sought advantage from the absence of the tax, if serious efforts are not made to ensure it is a universal tax? Critics of the tax point to the experience of Sweden, which in the 1980s introduced a tax on the trading of equities and, several years later, on fixed income securities. Because a significant share of trading in the Swedish market moved to London and New York, tax revenues were smaller than anticipated and the authorities ultimately opted for reducing the taxes and finally eliminating them altogether.

Other countries, however, have had much better experiences, including Japan, Korea and Switzerland, where a variety of taxes have been in place for many years and have not prevented the emergence of strong, deep financial sectors. Obviously, consideration of the tax would require the balancing of several objectives, from the desirability of generating additional revenue to promote economic development objectives (and addressing intensifying global catastrophic risks) to ensuring that implementation of the tax is feasible, and that it involves appropriate levels of international coordination and cooperation to ensure its success. In any case, given the size of today's United Nations budget and the potential revenue to be collected through a Tobin tax, we think there is merit in Tobin's idea that countries could be presented with a menu of choices as to how to allocate the proceeds of the tax, including, of course, a substantial allocation to the United Nations.

Indeed, in the longer term a Tobin tax or something similar, taking advantage of the substantial opportunities generated by economic globalization for government revenue generation, could be a promising avenue to provide funding to the United Nations, over and above the levels contributed from national treasuries linked to a fixed percentage of GNI. However, political opposition could be strong, given powerful anti-tax sentiments in many countries such as the United States, where even a carbon tax remains a distant prospect.[25] Financial sector interests in many countries are powerful and it is not difficult to imagine armies of lobbyists pressuring (or intimidating) lawmakers not to support the tax. Eichengreen makes the important observation that one would have to address in some way the issue of the mismatch between the volume of the tax that would be collected in particular jurisdictions and the ability or willingness of those countries to provide the concomitant levels of aid linked to the tax.[26] London accounts for a large share of foreign exchange transactions worldwide but the United Kingdom, though a generous

[25] Although, as of mid-2019, there are early indications that some states may consider doing this on their own, absent leadership from the federal government.
[26] Eichengreen, Barry. 1996. "The Tobin Tax: What Have We Learned?" in Mahbub ul Haq, Inge Kaul, and Isabelle Grunberg (eds.), *The Tobin Tax – Coping with Financial Volatility*, Oxford, Oxford University Press, 1996, pp. 273–287.

donor, accounts for a much smaller share of total donor funding to the United Nations and other development initiatives. The point is a valid one, but it simply highlights that one would have to implement the tax in the context of international agreements that addressed the issue of burden-sharing through the balancing of multiple national and global objectives.

Schwartzberg has a different set of arguments against the introduction of a Tobin tax to fund the United Nations, some of which are relevant and cannot be ignored. One obvious consideration is that under existing chaotic financing arrangements, the United Nations does not have (for now, anyway; this could change, obviously) the capacity to spend in an efficient, value-creating way the large sums of money that could be collected through a Tobin-tax type of instrument. This is currently true, but it is not an argument against the tax itself; it is rather a commentary on the state of the United Nations, and the "benign neglect" it has suffered. He is also concerned that in the foreseeable future the United Nations will not have the administrative capacity to collect such a tax. This, in our view, is not a persuasive argument because, as already argued, there would be no need for the United Nations itself to be involved in the collection of such a tax through the creation of some UN fiscal agency. The tax would be collected – as suggested by Tobin – by the tax authorities in the countries where the transactions would take place and simply passed on to the United Nations or other recipients, as EU members do with the share of VAT contributions and customs duties that go to the European Commission in Brussels.

UN BUDGET INDEPENDENCE?

Far more persuasive is the argument Schwartzberg puts forward that the world is perhaps not yet ready to give the United Nations the kind of independence that having a direct revenue stream would theoretically provide. Empowering the United Nations by delinking its income from the discretion of its contributing members could feed into a narrative that argues that what is being created is a world government. The main response to this concern argues that giving the United Nations an independent source of funding could come with a shift to a system of weighted voting in the General Assembly, correcting the historic imbalance previously described. In any case, the experience of the EU in this respect is clearly relevant; giving the EU an independent source of funding has co-existed with a considerable degree of latitude for member states to exercise sovereignty in those areas not directly the responsibility of EU institutions.

Second, as described, the members of the United Nations themselves would determine what share of the global Tobin-like tax is allocated to the United Nations and what share goes to other ends, outside of the UN framework. This argument also applies to the first two funding proposals outlined previously. We have used, in the Schwartzberg proposal, a 0.1 percent of GNI contribution rate, but this rate could be agreed upon by members, in light of perceived needs and the desirability of creating a reserve for future contingencies. In principle, it could be reduced or increased, *pari passu* the likely need for global action in the future across a range of areas. Should, for instance, the international community finally get serious about global disarmament (as we have proposed in Chapter 9, in the context of the bringing into being of an International Peace Force), the contribution rate could be raised to finance some of the transition costs associated with the retraining and redeployment of the millions of people currently employed in the military-industrial complex.

The point here is that the ultimate authority for funding levels remains with United Nations members, but in a way that is more transparent and efficient than the current system, which has distributed power over the budget in a very uneven way and has rendered the United Nations increasingly irrelevant in a number of areas.

Third, a United Nations with a more reliable and larger income stream will be a more effective organization, at a time when budgets everywhere are going to come under pressure because of demographic trends (e.g., aging populations in much of the developed and emerging world), the costs associated with the impact of climate change and, sooner or later, the need to deal with the effects of the next global financial crisis. As the United Nations is empowered not only to come to the assistance of low-income countries, but becomes a truly global organization with something to offer to all its members, public perceptions of the organization's usefulness could shift in a fundamental way. For example, we think that the business community could be a strong advocate for the creation of a dependable system of revenue generation for the United Nations, given the large economic costs associated with economic and political instability in many parts of the world, as indicated in Chapter 8 on the establishment of an International Peace Force or, more recently, the concerns expressed by senior policy-makers (e.g., the Governor of the Bank of England) about the potential financial shocks of climate change.

OUR PREFERRED OPTION FOR NOW

We think that in the short term, the Schwartzberg proposal of setting contribution rates at a small fixed share of each country's GNI has multiple merits.[27] Something like 0.1 percent of GNI would not be onerous. It would create a sense of ownership of the organization across the membership, in a way that would have numerous long-term benefits for the United Nations' relevance and credibility. It would be transparent and easy to administer and would relieve the General Assembly from constantly having to come up with novel schemes that in the end violate the principle of even-handedness of treatment across members. A move to a new

---

[27] For the reasons outlined in Chapter 4, on the determination of voting shares in the General Assembly, there would be advantages as well to linking contribution rates to the weighted average of GDPs at market exchange rates and adjusted for PPP, respectively.

funding mechanism would also have to be accompanied by a recommitment from UN members to the principle that contributions to the budget are a legal obligation of membership, not a choice that members make based on other considerations, such as whether they like or support (or not) particular programs or activities. Using budget contributions as leverage (particularly by the larger countries) to encourage reforms within the United Nations system is not consistent with the cooperative nature of the organization, where change should come as a result of deliberations and consultations among members and the forging of consensus for change.

With a system of weighted voting in the General Assembly, it could also allow a return to a budget where the United Nations itself (rather than donors) had ultimate say on the uses that are made of the resources collected, as opposed to the present system where, de facto, the General Assembly has lost control of the lion's share of the budget to its wealthier members through the use of voluntary earmarked contributions, where national donor priorities take precedence over the interests of the whole membership.

Over the medium term the above proposals are not mutually exclusive. There is no reason why the Schwartzberg proposal could not in time be complemented by something like a Tobin tax. As the United Nations established a track record of fiscal prudence and efficiency in the management of financial resources, there is reason to believe that members might be ready at some point to entrust it with a larger body of funding, particularly if by then all the members of the UN, not just its low-income members, can have access to its various programs and facilities.

In connection with the goal of a properly resourced and enhanced UN system, a high-level panel of experts should be convened to explore additional international revenue generation mechanisms, including, for example, an international carbon tax on fossil fuel consumption, a global tax on certain types of mineral resource extraction, an internationally tradable system of pollution permits, duties on alcohol and tobacco, a global wealth tax or other workable ideas, whether based on effective existing international schemes (e.g., that of the International Maritime Organization) or otherwise. In respect of the taxation of fossil fuels, it is noteworthy that according to a 2015 IMF study, at present, on a global scale, some US\$5.3 trillion is spent annually subsidizing the consumption of gasoline, coal, electricity and natural gas – a sum equivalent to 6.5 percent of world GNP. Sixty percent of the benefits of the subsidy for gasoline go to the top 20 percent of the income distribution, highlighting the deeply regressive nature of such subsidies, which have become an instrument for worsening income disparities, at a time when such inequities have reached unprecedented levels. According to the IMF, the elimination of such subsidies would result in a 20 percent drop in emissions of CO_2, contributing to mitigation of the impacts of climate change.

One important element in empowering the United Nations by expanding the envelope of resources available to it and reducing the uncertainty of resource flows, which has been a central characteristic of its history, is to signal to its member countries that resources will be used responsibly and transparently, to build trust in the organization's capacity to enhance the efficiency of resource use.[28] This would strengthen the hand of those who have long argued that contributions to the UN budget are an inseparable obligation of membership, not to be used to blackmail or coerce the organization in the interests of national prerogatives. Indeed, in tandem with such reforms, the UN should play a crucial role in helping its members address a number of serious problems that currently afflict member country tax systems, such as the "race to the bottom" that results from tax competition and that, if allowed to continue, is likely to limit further the ability of governments to respond to vital social and economic needs.[29] We also refer the reader to the discussion on the relationship between corruption and the ability of governments to collect tax revenues presented in Chapter 18, which includes a proposal for the creation of an International Anti-Corruption Court.

---

[28] See also Chapters 18–20 on comprehensive anti-corruption policies, enhanced international leadership and the implementation of norms of modern international good governance, including transparency

[29] This has been recognized in official circles as a serious international problem; see, e.g., www .businesstimes.com.sg/government-economy/the-panama-papers/imf-world-bank-un-oecd-form-new-group-to-stop-tax-erosion.

PART III

Governance and the Management of Multiple Global Risks

13

UN Specialized Agencies and Governance for Global Risks

For the first time in human history, we have reached a level of scientific knowledge that allows us to develop an enlightened relationship to risks of catastrophic magnitude. Not only can we foresee many of the challenges ahead, but we are in a position to identify what needs to be done in order to mitigate or even eliminate some of those risks. Our enlightened status, however, also requires that we ... collectively commit to reducing them.

Allan Dafoe and Anders Sandberg[1]

The United Nations has grown far beyond the institutions directly provided for in the UN Charter. This chapter and those immediately following review a number of global issues and risks that have emerged largely since 1945 and the responses through the UN family of specialized agencies, programs and convention secretariats. We consider the efforts of the UN to develop more strategic and integrated approaches to the range of interrelated problems in sustainable development facing the world today. We then consider examples of reform in the economic, environmental and social dimensions, without attempting to be comprehensive. We first look at governance for the global economy, especially to address the major challenges of growing inequality and the need for a level playing field for business. For the risks of instability in the financial system, we propose reinforcing the role of the International Monetary Fund (IMF) for enhanced financial governance. We then review global environmental governance, including climate change, as well as population and migration as significant global social issues.

ADDRESSING CRITICAL RISKS

While the first impetus for creating institutions of global governance was to prevent inter-state war as the principal risk to global security, many other issues have

---

[1] Dafoe, Allan and Anders Sandberg. 2018. "Why Care Now?" *Global Challenges Foundation Annual Report* 2018. https://globalchallenges.org/en/our-work/annual-report/annual-report-2018/why-care-now.

emerged requiring global collaboration, and the UN system has expanded with a variety of specialized agencies and other entities to address the different issues. Issues in need of focused and coordinated international attention can be expected to evolve in the future, and global governance mechanisms will likewise need to be flexible and adaptable.

Currently some of the most significant and threatening possible global risks are poorly understood and seriously underestimated by both political leaders and the general public. They tend to be complex and diffuse, and somehow are not considered short-term priorities. Global environmental challenges such as climate change and loss of biodiversity fall into this category. Risk assessment is always difficult – relying both on technical data and abstract probabilities – and even more so for problems that seem distant or infrequent, but with catastrophic consequences that we prefer not to think about. Improved scientific research on such risks and their interrelationships will be an important starting point, to assess more clearly their probability, magnitude and consequences. This should feed through assessment processes (see Chapter 6) into the deliberations of the the the General Assembly (and associated bodies), or the other relevant UN organ, specialized agency or affiliated international organization. Contingency planning for relevant countermeasures can then follow to reduce the risks. Similar scientific advisory processes are needed at national and local government levels coherent with the global level.

The many risks on the horizon are also increasingly interrelated, as any one crisis is likely to precipitate others in our globalized society.[2] For too long we have hoped that the specter of nuclear war had receded, but recent political changes have perhaps brought us closer than ever. The present generation of leaders has apparently forgotten about the studies of nuclear winter and other horrors for the entire planet that would result from a nuclear exchange, in which there would be only losers, and no winners. Moreover, the increasingly integrated global economic system of production is much more vulnerable than in the past, and the reduced capacity for self-sufficiency with the larger urban populations in most countries would mean that any large-scale war or other politically motivated violence that interrupted world trade would precipitate human catastrophes on a massive scale. The repeated small-scale wars of recent decades have inured the public in many places to the suffering of violence as something that happens only to others far away. The ease with which the world slipped into World War I should serve as a reminder of how easily it could happen again without the safeguards that only global governance can provide (see Chapters 8 and 9). A few countries have started a public debate on civil protection, including Sweden, and a recent referendum on increased self-sufficiency in Switzerland.

---

[2]   Laybourn-Langton, Laurie, Leslie Rankin, and Darren Baxter. 2019. *This Is a Crisis: Facing up to the Age of Environmental Breakdown*, London, IPPR: Institute for Public Policy Research. www.ippr.org/research/publications/age-of-environmental-breakdown.

For population growth (see Chapter 17), world overpopulation has been debated since Malthus, but improvements in agriculture, often unsustainable in the long term, have so far extended the limits of planetary carrying capacity, so people have stopped worrying about numbers. The focus is more on poverty, which is in fact partly a consequence of absolute numbers of people, as well as of an economic system that does not address the equitable distribution of wealth. Sooner or later, it is very likely that the global population crisis will emerge, perhaps when the world food supply, impacted by climate change or some other disaster, is no longer sufficient to feed everyone. By then, it will be too late. One immediate consequence of excessive numbers of people in some regions is migration, and this may be the issue through which to hold a broader debate on population growth. One partial solution to the population crisis is redistribution – moving people to where there are adequate resources and economic opportunities – but this needs to be presented as a positive solution to an inadequate workforce and replacements for an aging local population, not as an "invasion" of foreigners.

The globalized economy has brought with it a new scale of global risks, recalling the Great Depression of the 1930s, and more recently the financial system crisis of 2008. No effective mechanism to anticipate, prevent or prepare for an economic collapse has been developed at the global level, and existing institutions such as the IMF lack the resources necessary to face a major crisis (see Chapter 15).

Additionally, there are the new and emerging risks that are not yet on the global agenda. There are already worries about the next global influenza pandemic, comparable to the Spanish Flu of 1918–1919, with experts waiting for a virus to mutate to become easily transmittable between people, and which could in the worst-case scenario kill a third of the world population, particularly young people, through an excessive immune reaction. Beyond that, it would not be difficult to genetically engineer a dangerous virus or microbe in a laboratory, which might then be released accidentally or intentionally. Terrorist groups might be motivated to do this, or a criminal organization holding the world hostage to such a threat. Others worry about artificial intelligence becoming so powerful that it escapes from human control. Geoengineering, already debated as a solution to climate change but with the potential to destabilize the planetary system, has already been mentioned as posing significant risks. Many new chemical compounds are being invented, and are often manufactured in quantity and used without adequate study of their possible damaging effects on the environment or various forms of life, including humans. Chemicals that have been shown to be endocrine disruptors are one recent example. The reformed UN should have a strong Office of Technology Assessment with the capacity to follow all these developments and others that cannot now be anticipated, to research and evaluate the risks involved, and to advise the General Assembly and relevant specialized agencies as appropriate, so that measures can be taken rapidly to establish guidelines and precautions for research, and regulations and prohibitions as necessary, where the risks are identified as significant (see Chapter 6).

Similarly worrying is the increasing vulnerability of our globalized economy and society, because it has become a highly integrated system and is increasingly dependent on vulnerable information technologies.[3] Any one major disruption affecting global trade and communications would precipitate a series of other crises in a complex catastrophe. We have become so dependent on the digital society and the Internet that a major failure would leave many helpless. Such a disruption could be caused by cyber warfare, or even a giant solar flare.[4] Transportation systems could break down. Cities might be cut off from the flows of energy, food and water, and the removal of wastes, essential for the survival of their dense populations. If security breaks down and social cohesion is inadequate, societies could descend into anarchy. A reformed United Nations able to react rapidly to any emerging catastrophe with global reach or implications might be the last bulwark to maintain civilization on this planet.

UN SPECIALIZED AGENCIES

Just as a national government has central legislative, judicial and executive functions, with the executive function implemented through a variety of ministries or departments, so the United Nations has specialized agencies, convention secretariats, programs and other entities to address different areas of global concern. Unlike national governments, these often have both legislative and implementation functions in their areas of responsibility. The agencies and conventions have their own legislative charters and governing bodies or conferences of the parties that give them considerable autonomy. They may be financed both from the regular UN budget and/or from their own funding sources. All this is the result of states insisting on retaining complete national sovereignty, down to deciding what international legislation they are willing to accept, and what to ignore. The inefficiency of basing international governance on voluntary legislation is made evident if we imagine the result if each individual could choose what national laws to obey and opt out of others.

The United Nations, alongside its central functions in the Charter to maintain peace and security and control politically motivated violence, has incorporated mechanisms over the years to deal with a wide range of issues requiring a global approach across the economic, social and environmental fields and for collaboration in health, science and education, among others. Today, the United Nations system includes about two dozen specialized agencies that formulate programs and channel resources to a number of important areas that address the Charter's provisions for the promotion of economic and social development (see Figure 13.1, UN System Chart).

---

[3] MacKenzie, Debora. 2012. "Doomsday Book," *New Scientist*, No. 2846, January 7, 2012, pp. 38–41.
[4] A giant solar flare or coronal mass ejection could break through the protective magnetosphere around the Earth and send a surging electrical pulse through everything electrical and electronic with possibly disastrous consequences.

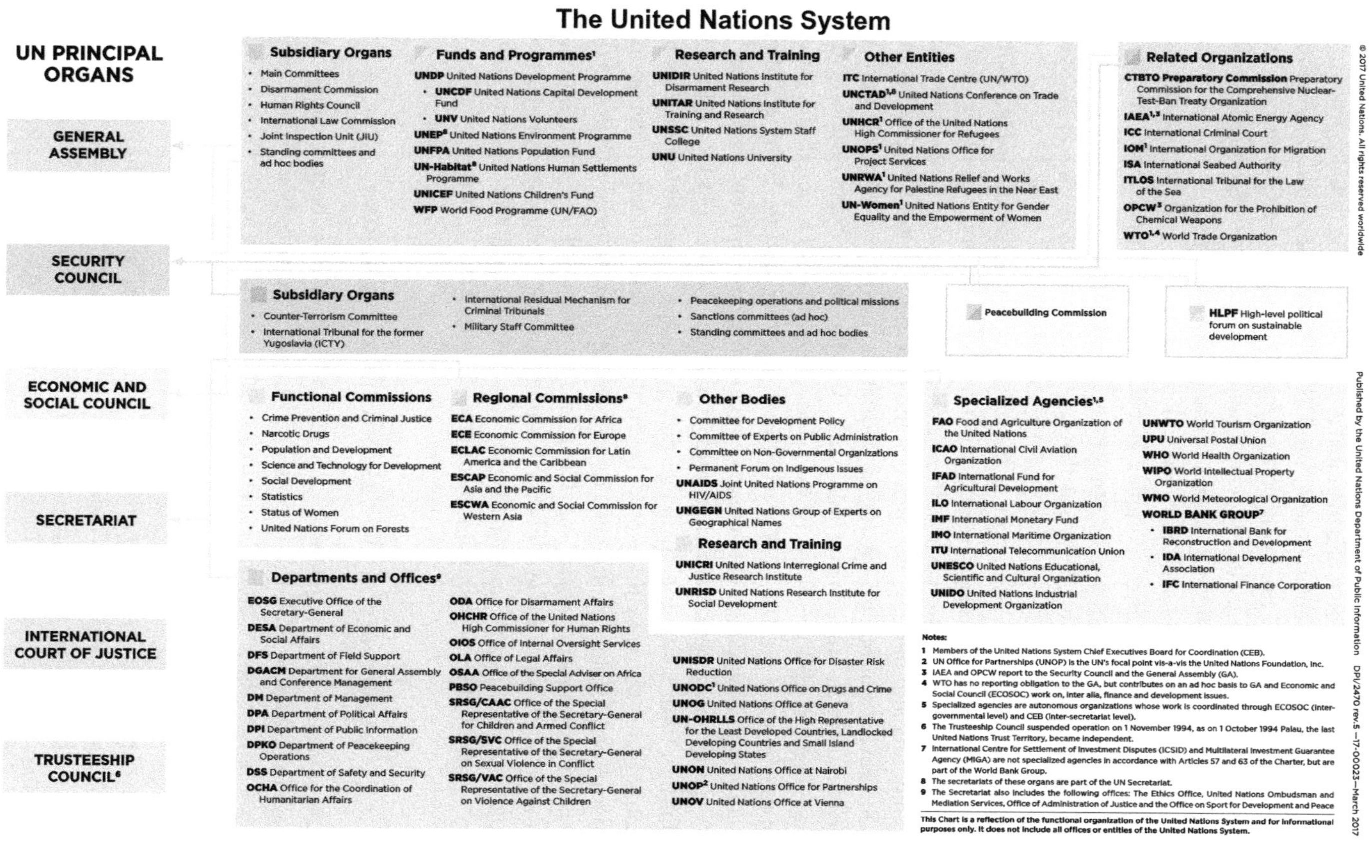

The United Nations System

Published by the United Nations Department of Public Information   DPI/2470 rev.5 —17-00023—March 2017

UN PRINCIPAL ORGANS

GENERAL ASSEMBLY

Subsidiary Organs
- Main Committees
- Disarmament Commission
- Human Rights Council
- International Law Commission
- Joint Inspection Unit (JIU)
- Standing committees and ad hoc bodies

Funds and Programmes[1]
- UNDP United Nations Development Programme
  - UNCDF United Nations Capital Development Fund
  - UNV United Nations Volunteers
- UNEP[1] United Nations Environment Programme
- UNFPA United Nations Population Fund
- UN-Habitat[1] United Nations Human Settlements Programme
- UNICEF United Nations Children's Fund
- WFP World Food Programme (UN/FAO)

Research and Training
- UNIDIR United Nations Institute for Disarmament Research
- UNITAR United Nations Institute for Training and Research
- UNSSC United Nations System Staff College
- UNU United Nations University

Other Entities
- ITC International Trade Centre (UN/WTO)
- UNCTAD[1,2] United Nations Conference on Trade and Development
- UNHCR[1] Office of the United Nations High Commissioner for Refugees
- UNOPS[1] United Nations Office for Project Services
- UNRWA[1] United Nations Relief and Works Agency for Palestine Refugees in the Near East
- UN-Women[1] United Nations Entity for Gender Equality and the Empowerment of Women

Related Organizations
- CTBTO Preparatory Commission Preparatory Commission for the Comprehensive Nuclear-Test-Ban Treaty Organization
- IAEA[1,3] International Atomic Energy Agency
- ICC International Criminal Court
- IOM[1] International Organization for Migration
- ISA International Seabed Authority
- ITLOS International Tribunal for the Law of the Sea
- OPCW[3] Organization for the Prohibition of Chemical Weapons
- WTO[1,4] World Trade Organization

HLPF High-level political forum on sustainable development

SECURITY COUNCIL

Subsidiary Organs
- Counter-Terrorism Committee
- International Tribunal for the former Yugoslavia (ICTY)
- International Residual Mechanism for Criminal Tribunals
- Military Staff Committee
- Peacekeeping operations and political missions
- Sanctions committees (ad hoc)
- Standing committees and ad hoc bodies

Peacebuilding Commission

ECONOMIC AND SOCIAL COUNCIL

Functional Commissions[5]
- Crime Prevention and Criminal Justice
- Narcotic Drugs
- Population and Development
- Science and Technology for Development
- Social Development
- Statistics
- Status of Women
- United Nations Forum on Forests

Regional Commissions[5]
- ECA Economic Commission for Africa
- ECE Economic Commission for Europe
- ECLAC Economic Commission for Latin America and the Caribbean
- ESCAP Economic and Social Commission for Asia and the Pacific
- ESCWA Economic and Social Commission for Western Asia

Other Bodies
- Committee for Development Policy
- Committee of Experts on Public Administration
- Committee on Non-Governmental Organizations
- Permanent Forum on Indigenous Issues
- UNAIDS Joint United Nations Programme on HIV/AIDS
- UNGEGN United Nations Group of Experts on Geographical Names

Research and Training
- UNICRI United Nations Interregional Crime and Justice Research Institute
- UNRISD United Nations Research Institute for Social Development

Specialized Agencies[1,6]
- FAO Food and Agriculture Organization of the United Nations
- ICAO International Civil Aviation Organization
- IFAD International Fund for Agricultural Development
- ILO International Labour Organization
- IMF International Monetary Fund
- IMO International Maritime Organization
- ITU International Telecommunication Union
- UNESCO United Nations Educational, Scientific and Cultural Organization
- UNIDO United Nations Industrial Development Organization
- UNWTO World Tourism Organization
- UPU Universal Postal Union
- WHO World Health Organization
- WIPO World Intellectual Property Organization
- WMO World Meteorological Organization
- **WORLD BANK GROUP[7]**
  - IBRD International Bank for Reconstruction and Development
  - IDA International Development Association
  - IFC International Finance Corporation

SECRETARIAT

Departments and Offices[8]
- EOSG Executive Office of the Secretary-General
- DESA Department of Economic and Social Affairs
- DFS Department of Field Support
- DGACM Department for General Assembly and Conference Management
- DM Department of Management
- DPA Department of Political Affairs
- DPI Department of Public Information
- DPKO Department of Peacekeeping Operations
- DSS Department of Safety and Security
- OCHA Office for the Coordination of Humanitarian Affairs
- ODA Office for Disarmament Affairs
- OHCHR Office of the United Nations High Commissioner for Human Rights
- OIOS Office of Internal Oversight Services
- OLA Office of Legal Affairs
- OSAA Office of the Special Adviser on Africa
- PBSO Peacebuilding Support Office
- SRSG/CAAC Office of the Special Representative of the Secretary-General for Children and Armed Conflict
- SRSG/SVC Office of the Special Representative of the Secretary-General on Sexual Violence in Conflict
- SRSG/VAC Office of the Special Representative of the Secretary-General on Violence Against Children
- UNISDR United Nations Office for Disaster Risk Reduction
- UNODC[2] United Nations Office on Drugs and Crime
- UNOG United Nations Office at Geneva
- UN-OHRLLS Office of the High Representative for the Least Developed Countries, Landlocked Developing Countries and Small Island Developing States
- UNON United Nations Office at Nairobi
- UNOP[2] United Nations Office for Partnerships
- UNOV United Nations Office at Vienna

INTERNATIONAL COURT OF JUSTICE

TRUSTEESHIP COUNCIL[9]

Notes:
1. Members of the United Nations System Chief Executives Board for Coordination (CEB).
2. UN Office for Partnerships (UNOP) is the UN's focal point vis-a-vis the United Nations Foundation, Inc.
3. IAEA and OPCW report to the Security Council and the General Assembly (GA).
4. WTO has no reporting obligation to the GA, but contributes on an ad hoc basis to GA and Economic and Social Council (ECOSOC) work on, inter alia, finance and development issues.
5. Specialized agencies are autonomous organizations whose work is coordinated through ECOSOC (intergovernmental level) and CEB (inter-secretariat level).
6. The Trusteeship Council suspended operation on 1 November 1994, as on 1 October 1994 Palau, the last United Nations Trust Territory, became independent.
7. International Centre for Settlement of Investment Disputes (ICSID) and Multilateral Investment Guarantee Agency (MIGA) are not specialized agencies in accordance with Articles 57 and 63 of the Charter, but are part of the World Bank Group.
8. The secretariats of these organs are part of the UN Secretariat.
9. The Secretariat also includes the following offices: The Ethics Office, United Nations Ombudsman and Mediation Services, Office of Administration of Justice and the Office on Sport for Development and Peace.

This Chart is a reflection of the functional organization of the United Nations System and for informational purposes only. It does not include all offices or entities of the United Nations System.

FIGURE 13.1   UN System Chart

Source: www.un.org/en/pdfs/18-00159e_un_system_chart_17x11_4c_en_web.pdf, ©2019 United Nations. Reprinted with the permission of the United Nations

Once the General Assembly is reformed to become a legislative body empowered to adopt binding legislation on issues of global concern including initially peace and security, and the planetary environment, the UN will have the capacity to reform and consolidate as necessary the many parts of the UN system (see Chapter 4). The General Assembly could legislate, allocate budgets and assign responsibilities for implementation, regulation and enforcement. Specialization is a necessary approach for any complex institution, but collaboration and integration are also increasingly necessary to address complex global problems. In addition, the independent funding mechanism for the renewed UN (see Chapter 12) would help to overcome the chronic funding shortages that have handicapped most UN agencies and programs.

Making a comprehensive assessment of the sorts of reforms that are needed in the UN's system of specialized agencies and other bodies is beyond the scope of this book. But because we feel strongly that these agencies can play a critically important role in promoting and bringing into practice the best ideals of the UN Charter, we do wish to provide the reader, by way of illustration, with a sense of the kinds of issues that emerge in undertaking this work. We provide a brief review of the governance challenges represented by the wide range of issues covered, the multiplicity of mechanisms created to deal with them and the need for better collaboration to address the integrated challenges of sustainable development. As examples, we then expand on a few particularly challenging issues for the risks they represent for the future of humanity: the challenge that increasing inequality represents for social stability and the risks that could be created by unregulated multinational corporations (see Chapter 14); financial issues in the global financial system and the risks of another financial crisis (see Chapter 15); the need for environmental governance to address the dangers of overshooting planetary boundaries, in particular through climate change and biodiversity loss (see Chapter 16); and the social challenges presented by population growth and migration (see Chapter 17).

UN AGENCIES, PROGRAMS AND CONVENTIONS

Many specialized intergovernmental agencies and bodies have been created over the last century, starting with the International Labour Organization (ILO) dating from 1919. Many of the global bodies, with a notable exception in the World Trade Organization (WTO), which was intentionally kept separate, are today part of the United Nations system. They can be grouped into three main categories:

a) **Conventions** and other multilateral agreements under the UN umbrella were negotiated independently by governments and are responsible to their Conferences of the Parties (COP) with their own secretariats, funds and subsidiary mechanisms. Among the international conventions born from UN processes, some, such as the

ILO conventions, have a single organization as secretariat, but many, including the UN Framework Convention on Climate Change (UNFCCC) and the Convention to Combat Desertification (CCD), have independent secretariats. The Convention on Biological Diversity (CBD), the Convention on International Trade in Endangered Species (CITES) and the Convention on Migratory Species (CMS) have their own secretariats directed by their COP, but are administratively under UN Environment (formerly UNEP).

b) **Specialized agencies** of the United Nations system have their own legal charters and intergovernmental bodies. In terms of the resources they receive from the UN budget through assessed annual contributions, the most important are the Food and Agriculture Organization (FAO), the World Health Organization (WHO), the ILO, the United Nations Educational, Scientific and Cultural Organization (UNESCO) and the International Atomic Energy Agency (IAEA).

c) **United Nations programs** such as the UN Development Program (UNDP), UN Women and UN Environment (UNEP) are under the UN Charter and considered part of the UN Secretariat under the ultimate responsibility of the UN General Assembly and the UN Secretary-General. They may have their own intergovernmental bodies and funds in addition to the regular UN budget.

The IMF and the World Bank were set up in 1944 at the United Nations Monetary and Financial Conference (also referred to as the Bretton Woods Conference), nearly a year before the San Francisco conference that adopted the UN Charter. These two agencies generate their own funding, have their own by-laws and founding charters and have traditionally had a considerable degree of independence from the UN Secretariat. They also have systems of weighted voting, unlike the one country–one vote approach within the UN General Assembly. In many ways, however, because the resources they deploy dwarf those of the entire UN system, they deserve particular attention.

Many other intergovernmental organizations, often regional in coverage or with a narrower focus, are outside the UN system. Since these were all independently negotiated, and may not have exactly the same governmental parties, they are quite independent, potentially making coordination or reform difficult.

Most of these agencies and programs receive direction from their own intergovernmental bodies, such as the World Health Assembly of the WHO representing health ministries, or the UN Environment Assembly of ministers of the environment. This can mean that the same national governments can take different and not always coherent positions in these specialized agencies. The UN itself has a range of subsidiary structures to coordinate across issue-areas and provide framing guidance where governments meet and make decisions, including the Economic and Social

Council, the Human Rights Council, the Statistical Commission, the Commission on the Status of Women and the High Level Political Forum charged with overseeing the 2030 Agenda and the Sustainable Development Goals, among many others.

The full range of UN bodies, commissions, programs, specialized agencies and other associated entities perform vital roles in promoting human welfare and prosperity. They represent institutional capital, a source of expertise and depth of experience that are essential for any effective system of international governance. They provide leadership on global issues, set global norms and give operational guidance and assistance to developing countries in particular. Whatever the direction of UN reform, it should preserve these important capacities and plan for their evolution into the new system.

At the same time, due to their diverse origins and heterogeneous arrangements, they are far from a coherent and efficient system at present. Coordination is difficult. There are significant gaps and overlaps, and the inevitable inefficiencies that come from such a multiplication of structures. In addition, their governing bodies have government representatives from different sectors, who may seldom coordinate at the national level, creating the potential for the same governments to give incoherent instructions to different parts of the UN system. Further their main problem is implementation, often because the means made available to them are inadequate to their mission, and sometimes because of government resistance and the general lack of a mandate and means for binding enforcement.

The challenge, then, is how to maintain and strengthen as necessary the existing UN agencies and bodies while making the transition to a more coherent and effective system of global governance. Indeed, in an increasingly interdependent community of nations facing a wide range of unresolved global problems, the need for an effective cluster of specialized agencies is more urgent than ever and is likely to intensify. A strengthened UN with a revised Charter, greater responsibilities in the areas of security, peace and management of the global commons, and a larger and steadier source of funding, will create new opportunities for international cooperation in a number of areas of global concern, including climate change and the environment, the global financial system, human rights, migration, poverty alleviation, income inequality, job creation, nuclear proliferation, corruption, terrorism and drug trafficking, among many others.

CREATING THE BASIS FOR REFORM

The first step to reform this complex but useful assemblage will be to create the necessary structures for binding international legislation in the reformed General Assembly (see Chapter 4), and for executive action in the Executive Council (see Chapter 7), through revisions to the UN Charter. The General Assembly would be mandated to adopt legislation in the different areas of specialized concern requiring international coordination and action as demonstrated by the existing institutional arrangements and as defined in the Charter. It would not start from scratch, but over time could consider all the existing charters and conventions in a particular field, build on their strengths and acquired experience, correct weaknesses, address new challenges and approve legislative texts that would substitute for and replace the existing international legal instruments. Such legislation would be binding on all countries, just as legislation is binding at the national level, without the need for complex processes of signature, ratification and accession as at present. This would also provide a mechanism for review and improvement in international legislation when required without the cumbersome process of ad hoc convention revision. The secretariats would transition into institutions within the new governance framework.

The legislative mandate of the General Assembly should ultimately include the ability to define and raise limited types of international taxes in its specific areas of responsibility (see Chapter 12). An effective system of governance must have some financial independence, and not be subject to the goodwill (and sometimes political pressure and leverage) associated with contributions from national governments. Taxation can be one of the tools of good management, requiring activities that damage the common interest or threaten its stability to cover the costs of their regulation. For example, this could initially simply involve a harmonization of specific taxes at the national level to reduce the harmful effects of tax competition, without the need to create a global system to collect taxes. Access to a reliable source of finance would also be a strong incentive for the specialized agencies, conventions and other entities to integrate into the new system.[5]

In the meantime, and as part of the evolving system of global governance, the Executive Council, with its management and system coherence mandate, could consider how to enhance the effectiveness of specialized UN agencies and conventions without waiting for legislative revision. The goals should be subsidiarity, coherence and efficacy.

There would still be a need for subject-specific intergovernmental consultations beyond the capacity of the General Assembly, presently carried out by the existing commissions, governing bodies and conferences of the parties. There are also scientific and technical advisory bodies, and mechanisms for the participation of

---

[5]　In Chapter 12 we presented a range of proposals for strengthening the UN system's capacity to respond to crises and to deliver on the responsibilities given to it in the UN Charter. None of these proposals envisaged the need for the UN to develop a revenue-generating machinery of its own, independent of its members. In this respect, our proposals are aligned with the system currently in operation in the European Union, where members have created an independent source of revenue for EU institutions, while maintaining revenue collection as a responsibility of member states. Potentially giving the UN taxing authority is a long-term objective that would need to be examined in light of the experience with the system(s) we have proposed. In particular, the UN would need to establish a fairly long track record of efficiency in the administration of the considerably larger volume of resources being made available to it under our proposals. In federal systems, all levels of government have some taxing authority and they have generally worked well, within a clearly defined legal framework.

civil society and other stakeholders. These could be attached to the relevant specialized agencies, or, if their function was legislative revision, become subsidiary commissions under the General Assembly (see Chapter 6).

THE SUSTAINABLE DEVELOPMENT GOALS: AN INTEGRATED APPROACH

The United Nations has always had a vital normative role, setting the global agenda and agreed standards, ranging from the 1948 Universal Declaration of Human Rights and other Declarations and Resolutions,[6] to Agenda 21 adopted at the 1992 Earth Summit.[7]

One of the remarkable recent steps forward in international consensus among states has been the adoption in 2015 at a UN General Assembly Summit of the 2030 Agenda and its Sustainable Development Goals (SDGs) (see Box).[8] The fact that unanimity could be achieved around such a broad and ambitious agenda covering and integrating so many issues of world concern and developed with such wide participation was already an achievement.[9] Its implications for global governance are also significant, as it maps out the wide range of areas where progress needs to be made globally, insisting that they are all integrated, indivisible, and must be addressed together.

Box: Sustainable Development Goals

Goal 1. End poverty in all its forms everywhere

Goal 2. End hunger, achieve food security and improved nutrition and promote sustainable agriculture

Goal 3. Ensure healthy lives and promote well-being for all at all ages

Goal 4. Ensure inclusive and equitable quality education and promote lifelong learning opportunities for all

---

[6] United Nations. 1948. *Universal Declaration of Human Rights*. www.un.org/en/universal-declaration-human-rights/index.html   www.ohchr.org/EN/UDHR/Documents/UDHR_Translations/eng.pdf.

[7] United Nations. 1992. *Agenda 21: Programme of Action for Sustainable Development*. United Nations Conference on Environment & Development, Rio de Janeiro, Brazil, June 3–14. New York, United Nations. https://sustainabledevelopment.un.org/content/documents/Agenda21.pdf.

[8] United Nations. 2015. *Transforming Our World: The 2030 Agenda for Sustainable Development*. Outcome document of the Summit for the adoption of the Post-2015 Development Agenda, New York, September 25–27. A/70/L.1. New York, United Nations. www.un.org/ga/search/view_doc.asp?symbol=A/70/L.1&Lang=E.

[9] United Nations. 2014. *The Road to Dignity by 2030: Ending Poverty, Transforming All Lives and Protecting the Planet*. Synthesis Report of the Secretary-General on the Post-2015 Agenda. Document A/69/700, December 4, 2014. New York, United Nations. www.un.org/ga/search/view_doc.asp?symbol=A/69/700&Lang=E.

Goal 5. Achieve gender equality and empower all women and girls

Goal 6. Ensure availability and sustainable management of water and sanitation for all

Goal 7. Ensure access to affordable, reliable, sustainable and modern energy for all

Goal 8. Promote sustained, inclusive and sustainable economic growth, full and productive employment and decent work for all

Goal 9. Build resilient infrastructure, promote inclusive and sustainable industrialization and foster innovation

Goal 10. Reduce inequality within and among countries

Goal 11. Make cities and human settlements inclusive, safe, resilient and sustainable

Goal 12. Ensure sustainable consumption and production patterns

Goal 13. Take urgent action to combat climate change and its impacts*

Goal 14. Conserve and sustainably use the oceans, seas and marine resources for sustainable development

Goal 15. Protect, restore and promote sustainable use of terrestrial ecosystems, sustainably manage forests, combat desertification, and halt and reverse land degradation and halt biodiversity loss

Goal 16. Promote peaceful and inclusive societies for sustainable development, provide access to justice for all and build effective, accountable and inclusive institutions at all levels

Goal 17. Strengthen the means of implementation and revitalize the global partnership for sustainable development

* Acknowledging that the United Nations Framework Convention on Climate Change is the primary international, intergovernmental forum for negotiating the global response to climate change.

The SDGs can be seen as a global framework for action toward sustainability. There are 17 goals that are action oriented, global in nature and universally applicable to all countries, rich and poor, unlike the previous Millennium Development Goals to 2015. There are goals that place humans at the center of a global development agenda to eliminate poverty, where environmental challenges represent threats to human health and well-being, and where environmental solutions can reinforce human progress. Another cluster of goals for environmental resources, processes and boundaries define the dimensions of planetary health on which human well-being and development depend. There are goals about transitioning to a green and circular economy that builds rather than undermines planetary sustainability. The final two goals are on institutional and governance issues including peace and security, and on the means of implementation. Along with the goals, 169 quantified targets were identified as a focus for action, and initially 241 global indicators have been adopted by the UN Statistical Commission to measure progress toward the targets.

As with any government-negotiated action plan, there are some contradictions and inconsistencies within the SDGs. A goal of sustained economic growth as currently measured, for example, is incompatible with environmental sustainability within planetary boundaries. Some targets need to be balanced or prioritized differently in each country; others are interdependent, with one, perhaps, a prerequisite for progress on another. One challenge in the UN is to coordinate and deal with the interactions in their implementation.[10]

The SDGs can be considered the most recent globally accepted definition of sustainable development, building on the Brundtland Commission definition of 1987, "development that meets the needs of the present without compromising the ability of future generations to meet their own needs,"[11] and then Agenda 21 adopted at the United Nations Conference on Environment and Development in 1992.[12] As such, they also can be considered an outline of what the responsibilities of governance should cover and the benefits governments should deliver to their populations. While much of the effort must be made at the national level and below, it is at the UN, acting today through the High Level Political Forum (HLPF) set up after the UN Conference on Sustainable Development in Rio de Janeiro in 2012,[13] that progress toward the global goals is assessed.

It is useful in the present context to consider, broadly speaking, the purpose of governance in light of the Secretary-General's summary in his synthesis report to the 2015 Summit which adopted the goals.[14] He called for a fundamental transformation of society and the economy, with the SDGs defining a paradigm shift for people and planet, inclusive and people-centered, leaving no one behind, integrating the economic, social, and environmental dimensions in a spirit of solidarity, cooperation, and mutual accountability, with the participation of governments and all stakeholders. How many governments today really see this remarkable and urgent vision as their core purpose and primary motivation?

At the 2015 Summit, heads of state and government committed:

---

[10] Nilsson, Måns, Dave Griggs, and Martin Visbeck. 2016. "Policy: Map the Interactions between Sustainable Development Goals," *Nature*, Vol. 534, pp. 320–322. DOI:10.1038/534320a; Nilsson, Måns, Dave Griggs, Martin Visbeck, and Claudia Ringler. 2016. *A Draft Framework for Understanding SDG Interactions*, ICSU Working Paper, Paris, International Council for Science. www.icsu.org/publications/reports-and-reviews/working-paper-framework-for-understanding-sdg-interactions-2016/SDG-interactions-working-paper.pdf.

[11] World Commission on Environment and Development. 1987. *Our Common Future*. Oxford, Oxford University Press.

[12] United Nations, *Agenda 21*.

[13] United Nations. 2012. *Report of the United Nations Conference on Sustainable Development*, Rio de Janeiro, Brazil, June 20–22. A/CONF.216/16. New York, United Nations. www.un.org/ga/search/view_doc.asp?symbol=A/CONF.216/16&Lang=E.

[14] United Nations, *The Road to Dignity by 2030*.

- to end poverty and hunger, in all their forms and dimensions, and to ensure that all human beings can fulfil their potential in dignity and equality and in a healthy environment.
- to protect the planet from degradation, including through sustainable consumption and production, sustainably managing its natural resources and taking urgent action on climate change, so that it can support the needs of the present and future generations.
- to ensure that all human beings can enjoy prosperous and fulfilling lives and that economic, social and technological progress occurs in harmony with nature.
- to foster peaceful, just and inclusive societies which are free from fear and violence. There can be no sustainable development without peace and no peace without sustainable development.
- to mobilize the means required to implement this Agenda through a revitalised Global Partnership for Sustainable Development, based on a spirit of strengthened global solidarity, focussed in particular on the needs of the poorest and most vulnerable and with the participation of all countries, all stakeholders and all people.[15]

It is encouraging that governments can sign up to such high ambitions, but they too often fall down in their implementation. The gap between principles and practice is still wide, as it is too often in intergovernmental processes. It is the responsibility of the UN system to take this agenda to heart and restructure itself as the best instrument to turn these ideals into actions. It should aim to catalyze "an organic change in the structure of society itself so as to reflect fully the interdependence of the entire social body—as well as the interconnectedness with the natural world that sustains it."[16] The 2030 Agenda calls for just such a fundamental transformation.

Indeed, among the transformational aspects of this agenda are its profound implications for approaches to governance. While the SDGs are intended to be met by 2030, they really define the scope of governance generally. Many proposals for sustainable development governance have been made, which are well summarized by Cruickshank, Schneeberger and Smith,[17] as well as in a recent study specifically on governance for the Sustainable Development Goals.[18] Governments

---

[15] United Nations, *Transforming Our World*.

[16] Bahá'í International Community. 2010. *Rethinking Prosperity: Forging Alternatives to a Culture of Consumerism*. Bahá'í International Community's Contribution to the 18th Session of the United Nations Commission on Sustainable Development, May 3. www.bic.org/statements/rethinking-prosperity-forging-alternatives-culture-consumerism.

[17] Cruickshank, Emlyn W., Kirsty Schneeberger, and Nadine Smith (eds.). 2012. *A Pocket Guide to Sustainable Development Governance*, 2nd edn., Commonwealth Secretariat/Stakeholder Forum. www.stakeholderforum.org/fileadmin/files/PocketGuidetoSDGEdition2webfinal.pdf.

[18] Monkelbaan, Joachim. 2018. *Governance for the Sustainable Development Goals: Exploring an Integrative Framework of Theories, Tools, and Competencies*, Tokyo, Springer. www.springer.com/us/book/9789811304743.

traditionally consist of ministries and departments responsible for different functions provided to citizens, such as health, education, welfare, finance, commerce, transport, energy, science, justice, security and defense. The United Nations similarly has specialized agencies and subsidiary bodies with a wide range of functions. The 2030 Agenda takes an integrated approach, in which all the goals must be addressed as an interrelated whole. Science is demonstrating how interrelated the physical, chemical and biological systems are at the global level, with biogeochemical cycles operating at a planetary scale, and human economic, technological and social systems now having global impacts. The world is a single integrated system in which every component and process influences, and is affected by, every other. This requires breaking down the traditional silos in which different functions have operated more or less independently, implying a radical restructuring, even for governments at the national level, and even more so for international governance.

It is not clear that anyone knows very well how to do this. Innovative new ways are needed to balance the values of specialization and of integration through new institutional structures and forms of coordination, as well as new skills and systems thinking. Such integrated, holistic governance will have to evolve organically through adaptive learning processes of action/experimentation, consultation and reflection. As a starting point, it will be necessary to agree on a framework of principles and values that would define the purpose of governance (see Chapter 20). Examples include ensuring justice and equity for every human being, defending the greater good and the common interests of all humanity, maintaining the sustainability of the biosphere, building resilience in human society, and encouraging learning, innovation and diversity. The people involved in governance, whether elected or appointed officials, should be conscious of the essential interdependence of humankind and operate with the common good in mind, rather than defending any unduly limited national perspective, ideology, selfish viewpoint or vested interest, as is too often the case in governments today. While much of the experimentation will need to be done at the national and even local levels, there will clearly be a role for the UN at the global level to coordinate these efforts, share best practices and encourage adoption and adaptation to the many different national circumstances.

The 2030 Agenda also specifies that no one should be left behind, so that governance should respond to the needs of all human beings, starting with the most deprived and marginalized. This will also be a challenge requiring new approaches. It is the economically deprived, the marginalized, minorities, those with disabilities, not infrequently migrants, women and girls, etc., that are most often left behind, frequently not captured or disaggregated in statistics, often not even legally recognized if unregistered at birth or without proper documentation, and thus invisible. The concept of statehood includes a state responsibility for its citizens, but not for non-citizens or the rest of humanity. There are also an increasing number of "failed states" and incompetent governments incapable of providing even the most rudimentary facilities and protections to which any citizen should have a right. Today an increasing number of migrants and displaced persons are escaping from any one state's responsibility and are not even covered in many cases by human rights protections. They are in an international limbo that only global governance can address; the system of a national citizenship for life is breaking down alongside the erosion of the nation-state. A renewed UN will have to consider adopting stronger measures to ensure that every human being has a recognized legal status regardless of where they are in the world. Leaving no one behind includes the poor whose births were never registered and the many undocumented refugees and migrants. Ultimately, the rights and opportunities of a human being should not be conditioned by something as arbitrary as where one is born.

Using the SDGs as a framework would also call for a number of other characteristics in governance, both in the UN and its specialized agencies and in governments at the national and local levels. This includes an important role for science and knowledge to support policy-making, both in describing the reality of the natural and human situation, and in generating indicators of the status and trends in actions to reach the goals. Furthermore, average statistics often give a misleading impression by covering over extreme differences, for example between a rich minority and a vast majority of the poor. The SDGs call for disaggregation of data, for example by gender, age, class, urban and rural, and including often-discriminated minorities, to ensure that all those that are being left behind are measured and monitored, and their needs identified and responded to. The lessons learned from the work coordinated by the United Nations after the 1992 Earth Summit to develop indicators of sustainable development can be a useful guide to the even greater effort needed to implement indicators for the SDGs.[19]

Cooperation and knowledge-sharing would be necessary to integrate all the goals and targets in a systems perspective, since some are dependent on others or are mutually reinforcing, while a few are contradictory and will require trade-offs.[20] Research is still needed on the best way to integrate indicators across all the domains of the SDGs, and to develop indicators of integration itself.[21]

Multilevel governance will be essential, since the global goals have to be translated to the national level for implementation, and many will require action at the

---

[19] Dahl, Arthur Lyon. 2018. "UNEP and the CSD Process for Sustainable Development Indicators," in Simon Bell and Stephen Morse (eds.), *Routledge Handbook of Sustainability Indicators and Indices*, London and New York, Routledge, pp. 347–363.

[20] Nilsson et al., *A Draft Framework*; Nilsson, Griggs, and Visbeck, "Policy: Map the Interactions"; International Council for Science (ICSU), 2017. *A Guide to SDG Interactions: From Science to Implementation*, ed. D.J. Griggs, M. Nilsson, A. Stevance, and D. McCollum, Paris, International Council for Science. www.icsu.org/cms/2017/05/SDGs-Guide-to-Interactions.pdf.

[21] Dahl, Arthur Lyon. 2018. "Contributions to the Evolving Theory and Practice of Indicators of Sustainability," in Simon Bell and Stephen Morse (eds.), *Routledge Handbook of Sustainability Indicators and Indices*, London and New York, Routledge, pp. 42–58.

subnational level and by other actors including business and civil society.[22] There will need to be continuing debate about the future of society and the visions and paradigms that will lead in the desired direction. In the modern world we have created, the past is no longer a good guide to the future, and we therefore need to learn from the emerging future. Innovation and experimentation should be encouraged, with both successful results and the lessons learned from failures shared so that society can keep advancing. All levels of governance from the global to the local will need to be involved in this process.

This book cannot review all the global risks requiring UN action. The important principle is to create the mechanisms through which reform can be pursued as and when needed. A few examples are developed in the following chapters, from the economic, environmental and social domains, as illustrations of how the reform process could work and the results that would be possible. These include governance of the global economy and business (Chapter 14), the global financial architecture represented by a reformed IMF (Chapter 15), global environmental governance including responding to the challenges of climate change and biodiversity loss (Chapter 16), and managing migrations and population displacements in an increasingly crowded world (Chapter 17).

---

[22] Karlsson-Vinkhuyzen, Sylvia, Arthur Lyon Dahl, and Åsa Persson. 2018. "The Emerging Accountability Regimesfor the Sustainable Development Goals and Policy Integration: Friend or Foe?" *Environment and Planning C: Politics and Space*, special issue on Integrative Governance. DOI: 10.1177/2399654418779995.

14

Economic Governance for Inequality and the
Private Sector

The outstanding faults of the economic society in which we live are its failure to provide for full employment and its arbitrary and inequitable distribution of wealth and incomes.[1]

John Maynard Keynes

Enabled by the technological revolution, the world economy has globalized. Yet despite an enormous increase in economic activity and world trade, and a significant reduction in poverty in some regions, inequality between and within countries has increased as economic returns go increasingly to capital rather than to labor, exacerbating social tensions. Addressing this inequality has become a global priority and is the first economic governance challenge discussed in this chapter. We then review the need for international governance and regulation of the business sector in the common interest and raise some general issues about global governance of the economy.

INEQUALITY

One function of governance is to address issues of inequality, as extreme differences create tensions and destroy the social cohesion necessary for stability and security. Income gaps are widening in many countries, while aspirations are growing. Social inequalities lead to apathy, alienation, social unrest, violence and the erosion of trust between individuals and the institutions of governance.[2] Inequality can occur at multiple levels: between individuals, between communities or cultural groups,

---

[1] This is the starting sentence in Keynes's chapter 24 ("Concluding Notes on the Social Philosophy towards which the General Theory might Lead"), 1936, for the *General Theory of Employment, Interest and Money*. Basingstoke, Palgrave Macmillan.

[2] Bahá'í International Community. 2012. *Beyond Balancing the Scales: The Roots of Equity, Justice and Prosperity for All*, Bahá'í International Community's contribution to the UN Global Thematic Consultation on "Addressing Inequalities," New York, October 12. www.bic.org/statements/beyond-balancing-scales-roots-equity-justice-and-prosperity-all.

between urban and rural areas, and between states. There can be inequality in wealth, in opportunities, in gender, in power, in status, in health and education, etc. There are also distributional issues between the highest and lowest levels, such as between a privileged minority and a deprived majority, or a well-off majority with excluded minorities on the margins. For this reason, average, mean or median statistics can be deceptive and hide significant inequalities.

The role of wealth distribution, including both in-country and global inequality, has emerged as a significant issue for development, with a number of influential books published on the subject since 2009.[3] Measures of public attitudes toward inequality suggest that people both prefer lower inequality than they imagine exists in their society, and underestimate the actual level of inequality. High levels of inequality tend to limit development. The 2030 Agenda, with its aim to achieve greater justice in the world and to leave no one behind, is an expression of the imperative need to reduce inequalities; goal 10 of the Sustainable Development Goals (SDGs) is specifically to *reduce inequality within and among countries*. The mandate for a vital role for global governance in addressing the issue is clear, but different approaches are required when addressing inequality between states, and inequality at the level of individuals within a given community.

This issue is so important that we recommend that a new multilateral specialized agency be created within the reformed UN system specifically to address growing economic inequality and to organize a more equitable distribution of the world's resources. Existing international economic institutions for poverty alleviation, financial system surveillance and trade regulation have failed to address this gap adequately. This will require novel approaches for funding, beyond those already used by institutions such as the International Monetary Fund (IMF) and the World Bank with mixed impact at best, and some options for this are considered in Chapter 12. The following sections address the rationale for and possible scope of such an agency.

If we start with the assumption inherent in the UN Charter and explicit in the Universal Declaration of Human Rights that "all human beings are born free and equal in dignity and rights" and are "endowed with reason and conscience," then equality is a fundamental aspect of what it means to be human. Dignity, reason and conscience are qualities common to every member of the human race. Therefore,

---

[3] Wilkinson, R. and K. Pickett. 2009. *The Spirit Level: Why More Equal Societies Almost Always Do Better*, London, Allen Lane; Stiglitz, Joseph E. 2012. *The Price of Inequality: How Today's Divided Society Endangers Our Future*, New York, W. W. Norton; Atkinson, A.B. 2015. *Inequality: What Can Be Done?* Cambridge, MA, Harvard University Press; Milanovic, B. 2016. *Global Inequality: A New Approach for the Age of Globalization*, Cambridge, MA, Harvard University Press; Scheidel, W. 2017. *The Great Leveler: Violence and the History of Inequality from the Stone Age to the Twenty-first Century*, Princeton, NJ, Princeton University Press.

equality is not something to be created, but is to be reflected in social structures and processes of governance as a matter of justice.[4]

While extreme inequality is clearly seen as unjust (except by some of those at the wealthiest extreme of the spectrum),[5] that does not of course mean that complete equality is the solution. It is often unfairness that is the issue. There are natural differences, whether between people or countries, that should be acknowledged. The concept of justice includes just rewards for talent, effort and accomplishments, and implies equality of opportunity. Differences are accepted if they are justified and earned or are the result of a random process such as a draw or lottery where everyone has an equal opportunity.[6] It is the extremes of inequality that need to be eliminated at both ends of the spectrum.

Inequality between Individuals

While hunter–gatherer societies were generally quite egalitarian, more complex settled societies tended to allow some people to acquire riches at the expense of others, and to perpetuate such differences.[7] The power to govern and to assemble riches often went together. Today, the extreme differences between the "haves" and "have nots" are rooted in a materialistic ideology, social norms and oppressive structures of power and production. In fact, despite progress in reducing poverty in some countries, income inequality has increased in recent decades to levels not seen in over a century, with wealth increasingly concentrated at the top while the poorest get less and even the middle classes see little benefit from growth in the economy. In the United States, middle-class incomes have been stagnant for the last

---

[4] Bahá'í International Community, *Beyond Balancing the Scales.*

[5] Many with considerable wealth also consider excessive economic inequality as repugnant and counterproductive. The "Patriotic Millionaires" of the United States, for example, advocate for fair taxes and a livable wage, among other things, with their stated values including the following: "We believe that the trend of growing economic inequality is both bad for society and bad for business. We believe revenue models that rely on human misery should be exorcised from our economy. We believe the government should mandate a liveable wage for all working Americans, rather than relying on 'the market' which has failed to realize that goal over 240 years of American history. We believe a national 'living wage' law will ensure a stable level of aggregate demand, which will fuel our economy more broadly, ushering in a new era of prosperity for all Americans, including rich ones ... We believe our nation's social and economic progress requires significant and constant public investment, and that the wealthy, who benefit the most from our country's assets and institutions, should naturally and gladly pay the greatest share of whatever taxes are needed to support that investment" (see: https://patrioticmillionaires.org/our-values/).

[6] Starmans, Christina, Mark Sheskin and Paul Bloom. 2017. "Inequality Isn't the Real Issue," *Wall Street Journal*, April 29–30, p. C3.

[7] See, e.g., recent research linking sex equality also to more egalitarian hunter–gatherer societies, before the emergence of agriculture: Dyble, M., G.D. Salali, N. Chaudhary, A. Page, D. Smith, J. Thompson, L. Vinicius, R. Mace, and A.B. Migliano. 2015. "Sex Equality Can Explain the Unique Social Structure of Hunter–Gatherer Bands." *Science*, Vol. 348, No. 6236, May 15, pp. 796–798.

40 years.[8] This has provided fertile ground for populist messages and the rejection of those considered to be elites or part of traditional political establishments.

In addressing the issue of inequality between people individually or in social or cultural groups, most of the focus has been on poverty in economic terms as differences in wealth, along with all the other inequalities in health, education, employment and opportunity that result from poverty. However, poverty, in our current global circumstances with significant accumulated global wealth, is an issue of justice. In a world without absolute scarcity, with adequate wealth to meet everyone's needs and enough food to feed everyone, it is unjust that people should go hungry or lack the basic necessities of life. The problem is one of equitable distribution, which effective systems of governance at different levels should be able to address, starting in each community and going up as necessary to the global level.

Some countries, particularly China and to some extent India, have done much to reduce extreme poverty, but much poverty still remains around the world, including in the most advanced economies. Despite the great growth in the world economy, poverty is actually increasing in some countries, often associated with conflict, government mismanagement or even climate change and natural disasters. Even wealthy countries that have minimized the interference of government in the economy for ideological reasons and implemented austerity programs to cut back on government expenditures, have seen poverty increase and the middle classes stagnating or regressing.[9] Similar effects have been produced by austerity measures necessitated by wasteful spending in the past and other causes of excessive debt burdens, requiring IMF bailouts when the authorities can no longer fund their budgets from revenues or by borrowing at reasonable rates from the markets. There is thus no guarantee that poverty will not increase in the future.

In the corporate search for ever-increasing profit and productivity, supported by technological innovation, workers are being squeezed out, with chronically high unemployment in many countries pushing more people into poverty, and fewer opportunities for young people, destroying social cohesion and the hope of younger generations. This could contribute to major planetary crises.[10] There are warnings that further automation, artificial intelligence and smart systems could replace many human occupations in the years ahead, creating further substantial unemployment, leading the OECD and the Bank of England's chief economist to highlight the challenges posed by the "technologically unemployed." Globalization has not

---

8   Krause, Eleanor and Isabel V. Sawhill. 2018. "Seven Reasons to Worry about the American Middle Class." Washington, DC, Brookings Institution, Social Mobility Memos, Tuesday, June 5. www .brookings.edu/blog/social-mobility-memos/2018/06/05/seven-reasons-to-worry-about-the-american-middle-class.

9   For reports and background materials on poverty, see the Office of the High Commissioner on Human Rights, Special Rapporteur on extreme poverty and human rights, www.ohchr.org/en/issues/poverty/Pages/SRExtremePovertyIndex.aspx.

10   Turchin, Peter. 2010. "Political Instability May Be a Contributor in the Coming Decade." *Nature*, Vol. 463, No. 7281, p. 608. DOI: 10.1038/463608a.

benefited everyone equally and has left many on the sidelines, embittered and drawn to populist rhetoric.

With all the emphasis on eliminating poverty, much less attention has been given to the other end of the spectrum, extremes of wealth. Yet the two are intimately related. Even where inequality at the rich end of the spectrum is measured, it is usually income inequality, not wealth inequality, where the disparities are more pronounced.[11] Levels of inequality have varied throughout history; in the period leading to the industrial revolution despotic leaders and economies based on slavery were not uncommon. With the arrival of new technologies and an acceleration in the pace of economic growth the standard of living rose, but income disparities persisted. Some narrowing of inequality between countries co-existed with generally high levels of inequality within countries. And global inequality, a concept used in recent decades that looks at income distribution for the world's entire population cannot be characterized as anything other than "sky high" or unacceptably high. Without doubt, inequality has become a source of political and social instability.

Inequality in income and wealth between individuals has been increasing rapidly for a few decades in the great majority of countries. Even though countries such as China and India have made progress in reducing extreme poverty, income and wealth disparities have widened. In economies where the financial sector has become dominant, wealth and earnings have increased at the top despite the failings of the industry during the 2008–2009 financial crisis, leaving unbelievable quantities of wealth in the hands of a privileged minority. This wealth concentration is clearly a consequence of the present economic system.[12] Most of the wealth created by development and resource exploitation in recent decades has gone to the already-rich as increases in capital, asset value and dividends, while wages for labor have stagnated and little or nothing has trickled down to the poor. The present global economic system selectively bestows advantage on the privileged few, while leaving the masses to make do with a small fraction of the world's resources.[13,14]

---

[11] Davies, J.B. and A.F. Shorrocks. 2000. "The Distribution of Wealth," in A.B. Atkinson and F. Bourguignon (eds.), *Handbook of Income Distribution*, Vol. 1. Amsterdam, Elsevier, pp. 605–675.

[12] Manning, Patrick. 2017. "Inequality: Historical and Disciplinary Approaches," AHA Presidential Address. *American Historical Review*, Vol. 122, No. 1, 1 February, pp. 1–23.

[13] Bahá'í International Community, *Beyond Balancing the Scales*.

[14] Reporting on the concentration of wealth in the United States, the *Washington Post* (February 9, 2019) highlights the conclusions of a recent paper by Gabriel Zucman, a University of California at Berkeley economist, who estimates that the 400 richest Americans, accounting for the top 0.00025 percent of the population, have tripled their share of the national wealth since the early 1980s and their net worth now exceeds the net worth of the 150 million Americans in the bottom 60 percent of the wealth distribution, whose share of the nation's wealth fell from 5.7 percent in 1987 to 2.1 percent in 2014. www.washingtonpost.com/us-policy/2019/02/08/wealth-concentration-returning-levels-last-seen-during-roaring-twenties-according-new-research/?noredirect=on&utm_term=.5b01d209ea95.

The concentration of wealth also leads to a concentration of power, sometimes directly when wealthy individuals run for political office, or less directly through control of the media and manipulation of public opinion, financing of political parties and campaign contributions, or corruption of political leaders and legislators.[15] Political power also creates possibilities to amass wealth that may be difficult for many to resist, resulting in turn in both a desire to cling to power and the means to do so. The recent rapid concentration of extreme wealth among a tiny fraction of the world's population, and their desire to protect their advantages, create strong forces to maintain the status quo that allowed them to reach the top, while resisting the transformation necessary to reduce inequalities, achieve social cohesion and move toward environmental sustainability. The social contract that brought significant progress in the second half of the twentieth century has been eroding, with inequality increasing again.[16] These same forces have fostered a nativist and populist backlash against progressive or socially minded elites (including scientific and other "experts"), carefully cultivated by unscrupulous leaders intent on eroding democracy to achieve and hold on to power, or simply the status quo. The legitimate frustrations of those who have been left behind or marginalized by economic globalization are channeled ironically to reinforce the present system and to block or reverse efforts for a more just, diverse and sustainable society.

Most economists consider that increasing disparities in income are normal, and the present economic system tends to allow corporations to achieve monopoly positions if the government does not intervene to maintain a reasonable level of competition. The lack of international governance in this area allows large multinational corporations to escape from much national control and to corner major shares of global markets. Shareholders demand a return on their investment, fund managers search for the placements with the highest returns and too many managers see the end of high profitability justifying any means, as perennial corporate scandals have demonstrated across the world. Growth is often promoted as the solution to inequality, as additional wealth is supposed to trickle down and benefit everyone, except that in practice this does not happen when the incentive is to increase productivity with technology, focus on returns on capital and reduce expensive labor inputs. Today's economic system, with its unbalanced

[15] A recent study by Martin Gilens and Benjamin Page found that wealthy elites in the United States have significant influence on national policy, while the middle classes and civil society have little or none (leading some to qualify the country as an oligarchy): "[m]ultivariate analysis indicates that economic elites and organised groups representing business interests have substantial independent impacts on US government policy, while average citizens and mass-based interest groups have little or no independent influence." Gilens, M. and B. Page. 2014. "Testing Theories of American Politics: Elites, Interest Groups, and Average Citizens." *Perspectives on Politics*, Vol. 12, No. 3, pp. 564–581. DOI: 10.1017/S1537592714001595.

[16] UNRISD. 2016. *Policy Innovations for Transformative Change: Implementing the 2030 Agenda for Sustainable Development*. UNRISD Flagship Report, Geneva, United Nations Research Institute for Social Development. www.unrisd.org/flagship2016.

focus on growth and consumer culture, is a fundamental cause of social and environmental unsustainability.

Different governance approaches are needed to address extreme wealth from those needed to reduce poverty. Laws can be designed to prevent an excessive accumulation of wealth, including the use of progressive income taxes aimed at improving equity. Tax authorities may also wish to consider some form of wealth tax for very high incomes, particularly in countries with a highly skewed income distribution.[17] Further incentives to encourage voluntary giving and philanthropy would be a useful complement. Also, given the proven ability and motivation of those with wealth to hide it in tax-free havens, only a globally coordinated approach harmonizing national legislation around the world can address this problem.[18] Beyond such necessary international measures, in application of the principle of subsidiarity, reducing inequality within countries should generally be a national responsibility, except, for example, where it reaches an extreme that affects fundamental human rights, is the result of extensive and uncontrolled corruption, or results from fundamental failures of governance or dictatorial rulers. In such cases, international legislation should authorize oversight by international mechanisms in the internal affairs of such countries.

Inequality between States

One of the challenges in any system of governance is how to deal with extreme inequalities between the subjects being governed, in this case between the states making up what has today globalized into a world system. Close to 60 states with a total population of more than 1 billion are falling behind, if not actually failing, creating chaos and suffering at home and driving economic migration.[19]

The range of diversity between states is enormous, whether in terms of population, surface area, size of the economy or natural resources. However, the differences are not always the same across all of these dimensions. The most and least

---

[17] According to Paul Krugman, commenting on a proposal put forward by economists Emmanuel Saez and Gabriel Zucman, a 2 percent annual tax on net worth in excess of US$50 million and an additional tax of 1 percent on wealth in excess of US$1 billion would only affect 75,000 households in the United States, and "because these households are so wealthy, it would raise a lot of revenue, around US$2.75 trillion over the next decade." He then asks: "Wouldn't it hurt incentives? Probably not much. Think about it: How much would entrepreneurs be deterred by the prospect that, if their big ideas pan out, they'd have to pay additional taxes on their *second* US$50 million?" Krugman, Paul. 2019. "Elizabeth Warren Does Teddy Roosevelt." *New York Times*, January 28, www.nytimes.com/2019/01/28/opinion/elizabeth-warren-tax-plan .html.

[18] The G7 has agreed in 2019 that there should be a global minimum corporate tax rate: www.ft .com/content/b74e8398-a944-11e9-984c-fac8325aaa04.

[19] See, for instance, the insightful discussion provided by Paul Collier in *The Bottom Billion: Why the Poorest Countries Are Failing and What Can Be Done About It*, Oxford, Oxford University Press, 2007.

populous UN member states are China and Tuvalu, with 1.39 billion and 11,000 people respectively. The largest land area is 17 million km² in Russia, versus 2 km² in Monaco. However, Kiribati, with a population of 108,000 on a land area of 811 km² spread over 21 inhabited and 12 uninhabited islands, has a sea area, including its exclusive economic zone, of 3.5 million km². Economically, China with a GDP of US$12 trillion contrasts with Tuvalu with a GDP of US$42 million. Before Tuvalu developed its fisheries resources, its most important export revenue earner was postage stamps for collectors.

Inequality between nations is often defined in economic terms or levels of development. For decades, the "developed" or "industrialized" countries have tried to help the "least developed" or "developing" countries, without much success, since other factors, such as debt repayments and disadvantageous terms of trade, have meant that financial flows out of poor countries have often been greater than foreign aid and foreign direct investment into them. Some estimates suggest that, in the present system, it may take centuries for poorer countries to catch up with richer countries, something that Thomas Homer-Dixon has termed "the dirty little secret of development economics."[20]

This situation of inequality between countries is exacerbated and further entrenched by rigid concepts of national sovereignty. Current ethical approaches are not consonant with, for example, a Rawlsian approach of "original position" behind a veil of ignorance, where we do not know and have no control over the circumstances of our birth. Human rights protections and relative wealth are conditioned by country of birth, and while everything else is globalized, the free movement of people is not allowed. Principles of justice are still primarily conceived as applying inside a sovereign state but not beyond. A state is responsible for its own citizens, but for others, charity is all that is usually called for. Countries are defined as equally sovereign and equally responsible for advancing their own populations' interests, often ignoring the question of whether they actually have the capacity to do so. Furthermore, there are domestic biases in which governments favor the elite or wealthy factions in their society that put them and keep them in power, which further compounds problems of (global) inequality, and the promotion of too narrow conceptions of "national" interest favoring the upper echelons in many countries, who are usually benefiting significantly from financial globalization.[21]

Inequality in wealth between countries is clearly a domain to be addressed through international governance, as it destabilizes the international system, entrenches debilitating injustice and blocks the realization of the fundamental well-being of vast numbers of people. Development aid by itself, as currently

[20] Homer-Dixon, Thomas. 2006. *The Upside of Down: Catastrophe, Creativity, and the Renewal of Civilization*, Toronto, Vintage Canada.

[21] Cabrera, Luis. 2017. "Global Government Revisited: From Utopian Dream to Political Imperative," *Great Transition Initiative* (October). www.greattransition.org/publication/global-govern ment-revisited.

practiced, is seldom the solution, and has generally failed to solve the problem over 70 years of effort. The root causes need to be addressed. One is the continuing effects of colonial systems of exploitation, where primary products from poor countries are exported at highly volatile and declining prices when all added value is created in importing countries, or by intermediaries in emerging market countries.[22] Cheap labor is similarly exploited, often in unhealthy conditions. If attempts are made to offer a living wage, production can simply be shifted elsewhere. If the poor migrate in search of better opportunities, they face opposition and rejection by nation-states defending their territorial borders and by nativist populations rejecting diversity. Another cause is the impact of agricultural subsidies in wealthy countries, usually in terms of price and output supports or other production-based measures of little real benefit to rural populations, which artificially lower the prices of agricultural exports from poorer countries.[23] In extreme cases, the dumping of subsidized excess production on the world market undercuts poor farmers around the world.

Another source of inequality between countries is the very unequal distribution of natural resources. Countries are inherently separate and unequal. Some have mineral resources, others agricultural potential or fisheries, or perhaps natural beauty as a basis for a tourism industry, while others may have little that is marketable. Those endowed with valuable resources may become wealthy without any particular effort on their part, while others without many resources struggle to meet basic needs. Indeed, some countries may not be viable at all in a longer-term perspective, in part due to very different resource endowments.[24] There is also the heritage left by colonizing powers creating mischief among nations by arbitrary (not to say irresponsible) border demarcations.[25] Countries may have vast untapped natural resources, but not the knowledge and capital to develop them, or there may be deficiencies in the quality and capacity of national governance. Their resources cannot be monetized because of mismanagement, lack of trust,

[22] Commodity dependence is generally negative for development, showing the need to diversity away from commodities. UNCTAD/FAO. 2017. *Commodities and Development 2017.* New York and Geneva, United Nations. https://unctad.org/en/PublicationsLibrary/suc2017d1_en .pdf.

[23] These payments amounted to US$257 billion in the 30 OECD countries in 2003 and had risen to some US$320 billion over the period 2015–2017. Tangermann, Stefan and Augusto López-Claros. 2004. "Agricultural Policy in OECD Countries Due for Reform," OpEd, November. http://augustolopezclaros.com/wp-content/uploads/2018/06/OpEdNov2004_IntlPub_A4.pdf? x28456.

[24] Collier, *The Bottom Billion.*

[25] Easterly, William. 2006. *The White Man's Burden: Why the West's Efforts to Aid the Rest Have Done So Much Ill and So Little Good,* New York, Penguin Press. Easterly writes: "There are three different ways that Western mischief contributed to present-day grief in the Rest. First, the West gave territory to one group that a different group already believed it possessed. Second, the West drew boundary lines splitting an ethnic group into two or more parts across nations, frustrating nationalist ambitions of that group and creating ethnic minority problems in two or more resulting nations. Third, the West combined into a single nation two or more groups that were historical enemies" (p. 291).

institutional weaknesses or corruption (see Chapter 18). Finally, there are countries that suffer from the "resource curse," where the money from resource development does not benefit the generality of the population but goes to support autocratic governments, finance corruption and fund civil wars. One challenge for global governance will be to ensure that the distribution of the products of economic activity is much more equitably regulated. Vast private sector resources may potentially become available through public–private partnerships under the aegis of a new, credible organization with a General Assembly mandate addressing global inequality that could guarantee and protect the interests of all parties.

As we have already explained, rapid population growth is both a cause and a consequence of poverty. Where children are the only form of social security available, or may be needed to herd animals, work the land or carry water, the incentive is to have as many as possible, especially if high infant mortality reduces the chances that all will survive to be useful. This poverty trap is itself the result of inequality. Enough of modern medical science has been shared globally to lower early childhood death rates and to control epidemics, but not enough wealth has been shared to reduce poverty, offer family planning services, establish some social security and achieve universal education, especially of girls, which would lower birth rates. This is what maintains high population growth rates among the poorer populations, especially (but not exclusively) in Africa. If these issues of inequality were addressed effectively, the high birth rate could be expected to drop more rapidly as it has in the rest of the world, and the problem of excessive population growth would be much attenuated.

States are also responsible for some share of the world's biodiversity and may not always have the capacity to care responsibly for something that is partly or mostly of global importance. Small island states in particular, because of the nature of evolutionary processes on islands, have some of the highest numbers of endemic species per capita in the world, sharing tiny land areas with their human populations. Yet microstates cannot easily attain all the technical competencies and financial means necessary to manage such responsibilities. One role of global governance should be to respond to the global crisis of biodiversity loss and species extinctions with assistance when and where it is needed. In this as in many other areas, the common interest is not evenly distributed around the world. Effective global governance would assure that all the necessary voices would be heard and taken into account in global decision-making processes, and human, technical and financial resources collected according to capacity and distributed according to need.

Addressing inequality is complicated by the challenges of planetary sustainability, as defined, for example, in the SDGs. It will not be enough simply to raise the income level of the poor and deprived, whether countries or individuals. The latest science shows objectively that it is impossible to give everyone a high material standard of living, as defined today by the levels of consumption in advanced materialistic societies, without overusing natural resources and exceeding planetary boundaries. Countries that are currently rated highly on measures of human well-being also break environmental limits, and those using resources within planetary boundaries are unable to meet the needs of their citizens, while some fail on both counts as dysfunctional over-consumers.[26] A fundamental transformation is needed to address global inequality in a sustainable way, with "over-consumers" changing their lifestyles and curbing excessive consumption to free up resources for those in need. This applies to both states and individuals.

To address the very dramatic current inequalities among states, deeper regional and global integration will likely be required: "[t]he ultimate goal of integration would be the creation of regional and global institutions that promote the interests and rights of all. Such higher-level institutions would also offer mechanisms to challenge repression and rights violations at the national level."[27] We suggest one such higher-level institution in the section on a new UN Agency for Inequality.

The European Union provides an example of states in a region addressing national inequality as a necessary accompaniment to allowing the free movement of people and goods (see Chapter 3). The wealthier countries provide structural funds for infrastructure and other projects to help less developed members catch up, in exchange for meeting common standards and regulations. The system is far from perfect, but it shows what is possible between states. And it has contributed to reducing inequality between countries within the Union, while also delivering some of the lowest Gini coefficients in the world for many members of the EU.[28]

NARROWING INCOME INEQUALITY

Lindert and Williamson raise an interesting and pertinent question with considerable relevance to the ongoing debate on the impact of globalization on inequality.[29] How unequal would a fully integrated world economy be? Imagine a world economy with a single currency, few if any barriers to trade, free mobility of labor and capital, and let's ask ourselves: "would such an economy be more unequal than the world of today?" The answer to this question has two dimensions. First, one must

---

[26] O'Neill, Daniel W., Andrew L. Fanning, William F. Lamb, and Julia K. Steinberger. 2018. "A Good Life for All within Planetary Boundaries." *Nature Sustainability*, Vol. 1, No. 2, pp. 88–95. https://doi.org/10.1038/s41893-018-0021-4.

[27] Cabrera, "Global Government Revisited."

[28] The Gini coefficient, developed by the Italian statistician Corrado Gini in 1912, is a variability measure designed to represent the income or wealth distribution of a group of people, such as a nation's inhabitants. It is the most commonly used measure of inequality. The coefficient is typically normalized to be between 0 and 1, with higher scores signifying higher levels of inequality.

[29] Lindert, Peter H. and Jeffrey G. Williamson. 2001. "Does Globalization Make the World More Unequal?" Cambridge, MA, National Bureau of Economic Research, NBER Working Paper No. 8228, April. www.nber.org/papers/w8228.

note that today we have large integrated economies – the United States, Japan, the EU – that are larger in size than was the global economy in 1950. These economies have Gini coefficients (47 for the United States, a lower 32 for Japan) that are much lower than the corresponding Gini coefficient for world inequality reported by Bourguignon and Morrisson (64)[30] or the higher (68) Gini calculated by Milanovic for 2010 on the basis of the latest purchasing power parity (PPP) exchange rates.

Globalization and other factors have not only contributed to a process of rapid convergence among high-income globalizing nations but have also delivered much lower levels of inequality within these countries than currently prevails in our barrier-filled world. A skeptic might argue that a barrierless global economy would still likely be characterized by large income disparities, reflecting the sharply different stages of development in places such as China, Africa and Latin America – witness the income disparities within the 50 states of the United States or the 28 members of the European Union. However, an important lesson from the past two centuries is that what matters most for economic and social transformation is what happens *at the margin* where proximity facilitates comparisons. As more countries adopted policies that facilitated their integration to the global economy, one would likely see set in motion the same class of convergence forces that have been in operation during the past century in the developed world. And this observation may contain within it an important piece of the puzzle as to how to reduce global income disparities in the future.

The second dimension concerns the speed with which growing inequality can be halted and reversed in a world where the injustice of inequality is apparent to everyone, creating social instability. When the top 10 percent of the world's population receive 58 percent of the world's income or, alternatively, when the bottom 60 percent do not even receive 10 percent of the world's income, we know that we have a serious problem of income distribution. It does not matter very much, in fact, if income inequalities might have "turned a corner" in the past decade because of feverish growth rates in India and China and other parts of the developing world. The current *levels* of inequality are unacceptably high and we cannot simply say to ourselves: within another 100 years or so, we will have returned to more socially acceptable and politically sustainable levels of inequality, closer to those seen in the nineteenth century. (It took Japan, starting in the 1870s, 100 years to catch up with the United Kingdom and other rich industrial democracies). The question is: what can we do to accelerate the process whereby income disparities are attenuated and we move to a more egalitarian world?

The answer to this question has many parts. First, it is necessary to say that the problem we face is one that admits solution; countries subject to some of the same forces shaping the global economic environment during the past century have

---

[30] Bourguignon, Francois and Christian Morrisson. 2002. "Inequality Among World Citizens." *American Economic Review*, Vol. 92, No. 4, September, pp. 727–744.

radically different levels of within-country inequality. The Nordic countries, for instance, are among the most competitive in the world, have managed to exploit effectively the opportunities provided by globalization, and yet have made considerable progress in creating more egalitarian societies – they have the lowest Gini coefficients in the developed world.[31] The relationship between economic growth and inequality may be a complex one, and there may be forces affecting the direction of inequality that have an exogenous character, but there is little doubt that inequality is also affected by policy, and policies are shaped by governments, sometimes increasingly within frameworks of international cooperation.

One way to frame this discussion is in terms of the future of globalization. Because globalization is mainly being driven by technological and scientific innovation, the profit motive and the uncoordinated actions of myriad players in the global economy, as well as what Thomas Friedman calls the democratization of technology, finance and information, it is very probably an irreversible process.[32] Policy-makers are not likely to be any more successful at stopping it than they have been at controlling the flow of capital across national boundaries. Thus, we would agree with those who suggest that all that can be hoped for is more effective *management* of the globalization process. In practice this would mean, for instance, reorienting government spending priorities – particularly in the developing world – so as to put greater emphasis on the protection of the economically vulnerable and other disadvantaged groups in society; and making sure that there are programs in place for temporarily displaced workers in declining industries – one of the inevitable consequences of a rapidly changing global economy – including those aimed at training and providing new skills. More generally, greater efforts need to be made in the developing world to build the social safety net institutions that were put in place in virtually all the developed countries during the twentieth century and that have been a key element behind the creation of more egalitarian societies.

Boosting the share of education budgets to broaden the range of opportunities available to women is likely to be a central component of this process, given the overwhelming scientific evidence linking female education and literacy to reductions in mortality rates for children, fertility rates and levels of poverty.[33] Benjamin Friedman observes:

> More widespread female education leads to fewer births per woman, not only because more educated women normally have more information about birth control but also because education creates alternative opportunities that are often

---

[31] The Gini coefficients of Denmark, Finland, Iceland, Norway, and Sweden hover around 25–27.

[32] Friedman, Thomas L. 1999. *The Lexus and the Olive Tree: Understanding Globalization*, New York, Farrar, Straus and Giroux.

[33] On these and related questions, see López-Claros, Augusto and Bahiyyih Nakhjavani. 2018. *Equality for Women = Prosperity for All: The Disastrous Crisis of Gender Inequality*, New York, St. Martin's Press.

more attractive than immediate childbearing. The resulting lower fertility apparently constitutes one of the principal ways in which the distribution of income and wealth affects economic growth in low-income countries.[34]

Intensified efforts are needed by donor governments and nongovernmental organizations (NGOs) engaged in assisting the developing world to encourage greater democracy and participation, to make people feel they are empowered, willing and knowledgeable participants in the development process. Pushing for more responsible behavior on the part of large global corporations vis-à-vis the environment, working conditions for their employees and as regards their relations with host governments would all be desirable components of a strategy aimed at better management of the globalization process.

While these points all sound ideal, the skeptic might ask: who will pay for all of these initiatives? The answer is twofold. First, the developing countries themselves, hosts to billions of people who feel left behind by the locomotive of globalization, can do a great deal more to improve economic management and to better use available resources. According to the World Bank's World Development Indicators, the emerging markets and developing countries, home to virtually all of the extremely poor, illiterate and malnourished people in the world, spend US$545 billion on their militaries every year. For many of these countries, more money is spent on the maintenance of military establishments every year than on health and education combined.[35]

That developing country governments bear a heavy burden of responsibility for the plight of the poor and the widening of income disparities does not exempt the donor governments – mainly in the industrial world – from their own share of culpability. First, wealthy countries' commitment to assisting the developing world is much weaker today than at any time in the postwar period. To cite a well-known example: the United States provided close to 3 percent of gross national income (GNI) in development assistance in 1946; by 2017 this figure had declined to approximately 0.05 percent of GNI or, proportionally, about 60 times less.

---

[34] Friedman, Benjamin M. 2005. *The Moral Consequences of Economic Growth*, New York, Alfred A. Knopf.

[35] There are just too many examples in the developing world that resemble the case of a relatively small country in Latin America that, during the 1990s, spent several hundred million dollars modernizing its air force. Not only is the figure painfully large in relation to the size of its economy, but the expense entailed a much larger claim on the budget over the next decade, because of the need to service the associated military debts, as well as ongoing expenses for maintenance, spare parts and training, all for a project with virtually zero social benefits. It boggles the mind to think how many hospitals could have been supplied, schools built and children provided with access to the Internet for the same sums. It is difficult to disagree with George Soros when he states: "By far the most important causes of misery and poverty in the world today are armed conflict, oppressive and corrupt regimes, and weak states – and globalization cannot be blamed for bad governments." Soros, G. 2002. *George Soros on Globalization*, Oxford, Public Affairs Ltd., p. 16.

According to the OECD, the rich industrial countries annually spent on average over the period 2015–2017 about US$317 billion subsidizing their agriculture and about US$141 billion in foreign aid.[36] Subsidies to relatively well-off farmers in the industrial world distort the markets for agricultural commodities and impose a heavy financial burden on farmers in the developing world. Second, what little aid is provided is often misspent, with little to show for it in terms of improved policies, living conditions and so on.[37] For this reason (and others) we also put a heavy emphasis on the significant enhancement of international anti-corruption efforts and institutions (see Chapter 18). Thus, the scope for improvements would appear to be enormous in both the volume and the efficiency of wealthy country aid flows and to support policies and institutional innovations that will help reduce income disparities.

But, beyond this, there are other instruments that we are not making use of – policies that, if implemented, could go a long way toward reducing the extremes of wealth and poverty within the existing economic system.

POLICIES AIMED AT HELPING REDRESS INCOME INEQUALITY

Countries that have managed to attain lower levels of income inequality within their national boundaries, such as the Nordic nations, Japan, France, Austria, the Nether-lands, Slovenia, Slovakia, the Czech Republic and other members of the European Union, to name a few, have actively used progressive taxation policies as an instrument of redistribution. There is no doubt that this is one of the more powerful tools at the disposal of policy-makers. The nation's budget is perhaps the largest pool of resources available in an economy, and governments typically have a chance, once a year, as the new budget is being prepared, to embed within it a range of national priorities, one of which can be to narrow the income gap – to boost the safety net that protects more vulnerable groups in society, to tax the income of high earners, to spend more on education and training, public health and so on. Different countries will have different priorities, depending on their current circum-stances, where they are located along the income distribution spectrum and what

---

[36] The aid figures for 2017 come from the OECD and comprise total Official Development Assistance (ODA) by the Development Assistance Committee's 29 members. This is the most reliable measure of aid and country-by-country numbers, and may be obtained from www.oecd .org. By a wide margin, the most generous countries are Luxembourg, Sweden, Norway, the United Kingdom, and Denmark. Moreover, by a wide margin, excluding relatively recent new entrants in Eastern and Central Europe, the least generous are the United States, Italy, Portugal, Korea and Spain.

[37] See Alesina, Alberto and David Dollar. 1998. "Who Gives Foreign Aid to Whom and Why?" NBER Working Paper No. W6612, June. See also the paper by Alesina, Alberto and Beatrice Weder, "Do Corrupt Governments Receive Less Foreign Aid?" *American Economic Review*, Vol. 92, No. 4, pp. 1126–1137, which finds no evidence that corrupt governments receive any less aid than countries with good policies and honest governments.

the preferences of voters are as manifested through the democratic process. Not all countries may be able to afford the high levels of social protection provided in the Nordic countries, with the associated high tax rates.

There are legitimate concerns about the kinds of incentives that can sometimes be unleashed when policies are extreme in some way. Ten years ago African countries had the highest tax rates on companies in the world, by a significant margin. Indeed, tax rates were so high that businesses found it more profitable to go underground, to become informal or to simply evade paying taxes, operating beyond the margins of legality. Tax collection levels in these countries were among the lowest in the world, severely undermining the ability of the state to generate enough revenue to fulfil essential social functions. Taxes on labor in some countries are so high that they discourage firms from hiring and the country ends up with higher rates of unemployment than would be the case under a more reasonable tax regime. Therefore, care must be taken not to implement policies that have exactly the opposite of their intended effects – this happens frequently across the world. Good intentions sometimes get kidnapped by attachment to incoherent policies, misguided ideologies or corruption and inevitably the people suffer, sometimes dramatically, as has happened in Venezuela in recent years. Over the past decade tax rates in African countries have come down and this, on the whole, has had a salutary effect on incentives and tax revenue.

The Nordic countries, with among the highest tax burdens in the world, are a special case. They have the lowest levels of corruption in the world. The taxes collected by the state are not leaked to offshore bank accounts of public officials or spirited away in some other fashion. The revenue collected is channeled back into the economy through high spending on education, on research and development, on boosting innovation capacity and investing in the modernization of the countries' infrastructure. This has contributed to the development of a virtuous cycle of development, where businesses and civil society largely trust their governments to use the taxes collected for the public good and, therefore, are willing to pay them – rather than, as happens in countless other countries, spending time and effort devising creative mechanisms to avoid paying the taxes due.

We live in a world in which one's prospects in life are very much a function of the nationality of our parents and, therefore, where we were born, which is, of course, a completely accidental event. If my parents are Norwegian, I will have a life of good health and opportunity, I will receive an excellent education and my future will be generously provided for because, among other things, the government has wisely invested more than US\$1 trillion of petroleum revenues in a Wealth Fund, the primary purpose of which is to ensure that the state is able to fulfil its obligations to future generations. And there are only 5 million Norwegians in the world! If I am born in Chad, Burundi, Sierra Leone or one of dozens of other sub-Saharan African countries, or I am one of several hundred million Indians living below the poverty line, I will have a life of onerous limitations. I may not make it to age one because of sky-high infant mortality rates, or I may become part of the close to 815 million people suffering from malnutrition across the world. Because of the incidence of early childhood diseases my IQ, on average, will be lower than that of children in Sweden, Singapore, Japan or South Korea and thus I will be limited in a number of other ways. Most people would not disagree with the statement that there is something profoundly unjust in this state of affairs.

One way to address this problem would be to provide what is called a "universal basic income" to every human being, as a right of citizenship, independently of a person's particular circumstances.[38] One could argue, on purely ethical grounds, that every human being should have access to an adequate caloric intake that will ensure the avoidance of hunger, to essential public health services independently of one's level of income, to free education at least through secondary school, to shelter to avoid homelessness and so on. Indeed, many countries, particularly wealthy ones, already provide key elements of this bundle of goods, but this is done in a haphazard way and largely as a matter of public policy, not because these basic forms of support are seen as a right of citizenship, as something that one is entitled to because one is a member of the human race.

There is a fascinating recent case study of a Native American tribe in North Carolina on whose reservation a casino was built. The casino generated some tax revenue and the authorities decided to split the after-tax profits among the reservation's population – every man, woman and child was entitled to a share. As the casino prospered and the size of the payoff grew, social scientists began to gather interesting data and discovered that the incidence of crime had come down, graduation rates for youngsters had gone up, and the incidence of domestic violence within families had decreased as well, as had rates of alcohol and substance abuse. Youngsters decided to get a college education, others decided to open small businesses and become entrepreneurs. This is not to say that gambling and casinos should be at the center of social policy; this was an accidental feature of this particular reservation. The point is that the existence of something like a universal basic income had all kinds of economic, social and psychological repercussions, all of them positive, suggesting that at least some of the crime, substance abuse, domestic violence and other social dysfunctions are linked to the psychological burdens of economic insecurity. Provide individuals with a reliable safety net, and we will see tangible improvements in social conditions.[39]

In 2016 Switzerland held a referendum on the introduction of a universal basic income. The measure was defeated, partly because of concerns about affordability and the impact on the budget, but also because there is concern in some circles

[38] Bregman, Rutger. 2018. *Utopia for Realists: And How We Can Get There*, London, Bloomsbury Paperbacks.

[39] Lapowsky, Issie. 2017. "Free Money: The Surprising Effects of a Basic Income Supplied by Government." November 12, www.wired.com/story/free-money-the-surprising-effects-of-a-basic-income-supplied-by-government/.

about the implications for people's incentive to work. Would the introduction of such a benefit lead to an increase in idleness and undermine people's desire to work and to be economically productive?

The issue goes far beyond a simple question of income. Everyone has skills and wealth-creating capacities that should be developed, and all should be provided with opportunities to work and to contribute some service to society. Dignity requires that everyone have a place in society, and not be forced to be idle and dependent. Unemployment is a social curse. In a world that can produce all the goods and services we need without creating employment for everyone in traditional occupations, equity requires that the benefits be shared in other ways. However, the poor do not need aid so much as more capacity to generate their own wealth. A fundamental transformation in the economic system is needed so that one priority is ensuring meaningful employment for everyone. This is a major challenge for economic thinkers, and should be enabled as one responsibility of governance, nationally and internationally.

Our own view is that, as a matter of priority, as part of our global efforts to reduce the incidence of poverty and encourage what the World Bank calls "shared prosperity," which means narrowing the extremes of wealth and poverty in the world, we should endeavor to introduce a universal basic income in those countries with the largest numbers of poor in the world. This could be done in stages. We might focus our attention first on those countries that account for the lion's share of the extremely poor, those close to 800 million people currently living on less than US$1.90 per day. This could subsequently be expanded to take care of those falling under a less onerous poverty line; there are, for instance, close to 2 billion people living on less than US$3.20 a day. The issue of affordability is obviously key. There are serious questions linked to implementation as well, but the details are beyond the scope of this discussion (see Chapter 12). It is worthwhile saying, however, that we live in a world in which there is massive waste of budgetary resources. We subsidize energy (gasoline/petrol, electricity, coal, natural gas) to the tune of US$5.3 trillion per year on a global scale (6.5 percent of world GDP according to a 2015 IMF study), resources that worsen income distribution because the primary beneficiaries of the subsidies are the car-driving middle classes, not poor illiterate women villagers. Indeed, according to the IMF, 60 percent of the subsidies end up with the top 20 percent of the income distribution. Furthermore, these particular subsidies make climate change worse. Also we spend trillions of dollars maintaining military establishments and a military-industrial complex because we have not organized our affairs so as to devise mechanisms of collective security, so there is massive overspending on defense, as noted in Chapter 8.

Profit sharing is another idea that should be explored more fully as a means to address income inequality, and could be encouraged by incentivizing legislation or other programs at the national and international levels. It is a way to supplement the income of workers that would align their interests with those of owners. By becoming stakeholders in the enterprise, workers would have powerful incentives to be more productive, to see their jobs not merely as a means to earn a daily living, but also as an investment in the future and as a way to accumulate wealth. This would likely be a policy to be implemented or spearheaded from within the private sector. As can be seen with the plethora of business community-led initiatives on ethical, sustainable, "triple bottom line" and similar values-based principles (see, e.g., the B Corp movement, which includes such companies as Patagonia and Ben and Jerry's Ice Cream), there should be an intensifying global appetite to explore such solutions to address economic inequality issues.

Beyond progressive taxation, universal basic income and profit sharing, there are other public policies that can contribute to empowering the poor and narrowing the income gap. Encouraging a culture of integrity and honesty in the public sector is of prime importance. As we will see in Chapter 18, corruption can have deleterious effects on the development process and severely undermine the ability of the government to deploy resources for socially productive ends. It reduces government revenue and thus adversely affects the interests of the disadvantaged, who seldom have the power to ensure that public policies promote their interests, as is the case with ruling elites. Education and training remain central to poverty alleviation; that we should have close to 800 million illiterate people in the world – amid the highest-ever levels of productive capacity in the global economy – is an eloquent indictment of the extent to which we have failed in helping to narrow the extremes of wealth and poverty.

One final area where there is huge scope to implement policies that could contribute to reducing income disparities concerns the hundreds of discriminations against women that are embedded in the laws (the constitution, the civic code, family law, the labor and tax codes, among others) of countries all over the world.[40] There is ample empirical evidence that a reduction in gender inequality can directly translate into a decrease in income inequality. Women make up more of the vulnerable segments of the population relative to men; since they are overwhelmingly in the lower end of the income distribution, an increase in the gender wage gap would further exacerbate the degree of inequality in the economy. Studies using microeconomic data have generally indicated that female labor force participation has had an equalizing effect on earnings. This has been found to be the case for the United States.[41] At the macroeconomic level, an empirical study from the IMF has

---

[40] For a comprehensive list of these restrictions, see recent editions of the World Bank's *Women, Business and the Law Report*, a database covering 189 countries.

[41] Maxwell, Nan. 1990. "Changing Female Labor Force Participation: Influences on Income Inequality and Distribution," *Social Forces*, Vol. 68, No. 4, 1 June, pp. 1251–1266; Pencavel, John. 2006. "A Life Cycle Perspective on Changes in Earnings Inequality Among Married Men and Women." *Review of Economics and Statistics*, Vol. 88, pp. 232–242; Chen, Wen-Hao, Michael Förster, and Ana Llena-Nozal. 2013. "Demographic or Labour Market Trends: What Determines the Distribution of Household Earnings in OECD Countries?" *OECD Journal: Economic Studies*, Vol. 2013, No. 1, 2014.

provided some basis for the link between gender inequality and income inequality. Gonzales et al. uncover three main ways gender inequality leads to worsening income inequality.[42] Gender wage gaps contribute directly to inequality, with gender differences in labor force participation likely to lead to lower wages for women, further increasing income inequality. Finally, there are some enabling conditions that create unequal opportunities for women, for instance unequal access to education, health and finance, leading to greater income inequality.[43]

TRANSFORMING THE ECONOMY

Given the tendency of the present economic system to foster inequality, what might an alternative look like? It is not possible to design a new economic system from scratch, or to create one within a rigid ideological framework. It will have to evolve, with some global characteristics defined in global legislation to create a level playing field for economic actors, and diverse applications at the national and local levels adapted to the conditions of each country and community.

However, if the overall goal is social cohesion and an economic system which is inclusive of all, it is possible to lay out some design criteria. Our economic systems should encourage strong entrepreneurial cultures and capacities for innovation, with robust and vibrant business sectors. A transformed economic system should also be socially just, more altruistic and cooperative in nature, create meaningful employment for all and eliminate poverty.[44] Its aim should be human health and well-being, and moderation, a value that aligns with the SDGs. Additionally, recent social science research has shown that, on the individual level, a more moderate income and lifestyle marked by good social relationships and meaningful work may be more conducive to happiness and satisfaction, with diminishing marginal returns in relation to well-being for lifestyles devoted to excessive wealth accumulation.[45] While growth is still needed in areas affected by poverty, consumption of material goods needs to be reduced in the most advanced economies, which should emphasize growth in intangible areas such as knowledge, culture, science, well-being and spirituality.

---

[42] Gonzales, C., S. Jain-Chandra, K. Kochhar, and M. Newiak. 2015. "Fair Play: More Equal Laws Boost Female Labor Force Participation." International Monetary Fund Staff Discussion Note SDN/15/02. Available at: www.imf.org/external/pubs/ft/sdn/2015/sdn1502.pdf.

[43] Gonzales, C., S. Jain-Chandra, K. Kochhar and M. Newiak. 2015. "Fair Play: More Equal Laws Boost Female Labor Force Participation." International Monetary Fund Staff Discussion Note SDN/15/02. www.imf.org/external/pubs/ft/sdn/2015/sdn1502.pdf.

[44] Bahá'í International Community. "Valuing Spirituality in Development: Initial Considerations Regarding the Creation of Spiritually Based Indicators for Development." A concept paper written for the World Faiths and Development Dialogue, Lambeth Palace, London, February 18–19, 1998. London, Bahá'í Publishing Trust.

[45] See, for instance, http://home.uni-leipzig.de/diffdiag/pppd/wp-content/uploads/Manuscript-Pursuit-of-Happiness_final.pdf.

Considerable research has gone into the policy innovations necessary for transformative change, as called for in the 2030 Agenda. Such change requires a reversal of the hierarchies of norms and values that subordinate social and environmental goals to economic objectives. In the immediate aftermath of the 2008 global financial crisis, Nobel laureate Amartya Sen wrote that "the question that arises most forcefully now is not so much about the end of capitalism as about the nature of capitalism and the need for change."[46] Sen reminded his readers that in *The Wealth of Nations*, Adam Smith "talked about the important role of broader values for the choice of behavior, as well as the importance of institutions." "But it was in his first book," Sen added, "*The Theory of Moral Sentiments*, published exactly 250 years ago, that he extensively investigated the powerful role of non-profit values. While stating that 'prudence' was 'of all virtues that which is most helpful to the individual', Smith went on to argue that 'humanity, justice, generosity, and public spirit, are the qualities most useful to others.'"

To break the vicious circle that produces poverty, inequality and environmental destruction, change should directly attack the root causes of these problems instead of the symptoms. It should combine social policies directed to marginalized populations; strengthened social care across health, education, infrastructure and social protection; more emphasis on the social and solidarity economy; framing climate change as a social and political issue; increased domestic resource mobilization; and improved national and international governance and inclusive political processes. This will require innovative policies that overcome palliative and compartmentalized approaches and are grounded in normative values such as social justice and sustainability, forged through inclusive political processes, new forms of partnership, multilevel governance reforms and increased state capacity.[47]

While redesigning the economy is likely beyond what global governance should attempt at present, growing income inequality – between countries and within countries – is one major global governance challenge, as exemplified in UN SDG 10. Income gaps are widening in many countries while aspirations are growing and the effects of climate change threaten the poor disproportionately. A large number of countries are fragile and conflict-ridden, becoming dysfunctional as sovereign states while serving as fertile sources of regional instability and out-migration. Climate-induced migration will accelerate, and recipient countries are already experiencing a political backlash from an unmanaged international migration crisis. Hundreds of millions of people are expected to be displaced in coming decades by environmental, social and economic pressures including climate change and sea level rise. This migration challenge is addressed in Chapter 17.

A variety of transformations are needed in governance to address the root causes of inequality. International governance has largely been dominated by an economic

---

[46] Sen, Amartya, "Adam Smith's Market Never Stood Alone," *Financial Times*, March 11, 2009.
[47] UNRISD, *Policy Innovations for Transformative Change*.

rationale that now – of necessity – should be subordinated to the social and ecological objectives of the 2030 Agenda, for example through sustainable economic policies that are conducive to employment creation and decent work, investment incentives that reward environmentally and socially sustainable activities, social policies that combine social and environmental goals, and environmental norms that rectify social and climate injustices. It is necessary to establish an international regulatory regime that establishes a level playing field and, as necessary, holds transnational corporations and financial institutions accountable so that they respect human rights, obey national tax laws and avoid environmental harm. Beyond public–private partnerships, partnerships are needed with communities and civil society, facilitating the political empowerment and activism of civil society, and providing real options for participation beyond "having a seat at the table."[48]

A UN MANDATE FOR INEQUALITY

Filling this gap in global economic governance requires a multilateral organization with a primary mandate to help redress global inequalities in income and wealth in a way that present international economic institutions for poverty alleviation, financial system surveillance and trade regulation have not been able to do. This will require novel approaches for funding beyond those already being used by institutions such as the IMF and the World Bank with mixed impact at best. Civil society will play an increasing role. Creative approaches to taxation, including certain kinds of global taxes, will also have their place. It should no longer be possible for the very wealthy, whether corporations or individuals, to profit from globalization while at the same time avoiding their social and fiscal responsibilities. To address individual inequality, global standards should be set for social security, minimum wages and employment creation, which will also reduce the motives for crime and corruption.

The heart of the present global system is too weighted toward political and economic power, which reflects historical factors and an unjust distribution of resources that should be corrected rather than enshrined in the structures of governance. In national governments, one solution to balancing different voices has been a bicameral legislature, with one house representative of the different states, cantons or provinces, and the other with representation weighted by population. It is clear that one country–one vote, as in the present UN General Assembly, would be unjust to the most populous states, while even the smallest states have something to contribute to the rich human and natural diversity of our planet. The governance structure is one part of addressing different kinds of inequalities. A bicameral legislative process is one approach that could be adapted to the limited range of responsibilities appropriate to a global government, balancing a voice for each state, some weighted by population, and an opportunity for non-state actors

[48] Ibid.

from civil society to contribute to the consultative process. This is discussed in detail in Chapter 4 on the General Assembly, Chapter 5 on the establishment of a World Parliamentary Assembly and Chapter 6 on advisory mechanisms, including a Civil Society Chamber.

More fundamentally, while the system should ensure that the widest range of perspectives is represented and contributing to the legislative debate, there needs to be an important step forward from the current excesses of partisan and representative democracy as it is usually practiced, where legislators consider themselves in quid pro quo relationship with their electorate, fighting for their particular interests, and also in unhealthy fights for power against other political factions. If global governance is to evolve from diplomats (too often) from competing nation-states defending their own interests, to elected representatives searching for the common good while considering the human interests and environmental boundaries of the entire planet, then the legislators should be selected for their competence, their mature experience and their adherence to basic principles and values. They should be united in their search for the common global interest in a consultative process guided by the core values of the Charter, the best scientific advice, careful attention to all the diverse perspectives shared in the debate and the long-term interests of a planetary society. In this way, they should see themselves as the trustees of all humanity rather than representatives of special interests. This will be the most effective way to overcome the inevitable inequalities in any legislative process.

GLOBAL MANAGEMENT OF THE PRIVATE SECTOR

One of the major challenges in designing a system of global governance is in extending its reach beyond the intergovernmental sphere to other areas of the emerging global system of institutions apart from governments themselves. Multinational corporations, for example, and the economic systems within which they operate are often now richer and more powerful than many governments. The economy and its associated world trade and financial flows are perhaps the first dimension of social organization to have globalized so completely, yet it is a domain in which global governance is particularly lacking.[49] This has allowed the private sector to expand beyond any national control or regulation in its goal to maximize profits and its return on investment, and to reduce its tax liabilities. It has increased its power to lobby national governments to protect its own interests and to play governments off each other to obtain the most favorable treatment with the least constraints and regulations. One consequence has been to increase returns on capital and reduce the dependence on labor, with the wealth created going largely

---

[49] Childers, Erskine with Brian Urquhart. 1994. *Renewing the United Nations System*, Uppsala, Sweden, Dag Hammarskjold Foundation. www.daghammarskjold.se/wp-content/uploads/1994/08/94_1.pdf.

to wealthy owners, shareholders and investors, and not to governments for redistribution as public services, or to the general public as wages. While development has reduced poverty in some parts of the world, the recent economic trend has been to increase inequality within and between countries as discussed above, and to see wealth concentrated among a few super-rich heads of enterprises at the top. This private wealth is largely beyond the reach of any governance mechanism or any goal of more equitable distribution.

National governments generally have a ministry or department of commerce and industry that sets the framework for, and encourages the development of, the private sector and state enterprises as well. It often intervenes to prevent the formation of monopolies or cartels that distort markets, and to ensure good business practices in the common interest. This is an important gap in the present system of international governance, with only the UN Industrial Development Organization (UNIDO) focused on developing countries, informal arrangements with business through the Global Compact, and the World Trade Organization (WTO) outside the UN system dealing with trade issues. Many core aspects of the global economy and business have been left unaddressed because of governments wanting to give the advantage to their own business sector,[50] and powerful lobbying by industries wanting a free hand to maximize their profits by exploiting opportunities around the world, with the ends justifying any means, as with the petroleum industry's denial of climate change.[51] Businesses have too often replaced governments as "colonial" powers looking around the world for resources and cheap labor to exploit.

An ideological approach to minimize government interference in the economy has led both to a reduction in some countries of government regulation of business at the national level, and to powerful lobbies effectively blocking any attempts at governance of the economy internationally. There is no United Nations economic organization. After the Great Depression of the 1930s, the anarchy of national currencies competing in a race to the bottom led to the creation of the IMF to stabilize relationships between central banks in the management of their currencies (see Chapter 15), in the absence of any willingness to consider a single global currency that would no longer be subject to national manipulations. Similarly, the General Agreement on Tariffs and Trade (GATT) and the WTO emerged out of the need to resolve trade disputes amicably rather than by trade wars. Beyond that, the wealthier countries set up the Organization for Economic Cooperation and Development (OECD), and ad hoc discussions of economic policy take place in the G7 or G20 groups of countries, but these are more for voluntary cooperation rather than actual governance. The economy is still an area where the raw exercise of

---

[50] Blackwell, David. 1995. "*Renewing the United Nations System: A Summary.* A review of *Renewing the United Nations System* by Erskine Childers with Brian Urquhart," Dag Hammarskjold Foundation, Uppsala, Sweden, 1994. Global Policy Forum. www.globalpolicy.org/component/content/article/225/32382.html.

[51] McKibben, Bill. "Life on a Shrinking Planet," *New Yorker*, November 26, 2018, pp. 46–55.

power is dominant, rather than considerations of fundamental justice, equity or the rule of law in service to shared and sustainable prosperity.

Furthermore, the heritage of the old colonial systems, where the resources of the world were raped and pillaged for the benefit of colonial powers, has often continued in other forms through multinational corporations and governmental and intergovernmental loan programs, with enormous net wealth transfers still taking place out of Africa and other poor developing areas of the world.[52]

National economic systems are already very diverse, ranging from unfettered free enterprise to majority state control and ownership. Good management is probably more important than the nature of the system itself, so this diversity is probably healthy and should continue, leaving room for continuing innovation. When economies were still national in scale, businesses operated within that framework, and were subject to national legislation. A brief summary of the forms of economic governance that have emerged at the national level may help to identify those functions that may now need to be extended or transposed to the international level.

National legislation has defined the legal forms that economic enterprises can take, such as partnerships, cooperatives, limited liability companies and corporations, defining principles of ownership, shareholding and legal standing. Systems of intellectual property have been created for patents, trademarks and copyrights to stimulate innovation and protect trade secrets. Frameworks for business accountability, management oversight and taxation have evolved, along with those for responsibility and liability. Abuses have led to labor laws, and regulations to protect health and the environment and to reduce social impacts, as well as product standards and labeling requirements for consumer protection. The scope of national governance of the economy is indeed very broad. These systems are still far from perfect, as evidenced by the frequent use by businesses of legal loopholes, lobbying, "creative" accounting, tax evasion, fraud and corruption.

With globalization, multinational corporations have been able to escape in large part from those controls, with many forms of behavior that would be considered illegal nationally perfectly "legal" internationally because of the lack of international legislation. Companies can choose the best legal regime for each activity, hide true ownership and control, locate their profit centers in tax-free havens and practice transfer pricing to minimize tax liabilities wherever they operate. They may also bribe public officials in developing countries when they would never do so at home. The natural tendency in a liberal economy for the biggest companies to outcompete or buy out their competitors leads to monopoly positions, which even the most liberal governments have legislated against at the national level to ensure

---

[52] Hickel, Jason, 2017. "Aid in Reverse: How Poor Countries Develop Rich Countries," *The Guardian*, January 14, www.theguardian.com/global-development-professionals-network/2017/jan/14/aid-in-reverse-how-poor-countries-develop-rich-countries; Curtis, Mark and Tim Jones. 2017. *Honest Accounts 2017: How the World Profits from Africa's Wealth*, Global Justice Now, May, www.cadtm.org/Honest-Accounts-2017-How-the-world.

some level of competition, but for which there is no equivalent capacity to manage this risk internationally. Corporations and financial institutions have become "too big to fail," larger in economic weight than many countries. Not only are global monopolies growing in different economic sectors, but vertical integration is allowing them to control everything between the primary producers to the final consumers with the aim to maximize their profits. The agriculture and food sector,[53] and information and communications technologies, are some examples.

It is also a waste of resources to duplicate in many countries the same process of determining standards for protecting health and the environment, when issues of human health are universal and a chemical's toxicity does not vary from one national jurisdiction to another. Wealthy countries can afford to research and determine high standards of protection, while poorer countries lack the resources to give their populations the same levels of protection. This is an obvious area for harmonization at the global level to the benefit of everyone everywhere. The best technical competences in the world could be harnessed to determine the levels of protection and regulation required. At the same time, global standards can create a level playing field for business that would greatly simplify commerce and reduce the bureaucratic burdens of dealing with a wide variety of national legislative requirements and regulations.

While it is relatively easy to define the scope of the problem of governance in this area, finding solutions is not so evident, since existing mechanisms of economic governance are often rudimentary or ineffective, as evidenced by the repeated economic crises that the world has experienced. Some elements of global governance will be necessary to provide a level playing field for economic actors and to prevent the present competition between countries for the lowest social and environmental standards and most advantageous fiscal arrangements (for the companies, not the countries). This need has long been recognized as a fundamental gap in the UN system.[54] Creating a UN Organization for the Economy would be one option.

Some of the options for areas of global economic governance would be common legal frameworks for the different types of enterprises, harmonized levels of taxation and common standards for fiscal systems and accounting to ensure transparency and comparability. Minimum social and environmental standards could ensure that the planetary environment is properly protected, human rights are respected and social cohesion within and across countries is maintained, while allowing some flexibility to adapt to local particularities and priorities. Intellectual property regimes that disproportionately favor private profits over the common good need to be considered and adjusted so that innovations do not benefit only the rich but are widely

---

[53] Berne Declaration/EcoNexus. 2013. *Agropoly: A Handful of Corporations Control World Food Production*, Zurich, Berne Declaration.
[54] Childers with Urquhart, *Renewing the United Nations System*; Commission on Global Governance. 1995. *Our Global Neighbourhood: Report of the Commission on Global Governance*, Oxford, Oxford University Press.

distributed to all who need them. More fundamentally, legal and institutional frameworks that make profits the sole objective of corporations should be replaced with statutes that adjust the primary purpose and driving force of the enterprise as some service to society, providing sustainable value for all stakeholders and the common good, with profitability one measure of efficiency among others (see, e.g., the Benefit Corporation model, which currently exists in more than 30 US states).[55]

THE WORLD ECONOMY

Since the Bretton Woods Conference, there has not been a significant step forward in designing a framework for the world economy. In 1944, Keynes wanted a global currency as the stable foundation for global markets, but the United States and United Kingdom were too intent on defending the dollar and the pound, so the IMF was the second-best option.[56] Since then, too many vested interests, both governmental and in the banking system, have sought to limit the extent of regulatory interference, with their aim to maximize financial power and profits. More recently, inadequacies in our global financial architecture – including, for instance, poorly regulated financial markets in the private sector – were central to the 2008–2009 world financial crisis and the associated costly disruptions. There seems to be little confidence that the vulnerabilities exposed by that crisis have been adequately addressed and that the global economy is thus protected from an even bigger future financial shock (see Chapter 15).

A greater concern is that the whole framework of the world economic system is fundamentally faulty, starting with the indicators for success that it uses. GDP measures financial flows, but not what they are used for in relation to the common good. Disasters and the subsequent reconstruction, and wars (at least for the victors), contribute positively to GDP. Profit as the ultimate objective and measure of success in the current prevailing economic paradigm is pursued as an end that can justify any means, such as the sale of tobacco and other harmful and addictive products.[57] The maximization of shareholder value has produced a shift of profits away from investment and toward dividends. The resulting underinvestment hurts employment and contributes to economic stagnation, while the top 1 percent of wealthy investors and corporate leaders with stock options become ever richer. They manipulate the system for their own advantage. Government and central bank efforts to stimulate the economy with quantitative easing and borrowing are ineffective when the money mainly inflates capital and market valuation rather than going into real

---

[55] See https://benefitcorp.net/what-is-a-benefit-corporation.

[56] López-Claros, A. 2004. "Sixty Years After Bretton Woods: Developing a Vision for the Future." http://augustolopezclaros.com/papers/.

[57] On the many limitations of GDP as a measure of human welfare see López-Claros, 2018, "Is There a Spiritual Dimension to Economic Development?" http://augustolopez-claros.blogspot .com/2018/04/is-there-spiritual-dimension-to.html.

investment, leaving ever-growing government debt and the resulting need for austerity in their wake. These economic inefficiencies are unsustainable.

In our interconnected world, the banking system does not exist in isolation. The Governor of the Bank of England warned before the 2015 Paris Climate Change Conference that climate change could bring down the whole world financial system, since banks were overextended in their lending to fossil fuel development, and if investors suddenly panicked over potential stranded assets, the system could collapse.[58] Today, the greatest risk may be excessive government borrowing for quantitative easing and reducing taxes. Austerity measures are imposed on the poor and middle classes to prevent governments from defaulting, and interest rates must be kept low, below the growth rate in the economy, to prevent debt servicing from becoming unmanageable. The realization that governments cannot go on expanding borrowing forever and are unlikely to ever pay back their debts, perhaps triggering a wave of government defaults, would be far more serious in its repercussions than the last global financial crisis, and would itself prevent governments from responding as they did in 2008–2009. No existing institution is currently capable of addressing this global risk, which is not negligible, as discussed in Chapter 15.

This is another challenge for global governance, which will need to create a new economic and financial architecture that will ensure productive investment and innovation, while also providing for better wealth redistribution so that everyone benefits from economic activity and no one is left behind. The IMF is only partly responsible for this (Chapter 15). The 1995 Commission on Global Governance proposed the creation of an Economic Security Council to assess the state of the world economy, provide a long-term strategic policy framework, ensure consistency between the parts of the system, and give political leadership and promote consensus on international economic issues.[59] It would be highly desirable to convene a new "Bretton Woods" conference to adopt preventive measures, build more resilience into the global financial system and ensure more social cohesion, before a serious crisis occurs that could see major currencies collapse, potentially shut down global trade and badly cripple the world economy.

---

[58] Carney, Mark. 2015. Quoted in Paul Brown, "Climate Change Threatens Global Financial Crash." *Climate News Network*, October 2. http://climatenewsnetwork.net/climate-change-threatens-global-financial-crash/?utm_source=Climate+News+Network&utm_campaign=1bd3656d6b-Carney_s_crash_warning10_2_2015&utm_medium=email&utm_term=0_1198ea8936–1bd3656d6b-38775505.

[59] Commission on Global Governance, *Our Global Neighbourhood*, chapter 7.

15

Global Financial Architecture and the International Monetary Fund

Multilateral institutions have hitherto worked in two ways. One approach is the quasi-legal one followed by the World Trade Organization (WTO), which regulates trade between participating countries. The WTO bases its actions on a set of agreements that limit barriers to trade. These agreements have been signed and ratified by member governments after long and arduous negotiations. The WTO has a dispute-resolution process aimed at enforcing participants' adherence to the agreements, and because the rules are relatively clear, adherence can be judged in a quasi-legal setting. A second approach, one that is far less effective because of the nature of the task, is the way the IMF goes about international macroeconomic management and coordination: essentially through a process of exhortation that fails to move anyone except those who need the Fund's money. The problem here is that the rules of the game are not clear at all. When does a pattern of actions by a country create global harm? When the Fed cuts interest rates to the bone, and thus sets off a global wave of risk taking, do countries elsewhere have the right to protest?[1]

Raghuram G. Rajan, former IMF Chief Economist

This chapter is divided into two parts. We will first review the role the International Monetary Fund (IMF) has played over the past few decades in managing financial crises and suggest possible areas for reform. We will then review the background to the 2008–2009 global financial crisis and analyze many of its implications, particularly the sharp increase in the burden of public debt that was a consequence of the crisis. We do this partly because we think there is a high likelihood that the next financial crisis will be fiscal in nature (more precisely, fiscal policies that trigger instability in the global financial system), but also because our current financial system has a number of vulnerabilities that pose a major threat to financial stability and economic prosperity and could, in a crisis, interact in highly destabilizing, destructive ways with other aspects of our governance system. The UN Charter

---

[1] Rajan, Raghuram. 2010. *Fault Lines: How Hidden Fractures Still Threaten the Global Economy*, Princeton, NJ, Princeton University Press, p. 210.

clearly introduced the concept of economic and social development as a key responsibility of the international community, and two of the leading UN agencies, the IMF and the World Bank, are very much at the center of implementing the UN's mandate in this area. The first part of this chapter will focus on the IMF because of the central role the organization plays in the management of the global monetary system, a system whose weaknesses were dramatically revealed during the 2008–2009 financial crisis. We will present several proposals for reforms aimed at improving the global financial architecture.

THE IMF AT THE CENTER

A number of questions have been raised over the past few decades (perhaps beginning with the 1997–1998 Asian financial crisis) about the IMF's approach to crisis management in emerging markets and other economies (e.g., Greece in 2010), the chief characteristic of which seems to be large-scale improvisation and ad hoc arrangements with at times costly social and political repercussions. The IMF has found itself in the middle of many of these episodes, and questions about its effectiveness have been raised each time; indeed, some have argued that the organization is no longer needed in an environment of largely floating exchange rates. It is clear, however, that because today's world is one of closely integrated markets, in which linkages are becoming increasingly complex, an institution that will have sufficient resources to deal with more frequent and recurrent episodes of financial instability, and that will help to cushion or prevent the effects of future crises, is indispensable. Some ideas follow on the sort of reforms that could make the world's only "financial peacekeeper" a more effective crisis manager.

As presently structured, the IMF falls far short of the role played by central banks in national economies. Like a national central bank, it can create international liquidity through its lending operations and the occasional allocations to its members of Special Drawing Rights (SDRs), its composite currency. Thus, as Richard Cooper has pointed out,[2] the IMF already is, in a limited sense, a small international bank of issue. As has often been seen, beginning with the Mexican crisis in 1994–1995, the Fund can also play the role of "lender of last resort" for an economy experiencing debt-servicing difficulties. But the amount of support it can provide has traditionally been limited by the size of the country's membership quota, and there is obviously an upper limit on total available resources; as of March 2019, the IMF's "lending capacity" was equivalent to SDR 715 billion (or around US\$1 trillion) consisting primarily of IMF quotas and multilateral and bilateral arrangements that the IMF has negotiated with member countries and institutions to provide so-called second and third lines of defense, to supplement quota resources.[3]

---

[2]   Cooper, Richard N. 1984. "A Monetary System for the Future," *Foreign Affairs*, Fall, pp. 20–30.
[3]   Since the late 1990s the IMF has been forced to substantially relax its long-standing parameters that established the extent of a country's access to Fund resources. Following the onset of the

While this sum may seem large, in early 2019 it was equivalent to about 3 percent of cross-border claims of Bank of International Settlements (BIS) reporting banks, 0.4 percent of total global debt and 1.2 percent of world GDP. It is, hence, a relatively modest sum, adequate to deal with a handful of crises in a few middle-income countries but, as we will argue, possibly a puny amount in the middle of a global financial crisis.[4] Furthermore, in the absence of additional progress in currently frozen negotiations on a quota increase, it is expected that more than half of the total IMF firepower will be gone by 2021.

Beyond the issue of the adequacy of resources, there are other serious structural flaws in its lender-of-last-resort functions. To begin with, its regulatory functions are extremely rudimentary. Its members are sovereign nations that are bound, in theory, by the Fund's Articles of Agreement, but the institution has no real enforcement authority, other than some limited functions through the "conditionality" it applies to those countries using its resources. In particular, the Fund has no authority to enforce changes in policies when countries are engaged in misguided or unsustain-able policy paths but are otherwise not borrowing from the Fund – this was the case with the Asian countries in 1997. What little enforcement authority the IMF does have is sometimes eroded when the country in question has a powerful sponsor, who may try to persuade the Fund and its managers to exercise leniency or "turn a blind eye" if policies appear to be going awry. Contrast this situation with that of a typical national central bank, which has enormous leverage vis-à-vis the commercial banks under its jurisdiction when making resources available to them, particularly in the midst of a crisis. The IMF simply does not have an analogous authority at the international level in relation to the countries that are eligible to use its resources.

There are a number of possible ways to deal with these shortcomings. One proposal put forward in the early 2000s was to create an International Financial Stability Fund, to supplement IMF resources. This would be a facility that could be financed by an annual fee on the stock of cross-border investment; a 0.1 percent tax could generate, according to Edwin Truman, a former Assistant Secretary at the US

Asian financial crisis in 1997 there have been a growing number of examples of "large access" IMF programs, such as Korea in 1997–1998, Turkey in 2000–2001, Uruguay in 2001 when the country received the equivalent of 16 percent of GDP, a similar program for Greece in 2010 and more recently Argentina, receiving almost 13 times its quota in 2018.

[4] In recent years there has been a proliferation of "windows" or facilities through which these resources are made available to member countries. Currently, in addition to the more traditional Stand-by Arrangements (SBA) and the Extended Fund Facility (EFF), the IMF also offers a Flexible Credit Line (FCL) introduced in 2009, very much in response to the crisis; a Precautionary and Liquidity Line (PLL) introduced in 2010, also against the background of the crisis; an Extended Credit Facility (ECF); an Exogenous Shocks Facility – High Access Component (ESF–HAC); a Rapid Financing Instrument (RFI); a Rapid Credit Facility (RCF); and a Stand-by Credit Facility (SCF), among others, all with differing eligibility criteria and terms. In 2016 the IMF approved an FCL for Mexico in the amount of US$88 billion, or about 700 percent of its IMF quota; one upper middle-income country and one facility, accounting for a sizable share of total IMF firepower.

Treasury, some US$25–30 billion per year, which could then be used over time to create a US$300 billion facility.[5] Using more updated figures and shifting the focus from cross-border investments to foreign exchange transactions, we saw in Chapter 12 on the development of new funding mechanisms for the UN that a relatively small Tobin-like tax could generate some US$600 billion annually, some of which could be used to strengthen the IMF's lending capacity. This would partly address the issue of the adequacy of IMF resources and would partially delink its lender-of-last-resort functions from the cumbersome, sometimes heavily politicized periodic allocations of national currencies, in the context of its quota reviews, that currently form the basis of IMF liquidity growth. An alternative and possibly more promising approach would give the Fund the authority to create SDRs as needed, as most national central banks can, to meet the calls of would-be borrowers. The IMF Articles envisaged the SDR to ultimately emerge as the "principal reserve asset" in the global economy. There is at the moment about US$280 billion outstanding in SDRs, or less than 0.4 percent of world GDP; thus the SDR has not fulfilled the promise that it held at the time of its creation. A national central bank does not seek the approval of parliament to make liquidity available to the financial system in the middle of a financial crisis; in most countries such attributes are already embedded in the existing legal framework. Hence the compelling need to overhaul and simplify the system under which the Fund may issue SDRs under exceptional circumstances, such as during times of crisis.[6]

When this idea was first put forward, in the early 1980s, concerns were raised about the possibly inflationary implications of such liquidity injections; however, international inflation was a serious problem at that time in ways that it clearly is not today, and measures could be introduced to safeguard against this. Furthermore, the size, integration and complexity of financial markets today dwarfs what we had in the 1980s, and the costs of an unresolved systemic crisis today are too high to even contemplate. This, of course, would involve giving the Fund considerably more leverage vis-à-vis the policies of those countries willing to have much larger potential access to its resources. Nobody questions the right of central banks to have a major say over the prudential and regulatory environment underlying the activities of the commercial banks under their jurisdiction; it is seen as a legitimate counterpart of its lender-of-last-resort functions. A much richer Fund would, likewise, have to have much stronger leverage and independence.

This says nothing, however, about the kinds of policies that the IMF advocates and whether these are generally welfare enhancing or not. A number of emerging

---

[5] Truman, Edwin M. 2001. "Perspectives on External Financial Crises," Institute for International Economics, December.

[6] Regular SDR allocations to supplement the systemic demand for "owned reserves" were also periodically recommended by some IMF members to enhance the role of the SDR. The IMF could also encourage the use of the SDR as a unit of account – invoicing of international trade in commodities, for instance, or for use in balance of payments statistics.

market crises in recent years (e.g., Asia in 1997, Russia in 1998, Turkey and Argentina in 2001, Greece in 2010 and thereafter, to name a few) have generated heated debates as to whether the IMF is part of the problem, part of the solution or a bit of both. Whatever the justice of these respective positions, it is clear that giving the Fund potential access to a much larger volume of resources would have to be accompanied by significant internal reforms, both in terms of the content of the policies it advocates, as well as its internal management. Both areas have received scant attention since 2009, with the focus having largely been on the types of facilities through which resources are made available and the bureaucratic underpinnings of each.

It is becoming increasingly clear, however, that at least some of the instances of unsuccessful intervention by the IMF since the late 1990s may reflect less a lack of resources and more old fashioned policy mistakes, arising from the Fund's own intellectual biases, its particular views as to what makes for good economic policy and the vagaries of its internal decision-making processes, which suffer from a number of flaws.[7] Thus, if the Fund is to be given more of the functions of a lender of last resort, then it needs an expanded philosophy, bringing into the center of its programs (and its conditionality) the kinds of concerns and policies that, so far, it has only tended to espouse in theory. In public speeches the Fund's top managers speak of transparency, social protection, good governance and "high quality growth," but, by and large, they have not yet managed to incorporate these laudable aims into IMF program design.[8] Indeed, it is becoming increasingly evident that only programs perceived as meeting actual needs and as being just and equitable in their objectives can hope to engage the commitment of citizens of countries around the world upon whom successful implementation ultimately depends. By this yardstick, most IMF programs yield distressingly disappointing results. Not surprisingly, the Fund has often found itself at the center of ineffective programs, blamed for the failure of its policy prescriptions.

A recent example will be useful to illustrate this point. Its financial power and the widely acknowledged professionalism of its staff notwithstanding, the IMF's *Global Financial Stability Report* of April 2006 set out an enthusiastic vision of the wonders of efficient financial markets:

---

[7] To take an example, in Russia the IMF disbursed some US$22 billion of debt between 1992 and 1999, with a mixed record of reforms at best. Indeed, six years of IMF involvement imploded in August 1998 with debt default and the collapse of the ruble. Simultaneously the Russian population endured a more pronounced decline in living standards than was warranted by the elimination of some of the distortions of the central plan, undermining public support for market-oriented reforms and, as Anne Applebaum convincingly argues, fueling the resentments and populism that are in full evidence today. Applebaum, Anne. 2018. "A Warning from Europe," *The Atlantic*, October, pp. 53–63.

[8] And, under the leadership of Christine Lagarde, the former IMF managing director, they also gave growing attention to gender equality, climate change and the dire consequences of corruption.

There is growing recognition that the dispersion of credit risk by banks to a broader and more diverse group of investors ... has helped to make the banking and overall financial system more resilient ... The improved resilience may be seen in fewer bank failures and more consistent credit provision ... It is widely acknowledged, meanwhile, that holding of credit risk by a diverse multitude of investors increases the ability of the financial system as a whole to absorb potential shocks ... Beyond risk diversification, the unbundling and active trading of risk, including through credit derivative markets, seem to have created an efficient, timely, and transparent price discovery process for credit risk ... All these structural changes, taken together, have made financial markets more flexible and resilient. As former U.S. Federal Reserve Chairman Alan Greenspan said: "These increasingly complex financial instruments have contributed to the development of a far more flexible, efficient, and hence resilient financial system than the one that existed just a quarter-century ago.[9]

While, after the 2008–2009 global financial crisis several years later, the IMF was in the forefront of critical assessments of what had gone wrong, one could argue that it was too late. The damage had been done. This led many critics to argue that we don't need an IMF that will act as a cheerleader for conventional wisdom, or that will see its role mainly in terms of buttressing the interests of its largest members. Ideally, we need an IMF that will admonish, alert, caution, illumine and, in general, protect its membership – and thereby the global economy – from flawed thinking, from unwarranted faith – in this particular case – in the self-correcting nature of financial markets or in the ability of credit derivatives to "provide valuable information about credit conditions and increasingly set the marginal price of credit."[10]

In response to a question raised by Queen Elizabeth during a visit to the London School of Economics about how economists had failed to anticipate the crisis, a group of them sent her a letter saying: "In summary, your majesty, the failure to foresee the timing, extent and severity of the crisis and to head it off, while it had many causes, was principally a failure of the collective imagination of many bright people, both in this country and internationally, to understand the risks to the system as a whole."[11]

---

[9] International Monetary Fund. 2006. *Global Financial Stability Report*, Washington DC, pp. 1, 51.

[10] "The IMF's ability to correctly identify the mounting risks was hindered by a high degree of groupthink, intellectual capture, a general mindset that a major financial crisis in large advanced economies was unlikely, and incomplete analytical approaches ... Bilateral surveillance of the US economy failed to warn the authorities of the pertinent risks and policy weaknesses. The IMF often seemed to champion the US financial sector and the authorities' policies, as its views typically paralleled those of the US Federal Reserve" is how the Fund's Independent Evaluation Office put it in an assessment made of the organization's role in anticipating the global financial crisis. See "Watchdog Says IMF Missed Crisis Risks," *Financial Times*, February 10, 2011.

[11] "Queen Told how Economists Missed the Financial Crisis," *Daily Telegraph*, July 26, 2009.

Easing the task of evolving new paradigms of intervention, a wealth of illuminating material already exists in the field. A perusal of Sen's *Development as Freedom*,[12] for instance, provides a compelling list of the ingredients for a successful approach to economic development, making clear to the reader that fiscal austerity is not the sole remedy available. Indeed, as former UK Chancellor of the Exchequer Gordon Brown noted in the middle of a wave of emerging market crises in 2001, the assumption that "just by liberalizing, deregulating, privatizing and simply getting prices right, growth and employment would inevitably follow" has "proved inadequate to meet the emerging challenges of globalization."[13] Eighteen years later this assessment remains broadly on target.[14]

A broadening of the policy content of Fund programs, to meet the challenges of Sen's much wider vision of successful development, to be credible, would need to be accompanied by a structural reorganization, whereby the Fund's shareholders assigned it a greater measure of intellectual independence, making it at the same time more accountable for the consequences of its decisions. It would seem desirable to separate the Fund's surveillance activities from its decisions in respect of lending, so that glaring conflicts of interest might be avoided. Gordon Brown's call for a "more transparent, more independent and, therefore, more authoritative" Fund is certainly a step in the right direction, and his call for new approaches to sovereign debt restructuring and the implementation of code standards for fiscal, monetary and other policies, to diminish the likelihood of future crises, remains relevant, notwithstanding the progress made in these areas in recent year. In these discussions the focus should overwhelmingly shift to crisis prevention rather than crisis resolution.

But even an updated set of policy prescriptions is unlikely to suffice without corresponding reforms in the internal workings of the organization aimed at improving its effectiveness, representativeness, legitimacy and accountability. As a preliminary measure, the international community might finally break with the convention adhered to since the IMF's creation, which establishes that its managing director must be European. (A similar recommendation applies to the World Bank, whose president has traditionally been a US citizen). The organization is too important and

---

[12] Sen, Amartya. 1999. *Development as Freedom*. Oxford, Oxford University Press.

[13] Speech given by Chancellor of the Exchequer Gordon Brown to the Federal Reserve Bank of New York, November 16, 2001.

[14] Many IMF staff and country authorities might not necessarily object to this more expansive view of the Fund but might ask: "with what instruments will these additional concerns be addressed by the Fund?" The experience with cross-conditionalities in Fund programs has been mixed, with too many conditions sometimes being counterproductive. In this respect the issue of "the Fund's comparative advantage" in dealing mainly with macroeconomic issues often arises. But, in our view, given the integrated nature of the global economy and the interactions between seemingly purely macroeconomic issues and other factors outside the traditional Fund mandate (e.g., the environment, income inequality), the solution may not be to stick to its traditional comparative advantage, but to expand its expertise and engagement beyond, for instance, analyzing issues of fiscal policy sustainability.

its mistakes too socially costly for the nationality of the candidate for managing director to be the determining factor in assessing suitability for the job.

The unseemly negotiating process that is entered into every few years as efforts are once more set in motion to locate the most suitable candidate from a specific country is inherently offensive to the peoples of those countries who have had to endure the rigors of IMF austerity, not to mention that it exemplifies the very inefficiency that IMF officials are quick to condemn in dealings with the Fund's member countries. (The practice reflects the position of the economic powers emerging from World War II and could not be justified under the ethical principles and best-practice management codes of the world of today.) Another desirable reform along these lines would be to accord the Managing Director a non-renewable fixed term of service, thereby freeing him or her from the conflict that may otherwise result between the interests of those who hold the appointment in their hands, and the countries which it is his/her mission to serve: in this way, the MD may never feel pressured to place personal interest above the function of the office.[15]

On this question of the controlling interest in the organization, it may be noted that the salaries of the Fund's MD and of its entire staff (as well as other administrative expenditures) are financed precisely by the interest paid by taxpayers in countries (mainly in the developing world) that are users of Fund resources. Whereas IMF lending operations have no budgetary implications for members such as the United States and the European Union – indeed, they earn a return on their SDR reserve assets – borrowing countries can end up paying billions of dollars in interest charges on previous Fund loans. Such a circumstance alone, one would think, might go some way to counter the existing notion that, because the large shareholders "contribute" more to the organization, they are in some manner

---

[15] In a piece in the *Financial Times* published in 2009, Jorge Castaneda, Mexico's former foreign minister, and Augusto López-Claros made the following proposal: "Let's do away with the job of the MD and replace it with a Supreme Management Council, a group of nine wise men and women appointed for life (or until a suitable retirement age). Think of all the benefits. First, they would not be beholden to the interests of the richer members and would operate with independence of mind and the interests of the international community at heart. Second, as members retired they would be replaced with younger blood and the council would thus become a repository of decades of relevant experience on the issues that matter for management of the global economy. Contrast this with the present system where each new MD has to spend a couple of years catching up before the pressures of work or other factors tempt them to bail out. Both Horst Köhler and Rodrigo Rato – the two preceding MDs – left before the expiration of their five-year terms. Nine members working in a spirit of consultation, not worried about the length of their tenure, would bring more mental firepower to the job than an individual. Unanimous decisions would be favoured but, as needed, majority voting would do. Instead of having central bank governors and finance ministers nominate their own favourite peers, the council could be filled via international recruitment. Such a system would go a long way towards strengthening the much-diminished credibility of the IMF, at a time when that scarce asset is most in need." "Nominate Nine Wise Men and Women to Restore IMF's Credibility," *Financial Times*, May 4, 2009.

entitled to oversee its operations as well, particularly since they, in any event, already have the largest voting shares at the IMF Board.

This leads to a second observation: namely, that increasingly there is a tendency for the markets, borrowers and other economic agents to view the Fund as subservient to its main shareholders, a proxy of G7 foreign policy or, worse, as has been noted by some scholars, "a branch of the US treasury" or, more recently, in the context of the euro crisis, the European Central Bank.[16] Such a perception is deeply damaging to the organization's ability to act effectively. It encourages countries to gauge their relationship with the IMF in terms of short-term political advantage rather than lasting economic gain.

The present organizational structure has implications too for the Fund staff, who cannot under the present regime be held accountable for policy miscalculations. Deprived of full freedom to make intellectually independent assessments, inasmuch as the controlling influence rests with the large shareholders, who, as indicated, may be answerable to various "strategic" (meaning political) interests of their own, they are constrained to represent themselves merely as executors – not a role calculated to enhance their standing with their counterparts in the Fund's member countries. And to the extent that they are viewed by the countries concerned as mere functionaries, their ability to act more generally as advocates for change will be impaired.

Emerging from the 1944 Bretton Woods Conference at which both the IMF and the World Bank were created, John Maynard Keynes expressed the view that: "As an experiment in international cooperation, the conference has been an outstanding success."[17] The world has changed beyond recognition in the meantime, and, with the emergence of one global economy, the case for an institution that will help further the cause of international cooperation and be identified with the promotion of economic policies supportive of improved efficiency and equity has only become stronger. Conditions now seem propitious for the convocation of a global conference of heads of state to consult upon the policy and institutional requirements for a more stable world financial system in the era of globalization. How to promote better ownership of programs, and how to engage more effectively in the decision-making process with the countries most affected by such crises, are clearly two central questions that would need to be addressed. Indeed, the time may be fast approaching for a new "Bretton Woods" conference aimed at turning the two premier development organizations into more flexible and effective instruments for the promotion of global welfare.

---

[16] See Krugman, Paul. 2002. "Argentina's Crisis Is a U.S. Failure," *International Herald Tribune*, January 21.

[17] See López-Claros, A. "Sixty Years after Bretton Woods: Developing a Vision for the Future." http://augustolopezclaros.com/wp-content/uploads/2018/06/BrettonWoods_RomeSummary_Jul2004_A4.pdf?x28456.

THE 2008–2009 FINANCIAL CRISIS AND WHAT IT SAID ABOUT THE WORLD'S FINANCIAL SYSTEM

The world's financial system unraveled very quickly after the collapse of Lehman Brothers in September 2008, the rescue of AIG and other interventions in the United States and Europe. A large increase in uncertainty linked to sharp swings in risk, as banks witnessed a collapse in the value of their assets, raised questions about the solvency of major participants in the global financial markets. As market volatility surged there was a shift to high-quality assets, with yields on liquid government securities falling quickly. The virtual disappearance of credit led to rapid and chaotic attempts to reduce debt levels and the sale of liquid assets at rapidly declining prices precipitated a downward spiral in equity markets worldwide. At the outset of the crisis there was short-lived optimism that emerging markets would be spared the worst effects of the crisis. But emerging markets were hit as well, highlighting, convincingly, the highly integrated nature of global financial markets.[18]

Initially many felt that a combination of a strong reserve position and low exposure to toxic assets would shelter them from the crisis, but as financing dried up they came under heavy pressure as well. Particularly hard hit were countries that had relied heavily on foreign investments or debt to finance large current account deficits; there was a sharp reversal of capital inflows. In the first year of the crisis gross capital flows plunged by about 90 percent. In parallel to these financial market developments, there was a vast synchronized collapse of international trade, which exceeded that seen following the crisis of 1929, reflecting the close integration of global supply networks. In the United States unemployment rose by some 8 million people and, by 2015, more than 9 million homes had been lost to foreclosures. There seems to be fairly broad agreement as well, as recently noted by *The Economist*, that the crisis "turbocharged today's populist surge, raising questions about income inequality, job security and globalization."[19,20]

---

[18] For a detailed account of the crisis, see the April 2009 issue of the IMF's World Economic Outlook. International Monetary Fund. 2009. *World Economic Outlook: Crisis and Recovery*, April, Washington, DC.

[19] *The Economist*, lead editorial, September 8, 2018.

[20] *The Financial Crisis Inquiry Report* (2011) issued by the National Commission on the Causes of the Financial and Economic Crisis in the United States stated: "We conclude this financial crisis was avoidable. The crisis was the result of human action and inaction, not of Mother Nature or computer models gone haywire. The captains of finance and the public stewards of our financial system ignored warnings and failed to question, understand, and manage evolving risks within a system essential to the well-being of the American public. Theirs was a big miss, not a stumble. While the business cycle cannot be repealed, a crisis of this magnitude need not have occurred. To paraphrase Shakespeare, the fault lies not in the stars, but in us." https://archive.org/stream/355893-the-financial-crisis-inqury-report-jan-2011/355893-the-financial-crisis-inqury-report-jan-2011_djvu.txt.

The authorities took extraordinary measures intended to stabilize markets, including: massive provision of liquidity, the takeover of several institutions perceived to be weak, the extension of deposit insurance, the introduction of legislation in the United States to use public funds to buy troubled assets from banks, the infusion of capital to the banking system which, de facto, turned the US and other governments into major shareholders of large portions of the banking system, and the announcement by the United States of an US$800 billion package to directly stimulate borrowing by homebuyers and small businesses, among others. Between December 2007 and October 2010 the Federal Reserve provided temporary swap lines to a group of 14 central banks amounting to some US$4.5 trillion. This was part, according to IMF estimates, of the US$12 trillion in interventions in the immediate aftermath of the crisis.[21] In addition, prodded by the IMF, the authorities also announced large programs of fiscal stimulus that were expected to lead to a huge jump in public indebtedness over the next several years.[22]

There are several reasons why we should worry about the remarkable increases in public debt that followed the crisis. One has to do with the constraints on government policy that high levels of debt normally imply. With debt levels in many developed and advanced countries in excess of 100 percent of GDP, governments are less able to invest in education, infrastructure and other productivity-enhancing areas, to say nothing of moving to a lower-tax environment. This leads to reduced "fiscal space" – also entailing a crowding out of private investment – and undermines economic growth. High debt service becomes an important constraint on the ability of governments to respond to pressing social and other needs, including possibly responding to other unforeseen crises in the future. For example, in the case of the US, a recent Congressional Budget Office (CBO) study (2018) shows that the federal government may soon pay more annually to service debt interest payments than on the military or Medicaid. The federal deficit is rising more quickly due to recent tax cuts, and rising interest rates make borrowing to finance such a deficit more expensive. The government may see an erosion in its capacity to complete mundane tasks such as infrastructure repair or its ability to respond to emergencies

---

[21] See the 2010 paper by Stijn Classens and his colleagues at the IMF, which identifies more than US$12 trillion of interventions in the advanced economies alone, including capital injections, purchases of assets and lending by the treasury, guarantees, liquidity provisions by central banks and upfront government financing. Classens, Stijn, Giovanni Dell'Ariccia, Denis Igan, and Luc Laeven. 2010 "Lessons and Policy Implications from the Global Financial Crisis." IMF Working Paper, WP/10/44, Washington, DC.

[22] Even the IMF, the world's traditional guardian of sound public finances, came out strongly in favor of fiscal loosening, arguing through its Managing Director that "if there has ever been a time in modern economic history when fiscal policy and a fiscal stimulus should be used, it's now" and that it should take place "everywhere where it's possible. Everywhere were you have some room concerning debt sustainability. Everywhere where inflation is low enough not to risk having some kind of return of inflation, this effort has to be made." Press briefing by Dominique Strauss-Kahn, IMF Managing Director, November 15, 2008, available at www.imf .org/external/np/tr/2008/tr081115.htm.

such as a recession. According to the CBO, interest payments will hit US$390 billion in 2019 – 50 percent higher than in 2017 – and are on track to hit US$900 billion within a decade, a figure that highlights the geopolitical implications of high public debt. Faced with onerous budget constraints, the United States may no longer be able to underwrite the global security arrangements that have under-pinned half a century of buoyant economic growth. In such scenarios, instead of worrying about reforms aimed at boosting productivity, governments increasingly have to worry about debt dynamics, market sentiment, credit ratings and where the money will come from to deal with the next crisis.[23]

Nor are emerging markets exempt from the risks associated with high debt. The level of debt that is regarded as prudent in emerging markets – about 40 percent of GDP – is generally considerably lower than in the advanced economies, with their much deeper financial markets and better track records of debt management. Emerging markets tend to have lower revenue ratios; they sometimes are more dependent on financing by nonresidents and have a much more uneven history of debt defaults. According to the IMF, countries such as Brazil, India, Pakistan, Poland, Turkey and Thailand, among others, already have debt levels above 40 percent of GDP, sometimes substantially so.

Second, in a large number of the bigger economies there are unfavorable demographic trends that are resulting in the aging of populations. Increases in life expectancy combined with declining fertility will have systemic implications for the sustainability of pension systems and the ability of governments to remain faithful to the key elements of the social contract. In some countries (e.g., Italy) unfunded pension liabilities exceed 100 percent of GDP, raising questions about the sustain-ably of pension systems and the likely need to significantly increase the retirement age as a way of propping up their financial position. The cost of pensions, health care and other social benefits is projected to rise rapidly over the next several decades. In the United States, for instance, 78 million people were born between 1946 and 1964 (the "baby boomers") and this cohort started retiring in 2011. In France and Germany pension and health spending by 2050 is expected to be well above the 17 percent of GDP registered in 2000.

But there is more. Climate change will be a feature of the global environment in the years ahead (see Chapter 16). Increases in sea levels could well require heavy investments in infrastructure, such as sea barriers. As many regions become drier,

---

[23] In *This Time Is Different: Eight Centuries of Financial Folly* (Princeton, NJ, Princeton University Press, 2009, p. 292) Carmen Reinhart and Kenneth Rogoff state: "All too often, periods of heavy borrowing can take place in a bubble and last for a surprisingly long time. But highly leveraged economies, particularly those in which continual rollover of short-term debt is sustained only by confidence in relatively illiquid underlying assets, seldom survive forever, particularly if leverage continues to grow unchecked. This time may seem different, but all too often a deeper look shows it is not."

outlays for irrigation networks and other investments to deal with water scarcity will be needed. In some cases it may be necessary to resettle populations no longer able to live in low-lying areas; roughly 1.2 billion people live within 100 km of the shore. The increasing incidence of extreme weather events (such as we saw in the summers of 2017–2018 in the Caribbean and the southern United States) will also require budgetary outlays that will, by definition, be difficult to plan for. To the extent that weather-related catastrophes put a dent in economic growth, there will be adverse repercussions for government revenue as well, putting additional pressures on budget deficits.

The risk, obviously, is that markets will not wait until a government is insolvent before significantly increasing the costs of borrowing. In 2010 we saw how systematically destabilizing the prospect of default by a small country such as Greece could be; how losses of confidence in the debt-carrying capacity of the country can, through an increase in risk premia, dramatically reduce the government's room for fiscal maneuver. The point here is that the fiscal consequences of climate change and population aging could at some point interact with financial markets in highly destabilizing ways, which could significantly worsen an already difficult fiscal situation. To make matters worse, there has also been a huge increase in private sector indebtedness since 2009. According to the Institute of International Finance's July 2018 *Global Debt Monitor*:

> The global debt mountain topped $247 trillion in Q1 2018, with the non-financial sector accounting for $186 trillion of that. Global debt-to-GDP exceeded 318% in Q1 2018—the first quarterly increase since Q3 2016. Borrowers reliant on variable-rate debt are most at risk—especially non-U.S. borrowers hit with higher USD funding costs. EM USD refinancing risk is also on the rise: almost $1 trillion in USD-denominated bonds/syndicated loans matures by end-2019.

There are credible economists (Nobel laureates even) who argue that the global financial system is inherently unstable, that there is no guarantee that it will not crash in the future as a result of abuse, misbehavior or other factors unrelated to those that caused the last crisis. Robert Shiller, a leading observer of financial markets and one who issued repeated warnings about the real estate bubble in the United States, thinks that "capitalist economies, left to their own devices, without the balancing of governments, are essentially unstable."[24] There is no certainty, thus, that we will not again face what we saw in 2008: the sharp contraction of equity markets as a result of sales of liquid assets at rapidly collapsing prices and the drying up of credit lines to financial and non-financial institutions, all of it followed by growing unemployment, falling incomes and a widening of budget deficits. What makes this a nightmare scenario is that the ability of governments to prevent an

---

[24] Shiller, Robert. 2009. "A Failure to Control the Animal Spirits," *Financial Times*, 9 March.

economic depression through a variety of interventions, such as those deployed in 2008–2009, will be very much a function of the health of their own finances and their being on a sustainable path. Absent this, what is left is the Latin American scenario of the 1980s: debt default and potentially very high inflation and a lost decade of growth, except that this time around the impact would be global and highly destabilizing. The point here is that there is no guarantee that the financial system might not itself become a wholly independent source of pressure on government resources, increasing the vulnerability of already strained long-term budgets.

The sooner we return to cautious management of the world's public finances, the sooner will we be in a position to respond effectively to the crises that, surely, will remain a feature of our economic landscape for years to come. More importantly, sound public finances empower governments to move away from day-to-day cash management in the middle of a crisis, to more proactive policies aimed at boosting the quality of education, improving infrastructure and spending more in competitiveness-enhancing areas.

The question that all of these recent developments raise is: can we immunize the global economy against a future crisis? And what is the role of regulation, and the kinds of monitoring mechanisms that are developed by organizations such as the IMF? This is a vast subject, and here we will be brief. We begin by outlining some problems and possible solutions.

Our model of financial regulation before the crisis was misconceived. Loan brokers had few incentives to assess risk that they sold on to others more realistically. Investors relied too heavily, in assessing asset quality, on sometimes optimistic analyses by credit rating agencies, who were themselves sometimes plagued by conflicts of interest. Regulation and supervision were too focused on firms and not sufficiently mindful of systemic risk. The shadow banking system – investment banks, mortgage brokers, hedge funds – were (and remain) lightly regulated by numerous agencies sometimes working at cross purposes. The assumption was that only deposit-taking institutions needed to be regulated and supervised, thereby encouraging "financial innovation" in the rest of the system (what investor Warren Buffet referred to as "financial weapons of mass destruction"), which, the thinking went, would act under a regime of self-imposed market discipline. Obviously, the system had (and still has) a huge amount of moral hazard built in.

On the consumers' side, it is known that financial markets intrinsically suffer from informational asymmetries and overall imbalances of power between individuals and financial institutions. Market failures allow the transfer of risk to consumers during the rent-seeking transactions performed by financial service providers. The financial crisis showed that the lack of regulatory frameworks that required transparency in the delivery of financial products and the sound assessments of consumers' affordability and suitability, among others, contributed to inflating wildly those intrinsic risks. As a result, irresponsible lending practices characterized by the mis-selling of subprime mortgages, complex financial products and promotion of over-indebtedness were pointed to as the main causes of the financial collapse.[25]

We need to move to a system where, as noted by the IMF, "all activities that pose economy-wide risks are covered and known to a systemic stability regulator with wide powers."[26] This would include investment banks, special investment vehicles selling collateralized debt obligations (CDOs) and insurance companies selling credit default swaps. Disclosure obligations within this broader circle should then allow the authorities to determine relative contributions to systemic risk and to differentiate the scope of necessary prudential oversight. For instance, one could discourage the emergence of mega-institutions, via capital ratios that increase with the contribution to systemic risk. Unfortunately, the crisis brought about a sharp increase in the concentration of the financial system.[27] It would also be desirable to mitigate pro-cyclical behavior, for instance by raising minimum capital requirements during periods of economic expansion and reducing them during periods of contraction or slowdown. A similar approach could be taken for leverage – introduce a supplementary leverage ratio for banks, to discourage excessive borrowing, which at times can border on recklessness, as we saw in the period leading to the 2008–2009 crisis. There is also a need to reform the system of incentives for employee compensation, making it more risk based and consistent with the long-term objective of sustainably maintaining the firm. Or we could delink compensation from annual results and link it more to medium-term return on assets.[28]

The IMF's call for greater transparency about techniques, characteristics and other dimensions of valuation of complex financial instruments, more information about the over-the-counter derivatives markets and clearing arrangements in ways that make it possible for regulators to aggregate risks for the system as a whole is a

---

[25] Melecky, Martin and Sue Rutledge. 2011. "Financial Consumer Protection and the Global Financial Crisis," MPRA Paper 28201, University Library of Munich, Germany.

[26] International Monetary Fund. 2009. "Initial Lessons of the Crisis," Washington DC, p. 3.

[27] According to a JP Morgan Chase 2015 study on the financial crisis, "Since 1992 the total assets held by the five largest U.S. banks has increased by nearly fifteen times! Back then, the five largest banks held just 10 percent of the banking industry total. Today, JP Morgan alone holds over 12 percent of the industry total, a greater share than the five biggest banks put together in 1992. Even in the midst of the global financial crisis, the largest U.S. banks managed to increase their hold on total bank industry assets. The assets held by the five largest banks in 2007 – $4.6 trillion – increased by more than 150 percent over the past 8 years. These five banks went from holding 35 percent of industry assets in 2007 to 44 percent today." http://theeconomiccollapse blog.com/archives/tag/jpmorgan-chase.

[28] According to *The Economist* (September 8, 2018), "The salaries for high-ups remain phenomenal. In 2017 AIG's new boss, Brian Duperreault, was paid $43 million, Mr. Dimon $29.5 million, Goldman Sachs' Lloyd Blankfein $24 million and Bank of America's Brian Moynihan $23 million." The total compensation of these four bankers thus exceeds by 61 percent the total annual budget contributions received from the UN budget by UN Habitat, UNHCR (the Refugee Agency) and UN Women, three important UN agencies doing vital work in a number of areas.

sensible recommendation. Central banks need to broaden their definition of "financial stability" from an often exclusive concern with stabilizing inflation to looking at asset price increases, credit booms and debt. This is to avoid the buildup of huge risks that escape the notice of the supervisory authorities, particularly in the shadow banking system. It matters a great deal whether a boom is associated with high borrowing. For instance, the dotcom bubble of the late 1990s was associated with limited indebtedness and thus its bursting had limited impact on economic growth. In the latest crisis, asset price declines greatly affected the balance sheets of financial institutions.

In addition, consumer protection needs to be a focus of the strategic plan of every central bank. The assessment of risk should go beyond financial stability to also pay prominent attention to societal risks related to inadequate practices from regulated entities. A step beyond would be setting the agenda to include financial inclusion efforts to enable access to the financial services to the 1.7 billion unbanked individuals around the globe.[29]

WHAT ABOUT THE INTERNATIONAL MONETARY SYSTEM?

Beyond building a better regulatory framework that addresses many of the vulnerabilities revealed by the 2008–2009 financial crisis, there are other reforms that are very important and that pertain to other aspects of the operation of the international monetary system. We will address three aspects of this vast subject: (1) the need for reforms in the area of multilateral peer review of national policies – also known as "surveillance"; (2) aspects of the management of global liquidity and risks stemming from the absence of a lender of last resort for the international monetary system; and (3) the governance of the international monetary system and the extent to which flaws in the system are undermining the credibility of the system itself by providing perverse incentives for some countries to create competing structures.

Surveillance

The problem here, as noted earlier, is that the IMF has very little real leverage to influence the policies of countries not borrowing from it. The process of surveillance is deeply asymmetric. The Fund is able to extract numerous concessions (mainly from developing countries) as part of its loan negotiations, with all of them, at least in theory, intended to improve the policy framework and make it more sustainable. However, it is usually the bigger countries that do not borrow that pose systemic risks to the global economy, as we saw during the last crisis. The IMF

---

[29] On this, see Findex 2017: https://globalfindex.worldbank.org/.

may feel strongly that a systemically important country is pursing unsustainable economic and financial policies, but it has no effective way to induce the country to change course. The question here is: what to do?

One option would be to amend Article IV of the IMF Articles of Agreement ("Obligations Regarding Exchange Arrangements") to broaden the focus to all policies that have an impact on stability of the global economic, monetary and financial system. The IMF already assesses a broad range of economic and financial policies among its members, but it could be more forceful in the public identification of policies that are a danger to the stability of the global financial system. On the general obligations of IMF members, Article IV (Section 1) states:

> Recognizing that the essential purpose of the international monetary system is to provide a framework that facilitates the exchange of goods, services, and capital among countries, and that sustains sound economic growth, and that a principal objective is the continuing development of the orderly underlying conditions that are necessary for financial and economic stability, each member undertakes to collaborate with the Fund and other members to assure orderly exchange arrangements and to promote a stable system of exchange rates. In particular, each member shall: (i) endeavor to direct its economic and financial policies toward the objective of fostering orderly economic growth with reasonable price stability, with due regard to its circumstances; (ii) seek to promote stability by fostering orderly underlying economic and financial conditions and a monetary system that does not tend to produce erratic disruptions; (iii) avoid manipulating exchange rates or the international monetary system in order to prevent effective balance of payments adjustment or to gain an unfair competitive advantage over other members; and (iv) follow exchange policies compatible with the undertakings under this Section."

And specifically on the issue of surveillance, it states: "the Fund shall oversee the international monetary system in order to ensure its effective operation, and shall oversee the compliance of each member with its obligations under Section 1 of this Article.[30] The 2008–2009 crisis was obviously, as already noted, a glaringly painful example of the Fund failing in the oversight role entrusted to it in Article IV, with dramatic consequences for global economic welfare.

IMF members could also amend Article VI ("Capital Transfers") to give the IMF jurisdiction over capital account transactions, to monitor, assess and discuss capital flows with members. This would appear to be necessary given the magnitude of capital flows today and the influence that these have on exchange rate movements

---

[30] The requirements for Amendments of the Articles are specified in Article XXVIII. It states in part: "When three-fifths of the members, having eighty-five percent of the total voting power, have accepted the proposed amendment, the Fund shall certify the fact by a formal communication addressed to all members."

(and hence the real economy), which by now dwarf by several orders of magnitude those linked to current account flows, such as merchandise trade and service-related transactions.

One way to make the surveillance process more symmetric would be for the IMF to adopt norms on such variables as current account deficits, real exchange rates, capital inflows and outflows, changes in the composition of reserve assets, inflation, budget deficits and debt levels, to name a few, and establish thresholds that, if breached, would trigger consultations and various remedial actions. Candid assessments of policy failures in systemically important countries should be made public. In practice these norms would reward countries that stayed within them by, for instance, giving them automatic qualification to various liquidity facilities. As part of this system, punitive measures against countries in breach of them, such as financial penalties, waiving of voting rights, and depriving them of their share of SDR allocations could be contemplated, quite independently of whether the country in question was or was not using the Fund's resources. Obviously, it is not enough to have voluntary or so called indicative norms.

The EU has tried these at various times through, for instance, the introduction of Maastricht criteria for levels of public indebtedness, or the Stability and Growth Pact for other, mainly fiscal, variables brought about in the late 1990s that were supposed to steer members' policies within acceptable thresholds. In the absence of meaningful penalties, however, countries simply violated the rules with glaring impunity. Given the dire real economy costs of globally systemic crises, pure volunteerism clearly will not work. In this respect, we are proposing to bring into management of the global financial system the same kind of binding mechanisms that we are advocating in the area of peace and security. It is more sensible to complement the creation of, for instance, a United Nations International Peace Force to ensure that the UN is actually able to deliver on its peace and security responsibilities, with international monetary arrangements that provide adequate insurance against systemic financial crises, the impact of which can be devastating, impoverishing and politically calamitous.

In this respect, it would also be desirable to develop globally consistent exchange rate norms, bearing in mind countries' key structural characteristics. Under enhanced surveillance practices, there would be stricter review of policies that contribute to volatility in foreign exchange markets. This is an issue that has acquired particular importance in recent decades because sharp swings in exchange rates, delinked from economic fundamentals, can be very destabilizing for market participants, especially the business community. Exchange rate volatility makes it very difficult for businesses that now operate at the global level in respect of the markets for their products and their sources of supply to assess costs and to plan for the future in the context of a globalized economy. We are also of the view that it would be worthwhile to consider the introduction of a Tobin-like tax as a stabilizing mechanism to dampen speculation. As noted in Chapter 12, the revenue thus generated could be an important source of development finance and could also go some way to buttress IMF resources.

Global Liquidity

The aim of reform in this area is to turn the IMF into a global lender of last resort, ready to act in a rules-based way, as opposed to the ad hoc arrangements that have characterized policy interventions in times of crisis, such as the 2008–2009 financial crisis. Some might argue that the global economy already has a lender of last resort: the US Federal Reserve; and the temporary liquidity swap arrangements that were introduced in 2008 did much to prevent the collapse of the financial system in countries desperately in need of dollar credits.[31] While indeed very clearly helpful, such arrangements were ad hoc and were limited to 14 central banks (not including those of China, Russia and India), with the choice dictated by the US monetary authorities, presumably involving an element of "national interest" criteria, such as the exposure of US banks to those countries. For those countries lucky enough to be part of this lifeline it was greatly beneficial, but not otherwise. This is obviously not ideal; no individual IMF member, no matter how powerful, should have to play the role of lender of last resort to the global economy. More worryingly, it is not clear that such interventions would work in a future crisis, since US legislators might wish to interfere and politicize the process (in a way that did not happen in 2008 because the Federal Reserve acted with great discretion), depriving it of its first and most important attribute, which is speed and automaticity.

In any case, reforms in this area should also introduce protections to limit moral hazard. The idea is to put in place well-funded crisis financing mechanisms available to all IMF members as an alternative to precautionary reserve accumulation, which is what countries have done in recent decades in a very substantial way. There are enormous inefficiencies in the accumulation of war chests denominated in hard currencies as a way of providing a protective barrier during periods of market volatility. There is an interesting analogy here between the need for reserve accumulation in the international financial system and the absence of collective security mechanisms, where almost 200 independent countries worldwide feel the need to

---

[31] Two additional aspects worth keeping in mind are: (1) The United States established the Exchange Stabilization Fund (ESF) in the 1930s enabling credit line support to crisis-hit foreign governments. The US Federal Reserve can also provide currency swaps to foreign central banks through its System Open Market Account (SOMA). During the 2008 financial crisis resort to SOMA was intensive, and more than US$500 billion was provided to foreign central banks at the height of the crisis. Activation of the US Treasury's ESF and the Fed's SOMA does not require US congressional approval and (2) important new mechanisms of last resort liquidity supplementation (LORs) have also appeared in the system; i.e., China increased its currency swap line to Argentina to US$20 billion in 2018, and other regional reserve supplementation agreements were augmented in the EU and Asia–Chiang Mai, among others. (We are indebted to our colleague Guillermo Zoccali for bringing these facts to our attention.)

equip their respective armies and put in place various security establishments that end up involving excessive defense spending. As part of its efforts to improve global liquidity management, the IMF should be allowed to mobilize additional resources by: tapping capital markets, issuing bonds dominated in SDRs, doing emergency SDR allocations under considerably more streamlined procedures, and expanding its program of loan/swap arrangements with key central banks and, as noted previously, allocate regularly SDRs to supplement the demand for "own reserves."[32]

Governance

Unlike the United Nations, both the World Bank and the IMF were established with a system of weighted voting within their governance structures. There is no evidence that the one country–one vote system adopted for the General Assembly at the San Francisco Conference in 1945 was ever contemplated at the Bretton Woods Conference that launched these organizations in 1944. Weighted voting has served them well, has contributed to boosting their credibility, and has been reflected in the importance and attention that their large shareholders have given to their operations. Voting shares have been updated from time to time, but with the rapid pace of economic growth in emerging and developing countries such as India and China in recent years, a sizable gap has emerged between the relative weight of particular countries in the global economy and their voting share within the IMF governance structure. The gap has been particularly glaring in the case of China, whose voting power is less than 7 percent (compared with 17.5 percent for the United States), even though by 2018 the GPD gap had virtually disappeared and China was well on its way to overtaking the United States as the world's largest economy.[33]

Quota shares at the IMF are allocated by a formula that captures aspects of each member country's position in the world economy at a particular moment in time.[34]

---

[32] At the time of writing there is a fairly intense debate in the media and policy-making circles about the emergence of new digital currencies and this, in turn, raises the question of the role the IMF might play in the future in the evolution of such new forms of money. Facebook and several dozen corporate partners have proposed the introduction of the Libra, to be pegged to a basket of currencies and to be fully backed by safe assets. It is outside the scope of this chapter to analyze the case for such initiatives. At present a number of concerns have been raised about possible volatility in the value of such currencies, how they would co-exist with other forms of digital payment, issues of privacy and the extent to which these currencies might serve as a conduit for money laundering, tax evasion and other forms of malfeasance. The related question of whose responsibility (and how) it would be to monitor and regulate an activity that presumably would involve some 200 sovereign states is equally important.

[33] Indeed, on a PPP basis, China has already overtaken the United States.

[34] The so-called Calculated Quota Shares (CQS) are determined by the formula:

$$CQS = (0.5 * Y + 0.3 * O + 0.15 * V + 0.05 * R)$$

where Y is a blend of GDP estimated at market exchange rates and PPP rates, O is an openness measure defined as the annual average of the sum of current payments and currents receipts over a five-year period, V is the variability of current receipts and net capital flows, and R is the

This quota, in turn, establishes the country's subscription (its maximum financial obligation to the IMF), voting power within the Fund and access to Fund financing.[35] GDP is given the largest weight in the determination of a country's quota as it captures its ability to contribute to the Fund, linking it to a measure of its size and influence in the global economy. In this respect, the Calculated Quota Share (CQS) formula reflects some of the spirit of the current formulas used to determine countries' contributions to the UN budget and our own proposals for newer and better UN funding mechanisms. The openness metric reflects a member's integration with the global economy, an important metric that attempts to measure its stake in global economic and financial stability. The variability measure is intended to be a proxy for a member's vulnerability to balance of payments shocks and subsequent need for the Fund's assistance. Finally, reserves are also an indicator of a country's ability to contribute to the Fund. Quotas are supposed to be reviewed every five years by the IMF's Board of Governors. Changes to members' quotas must be approved by an 85 percent majority vote.

The figure below shows, on the left-hand side, for a group of ten selected countries the voting shares in 2019 following the update that was done in 2010, based on 2008 data. While, at the time of writing, quotas had not been updated since 2010, this has not prevented the IMF staff from preparing a variety of illustrative simulations using more recent data and under different assumptions. There seems to be broad-based support within the IMF membership to drop the variability measure on the occasion of the next quota review and to allocate its weight to the other variables. The figure on the right-hand side shows quota shares under one such simulation, in which all of the 15 percent weight currently allocated to the variability metric is allocated to the GDP blend, with GDP at market exchange rates assigned a weight of 39 percent and purchasing power parity (PPP) GDP a weight of 26 percent. In this simulation China's quota rises from 6.4 percent to 11.4 percent, and India's rises from 2.7 percent to 3.4 percent. While the US quota falls from 17.4 percent to 15.7 percent, there are drops in the shares of other advanced economies as well.[36]

12-month average over one year of international reserves (foreign exchange, SDR holdings, the Fund's reserve position and gold). The formula also imposes a so-called compression factor by raising the CQS that fall out from the above calculation to the nth power, where n is typically set at 0.95. The purpose of this ad hoc arrangement is to reduce somewhat the dispersion of quota shares among the IMF's 189 members.

[35] According to the IMF, "Member country voting power at IMF is calculated by aggregating quota-based votes and basic votes. The total number of basic votes are divided equally among all members. Thus, the allocation of basic votes ensures a minimum voting power for all members." Thus, for instance, while the quota share of the United States is 17.46 percent, its voting power is 16.52 percent. International Monetary Fund, *Governance and the IMF— Evaluation Update 2018*, Independent Evaluation Office of the International Monetary Fund, Washington DC, p. 6.

[36] For illustrative purposes we have done a simulation using GDP and population shares weighted equally as the criteria for the determination of quota shares. We are not necessarily

Serious consideration should also be given to lowering voting thresholds for important decisions from 85 percent (which effectively gives the United States veto power since it is the only country among the IMF's 189 members with a voting share in excess of 15 percent) to something like 60 percent, as being more consistent with sound democratic principles.

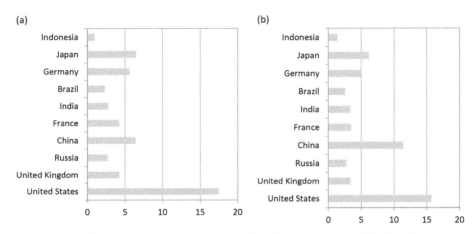

FIGURE 15.1 (a) Current voting shares in IMF: selected countries (%). (b) Alternative voting shares in IMF: selected countries (%).

In respect of other internal governance reforms we find the recommendations made by former IMF Managing Director Michel Camdessus to be a sensible set of proposals, moving the IMF in the right direction.

> In a lecture delivered a few years after leaving the Fund, the former IMF Managing Director outlined an ambitious reform agenda for IMF governance. He identified three values that, in his view, the IMF and other international financial institutions must embrace if they are to tackle successfully global economic challenges: (1) good governance, including transparency, openness, and accountability; (2) public ownership of policies, and (3) partnership between developing and developed countries. Camdessus recommended replacing the International Monetary and Financial Policy Committee (IMFC) with the Council, a formal decision-making body. Major strategic decisions would be transferred from the Executive Board to the Council. Working on the basis of staff analysis and Board deliberation, the Council, argued Camdessus, would be the ideal place for a global membership to discuss policies to address systemic issues. Camdessus ... also called for strengthening

recommending that shares be determined using these two factors (important as they are), but do wish to highlight the fairly dramatic changes in voting shares implied by this exercise, with China, the United States, India and Indonesia emerging as the IMF's largest shareholders, in that order.

surveillance by submitting preliminary conclusions of staff missions to broader public debate before transmission to the Executive Board. On Management, the main recommendation was to change the rules and practices that govern the selection of the Managing Director. Europe and the US should renounce the nomination 'privilege', and the process should be open to all candidates.[37]

In this chapter we have focused on some of the reforms that may be needed in coming years to better prepare the IMF to confront the challenges and risks associated with the emergence of a fully integrated global financial system in which, as of this writing, its two largest shareholders are engaged in an escalating trade war. The global financial crisis in 2008–2009 and its after effects, not only raised fundamental questions about the sustainability of an economic system based on various combinations of liberal democracy and the market but it also was a powerful catalyst for the emergence of various forms of populism and a questioning of the benefits of multilateralism and international cooperation which have been at the basis of economic growth during the past half a century.

The global financial system today is more fragile than it was in 2007, on the eve of the last crisis. Dealing with the next global financial crisis in the context of sharply reduced fiscal space, when the traditional responses to managing downturns (such as reducing interest rates, unleashing fiscal stimulus) will largely no longer be there as weapons in the arsenal of policymakers will clearly be a crucial challenge for the world's largest economies. There is no doubt in our minds that the IMF will be forced to play a central role in crisis management during the next global financial implosion. Whether the organization is ready and empowered, with the appropriate instruments at its disposal is a highly consequential question. If our proposals for reform appear somewhat ambitions, it is because the stakes are remarkably high, both in terms of the social and economic costs associated with a preventable global financial crisis, but also in terms of the IMF's future reputation and public perceptions of its role in contributing to establish a solid foundation for a sustainable economy.

---

[37] Quoted in "Background Document 4: External Recommendations for IMF Governance Reform," for the Independent Evaluation Office Report: *Governance of the IMF: An Evaluation*. 2008. The full text of the speech by Michel Camdessus is contained in: "International Financial Institutions: Dealing with New Global Challenges," Washington, DC, Per Jacobsen Foundation. An argument can be made that moving away from such nomination "privileges" should be done in respect of all international organizations, as part of a systemic effort to set aside nationality considerations in favor of experience, competence and merit in the appointment of the leadership of all such agencies.

16

Responding to Global Environmental Crises

As trustees, or stewards, of the planet's vast resources and biological diversity, humanity must learn to make use of the earth's natural resources, both renewable and non-renewable, in a manner that ensures sustainability and equity into the distant reaches of time ... Therefore, sustainable environmental management must come to be seen not as a discretionary commitment mankind can weigh against other competing interests, but rather as a fundamental responsibility that must be shouldered.[1]

Bahá'í International Community, 1998

In this chapter, we review the contemporary imperative of global environmental governance that did not exist when the United Nations was founded. After a brief historical summary, we confirm the need for a reinforced global environmental organization,[2] consider the existential challenges of climate change and threats to global biodiversity, make a case for global regulation of dangerous chemicals, and for equitable management of natural resources.

Our planet functions as a single global system, a biosphere with many interacting components and cycles of materials in the atmosphere, on land and in the oceans, that pay no attention to national boundaries, but instead define planetary boundaries

---

[1] Bahá'í International Community. 1998. *Valuing Spirituality in Development: Initial Considerations Regarding the Creation of Spiritually Based Indicators for Development*. A concept paper written for the World Faiths and Development Dialogue, Lambeth Palace, London, February 18–19.

[2] For example, the Secretary-General proposed in 1997 that the Trusteeship Council "be reconstituted as the Forum through which Member States exercise their collective trusteeship for the integrity of the global environment and common areas such as the oceans, atmosphere and outer space. At the same time, it should serve to link the United Nations and civil society in addressing these areas of global concern, which require the active contribution of public, private and voluntary sectors." UN General Assembly. 1997. "*Renewing the United Nations: A Programme for Reform*," 14 July, A/51/950, New York, United Nations, para. 85.

that we must respect to maintain an environment suitable for human life and well-being.[3] Through our actions and consumption patterns, we have already overshot some of these planetary boundaries, threatening the future human carrying capacity of the planet. Many dimensions of this system can only be managed at the global level through close cooperation of all countries, first through reducing damaging activities to a sustainable level, and then through collaboration to restore and eventually extend that carrying capacity in an ever-advancing civilization. The reform of the UN system should incorporate the necessary dimensions of environmental governance, particularly as they concern climate change and biodiversity resilience, as a central rather than peripheral responsibility.

While the conservation of nature has been a concern for well over a century, and the International Union for the Conservation of Nature (IUCN), with both state and not-state members, was founded in 1948, it was only in the 1960s, in light of warnings such as Rachel Carson's *Silent Spring* and the Torrey Canyon oil spill in 1967, that the environment became a political issue and governments began to create agencies and ministries for environmental protection.[4] It was already obvious that environmental problems often escaped from national control, and that environmental cooperation was needed at the international level. In 1972 the US National Academy of Sciences prepared a report for the US Department of State on *Institutional Arrangements for International Environmental Cooperation*,[5] recommending a new environmental unit within the UN supported by an intergovernmental advisory body, a science advisory and research board, a monitoring and surveillance network and an environment fund.

The 1972 United Nations Conference on the Human Environment in Stockholm, Sweden, adopted a Declaration and Action Plan for the Human Environment,[6] which created the UN Environment Programme (UNEP) with an environmental assessment (Earthwatch) component including a Global Environment Monitoring System (GEMS),[7] an environmental management component and an Environment Fund, intended to catalyze environmental action across the UN system.

---

[3] Rockström, Johan et al. 2009. "A Safe Operating Space for Humanity." *Nature*, Vol. 461, pp. 472–475. DOI: 10.1038/461472a; Steffen, Will et al. 2015. "Planetary Boundaries: Guiding Human Development on a Changing Planet." *Science*, Vol. 347, No. 6223. DOI: 10.1126/science.1259855.

[4] Carson, Rachel. 1962. *Silent Spring*, Boston, Houghton Mifflin.

[5] National Academy of Sciences. 1972. *Institutional Arrangements for International Environmental Cooperation*. A report to the Department of State by the Committee for International Environmental Programs, Environmental Studies Board, Washington, DC, National Academy of Sciences.

[6] United Nations. 1972. *Report of the United Nations Conference on the Human Environment*, held at Stockholm, June 5–16, 1972. A/CONF.48/14. New York, United Nations.

[7] Gosovic, Branislav. 1992. *The Quest for World Environmental Cooperation: The Case of the UN Global Environment Monitoring System*, London and New York, Routledge.

Since the Stockholm Conference, there has been considerable progress in elements of international governance of specific environmental problems ranging from conservation of species and biodiversity, managing chemical pollution, depletion of the ozone layer and climate change, to transboundary air pollution, shared river basins and regional seas. The result has been hundreds of multilateral environmental agreements, both global and regional, usually with separate secretariats, some within the United Nations system and many outside of it. While some subsidiarity is appropriate for specific geographic realities or shared resources, the overall patchwork, with gaps and overlaps, has become increasingly unwieldy and has placed an increasing burden on governments to participate in, apply and report to all these separate mechanisms.

The next major step forward in international environmental governance occurred 20 years later in 1992, at the UN Conference on Environment and Development (UNCED), the Rio Earth Summit, in Rio de Janeiro, Brazil. The Rio Declaration established new principles in international soft law, and its action plan, Agenda 21, with 40 chapters negotiated and agreed by governments,[8] became the global blueprint for sustainable development. Conditions for progress were less favorable at the World Summit on Sustainable Development in Johannesburg in 2002, which in many ways was a holding action to maintain the advances achieved in Rio, with calls for revitalizing global environmental governance.[9] The UN Conference on Sustainable Development, again in Rio de Janeiro in 2012, was less ambitious, but it succeeded in launching a wide participatory process that led to the adoption in 2015 of the UN 2030 Agenda and its Sustainable Development Goals (SDGs), to be achieved by 2030.[10]

These and many other intergovernmental processes have resulted in a fragmented assemblage of hard and soft law, legally binding or increasingly accepted as customary. Many agreements are often difficult to apply, particularly at the national level where both legal capacity and technical expertise are limited. The Earth Charter was one attempt after the 1992 Earth Summit to assemble fundamental values and principles for a just, sustainable and peaceful global society,[11] but its origins in civil society meant that it had little weight with governments.

---

[8] United Nations. 1992. *Agenda 21: Programme of Action for Sustainable Development.* United Nations Conference on Environment and Development, Rio de Janeiro, Brazil, June 3–14. New York, United Nations. https://sustainabledevelopment.un.org/content/documents/Agenda21.pdf.

[9] Esty, Daniel C. and Maria H. Ivanova (eds.). 2002. *Global Environmental Governance: Options & Opportunities*, New Haven, CT, Yale School of Forestry and Environmental Studies.

[10] United Nations. 2015. *Transforming Our World: The 2030 Agenda for Sustainable Development.* Outcome document of the Summit for the adoption of the Post-2015 Development Agenda, New York, September 25–27, 2015. A/70/L.1. New York, United Nations. www.un.org/ga/search/view_doc.asp?symbol=A/70/L.1&Lang=E.

[11] Launched by the Earth Charter Commission in The Hague on June 29, 2000. See http://earthcharter.org/.

To bring some legal coherence, a group of 80 experts from 40 countries recently prepared a draft Global Pact for the Environment that assembles and codifies the main principles of international environmental law, supplemented in light of current challenges.[12] It consolidates the principles already agreed in the Stockholm Declaration of 1972, the Rio declarations of 1992 and 2012, the environmental SDGs and the Paris Climate Change Agreement of 2015. They propose this as the basis for negotiating a legally binding international treaty that would supplement the existing conventions, filling gaps and providing a coherent text that would be easier to implement at the national level. The 1966 UN Covenants, one dedicated to civil and political rights, the other to economic, cultural and social rights, and enshrining fundamental and comprehensive human rights norms in binding treaties, may be a useful precedent in thinking about the development of similar binding and consolidated treaties in the environmental field. The government of France organized a Summit for the Global Pact on the sidelines of the UN General Assembly in September 2017 with some 40 heads of state and government and ministers who called for support to the project. An intergovernmental working group is now negotiating a final text.

Even in its draft form, the Global Pact is a useful summary of international environmental law. It has a preamble and 26 articles, each devoted to one aspect of international law and development – most of which enjoy consensus. In particular, it includes the right to an ecologically sound environment; the duty to take care of the environment, to exercise prevention and precaution; to remediate environmental damages; to enforce the principle that "polluters pay"; to establish intergenerational equity; to ensure public information and participation, access to environmental justice, education and training in environmental protection. The Pact also provides for the vital role of nongovernmental stakeholders; the effectiveness of environmental standards; resilience; non-regression of standards; and shared but differentiated responsibilities. It also suggests mechanisms for implementation and follow-up.

This illustrates the need for consolidation in the area of environmental protection and management as in so many other fields where the continuation of ad hoc independent negotiating and legislative processes between multiple states ultimately can only lead to international legal gridlock, overload governments and make environmental responses ever harder to implement at the national level. One challenge for strengthened global governance will be to organize the transition to a more coherent international system, which is easier for all countries to participate in and adhere to.

---

[12] See http://pactenvironment.org/.

AN ENVIRONMENTAL ORGANIZATION

It is too early to say whether other multilateral environmental agreements should lead to specialized agencies or be grouped within a strengthened UN Environment Organization. UN Environment is just a program within the United Nations, with limited resources and only administrative responsibilities for some biodiversity and chemicals conventions, while climate change has a separate convention, and the wetlands convention is not even within the UN system. It has even been suggested that the multiplicity of environmental agreements with secretariats scattered around the world was intended to prevent them from being effective and thus interfering with profits and the growth of the economy. In many cultures, humanity is an integral part of nature, or Mother Earth. The Western concept of the environment as something outside of us has made it easier to consider environmental issues as externalities and not really central to the economy. For economists, natural resources have traditionally had no value until they were exploited and marketed, with a range of pernicious consequences. Faced with the pressure of commercial interests, efforts to adopt a convention on forests have failed. Plastic pollution has become a global crisis, and many environmentally damaging chemicals remain unregulated. Now that we understand our fundamental dependence on natural capital and planetary life support systems, and the need for sustainable use of resources as we overshoot planetary boundaries,[13] a coherent approach has become a priority for global governance.

This challenge is particularly acute because there is no easy way to achieve the current concept of a high quality of life for the entire world population without destabilizing critical planetary processes. A recent study using indicators designed to measure a "safe and just" development space between social thresholds and bio-physical boundaries for over 150 countries quantified the resource use associated with meeting basic human needs and compared this with downscaled planetary boundaries. No country met basic needs for its citizens at a globally sustainable level of resource use. Physical needs such as nutrition, sanitation, access to electricity and the elimination of extreme poverty could likely be met for all people without transgressing planetary boundaries, but the level of necessary resource use must be dramatically reduced.[14] However, the universal achievement of more qualitative goals such as high life satisfaction, as presently defined in our consumer society, would require a level of resource use that is two to six times the sustainable level. For these goals, non-material means should be used such as social support, generosity, freedom to make life choices and absence of corruption. Meeting this challenge will

---

[13] Rockström et al., "A Safe Operating Space for Humanity"; Steffen et al., "Planetary Boundaries."

[14] Hanley, Paul. 2014. *Eleven*, Victoria, BC, Friesen Press.

require strategies that improve physical and social provisioning systems, with a focus on sufficiency and equity, in order to move nations toward sustainability.[15] Global mechanisms need to be strong enough to give priority to the common good of all with justice and equity, and to use various policy tools, including more responsible tax and expenditure policies, to shift incentives in a way that puts consumption levels, particularly of the wealthy and powerful, on a more sustainable path.

One necessary innovation will be to create a global legal framework for those areas, resources, planetary processes and biogeochemical cycles that are essential to maintaining a global environment conducive to human life and well-being. They should be considered the common property of humankind and could be managed as a condominium, just as individual owners in an apartment building share responsibility for the common public areas and utilities that service the whole building.[16] All states and peoples would be expected to contribute to the upkeep and protection of these common property resources, including the atmosphere, the oceans, the climate and cycles of nitrogen, phosphorus and other elements that support all life, among others.

The above reference to natural cycles illustrates that the environmental dimension of international governance has some specific characteristics, as it concerns not just human society and the built environment created by humanity for its own needs, but the natural environment and planetary life support systems that are essential for human well-being and survival. One requirement of environmental governance is ensuring that the scientific input to policy-making is adequate and objective, that the risks and uncertainties are presented correctly, and that sufficient attention is devoted to long-term as well as short-term priorities. This requires coordinated and sustained research, monitoring and scientific advisory procedures appropriate to each environmental process, with structures for multi-level governance at the scales most relevant to each characteristic or problem. Decision-makers also need to be scientifically literate to be able to understand scientific advice.

---

[15] O'Neill, Daniel W., Andrew L. Fanning, William F. Lamb, and Julia K. Steinberger. 2018. "A Good Life for All within Planetary Boundaries." *Nature Sustainability*, Vol. 1, No. 2, pp. 88–95. https://doi.org/10.1038/s41893-018-0021-4.

[16] The Common Home of Humanity (CHH) project proposes a new legal condominium framework for science-based governance of the global Earth System to ensure a sustainable "Safe Operating Space" for humanity, given planetary boundaries. Initiated in 2016, CHH has convened a global and interdisciplinary network to develop and build "a new theoretical and operational model of just and sustainable global governance, through a decision-making structure based on an improved knowledge of Earth System functioning and in harmony with the sovereignty of states." See www.commonhomeofhumanity.org/. It has been suggested that the facility to manage the global environment under this paradigm could replace the now-defunct Trusteeship Council under the Charter.

CLIMATE CHANGE

The challenge of climate change has been defined as a "super-wicked" problem. It needs urgent responses. It needs those responsible to accept responsibility and provide solutions and support. It requires aspects of sovereignty to be ceded to an international body, or that wide-ranging powers be conferred to a central body at the national level. And it carries perverse incentives to push action into the future.[17]

Leena Srivastava

A priority area for coherent international action is climate change, and the UN Framework Convention on Climate Change (UNFCCC) signed in 1992 bears this responsibility. The scientific evidence is frightening, with global warming accelerating, impacts such as extreme storms, wildfires, droughts and sea level rise increasingly costly in human and financial terms, and fears of tipping points that could cause runaway acceleration of damaging processes.[18] Parts of the planet will become less able to support a human population, or even uninhabitable, due to excessively high temperatures, whereas other regions presently too cold could become more habitable, requiring significant displacement of human populations across national borders. Failure to act in time could lead to a reduced capacity of the planet to support human life, with mass fatalities.[19] Yet the response from governments is too little, too late, with some even denying the reality of climate change and encouraging economic activities that increase the release of greenhouse gases.

The reason for this is that climate change is a complex and diffuse risk that has long seemed somehow to lie outside short-term priorities.[20] Because of its political sensitivity and economic implications, scientists have tended to make conservative evaluations of the scientific data, while there have been unanticipated accelerations in various scientific processes.[21] It is not easy to assess the probability of tipping points beyond which runaway processes become uncontrollable but with timing that is uncertain. In addition, there have been massive attempts to deny and discredit the

---

[17] Leena Srivastava. 2018. "Governance of Catastrophic Climate Change." *Global Challenges Foundation Annual Report 2018.* https://globalchallenges.org/en/our-work/annual-report/annual-report-2018/governance-of-catastrophic-climate-change.

[18] IPCC. 2018. *Global Warming of 1.5°C* (SR15), Special Report. Summary for Policy Makers. Geneva, Intergovernmental Panel on Climate Change, October 2018. www.ipcc.ch/report/sr15/.

[19] Ripple, William J., Christopher Wolf, Thomas M. Newsome, Mauro Galetti, Mohammed Alamgir, Eileen Crist, Mahmoud I. Mahmoud, William F. Laurance, and 15,364 scientist signatories from 184 countries. 2017. "World Scientists' Warning to Humanity: A Second Notice." *BioScience* Vol. 67, No. 12, pp. 1026–1028. https://doi.org/10.1093/biosci/bix125; Meadows, Donella, Jorgen Randers, and Dennis Meadows. 2004. *Limits to Growth: The 30-Year Update,* White River Junction, VT, Chelsea Green Publishing Company; McKibben, Bill. 2018. "Life on a Shrinking Planet," *The New Yorker,* November 26, 2018, pp. 46–55.

[20] Marshall, George. 2014. *Don't Even Think about It: Why Our Brains Are Wired to Ignore Climate Change,* London, Bloomsbury.

[21] IPCC, *Global Warming of 1.5°C.*

science for ideological and political ends and to protect vested interests. It is already difficult enough to educate the public on such issues without the headwind of such negative forces that stoop to anything to win their argument, even to the extent of denying the validity of expert scientific opinion. Much of the world is in denial.

The human-induced causes of climate change are well known, with the release of greenhouse gases from fossil fuels, intensive agriculture and deforestation primarily responsible.[22] Unfortunately these activities are fundamental to the present model of development and high consumption, meaning that everyone is responsible, with increasing responsibility with greater wealth and power. The only solution is a fundamental transformation in the system, but there is great inertia and resistance from vested interests. A global approach is the only option, since the failure of some countries to cooperate can doom the efforts of all the rest. However, a system of global governance still dominated by great powers defending national interests has proved itself incapable of responding to the problems of such interdependence.[23]

While there are many positive signs of change, and technological solutions are largely available, the transition is not occurring quickly enough. After the failure at the UN Climate Change summit in Copenhagen in 2009, the 2015 Paris Climate Change Agreement succeeded in mapping out a way forward, agreeing to hold global warming to 2°C and aiming for 1.5°C, which is the level that might ensure the survival of some small island developing states that would otherwise drown with rising sea levels. In Paris, almost all governments promised voluntary nationally determined contributions to greenhouse gas emission reduction, but even if all of these are effectively implemented, which is far from certain, they would only limit warming to about 3°C. The Agreement therefore includes provisions for the regular review of progress and a ratcheting up of commitments to try to reach the target.[24]

There are already some other elements of international governance for climate change in place. These include an effective scientific advisory process in the Intergovernmental Panel on Climate Change (IPCC) under the World Meteorological Organization (WMO) and UN Environment. With the rapid acceleration in the signs of climate change, it may need to increase the frequency of its reports (the next one is due in 2022), or to supplement them with near-real-time reporting where appropriate, to stimulate policy action. The Secretariat of the UNFCCC, supported by the host country France and many others, demonstrated its effectiveness in achieving the Paris Climate Change Agreement. However, as with most international agreements today, there is no enforcement mechanism. While the

---

[22] IPCC. 2014. *Climate Change 2014: Synthesis Report. Contribution of Working Groups I, II and III to the Fifth Assessment Report of the Intergovernmental Panel on Climate Change* [Core Writing Team, R.K. Pachauri and L.A. Meyer (eds.)], Geneva, IPCC.

[23] Viola, Eduardo, Matias Franchini, and Thais Lemos Ribeiro. 2012. "Climate Governance in an International System under Conservative Hegemony: The Role of Major Powers." *Revista Brasileira de Política Internacional*, Vol. 55 (special edition), pp. 9–29.

[24] The first review and recommitment is in 2020.

reporting mechanism is legally binding, the national commitments to reductions in emissions are explicitly voluntary both in the levels set by governments and in their implementation. The Conference of the Parties functions by consensus, so any one country can block decisions not in its national interest, and some frequently do so. The mechanisms of accountability are very weak,[25] relying largely on moral peer pressure to have any impact. A simple change in a national administration can easily lead to abandoning such commitments, and even to withdrawing entirely from the agreement, as we have already seen. Given the evident risks and even actual costs from climate change, and the threats to universal human well-being, this is not sufficient. Similarly, discussions of a mechanism for liability and compensation are blocked because some governments are well aware that they have contributed most to the problem and eschew accepting responsibility. Principles of good governance and responsibility that are widely accepted at the national level are rejected internationally as interference with national sovereignty and against national interests.[26]

Given the recent evidence that the climate is already changing rapidly with negative consequences for humans and the environment, and the calls from the scientific community for urgent and immediate action,[27] what is really needed is a massive global campaign to transform energy, transportation and agricultural systems and the economy on what might be comparable to a war footing. There is no time to wait for fundamental improvements in global governance, but climate change could be the impetus for some first steps toward the collective global management of a significant dimension of the biosphere.

Ultimately, possibly not even waiting for the General Assembly to be reformed to give it a legislative responsibility, the UNFCCC Secretariat should be expanded into a UN Climate Change Organization with the authority to set global limits on greenhouse gas emissions necessary to keep global warming below 1.5°C or another boundary as determined by its scientific advisory process, and then to negotiate the assessment of risks and how the necessary actions will be shared among countries, with binding application and fines or other penalties for failure to respect the agreed limits. This will leave scope for different states to experiment with and evolve various approaches to returning to and staying within this planetary boundary, such as a global price for carbon or carbon tax, incentives for carbon capture and storage with both natural and technological methods, and accelerated implementation of renewable energy sources. The organization should have the financial means and technological capacity to assist poorer countries and small states to meet their mitigation obligations.

---

[25] Karlsson-Vinkhuyzen, Sylvia I., Maja Groff, Peter A. Tamás, Arthur L. Dahl, Marie Harder, and Graham Hassall. 2018. "Entry into Force and Then? The Paris Agreement and State Accountability." *Climate Policy*, Vol. 18, No. 5, pp. 593–599.

[26] In 2017, the United States announced its withdrawal from the Paris Agreement, has been gutting environmental regulation, and stimulating fossil fuel development.

[27] IPCC, *Global Warming of 1.5°C*.

Another part of the solution is educational. Formal educational systems should teach a proper understanding of science, complex systems and integrated approaches, and ethical values that favor solidarity, cooperation and service to the common good, as discussed in Chapter 19 on education and Chapter 20 on values. Media campaigns can also relate peoples' lived experience of the signs and symptoms of climate change to the larger scale of the problem and the causal factors in everyone's lifestyles and consumption patterns, including the more restrained use of natural resources, to build a sense of responsibility for action. This should be on the policy agenda of countries everywhere.

Climate-Induced Migration

It is probable, given the delays already in implementing controls to mitigate greenhouse gas emissions, that the organization will also need capacity to assist countries with adaptation to the already inevitable consequences of climate change, such as climate-induced migration (see Chapter 17). This will include anticipating the need to displace populations threatened by sea level rise or the permanent loss of essential water resources, so that this can be done proactively and not only after disaster strikes, to prevent human suffering. Since about 100 million people currently live less than 1 meter above sea level, and many others will be threatened, the magnitude of these forced permanent migrations will exceed anything the world has previously experienced on this time scale. Recent estimates of possible sea level rise from climate change now suggest that this could reach several meters by the end of the century if greenhouse gas emissions are not curtailed rapidly, displacing hundreds of millions of people and drowning coastal cities and infrastructure. The chaos this would create if not properly managed is incalculable, but holding back the waters is not an option.

Other parts of the UN system should collaborate in planning and executing the necessary migrations, many of which will have to cross national boundaries, and it may prove necessary to expand the mandate and resources of the International Organization for Migration, recently incorporated into the United Nations, to manage this process (see Chapter 17). While the need to help climate-displaced populations pull up roots, settle elsewhere and reestablish stable and productive lives is already daunting, an equally great challenge will be to prepare the receiving countries and populations, who have contributed to causing the climate to change, to welcome these immigrants and to help them integrate into their new situations.

Other Impacts

Climate change is already having a major impact on agriculture, forestry and fisheries, and thus on national economies and subsistence. First, there are the obvious impacts of droughts, floods, major storms and forest fires triggered or accentuated by climate change. Responding to such natural disasters is usually seen as a national responsibility, but their increasing frequency and severity will push countries beyond their capacity to recover, requiring international assistance. A second dimension of climate change impact is on the very nature of these economic activities. Staple crops may no longer grow where they had previously been mainstays of local populations. Trees may be subject to new attacks by insects or diseases that the climate had previously kept under control, and tree species may no longer be adapted to changing local conditions of temperature and rainfall, such that forest types may have to be completely transformed. Trees cannot get up and walk to a better environment, so human intervention will be necessary to displace forests around the world, a process that will take many decades, often again crossing national boundaries. Ocean fish populations are already migrating in response to changing oceanographic conditions, sometimes out of reach of local fishermen and inshore fishing industries. The UN Food and Agriculture Organization (FAO) will need to add to its responsibilities the management of these large-scale transformations in the productive resources of the planet and help countries and local populations to adapt.

The same organization for managing global climate change should address another planetary boundary, that of ocean acidification, since this is caused by carbon dioxide dissolving in sea water and becoming carbonic acid. This acidification is already occurring and will impact all marine life that depends on calcified shells or skeletons, from fish and shellfish to plankton. Coral reefs are already under threat from coral bleaching due to excessively hot water, and acidification reducing coral growth will only make things worse. Efforts to control CO_2 as a greenhouse gas will also be relevant to ocean acidification, and the measures adopted for climate change mitigation and the assessment of impacts should explicitly take this other dimension into account.

At the largest scale, with our failure to respond in time to climate change, proposals are now being considered seriously for geoengineering as a last resort to stop runaway global warming. Seeding the oceans with iron to stimulate plankton blooms that might capture carbon and take it to the seabed has been proposed, but small-scale experiments have not demonstrated its effectiveness. Other proposals are to inject materials into the atmosphere that could reflect some of the sun's energy and thus cool the atmosphere, but this would also reduce photosynthesis and thus forest and crop growth. Atmospheric circulation driven by temperature differentials would be affected in unknown ways. The risks are high, the impacts uncertain and possibly catastrophic, and the effects not easily reversible in the short term. The idea that at present anyone can undertake such experiments is frightening, and businesses might see this as a new opportunity for profits. The reformed UN should have a strong technology assessment capacity to review all such proposals, to identify the risks involved and to advise the General Assembly on measures to be taken to protect the common global interest. Global legislation should be adopted to regulate all geoengineering, to determine the necessary scientific research and development, to define the essential safeguards, and to authorize experiments or even implementation only once all risks have been addressed and minimized. It would be much more reasonable to control our greenhouse gas emissions.

Energy

The other face of the climate change challenge is energy, and specifically our present dependence on fossil fuels (coal, oil, gas) to power our material civilization. Fossil fuels represent solar energy trapped eons ago in organic matter (carbon compounds) buried in geological formations, providing a relatively cheap and concentrated form of energy. Releasing carbon dioxide to the atmosphere is a side effect of our use of these energy sources. We have become deeply dependent on (some may say addicted to) fossil fuel use, and much of our technology, from transport to petrochemicals, depends on these resources. The investments we have made in these technologies are enormous, and while alternatives now exist for much of this, managing the transition is proving very difficult. Economically, it means significant short-term costs associated with replacement of our massive investments in fossil fuels for everything from airplanes to road transport to ships to power plants, compensated by the huge economic growth that will result from investments in clean technologies and energy (with part of the funds coming from money currently spent on fossil fuel subsidies). Politically, it means depriving a range of countries that produce fossil fuels of their means of livelihood and status in the world. In human terms, there will be significant short-term unemployment across many industries, requiring retraining and new job opportunities.

Most urban infrastructure and many human habitations will have to be rethought and rebuilt. It might seem reasonable to allow many decades for this transition, but the rapid acceleration of climate change shows that this is not possible, and urgent action is required to avoid disaster. Inevitably, the inertia of the present system, vested interests in all these technologies and general resistance to change are throwing up obstacles that may seem impossible to overcome. Global governance will clearly have to play a significant role in preparing for, planning, accompanying and compensating for such fundamental changes in our civilization, yet there is presently no UN Energy Organization, only an International Energy Agency outside the UN system with 29 state members. More recently, in 2011 an International Renewable Energy Agency was established with 154 members that is supporting countries in their transition to a sustainable energy future.[28] The International Solar Alliance (ISA), a treaty-based intergovernmental organization of more than 121 countries within the Tropics, was initiated by India in 2015.[29]

---

[28] Now 160 members. www.irena.org/.
[29] See www.isolaralliance.org/.

ENVIRONMENT AND THE BIOSPHERE

Biosphere Integrity

The Convention on Biological Diversity (CBD), the Convention on International Trade in Endangered Species (CITES), the Convention on Migratory Species (CMS), the Ramsar Convention on Wetlands and other conservation agreements, as well as many regional agreements, suggest the need for a coherent approach to the protection and ultimately restoration of the biological heritage of the planet and the integrity of the biosphere on which we all depend for survival. This includes both the functional diversity of ecosystems and life support systems, and genetic diversity represented by species or genetic resources. These are all interrelated and must be treated together. Much conservation action is implemented at the national level through endangered species protection, parks and other conservation areas, but there are also dimensions requiring an international approach, as is already the case for migratory species and trade in endangered species and their parts.

There is evidence that the sixth mass extinction event is already beginning,[30],[31] with 60 percent of all animals on the planet lost in recent decades and pressures growing as available habitats are shrinking.[32] This will have inevitable consequences for the loss of ecosystem services and the future carrying capacity of the planet for human society. Saving what is left and eventually trying to restore essential ecosystems will require international efforts beyond the national capacity of many countries. Global levels of coordination, scientific research and advice, and often financial support, will be necessary to assist countries to preserve what is left of their natural heritage.

Another related problem requiring an international approach concerns invasive species, which need to be identified, quarantined and controlled where they get out of hand. Invasive species can cause conservation catastrophes wiping out endemic species, upset the balance of ecosystems, impact human health and require expen-

---

[30] Previous mass extinctions include the Late Devonian, 375 million years ago, 75% of species lost; end of the Permian, 251 million years ago, 96% of species lost; end of the Triassic, 200 million years ago, 80% of species lost; and end of the Cretaceous, 66 million years ago, 76% of species lost.

[31] Ceballos, Gerardo, Paul R. Ehrlich, and Rodolfo Dirzo. 2017. "Biological Annihilation via the Ongoing Sixth Mass Extinction Signaled by Vertebrate Population Losses and Declines." *PNAS – Proceedings of the National Academy of Sciences* Vol. 114, No. 30, e6089-e6096. DOI: 10.1073/pnas.1704949114; published ahead of print July 10, 2017. https://doi.org/10.1073/pnas.1704949114; IPBES. 2018. "Summary for policymakers of the thematic assessment report on land degradation and restoration of the Intergovernmental Science-Policy Platform on Biodiversity and Ecosystem Services," ed. R. Scholes et al., Bonn, IPBES Secretariat.

[32] WWF. 2018. *Living Planet Report – 2018: Aiming Higher*, ed. M. Grooten and R.E.A. Almond, Gland, Switzerland, WWF.

sive control measures – if they can be controlled at all.[33] The International Maritime Organization has taken the lead on invasive marine species spread in ships' ballast water, but much still needs to be done in other areas.

A further international issue is the conservation of biodiversity in areas beyond national jurisdiction. The International Whaling Convention (IWC) started as an instrument to regulate whaling, but since it failed to avoid the near-extermination of whales, it serves now primarily to conserve remaining whale populations and foster their recovery. There is a Convention for the Conservation of Antarctic Living Marine Resources, and protected areas on the high seas are now being considered under the Law of the Sea. There is no mechanism to protect the seabed and its biodiversity from proposals for seabed mining, which are being actively considered, by various companies.

Since the aims of all these processes are similar, there may be scope here for a more collective international approach in the future.

Another challenge requiring similar kinds of expertise is genetic engineering, at least in its environmental dimension (with human genetic engineering more the responsibility of the World Health Organization (WHO)). The capacity to create genetically modified organisms (GMOs) has largely been pursued by multinational agroindustries in a search for profits, with little attention to safeguards or the precautionary principle, producing a backlash against all GMOs in some regions. There is certainly a potential in genetic engineering to produce, for example, more drought-resistant crops to adapt to climate change, and other more constructive uses. A neutral science-based global mechanism is needed to review research in the field, screen proposals to release GMOs into the environment, authorize those that meet essential criteria of safety and usefulness, and monitor releases for unexpected side effects, just as is done with medicines. The mechanism should likely be global and within the UN system, carefully designed to be shielded against pressures from commercial interests.

Chemicals

The threats to human health and the environment from chemical pollution and similar human innovations and novelties such as nanomaterials represent another set of planetary boundaries to be respected. There are already the Basel, Rotterdam and Stockholm conventions that have recently been grouped as a chemicals cluster within UN Environment, with major interests also from the WHO for human health, and from the FAO for agricultural chemicals. The new Minimata

---

[33] For example, the predatory rosy wolf snail (*Euglandina rosea*) was introduced to French Polynesia to control the introduced giant African snail; instead it caused the extinction of 57 of 61 species of endemic snails in French Polynesia. The cane toad (*Rhinella marina*), introduced to many tropical areas to control pests in sugar cane, multiplies rapidly and its toxic skin threatens many animals that try to eat it.

Convention is now addressing mercury. The same framework might also take responsibility for the planetary boundaries for biogeochemical flows, in particular the global cycles for fixed nitrogen and phosphorus compounds, which have already been exceeded.

The current mechanisms to assess chemicals for their toxicity and the danger they represent to human health and the environment are largely national, or regional in the case of the European Union. Thousands of new chemical compounds are invented every year and must be tested and, if necessary, regulated. Many compounds and molecules created before modern testing was introduced have never been properly assessed. Coordination between these national processes is insufficient, and there is evidence that they are too easily subjected to lobbying from commercial interests. Chemicals may be banned in one country and still be freely available elsewhere. Research may suddenly demonstrate that a chemical previously thought innocuous has hidden damaging effects, as was discovered with the endocrine-disrupting compounds that upset hormonal balances in the body. The great multinational chemical companies are notorious for their efforts to protect their markets from regulation, in total disregard of the environmental and health impacts of the chemicals concerned, which have often been concealed from the public and regulators. Human susceptibility to a toxin does not depend on nationality, and chemicals, once released, do not respect national boundaries. Global governance of dangerous chemicals will be an obvious area to develop, producing considerable economies in overlapping national testing and regulatory processes, and filling gaps where countries do not have the technical means to manage such dangerous products.

Atmosphere

As much as some politicians might regret it, national boundaries do not extend into the atmosphere, and no policy or legislation can determine where the wind blows or where the air goes. The World Meteorological Organization observes the atmosphere to support weather forecasting but does not have a mandate for the composition of the atmosphere or its contaminants. Yet we know today that the atmosphere links all nations together in a global system. Pesticides used in the tropics evaporate, are carried by air currents toward the poles and condense out of the cold air to contaminate wildlife and affect human health. Vehicle traffic in the Sahara desert breaks up the surface crust, feeding dust storms that deposit iron and cause plankton blooms in the Black Sea and deliver fungal contaminants that attack marine life on Caribbean coral reefs. Dust from wind erosion on the loess plateau of northern China can reach as far as North America.

Transboundary air pollution has both regional and planetary implications. For stratospheric ozone, there is already the International Convention on the Ozone

Layer, with its Montreal Protocol on substances that deplete the ozone layer that is often cited as a great success for multilateral environmental diplomacy. Atmospheric aerosols can be transported long distances, even affecting the amount of sunlight reaching the Earth's surface. Europe has a regional Convention on Transboundary Air Pollution that has helped to control acid rain. Asia, however, has a significant problem with transboundary air pollution that has not yet been addressed, with clouds of particulate matter from East Asia reducing sunlight in India and as far away as the Maldives in the Indian Ocean. The illegal burning of tropical forests in Southeast Asia has spread smoke across the region, affecting human health and even air traffic. There is scope here for a more coherent global approach, as problems are certain to emerge in other regions with development. A global framework agreement on atmospheric pollution could encourage subsidiary regional agreements to address particular problems.

Managing Natural Resources

As a global community, we have been so focused on industrialization and now the post-industrial economy of services that we tend to forget that all of this ultimately depends on the natural resources of the planet: its soil, fields, forests and biodiversity; its air, winds and water; its minerals and fossil fuels. Our food and drink, and everything we manufacture, come ultimately from natural resources. Yet economists found it convenient to ignore them until they were exploited and turned into raw materials for products that could be marketed. Only on the fringes did some say that natural resources should be considered as natural capital, just as we have industrial capital or financial capital, and that we should try to live off the interest and maintain the capital resource sustainably. Some natural resources are renewable, and their productivity should be maintained, rather than mining them like forests for short-term profit. Others, such as some minerals or fossil fuels, are non-renewable; when they are used up, they are gone or degraded beyond use. Still others, including some metals, could be used over and over again if we recycle them in closed systems or a circular economy.

Since natural resources are not evenly distributed, they are a principal object of world trade, and this links them into a global pool of resources that requires global management. For example, the global trade in wood, pulp for paper and other forest products generates pressure to cut down forests everywhere, regardless of their importance for biodiversity conservation, watershed management, soil restoration, carbon storage, climate moderation and other ecosystem services not valued by the market. In the present economy, only marketed resources have value, so forests are logged. Clear-cutting for maximum profit may be favored over more sustainable forestry practices, and illegal logging and forest clearing are widespread, feeding corruption. National governments are often too weak to resist these pressures. There is no mechanism to determine which forests are best conserved in the global interest, and to provide compensation or protection if necessary. Only by looking at forests as a global resource can the best uses be determined for each area, with some having their highest global value for biodiversity conservation, others for water supply and erosion control, and others suited for timber production. A share of the profits from the global timber trade could be used to finance the protection of forests with higher value for ecosystem services in their natural state.

What resource management there is today is done by multinational corporations, major traders and the market, with profit as the primary motive and the short term the temporal framework. Nations have largely lost sovereignty over their resources under global market pressures. All the non-market values of natural resources, such as the ecosystem services they provide and the maintenance of the biosphere suitable for life, are ignored. National boundaries do not correspond to natural features or ecoregions, and do not facilitate the management of shared resources. Natural resources are also unjustly distributed, with some countries well endowed and others very limited, requiring a global approach to redress inequities (see Chapter 14). In any federation or union of states, such as the United States or the European Union, it is normal for resources to be distributed where they are needed the most to reduce inequalities. The reformed United Nations should be able to earn the trust necessary to achieve this rebalancing in the common interest.

Ultimately, from a global perspective of equity and leaving no one behind, the natural resources of the planet should be seen as global assets from which everyone may benefit. They should be managed for sustainability and their distribution should be equitably regulated, which can best be done from a global perspective. The interconnectedness of energy and food systems, for example, is beyond market regulation, as when the conversion of crops to biofuel production for wealthier countries raised prices for food beyond the reach of the poor.

It will thus be necessary to replace gradually the present system of absolute national sovereignty over resources and their private or corporate ownership for profit. Accounting systems need to include natural resources, assets and processes as global natural capital to be maintained for planetary sustainability, with only the interest on that capital considered an available economic resource. Countries could be compensated for the use of resources within their territories to meet global needs, especially when there are negative impacts or trade-offs when the exploitation prevents other forms of development or benefit. They could also be compensated when a resource that could be developed has a higher use in its natural state for planetary welfare as a biodiversity conservation area or essential component of a life support system. Private enterprises could be licensed to develop resources within whatever limits are defined to protect the common interest. Institutionally, the altruistic motivation to create wealth for everyone can be just as powerful as, and should replace, profit making for individuals or corporate entities. Profits are one sign of economic efficiency but should not become ends in themselves. Natural capital should take its place alongside financial capital and human capital and be managed and measured as such, as explained above. Costs and impacts presently treated as externalities should be incorporated in more complete accounting of costs and benefits.

Countries often sit on vast untapped natural resources that cannot be monetized or developed sustainably because of mismanagement, lack of trust, institutional weaknesses or corruption. Vast private sector resources might potentially be made available through public–private partnerships, within a framework of regulations in the common interest and providing for the equitable sharing of benefits, overseen by a credible organization or a renewed and expanded FAO with a General Assembly mandate in this area (see Chapter 14). This organization could also be given authority for the management of some resources beyond national jurisdictions, such as high seas fisheries and minerals found in the international seabed, presently a source of growing insecurity. Once some confidence is built in the global capacity to manage natural resources and ensure their equitable distribution, states may be ready to widen the scope of global management of the planet's resources where required to maintain and possibly improve planetary carrying capacity, and to remain within planetary boundaries.

Recommendations

The previous sections on global environmental challenges demonstrate the need for a strengthened global capacity for environmental governance, whether in one or several specialized agencies, supported by international scientific advisory and technology assessment processes designed to be protected from partisan national interests and industrial lobbying. This should cover climate change and ocean acidification, energy, atmospheric pollution, chemicals, and wastes such as plastics impacting the environment and human health, biodiversity and ecosystem services, and the global dimension of natural resources management. Some flexibility will be needed to take on new environmental risks that may be identified in the future. The many existing environmental programs, conventions and other bodies should be gradually integrated into this framework, retaining their competences and successes while reducing fragmentation and overlap. There will be a growing need for environmental restoration, requiring a global agency for knowledge sharing, technical assistance, and financial support to repair the damage done to our life support systems by the pillage of our planet by past and present economic activities.

Above all, an integrated approach is needed, since all environmental problems are interrelated in one global system, and they interact in complex ways. The acceleration of environmental decline – if not the collapse of essential ecological processes – is a catastrophic risk that is far from appreciated today. Through the rising costs of natural disasters and destabilization of the resources on which our civilization depends, it could trigger social and economic crises and a downward spiral into collapse, chaos and anarchy.[34] Again, a rapid strengthening of global governance would be our best hope to avoid the worst outcome.

---

[34] Laybourn-Langton, Laurie, Leslie Rankin and Darren Baxter. 2019. *This Is a Crisis: Facing up to the Age of Environmental Breakdown*, London, IPPR: Institute for Public Policy Research. www .ippr.org/research/publications/age-of-environmental-breakdown.

17

Population and Migration

We recognize the positive contribution of migrants for inclusive growth and sustainable development. We also recognize that international migration is a multi-dimensional reality of major relevance for the development of countries of origin, transit and destination, which requires coherent and comprehensive responses. We will cooperate internationally to ensure safe, orderly and regular migration involving full respect for human rights and the humane treatment of migrants regardless of migration status, of refugees and of displaced persons. Such cooperation should also strengthen the resilience of communities hosting refugees, particularly in developing countries.[1]

While there are many compelling social issues that could be considered at least in part at the global level, this chapter takes as a specific example the related issues of population and migration. It is rapid population growth that has brought society up against planetary boundaries. While people have always migrated, the flow of migrants has accelerated, with environmental displacement from climate change adding to economic migration and the flood of refugees from war and persecution, making this a priority for global governance.

The United Nations has had a Population Commission since 1946, later renamed the Commission on Population and Development to follow up on the International Conference on Population and Development in Cairo in 1994, and established the United Nations Population Fund (UNFPA) in 1969. It is supported by the Population Division within the Department of Economic and Social Affairs in New York. While the UN has played an important role in assembling population statistics and debating related issues, it has not always been very successful because of the strong ethical, religious and ideological differences between nations over the issues of reproductive rights, birth control, abortion and other factors relevant to the rate of population growth. There is no independent UN agency charged with

---

[1] UN. 2015. "Transforming Our World: The 2030 Agenda for Sustainable Development." para. 29.

the larger issues of the human carrying capacity of the planet, the relationship of population to resources or questions of population concentration and movement.

The most invasive species on the planet today is *Homo sapiens.* The human population has at least tripled within living memory.[2] A principal role of governance should be to find a place for, and ensure the welfare of, every human being on this planet. There are a number of dimensions to this challenge: the total number of people, their age structure and rate of growth or decline, their locations relative to the carrying capacity of their environments, and their movements or migrations.

These problems have been aggravated, if not created in part, by the relatively recent emergence of the concept of national sovereignty over a national territory with fixed borders inhabited by legally recognized citizens whose movements can be controlled. We tend to forget that the concept of the modern passport as a permission to travel is only a hundred years old, dating back in Europe to World War I, 1914–1918.

Not all of these problems need to be addressed by global governance. This is clearly an issue where subsidiarity applies (that is, the principle that decisions should be taken at the lowest possible level of organization or closest to where they will have their effect), and a diversity of approaches will need to evolve naturally in each community, country and geographic entity with physical rather than political boundaries, such as islands or river basins. Nevertheless, the total world population is on track to overshoot our planetary carrying capacity, and natural, political, and economic pressures are displacing large numbers of people across national frontiers, requiring a planetary response beyond what any country can manage.

POPULATION GROWTH

Population growth is often depicted as a major global problem and a threat to planetary stability, and extreme measures are sometimes suggested to prevent "others" from multiplying excessively. Certainly, the still rapidly growing world population, projected by the UN to reach perhaps 11 billion people by the end of this century, is creating political, social and environmental stresses of major proportions.[3]

---

[2] The world's population surpassed the 1 billion mark around the year 1800. It has grown at an exponential rate since then, reaching 2.3 billion in 1939, at the outset of World War II, and is estimated to have reached about 7.5 billion in 2018.

[3] Some of that growth is built into the age structure, where recent growth has been rapid and a significant part of the population is only now reaching reproductive age, but the official projections (some argue) may underestimate the impacts of urbanization and the spread of cellphones and other information technologies accelerating female education and precipitating a fast drop in birth rates where they are still high. See Bricker, Darrell and John Ibbitson. 2019. *Empty Planet: The Shock of Global Population Decline*, New York, Penguin Random House.

When combined with the excessive consumption of a consumer society, there is no way with present resources and technologies to both maintain the standard of living of the rich and meet the essential needs of the poor in the decades immediately ahead as the world population peaks and then starts to decline.[4] It is not that this would be technically impossible, but it would require fundamental changes in our lifestyles, consumption patterns, social relationships, institutional structures and value systems.[5]

The present rapid population growth is a symptom of the extreme inequality in the world. Attempts to limit birth rates through legislation or constraint raise serious issues of human rights. The reasonable solution lies in addressing the root causes of rapid population growth. It is extremes of wealth and poverty, coupled with the lack of empowerment of women, that have maintained the world for so long in an unstable intermediate state between high and low birth and death rates. Modern health advances have been widely shared to prevent or control epidemics, and to reduce infant mortality, bringing down death rates around the world. At the same time, we have not shared enough wealth with the poor to reduce poverty, educate girls and women and provide meaningful employment, which would reduce the incentive to have many children. It is well-known that countries go through a demographic transition as the standard of living rises. A better distribution of wealth, coupled with universal education and social security, would be the best route to stabilizing the world population. The population could then grow in balance with our efforts to restore and then raise the human carrying capacity of the planet.[6]

From this perspective, the sustainable solution to the world's population problem lies in the transformation of the world economy so that it is more firmly based on principles of social justice and equity, reducing the present extreme inequality within and between states (see Chapter 14). The world today generates sufficient food and wealth to meet everyone's basic needs. The challenge is one of distribution, which improved global governance could address. Economic systems need to be redesigned to enhance their altruistic and cooperative attributes, to create meaningful employment for all and to eliminate poverty in the world, as this is now a realistic possibility, given global wealth.[7] There are already many small-scale experiments in alternative economics that global governance mechanisms could

[4] Randers, Jorgen. 2012. *2052: A Global Forecast for the Next Forty Years*. A Report to the Club of Rome. Commemorating the 40th Anniversary of The Limits to Growth. White River Junction, VT, Chelsea Green Publishing.

[5] Hanley, Paul. 2014. *Eleven*. Victoria, BC, Friesen Press.

[6] Dahl, Arthur Lyon. 1996. *The Eco Principle: Ecology and Economics in Symbiosis*, London, Zed Books Ltd. and Oxford, George Ronald.

[7] Bahá'í International Community. 1998. *Valuing Spirituality in Development: Initial Considerations Regarding the Creation of Spiritually Based Indicators for Development*. A concept paper written for the World Faiths and Development Dialogue, Lambeth Palace, London, February 18–19, 1998.

help bring into the mainstream.[8] It is the same excessive differences between wealthy and poorer countries, maintained by barriers of excessive national sovereignty and an exploitative international economic system, that are behind the global pressures for economic migration.

POPULATION AGE STRUCTURE

Many of the most industrialized countries, including China, are faced with aging populations as birth rates have declined below replacement levels. The costs of caring for old people are rising, while there are proportionally fewer young people of working age to support the necessary social services. In addition, China, because of the one child per family policy that it maintained until recently, and a strong cultural preference for male offspring, has a large excess of men who cannot find spouses, adding to social tensions.[9] Other countries see half or more of their population under age 21, although many have now passed "peak children" and are now at or beyond "peak youth." These are population trends with large economic and social repercussions that take decades to work through.

The logical solution would be for those countries with large younger populations of working age to more substantially "share" them with countries which lack enough younger people in the work force to maintain a demographic balance. Yet today, what country would open its doors to migration on such a scale, when facing seemingly insurmountable political, social and cultural barriers at home?

CARRYING CAPACITY

Carrying capacity refers to the ability of a geographic area and its resources to support the population living there on a sustainable basis. In nature, some animal species will multiply to the extent that their food supply will allow, until they finally consume all the food available and the population crashes. Only when the food supply regenerates will the cycle begin again. However, in most mature ecosystems, there are multiple control mechanisms and predator–prey relationships that keep

---

[8]   See for example: Schumacher, E.F. 1973. *Small Is Beautiful: A Study of Economics as If People Mattered*, London, Blond & Briggs; Brown, Peter G. and Geoffrey Garver. 2009. *Right Relationship: Building a Whole Earth Economy*. San Francisco, Berrett-Koehler Publishers; Jackson, Tim. 2017. *Prosperity without Growth: Foundations for the Economy of Tomorrow*. 2nd ed. London, Routledge; Beinhocker, Eric D., 2006. *The Origin of Wealth: Evolution, Complexity, and the Radical Remaking of Economics*. Cambridge, MA: Harvard Business School Press, and London, Random House Business Books; and the B-corp movement https://benefitcorp .net/what-is-a-benefit-corporation.

[9]   For a detailed discussion of the multiple implications of slanted sex ratios, see López-Claros, A. and Bahiyyih Nakhjavani, 2018. Chapter 1, "The People Problem," in *Equality for Women = Prosperity for All: The Disastrous Crisis of Global Gender Inequality*, New York, St. Martin's Press.

the system more or less in balance. Human populations were also regulated traditionally by war, famine, and pestilence. Modern technology has pushed back those threats but not eliminated them as ultimate forms of control, if we do not consciously prevent them.

One difficulty in determining carrying capacity and planning to identify and respect environmental limits is the frequent time lag between an action and its observable consequences. This often happens when excessive consumption of a resource does not yet exhaust the resource but reduces the capacity to produce the resource, so that we are living off the capital rather than the interest on that capital, leaving a debt or future impact for later generations to pay back or experience. With intensive agriculture, for example, every ton of grain produced in the American Midwest means a ton of topsoil is lost to erosion. At a planetary level, we have degraded 37 percent of all the world's arable land since World War II.[10] By some calculations, our present civilization already consumes the current annual production of planetary resources in the first seven months of the year, so for the last five months we are living off of the planet's capital and reducing its long-term productive capacity.[11]

The integration of the global system through trade and transport has added some resilience to the human capacity to resist or recover from disasters, most of which are local or regional in scope, so aid can be provided from elsewhere. This does not mean that a large-scale disaster could not push us over planetary limits and result in massive loss of life. Already in 2008 and 2012, widespread crop failures meant that the world produced less food than it consumed, drawing down food reserves. The possibility of a global catastrophe is in fact not remote, and one aim of global governance should be to anticipate and prevent such a catastrophic situation from materializing. The 2018 New Shape Prize of the Global Challenges Foundation was specifically aimed to award innovative ideas for global governance able to avoid risks that might annihilate 10 percent or more of the world population.[12]

POPULATION DISPLACEMENT AND MIGRATION

Migration and growing mass movements of refugees have become a defining issue of the first years of this century, and the subject of great political controversies. Recipient countries are already experiencing a political backlash from this

---

[10] Montgomery, David R. 2007. *Dirt: The Erosion of Civilizations*, Berkeley, University of California Press.

[11] WWF. 2018. *Living Planet Report 2018: Aiming Higher*, Gland, Switzerland, WWF International. http://wwf.panda.org/knowledge_hub/all_publications/living_planet_report_2018/.

[12] Global Challenges Foundation. 2018. New Shape Prize. https://globalchallenges.org/en/our-work/the-new-shape-prize. Awardees: https://globalchallenges.org/en/our-work/the-new-shape-prize/awardees.

unmanaged international crisis. No proposals for global governance can ignore this issue threatening the stability of many countries and regions. As in the Middle Ages in Europe, when the rich barricaded themselves behind castle ramparts, wealthier countries are today closing their frontiers, even behind walls and high fences, to keep migrants out, often exacerbating the human suffering of already distressed people.

Yet it is important to place migration in its proper context. The human race has always migrated, from the first migrations out of Africa to the gradual colonization of all the inhabited places on Earth, even to the most remote Pacific islands. Empire building and migration went together. The great religions, too, spread by migration. Moses led the migration of the Hebrew people out of Egypt. Islam migrated out of Arabia as far as Spain and Indonesia. National borders changed often in the past, and, as mentioned, passports for travel are a recent phenomenon. The great economies of America, Canada, and Australia were largely built through the hard work of immigrants, and even today, with many countries experiencing aging populations and birthrates below replacement levels, their future will depend on migration. Migration therefore can be a positive phenomenon for receiving countries, even if the migrants have been forced to leave because of various traumas or lack of opportunity at home. As the distribution of the world carrying capacity and resources changes in future years due to changing environmental conditions, it will be necessary to reduce the number of people living in some regions under stress and to populate other areas that become newly inhabitable.

It can be helpful to distinguish different categories of migrants, including those that choose to leave their country for better opportunities elsewhere, sometimes called economic migrants, and those refugees that are forced to leave their homes because of war, violence or persecution. Religious intolerance is another leading cause of forced displacement by denying equal citizenship rights on religious grounds. A new category of environmentally displaced persons includes those who migrate because rising sea levels, drought, storms, flooding and other disasters, often associated with climate change, have permanently rendered their former homes uninhabitable. Their numbers are expected to increase substantially in the years ahead.

The UN responded to the refugees created by World War II and subsequent events by creating the UN High Commissioner for Refugees and adopting the 1951 Convention Relating to the Status of Refugees, including rights of asylum and an assumption that refugees would return home once the cause of their displacement was removed. The International Organization for Migration was created at the same time to resettle the millions of people uprooted by the war. There is no equivalent normative framework for economic migrants or the environmentally displaced, a major gap in international legislation that needs to be filled, and that is acknowledged in the Sustainable Development Goals target 10.7.

In 2018, the UN negotiated and endorsed two new texts to consolidate and clarify the international approach to migrants and refugees, the Global Compact for Safe, Orderly and Regular Migration, and the Global Compact on Refugees.[13]

As described above, economic migration is driven largely by the income gap between the origin and destination countries, with average incomes 70 times larger in the latter, and the lack of educational and employment opportunities at home.[14] Migrants have always left homes and families in search of a better life and have generally been successful. As mentioned above, a second driver today is the demographic divergence between regions with a high proportion of young people and the aging populations of the advanced economies that need workers and a larger working population to support the rising costs of supporting the elderly.[15]

Contrary to much contemporary popular opinion and political discourse, migration is usually beneficial for all concerned. Migration is integral to development; people need to move to where the jobs are. For economically deprived populations, migration can provide the best opportunity to escape quickly from poverty and unemployment. Increasing migration can produce greater economic gains than trade liberalization. Migrants see increases in income and child education and reduced infant mortality, with additional benefits for women and minorities. For countries of origin, migration lowers unemployment and creates more productive, higher paying jobs, and is thus a powerful force for development. Remittances from migrants can be an important source of foreign exchange, investment capital and direct support to the poor. According to the World Bank, remittances to developing countries in 2018 were US$528 billion, nearly four times larger than Official Development Assistance.[16] Migrants can also transfer knowledge and technology, with a diaspora supporting development at home. For receiving countries, migration has a positive fiscal effect, increasing goods and services and lowering prices for consumers. It addresses labor shortages at both the high and low ends of the job market. Prices for health care and university education are also lower because of the high number of immigrants employed in these sectors. There are labor market complementarities, and a high number of inventors, innovators and entrepreneurs

---

[13] Global Compact for Safe, Orderly and Regular Migration, endorsed by the UNGA on December 19, 2018, https://refugeesmigrants.un.org/migration-compact. Global Compact on Refugees, affirmed by the UNGA on 17 December 2018. www.unhcr.org/the-global-compact-on-refugees.html.

[14] The ratio of the average income per capita in the high-income countries to that of the low-income countries is about 70, using the latest data from the World Bank's World Development Indicators.

[15] For a good overview of the links between migration and development, including the trade link in developing economies, see Robert E.B. Lucas (ed.). 2014. *International Handbook on Migration and Economic Development*, Northampton, MA, Edward Elgar.

[16] World Bank. 2018. "Migration and Remittances: Recent Development and Outlook." Washington, DC, World Bank Group, December.

among migrants. The more the host community facilitates integration and assimilation, the greater the benefit.[17]

Despite these overwhelming advantages, popular opinion is easily turned against migrants, with people's perceptions of the percentage of migrants in their countries greatly exaggerated. Crime rates among migrants are actually lower than among the native population. Moreover, most efforts to control migration, especially irregular migration, are ineffective. However, large-scale immigration can challenge governments to provide social and physical infrastructure and confronts civil society with issues of adaptation and assimilation.

Two things have changed in recent years to give migration a bad name. First, a reaction against economic globalization, with the rise of nationalisms for political ends built on nativism and xenophobia, coupled with the revival of ancient tendencies toward racism and religious intolerance, have led in many countries to increasing divisions and social fragmentation, if not violent rejection of those who are different, even in places where peaceful coexistence had long been the rule. The resulting negative view of migration is quite recent.

Second, the rapid growth of the human population pressing against planetary limits and its globalization with the support of new technologies is stressing if not seriously eroding the carrying capacity of the planet. When people feel forced to emigrate, there is no place on the planet left to migrate to that is not already well occupied. Furthermore, our environmental impacts, first among them accelerating climate change, are going to displace hundreds of millions of people in the decades ahead, forcing them permanently from their homes due to rising sea levels, increasing drought, agricultural failures, violent storms and other catastrophes. In these situations, it is always the poor who have the fewest options. These displacements do not fall under the current criteria for refugees, since they have no hope of returning once the cause of the displacement is removed. The most extreme case is that of the Small Island Developing States on low atolls that risk losing their entire national territory, and thus not only their homes and occupations but their culture and national identity, becoming citizens without a state.

All of this is in addition to the migrations and displacements caused by social and political factors, from war and violence to terrorism, failed states and persecution of minorities, generally covered by the present Refugee Convention. We must anticipate greatly increased flows of migrants.

The fear of migrants cultivated by certain politicians and the media has important consequences for human rights. Many human rights violations today are against migrants, and illegal migrants are often denied even the most fundamental human rights protections. The label "illegal" from the simple fact of crossing a border may be seen by some to withdraw their right to exist as human beings, and can be thrown

---

[17] World Bank. 2016. "Migration and Development: A Role for the World Bank Group." Washington, DC, World Bank Group, September.

up as a barrier to defend a "national interest." Even those who are legally in another country face discrimination. One of the issues raised at the 2010 UN Human Rights Council Social Forum on Climate Change and Human Rights was the need to extend concern beyond those migrants who are victims of climate-induced violations of their human rights, to focus on the education of receiving communities.[18] Forced migrants need to be seen as human beings, as victims of events beyond their control. Since we are all generally, through our lifestyles, part of the cause of climate change and environmental degradation, we have a duty of solidarity to those who are its victims. By educating those in the communities receiving migrants to have sympathy for their circumstances and a sense of responsibility toward them, welcoming them and assisting in their settlement, many human rights violations could be avoided.

THE RESPONSE NEEDED

From the perspective of global governance, greatly increased environmentally induced migrations can be anticipated. They should thus be planned for and well organized; we should not wait until a natural disaster or catastrophe forces such displacement, no doubt with great misery and suffering. This also means determining where such displaced persons could best be settled: where adequate resources are available, and perhaps with a situation and climate not too different from what they have known. Where whole communities are displaced, it should be possible for them to migrate as a unit, keeping families together and retaining as much as possible of their social capital. The UN International Organization for Migration could have expanded responsibilities in this area. The UN is presently adopting Global Compacts on Migration and on Refugees, and pressure is building for strengthened UN mechanisms to manage migration from a global perspective.[19]

Special educational programs need to be developed both for migrants and for their receiving communities. Among the issues to be addressed is that of assimilation or cultural preservation. Should migrants be encouraged to abandon their culture, traditions and faith and assimilate completely into the receiving community? Should they be allowed to cluster in their own in-group, maintaining their differences in a kind of cultural ghetto? Neither extreme is desirable. If the receiving community is welcoming and offers all the necessary opportunities for education, employment and participation, each person can choose the balance he or she feels comfortable with. Ideally, those migrating should see the culture and faith that they bring with them as enriching the diversity in their new community, something to

---

[18] International Environment Forum. 2010. *Climate Change and Human Rights.* https://iefworld .org/node/249.

[19] Bahá'í International Community. 2018. *Migration: A Chance to Reflect on Global Well-Being.* Statement for the Sixth Intergovernmental Negotiations on the Global Compact for Migration, Geneva, July 12, 2018. www.bic.org/statements/migration-chance-reflect-global-well-being.

offer on equal terms as they also receive new perspectives from the community they have joined. Children can share the richness of multiple heritages, and young people, as they intermarry, will pass this human richness on to their offspring. Learning diverse languages as an infant has been shown to increase intelligence. With a proper understanding of shared values on both sides, migration can be an enriching experience for everyone, as demonstrated by the experience of millions of people during the past century.

Finally, given what we now know about the changes to come in the world, not to mention other potential crises and catastrophes that past experience suggests could well be on the horizon, we could all find ourselves as migrants, refugees or displaced persons; no country or group within a given country is immune. The golden rule of doing unto others as we would have them do unto us certainly applies.

PART IV

Cross-Cutting Issues

18

Corruption as a Destroyer of Prosperity and the Need for International Enforcement

Corruption kills ... The money stolen through corruption every year is enough to feed the world's hungry 80 times over ... Corruption denies them their right to food, and, in some cases, their right to life.[1]

Navi Pillay, Fifth UN High Commissioner for Human Rights

The successful prosecution and imprisonment of corrupt leaders would create opportunities for the democratic process to produce successors dedicated to serving their people rather than to enriching themselves.[2]

Judge Mark Wolf

If the purpose of governance is to execute collective functions in the common interest, its essential foundation is trust in the institutions of government and confidence that the functions will be carried out justly and effectively. Corruption is the antithesis of this, turning institutions against their intended purpose, plundering the resources available, undermining confidence in government and destroying human prosperity. While previously underappreciated for its widespread and insidious effects, corruption has finally emerged as a problem involving enormous social and economic costs – no approach to governance today can avoid addressing it head on.

The pernicious and systemic ramifications of corruption have now been well documented, with corrupt officials often being the worst human rights abusers and even linked to war crimes. Economically speaking, it is estimated that trillions of

---

[1] Pillay, Navi. 2013. "The Negative Impact of Corruption on Human Rights," Opening Statement to the Office of the United Nations High Commissioner on Human Rights, March 13. In *The Human Rights Case against Corruption*. Geneva, Office of the High Commissioner, United Nations Human Rights, 2013, pp. 8–9. www.ohchr.org/Documents/Issues/Development/GoodGovernance/Corruption/HRCaseAgainstCorruption.pdf

[2] Wolf, Mark L. 2018. "The World Needs an International Anti-Corruption Court." *Daedalus, the Journal of the American Academy of Arts & Sciences*, Vol. 147, No. 3, p. 144.

dollars in bribes are paid globally on an annual basis, with more than 5 percent of global GDP likely being lost to all forms of corruption every year.[3] Moreover, as has been powerfully argued in recent analyses, the international security consequences of endemic corruption in various states are ignored at our own peril.[4] As expressed by then US Secretary of State John Kerry, "the quality of governance is no longer just a domestic concern."[5]

It has also been argued recently that *the key* to economic prosperity, across societies, is the creation and maintenance of "inclusive" economic and political institutions, rather than those engineered in the service of ruling elites bent on extractive behaviors.[6] Acemoglu and Robinson argue that it is only through inclusive and fair institutions that conditions for collective prosperity are achieved, as such institutions, among other things, provide the appropriate incentives to reward the innovation and hard work required to drive economic development.

In the first part of this chapter we provide a broad definition of corruption and discuss why it is so toxic to effective governance. We then address how corruption has emerged as a key issue in the development process after being ignored for many decades. We explore the ways that, without proper vigilance, government and corruption can become intertwined and feed off each other, destroying the foundations of human prosperity and the very purpose of governance. We review existing efforts to tackle corruption at the national, regional and global levels, and suggest additional ways forward. Finally, we support proposals for the establishment of an International Anticorruption Court (IACC), to greatly strengthen and better implement a range of legal instruments that are already in place, but that have had limited success in arresting the growth of multiple forms of corruption across the planet – affecting developing and developed countries alike. We consider the setting up of an IACC as a necessary adjunct to existing tools to check the spread of what many now regard as a global epidemic.

DEFINING CORRUPTION

Corruption is traditionally defined as the abuse of public office for private gain, including bribery, nepotism and misappropriation; extra-legal efforts by individuals or groups to gain influence over the actions of the bureaucracy; the collusion between parties in the public and private sectors for the benefit of the latter; and more generally influencing the shaping of policies and institutions in ways that

---

[3]   See Pillay, "The Negative Impact of Corruption," and Wolf, "The World Needs an International Anti-Corruption Court," pp. 144–146.

[4]   See, e.g., Chayes, Sarah. 2015. *Thieves of State: Why Corruption Threatens Global Security,* New York and London, W. W. Norton & Company.

[5]   Kerry, John. 2016. "Remarks at the World Economic Forum," US Department of State, January 22. https://2009-2017.state.gov/secretary/remarks/2016/01/251663.htm.

[6]   See, e.g., the hypotheses set forth in Acemoglu, Daron and James A. Robinson. 2013. *Why Nations Fail: The Origins of Power, Prosperity, and Poverty,* London, Profile Books.

benefit the contributing private parties at the expense of the broader public welfare.[7] The benefits are customarily seen as financial, and many people become rich through corruption.

However, the corruption that is eating into the vitals of global society today is more than just the material corruption of bribery, extortion or embezzlement for personal gain. It is any undue preference given to personal or private gain at the expense of the public or collective interest, including the betrayal of a public trust or office in government, but also the manipulation of a corporate responsibility for self-enrichment, the distortion of truth and denial of science to manipulate the public for ideological ends, and even the misuse of a religious responsibility to acquire power and wealth. Corruption is just one expression of the priority given to oneself over others, of egoism over altruism, of personal over collective benefit.[8] It is often said that power corrupts, and absolute power corrupts absolutely. One of the first effects of corruption in government is to reduce the capacity of a public administration to fight corruption, creating a vicious circle from which a government has difficulty extricating itself. Corruption at the governmental level is now so widespread that it is an obvious area for international governance to set standards and intervene in the common interest.

A related issue is organized crime, which exists largely through collusion with governments. This can take the form of turning a blind eye to criminal behavior, perhaps for kickbacks or other advantages, directing government procurement or other contracts to criminal enterprises in return for a share of inflated contracts, and interfering with the course of justice to the benefit of criminals. There is potential for such corruption at all levels, from the individual police officer who rents a gun to robbers at night, to heads of state who accept large cash donations in return for favors. Where governments are incorruptible and prosecute criminal activity with vigor, organized crime has difficulty gaining a foothold.

Corruption and associated organized crime are not just a marginal issue. The illegal economy from organized crime is now estimated at US$2 trillion per year, roughly equivalent to all the world's defense budgets. Bribery has been estimated to amount to US$1 trillion,[9] with the vast majority of bribes going to people in wealthy countries. Ten percent of all public health budgets are lost to corruption.[10] Much of

---

[7] López-Claros, Augusto. 2015. "Removing Impediments to Sustainable Economic Development: The Case of Corruption." *Journal of International Commerce, Economics and Policy* Vol. 6, No. 1, 1550002. 35 p. DOI: 10.1142/S1793993315500027.

[8] Dahl, Arthur Lyon. 2016. "Corruption, Morality and Religion." International Environment Forum blog, http://iefworld.org/ddahl16l.

[9] Kaufmann, Daniel, Aart Kraay, and Massimo Mastruzzi. 2007. "Governance Matters VI: Governance Indicators for 1996–2006 (July)." World Bank Policy Research Working Paper No. 4280. Available at SSRN: https://ssrn.com/abstract=999979.

[10] Anello, Eloy. 2008. *A Framework for Good Governance in the Public Pharmaceutical Sector.* Working draft for field testing and revision. April. World Health Organization, Geneva. www.who.int/medicines/areas/policy/goodgovernance/GGMFramework2008-04-18.pdf.

this money escapes from national control and oversight along with many international financial flows, as another negative dimension of globalization.

The impacts of corruption are not limited to financial losses and diversions or political inefficiency or failures. If leaders are corrupt, others will be inspired to follow the same model. There are many secondary effects of corruption that spread throughout society. For example, the impact of corruption on environmental destruction and mismanagement is often underestimated because, as an illegal activity, it escapes from statistics; yet it is a principal reason for the failure of many efforts at environmental protection and management, whether from traffic in endangered species, illegal logging and fishing, or ignoring or evading environmental regulations. Both the public and private sectors are heavily implicated in this form of corruption, as is organized crime.

Normally it is a government's responsibility to prohibit, investigate and prosecute corrupt behavior within its borders or for which its nationals are responsible. However, there are frequently cases where the highest levels of government are themselves corrupt, or where corruption has become so widespread that it is seen as a normal and legitimate part of politics and simply a cost of doing business.[11] In many cases, the police and courts that should be investigating and prosecuting corrupt behavior are themselves caught up in the system. Criminal prosecutions may then simply become an instrument for eliminating political opponents. Guarantees of immunity from prosecution are another tool used by the corrupt for their own protection. In such situations, national sovereignty becomes a shield behind which to hide illegal activity from international scrutiny.

It is not unknown for a government motivated by corrupt intentions to use legislation or judicial interpretation to render legal those practices that in other states or contexts would be considered corrupt and illegal. For example, removing all limits to the amount of money that individuals or corporate enterprises can donate to the campaign funds of politicians essentially amounts to vote-buying, with politicians becoming dependent on and beholden to the highest bidder.

Only international standards of honesty and definitions of corruption with appropriate means of enforcement will make it possible to intervene in the general public interest where a government has opened the door to corrupt behavior at the expense of its own people. To prevent the rot from spreading, and to protect the public who ultimately pay the price for such corruption, global standards and mechanisms for international intervention are essential.

CORRUPTION WITHIN THE DEVELOPMENT PROCESS

After many years of authorities turning a blind eye, corruption has finally emerged as a central issue in discussions about the effectiveness of development policies. It is

---

[11] López-Claros, "Removing Impediments to Sustainable Economic Development."

now recognized that corruption comes from many sources and undermines the development process in multiple ways. While various remedies have been proposed and are being used in various parts of the world, the results are mixed.

The period since the late 1990s has witnessed a remarkable change in the understanding of what factors matter in creating the conditions for sustainable economic development. The economics profession has come to a new comprehension of the role of such factors as education and skills, institutions, property rights, technology, transparency and accountability. With this broader outlook has come an implicit recognition that promoting inclusive growth requires tackling an expanding set of nontraditional concerns.

One of these concerns is corruption, a subject that has gone from being very much on the sidelines of economic research to becoming a central preoccupation of the development community and of policy-makers in many countries. Experiences and insights accumulated during the postwar period, and reflected in a growing body of academic research, throw light on the causes and consequences of corruption within the development process and on the question of what can be done about it.

Within the development community, the shift in thinking about the role of corruption in development was tentative at first; multilateral organizations remained reluctant to touch on a subject seen as largely political even as they made increasing references to the importance of "good governance" in encouraging successful development. What factors contributed to this shift? One was linked to the fall of the Berlin Wall and the associated collapse in the late 1980s of central planning as a supposedly viable alternative to free markets. As the international community faced the need to assist formerly socialist countries in making a successful transition to democratic forms of governance and market-based economies, it was clear that this would take far more than "getting inflation right" or reducing the budget deficit. Central planning had collapsed not because of inappropriate fiscal and monetary policies but because of widespread institutional failings, including a lethal mix of authoritarianism (with its lack of accountability) and corruption. Overnight, the economics profession was forced to confront a set of issues extending far beyond conventional macroeconomic policy.

Related to the demise of central planning, the end of the Cold War had clear implications for the willingness of the international community to recognize glaring instances of corruption in places where ideological loyalties had earlier led to collective blindness. By the late 1980s, the donor community cut off President Mobutu of (then) Zaire, for instance, no longer willing to quietly reward him for his loyalty to the West during the Cold War.

A second factor was growing frustration with entrenched patterns of poverty in Africa in particular, as well as in other parts of the developing world. The global fight against poverty had begun to produce gains, but these were concentrated largely in

China; in Africa, the number of so-called extremely poor people was actually increasing.[12] During the late 1980s and early 1990s, staff at the International Monetary Fund (IMF) began to look beyond macroeconomic stabilization to issues of structural and institutional reform. Corruption could no longer be ignored.

A third factor had to do with developments in the academic community. Research began to suggest that differences in institutions appeared to explain an important share of the differences in growth between countries. An increasing number of economists began to see corruption as an *economic* issue, and this led to a better understanding of its economic effects.

An important role was also played by the intensifying pace of globalization beginning in the 1980s. Globalization and its supporting technologies have led to a remarkable increase in transparency as well as to growing public demand for greater openness and scrutiny. The multilateral organizations were not immune to these influences. How could one overlook the hoarding of billions of dollars of ill-gotten wealth in secret bank accounts by the world's worst autocrats, many of them long-standing clients of these organizations?

Paralleling these developments, and further raising international public awareness of corruption, were the many corruption scandals in the 1990s involving major political figures. In India and Pakistan, incumbent prime ministers were defeated in elections largely because of corruption charges. In South Korea, two presidents were jailed following disclosures of bribery. In Brazil and Venezuela, bribery charges resulted in presidents being impeached and removed from office. In Italy, magistrates sent to jail a not insignificant number of politicians who had ruled the country in the postwar period, exposing the vast web of bribery that had bound together political parties and members of the business community. In Africa, there was less progress in holding leaders to account, but corruption became harder to hide as new communication technologies supported greater openness and transparency.

Globalization also highlighted the importance of efficiency. Countries could not hope to continue to compete in the increasingly complex global market unless they used scarce resources effectively. And rampant corruption detracted from the ability to do this. Meanwhile, business leaders began to speak more forcefully about the

---

[12] As noted in Chapter 1, World Bank data show that between 1990 and 2015 the number of poor people living on less than US$1.90 per day (the poverty line used f or the definition of extreme poverty) fell from about 2 billion to about 740 million. The reduction in extreme poverty, however, was largely accounted for by the very high economic growth rates in China and, to a lesser extent, in India. In sub-Saharan Africa, for instance, the number of extremely poor people actually rose from 276 million in 1990 to 389 million in 2015. Furthermore, using a less austere poverty line of US$3.20 per day, the number of poor is closer to 2 billion people, which is still an unacceptably high number. At this higher poverty line, the number of poor in Africa in 2015 was about 620 million. More disturbingly, on a US$5.50 poverty line, which still leaves people struggling to cope with the challenges of low income, close to 50 percent of the world's population can be classified as poor.

need for a level playing field and the costs of doing business in corruption-ridden environments.

In the 1990s, the US government made efforts to keep the issue of corruption alive in its discussions with OECD partners, further raising international awareness. The US Foreign Corrupt Practices Act of 1977 had forbidden American executives and corporations to bribe foreign government officials, introducing stiff penalties, including prison terms, for those doing so. Because other OECD countries did not impose such restrictions – in fact, most continued to allow tax deductions for bribe payments, as a cost of doing business abroad – American companies began to complain that they were losing business to OECD competitors. Academics sifting through the data showed that US business activity abroad declined substantially following passage of the law. These developments gave impetus to US government efforts to persuade other OECD members to ban bribery practices, and in 1997 the OECD adopted the Anti-Bribery Convention, an important legal achievement.

Another factor contributing to this shift in attitude was the work of Transparency International, including the publication, beginning in 1993, of its Corruption Perceptions Index. That corruption existed everywhere was a well-known fact. What Transparency International showed was that some countries had been more successful than others in curtailing it. The organization's work helped to focus public attention on corruption and legitimize public discourse on the issue, easing the transition of the multilateral organizations into doing the same.

Transparency International was soon assisted in its efforts by the international organizations themselves. In a speech at the IMF–World Bank annual meeting in 1996, then World Bank President James Wolfensohn did not mince words, saying that there was a collective responsibility to deal with "the cancer of corruption." More importantly, Wolfensohn gave strong backing to efforts by Bank staff to develop a broad range of governance indicators, including indicators specifically capturing the extent of corruption. This made it possible for the Bank, through the use of quantified indicators and data, to focus attention on issues of governance and corruption while not appearing to interfere in the political affairs of its member countries.

POOR GOVERNMENT AND CORRUPTION: INTIMATE BEDFELLOWS?

What are the sources of corruption, and what factors have nourished it and turned it into such a powerful impediment to sustainable economic development? Economists seem to agree that one important source of corruption stems from the distributional attributes of the state.

For better or for worse, the role of the state in the economy has greatly expanded over the past century. In 1913, the world's 13 largest economies had public expenditure averaging around 12 percent of GDP. By 1990, this ratio had risen to 43 percent, and in some of these countries to well over 50 percent. Many other countries saw similar increases. Associated with this growth was a proliferation of benefits under state control and also of the ways in which the state imposes costs on society. A larger state need not be associated with higher levels of corruption – the Nordic countries illustrate this. The benefits range from improved infrastructure, public education, health and welfare, to environmental protection and reining in the monopolistic tendencies of corporations. It is not the size of government itself that is the problem. But the larger the number of interactions between officials and private citizens and the weaker the ethical framework determining socially acceptable behavior, the more opportunities there are for citizens to pay illegally for benefits to which they are not entitled or to avoid costs or obligations for which they are responsible.

From the cradle to the grave, the typical citizen has to enter into transactions with government offices or bureaucrats for countless reasons – to obtain a birth certificate, get a passport, pay taxes, open a new business, drive a car, register property, engage in foreign trade. Indeed, governing often translates into issuing licenses and permits to individuals and businesses complying with regulations in myriad areas. The World Bank's *Doing Business* report, a useful annual compendium of the burdens of business regulations in 190 countries, paints a sobering picture. Businesses in many parts of the world endure numbing levels of bureaucracy and red tape. In fact, the data in the report eloquently portray the extent to which many governments *discourage* the development of entrepreneurship in the private sector.

Not surprisingly, the prevalence of corruption is strongly correlated with the incidence of red tape and cumbersome, excessive regulation, which is not generally linked to the public interest. Figure 18.1 compares the rankings of 177 countries on Transparency International's 2018 Corruption Perceptions Index with their rankings on the *Doing Business* report's Ease of Doing Business Index for the same year. The figure speaks for itself: the greater the extent of bureaucracy and red tape, the greater the incidence of corruption – the correlation coefficient is close to 0.80.

As many surveys have shown, businesses allocate considerable time and resources to dealing with unnecessary bureaucracy. They may often perceive paying bribes as a way to save time and enhance efficiency – and, in many countries, as possibly the only way to get business done without undermining their competitive position relative to those that routinely pay bribes. The more dysfunctional the economic and legal system and the more onerous and ill-conceived the regulations, the greater the incentives to short-circuit the system by paying bribes. The literature is full of examples: the absurdities of central planning in the Soviet Union induced "corruption" on the part of factory managers, to add some flexibility to a system that made a mockery of efficiency in resource allocation. The more irrational the rules, the more likely that participants in the system will find themselves breaking them.

In an insightful analysis in 1964, the Harvard researcher Nathaniel Leff argued that those who viewed corruption as an unremittingly bad thing were implicitly assuming that governments were driven by benevolent motivations and committed to implementing policies that advanced the cause of economic development. In

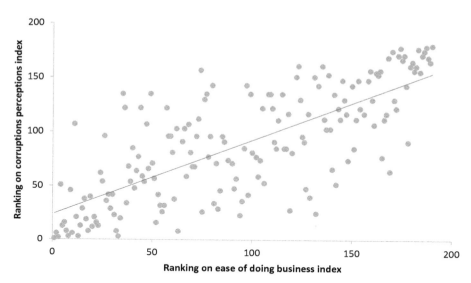

FIGURE 18.1. Rankings of 177 countries on the Corruption Perceptions Index and Ease of Doing Business Index, 2018.
Sources: Transparency International data; World Bank, *Doing Business 2018* (Washington, DC: World Bank, 2017)

reality, Leff thought, policies in many countries were geared largely to advancing the interests of the ruling elite. Leff and his Harvard colleague Joseph Nye both suggested that corruption was partly a response to market distortions, red tape, excessive and unreasonable regulation and bad policies, but that these were themselves affected by the prevailing levels of corruption – in a symbiotic two-way form of causality that turned corruption into an intractable social and economic problem.[13]

Features of government organization and policy may (wittingly or unwittingly) create incentives for corrupt behavior in numerous ways. The tax system is often a source of corruption, particularly where tax laws are unclear or otherwise difficult to understand. This lack of clarity presumably gives tax inspectors and auditors considerable leeway in interpretation, allowing unwholesome "compromises" with taxpayers. The provision of goods and services at below-market prices also creates fertile ground for corruption. It invariably gives rise to some form of rationing mechanism to manage excess demand, requiring the exercise of discretion by government officials. At a meeting at the Central Bank of Russia in May 1992, IMF staff were shown a several-page list of the exchange rates that applied for importing items, from medications and baby carriages to luxury cars. Bureaucrats had managed to come up

---

[13] Leff, Nathaniel. 1964. "Economic Development through Bureaucratic Corruption." *American Behavioural Scientist* Vol. 8, No. 3, pp. 8–14; Nye, Joseph. 1967. "Corruption and Political Development: A Cost-Benefit Analysis." *The American Political Science Review* Vol. 61, pp. 417–427.

with criteria for establishing dozens of different prices for foreign exchange. Needless to say, the list allowed considerable latitude for discretion.

A similar regime existed for export quotas, allowing those who obtained an export license to benefit from the huge gap between the domestic and international price. Another legacy of the Soviet Union was a system of directed credits, essentially highly subsidized loans to agriculture and industry. At rates of interest that were absurdly negative in real terms, these credits were in strong demand and, of course, the criteria for allocating them were extremely opaque.

The incentives for bribes provided in these examples are easy to see; the resulting losses in economic efficiency are similarly evident. Directed credits in Russia did not generally end up with farmers. Instead, they ended up with the highest bidder, who then used the proceeds to buy foreign exchange and finance capital flight (while never repaying the credits or doing so only in deeply depreciated rubles). Export quotas resulted in massive losses for the Russian budget, at a time when the country was going through a severe economic contraction and there were therefore enormous pressures for increased social spending. Susan Rose-Ackerman, one of the leading experts on corruption, refers to the kinds of bribes in these examples as those that clear the market or that equate supply and demand.

Some bribes are offered as incentive payments for bureaucrats. These can take a variety of forms. One is "speed money," ubiquitous in many parts of the world and typically used to "facilitate" some transaction or to jump the queue. Some economists have argued that this kind of bribery could improve efficiency, since it provides incentives to work more quickly and allows those who value their time highly to move faster. Gunnar Myrdal, writing in 1968, pointed out that, over time, incentives could work the other way: bureaucrats may deliberately slow things down or, worse, find imaginary obstacles or create new ones in order to attract facilitation fees. So, in the end, "speed money" is paid not to speed things up but to avoid artificial delays created by corrupt bureaucrats.

Indeed, some of the regulations enforced in many parts of the world are so devoid of rationality that one can only infer that they were introduced to create opportunities for bribery. Far from being a way to enhance efficiency, paying bribes preserves and strengthens the bribery machinery.

All this is not to say that government regulation is inherently wrong. On the contrary, the World Economic Forum has shown that appropriate environmental and social regulations, fairly enforced, can increase business competitiveness and efficiency in meeting social goals. Where corruption makes it possible to get around the regulations, the result is bad for both business and the public welfare.[14]

---

[14] Dahl, Arthur Lyon. 2004. "The Competitive Edge in Environmental Responsibility," in Michael E. Porter, Klaus Schwab, Xavier Sala-i-Martin, and Augusto López-Claros (eds.), *The Global Competitiveness Report 2004–2005.* World Economic Forum. Basingstoke and New York, Palgrave Macmillan, pp. 103–110.

NINE REASONS WHY CORRUPTION IS A DESTROYER OF PROSPERITY

No matter its source, corruption damages the social and institutional fabric of a country in ways that undermine sustainable economic development. A review of some of its consequences helps show why corruption destroys human prosperity.

First, corruption undermines government revenue and therefore limits the ability of the government to invest in productivity-enhancing areas. Where corruption is endemic, people will view paying taxes as a questionable business proposition. There is a delicate tension between the government as tax collector and businesses and individuals as taxpayers. The system works reasonably well when those who pay taxes feel that there is a good chance they will see a future payoff, such as better schools, better infrastructure and a better-trained and healthier workforce. Corruption sabotages this implicit contract.

When corruption is allowed to flourish, taxpayers will feel justified in finding ways to avoid paying taxes or, worse, become bribers themselves. To the extent that corruption undermines revenue, it undermines government efforts to reduce poverty. Money that leaks out of the budget because of corruption will not be available to lighten the burden of vulnerable populations. Of course, corruption also undermines the case of those who argue that foreign aid can be an important element of the fight against global poverty – why should taxpayers in richer countries be asked to support the lavish lifestyles of the kleptocrats in corrupt states?

Second, corruption distorts the decision-making process connected with public investment projects, as the IMF economists Vito Tanzi and Hamid Davoodi demonstrated in a 1997 analysis. Large capital projects provide tempting opportunities for corruption. Governments will often undertake projects of a greater scope or complexity than is warranted by their country's needs – the world is littered with the skeletons of white elephants, many built with external credits. Where resources are scarce, governments will find it necessary to cut spending elsewhere. Tanzi plausibly argued in 1998 that corruption will also reduce expenditure on health and education, because these are areas where it may be more difficult to collect bribes.

Third, there is solid empirical evidence that the higher the level of corruption in a country, the larger the share of its economic activity that will go underground, beyond the reach of the tax authorities. Not surprisingly, studies have shown that corruption also undermines foreign direct investment, because it acts in ways that are indistinguishable from a tax; other things being equal, investors will always prefer to establish themselves in less corrupt countries. Shang-Jin Wei, in a 2000 analysis of data on direct investment from 14 source countries to 45 host countries, concluded that "an increase in the corruption level from that of Singapore to that of Mexico is equivalent to raising the tax rate by 21–24 percentage points."

Fourth, corruption discourages private sector development and innovation and encourages various forms of inefficiency. Budding entrepreneurs with bright ideas will be intimidated by the bureaucratic obstacles, financial costs and psychological burdens of starting new business ventures and may opt to take their ideas to some other, less corrupt country or, more likely, desist altogether. Thus, whether corruption is a barrier to entry into the market or a factor in precipitating early departure, it harms economic growth.

A high incidence of corruption will also mean an additional financial burden on businesses, undermining their international competitiveness. Unlike a tax, which is known and predictable and can be built into a company's cost structure, bribes are unpredictable and will complicate cost control, reduce profits and undermine the efficiency of companies that must pay them to stay in business. In a 1995 analysis using indices of corruption and institutional efficiency, the IMF economist Paulo Mauro showed that corruption lowers investment and thus economic growth.

Fifth, corruption contributes to a misallocation of human resources. To sustain a system of corruption, officials and those who pay them will have to invest time and effort in developing certain skills, nurturing certain relationships and building up a range of supporting institutions and opaque systems, such as secret bank accounts and off-the-books transactions. Surveys of businesses have shown that the greater the incidence of corruption in a country, the greater the share of time that management has to allocate to ensuring compliance with regulations, avoiding penalties and dealing with the bribery system that underpins them – activities that draw attention and resources away from more productive tasks.

Sixth, corruption has disturbing distributional implications. In empirical work done at the IMF in 1998, Gupta, Davoodi and Alonso-Terme showed that corruption, by lowering economic growth, perceptibly pushes up income inequality. It also distorts the tax system, because the wealthy and powerful are able to use their connections to ensure that this system works in their favor. And it leads to inefficient targeting of social programs, many of which will acquire regressive features, with benefits disproportionately allocated to the higher income brackets – as with gasoline subsidies to the car-owning middle classes in India and dozens of other countries.

Seventh, corruption creates uncertainty. There are no enforceable property rights emanating from a transaction involving bribery. A firm that obtains a concession from a bureaucrat as a result of bribery cannot know with certainty how long the benefit will last. The terms of the "contract" may have to be constantly renegotiated to extend the life of the benefit or to prevent its collapse. Indeed, the firm, having flouted the law, may fall prey to extortion from which it may prove difficult to extricate itself. In an uncertain environment with insecure property rights, firms will be less willing to invest and plan for the longer term. A short-term focus to maximize short-term profits will be the optimal strategy, even if this leads to deforestation, say, or to the rapid exhaustion of non-renewable resources.

Very importantly, this uncertainty is partly responsible for a perversion in the incentives that prompt individuals to seek public office. Where corruption is rife, politicians will want to remain in office as long as possible, not because they are even remotely serving the public good but because they will not want to yield to others the pecuniary benefits of high office, and may also wish to continue to enjoy immunity from prosecution. Where long stays in office cease to be an option, a new government, given a relatively short window of opportunity, will want to steal as much as possible as quickly as possible.

Eighth, because corruption is a betrayal of trust, it diminishes the legitimacy of the state and the moral stature of the bureaucracy in the eyes of the population. While efforts will be made to shroud corrupt transactions in secrecy, the details will leak out and will tarnish the reputation of the government. By damaging the government's credibility, this will limit its ability to become a constructive agent of change in other areas of policy. Corrupt governments will have a more difficult time remaining credible enforcers of contracts and protectors of property rights.

Ninth, bribery and corruption lead to other forms of crime. Because corruption breeds corruption, it tends soon enough to lead to the creation of organized criminal groups that use their financial power to infiltrate legal businesses, to intimidate, and to create protection rackets and a climate of fear and uncertainty. In states with weak institutions, the police may be overwhelmed, reducing the probability that criminals will be caught. This, in turn, encourages more people to become corrupt, further impairing the efficiency of law enforcement – a vicious cycle that will affect the investment climate in noxious ways, further undermining economic growth. In many countries, as corruption gives rise to organized crime, the police and other organs of the state may themselves become criminalized. By then, businesses will not only have to deal with corruption-ridden bureaucracies; they will also be vulnerable to attacks from competitors who will pay the police or tax inspectors to harass and intimidate.

In fact, there is no limit to the extent to which corruption, once unleashed, can undermine the stability of the state and organized society. Tax inspectors will extort businesses; the police will kidnap innocents and demand ransom; the prime minister will demand payoffs to be available for meetings; aid money will disappear into the private offshore bank accounts of senior officials; the head of state will demand that particular taxes be credited directly to a personal account. Investment will come to a standstill, or, worse, capital flight will lead to disinvestment. In countries where corruption becomes intertwined with domestic politics, separate centers of power will emerge to rival the power of the state.

At that point, the chances that the government will be able to do anything to control corruption will disappear and the state will mutate into a kleptocracy, the eighth circle of hell in Dante's *Divine Comedy*. Alternatively, the state, to preserve its power, may opt for warfare, engulfing the country in a cycle of violence. And corrupt failed, or failing, states become a security threat for the entire international community – because, as Heineman and Heimann wrote in *Foreign Affairs* in 2006, "they are incubators of terrorism, the narcotics trade, money laundering, human trafficking, and other global crime – raising issues far beyond corruption itself."[15] More recently, Chayes has tracked the regional and international security implications of kleptocracies in such countries as Afghanistan, Egypt and Nigeria, among others, noting the transnational effects of systemic corruption as akin to an "odourless gas" fueling the various identified threats "without attracting much policy attention."[16] "When every government function is up for sale to the highest bidder," she notes, "violations of international as well as domestic law become the norm."[17] The sale of Pakistani nuclear technology to Iran, North Korea and Libya is just one dramatic example.

TACKLING CORRUPTION

As all of these points demonstrate, corruption is a major impediment to effective governance, transparency, economic development and the proper allocation of public funds for public good, as well as the source of a range of very serious transnational security risks. As corruption in governments and the private sector has globalized, so must the efforts to tackle it. An international legal framework for corruption control is essential to deal with its cross-border effects, and fortunately a strong foundation already exists.

New, well-designed international implementation and enforcement tools should give significantly greater effect to existing international conventions in this field, such as the United Nations Convention Against Corruption (UNCAC), with 186 parties (entry into force December 2005), and the 1997 OECD Convention on Combating Bribery of Foreign Public Officials in International Business Transactions, with 43 states parties (entry into force February 1999). In addition to these conventions, there are also a range of regional treaties covering Africa, Europe, and the Americas.

Unlike the OECD convention, the UNCAC creates a global legal framework involving developed and developing nations and covers a broader range of subjects including domestic and foreign corruption, extortion, preventive measures, anti-money-laundering provisions, conflict-of-interest laws and means to recover illicit funds deposited by corrupt officials in offshore banks. As UNCAC only possesses a weak monitoring mechanism, and the implementation of its provisions in effect has been "largely ignored,"[18] enforcement should be a priority in strengthened international governance. Until such enhanced tools are developed, the effectiveness of the UNCAC as a deterrence tool will very much depend on the establishment of adequate national monitoring mechanisms to assess government compliance. Many

---

[15] Heineman, Ben W. and F. Heimann. 2006. "The Long War against Corruption." *Foreign Affairs* 85 (May/June), pp. 75–86.
[16] Chayes, *Thieves of State*, p. 184.
[17] Ibid.
[18] Wolf, "The World Needs an International Anti-Corruption Court," p. 148.

countries need technical assistance to develop the capacity to comply with the UNCAC's provisions. Multinational corporations are both originators of bribery and frequent victims of extortion, and need strong internal controls and sanctions to protect themselves against malfeasance with its resulting damaging revelations and large fines. Additional international legislation may also be required for types of corruption that are insufficiently regulated, and for novel forms of corruption enabled by new technologies.

Others have argued that another workable approach to fighting corruption may be more robust implementation of the anticorruption laws in the 43 states that have signed the OECD's Anti-Bribery Convention. Governments will need to do better in holding to account companies that continue to bribe foreign officials. They have at times been tempted to shield companies from the need to comply with anticorruption laws, in a misguided attempt to avoid undermining their competitive position in other countries. Trade promotion should not be seen to trump corruption control. Governments continue to be afflicted by double standards, criminalizing bribery at home but often looking the other way when bribery involves foreign officials in non-OECD countries.

Another international dimension that is closely related to corruption is the necessary monitoring of international financial flows, only a small part of which reflect real investment in the economy. Apart from speculation, these flows represent major channels for the profits of international organized crime and money laundering, which might be detected with better regulation and monitoring. There is also the crucial issue of offshore financial havens used for tax evasion, transfer pricing and unethical minimization of tax liabilities.[19] A surprising number of wealthy countries also have their own tax-free havens (domestic and in overseas territories) allowing secret ownership, front corporations, little or no reporting, and other mechanisms to facilitate accumulating and hiding wealth. Only international legislation to plug such loopholes will allow more transparency and accountability for the world's wealth.

One other issue requiring international attention is a more ethical approach to the residual liabilities from past corruption. Too many poor and indebted countries have been drained of their resources and wealth for years by corrupt leaders.[20] When the leaders eventually fall, successor governments are still expected to pay back all the accumulated debt with interest. This is one cause of the continuing net transfer of wealth from poor to rich countries, undermining efforts to reduce poverty by 2030 as called for in the Sustainable Development Goals. On the one hand, countries that make effective efforts to stamp out corruption should be rewarded with debt forgiveness, in the context of a program of coherent economic reforms.

---

[19] For a chilling account of this global problem generally, see Shaxson, Nicholas. 2016. *Treasure Islands: Tax Havens and the Men Who Stole the World*, London, Vintage.

[20] See López-Claros, Augusto. 2003. "Drowning in a Sea of Debt," *The New Times*, May, Moscow.

On the other hand, much stronger international mechanisms are required to track down and recuperate the ill-gotten gains stashed abroad by corrupt leaders and their families.[21]

GENERAL STRATEGIES TO FIGHT CORRUPTION

The best defense against corruption is to avoid it happening to begin with, and to reduce or eliminate those situations in which corruption breeds. Much of this is best accomplished at the national level where the will exists, but much can be done within the framework of international governance to facilitate and reinforce national processes. Beyond increasing the benefits of being honest and the costs of being corrupt, one of the present authors has recently summarized some of the options.[22]

For governments that can still hope to reduce corruption, what are some options for reform? Rose-Ackerman, writing in 2016, recommended a two-pronged strategy aimed at increasing the benefits of being honest and the costs of being corrupt, a sensible combination of reward and punishment as the driving force of reforms. While this is a vast subject, some complementary approaches can be proposed.

Pay civil servants well. Whether civil servants are appropriately compensated or grossly underpaid will clearly affect their motivation and incentives. If public sector wages are too low, employees may find themselves under pressure to supplement their incomes in "unofficial" ways. The IMF economists Caroline Van Rijckeghem and Beatrice Weder's 2001 empirical work revealed that in a sample of developing countries, lower public sector wages are associated with a higher incidence of corruption – and higher wages with a lower incidence.[23]

Create transparency and openness in government spending. Governments collect taxes, tap capital markets to raise money, receive foreign aid and develop mechanisms to allocate these resources to satisfy a multiplicity of needs. Some do this in ways that are relatively transparent, with a clear budget process with fiscal targets and priorities, clear authorizations and execution, public disclosure of performance, and independent reviews and audits, and try to ensure that resources will be used in the public interest. The more open and transparent the process, the less opportunity it will provide for malfeasance and abuse. The ability of citizens to scrutinize government activities and debate the merits of public policies also makes a difference.

---

[21] In this respect, more could be done to boost the effectiveness of initiatives such as the Stolen Asset Recovery Initiative (StAR), which is a partnership between the World Bank Group and the United Nations Office on Drugs and Crime (UNODC). Their aim is to "support international efforts to end safe havens for corrupt funds" by bringing together developing country authorities and financial centers "to prevent the laundering of the proceeds of corruption and to facilitate more systematic and timely return of stolen assets."

[22] López-Claros, "Removing Impediments to Sustainable Economic Development."

[23] Van Rijckeghem, Caroline and B. Weder. 1997. "Corruption and the Rate of Temptation: Do Low Wages in the Civil Service Cause Corruption?" *IMF Working Paper* 97/73. Washington, International Monetary Fund.

Thus, press freedoms and literacy levels will shape the context for reforms in important ways. An active civil society with a culture of participation can also be important in supporting strategies to reduce corruption.

Cut red tape. The strong correlation between the incidence of corruption and the extent of bureaucratic red tape suggests the desirability of eliminating needless regulations while safeguarding the essential regulatory functions of the state necessary for environmental and social protection, health and safety. The sorts of regulations on the books of many countries – requiring certifications and licenses for a plethora of reasons – are sometimes not only extremely burdensome but also no longer relevant. Rose-Ackerman suggests that "the most obvious approach is simply to eliminate laws and programs that breed corruption."

Replace regressive and distorting subsidies with targeted cash transfers. Mindless subsidies, often benefiting the wealthy and vested interests, are another example of how government policy can distort incentives and create opportunities for corruption. As noted previously, according to a 2015 IMF study, consumer subsidies for energy products amount to some US$5.3 trillion a year, equivalent to about 6.5 percent of global GDP.[24] These subsidies are very regressively distributed: for gasoline, over 60 percent of benefits accrue to the richest 20 percent of households. Subsidies often lead to smuggling, to shortages and to the emergence of black markets. Leaving aside the issue of the opportunity costs (how many schools could be built with the cost of one year's energy subsidy?), and the environmental effects associated with artificially low prices, subsidies can often put the government at the center of corruption-generating schemes. It would be much better to replace expensive, regressive subsidies with targeted cash transfers.

Deploy smart technology. Frequent, direct contact between government officials and citizens can open the way for illicit transactions. One way to address this problem is to use readily available technologies to encourage a more arm's-length relationship between officials and civil society. The use of online platforms has been particularly successful in public procurement, perhaps one of the most fertile sources of corruption. Purchases of goods and services by the state can be sizable, amounting in most countries to somewhere between 5 and 10 percent of GDP. Because the awarding of contracts can involve bureaucratic discretion, and because most countries have long histories of graft, kickbacks and collusion in public procurement, more and more countries have opted for procedures that guarantee adequate openness and competition, a level playing field for suppliers, clear bidding procedures and the like.

Chile has used the latest technologies to create one of the world's most transparent public procurement systems. ChileCompra, launched in 2003, is an Internet-based public system for purchasing and hiring that serves companies, public

---

[24] Coady, David, I. Parry, L. Sears, and B. Shang. 2015. "How Large Are Global Energy Subsidies?" IMF Working Paper WP/15/105. International Monetary Fund. Washington, DC.

organizations and individual citizens. It is by far the largest business-to-business site in the country, involving 850 purchasing organizations. In 2012, users completed 2.1 million purchases totaling US$9.1 billion. The system has earned a worldwide reputation for excellence, transparency and efficiency.

Many other areas of reform can contribute to reducing corruption. A viable legal system with clear laws, independent judges and credible penalties, supported by a tough anticorruption agency and an ombudsperson to investigate requests for bribes, can show that a government takes the issue seriously. In aid programs, donors can do much more to ensure that the funds provided are used properly and achieve the intended results.

More generally, the types of development projects that are encouraged or supported should also be examined critically from an anticorruption perspective. For example, the tax-free zones and similar arrangements that have been established in many countries to attract foreign businesses and create employment require government subsidies and tax breaks with often ephemeral results that are not cost-effective, but local politicians love them because it is so easy to siphon off money from both government and business.

In many of these measures, the underlying philosophy is to remove the opportunity for corruption by changing incentives, closing loopholes and eliminating misconceived rules that encourage corrupt behavior. But an approach that focuses solely on changing the rules and incentives, along with imposing appropriately harsh punishment for violating the rules, is likely to be far more effective if it is also supported by efforts to buttress the moral and ethical foundations of human behavior. One of the underlying causes of corruption is the general decline or vacuum in moral standards and ethical values, and the corollary glorification of greed and excessive wealth across many societies. Efforts, whether in education, local communities or faith-based organizations, to strengthen values such as honesty, trustworthiness and aspirations that reach beyond the purely material, will always be the best defense against corruption. Such stronger ethical standards will provide a new source of strength in the struggle against corruption, complementing the progress made in recent years in improving the legal framework designed to combat bribery and corruption.

AN INTERNATIONAL ANTICORRUPTION COURT

To support and enhance all of these efforts to fight corruption at lower levels, binding international juridical oversight must also be established. Supranational judicial mechanisms are necessary to prosecute individuals and entities violating established norms on corruption when nations are unable to carry out such prosecutions; such a state of affairs is all too frequently the case when the political establishment and the justice system have been captured by corrupt elites. Such mechanisms could also ensure the effective adjudication of cases of corruption at the international level that escape from or fall between national jurisdictions, or that involve multinational corporations, international criminal syndicates or other trans-national actors that may be difficult for any one nation to prosecute. New inter-national mechanisms could take the form of a free-standing international court focusing on anticorruption, a special chamber of the International Criminal Court (ICC) or of an International Human Rights Tribunal, in combination with a companion technical training and implementation body.

Among the most promising proposals that has emerged to date is for a new, stand-alone International Anticorruption Court that would generally follow the model of the ICC, as currently advocated by US Senior Judge Mark Wolf and others engaged in the Integrity Initiatives International (III).[25] Judge Wolf notes that federal juris-diction at the US national level is commonly employed to address state-level corruption, to deploy appropriate expertise, resources and independence to tackle embedded corruption effectively at the more local level. By analogy, to ensure meaningful prosecutions of corrupt national officials around the world, a higher level of oversight and enforcement is required at the international level.

The IACC model proposed by Wolf and colleagues would embrace the comple-mentarity principle of the ICC, only stepping in with investigations and prosecu-tions when national courts are unwilling or unable to prosecute. Such a court could in particular target "grand corruption," or the abuse of public office for private gain by a country's leaders, which often translates directly into entrenched systemic national norms of corruption, and impunity for the same, as those same leaders control the law enforcement and justice apparatus.[26]

A companion technical institute established at the same time as the proposed IACC could moreover have the capacity to provide innovative and unprecedented internationalized (or "hybrid") ad hoc technical bodies for review and enforcement audits and support of prosecutions at the national level, when appropriate, in addition to general technical training. Such a body could make assessments about whether technical assistance and training would be effective in a given country (and, if so, to whom and when to deliver such training), and could consider possible hybrid prosecutions or "loaning" of highly skilled international staff in service of national prosecutions, according to specific country conditions. An international anticorruption technical institute could build on sound initiatives already begun at the international level, for example, the International Anti-Corruption Coordination Centre (IACCC), recently established and initially seated in the United Kingdom, with the goal of facilitating international cooperation and information exchange on

---

[25] See Wolf, "The World Needs an International Anti-Corruption Court," pp. 149–153. Infor-mation on the III, including other prominent supporters (such as South African jurist Richard Goldstone), can be found at www.integrityinitiatives.org/.

[26] Wolf, "The World Needs an International Anti-Corruption Court."

the prosecution of grand corruption.[27] An international institute could also develop and consolidate crucial techniques and cooperative approaches to international asset location and recovery.

In order to set up an IACC (and a supporting technical institute), a transnational network could be established, akin to that which was instrumental in setting up the ICC, to advocate for this new, badly needed international institution. The global public is yet to become sufficiently aware of the comprehensive dimensions of the issue of grand corruption, including the persistent risks of cross-border infection across a range of serious issues of public concern (transnational organized crime, tax evasion, the theft of foreign development aid, sale of weapons of mass destruction, etc.). The III has set out to raise such transnational public awareness, working in particular to establish a global network of youth and young professionals throughout the world who are dedicated to fighting corruption in their home countries and at the global level.

As with proposals for the establishment of other significant international institutions, a concern commonly raised in relation to an IACC is its cost. However, corruption at the international level involves the loss of trillions of dollars every year; this staggering sum would make the funding of a new international court pale in comparison (the ICC, for example, currently costs about US$167 million annually). Moreover, convictions at the IACC would likely normally also entail the restitution of stolen funds or assets, as well as the imposition of fines, which might be used to subsidize the costs of the court.[28]

---

[27] Members of the IACCC initiative, as of late 2017, included governmental agencies from Australia, Canada, New Zealand, Singapore, the United Kingdom and the United States. Interpol and the US Department of Homeland Security, Immigration and Customs Enforcement, and Homeland Security Investigations were also slated to join.

[28] See Wolf, "The World Needs an International Anti-Corruption Court," p. 150.

19

Education for Transformation

All people ... should have access to life-long learning opportunities that help them acquire the knowledge and skills needed to exploit opportunities and to participate fully in society ... The spread of information and communications technology and global interconnectedness has great potential to accelerate human progress, to bridge the digital divide and to develop knowledge societies.[1]

Transforming Our World: The 2030 Agenda for Sustainable Development, UN

Reforming legal texts, institutions and procedures, however well-conceived the reforms may be, will be inadequate to achieve significantly strengthened, effective international governance if attention is not also paid to engage the support and the participation of all those inhabitants of the planet, whom the institutions of governance, are meant to serve. The foundation for a renewed United Nations must be the shared values of all those who support it, as well as solid "civics" understanding of the nature and functions of key global institutions. Public education to understand our common humanity and the global good for all, both formal and informal, and extensive engagement with the mass media, will be an essential support to the success of proposals such as those contained in this book. Populations around the world will need to be grounded better in key principles of the international order – such as peaceful settlement of disputes and universal respect for human rights – in order to uphold these values and the relevant institutions, no matter where they are located throughout the world.

Crucially, relevant education is also needed for all those who will be called upon to serve in the institutions of global governance, and who will provide leadership or participate in governance processes. Many will need new skills, new ways of

---

[1] United Nations. 2015. *Transforming Our World: The 2030 Agenda for Sustainable Development.* Outcome document of the Summit for the adoption of the Post-2015 Development Agenda, New York, September 25–27. A/70/L.1. New York, United Nations, paras. 15 and 25. www.un .org/ga/search/view_doc.asp?symbol=A/70/L.1&Lang=E.

thinking and particular qualities of evolved leadership relevant to their roles in strengthened international institutions. This chapter sketches the multiple forms of education and the related sharing of knowledge that should accompany the proposed processes of reform, to ensure the correct general cultural and practical circumstances needed for functional global governance, requiring new levels of complexity and investment of resources (financial and otherwise). Chapter 20 on values and principles shares more detail on a range of the values, already inherent or agreed within the current international system, to be incorporated in new educational efforts.

BUILDING PUBLIC SUPPORT

A government of "we the peoples" needs to have the full understanding and general support of the populations governed. Any system of governance that becomes too remote from those benefitting from the governance will fail to gain support and ultimately become ineffective. At the global level, it is particularly challenging to ensure that the entirety of the world's population is educated in the imperative necessity of global governance in particular areas of international responsibility, and to the relevance of proposals such as those presented in this book. This should be the subject of public debate with wide participation. Early attempts to assemble popular support for efforts at substantial UN reform failed because they lacked the "immense works of *preparing world public opinion* for new political leadership."[2]

Fortunately, with information technologies, this is no longer an unrealistic goal. One prerequisite may be the initial support of a range of governments, as their cooperation will be important in reaching their populations through, among others, the formal school system and national media. Engagement of at least some governments would add significant weight to an influential international campaign for strengthened global governance, which could be planned and implemented with the support of the relevant educational institutions, mass media, information platforms and organizations of civil society. In particular, any model including a legislative mechanism based ultimately on universal suffrage must be supported by international civics education, and a generally well-educated and informed global public.

Even before the point of government adoption, civil society organizations, citizen and youth groups, and groups active in social media can increase and coordinate their actions to sensitize the public to the issues at hand and to encourage government action. Efforts are needed to create collective consensus and multiple global fora for vital dialogue and exchange, based on wide partnerships in favor of effective global governance (see Chapter 21). This may in turn catalyze a wide range of governments to act through more formal channels.

---

[2] Baratta, J.P. 2004. *The Politics of World Federation*, Vol. 1. Westport, CT, Praeger, p. 531.

Even if some governments are not fully engaged or committed to international cooperation, their citizens will often still have access to the Internet and to radio and television broadcasts from outside their borders, bringing positive messages to their populations. It will be important to reveal and refute disinformation spread by those who may be opposed to certain institutional reforms for reasons of self-interest.

CENTRAL MESSAGES

At the heart of public education for global governance lies the concept of the interdependence and unity in diversity of the global human community, as discussed in Chapter 20. Shared human identity is a biological fact, and greater international solidarity among peoples has become technologically possible in a world physically reduced to a neighborhood.[3] The advantages of thinking in a more unified manner at the global level and the many merits of establishing a workable "peace system" through international institutions (see Chapter 10) will need to be explained clearly. People should be reassured that their national autonomy, cultural diversity and personal freedom and initiative will be safeguarded through secure institutional checks and balances, and that no one will be left behind. There should be a collective expectation that, around the world, leaders and civil servants will be held to the highest standards of integrity and accountability (see, e.g., Chapter 18).

Public education also needs to take account of the emotional and psychological dimensions of reform processes, whether these are in the form of opposition that comes from the fear of change, or the positive desire to contribute to a better world. Conspiracy theories in some countries about the threat of a "New World Order" or global government revoking their freedom, disarming and enslaving them, need to be addressed. The frustrations of those who have not benefited from globalization or who have lost their dignity and place in society, leaving them open to populist messages, should be resolved. Fundamental global economic, social, cultural and humanitarian goals, already embedded in the UN Charter, must be emphasized and also meaningfully realized in new approaches and institutions, to correct the deficit in current economic globalization that has given "globalism" a bad name (see Chapter 14).

Today's nationalism, nativism and xenophobia are rooted in fear of the "other," which can be prevented and countered through education. Fear generally comes from ignorance. Usually the "other" is a fantasized caricature of the unknown, as once people get to know each other personally, prejudices and misconceptions are usually dispelled. As E.B. White satirically wrote in 1946 (criticizing what he viewed as a too-weak UN):

---

[3] Commission on Global Governance. 1995. *Our Global Neighborhood: Report of the Commission on Global Governance*, Oxford, Oxford University Press.

A world made one, by the political union of its parts, would not only require of its citizen a shift of allegiance, but it would deprive him of the enormous personal satisfaction of distrusting what he doesn't know and despising what he has never seen. This would be a severe deprivation, perhaps an intolerable one. The awful truth is, a world government would lack an enemy, and that is a deficiency not to be lightly dismissed.[4]

Opportunities should be created for nations, races, classes and creeds to mix, work and socialize with one another, with, for example, their children growing up together, as is already happening in many parts of the world. The inevitably increasing migrations driven by climate change and sea level rise, among other driving forces, might be viewed as a constructive mixing of peoples if supported by education that presents human diversity in a positive light. Relatively successful national policy approaches to build cultures of diversity proactively, such as those employed in Canada or Singapore, should be meaningfully explored as models and improved upon at the international level.

Education lies at the very heart of community building, at whatever scale, whether it concerns how we welcome new neighbors from foreign countries, or how we consider the consequences of our own actions and those of our own cities or countries on citizens of other nations. Learning about our shared human identity and basic human rights, values and responsibilities is central to creating a sense of community, including a community of nations (see Chapter 20).[5] Such education needs to start at a very early age, and will be necessary in the context of the global implementation of shared human rights norms, among the range of other reforms suggested.

While global governance may seem very distant from local communities through-out the world, communities are in fact the ultimate foundation for all levels of governance. The expression "think globally, act locally" captures this idea well. Our proposals for a reformed General Assembly, a World Parliamentary Assembly and a Chamber of Civil Society would help to provide better linkages and public account-ability. The steadily increasing involvement of civil society organizations in UN processes already represents a remarkable level of public and grassroots engagement helping to drive UN policy change. The healthier local communities are, the stronger the foundation will be. When principles of participation in local govern-ance, and collective reflection, consultation and common action, are implemented in neighborhoods, villages and communities, they provide a bottom-up complement to, and understanding of, government at higher levels. The values of unity in diversity, solidarity, moderation and service to others are as important at the local

---

[4]   White, E.B. 1946. *The Wild Flag*, Boston, MA, Houghton Mifflin, p. xii.
[5]   Karlsson-Vinkhuyzen, Sylvia. 2017. "Contribution to 'Roundtable on Global Government,'" *Great Transition Initiative*, October. www.greattransition.org/roundtable/global-gov-sylvia-karlsson.

as at the global level and should be reflected in educational activities for all age groups in communities. Local action can be linked to global awareness by emphasizing the idea that each person is playing a small part in the global enterprise of constructing a positive, sustainable peace in the world.

FORMAL EDUCATION

UN member states have pledged to promote education for human rights and global understanding, and a detailed plan of action was approved in 1993 that can equally be applied today to education for global governance.[6] It identifies all the levels of education that should be included, the variety of non-formal settings where such education should be carried out, the specific contexts and difficult situations where relevant education should be targeted to people whose rights are in danger and the specific vulnerable groups to be included.

The Universal Declaration of Human Rights requires governments to "strive by teaching and education to promote respect for these rights and freedoms" (see Preamble and Art. 26).[7] Article 29 of the 1989 Convention on the Rights of the Child requires that states parties – which include virtually every nation of the world – provide children with education directed to:

- The development of respect for human rights and fundamental freedoms, and for the principles enshrined in the Charter of the United Nations;
- The development of respect for the child's parents, his or her own cultural identity, language and values, for the national values of the country in which the child is living, the country from which he or she may originate, and for civilizations different from his or her own;
- The preparation of the child for responsible life in a free society, in the spirit of understanding, peace, tolerance, equality of sexes, and friendship among all peoples, ethnic, national and religious groups and persons of indigenous origin.[8]

The United Nations Educational, Scientific and Cultural Organization (UNESCO) and many other international agencies seek to nurture our common humanity and to help learners become active global citizens.[9] However, the

---

[6] United Nations. 1993. *World Plan of Action for Education on Human Rights and Democracy*, Montreal. http://un-documents.net/wpa-ehrd.htm.

[7] United Nations. 1948. *Universal Declaration of Human Rights*. www.un.org/en/universal-declar ation-human-rights/index.html. www.ohchr.org/EN/UDHR/Documents/UDHR_Translations/ eng.pdf.

[8] UN Convention on the Rights of the Child, Article 29. UN General Assembly, *Convention on the Rights of the Child*, 20 November 1989, United Nations, Treaty Series, Vol. 1577, p. 3.

[9] UNESCO. n.d. *Global Citizenship Education*. https://en.unesco.org/themes/gced.

implementation of these promises, which is currently left to the national level without sufficient monitoring or support, falls short, and people in most of the world receive no education or information about human rights, global issues or the role of global institutions.

The essential foundation for an active citizenry, of course, is universal basic education, so that the entire world population becomes literate in line with the Quality Education Goal 4 of the 2030 Sustainable Development Goals (SDGs). A literate and educated public is essential for the effective functioning of democratic processes and public participation at any level. While progress has been made in many countries, there were still 745 million illiterate people in 2015.[10] As required in SDG4, every child should be taught about her or his common humanity, global issues and governance. UNESCO has focused on global citizenship education for over a decade,[11] and has also prepared objectives and competences for a universal core curriculum for the SDGs in general and sustainable development in particular.[12] The challenge is universal implementation by governments in their school systems. Schools across the world can now be linked online to share experiences of global issues so that students come to understand their shared humanity and the planet they all inhabit. Universal quality education must be a priority for all governments. Where governments are unable to provide this, it should become a responsibility of the international community and the UN system to supply the necessary means. A small fraction of the amount presently spent on arms would be sufficient.

States have already obligated themselves to work on education to address specific global risks. For example, in the UN Framework Convention on Climate Change, Article 6 states that parties "shall promote and facilitate … the development and implementation of educational and public awareness programmes on climate change and its effects."[13] If parties had taken this obligation seriously, the Paris Agreement would have a more solid foundation, as the publics and policy-makers at various levels in all countries, which need to identify their own ambition levels, would have been much better informed about what is at stake.[14]

A second, later step will be to define a more systematized universal core curriculum for the different levels of formal education that would include essential ethical

---

[10] UNESCO. 2017. *Reading the Past, Writing the Future: Fifty Years of Promoting Literacy*, Paris, UNESCO, pp. 21–23, 26.

[11] https://en.unesco.org/themes/gced.

[12] UNESCO. 2017. *Education for Sustainable Development Goals: Learning Objectives*, Paris, UNESCO. https://unesdoc.unesco.org/ark:/48223/pf0000247444.

[13] United Nations. 1992. *United Nations Framework Convention on Climate Change*, New York, United Nations. https://unfccc.int/sites/default/files/conveng.pdf.

[14] Karlsson-Vinkhuyzen, "Contribution to 'Roundtable on Global Government.'"

principles, human rights, civic responsibilities, grounding in the roles and functions of international institutions (and the ideals on which they are founded) and the SDGs as long as they are in effect. This would be integrated into the formal educational systems of all countries, both as a separate subject and integrated into other disciplines, while leaving ample space for cultural, national, and regional specificities to maintain the richness of human diversity.

Even once content appropriate to living in a globalized world has been developed, there will be practical and institutional challenges in its translation into all the necessary global languages and its integration into the curriculum of schools at the national level. Education ministries are notably conservative about change, requiring special efforts to help them to understand their important role. This should be one essential component of the commitments governments make to support steps to strengthen global governance. There would also be the need to train millions of teachers in the use of the materials through focused in-service training. Several years would then be required for students to have passed through a sufficient part of the curriculum to have grasped its essential messages. Given the inevitable time required for educational reform to have an impact, such changes should begin as soon as possible so that their effects will influence and reinforce the processes needed to transform global governance systems.

In tertiary education, there will be significant educational and research opportunities across the range of areas requiring global governance. International institutions will need well-trained civil servants, and national governments will also need to strengthen their structures that interface with global institutions. This may challenge academic institutions structured along disciplinary lines, as many governance issues are transdisciplinary and require integration across many fields. Certain core skills such as systems thinking and the ethical principles upon which governance is founded need to be widely taught as part of general education. Student exchange programs between universities at the international level (which are already occurring with unprecedented frequency) can be further systematized, also reinforcing a sense of global citizenship, as the European Union has employed the Erasmus inter-European student exchange program, building a new generation of European citizens.

The time may well come in the future when governments will see the need for an official international auxiliary language (e.g., a shared, common global language, spoken by all, in addition to local language(s)) that could be chosen or created to provide everyone with a means for inter-communication within an evolving global system, while still protecting national and subnational language diversity. Research could already be undertaken on what would be the most desirable characteristics for such a language, how it might be developed or selected, and how it could be introduced gradually to support better communication and understanding.

INFORMAL EDUCATION

One important group to reach and educate about global governance is the members of the world's parliaments and political assemblies, political leaders and influential personalities. Despite their responsibilities, they may often be behind even the majority of the citizens they should be serving in their understanding of global issues and priorities. Since such leaders and influencers are often isolated within their groups of advisors or entourage and access to them is limited, special events to reach such circles will need to be organized, where objective information, relevant ethical principles, and the issues and challenges can be discussed frankly.

Moreover, there are many other channels for education beyond the formal school system. Many civil society organizations have great capacities to reach their own target groups. They can find their particular messages within the global governance framework and add their support to the educational process. Religious organizations, in particular, have both formal educational institutions and Sunday schools, madrasas, children's classes or other community educational activities. The moral and ethical values behind a more peaceful, just and sustainable world, including good governance, social justice, respect for others, moderation and other spiritual values, can easily find their place in these educational programs.[15]

Generations that are beyond formal schooling will need to be reached with public education campaigns. Their fears and doubts should be addressed and reassurance provided that a strengthened layer of governance at the planetary level will not be threatening, but will contribute fundamentally to ensuring peace and prosperity for all. Their justifiable skepticism based on poor experiences with discredited national governments will have to be overcome. This is a formidable challenge but an important support to the necessary transformation.

Special attention should be given to all those whose livelihoods are linked to those parts of the economy that will be negatively impacted by the transition to a true collective security system with the peaceful settlement of disputes at the international level, as discussed in Chapter 9 on disarmament. They will need guarantees of retraining for new, more constructive forms of employment.

INFORMATION TECHNOLOGIES AND SOCIAL MEDIA

The potential of the Internet to reach the vast majority of humanity has expanded so rapidly that we are far from understanding the best ways to employ this potential for the common good. The UN Secretary-General's High-level Panel on Digital

---

[15] See arguments for the greater involvement of diverse religious communities in the promotion of human rights in Penn, Michael, Maja Groff, and Naseem Koroush. 2019. "Cultivating Our Common Humanity: Reflections on Freedom of Thought, Conscience, and Religion," in Neal S. Rubin and Roseanne L. Flores (eds.), *The Cambridge Handbook of Psychology and Human Rights*, Cambridge, Cambridge University Press, chapter 13.

Cooperation has recommended a strengthening of international governance of this new potential in order to foster global digital cooperation, build an inclusive digital economy and society, develop human and institutional capacity, protect human rights and human agency, and promote digital trust, security and stability.[16]At present it is excessively dominated by too few companies in a near-monopoly position motivated primarily by profit, without due regard for public service. At the same time, there is enormous capacity to use social media and Internet platforms, together with the wide spread of mobile phone technologies extending their reach even in least developed countries, to provide most of the world's population with access to information at a scale never before imagined. As mentioned previously, it is the new information and communications technologies that bring universal education into the realm of practical possibility. This potential should be developed in positive service to the shared ideals that will emerge as global governance is strengthened and becomes more effective. The popularity of social media should be harnessed to spread the main messages about the cultivation of global solidarity, the ethical principles being applied and the practical steps being taken to make enhanced and functional global governance a reality for everyone – delivering on the various promises enshrined in the Charter with respect to social and economic development, human rights, peace and security, and so on. Public institutions and civil society organizations should be increasingly proactive in using modern media for public education, countering forces driven exclusively by the profit motive, movements manipulating public opinion and the excesses of youth or immaturity. A well-informed public is in a better position to hold governments to account for the commitments they have made.[17] There are already many small-scale efforts in this direction that could be scaled up.

Resources on UN reform and global governance should be freely available on the Internet and the range of social media platforms in forms and languages accessible to many audiences, with coverage and explanations of the main events as reform is discussed and implemented. Transparency is an essential part of building public confidence that the global transformations are in the collective best interests.

The capacity of online education, whether in courses offered by formal educational institutions, massive open online courses (MOOCs) that can reach many thousands, or less formal opportunities for continuing education, all have great potential to build human capacity with a minimum of resources. Reform processes should be accompanied by a wide range of online educational opportunities, both to build public understanding and to prepare people for the many emerging opportunities for service and employment.

---

[16] UN Secretary-General's High-Level Panel on Digital Cooperation. 2019. *The Age of Digital Interdependence*. Report presented June 10, 2019. New York: United Nations. www.un.org/en/pdfs/DigitalCooperation-report-for%20web.pdf.

[17] Karlsson-Vinkhuyzen, "Contribution to 'Roundtable on Global Government.'"

THE MASS MEDIA

As public opinion in most countries is formed by the mass media, it is clear that the media should have an important role in covering and explaining the various steps taken to reform and strengthen the United Nations system. Better education of journalists on these issues would be one important measure, along with the provision of access to reliable sources of information for journalistic communities. The media could also be encouraged not only to report the negative news regarding all the problems of the world, but also to tie them to some discussion of workable solutions. Widespread debate will be essential to inform the decisions to be taken by the governments of the world as they move forward to transform governance at the international level. Transparency is important to build public trust. The media themselves will need to rise above traditional roles that may include the defense of national interests and insular views. Journalists should be kept well informed of each step in the process through newswires and accessible reports, both from official sources and from civil society.

Given the importance of the mass media and news organizations in informing the public and shaping public opinion, the UN should consider the adoption of a universal ethical code for objective and responsible reporting,[18] also assuring the independence of journalists, initially as voluntary guidelines and later after General Assembly reforms with mechanisms for its enforcement. It is important to ensure protection of the media from manipulation by special interests while encouraging transparency and the expression of a full range of viewpoints and perspectives. There are challenges today from journalists who are killed or imprisoned; authoritarian regimes that stifle debate; hidden filters in search engines that facilitate confirmation bias; the fabrication of alternative facts and false news; the intentional spread of rumors and conspiracy theories to create fear, mistrust and disunity; the covert infiltration of the media by foreign powers for political ends including the destabilization of states; and the monopoly position of a few multinational corporations profiting from information technologies. Many of these problems escape today from national legislation and control and require an international framework.

RESPONSIBILITY IN THE UN

The United Nations should itself play a leading role in building public understanding of its purpose and actions in the common global interest. It already has

---

[18] There are many professional codes of ethics for journalism, and the Council of Europe adopted a resolution on the topic, but these are voluntary and geographically limited in scope. With rapidly evolving media through which anyone can transmit information, including "fake news" for profit or vested interests without adequate regulation or control, together with political repression and manipulation of journalism and the media, existing codes are clearly inadequate to the challenges of the globalized world of information.

UNESCO, with extensive experience in education but limited means or influence on governments. There is a problem in terms of the coordination of international educational programming within the present UN system, where efforts are fragmented. The UN produces excellent publications but they are poorly distributed. A reformed UN system will therefore need a coherent collective strategy for education for global citizenship and civic engagement. It should build networks and partnerships with all those involved in the creation, communication and transmission to future generations of knowledge relevant to global governance and planetary sustainability.

Its functions should be to:

- strengthen cooperation between knowledge centers in the UN system and governments, universities, business, Internet companies and civil society, and ensure that Internet access is accessible, secure and trustworthy;
- increase capacity in all countries to take part in global governance, and provide leaders, civil servants and other actors with the necessary abilities and qualities;
- ensure equal access to knowledge, particularly in developing countries;
- connect global knowledge platforms to every government and parliamentary website to give policy-makers, politicians and citizens direct access to global knowledge through their own governance portals;
- promote information in ways that enable citizens and decision-makers to find and use knowledge effectively.

Educational outreach by the UN system should be linked to its own internal efforts at knowledge management, which recognize knowledge as a strategic asset.[19] The UN has an enormous pool of information and experience relevant to global governance that should be maintained and transmitted as reforms are instituted and the system is upgraded for its new responsibilities.

The current UN News Service should be significantly expanded in order to provide impartial and quality information on UN programs and processes to populations worldwide, so that this knowledge becomes commonplace and enhanced UN powers are understood.

Without undermining the complementary role of independent journalism, the UN News Service should explain the sometimes-arcane ways of international diplomacy in stories that the general public can understand. It should earn the confidence of people everywhere, so that questions concerning the veracity of other reports can be compared with a reliable and objective global source. The built-in

---

[19] Dumitriu, Petru. 2016. *Knowledge Management in the United Nations System*, Geneva, UN Joint Inspection Unit. www.unjiu.org/sites/www.unjiu.org/files/jiu_document_files/products/en/reports-notes/JIU%20Products/JIU_REP_2016_10_English.pdf.

bias of national perspectives is well known, particularly where there are issues of conflict between states. This could be neutralized with facts from the UN itself. A reinforced and adequately funded UN would have the means to do this.

The constructive role of the UN and its agencies around the world also needs to be told more clearly, so that people can see the benefits that they will derive from UN action as well. A global sense of solidarity needs to emerge concerning people in need, the victims of disaster and the constructive actions that have overcome past problems and built resilience and reassurance in formerly suffering communities. Positive stories are needed to counterbalance the negative news that frequently makes headlines.

LEADERSHIP

Leadership and governance are often closely associated, as most forms of national governance have featured strong individual leaders such as kings or queens, auto-crats, dictators or presidents. Unfortunately, this focus on personal leadership too often brings to the top people (historically mostly men) with strong egos and a desire for power and wealth, who will often employ any means to achieve their ends and then wish to hold on to power indefinitely. Many political processes reinforce this selective pressure. The characteristic old leadership styles, whether authoritarian, paternalistic, "know-it-all," or manipulative, all commonly seek to dominate decision-making, serve an egoistic need for power and neglect to develop the potentialities of the group being led.[20] The result is governance that is generally not in the best interest of those being governed. This bad reputation is one reason why some are opposed to the concept of a world government, since they assume that any such government could be taken over by an autocrat or an elite or corrupt class that could never be dislodged.

Nor is the world and its citizenry protected from politicians, seemingly mentally healthy when they first come to high office, who may become thoroughly corrupted by the exercise of power and increasingly detached from reality, trying to hold on to office as they come to believe that they are indispensable to their respective nations' stability and prosperity.[21] Narcissistic personality traits may push people to seek

---

[20] Anello, E. 1997. "Distance Education and Rural Development: An Experiment in Training Teachers as Community Development Agents." Doctoral dissertation. Amherst, University of Massachusetts. Doctoral dissertations available from Proquest. AAI9721427. https://scholar works.umass.edu/dissertations/AAI9721427.

[21] See, Kelly, E., Elizabeth W. Morrison, Naomi B. Rothman, and Jack B. Soll. 2011. "The Detrimental Effects of Power on Confidence, Advice Taking, and Accuracy." *Organizational Behavior and Human Decision Processes*, Vol. 116, No. 2, pp. 272–285. https://doi.org/10.1016/j .obhdp.2011.07.006; Guinote, Ana. 2017. "How Power Affects People: Activating, Wanting, and Goal Seeking." *Annual Review of Psychology*, Vol. 68, pp. 353–381. https://doi.org/10.1146/ annurev-psych-010416-044153.

leadership but are not conducive to effective leadership.[22] As citizens we are not entrusted with the responsibility of driving a car without providing evidence to the relevant authorities that we are familiar with traffic rules and the workings of an automobile. We think nothing, however, of entrusting vast responsibility and, in some cases, the possibility of wreaking havoc on the world through the misuse of that power, without any evidence of suitability (mental, moral, psychological) for the job. An improved system of global governance should consider implementing proper checks on potential leaders, to be embedded in various institutional processes (e.g., through expert psychological review panels, which are now being employed in the private sector and for many leadership roles). It does not require much imagination to think about the calamities that could have been averted if such safeguards had been in place during our blood-soaked twentieth century.

To avoid these risks, any system of global governance needs safeguards to prevent any tendency to autocracy, both by ensuring that the roles of individuals with power and authority are minimized and properly limited, and by a strong program of selection and ongoing education to ensure that all those within the system reflect attributes of altruism, service and dedication to the common good.

This means that the qualities of good leadership in institutions of global governance may be quite different from leadership as currently understood or commonly tolerated in some governments or businesses. In studies about leadership competencies, the most important were to have high ethical and moral standards and humility, and to be focused on the truth.[23] This would be particularly important in global governance, where giving priority to the global collective good will be of great importance.

There has been considerable work on values-based leadership, or "moral leadership," which can suggest some of the qualities to be sought in selecting and

[22] Nevicka, Barbara, Femke S. Ten Velden, Annebel H.B. De Hoogh, and Annelies E. M. Van Vianen. 2011. "Reality at Odds with Perceptions: Narcissistic Leaders and Group Performance." *Psychological Science*, Vol. 22, No. 10, pp. 1259–1264. DOI: 10.1177/0956797611417259; Nevicka, Barbara, Annebel H.B. De Hoogh, Deanne N. Den Hartog, and Frank D. Belschak. 2018. "Narcissistic Leaders and Their Victims: Followers Low on Self-Esteem and Low on Core Self-Evaluations Suffer Most." *Frontiers in Psychology*, Vol. 9, Article 422. DOI: 10.3389/fpsyg.2018.00422.

[23] Collins, Jim. 2001. "Level 5 Leadership: The Triumph of Humility and Fierce Resolve," in Peter Ferdinand Drucker, Clayton M. Christensen, Daniel Goleman, and Michael E. Porter (eds.), *HBR's 10 Must Reads on Leadership*, Boston, MA, Harvard Business Review Press, 2011, pp. 115–136; Cooke, David and William R. Torbert. 2005. "Seven Transformations of Leadership," in *HBR's 10 Must Reads on Leadership*, Boston, MA, Harvard Business Review Press, 2011, pp. 137–161; Giles, Sunnie. 2016. "The Most Important Leadership Competencies, According to Leaders Around the World." *Harvard Business Review*, March 15. https://hbr.org/2016/03/the-most-important-leadership-competencies-according-to-leaders-around-the-world.

educating leaders for global governance.[24] In summary, these explore three aspects of leadership: the objective or mission of leadership, the style of leadership, and the individual morality and motivational drive needed for a leadership role in societal change. Motivation concerns the personal values of the leader, and whether they are driven primarily by self-interest or altruism.

Education at all ages can cultivate in people the ability to move away from the all-too-common "cultures of contest," where egos strive for themselves or their own group, to a culture of cooperation for the benefit of themselves and all others.[25] It is possible to nurture a culture of global solidarity through education or processes of cooperative interaction.[26] A moral leadership framework can have considerable potential to clarify or change people's motivation to serve their communities.[27] The need to consider the implications of actions with consequences for many generations brings a spiritual, ethical or philosophical dimension to leadership.[28]

One "moral leadership" framework that has been developed since the late 1990s is based on interrogating and transcending traditional, unconscious mental models and developing new capabilities, such as utilizing participatory techniques as well as practicing more horizontal and less vertical power structures. It is a model of leadership dedicated to personal and collective transformation, committed to moral values and principles, based on the value of truthfulness and guided by the exercise of capabilities in service of the common good. It has a clear vision of the society it wishes to create and the strategies that will help bring it into being, and acts on the basis of this vision and these strategies. It entails a deep personal commitment to strive for individual transformation through the development and exemplification of a life based on ethical principles, characterized by qualities of integrity and empathy. It aims for collective transformation through actions that promote community cohesion and justice. In summary, it is leadership characterized by service to the common good, selfless, listening, reflective and persevering.[29] Such a framework at the core of education for leadership in global governance, combined with high levels of technical and administrative capacity of officials, could ensure the efficacy of any institution.

[24] Vinkhuyzen, Onno M. and Sylvia I. Karlsson-Vinkhuyzen. 2014. "The Role of Moral Leadership for Sustainable Production and Consumption." *Journal of Cleaner Production*, Vol. 63, pp. 102–113. http://dx.doi.org/10.1016/j.jclepro.2013.06.045.

[25] Karlberg, M. 2004. *Beyond the Culture of Contest*, Oxford, George Ronald.

[26] Jäger, J. et al. 2007. "Vulnerability of People and the Environment: Challenges and Opportunities," in UNEP (ed.), *Global Environmental Outlook*, Vol. 4: *Environment for Development*, Nairobi, United Nations Environment Programme, pp. 301–394.

[27] Anello, "Distance Education and Rural Development."

[28] Allen, K.E., S.P. Stelzner, and R.M. Wielkiewicz. 1998. "The Ecology of Leadership: Adapting to the Challenges of a Changing World." *Journal of Leadership & Organizational Studies*, Vol. 5, No. 2, pp. 62–82.

[29] Anello, E. and J.B. Hernández. 1996. "Moral Leadership." Núr University, Santa Cruz, Bolivia. Unpublished translation from the Spanish. Summarized in Vinkhuyzen and Karlsson-Vinkhuyzen, "The Role of Moral Leadership for Sustainable Production and Consumption."

Complementary to the proactive training of good leaders with requisite qualities is the establishment of safeguards to hold leaders and governments to account for the most serious violations of international standards, including the proposed International Anticorruption Court (Chapter 18), the International Criminal Court (Chapter 10) and the proposed International Human Rights Tribunal (Chapter 11).

Another complementary approach is to favor group leadership, in which authority is vested in a consultative body that brings diverse perspectives together in a common search for the global interest. This can draw on the strengths of each individual present, while neutralizing their shortcomings. The ideal would be to reach a consensus, but majority voting would also be possible. Since no individual would have power or authority, many of the risks of individual leadership would be avoided. This more collaborative model has some common features with the consensual system of government in Switzerland, and with some religious systems of governance.[30]

It will also be important that leadership in international organizations be gender balanced and fully reflect human cultural differences, moving further away from the political interests and power politics of some of the present United Nations appointment processes for leadership positions, to rather emphasize competence and commitment to the global common good.

FORMING AN INTERNATIONAL CIVIL SERVICE

The staff of the UN Secretariat, its programs and specialized agencies, is recruited from all parts of the world, with certain guidelines to respect a balance of nationalities. If international governance is to respect the principles of unity in diversity and leaving no one behind, then the people within the system need to reflect the spectrum of human diversity and to bring their unique perspectives to the administration of the global community.

One of the enabling mechanisms to ensure coherence and efficiency in the international civil service will be education on the principles of the UN Charter and other founding documents, the core values and ethical principles that every civil servant should respect and the basic procedures of administration. Since such education will not necessarily be available to every recruit, and setting standards too high may exclude more disadvantaged groups from such opportunities for service, the UN system itself should provide enhanced more educational opportunities on recruitment and through regular in-service training. The UN Staff College should also give existing staff new skills as they move up to higher responsibilities.

Special training would also be needed for the personnel of an International Peace Force and its reserves (see Chapter 8), so that volunteers receive not only the

---

[30] This is the model used, for example, in the administration of the Bahá'í Faith or in Quaker business meetings.

necessary military skills but also a clear understanding of the high purpose of their missions and the ethical principles that should guide all their actions in the common interest, in the performance of such a sensitive function. Accepting that the use of force may sometimes be necessary to bring or restore peace will always involve careful operations to achieve enforcement without a motive of retribution or harming the innocent.

An International Judicial Training Institute (see Chapter 10) is likewise imperative to ensure that members of the international judiciary have the requisite levels of independence, knowledge base and technical skill required for the enhanced new international legal institutions that are crucial for effective, balanced and fair global governance.

The UN has always aimed to recruit the most able staff available. The Noblemaire principle, first formulated in the early days of the League of Nations, states that:

> for the international civil service, only a global salary system could ensure both equity and the necessary mobility of staff. In line with the principle of 'equal pay for equal work', no distinction could be admitted in the remuneration of internationally recruited staff on the grounds of their nationality or of salary levels in their own countries. Since the organisations must be able to recruit and retain staff from all Member States, the level of remuneration must be sufficient to attract those from the countries where salary levels are highest.[31]

By extension, every effort should be made to recruit the most able staff from everywhere in the world, compensating through education where necessary the deficiencies in training available in more disadvantaged countries.

Service in international governance should be seen as a highly attractive vocation if it is to attract the most able candidates. The combination of general education on governance and civic responsibility and on the high ideals of the UN system throughout the world will enhance its attractiveness for the most able and highly motivated people to join the international civil service, increasing its effectiveness even further.[32]

INFORMATION AS AN INTERVENTION

A global government needs means of enforcement if it is to resolve key global problems. The ultimate means is the use of force, which could be justified in extreme situations, for example, against a government that has itself resorted to force in a serious breach of international law or to aggress its neighbors. Obviously, any

[31] ICSC. n.d. "The Noblemaire Principle," in *Compendium*, International Civil Service Commission. https://icsc.un.org/compendium/display.asp?type=22.12.1.10.
[32] Katirai, Foad. 2001. *Global Governance and the Lesser Peace*, Oxford, George Ronald.

other means of intervention short of force should be used whenever possible. Information and education should be considered among those options.

One specific challenge in the implementation of UN actions for peace and security, and other relevant global issues, is the need to counteract disinformation, propaganda and hate speech, which can too easily incite violence. The case of Rwanda, where extremist radio stations incited the population to genocide with great effect,[33] shows the importance of a UN capacity to neutralize or counter such messages, providing alternative sources of information in which the population can have confidence. This can be one form of intervention among others in crisis situations.

There may be many other situations where governments malfunction, or extremist movements try to hold sway over a population, where objective information from a neutral UN source could defuse a dangerous situation and restore order. Educational countermeasures could be employed for preventive action within vulnerable groups, for example, to counter terrorist organizations which use information channels to attract recruits.

ACCESS TO KNOWLEDGE

Behind every educational effort lies the basic principle of access to knowledge for everyone. Education both conveys knowledge and teaches how to access it. Global governance must ensure that every person on the planet can acquire the knowledge needed to be a constructive and informed member of society. Every community should be invited to collect, preserve and transmit the knowledge of its history, culture, arts, agriculture and industries, and every nation has its own rich heritage. The advancement of science depends on the free exchange of knowledge, in which everyone, everywhere should participate. An evolving global civilization will increasingly reflect the knowledge required to live peacefully and sustainably on this planet.

One challenge that will require some innovative global legislation and regulation in the framework of the World Intellectual Property Organization (WIPO) will likely be to modify the present regimes for intellectual property to ensure and facilitate a universal global right of access to knowledge. The present regimes are too slanted to favor private interests profiting from knowledge and artistic creations sold for the highest price the market can bear. The patent system for inventions and chemical or medical innovations also places too much emphasis on the profits of the holders of the patents above widespread sharing for the general good. The limited time of a patent's validity is intended to allow the inventor a reasonable return for the effort of discovery and development to market, but under current systems this often excludes the poor majority of humanity from any benefit until the patent has expired. In the case of life-saving medicines at least, this is ethically questionable.

---

[33] Akhavan, Payam. 2017. *In Search of a Better World: A Human Rights Odyssey*, Toronto, House of Anansi Press.

Before the development of the Internet, knowledge was distributed on material supports that had a cost, such as books, journals, records, films or compact discs, or performed in theaters or shown in galleries or museums. With new information technologies, knowledge and creative works have dematerialized, and can be made available at little or no cost to everyone around the world with the necessary technology to access them. Information should not be a scarce resource to be rationed through the market. On the contrary, it gains in value to society the more it is shared.

A helpful distinction may be made between two types of knowledge and creative works. Universal access should generally be facilitated or guaranteed to those that serve to inform, educate, enlighten and uplift the individual through the arts and culture, or that advance scientific knowledge and understanding, furnish citizens with news and necessary information, improve health and well-being, provide a basis for policy-making, and facilitate technological innovation and thus contribute to the general good. On the other hand, it is appropriate for the entertainment industry to charge for its productions. The knowledge necessary to be good global citizens and to develop each individual's capacity to be of service to society should always be accessible, regardless of ability to pay.

Today the intention of intellectual property rights to reward the creators has in many quarters been captured by corporate actors focused too narrowly on profit. One salient example is scientific knowledge. If scientists want to publish their findings in reputable journals or books, they must sign away their intellectual property rights to the publisher while receiving no remuneration, only the recognition that comes from having their work read by others. In some cases, they must pay high page charges for open access. Peer reviewers also contribute their knowledge and judgment without any personal benefit as part of the open culture of science. Currently the major scientific publishers have bought up the journals of scientific societies and consolidated into a few large multinationals. Expensive books and journal subscriptions go only to the best-endowed university libraries. Individual scientists outside such institutions, or in economically disadvantaged countries that cannot afford to buy the literature, can access the scientific literature online, but only by paying a high fee to read each article, even those that they have authored, which is generally beyond their means. This recent privatization of the commons of scientific knowledge effectively restricts cutting-edge science to only the wealthiest countries and researchers in institutions.[34] A new kind of scientific poverty is thus spreading around the world; this trend must be actively countered and reversed at the international level to ensure the steady advancement of science, knowledge

---

[34] Dahl, Arthur Lyon. 2018. *Information: Private Property of Public Good?* International Environment Forum blog, April 12. https://iefworld.org/node/921; Lawton, Graham. 2018. "The Scandal of Scholarship" (review of the film *Paywall: The Business of Scholarship*, directed by Jason Schmitt). *New Scientist*, Vol. 240, No. 3201, October 27, p. 46. The European Union and some other jurisdictions are beginning to require open access publication for research they fund, but their influence is regional, not global.

generally and innovation at the global level. There is a counter-movement toward open access, but it still covers only a fraction of the scientific literature, and not the most significant part.[35]

RECOMMENDED ACTIONS

It is clear that a reformed United Nations needs capacities in a range of domains relevant to education, including support to public education for global citizenship, a news flow on UN reform and actions around the world, a significant presence on the Internet and in social media, and close links with the national governments it serves. Internally it needs to give more profound education in UN values to new recruits and all staff, and continuing education to build staff capacities. It should create a global framework for ethical journalism, the free access to science and other knowledge necessary for the good functioning of global governance, and safeguards against any infringements on every individual's rights to education, general knowledge and objective information. As the global system matures, the UN could become a guarantor of the quality of leadership at the national level in service to the common good, both nationally and internationally.

[35] Suber, Peter. 2012. *Open Access*, Cambridge, MA, MIT Press.

PART V

Foundations for a New Global Governance System

20

Values and Principles for an Enhanced International System: Operationalizing Global "Good Governance"

The United Nations should transform itself from a large community of governments, diplomats and officials into a joint institution for each inhabitant of this planet ... The most important thing that we should seek to advance in the era of globalization is a sense of global responsibility. Somewhere in the primeval foundations of the world's religions we find, basically, the same set of underlying moral imperatives. It is in this set of thoughts that we should look for the source, the energy and the ethos for global renewal of a truly responsible attitude towards our Earth and all its inhabitants, as well as future generations. Without the ethos emanating from a rediscovered sense of global responsibility, any reform of the United Nations would be unthinkable, and without meaning.[1]

Vaclav Havel, President of the Czech Republic

At the foundation of any effective institution must be a common understanding of its purpose, basic values and operating principles. If we are to reform the United Nations and take it to the next significant evolutionary step in global governance, we need to start with the values and principles already grounded in UN declarations, statements and existing materials.[2] In this chapter we briefly discuss several clusters of substantive values and principles relevant to international governance. Whether rooted in the core precepts of global philosophies or religions (as Havel notes), or in international secular sources, the range of widely affirmed values and principles on which governments have agreed at the UN and in associated processes represent a repository of common global aspirations. Collective action on the basis of shared,

---

[1] Vaclav Havel, President of the Czech Republic, Statement at Millennium Summit, General Assembly Plenary 3, Press Release GA/9758 8th Meeting (PM), September 8, 2000. www .un.org/press/en/2000/20000908.ga9758.doc.html.

[2] See, e.g., Spijkers, Otto. 2011. *The United Nations: The Evolution of Global Values and International Law*, Cambridge, Intersentia. See also Ignatieff for a practical-philosophical exploration of what international "ordinary virtues" might bind us. Ignatieff, Michael. 2017. *The Ordinary Virtues: Moral Order in a Divided World*, Cambridge, MA and London, Harvard University Press.

internalized values and principles is crucially important, facilitating trust among diverse actors, engendering productive consultation and intelligent, good-faith exchange.[3] When institutions and communities at all levels of governance are guided by shared values and common goals, they function effectively and do not require heavy-handed enforcement. Moreover, internalized, shared values at the international level facilitate addressing global complexity and the vast, diverse field of actors associated with our new global governance landscape in which decentralized and networked globalization also engages a wide range of private, non-state actors.[4] Values and principles are not cosmetic, but rather provide a basis for designing "hard" obligations, as well as effective, legitimate institutions and governance processes with appropriate checks and balances.

In this chapter we also review operational values associated with the processes of "good governance," as we feel strongly that the international community should commit to and genuinely realize *good* governance as a key value at the international level. There should be a shared international aim for genuinely functional global governance, achieving the goals the international community has set out for itself, including the full implementation of the "peace system" vision,[5] as well as other laudable aims of the Charter such as social and economic progress. These efforts must be grounded in values conducive to general human well-being, to be achieved within the parameters of planetary boundaries, while addressing the existential crises that we now confront caused by exceeding these boundaries.[6] Tireless and painstaking efforts should be employed until these aims are realized.

A common and mundane criticism of the UN is that it is "all talk," and that there is significant hypocrisy when the organization's explicit aspirations and declarations and other statements are adopted but not implemented. We call for a new phase of implementation of agreed international norms, and the concrete realization of stated international aspirations, through enhanced international institutions and processes, such as those described in this book. However, as Havel notes, a new ethical commitment and a much deeper sense of global responsibility are required if we are to build these institutions and to confront the global challenges we now face. New international mechanisms must be developed that are equipped to solve our

---

[3]   Hence the emphasis and the practical importance we put on education, including the moral dimension, for a renewed international system (see Chapter 19 on education for transformation).

[4]   The Sustainable Development Goals (SDGs), the UN 2030 Agenda and the UN Global Compact initiative explicitly invite companies and individuals to become actively involved in implementing the relevant goals and principles of these initiatives.

[5]   That is, the collective security, obligatory supranational dispute resolution, the prohibition on the international use of force and the attendant opportunity for disarmament that the Charter sought to establish (see Chapter 10). For an anthropologist's perspective on the necessary features of "peace systems," see Fry, Douglas P. 2012. "Life without War." *Science*, Vol. 336, No. 6083, pp. 879–884.

[6]   E.g., climate change (and a possible "hothouse earth" tipping point) and catastrophic biodiversity loss. See also the risks and emerging crises sketched in Chapter 1.

unavoidable collective problems, which also incarnate a basic coherence and legitimacy in a reliable, values-based international system. To this end, in the final part of this chapter we describe how our reform proposals might be "operationalized," clustered around various substantive and process values for sound international governance.

Grenville Clark, at the time of the framing of the 1945 UN Charter, criticized those leading the negotiations for repeating the same errors seen in the League of Nations, in terms of what was needed in order to correct the Charter's key flaws. He noted that "We must recognize, indeed, that in comparison with the unique galaxy of our [US] Revolutionary statesmen, our generation lacks maturity for the framing of great institutions."[7] A certain broadness of vision, as noted by Habermas (see Chapter 10), is now required to design systems and great institutions for the twenty-first century that serve all.

THE UN LEGACY: A VALUES-RICH LANDSCAPE

The principles of the Charter are, by far, greater than the Organization in which they are embodied, and the aims which they are to safeguard are holier than the policies of any single nation or people.[8]

– Dag Hammarskjöld

From the Preamble and text of the UN Charter through the Universal Declaration of Human Rights (UDHR), to numerous other treaties, declarations and statements on wide-ranging topics, the UN system has, since its inception, had a powerful normative role in defining and building global consensus on the principles and values that unite the human race.

One can indeed argue that the principal goal of the 1945 Charter was to enable a watershed moment in human history, as it unapologetically sought to establish clear new principles for a values-based international order to replace the muddled, precarious and amoral circumstances that preceded it. If "[h]istory ... is a nightmare from which [we are] trying to awake,"[9] the San Francisco conference determined "to save succeeding generations from the scourge of war" and to awaken the peoples of the world from its repetitive nightmare.

The Charter's Preamble and Chapter I most notably set out the framing ideas of the new international order, with purposes and general binding "principles" to guide

[7] Clark, Grenville. 1944. "Dumbarton Oaks Plans Held in Need of Modification: Viewed as Repeating Essential Errors of League of Nations and Offering No Assurance of International Security – Some Remedies Suggested," *New York Times*, October 15: ProQuest Historical News Papers; The New York Times, pg. E8.

[8] Statement during the Suez Crisis, October 31, 1956. Official Records of the Security Council, 751st meeting. Quoted in Urquhart, Brian. 1973. *Hammarskjold*, London, Sydney and Toronto, The Bodley Head, p. 174.

[9] Joyce, James. 1961. *Ulysses*, New York, Random House, p. 34.

member state behavior under Article 2, seeking to establish an international "peace system" (see Chapter 10). Various other related "values" and interdependent obligations are interlaced throughout the rest of the document. Since 1945, now endowed with this new "Great Charter," states and their representatives, and other relevant actors, have struggled to implement the high ideals of the new instrument, listening to or fighting against "the better angels of our nature," with varying degrees of success.

The lack of a truly effective institutional and juridical architecture that would support the ideals of the Charter, and the problem of the Security Council vetoes, were roundly criticized by a range of actors at the time of its adoption, with, however, the hope and symbolism it represented still acknowledged:

> For those of us who have fought not for power but because we believe in the possibility of peace, the Charter is more than a series of harmless platitudes. Weak and inadequate as it stands today, it is all that we shall have won from the war. By our effort, it may yet become a symbol and instrument of a just order among men. No matter how remote our chances or how distant our success, we have in simple honesty no alternative but the attempt to make it that.[10]

Regardless of evident failures, setbacks and even the simple lack of implementation of important Charter provisions and other international treaties since 1945,[11] they have established core international values, principles and obligations under international law. The Charter itself has been ratified by virtually every state in the world – an astounding accomplishment in universality. Charter values are already covenanted to by the nations of the world, notably also embracing the international human rights *acquis* that has grown out of the relevant Charter provisions. Together, the shared international norms issuing from the UN system are a priceless heritage of humanity and a remarkable collective achievement.

The Sustainable Development Goals (SDGs) and the UN 2030 Agenda provide a recent, wide-ranging statement of unanimously shared values and principles of all members of the international community. They represent a recent broadening of the universally accepted aims of international action including the need to eliminate poverty, achieve universal education and reduce inequalities, leaving no one behind. Adopting such goals implies a moral obligation to achieve them. It clearly follows that an essential purpose of global governance should be to create the enabling conditions for the achievement of these goals globally and the implementation of the principles on which they are based, together with governments and all the actors of civil society.

---

[10] Meyer, Cord. 1945. "A Serviceman Looks at the Peace." *The Atlantic Monthly*, Vol. 176, No. 3, p. 48.

[11] For example, responsibilities of the Security Council to conclude military agreements for collective security action under Article 43, or in relation to disarmament under Article 26 (see Chapters 8 and 9).

Recent scholarship has sought to analyze what might now be deemed "global values," tracking a maturation of the UN system in this respect.[12] Regardless of what exactly might be considered to be the full corpus of shared international values or norms, whether binding international law or "soft law," we now find ourselves in a happy state of being "norm rich" at the international level – with, however, challenging or incomplete implementation of those norms, and a deficit in institutional capacity for judicial interpretation and enforcement.

However, there are now calls for the defense of the "rules-based" international order that was sought to be established in 1945 against serious emerging threats. A recent meeting of the G20 underlined a renewed shared "commitment to work together to improve a rules-based international order that is capable of effectively responding to a rapidly changing world."[13] There are even proposals for a "G9" made up of "middle power" democracies as a "Committee to Save the World" if the United States is no longer prepared to support and further the post-World War II "liberal international order" that it centrally assisted in creating.[14]

The current "crisis in multilateralism" presents an important opportunity to take stock of the multilateral system as it now stands, and to work to strengthen it significantly. The existing shared values and principles form a sound basis for the types of Charter and institutional enhancements we call for in this book, achieving new levels of implementation and enforcement of international norms and a higher standard of excellence in global governance. International values and principles must match a reality in action and in concrete institutions, with trust in and legitimacy of global governance organizations firmly established.

ETHICAL FOUNDATIONS FOR COLLECTIVE ACTION: HUMAN DIGNITY AND CAPABILITY

Chapter 11 describes the principles and values found in the Universal Declaration of Human Rights, and subsequent human rights instruments enabled by provisions of the Charter, from a primarily juridical perspective. Here we further explore the ethical foundations for global collective action, and the important role of the values held and lived by each individual in contributing to social cohesion and advancement from the bottom up, as well as to the institutions within which they are active.

---

[12] Spijkers, *The United Nations*.

[13] G20 Leaders' declaration: Building consensus for fair and sustainable development. Buenos Aires, Argentina, November 30–December 1, 2018. www.g20.utoronto.ca/2018/buenos_aires_leaders_declaration.pdf.

[14] Daalder, Ivo H. and James M. Lindsay. 2018. "The Committee to Save the World Order: America's Allies Must Step Up as America Steps Down." *Foreign Affairs*, Vol. 97, No. 6, November/December, pp. 72–83. www.foreignaffairs.com/articles/2018-09-30/committee-save-world-order.

The starting point is the fundamental concept of human dignity and purpose, implicit in the rights to which each human being is entitled from birth. The UDHR and other human rights instruments acknowledge that human reality includes dimensions that are material, social, rational and intellectual, and for many people spiritual, as articulated in the human right to freedom of religion or belief.[15] To fulfil that human purpose is for each individual to develop all those dimensions as far as they are able, within the inevitable limitations of any human life. This means starting life within the protection of a secure family; benefiting from adequate food, water, shelter, health services and other means of life; receiving both a moral and material education; acquiring skills and capacities to be able to work and contribute in some way to society and wealth creation; marrying or having a partner and raising a family; living in security and dignity within a social framework; and ultimately aging and dying without too much suffering. It is commonly accepted that government has an important role either in the direct provision of the necessary services or in ensuring that they are made available through others; hence the major place given to health services, education, social security, protection from internal and external threats, economic development and environmental management, among other government services.

From this shared human identity – the inherent dignity of all persons, our general life-cycle needs and our interdependence with the social spheres in which we live – it follows that everyone needs a moral education in those values conducive to social cohesion and constructive contributions to their community, country and world civilization, within the frame of what might be called the common ethical heritage of every human being.[16] Everyone needs to understand her or his individual and collective rights *and* responsibilities. It has been correctly noted that too much emphasis has been placed on individual rights in isolation, and insufficient attention paid to our responsibilities to each other, to cultivate the genuine solidarity needed, within and among societies, to tackle together the very serious challenges that now lie before us.[17]

---

[15] See, e.g., Penn, Michael, Maja Groff, and Naseem Koroush. 2019. "Cultivating Our Common Humanity: Reflections on Freedom of Thought, Conscience, and Religion," in Neal Rubin and Roseanne Flores (eds.), *The Cambridge Handbook of Psychology and Human Rights*, Cambridge, Cambridge University Press, chapter 13.

[16] See ibid.; Falk, Richard. 2001. *Religion and Humane Global Governance*, New York, Palgrave Macmillan.

[17] Various authors have recently explored how social cohesion and cultures of cooperation ("the connections among individuals' social networks and the norms of reciprocity and trustworthiness that arise from them," in the words of Putnam), including on a mass scale, are a type of crucial social capital required for healthy and successful societies with problem-solving ability. Turchin, Peter. 2016. *Ultrasociety: How 10,000 Years of War Made Humans the Greatest Co-operators on Earth*, Chaplin, CT, Beresta Books; Putnam, R.D. 2000. *Bowling Alone: The Collapse and Revival of American Community*, New York, Touchstone Books/Simon & Schuster, p. 19.

These lived "everyday virtues" need to be more consciously internalized. This would give effect to the aims of the UDHR, to Eleanor Roosevelt's vision of "human rights in small places" embedded throughout our daily environments (see Chapter 11), and to the type of peace system that the Charter envisions "to practice tolerance and live together in peace with one another as good neighbours."[18] Some examples are living by principles of justice and equity, showing generosity and solidarity, and the need to leave no one behind (as enshrined in the UN 2030 Agenda). Other social principles and goals could include the essential shared identity of humankind in all its diversity, an appreciation of cultural differences, trustworthiness, avoiding conflict and contention, and replacing feelings of fear or hate with stronger feelings of compassion. Economic principles include the importance of the economy as a service to society, beyond narrow materialism, applying moderation, building a just and sustainable civilization, and creating the means to achieve higher purposes such as revealing the unlimited potentials in human learning and consciousness. The growing global impact of human society on the environment leads to some essential environmental principles, such as the preservation of life-support systems of the biosphere, acknowledging the criminal nature of serious environmental damage and perhaps developing ways to give nature legal standing, respecting nature or notions of Mother Earth found in a range of indigenous cultures, and appreciating the material, cultural and spiritual dimensions of human relationships to the natural world. There are sources of such principles in all the great religious traditions, many philosophies and moral treatises, and the rich traditions of indigenous peoples, among others.[19] Principles such as these are what give each of us our individual moral or ethical framework, whether conscious or unconscious and simply taken for granted. Because of our by now inescapable interdependence and the gravity and uncertainty of the threats to our common future, sincere and lived ethical frameworks are more important than ever, and are perhaps our only hope.

The foundation of any system of justice is reward and punishment. Yet a legal system that relies primarily on police systems, courts and prisons is inefficient, expensive and socially damaging, locking people away when they could be contributing to society. A citizenry motivated by high ideals, educated to good morals and with a conscience regarding right and wrong has little need for such machinery of justice; the same is true at the international level and with respect to the highest levels of political leadership (see Chapter 19).[20] An ethical motivation to do good

---

[18] Fry, "Life without War."

[19] See, e.g., the prominent interfaith declaration "Towards a Global Ethic," drafted at the 1993 Parliament of the World's Religions in Chicago, IL. https://parliamentofreligions.org/parliament/global-ethic/about-global-ethic.

[20] The United States, for example, has some of the most strict and onerous lobbying regulations in the world, yet is still plagued by dramatic policy-making distortions due to corporate lobbying, with an estimated US$3.4 billion spent per year on this pursuit.

and to be of service to all humanity is much cheaper and more effective than the threat of punishment, which is then only needed as a last resort. The higher are the ethical standards in a society, with the attendant investments in the health and education of its peoples, the less the need for heavy systems of justice. An authentic belief in a transcendent being, for example, which includes a notion of higher accountability for one's deeds, can also provide an internal motivation to be honest.[21] Community social sanctions for unethical behavior are a powerful force as well. Such motivations are also the best response to corruption, which flourishes – at times even despite strong legal regulation – when a society lacks ethical standards.

As we reconsider the roles of governance for the twenty-first century, we must explore ways to extend to the institutions of governance a similar foundational moral framework. The existing set of UN declarations and principles is an important starting point. Just as selfless service is an expression of an individual ethical stance, so should governance in service to the collective be the high standard of an international system. Governance should never be seen as an end in itself, but as a tool to achieve social goals. Collateral principles would, of necessity, include efficiency, subsidiarity, moderation and achieving an optimal size rather than an endless bureaucracy. We discuss below certain good governance "process" values, which are important for efficient systems.

Inherent in the notion of human dignity and the endowments of moral reasoning is the importance of human capability, innate capacities, and ingenuity. Investments in human capital are crucial for national and international development, economic and otherwise.[22] Generally, there is a need to resuscitate our faith in human capacities for large-scale collective action, and our ability to solve global problems, peacefully and competently, on a scale heretofore not attempted. If we have sincere common ethical values, shared international goals and faith in our abilities, we shall be equal to the tasks before us. As economist Jeffrey Sachs has noted, global poverty is not a resource issue, as internationally we have unprecedented wealth; it is at root an ethical issue.[23] We should consciously cultivate ambitious, solution-oriented and innovative mindsets in addressing global governance and resolving global problems. This is part and parcel of a movement, at the macro level, away from zero-sum to collaborative approaches in international affairs, based on human solidarity around

---

[21] See, e.g., Sheiman, Bruce. 2009. *An Atheist Defends Religion: Why Humanity Is Better Off with Religion than without It.* New York, Alpha (Penguin Group), chapter 2, p. 23 et seq.

[22] World Bank. 2007. World Development Report: Development and the Next Generation. Washington DC, World Bank Group.

[23] He notes, for example, that "[t]he world has not developed a political or ethical sensibility of a global society . . . Most of the institutions that are charged to deal with these problems are post-World War II institutions like the United Nations, or departments of government that were created in the 20th century along structural lines that are not equipped to understand these challenges or to treat them in a holistic way." Nee, Eric. 2010. Interview with Jeffrey Sachs (Environment), *Stanford Social Innovation Review*, Summer. https://ssir.org/articles/entry/qa_jeffrey_sachs.

shared values, employing our very significant aggregate technical skill and expertise in service of collective well-being. As affirmed in the SDGs, all actors across society have an important role to play in service of our shared goals.

ABSOLUTE SOVEREIGNTY IN AN AGE OF GLOBAL CHALLENGES

The Age of Nations is past. It remains for us now, if we do not wish to perish, to set aside the ancient prejudices and build the earth. ... The more scientifically I regard the world, the less can I see any possible biological future for it except the active consciousness of its unity.[24]

– Pierre Teilhard de Chardin, S.J.

Behind current global governance failures is, among other things, what has been understood as the concept of "absolute sovereignty."[25] A rigid notion of national sovereignty has become an inadequate foundational principle.[26] It may have been useful for an earlier scale of human organization, and the rise of modern nations has shown how it worked at its best. During decolonization, it became the rallying cry of newly independent nations taking control of their own land and resources. Addressing this issue in the context of UN reform is highly sensitive and will trigger initial push-back by many countries. However, in a globalized world it is increasingly leading to failures. Non-interference in the internal affairs of states is often used as a screen for national abuse, corruption and the individual aspirations and egos of national leaders. The twentieth century has shown how the sovereign right to make war in defense of national interests or to extend power led to the ruinous world wars. With the advent of nuclear weapons, their use in the next war would not only lay waste the countries directly involved but would precipitate planetary contamination, undermining civilization as we know it, if not exterminating the entire human race. Lack of effective international coordination and supranational policy enforcement on climate and other key planetary systems likewise threatens our general survival.

---

[24] Pierre Teilhard de Chardin, S.J., in his essay, "The Spirit of the Earth," cited in Teilhard de Chardin, P. 1969. *Human Energy*, London, Collins, p. 37.

[25] Some authors, however, have contradicted traditional narratives of the autonomous sovereign states in relation to international organizations, underlining, for example, the interdependence of individual state construction or reform and the activities and growth of international organizations in the modern era. Sinclair, Guy Fiti. 2017. *To Reform the World: The Legal Powers of International Organizations and the Making of Modern States*, Oxford, Oxford University Press.

[26] Indeed, the normative construct of sovereignty has come under increasing question and debate in light of increasing international cooperation and integration. Besson discusses a number of these debates and proposes the concept of "cooperative sovereignty" with the framework of the European Union in particular: "[i]n the European context, cooperative sovereignty provides the normative framework for the development of a dynamic and reflexive form of constitutionalism." Besson, Samantha. 2004. "Sovereignty in Conflict." European Integration online Papers (EIoP), Vol. 8, No. 15. Available at SSRN: https://ssrn.com/abstract=594942.

Cord Meyer, fresh from World War II, in "A Serviceman Looks at the Peace" in *The Atlantic Monthly*, describes the irrationality of absolute sovereignty as follows:

> Our present world is composed of more than fifty separate sovereign and independent nations. Each one of them jealously guards its twofold sovereignty, through which it proclaims itself free from any interference by others in its internal affairs and equally free in its external affairs to make any decisions that it wishes ... We should frankly recognize this lawless condition as anarchy, where brute force is the price of survival.[27]

A second dimension of the obsolescence of national sovereignty as the central principle of governance is its failure even in the best-governed states, given powerful international forces. What is the use of high principles and effective governance at the national level when there is anarchy at the global level? More and more domains of governance are escaping from national control or even influence in a globalized world, from the economy to migration to the flow of information. In too many cases, states are pushed by unrestrained global competition into a race to the bottom, trying to retain or attract corporations and investments by lowering corporate taxation, reducing environmental and social regulations or safeguards, and offering special exemptions to the economically powerful, as discussed in Chapter 14. The real independence and well being of nation states can only be assured today by interstate collaboration in supranational mechanisms, just as the freedom of individuals is best guaranteed by the protections of an effective national government.

In the emerging framework of global governance, various useful features of national governance should also be employed at the global level (e.g., adequate legislative, judicial and executive functions, discussed in various chapters of this book), while refining our concept of national sovereignty to ensure it is suitable to our era (e.g., employing notions of "cooperative sovereignty"), and still being sure to safeguard vital aspects of national autonomy. In any federal system, for example, many crucial responsibilities are, as much as possible, left to lower levels of government. A reformed UN system would need to carefully protect national autonomy, and may need, for example, an explicit Declaration of National Rights and Responsibilities as a protection from overreach at the global level, and judicial oversight to uphold that protection. At the same time, it will need to evolve a clear definition of those extreme conditions that would justify global institutions interfering in the internal affairs of countries (as has already begun to be developed, including under the International Criminal Court (ICC) and under the Responsibility to Protect norm, to name two examples), which might include uncontrolled corruption, extreme abuse of power, a failed government, and the responsibility to protect citizens or a significant minority against criminal behavior or abuse by a government.

---

[27] Meyer, "A Serviceman Looks at the Peace," p. 44.

A related problem is the present narrow definition of the responsibility of a sovereign government only for its citizens, however it chooses to define this. This allows governments to ignore, neglect or persecute those within its borders who fall outside their definition of citizenship. In a world where every government was equally efficient and responsible in providing for their citizens (including when out of their country), this might work, but today this is the exception rather than the rule. Many governments are too poorly resourced, autocratic, corrupt or incompetent (or all of these), if not a failed state, excluding many millions at home from the benefits that a government should provide, while driving many to flee the impossible conditions in their country of origin with no hope that their nationality, if they have one, will provide any protection abroad. Enhanced and legitimate global institutions, such as those proposed in this book, should seek to close this gap in uneven international protection and current governance deficits at the national level.

Indeed, an increasing proportion of the world population is not being represented or defended by any national government, if not actively persecuted or expelled. In a system relying excessively on national sovereignty, what government is responsible for and speaks on behalf of those it fails or refuses to recognize within or outside its national borders: non-citizens, refugees, migrants (legal or illegal), and those with no legal existence, either stateless or whose birth was never registered? These are the invisible masses often not captured in official statistics or masked by aggregated measures, who have too frequently been left behind. In an effective global system, no human being should be left in limbo.

CONTEMPORARY APPROACHES TO GOOD GOVERNANCE

Since the late 1980s there has been a vibrant debate within the academic community and in policy-making circles about the role of government in creating the conditions for sustainable economic development and well-being for all citizens.[28] There have been at least two dimensions to this debate. One has focused on the nature and content of public policies that create an environment conducive to security, economic growth and prosperity, whether in the overall management of the macroeconomy or in a broad range of complementary sectoral and institutional factors and policies. The second has focused on the exercise of political authority in a society for the management of its resources, and the *quality* of government in this process, identifying the key building blocks of good governance. The broadening of development objectives to include equity and social justice, civil and other basic human rights, peace and security, has thus established a natural linkage between governance on the one hand and development on the other. The insights of modern good governance thinking apply equally to the national and international levels,

---

[28] Kaufmann, D. and A. Kraay. 2002. "Growth without Governance." *Economia*, Vol. 3, No.1, pp. 169–229.

with of course key governance institutions, that are taken for granted at the national level, found deficient or absent at the international level (hence the international reform proposals of this book).

One approach to the question of what constitutes good governance has been to refer to a minimal set of characteristics on which there might be broad international agreement, including in relation to international human rights standards (see Chapter 11). Attempts have been made to link such a minimal set to the UDHR, as representing the consensus of the international community on some fundamental, broadly held values.[29] Various articles of the Declaration address such concepts as: the will of the people as the basis of government authority and hence the need for the periodic establishment of the legitimacy of governments through elections (Article 21); the safety of citizens and the right to equal protection under the law (Article 7); the availability of information, and freedoms of association and expression (Article 19); the ownership of property (Article 17); and the right to a standard of living adequate for the health and well-being of the individual and his/her family (Article 25). All of these would appear to be essential components of good governance and have been used as the "raw material" with which to formulate the underlying conceptual framework.

Daniel Kaufmann and his colleagues at the World Bank put forward a useful definition of governance as "the set of traditions and formal and informal institutions that determine how authority is exercised in a particular country for the common good, thus encompassing: (1) the process of selecting, monitoring, and replacing governments; (2) the capacity to formulate and implement sound policies and deliver public services; and (3) the respect of citizens and the state for the institutions that govern economic and social interactions among them."[30] For measurement purposes and to facilitate analysis, they further introduce two concepts for each of these three dimensions: voice and external accountability; political stability and lack of violence, crime and terrorism; government effectiveness; lack of regulatory burden; rule of law; and control of corruption. While not explicitly mentioning the UDHR in their definition, it is clear that they draw content and nourishment from it. The utility of developing a framework for governance with reference to a set of principles such as those contained in the Declaration is obvious. It makes unnecessary the need to build consensus on a new set of guiding principles, likely a difficult task in the context of a diverse community of nations with often diverging interests. As this thinking has evolved, a consensus has gradually emerged as to what are some of the central, core characteristics of good governance. It is useful to identify briefly four such factors judged to be of fundamental importance, drawing

---

[29] Landell-Mills, P. and I. Serageldin. 1991. "Governance and the External Factor." *The World Bank Economic Review*, Vol. 5, pp. 303–320.

[30] Kaufmann, Daniel, Aart Kraay and Massimo Mastruzzi. 2010. *The Worldwide Governance Indicators: Methodology and Analytical Issues*. Draft Policy Research Working Paper, World Bank, September. http://info.worldbank.org/governance/wgi/pdf/WGI.pdf.

in particular on the valuable work of Amartya Sen in this field.[31] These are accountability, transparency, consultation and the rule of law.[32]

Accountability

One factor pertains to the exercise of power, which must take place within a framework of *accountability*. Adequate safeguards are introduced to prevent the abuse of that power where, for instance, ruling elites use it for personal gain rather than public benefit. Recent trends toward democracy and political pluralism in all regions of the world are seen as facilitating this task, which will at a minimum involve the periodic legitimization of governments through popular choice, making them more responsive to the needs of society.[33] The issue of accountability is closely linked to that of participatory development and democracy. Unless people feel that they have a say in whom they are ruled by, they cannot be expected to fully support the government's policies. Without such public support, even well-designed plans will in the end amount to very little. Furthermore, while democracy is a necessary ingredient of creating an economy based on the rule of law (see section below), it is not a sufficient condition to ensure responsible governments that will work in the interests of the majority.[34] Many have pointed to the successful development experiences of economies such as the Republic of Korea, Singapore, and Taiwan – non-democratic regimes during the periods of highest economic growth – to highlight the complex nature of the relationship between democracy and development.

Much is at stake here. Sen convincingly argues that those countries in which governments operate in an environment of political legitimacy tend to be much better at allowing the formation of vital understandings and beliefs among the population that directly impinge upon aspects of the development process – for

---

[31] Sen, Amartya. 1999. *Development as Freedom*, Oxford, Oxford University Press.

[32] For an early look at the concept of good governance and the role of external agencies and donors in promoting it, see Landell-Mills and Serageldin, "Governance and the External Factor."

[33] It is important, however, to note that there is a distinction between safeguarding the *principles* of democracy or participatory governance – giving voice to the people, ensuring that governments are made legitimate through popular choice – and many of the habits, taken to excess, that are too often attached to the contemporary *practice* of democracy, such as extreme partisanship, adversarial political campaigns, vast financial contributions to political parties, the role of the media and, more generally, the circus that sometimes surrounds the election of public officials in many parts of the world and that has done so much to turn many citizens away from participation in the political process and resulted in low voter turnouts during national and local elections.

[34] Easterly notes a number of reasons why democracy may not take hold, including "elite manipulation of the rules of the political game, weak social norms, landed wealth, natural resources, high inequality, corruption, and ethnic nationalism and hatreds." Easterly, William. 2006. *The White Man's Burden: Why the West's Efforts to Aid the Rest Have Done So Much Ill and So Little Good*, New York, Penguin Press, p. 129.

instance, the notion that female education, employment and ownership rights exert powerful influences on a woman's ability to control her environment and improve her condition.[35]

Transparency

A related aspect of good governance is *transparency*, the willingness of governments to open to public scrutiny the accounts and activities of public institutions and to institute reliable systems of auditing and financial management. Lack of openness, more often than not, does not serve useful public ends but has instead been used to hide unlawful practices and abuse. Transparency is particularly important in the case of the tax system, where the ability of governments to collect revenues will depend on public perceptions of the fairness of its operation and the proper use that is made of public funds. The experience of the Nordic countries fully bears out these observations. These countries have the lowest levels of corruption in the world (they consistently are top performers in Transparency International's Corruptions Perceptions Index) and some of the highest tax burdens in the world – and yet they have no major problems with tax compliance. Businesses and citizens may *wish* for a lower tax regime, but ultimately they understand that tax revenues get translated into high investments in education and training that boost innovation capacity, in excellent infrastructure and in extensive safety nets providing ample social security. Sen notes that societies operate better under some presumption of trust and that, therefore, they will benefit from greater openness. The freedom for society's members to deal with one another under "guarantees of disclosure and honesty" are essential to prevent corruption and other abuses.[36]

Consultation

Peace and security and sustainable social and economic development depend to a great extent on the government's ability to generate a broad consensus for change. A process of good faith *consultation* whereby the government elicits the views of various sectors of society – businesses, professional organizations, academics and researchers, nongovernmental organizations (NGOs) and other organizations of civil society, local communities and indigenous peoples, etc. – is likely to result in greater understanding of and commitment on the part of the population to the sometimes painful measures that accompany the implementation of various development or environmental protection strategies. Consultation is also likely to result in a more equitable distribution of the costs of adjustment and thereby enhance the

---

[35] López-Claros, Augusto and Bahiyyih Nakhjavani. 2018. *Equality for Women = Prosperity for All: The Disastrous Global Crisis of Gender Inequality*, New York, St. Martin's Press.

[36] Sen, *Development as Freedom*, p. 39.

chances of sustainable reforms. The building of consensus through consultation is at the root of participatory governance and facilitates transparency and accountability. In this respect, the development of a thriving non-profit sector since the mid-1990s has greatly contributed to enhancing the possibilities for meaningful consultation between government and civil society.

One challenge in consultation is determining the circle of who is consulted, and who participates in decision-making. The adoption in the UN 2030 Agenda of the principle of "no one left behind" implies a wider circle of participants than just those already with some power or influence.

Rule of Law

Closely linked to the issue of accountability is the need for the *rule of law*, the notion that the rules that govern a society are applicable to all. As noted in Chapter 10, the rule of law, at both the national and international levels, has been affirmed as a key international value and operational principle multiple times at the UN, and by the highest levels of political leadership. There is increasing recognition that without a reasonably objective, efficient and predictable judicial system and legal framework, accountability will have no legal underpinnings and the goals of good governance will be undermined. The absence of an adequate legal framework and judicial system will encourage corruption and crime, diminish peace and security, increase business costs, discourage investment and introduce an element of uncertainty that will be detrimental to the development process. This is true at both the national and international levels.[37]

There have been a number of attempts to provide a meaningful definition of the rule of law, which has meant any of a number of things including, as noted by Trebilcock and Daniels, government bound by law, equality before the law, law and order, the presence of a predictably efficient system of justice and the existence of a state that safeguards human rights.[38] Some have argued that the concept is linked to notions of liberty and democracy, necessarily implying constraints on the power of the state and the guaranteeing of basic freedoms for citizens, such as those of speech and association. In this view, the rule of law has elements of political morality and is very much a foundation for a just society. It is certainly inseparable from the morality underpinning contemporary democracy, with its emphasis on the protection of

[37] Groff, Maja and Sylvia Karlsson-Vinkhuyzen, 2019. "The Rule of Law and Accountability: Exploring Trajectories for Democratizing Governance of Global Public Goods and Global Commons," in Samuel Cogolati and Jan Wouters (eds.), *The Commons and a New Global Governance*, Cheltenham, Edward Elgar, pp. 130–159.

[38] Trebilcock, Michael J. and Ronald J. Daniels. 2008. *Rule of Law Reform and Development: Charting the Fragile Path to Progress*, Cheltenham, Edward Elgar, p. 15.

individual rights, including those of free expression, voting and the right to private property.[39]

UN Secretary-General Kofi Annan offered the following definition, supporting the inclusion of substantive rights and participatory governance, postulating "the rule of law" as:

> a principle of governance in which all persons, institutions and entities, public and private, including the State itself, are accountable to laws that are publicly promulgated, equally enforced and independently adjudicated, and which are consistent with international human rights norms and standards. It requires, as well, measures to ensure adherence to the principles of supremacy of law, equality before the law, accountability to the law, fairness in the application of the law, separation of powers, participation in decision-making, legal certainty, avoidance of arbitrariness and procedural and legal transparency.[40]

Interactions among Good Governance Attributes

From the previous discussion, it is clear that these various elements of good governance – accountability, transparency, consultation and the rule of law – are not independent. Further, interactions with various other governance vectors are inevitable and conflicts could arise in the short run. For example, participatory processes implemented in an environment of political pluralism and openness may add an element of unpredictability to the decision-making process. It may take longer to forge the necessary consensus around a particular strategy, as the views of various stakeholder groups are considered and possibly brought on board. Sen caricatures a "blood, sweat and tears" approach to development, where "wisdom demands toughness and a calculated neglect of 'soft-headed' concerns," such as the need for a safety net that protects the very poor, providing certain social services for the population at large, favoring political and civil rights at an early stage and regarding democracy as a "luxury" that can be put off for the distant future.[41] Transparency in the use of public resources may, likewise, impose some constraints on the spending priorities of government, particularly in the context of countries operating in a context of democracy.

---

[39] In some countries, many politicians may interpret the rule of law to be the rule *by* law, meaning that the there is no presumption of government subordination to the law, which is seen as a vehicle not to limit its power but rather to serve its purposes. (This is what is meant by the "dictatorship of the law – the government may wish to do as it pleases). This clearly is not consistent with contemporary and widely accepted notions of the rule of law, which is presumed to be embedded within a constitutional order with appropriate checks and balances.

[40] United Nations Security Council. 2004. *The Rule of Law and Transitional Justice in Conflict and Post-Conflict Societies.* Report of the Secretary-General, August 23, UN Doc. S/2004/616, p. 4, para. 6.

[41] Sen, *Development as Freedom.*

But these challenges do not detract from the intrinsic value of the core building blocks of good governance, including at the international level, and the overriding need to pursue them as essential ingredients of enlightened sustainable development. Only to the extent that all parties concerned jointly cooperate to nurture the growth of these key building blocks will the international community be able to contribute in a meaningful way to unleashing processes aimed at both improving the welfare of its most needy members and enhancing people's capacities to manage change. Furthermore, in the presence of these core elements of good governance, the credibility of government policies will be significantly strengthened. Government credibility is a precious commodity; without it the business community and civil society will act in ways that will undermine the effectiveness of policies, whether, as already noted, we refer to the paying of taxes or the entire range of other policies that require the participation of the private sector and the public for their successful implementation.

It is therefore possible to interpret the heartbreakingly disappointing fruits of economic development in many parts of the developing world during the last half-century in terms of the absence of the basic building blocks of good governance, including the strength to resist pressures of unsustainable exploitation from without.[42]

IMPLICATIONS FOR THE UNITED NATIONS: MAKING ENHANCED GLOBAL GOVERNANCE EFFECTIVE

We have dwelt at some length on the question of what some of the key values and attributes of good governance may be, in essence to reflect on the extent to which these are present in the United Nations as presently constituted. It should be fairly obvious to the reader by now that the system that came into being with the UN Charter in 1945 was more a reflection of the highly uneven distribution of power in the world at the time and the desire of the four largest founding members to entrench or preserve certain national prerogatives. Several examples already dealt with in other chapters include the one country – one vote rule for the General Assembly (GA) and, most importantly, the existence of veto power for the permanent members of the Security Council, the at times heavy-handed way in which large members have used the UN for the pursuit of national strategic objectives, and a whole range of practices and rules that have emerged over the past seven and a half decades. These make it abundantly clear that UN governance mechanisms do not conform to the standards of good governance identified here.

---

[42] This is not to say that the developed world is necessarily well-governed, in keeping with the above principles. We address multiple governance problems in the high-income countries in various forms in Chapters 13–18.

In the Box below we examine how a range of these flaws are addressed in the proposals we have put forward, based on established shared values and modern thinking on good governance. We sketch out how a reformed, values-based international governance system could work, "operationalizing" the various proposals set forth in the other chapters, in particular, if implementation of the reform proposals were to be effected through comprehensive Charter review (see Chapter 21 for a discussion on possible implementation pathways and scenarios).

Box

Operationalizing Key Attributes and Values of a New Global Governance System

Core Values

An amended UN Charter would assure and give central place to the fundamental human rights of all persons, the principle of binding international rule of law, the peaceful settlement of disputes, collective disarmament and security, certain core principles of environmental stewardship and sustainability, and other values deemed fundamental to the new international order.

One of the first tasks of the reformed GA could be to compile and enumerate the core values enshrining the good of all humankind and the equal value of all human beings, drawing from the significant current *acquis* of international law, both "soft" and "hard." These would be made explicit in legally binding texts to serve as the basis for legislation, judicial review and enforcement, with the frame of the revised UN Charter serving as a global constitution. This consolidated document would represent the coherent declaration of core values, rights and responsibilities for international governance and sustainability, complemented by a clear definition of the remaining scope of national autonomy, and an individual Bill of Rights as one of the foundations for accountability.

The 2030 Agenda and its SDGs provide a globally accepted example of the application of core values and their implementation, exemplifying a framework for adapting and focusing international governance structures, mechanisms and programs, as well as implementation at the national and local levels and by all economic actors and civil society.

Core values would be implemented dynamically by legislative and judicial interpretation, through legally binding acts of the GA in its areas of responsibility, and the international judicial mechanisms emerging from these reform principles. Norms of equality before the law, protection by law from arbitrary abuse of power, transparency and other fundamental values inherent in established rule-of-law structures would be implemented throughout the system. An Office of Ethical Assessment advisory to the GA would ensure that it is informed of the relevant core values underlying proposed legislation.

The envisioned reformed legislative dimension of the UN would manifest values of democracy and consultation, proportionally representing the world's populations in the reformed GA, and engaging recognized advocates of the global public interest in a Chamber of Civil Society.

Strong provisions against large-scale international criminality and corruption, beyond national responsibilities or enforcement capacities, would give the international community for the first time the necessary tools to fight criminal disregard for core values, and to prosecute the individuals and groups responsible. With such mechanisms and core values in place, the new international system would necessarily drive the creation of a new generation of uncompromised leadership, subject to the highest standards, whose efforts are devoted to good governance and the public good.

The core values of the common identity and interdependence of humankind, as well as those enshrined in the revised Charter, should also be incorporated in all international educational tools, and reflected, as much as possible, in national constitutions and education. They should be essential components in the training of heads of state and their cabinets, international civil servants, contributors to global institutions and the personnel responsible for enforcement mechanisms, so that much implementation of values is internalized in individual ethics and a responsible conscience. Relevant resource materials should be made available to all educational systems, and modern media used for their global distribution; an enhanced UN News Service can assist in this process, as it functions to build appropriate levels of popular understanding of international governance institutions.

The focus on wealth inequality within the frame of the broader reform proposals, for the first time seeking to address systematically national and international extremes of wealth and poverty, would further change the current, inefficient international order based on spending for a militarized notion of security, to focus on the well-being and practical needs of all individuals and populations of the world. The new rationalized and effective international order would be oriented toward human well-being and values of "human security," with a corollary international "right to peace," secured, inter alia, through greatly strengthened Charter provisions for collective security, disarmament and the peaceful settlement of disputes.

Decision-Making Capacity, Consultation and Rule of Law

The proposed reform of executive functions presently in the Security Council would significantly enhance decision-making capacity in international governance, as the use or threat of the use of the veto power has regularly caused crippling delays or failures to act. Abolition of the veto has been proposed multiple times in Charter history to enhance UN decision-making on crucial issues, most recently and prominently in humanitarian crises, where permanent members possessing the veto have been requested to abstain from its use. The new Executive Council, with its management function, would be preoccupied with taking regular and wide-ranging operational decisions in its oversight and coordination mandate for the entire UN system. A key task of the Executive Council would indeed be to enhance decision-making effectiveness throughout the system, including through internal management, leadership formation and administrative reforms.

The professionalization, systematization and clear lines of control and accountability of the International Peace Force, subject to protocols and objective criteria for its deployment and use, would likewise remedy the inefficient, under-resourced, ad hoc system currently used to conduct peacekeeping and collective security operations. Effective and mandatory mechanisms for, among others, mediation, conciliation, arbitration and judicial resolution would resolve most disputes, with force used only as a last resort.

With reform of the GA, there would now be a duly constituted, legitimate and representative body to take decisions on crucial issues of peace, security and environment in particular (and on other matters in the future). As with other legislative bodies at the national level, the GA would convene a suite of specialized committees on issues of core concern, such as collective security action, enforcement of international judgments, climate change, etc., with the assistance of specialized, advisory technical experts, as proposed. A possible advisory Chamber of Civil Society, composed of members of global civil society, would be a strong catalytic force driving UN decision-making, exerting active and vigorous pressure for ongoing change, innovation and reform. The Chamber would act as a watchdog on UN governmental decision-making and operations, applying scrutiny to hold governments and the international institution to account and to force it to take decisions on pressing issues.

The strengthened role of international judicial authorities would significantly enhance decision-making processes in the international system, as courts would be tasked with deciding upon issues of core concern to states, individuals and the international community, which too often now represent festering conflicts with no hope of decisive resolution. Likewise, binding protocols on the peaceful settlement of disputes would allow staged and clear decisions on issues related to international peace and security.

Effectiveness

With the foundations for this step already established in the existing system, the proposal suggests a substantial advance in establishing genuine, comprehensive rule of law at the international level. The international community would be equipped with the supplementary architecture and tools required to ensure that international decisions and policies are implemented and observed. Binding adjudication, compulsory, universal jurisdiction of the key international courts, and an effective range of enforcement mechanisms, including the use of the International Peace Force as a last resort, would ensure that there is no ambiguity in the enforceability of international law, decisions of international tribunals and implementation of the terms of the UN Charter itself – including its prohibitions on the use of force, save under narrow exceptions.

Ensuring adequate financing for international institutions would be a highly significant reform toward substantial gains in effectiveness of the UN and related bodies. Currently, effectiveness and the scope of operations are hampered by paltry, inconsistent funding. The ambitious and comprehensive collective security and disarmament components of the proposal would likewise free resources for international (and national) institutions in service of the public good, allowing for a true peace dividend. The disarmament agency, with robust and comprehensive inspection functions, would facilitate implementation of a general international disarmament process, overcoming traditional security dilemmas and costly arms races among states.

The Executive Council, with core management duties, would primarily be focused on operational efficacy and the coherent implementation of policy and programming decisions taken by the GA.

Tackling corruption is key to ensuring efficacy in global governance, as its prevalence perverts lines of implementation of international norms at the national level, leads to diversion of resources and constitutes a general drain on the system. The proposal suggests a model of complementary prosecution and oversight for addressing corruption at the national level, generally following the model of the ICC in this respect.

Ongoing system efficacy would be safeguarded with mandatory five-year reviews of GA powers, a ten-year mandatory General Conference for review of the UN Charter and, if necessary, bypassing the present Security Council if it chooses to block meaningful Charter reform in the first instance (see Chapter 21). Various individuals and bodies in the reformed UN institutions could regularly make suggestions for system reform and enhancement, based on operational experience.

Finally, the UN would now be a body with significantly enhanced democratic and representative legitimacy, with reformed legislative chambers, a representative Executive Council, a well-trained, independent international judiciary, and a UN Bill of Rights, to heighten the willingness of all actors to cooperate and comply with its decisions and accept its global management responsibilities. The focus on international basic education and quality access to information on UN institutions and activities would likewise strengthen this dynamic of legitimacy and participation in an international "social contract" for more effective governance.

Resources and Financing

The institutions underpinning the new mechanisms of global governance must be adequately resourced to provide a steady, predictable source of funding to finance its multiple operations. A system of funding that involves a level of automaticity is proposed, in order that the UN is insulated from the uncertainties associated with member state budgetary discretion. By allocating directly to the UN budget a fixed share of each nation's gross national income (GNI) (our preferred approach), the UN would be empowered to implement its work program reliably and formulate its strategies in a medium-term framework.

While there are, in principle, multiple sources of such funding, a relatively modest 0.1 percent of GNI would not only bring into being a transparent and fair system, but it would also make available to the UN an expanded envelope of resources that could be allocated to a broad range of economic and security needs, substantially strengthening the organization's capacity to deliver on its Charter responsibilities.

While it would be tempting to shift the burden of financing to high-income countries, universal participation in funding by all countries is an important principle, to encourage ownership by all member states of the new governance system.

If the system of funding envisaged is linked to national income, wealthier states will automatically make larger contributions in absolute terms than lower-income members. Additional sources of international funding based on principles of equity and progressive taxation, such as those suggested by some prominent economists (e.g., a Tobin tax), or those based on successful models employed by international organizations (e.g., the International Maritime Organization), would also be explored. Adequate and predictable funding would allow the UN to build a highly professional staff, including the creation of the International Peace Force.

General Security

The issue of security will be addressed from multiple perspectives. First, an International Peace Force would be created to act on behalf of the international community as reflected in the deliberations of the GA and Executive Council, under whose authority it would operate. While recognizing the need for national forces to safeguard internal national security, it would bring about the creation of a tool for the prevention of international aggression and other threats to peace, and ensure compliance with the revised Charter. Creating an International Peace Force would be an important confidence-building measure, enhancing the credibility of the UN in fulfilling its security responsibilities. It would also ensure, through the creation of a true system of collective security, a better allocation of global economic and financial resources, with states empowered to redirect resources now allocated to the maintenance of excessively large military establishments to socially productive ends.

Second, the reforms would ensure the mandatory and peaceful settlement of international disputes and the enforcement of international law. In particular, compulsory jurisdiction would be granted to the International Court of Justice (ICJ) over international legal disputes for all UN members, departing from the current system requiring states' agreement to adjudicate. Revisions to the Charter would also make mandatory acceptance by all UN members of the statute of the ICC. Third, there would be a significant strengthening of the current system of non-binding human rights oversight mechanisms through creation of an International Human Rights Tribunal. Fourth, a new Bill of Rights attached to the Charter would include fundamental human rights protections in specified areas. Finally, the process of international disarmament would be consistent with the transition to a global security model firmly anchored in the principle of collective security, the dignity of persons and the rule of law.

Flexibility

The proposed institutional mechanisms have levels of built-in review and revision procedures to ensure that international governance can be adapted to changing conditions and can learn from accumulated experience. Governance mechanisms should develop organically in response to needs, form following function, with change considered normal and necessary.

At the constitutional level, obligatory periodic review of the Charter would open the door for necessary revisions, and for relevant principles underlying widely accepted customary and soft law to be codified in the foundation text.

The Executive Council would have the mandate to review UN system performance, ensure good governance and management, and make necessary adjustments through administrative and UN system reforms.

As unnecessary posts are abolished and new needs defined, institutional flexibility requires complementary procedures for social security and human resource management to protect the rights of international civil servants and facilitate optimal use of their capacities. This could reduce bureaucratic blockage and resistance to change.

Some flexibility will be required in gradually implementing the components of substantial UN reform, depending on the willingness of governments to accommodate necessary changes. While collective adoption by consensus would be ideal, provisions are included to sidestep any blockage by recalcitrant governments and enable the larger community of common interests to go forward, while gradually building the trust necessary for more substantial changes (e.g., confidence-building is a major component of the disarmament proposals).

Accountability and Transparency

The core values provide the foundation for accountability at all levels, and the framework for legislative, executive and judicial action for their application. Charter revision should incorporate provisions for transparency and public access to information. As collective consultative bodies, the GA and Executive Council provide some protection from individual abuse of power and the ability of any one country to block international action. The revised Charter would create higher standards of government accountability and mechanisms for international action where necessary to intervene against security threats, abuse of power and human rights violations at the national level.

Once the GA is fully elected by popular vote, it would be directly accountable to its universal electorate through regular renewal of its membership. The Executive Council would have the mandate to ensure accountability within the UN system. The Chamber of Civil Society would provide a formal channel for civil society and global stakeholders to address accountability within and across the system.

A better educated global public electing its representatives to the GA would also provide a fundamental level of accountability, and should come to see the core values as essential criteria for the selection of candidates for international governance responsibilities.

An international press and media system freed from national hindrances and interference could express the diversified views of humankind and stimulate open, responsible and constructive debate on issues facing humanity, investigating abuses, ensuring transparency and supporting general public education. The GA would need to legislate on the necessary standards, responsibilities and safeguards for an independent world press and associated media, especially given the advent of universal media access and the temptation to manipulate public opinion for partisan political and ideological ends. The media could, rather, become a tool for increased public participation in international governance, a potential already exploited prior to Rio+20 and for the 2030 Agenda.

21

Some Immediate Steps Forward—Getting "From Here to There"

We are a movement for rationality. For democracy. For freedom from fear ... We are campaigners from 468 organisations who are working to safeguard the future, and we are representative of the moral majority: the billions of people who choose life over death.[1]

Beatrice Fihn, Nobel Peace Prize Lecture, International Campaign to Abolish Nuclear Weapons (ICAN)

As with any ambitious set of proposals for fundamental change, the obvious question is how to get from the lamentable present state of affairs to a substantially improved future condition. Is this just a utopian ideal and totally unrealistic, or are there practical ways forward? Dutch historian Rutger Bregman has recently called for a transcendence of the simplified or false dichotomy implicit in the labeling of all visionary or ambitious ideas as utopian, arguing that a range of "utopian" ideas are highly implementable and could result in significant social benefit.[2] Experience has shown that tinkering at the edges and marginal improvements have not succeeded in overcoming the fundamental problems with the present global governance paradigm that privileges an obsolete notion of the sovereignty of nations at any cost, and leaves the 1945 UN Charter essentially frozen in time. Furthermore, the urgency of many problems and the growing risks from issues left unaddressed do not allow time for the gradual change that might otherwise seem to be the reasonable way forward.

---

[1] Nobel Lecture given by the Nobel Peace Prize Laureate 2017, International Campaign to Abolish Nuclear Weapons (ICAN), delivered by Beatrice Fihn and Setsuko Thurlow, Oslo, December 10, 2017. www.nobelprize.org/prizes/peace/2017/ican/26041-international-campaign-to-abolish-nuclear-weapons-ican-nobel-lecture-2017/.

[2] Bregman, Rutger. 2018. *Utopia for Realists: And How We Can Get There*, London, Bloomsbury Paperbacks.

SCENARIOS OF POSSIBLE FUTURES

While we cannot predict the future, scenarios or storylines of possible futures can help us to imagine what possibilities lie ahead. It is customary to develop best- and worst-case examples, with some intermediate options in between. The most realistic scenarios are based on systems science that can help to model complex interacting processes. The classic economic myth of equilibrium is now replaced by the concept of a dynamic, constantly evolving system.[3] We can learn from nature that system change seldom follows a smooth trajectory, but generally what are termed "punctuated equilibria." Changing conditions or new pressures disrupt a relatively stable system, which goes through a period of turmoil and rapid change as it gradually adapts to the new situation and stabilizes, until external or internal changes push it again into a new transition.

This can help us to understand our own position in such a process. We are in the middle of the transition from social organization based on the scale of the isolated nation state to a global level of governance and organization based on what has become a physically united world. This change has created forces of disintegration that are tearing down old maladapted institutions and mindsets, and constructive forces that are building the elements of a global level of social organization and consciousness. Part of this challenge is to find the best balance of organization at each level – global, national and local communities – applying principles of subsidiarity, efficiency and participation. The following three scenarios sketch out possible ways ahead.

1. *The rational trajectory*. According to Richard Falk,[4] an enthusiastic admirer of Saul Medlovitz, the father of global constitutionalism studies, our choices for the future have narrowed. We can be rational about it and design new structures and come forward with creative proposals, just as Clark and Sohn did in the 1950s and 1960s, producing a detailed blueprint for a new or significantly enhanced United Nations Charter, as the basis for the establishment of institutions and governance arrangements that would not just lay the basis for international peace but also achieve other aims that are implicit in discussions about the kind of global order that we would wish.

Based on these proposals, a number of enlightened leaders could recognize that a determined collective effort by governments can resolve the flaws in the United Nations through an act of consultative will and adapt it to the needs of the diverse

[3]   Beinhocker, Eric D. 2006. *The Origin of Wealth: Evolution, Complexity, and the Radical Remaking of Economics*, Cambridge, MA, Harvard Business School Press, and London, Random House Business Books.
[4]   Falk, Richard, Robert C. Johansen, and Samuel S. Kim. 1993a. "Global Constitutionalism and World Order," in Richard Falk, Robert Johansen, and Samuel Kim (eds.), *The Constitutional Foundations of World Peace*. New York: State University of New York Press, chapter 1, pp. 3–12.

peoples of the world, seeing clearly the range of looming international crises close on the horizon. They rally the great majority of governments to convene a review conference on the UN Charter to adopt changes such as those proposed in this book.[5] The momentum is such that even the members with veto powers agree to go along. A set of transitional processes is implemented to increase trust, such as carefully organized confidence-building and mutual disarmament, and technical training and investment in capacity-building at the national level, before the new international institutions acquire binding jurisdiction. If one or more of the permanent members of the Security Council blocks revision of the UN Charter (e.g., by refusing to ratify the significant Charter amendments proposed at a general review conference), a majority of governments could hold an alternative Charter replacement conference instead, to set up a new United World Organization to succeed the United Nations.[6] An "Interpretative Declaration" approved at the plenary session of the San Francisco conference indeed noted that states would have a "right of withdrawal" from the UN "if an amendment duly accepted by the necessary majority in the Assembly or in a general conference fails to secure the ratification necessary to bring such amendment into effect" (para. 3).[7] Once the new mechanisms are in place and new financing creates an organization with more resources than the UN, such an entity could propose a "merger" with or "buy-out" of the UN, absorbing for example, the Secretariat and specialized agencies into the new system, and leaving recalcitrant governments to opt in or out. The reasonable possibility of this second option might be sufficient to convince all governments that it is better to be within the new system than outside of it.

This global order would also address the economic, social, environmental and other dimensions of creating a better world. In this scenario the United Nations or its successor would see a substantial enhancement of its role in the area of the peaceful settlement of disputes, general conflict prevention and peacekeeping; it would play a

[5] Article 109(3) of the UN Charter envisaged a general UN review conference that should be held within ten years of the Charter's adoption in 1945. This provision was added as a "compromise" for the majority of states at the global level who had significant reservations about the veto of power of the five permanent members of the Security Council, to which they only reluctantly agreed. The general review conference as provided for under Article 109(3) was never held. Article 109(1) of the Charter additionally allows for the holding of a general review conference on the Charter at any time, upon the request of the General Assembly (with a two-thirds majority) and the Security Council (by a vote of any nine members).

[6] Indeed, some legal scholars argue that if the changes proposed to the current Charter are too significant, international organizational precedent would call for setting up a whole new international successor organization, as occurred with the League of Nations and the United Nations, and the transition in 1960 from the OEEC to the OECD, among other examples. See, e.g., Frowein, J.A. 1998. "Are there Limits to the Amendment Procedures in Treaties Constituting International Organisations?" in G. Hafner et al. (eds.), *Liber Amicorum Prof. Seidl-Hohenveldern, in Honour of His 80th Birthday*, Leiden, Brill, p. 201.

[7] Witschel, Georg. 2012. "Ch.XVIII Amendments, Article 108," in Bruno Simma et al. (eds.), *The Charter of the United Nations: A Commentary*, Oxford Commentaries on International Law series, 3rd Edition, 2 vols., Oxford, Oxford University Press, Vol. II, pp. 2199–2231, at p. 2217.

much more critical role in the administration of the global commons, in environmental protection, in disarmament, in humanitarian responses to calamities whether natural or man-made; in a nutshell, it would move into the empty space created by our current global governance gap, that nebulous and dangerous area where no one is in charge.

There is an implicit optimism in this first option; it assumes that the forces of globalization and the coming of humanity into an age of greater maturity and capability are pushing us toward a more integrative political order, one that will set aside the neo-Darwinism of the state system that is at the heart of a wide range of unresolved problems and has been so damaging to the world over the past century. The proposals contained in this book have attempted to provide key elements of such a blueprint that, in essence, imply enhancement of governance capabilities on an international scale, many of them involving a significant strengthening of supranational institutions and mechanisms to put in place defenses to protect peoples and the global commons, and at the same time to ensure national autonomy. They include a first sketch of

> legislative organs to establish binding standards of behavior, administrative capacity to interpret these standards, financial powers, including revenue sources, and [eventually] taxing power, rules and procedures determining membership and participation in international institutions and the status of international actors, as well as modes to render all actors accountable ... regimes for protecting and managing the global commons, regulation of collective violence and supranational police, frameworks for world economic life, including trade, monetary and financial spheres ... and finally, a "global constitution" or, possibly, some invisible "document" that establishes an organic law for the community of states, nations, and peoples which frames and constitutes the political world.[8]

Maturing Capacities of Transnational Civil Society

For those who think that this scenario is not politically realistic because it ignores great-power politics, deep-seated nationalisms and narrow national interests, particularly among the veto-wielding members of the Security Council, one can point to the absence of (initial) great-power consent in a number of recent important initiatives in the area of international cooperation, including the adoption of the Anti-Personnel Mine Ban Convention (1997), the International Criminal Court (ICC) and its Rome Statute (1998), the development and acceptance of the Responsibility to Protect (R2P) norm and its implementation (ongoing), and the Treaty on

---

[8] Falk, Richard. 1993b. "The Pathways of Global Constitutionalism," in Richard Falk, Robert Johansen, and Samuel Kim (eds.), *The Constitutional Foundations of World Peace*. New York, State University of New York Press, chapter 2, pp. 13–38, at p.15.

the Prohibition of Nuclear Weapons (2017), among others. These innovations have come about with the significant involvement of international nongovernmental organizations (NGOs) working in concert, forming "smart coalitions" by creating alliances with a range of like-minded states in order to advance reforms in the global public interest. The negotiation of the 2006 UN Convention on the Rights of Persons with Disabilities has been held up as another dramatic achievement of transnational civil society and "smart coalitions," representing also a new form of engaged, proactive and concretely influential "citizen diplomacy."[9] Techniques for such transnational efforts are being progressively refined and articulated (see, e.g., the Box "What Does a Successful Civil Society Movement Look Like?" according to Nobel Peace Prize-winner Jody Williams of the International Campaign to Ban Land Mines).

Additionally, in two of the three cases where the Charter has been amended since 1945 (under its Article 108), agreement of all the permanent members of the Security Council was only achieved belatedly, after the amendments were proposed by the General Assembly. One can see similar patterns in normative shifts where some countries may initially vigorously resist a significant change, but then acquiesce or move to an actively supportive role of that change, as happened with the ICC in certain respects.[10] As David Bosco notes in relation to the ICC: "it is possible to construct institutions around power—and then leverage the normative power of those institutions to induce major-power support."[11] The 2015 Report of the Commission on Global Security, Justice and Governance, co-chaired by Madeleine Albright and Ibrahim Gambari (former US Secretary of State and Foreign Minister of Nigeria, respectively), indeed mentions the importance of smart coalitions in the context of key strategies for global governance reform.[12]

This growing list of international civil society successes echoes a recent observation by Jürgen Habermas, who calls for new efforts to tame the generally uneven effects of globalization: "[f]or it is only through new transnational capacities for political action that the *social and economic* forces unleashed at the transnational level can be tamed, i.e., the systemic pressures reaching across national borders, today above all those of the global banking sector," noting that economic dynamics

---

[9] See the description of this phenomenon in: White, J. and K. Young. 2008. "Nothing about Us without Us: Securing the Disability Rights Convention," in J. Williams, S.D. Goose, and M. Wareham (eds.), *Banning Landmines: Disarmament, Citizen Diplomacy, and Human Security*, Lanham, MD, Rowman and Littlefield, pp. 241–262.

[10] See, for example, a detailed narrative of the US relationship with the ICC in: Bosco, David. 2014. *Rough Justice: The International Criminal Court in a World of Power Politics*, Oxford, Oxford University Press.

[11] Ibid., p. 16.

[12] Commission on Global Security, Justice & Governance, *Confronting the Crisis of Global Governance*. Report of the Commission on Global Security, Justice & Governance, June 2015, The Hague, The Hague Institute for Global Justice, and Washington, DC, The Stimson Center, p. 105.

within international society have been "exacerbating a democratic deficit" for decades.[13] This is why we are, among other things, proposing enhanced legislative capacities of the UN, and a standing advisory Civil Society Chamber (see Chapters 4–6).

Box

What Does a Successful Civil Society Movement Look Like?[14]

- Know how to organize
- Maintain a flexible structure
- Need for leadership and committed workers
- Always have an action plan, deadline, outcome-oriented meetings
- Communication, communication and more communication
- Follow-up and follow through
- Provide expertise and documentation
- Articulate goals and messages clearly and simply
- Focus on the human cost
- Use as many forums as possible to promote the message
- Be inclusive, be diverse, yet speak with one voice
- Recognize that international context and timing do matter

---

2. *Business as usual.* Muddling through or "drift" is certainly a second possible scenario for the next half-century. As there is little sign of sufficient enlightened leadership to take us safely through the transition, where might inaction take us? This may appear to be the path of least resistance, but we should be wary of where it could lead. The voice of realism might say that populations should adapt to the "real world" and recognize that there is no political will among the key global powers to rethink in a major way the institutional structures that were put in place in 1945. States are not interested in working out the details of new global constitutional arrangements because they do not believe that the world can ultimately be better integrated. The permanent members of the UN Security Council will never want to give up the veto power because they value the absolute discretion on which it is based, the ability to exempt themselves (and their close allies) from scrutiny, even if they understand that it undermines the moral legitimacy of the system, and has

---

[13] Habermas, Jürgen. 2012. "The Crisis of the European Union in the Light of a Constitutionalization of International Law." *The European Journal of International Law*, Vol. 23, No. 2, pp. 335–348, at p. 338.

[14] This list is taken from: Williams, J. and S.D. Goose. 2008. "Citizen Diplomacy and the Ottawa Process: A Lasting Model?" in J. Williams, S.D. Goose, and M. Wareham (eds.), *Banning Landmines: Disarmament, Citizen Diplomacy, and Human Security*, Lanham, MD, Rowman and Littlefield, pp. 181–196.

hampered in important ways the adaptation of UN institutions to the demands of a radically different world than that which existed at the end of the last world war. Thus, "reforms" should be limited to tinkering at the edges, making small gains in efficiency (e.g., set up an Ad Hoc Working Group to study how to revitalize the General Assembly, explore ways to limit the use of the veto in cases involving mass atrocities, study ways to increase the relevance of the UN's Economic and Social Council, and so on), but not challenging in any fundamental way the essential infrastructure, not because such changes are not needed, but mostly because they will not be accepted. Indeed, the last US president to talk about a "new world order" was George H.W. Bush, in 1991, but few doubted that he simply meant a more cooperative approach in dealing with international problems at the end of the Cold War, but still within a rigid framework of maximally sovereign states.

Were they alive today, Clark and Sohn would still be preaching in the wilderness, it is claimed. Their proposals, 60 years after they were first made, would still be considered hopelessly optimistic. The problem with this scenario is that "drift" is itself hopelessly optimistic. It assumes that we are in a stable equilibrium, where tinkering at the edges will suffice to confront the existential crisis of climate change and global ecosystem degradation, to keep away the dangers of nuclear proliferation, to address the social, economic and (increasingly) political consequences of income inequality, to prevent the next global financial crisis from wreaking havoc with the livelihoods of hundreds of millions, to prevent now-globalized corruption from undermining the very basis of our institutions and our civilization, to name just a few of our current global challenges. It is unlikely that we shall just muddle through with governments always doing too little, too late, as Jorgen Randers, one of the authors of the original *Limits to Growth*, predicted in 2012.[15] We are close to too many breaking points, increasing the probability that one of them could push us over the edge.

Drift is a recipe for inevitable disaster. The only question is how long it will take before we crash into the wall and at what cost, in economic and human terms, and how long it will take to recover, assuming recovery is even possible following, for instance, multiple and large-scale climate-change-induced calamities.[16] A period of drift is what we entered into with the onset of the Cold War, when nuclear deterrence created a semblance of peace and security. We avoided World War III, but not the killing and maiming of millions in dozens of conventional conflicts across the planet. There have been countless other casualties involving human rights violations, autocratic repressions, Cultural Revolutions and the like. Meanwhile we

[15] Randers, Jorgen. 2012. *2052: A Global Forecast for the Next Forty Years.* A Report to the Club of Rome. Commemorating the 40th Anniversary of The Limits to Growth. White River Junction, VT, Chelsea Green Publishing.

[16] Steffen, Will et al. 2018. "Trajectories of the Earth System in the Anthropocene." *PNAS*, Vol. 115, No. 33, pp. 8252–8259. https://doi.org/10.1073/pnas.1810141115.

passively incubated a myriad of other problems, many of them ticking time bombs ready to explode in the twenty-first century.

A financial crisis or collapse might be the most benign of those time bombs, since it would not directly destroy infrastructure or wipe out masses of people, although the secondary effects could be quite serious if trade collapses. In fact, if trade in fossil fuels was interrupted, this might help us to avoid catastrophic climate change. A more limited war between a few major countries, or a pandemic killing a significant fraction of the world population and requiring the shutting down of most trade and transport to slow its spread,[17] are other plausible possibilities. A youth or popular rebellion against an economic system that has left them no hope has also been predicted.[18] In another intermediate scenario, a series of smaller crises could be used to catalyze significant step-wise improvements in global governance, rather than trying to do dramatic system renovation all at once.

3. **Rebuilding after disaster.** In the worst-case scenario, national leaders driven by ego stumble into World War III, which draws on many existing tensions and conflicts to also instigate a range of civil wars in parallel. In this cataclysmic upheaval, cities are laid waste and some nuclear arms are used, precipitating a nuclear winter that destroys agricultural production for several years. Or, Earth shifts into one of the worst-case "hothouse" scenarios due to unchecked climate change.[19] There is a catastrophic collapse in civilization, and billions of people die in the resulting famine. The survivors are mostly the poorest of the poor living outside the economy in remote areas far from the cities or sites of conflict, as well as communities with sufficient solidarity and resilience to survive until the crisis passes. With so much destruction, rebuilding is a slow and painful process, trying to salvage enough knowledge of communication technologies to establish materially simpler, potentially less urbanized societies. Only then could appropriate institutions of global governance be put in place to prevent any such catastrophe from occurring again.

What we did not do through rational design, when we had the means and the time to do it, we would have to do against the background of great adversity, worldwide dislocations, suffering and constrained resources because of a multitude of claims on already strained governments and public finances. Just as it is difficult to do economic reforms following a crisis – something that one of us learned early

[17] MacKenzie, Debora. 2008. "The Collapse of Civilization: It's more Precarious than We Realized," "The End of Civilization," pp. 28–31; "Are We Doomed? The Very Nature of Civilization May Make Its Demise Inevitable," pp. 32–35. *New Scientist*, Vol. 2650, cover story, 5 April.

[18] Turchin, Peter. 2010. "Political Instability May Be a Contributor in the Coming Decade." *Nature*, Vol. 463, p. 608. DOI: 10.1038/463608a.

[19] Watts, Jonathan. 2018. "Domino-Effect of Climate Events Could Move Earth into a 'Hothouse' State," *The Guardian*, August 7. www.theguardian.com/environment/2018/aug/06/domino-effect-of-climate-events-could-push-earth-into-a-hothouse-state; Steffen et al. "Trajectories of the Earth System in the Anthropocene."

on in his professional career as an international economist – it would be immeasurably more difficult to bring new, cutting-edge global institutions into being against the background of a collapsed social order.

Opinions are divided on what follows a global calamity; the implied scenarios hinge on one's beliefs about human nature under extreme forms of stress. Would such events bring out the best in us, would they lead to changes in behavior and psychological reflexes as we realized that we needed to explore new arrangements for global order? Or would they unleash a new dark age? Would the absence of a global hegemonic power lead to problems in the restoration of order and stability? Or perhaps, just as the European powers in the 1950s had no option but to put aside war as an instrument for the settlement of international disputes and opted instead for creating the European Union, we would have to find the courage and imagination to do the same on a global scale. And just as World War II precipitated a change in European consciousness, a global catastrophe would surely do the same on a world scale.

Regardless of the way in which an effective global order comes into being, the ultimate outcome will be a function of humanity's exertions, initiative and the strength of its will. Einstein was right when he wrote that "the destiny of civilized humanity depends more than ever on the moral forces it is capable of generating."[20]

SOME IMMEDIATE STEPS AHEAD

A first step is obviously to reopen the debate on the need for revision of the UN Charter and the options to make the UN fit for purpose in this century. This debate should extend beyond academic and specialist circles, and should involve governments on the one hand, and a wide range of professionals and the general public on the other. For the latter, clear messages will be needed comparing what the public naturally expects from government at the national level and what is lacking internationally, which leaves an anarchy that threatens their well-being in fundamental ways. As large an alliance as possible of like-minded people and organizations should be gathered around this public discourse, leaving the specifics to be considered and debated openly. It is hoped that many ideas will be championed by one organization or another. There will clearly be opposition to such discussion, with attempts to discredit and distort proposals, which should be anticipated and countered to the extent possible. A particularly strong reaction may be expected from at least some of the permanent members of the Security Council, given present trends.

---

[20] Einstein, Albert. 1990. *The World as I See It*, New York, Quality Paperback Books, p. 44.

A WORLD CONFERENCE ON GLOBAL INSTITUTIONS

One mechanism to expand the debate on global governance would be through world conferences on global institutions.[21] These could be intergovernmental conferences, also including wider participation from all stakeholders from civil society. The UN Conference on Sustainable Development (Rio+20) in 2012, with the subsequent negotiations of the 2030 Agenda and its Sustainable Development Goals, was a good example of an intergovernmental process supported by widespread consultation with, and contributions from, civil society. In 2015, the Commission on Global Security, Justice and Governance made a proposal to convene a world conference in 2020 to mark the 75th anniversary of the creation of the UN.[22] The aim would be to take up the issue of the reforms that need to be implemented to adapt our system of global governance to the needs and the challenges that we now face and which, if unaddressed, could well plunge the world into unprecedented crises and be hugely costly in economic and human terms. 2020 is also the year for the UN Framework Convention on Climate Change (UNFCCC) to review and increase the voluntary national commitments under the Paris Agreement on climate change—another opportunity to strengthen governance of an existential threat to global security and well-being. A major world conference may now realistically be held in 2025 for the 80th anniversary of the UN, allowing time for thorough preparation.

The 1944 Bretton Woods Conference, which led to the creation of a new international financial system, was a highly successful example of effective and productive international cooperation. The World Conference we have in mind would have a more ambitious agenda, reflecting the global and varied nature of the challenges we face. Unlike Bretton Woods, the World Conference would bring together representatives not only from governments but also civil society and the business community. The conference would be a rallying point, and also the start of a staged process intended to build momentum and consensus around the sorts of reforms that have been identified in this book. Building the institutions that will underpin our system of global governance in the coming decades could well be the most important project of this century, requiring imagination, persistence and confidence that, sooner rather than later, we will need to make the transition to vastly enhanced mechanisms of binding international cooperation if we are to avoid and address untold human suffering and catastrophe.

---

[21] Alexander, Titus and Robert Whitfield. 2018. "Creating a Global Consciousness." Blog on One World Trust, November 5. www.oneworldtrust.org/blogs.

[22] Commission on Global Security, Justice & Governance, *Confronting the Crisis of Global Governance*.

A COALITION OF THE WILLING AND LIKE-MINDED

There are an increasing number of governments that are convinced of the need for major changes and reinforcement in multilateral cooperation, largely in the middle range of countries, neither "great powers" with hegemonic ambitions, nor those struggling to meet basic needs. They can assemble into a like-minded "coalition of the willing," and not wait for universal acceptance.

A major effort should be directed to bring as many of these governments as possible around to serious consideration of Charter reform. The threat of blockage by veto should not be allowed to stymie informed debate. The aim should be to assemble, gradually if necessary, the majority of governments around the world with a common vision, ready to take a comprehensive reform agenda forward. The possibility of creating a new organization to replace the United Nations, if necessary, as a last resort, should not be excluded as a viable option in a scenario involving multiple crises across a range of fronts.

A series of expert groups or commissions could be charged to refine proposals such as those presented in this book and to draft the specific Charter language needed to capture a growing consensus. Once the revised (or new) proposed Charter was in reasonably complete form, a global Charter conference should be called under the UN Charter review provisions or otherwise, attended by heads of state and government, to conclude the binding amended or new Charter document, the provisions of which would be accepted by governments as a condition of membership. Ideally, all governments should join this organization voluntarily, as with the United Nations. But it is conceivable that some would wish to wait; as the new organization took off, it is likely that governments and citizens would gradually recognize that the benefits of being inside such an enhanced institution vastly exceed the costs of being outside, with the organization rapidly becoming universal in its coverage.

Once the central structure was operational, the many specialized agencies, associated organizations, and convention secretariats would be integrated gradually into the new global architecture without interrupting their continuing activity. A reliable mechanism for international funding would give the new organization far greater resources than the old UN. With its new legislative capacity, the General Assembly could review the conventions and other legal charters of the system components, and make recommendations for institutional consolidation, in the interest of greatly simplifying the global system. Since the governments are the same, and none of the specialized agencies and UN-related organizations has the same problem with permanent members with a veto, the will of a concerted majority of governments to transfer allegiance to a new organization should more readily prevail. The recent integration of the International Organization for Migration (IOM) into the UN system shows that this kind of fusion is certainly possible. After some years, as more and more governments withdrew from the old UN and joined the new organization, just as the UN replaced the League of Nations, the transition would be complete.

INCREMENTAL STEPS TOWARDS SUBSTANTIAL REFORM

Building on the many improvements in the UN system since 1945, and existing potentials for further reform that do not depend on UN Charter revision, there are a wide variety of further possible steps to break the ground for a more fundamental transformation.

We suggest two potential initial strategies – without prejudice to a range of other viable pathways – to respond to the concern about practical ways forward and to address various dimensions of the challenge to improve global governance. It is currently not clear which paths may have the best chance of succeeding, so a range of options likely should be tried; there is a need for learning and adaptation as we go along.

The World Parliamentary Assembly

It may take time before the community of nations is ready to reform the UN Charter and give the General Assembly the legislative powers and proportional representation necessary to increase its legitimacy and effectiveness. Establishing a World Parliamentary Assembly (WPA) as an advisory body to the General Assembly, as proposed in Chapter 5, would be a valuable learning process in both popular representation in UN decision-making and in selecting those to speak on behalf of "we the peoples" at the UN. The creation of a WPA and its evolution over time will make it possible to experiment with different processes and approaches, and to accumulate valuable experience to support eventually the formal consultations leading to Charter revision.

Additionally, the WPA, working in parallel with or catalyzed by transnational civil society coalitions and possibly a standing forum or Chamber for Civil Society (see Chapter 6), could champion key priority reform items, for example, ensuring that the International Court of Justice and the International Criminal Court are obligatory courts with compulsory jurisdiction for all UN members, advocating for reformed UN financing, designing ambitious and consolidated new disarmament proposals, and so on. Reforms that required Charter amendment could be made by way of the Charter's Article 108, outside of a general UN review conference.

The European Union Stepwise Approach

Chapter 3 on European Integration provided background and an analysis of the steps in the formation of the European Union as it exists today, as an example of a process focusing on building the trust and confidence necessary for governments to yield elements of national prerogative to supranational institutions. We summarize main milestones of this integration trajectory below, which may help to catalyze thinking as to possible trajectories at the international level.

Starting with a vision of the need for greater economic and political integration to make future wars in Europe impossible, a gradual approach was adopted. The first step in 1951 was to select the formation of the European Coal and Steel Community as a narrow area where the mutual benefits of the cooperation necessary for conflict prevention and reconstruction after the war were most obvious. Even then, the political leaders went over the heads of resistant government bureaucracies to take the first step in giving up sovereignty over a critical dimension of their economies. Building on the success of this step, and following an exploration of the issues of further integration, the Treaties of Rome were signed in 1957 establishing the European Economic Community and the European Atomic Energy Commission with six founding members. A 1979 decision of the European Court of Justice established the principle of mutual recognition of standards of product regulation among all European member states. Amendments were made to the Treaty of Rome to remove the requirement for unanimity for a range of decisions of the Council through the Single European Act ratified in 1987. While European trade greatly expanded, hidden barriers created pressures from business for further integration and deregulation, implemented in the Europe 1992 program. Border controls were streamlined and then eliminated. Variations in VAT rates were reduced. The European Parliament evolved from an advisory group of national parliamentarians to a directly elected body. The 1992 Maastricht Treaty called for a common European currency and gave legal meaning to the concept of Union citizenship. Finland, Austria and Sweden joined the Union in 1994. The 2009 Treaty of Lisbon made further reforms and expanded European competencies, strengthening the European Parliament, and creating the posts of President of the European Council and High Representative of the Union for Foreign Affairs and Security Policy. The Charter of Fundamental Rights was made legally binding. There have been ups and downs, and countries have advanced at different paces, yet the Union has expanded to 28 members to date. The eurozone does not cover all EU member states and the Schengen open-border area includes some states outside the European Union, showing institutional flexibility to cater to different national needs and concerns. Still, the process shows the benefits that can come from passing certain elements of national sovereignty to a supranational level.

Taking the European Union as an example, the international community could select an issue on which global unity is most likely and cooperation in the common global interest so clearly justified, as a first stepping-stone in a confidence-building process. Climate change could easily be such an issue, given the clear scientific evidence of the need for rapid action and the unanimity already achieved in the adoption of the Paris Agreement in 2015.[23] The next step could be to agree on a scientifically determined binding limit for global greenhouse gas concentrations, with legally enforceable responsibilities to respect those limits (and the institutional machinery to ensure compliance) to be shared equitably among all countries. This could be founded on the legal recognition that the atmosphere, the biosphere, the oceans and major biochemical processes such as the carbon and nitrogen cycles are common properties and responsibilities of all nations, much like the shared common spaces in a condominium building.[24] Once the mechanisms and institutions created for this purpose show their effectiveness and establish the necessary level of trust, the way would be open to extend these efforts to address other pressing global risks and needs, by further strengthening global institutions and capacities.

---

[23] IPCC. 2018. *Global Warming of 1.5°C* (SR15), Special Report. Summary for Policy Makers, Geneva, Intergovernmental Panel on Climate Change, October. www.ipcc.ch/report/sr15/.

[24] The Common Home of Humanity (CHH) project proposes such an approach, as mentioned in Chapter 16 of this book; see: www.commonhomeofhumanity.org/.

PART VI

Conclusions

22

Bridging the Governance Gap

Peoples and their governments around the world need global institutions to solve collective problems that can only be addressed on a global scale. They must be able to make and enforce global rules on a variety of subjects and through a variety of means. Further, it has become commonplace to claim that the international institutions created in the late 1940s, after a very different war and facing a host of different threats from those we face today, are outdated and inadequate to meet contemporary challenges. They must be reformed or even reinvented; new ones must be created.[1]

Anne-Marie Slaughter

As a review of past governance proposals has shown, there has been no shortage of persuasive arguments for stronger global institutions. Anne-Marie Slaughter has diagnosed "the globalization paradox," which consists in "needing more government and fearing it."[2] The United Nations was born in 1945 with fundamental flaws intended to make it weak enough to be acceptable to Stalin and the United States Senate. Of the initiatives for reform called for by Einstein and Russell in the early postwar period, and by Clark and Sohn a decade later, among others, none have led to concerted international action, and there is no evidence that this trend will reverse in the near future. Multilateralism is currently under attack, in part because of these failings. A multipolar world is – for now – replacing the superpower dominance of previous decades. However, a rising nationalism in many countries, and increased assertiveness, sometimes combined with protectionist tendencies, among the most powerful of the permanent members of the Security Council suggest that these nations wish to continue the trend of disproportionate military and other influence in the world, and have little interest in giving up their veto power or other anachronistic prerogatives. If anything, the spirit of national

---

[1] Slaughter, Anne-Marie. 2004. *A New World Order*, Princeton, NJ, and Oxford, Princeton University Press, p. 9.
[2] Ibid.

sovereignty, however maladapted to a globalized world, is currently strengthening rather than receding. The future of global governance, and perhaps of civilization itself, depends on our ability to reconcile somehow political realism, the scientific facts of a limited planet under serious stress, the fears generated by rapid change and the hopes of finally achieving a just and united world. Without reform in global governance, we risk a further downward spiral of disintegration into the anarchy of absolute national sovereignty in a deeply interdependent world, made more dangerous by our advanced technologies for destruction and the destabilization of the fundamental life support systems of our planetary environment.

Foreign policy experts and various wise women and men who have looked at the future of the United Nations – and have tried to imagine where it is headed in the twenty-first century – have inevitably come up against the issue of whether the UN will continue to be an organization founded on a rigid notion of the sovereignty of its component members, which was ultimately the expressed desire of the four major powers that created it in 1945. Can the UN evolve in some fashion, reflecting the changing role of the state in the context of a fully integrated global economy and a world facing a range of critical global problems, the solutions for which seem to be out of reach without a significant strengthening of our mechanisms of international cooperation? Richard von Weizsacker and Moeen Qureshi, co-chairs of the Independent Working Group on the Future of the United Nations, for instance, noted, as far back as 1995: "By the mid-twenty-first century, however, it is likely that the nature of statehood and assumptions about national sovereignty will have evolved in response to global needs and to an enlarged sense of world community."[3]

In this concluding chapter we acknowledge the realities of our present situation, highlight some of the general foundations for any system of governance and look also at some of the positive signs of change. Skeptics might point to the fact that the major initiatives taken during the twentieth century in the area of international cooperation were primarily in response to, and not to anticipate or prevent, the suffering and destruction of the two world wars. Indeed, the most far-reaching and ambitious of these, the creation of the European Union, brought together precisely the states at the center of those global conflicts. This suggests that truly global institutions are unlikely to emerge unless some sufficiently profound crisis, unparalleled in its intensity, permanently marks human consciousness with the notion of global interdependence and the dangers of remaining within an international institutional framework inadequate for and unresponsive to the needs of humanity as a whole. Infinitely preferable, of course, would be an act of mature and collective will, rather than the forces of adverse circumstances, to set a new stage in the political life of humanity. We hope that our proposals in this book will seed ideas, stimulate

---

[3] Von Weizsacker, Richard and Moeen Qureshi (co-chairs), Independent Working Group on the Future of the United Nations. 1995. *The United Nations in Its Second Half-Century*, New York, Ford Foundation, p. 7.

discussion and debate, show that there are reasonable ways forward and encourage positive developments to avoid the worst.

THE ROOTS OF PRESENT FAILURES

It is important to understand why developments over the past seven decades have led to so little progress. Even today, few people would say that there is a realistic possibility in the near term for nations to accept the ambitious vision of the United Nations advocated by the likes of Clark, Einstein, and Russell in the 1940s and 1950s, turning the organization into an effective and legitimate governance instrument, operating under the effective rule of international law, with a legislature passing laws imposing binding obligations on its members in areas of key international concern. With the end of the Cold War in the early 1990s, the fear of nuclear annihilation – so elegantly and eloquently portrayed in Jonathan Schell's *The Fate of the Earth*[4] – receded into the background and led to a false sense of security that the existing mechanisms of international cooperation embedded in the UN Charter, while flawed, would still allow us to muddle through the next century. The maintenance of international peace and security anticipated in Article 1(1) of the Charter has largely remained a responsibility of the major powers in the cases of countries or situations in which their strategic interests were affected, while being nobody's responsibility where no such interests were involved. Other problems with systemic implications for global welfare – management of the world's financial system, human rights violations, migration, to name a few – have either been nobody's responsibility or have been managed on an ad hoc basis by some of the UN agencies or other disparate international bodies, with all the associated inefficiencies and social costs, such as the near collapse of the world's financial system in 2008.

Few would argue that the present world order is fit for purpose, or that it is a solid basis to ensure security and prosperity for the future, whether in the developing or developed world. The idea that in a globalized world we need a higher level of government to deal with problems that straddle national boundaries has gained considerable traction in recent decades, and the European Union – with all its flaws – bears ample testimony to that. In any case, this line of thinking has been buttressed by the growing inability of national governments to solve global problems of concern to citizens everywhere. We do not yet have many politicians running for office making an informed case for more effective international governance, but the current system has few credible defenders willing to make the case that we can simply proceed on our present path, managing the world one crisis at a time, with the faith that a world order based on the sacred principle of national sovereignty provides, to use economic jargon, a stable equilibrium.

---

[4] Schell, Jonathan. 1982. *The Fate of the Earth*, London, Jonathan Cape.

It is difficult to disagree with those who have argued that we missed a great chance in the early 1940s, when, against the background of a world war, we could have opted for bringing into being an organization that would actually be able to deliver on the laudable promises contained in its first Article. Those noble sentiments seemed highly timely and appropriate, bearing in mind the untold suffering and calamity, the tens of millions of dead, the mindless killing of innocents in concentration camps, the destruction of entire cities, the collapse of the economy and social order. But, in the end, more pedestrian concerns prevailed. Would the US Senate ratify anything other than the creation of a largely harmless (or even useless) organization, with no teeth and no ability to interfere to the slightest degree with the prerogatives of American power? The ghost of Senator Henry Cabot Lodge, who led the US Senate rejection of the League of Nations, hovered over the Dumbarton Oaks proceedings, effectively neutralizing the emergence of anything other than a weak organization.

This is not to suggest that others were not at fault as well. Stalin was equally fierce in his determination not to allow a body of international laws and principles to interfere with his own repression and killing, his overwhelming determination to defeat Nazi Germany and the pursuit of his own nuclear ambitions. We have deep respect for the work done by Clark and Sohn in *World Peace through World Law*,[5] but by the late 1950s, when their admirable suggestions for UN Charter reform were put forward, the Cold War had set in and a new landscape for international relations had emerged. The Soviet Union had already begun to act in ways that went wholly counter to the foundational principles of the UN Charter (to say nothing of the Charter amendments suggested in the Clark and Sohn proposals).

Thus, in thinking about the future, it is evident that the political context matters a great deal; there must be a coming together of minds about the ends and the means of a reformed system of global governance, at least among the major powers and many of the countries that are now operating as full democracies. It is worth noting the role played by enlightened leadership at various critical moments during the past century, from President Wilson's strenuous efforts to bring into being the League of Nations, to President Roosevelt's vital role in pushing for the founding of the United Nations, to Jean Monnet's vision for a united Europe pledged to peace and prosperity in the Treaties of Rome. The creation of the United States of America itself would not have happened in the eighteenth century without the resolute leadership of its Founding Fathers.

Governments need to feel that whatever new system is brought into being, it will protect their peoples, safeguard their national autonomy and cultural distinctiveness,[6] and lead to objective improvements with respect to the status quo. The system

---

[5] Clark, Grenville and Louis B. Sohn. 1966. *World Peace through World Law: Two Alternative Plans*, Cambridge, MA, Harvard University Press.

[6] For example, through the employment of well-known federalist principles, or principles such as subsidiarity and proportionality, which are fundamental to EU operation (the former requires that decisions occur as closely as possible to the citizen, with checks made that

has to earn their trust, a rare commodity today among governments. How to get the process started and by whom is an important question. Some, including Clarence Streit in his 1939 classic *Union Now*, have suggested that the world's established democracies, with long traditions of rule of law, bear a special responsibility to lead the way.[7] But, eighty years later, India and China have emerged as global economic and political powers and it is difficult to think of any global governance initiative that could catalyze change without the participation of two countries that account for nearly 40 percent of the world's population. One may have reservations about including Russia in this list because, a quarter-century after the transition from the Soviet Union, to the world's 12th largest global economy, its claim to global power status seems to be based on the existence of its large nuclear arsenal and ability to disrupt and interfere, often on the margins of legality. This is not a substitute in any meaningful sense for a positive vision of what needs to be done to bring into being an improved global order.

Baratta argues that in the postwar era we found a middle way between World War III and world government.[8] We built nuclear arsenals, we developed a sophisticated military-industrial complex as an integral part of our economies (which, in the case of the Soviet Union, did much to bring about its collapse because of its unsustainable financial burdens), we put forward deterrence as the linchpin of our defense policies, we attempted to negotiate a range of arms control treaties – but we did not address in any fundamental way the main limitations in our state-based system.

According to Falk we continue to live in a world in which nation states "retain full control over their military capabilities"; in which they are not obliged to submit international disputes to some form of third-party procedure with high probability of effective implementation in cases involving war and peace; where international treaties remain the main mechanism of cooperation but are generally weak in settling disputes and even weaker in implementation; international institutions are poorly resourced and "lack any standing police or military forces;" "the peoples of the world remain overwhelmingly dependent on their domestic governments for protection against all forms of political violence and against abuses of human rights;" and nationalism remains a powerful force to mobilize people for narrow political ends.[9] Unfortunately for us, these flaws, which were evident at the San Francisco

---

decisions at the EU level are necessary given options available at the national, regional or local level; the latter requires that any action by the EU should not go beyond what is necessary to fulfil the objectives of the relevant EU treaties). See brief discussion of notions of subsidiarity in this chapter.

[7] Streit, Clarence, K. 1939. *Union Now: A Proposal for an Atlantic Federal Union of the Free*, New York and London, Harper & Brothers.

[8] Baratta, Joseph Preston. 2004. *The Politics of World Federation, United Nations, UN Reform, Atomic Control*, Westport, CT, Praeger Publishers.

[9] Falk, Richard. 1993. "The Pathways of Global Constitutionalism," in Richard Falk, Robert Johansen, and Samuel Kim (eds.), *The Constitutional Foundations of World Peace*, New York, State University of New York Press, chapter 2, pp. 13–38, at p. 23.

conference in 1945 for the world we had then, were greatly magnified in the decades that followed by growing interdependence, by the forces of globalization and the emergence of a multitude of new global problems for which our UN-based system was wholly unprepared. Hence the opening of what some experts call a "governance gap" – our inability to address global problems because our institutions are overwhelmed, as they were designed for a different world that has ceased to exist.

SEEDS OF SUCCESS

This is not to deny the great progress that has been made in the UN system since 1945. The scope of its action has enlarged greatly. New issues have been taken on board through international conventions and the activities of the specialized agencies, especially in the social and environmental fields. International law has deepened and extended its reach, both in formal texts and in customary international law. Collaboration has been successful in many technical areas, from transport and telecommunications to science and health. Smallpox was eradicated in 1980 and global epidemics brought under control. Working internationally is now the accepted norm. There is therefore much to build on for the further evolution of global governance. It is largely in collective security and disarmament, financing and effective progress on the environment that the system has been held back.

Much has been learned about multilevel sovereignty since the federation of 13 states into the United States of America in the eighteenth century. The European Union, despite its challenges today, has demonstrated the benefits of yielding some sovereignty to supranational institutions and opening borders. Recognition of the "responsibility to protect" (R2P) doctrine by the international community is another acknowledgment of the limitations of national sovereignty, and the evolution of key sovereign *responsibilities*, to protect and care for national populations. With advances in the theory of change and examples of punctuated equilibria, rapid transformation has been shown to be possible and to lead to positive outcomes even in complex systems. The dire situation in which we find ourselves today can be the motivation to trigger positive steps forward.

The great expansion of international civil society, organized around many themes and directly engaged with the United Nations and other structures of global governance, is another encouraging feature of our times. Civil society organizations are active in public discourses and have built mature international coalitions in support of critical issues. With new technologies of information and communications, this collaboration has only begun to fulfil its potential and can only increase in the future. Public expectations have also increased, fed by the media and the intensified cross-border movement of people, encouraging more global perspectives, particularly among the young. In a connected world, public education can also become more sophisticated and effective.

FOUNDATIONS FOR GLOBAL GOVERNANCE

The world of today is unlike anything in our past experience, and yet any future trajectory will necessarily have some roots in what we have learned. A starting point is our historical experience with the principles and institutions of governance expressed today in national systems. We also need to understand the accelerating change we are experiencing as existing and emerging technologies transform the scale of human interaction and our ability to educate, communicate and consult. Most importantly, we need some agreement on humanity's fundamental purpose, potential and inherent capacity for good if properly motivated.

National Sovereignty

The Treaty of Westphalia of 1648 that ended the Thirty Years War has commonly been interpreted as an important juncture for the birth of the modern nation state and the concept of national sovereignty that we have known in the nineteenth and twentieth centuries. So-called Westphalian notions of sovereignty have served a useful purpose as the relevant scale for governance for more than three centuries; but already during the last of those centuries, as new technologies of communication and transportation eroded the significance of national boundaries, the national scale of social organization and governance gradually became insufficient. The trauma of the two world wars of the twentieth century, which new technologies for warfare made increasingly destructive, forced nations to acknowledge the need for a supranational organization to prevent the repetition of such collective self-inflicted disasters. However, national sovereignty remained at the heart of the League of Nations and the United Nations, and the insistence of the great powers to give priority to their sovereign national interests over collective security led to fundamental flaws in the institutions created. The League of Nations had no independent power of enforcement, and Japan could simply withdraw to pursue its adventure in Manchuria. In the United Nations, the Security Council had the potential means to enforce its decisions, but these were largely neutralized by the veto retained by the five permanent members of the Security Council, who could also block any proposals for institutional reform. Both thus failed in their essential purpose to maintain peace and to pursue other worthwhile international goals.

These failures are also symptomatic of a fundamental flaw in any system based on closed and rigid approaches to national sovereignty, and on cultures of competition and zero-sum thinking: the lack of trust between national governments. Governments on the international stage have often proven themselves not to be trustworthy, whether because of the cunning and deception of autocratic regimes and their leaders' insatiable appetite for power, or the inconsistencies produced by democratic changes in leadership and ideology. The only area in which, practically speaking, a government signature is worth more than the paper it is written on, is the financial obligation for debts incurred, no matter how dubious in origin. Almost all other international obligations are still voluntary. This underlies the importance for any system of global governance to build trust that all decisions taken in the common interest will respect principles of justice and equity for all concerned.

A second flaw that can arise in giving primacy to national sovereignty, in which each state is considered equal, derives from the enormous differences, in fact, between nations – whether in geographic extent, population, economic power, military might or political influence. What chance could the tiny island state of Grenada have against the US military, which did indeed invade in 1983? How much does the population of Tuvalu (12,000) count in comparison with that of China (1.4 billion)? Perhaps more importantly, how can a Small Island Developing State with a tiny population carry out all the functions and international obligations expected of a modern nation? What is the hope for an economy that will never achieve economies of scale? Can a country such as Madagascar, a biodiversity hotspot with a population mired in poverty, be expected to meet both its human and nature conservation needs and obligations? The diversity of nations is part of the richness of humankind, and the autonomy of states needs to be preserved, but much greater flexibility and adaptability are required in intergovernmental processes to respond to the needs and to support the progress of all nations, leaving none of them behind.

At the other end of the scale, should the largest, wealthiest and most populous states continue to dominate the world, trampling on the rights of others? In essence, they often behave like bullies in a school yard, terrorizing others, grabbing whatever they want and competing to see who can be the most powerful at the top of the heap, imposing their hegemony on all the rest.

Furthermore, building the UN Charter around national sovereignty has produced an institution that addresses the aggregate of national interests, with nations too often jockeying for position to have their interests represented in the decision-making process. As in most power struggles, the stronger win out over the weaker. The present institution is poorly structured to protect and promote the collective global and human interests that must be the primary focus in the twenty-first century, and that are central to our proposals for Charter revision.

Governance

Nations have tried many systems of governance over the centuries, most of which can still be found somewhere in the world today. None could be said to be ideal. In fact, dysfunctional governments hide many of their misdeeds against their citizens behind a smokescreen of national sovereignty. If governance is to be just and equitable in service to their people at all scales, then the global framework should include a fuller definition of basic rights and responsibilities of all national governments, with the power to accompany and support, or to intervene in cases of flagrant and repeated failures to meet those standards at the national level.

Democracies, in principle, place the selection of leaders in the hands of the people. In representative democracies, those elected are expected to implement the platform on which they were elected (although this may seldom happen in practice) and thus to represent the majority. They are generally conceived to be only responsible to their electorate, rather than to any basic principles of justice or their own conscience. In most cases, political groups or factions within a society, once elected, try to govern while the other factions try to make them fail so that they, in turn, can take power. The interests of minorities are generally overlooked, as is, not infrequently, the long-term collective interest. In too many countries, winning the next election becomes more important than governing with the best interests of the people in mind. Lobbying and corruption give more influence to the wealthy and powerful. Many elected governments, once in power, have proven that they will stoop to anything to stay in power, undermining checks and balances, stifling opposition and dissent, and even sliding into despotism. As history and a number of current situations show, many autocrats were originally democratically elected, and may continue to go through the motions of irregular or sham elections.

Autocracy, whether by an absolute monarch or the head of an ecclesiastical hierarchy, was the dominant form of government for many centuries, and was the nearly universal form in Europe when the concept of national sovereignty was formulated. As history shows, a few exceptional leaders made great progress, but most were mediocre if not dangerously destructive in wielding their power. An aristocracy of hereditary landowners allowed for some decentralization, but it left the masses disenfranchised, if not completely subservient to the aristocratic classes.

One of the major objections to the creation of a global system of government is that it would "just be like national governments," only worse and more remote, with no way to go back if it gets out of hand. Despite our long history of the practice or malpractice of governance, there is no existing "perfect" system that could serve as *the* appropriate model for global governance, with fully comprehensive safeguards to protect it from those seeking power for selfish ends. We have therefore spent several chapters in this book also focusing on the importance of education and shared and internalized values and principles, to create the requisite cultures and individual qualities necessary for functional governance. However, we now collectively have the great luxury of a historical and comparative global vantage point to draw from the best mechanisms and design features of diverse governance systems, in order to fashion state-of-the-art institutions with the requisite qualities and checks and balances against various abuses of power at the international level. Similarly, modern good governance literature, as described in this book, provides much knowledge to guide the creation of sound, appropriate new institutions.

Some basic design criteria can be identified that can be used in conceiving of institutions of global governance, such as those proposed here. The legislative, executive and judicial functions necessary for any government should be separated, with checks and balances between them. No one function should be able to control and dominate the others, but they should collaborate to meet their common objectives. Safeguards should be built into the charter or constitution, with clear definitions of institutional, national and individual rights and responsibilities.

Given the frequent problems with individual leadership, and the complexities of governance today, it would be preferable to place the main administrative responsibility in a collective consultative body or council, to minimize the focus on personalities and to draw on a diversity of competencies. Power would be held collectively rather than individually.

One major challenge in an evolving system of global governance will be for national representatives, whether elected by the people or otherwise designated, to rise above merely representing national (or personal or ethnic) interests to see their role as seeking the welfare of all humanity and the planet as a whole. The ideal would be to set aside ideologies and political party platforms so as to select those with the personal qualities, mature experience and the basic values necessary for them to serve most effectively in the common interest. In this way, the rich diversity of perspectives and cultures so assembled could contribute to a collective consultative process in their search for the best solutions balancing the needs of all countries and peoples, with justice and equity, far from the conflict and raw exercise of power that mar present international relations.

A World Transformed (and Divided) by New Technologies

With the continuing process of rapid globalization, the world faces multiple potential instabilities.[10] Our systems of communication, transportation and finance are increasingly integrated, creating associated vulnerabilities from failures that can propagate through the system. Despite the wealth created by technological innovation in agriculture, industry and commerce, a major part of the world's population has failed to benefit sufficiently, and in recent years the concentration of wealth has accelerated.

Among the root causes of this socially destabilizing tendency is the primacy given to the profit motive as the exclusive end and purpose of the institutions (corporations and other business entities) creating economic wealth. Profit should be one measure of efficiency among others, but not a sole end in itself, enabling, for example, the destruction of the foundations of our collective prosperity and planetary life support systems. Important scientific knowledge and innovation thus, for example through distortions in our system of intellectual property, too frequently become walled-off private property, and access to them is restricted to those who can pay. This

---

[10] MacKenzie, Debora. 2008. "The Collapse of Civilization: It's More Precarious than We Realized," "The End of Civilization," pp. 28–31; "Are We Doomed? The Very Nature of Civilization May Make Its Demise Inevitable," pp. 32–35. *New Scientist*, Vol. 2650, cover story, 5 April.

reinforces the barriers between rich and poor and impedes human progress; when new technologies benefit poor populations, it is often as passive consumers rather than co-creators or innovators of technological advances. Even the scientific literature is increasingly privatized, making the latest discoveries inaccessible to researchers who cannot pay to access them, now producing a strong reaction from the European Union but not solving the problem at the global level. Companies may hide behind a wall of commercial secrecy to prevent interference, even when it should be in the common interest, as in health and safety or environmental impact.

On the human side, there seems to be a general failure of leadership in service of the global collective good, with a rise of populist movements and xenophobia in reaction to insufficient sharing of the benefits of economic growth and neglect of the general welfare, leaving too many behind. There are vast forces of inertia and corruption blocking change. The financial system has become the most significant generator of wealth, but much of the turnover in the sector is detached from the real economy, more focused on trading of increasingly complex financial instruments than on supporting tangible employment-creating activity. The planet faces demographic instabilities from a population still growing in poor areas while aging and shrinking in rich areas. Economically we are trapped between the growth paradigm and our consumer culture confronting planetary boundaries, with emerging environmental crises such as climate change raising social and economic costs and driving population displacements. Business as usual is not an option.

Beginning in the mid-nineteenth century with the telegraph and the railroad, a sequence of new technologies facilitated increasing scales of communication, exchange and social organization. On the one hand, this has created a more united world and made globalization possible. It has also opened up new potential for mechanisms of governance and public participation that are as yet far from being realized. As a compelling example of the shape of things to come, in the preparations for the UN Conference on Sustainable Development in Rio de Janeiro in 2012, 6 million people participated in the public online consultation on the themes of the conference. Hundreds of stakeholders apart from governments contributed to the documents considered at the conference and to the implementation of its results. These technologies are contributing to a sense of moral interdependence and responsibility and help everyone to see that Earth stewardship and human rights, among other things, are global norms to be respected everywhere.

However, we are also beginning to appreciate that the same technologies can be turned to pernicious ends. The genocide in Rwanda was fanned by extremist radio stations that incited neighbor against neighbor. The Internet lends itself to spreading conspiracy theories, terrorist recruitment, incitement to hate, confirmation bias and "alternative facts" with potential for mass manipulation, foreign political interference and the undermining of democracy. Systems of government are being destabilized. Cybercrime is spreading. Personal data are captured and used to target advertising and political messages for maximum impact, without people realizing that they are being manipulated. A few giant companies mastering information technologies have acquired near-monopoly positions and great financial power. These are global processes, and only global approaches to their regulation will be effective.

Shared Human Purpose and Potential

The most fundamental area in which to build consensus is the ultimate purpose of governance itself. Why do we need governance: to avoid anarchy and collective destruction, and/or to achieve some common purpose? What should be the ultimate outcome of effective governance?

From the perspective of the individual living beyond a remote subsistence lifestyle in complete autonomy, governance should ensure the ability to meet basic needs for food, water, health and shelter. To this would be added access to education, to culture, to employment, to security and to opportunities to contribute to society in some way.

Beyond the individual, governance should maintain a certain social cohesion, facilitate the development of peaceful communities and their organization, collect revenues to support common services, encourage a sense of common identity, and implement solidarity through assistance to abandoned or vulnerable children and those who through poor health, disability, old age or other constraints cannot fully provide for themselves.

Those with a purely materialist orientation would say it is sufficient for everyone to be properly fed, well housed, comfortable, in some security and appropriately distracted to achieve some superficial form of happiness. However, most cultures, all religions and many psychologists accept an ethical framework and a concept of a higher fundamental purpose and potential for the human person than just material satisfaction. If our goal is a more just and sustainable social order, we shall need to cultivate other qualities of character such as moderation, justice, love, reason, sacrifice and service to the common good, which are necessary to overcome the focus on ego, greed, apathy and violence behind many of the failures of governance today.

At the highest level, effective governance should enable each person to develop her or his inherent potential and to refine her or his character, while contributing to the advancement of civilization. For most of humanity, human experience is ultimately spiritual in nature, and cultivating our higher qualities and the endless potential in human consciousness is at the core of what it is to be human.[11]

---

[11] Approximately 84 percent of the global population expresses a religious belief or affiliation. *The Global Religious Landscape*, Pew Research Center: Pew Forum on Religion and Public Life, December 2012. http://assets.pewresearch.org/wp-content/uploads/sites/11/2014/01/global-reli gion-full.pdf.

In return, fulfilled human beings can better contribute to effective governance. A program of governance that includes a strong moral and ethical component, building commitment at the emotional as well as the intellectual level, can be highly motivating.

The second dimension is the role of governance in advancing human civilization in all its aspects – material, social, cultural and spiritual – primarily through facilitation. Government should not try to do everything, but its scope is very broad, including the legal system with legislation, enforcement and justice; and providing or enabling education and scientific research; health and police/security services; major cultural institutions; the instruments of the economy such as a stable money and supportive infrastructure, transport and communications systems; regulations for the environment, health and safety; disaster response; nature conservation; opportunities for recreation; etc.

One of the challenges in designing a system of governance is to determine which functions are best implemented at different levels from the global through national to local communities, and various other scales in between depending on circumstances. The principle of subsidiarity is important, leaving the maximum responsibility as close to the level of implementation as possible, and only taking to higher levels those things that cannot be dealt with at a smaller scale. Over-centralization should be avoided. In particular, the institutions of global governance should only concern those issues – such as world peace and security, protection of the global environment, ensuring basic human rights, aspects of management of the world economy and the equitable distribution of the world's resources – that are inherently global in nature.

In a world undergoing rapid change and transformation, it is particularly important to ensure enabling conditions for innovation at the community level. The future forms of society are far from fixed, and past experience is no longer an adequate guide to future possibilities. Communities forming their own vision of the life that they want, drawing strength from their diversity, combining well-established populations and new arrivals, building a strong sense of social cohesion and solidarity, will be the best placed to experiment with new forms of economic relations, social justice and governance. A strong focus on the education of children, motivating youth with the ideals of altruism and service, consulting together and sharing their intellectual and devotional life (inclusive of various backgrounds), can provide the foundations for lasting change. Strong communities will also be in a better position to pass through whatever trials and crises may now be facing us, accompanying the seemingly inevitable transition toward a more united and organized global society.

POSITIVE FORCES FOR GLOBAL GOVERNANCE

One question that quickly emerges in this debate about the future of global governance is: what are the factors in recent decades that have contributed to creating a stronger sense of "world citizenship" or shared human solidarity across national boundaries? This is an important question because people would be asked, in an evolved international political order, to assume certain obligations of expanded civic engagement. Several issues come to mind.

First, because of developments in transport and communications, the world is a fraction of the size that it was at the end of World War II. Our global order may be state-based, but there is a much stronger sense of belonging to a global community of interdependent nations or peoples, where individuals travel more freely, more cheaply and more frequently than their parents or grandparents ever did. National boundaries in many parts of the world are in the process of softening or disappearing; this is already the case among the members of the European Union, but other regions of the world have also significantly lightened the burdens of previous restrictions on the movement of peoples, goods, capital and labor, as policy-makers and businesses have seen the benefits for economic efficiency and prosperity of the freer mobility of the factors of production. The Internet, social media and the spread of mobile phones have linked people as never before. There are still, to be sure, isolated pockets of nationalistic sentiments, with, for example, many Catalans in Spain yearning to establish their own sovereign republic, and a proportion of citizens in some European countries identifying with the resentments promoted by political parties from the extreme right wing. But overall, the tendency to look beyond national frontiers is clearly well established and it seems to point to an increasingly integrated global community, facing a range of problems that straddle national boundaries. Businesses, in particular, are likewise even more rapidly "going global" in terms of the markets where they sell their goods, the countries where they source their supplies, where they finance their activities and where they hire their workers.

This is not only a matter of technological change and perceptions of a new global geography. Values are changing as well as; to use one of Bertrand Russell's famous phrases, peoples are forced to expand their mental horizons and to acquire broader loyalties. Most people today, regardless of cultural, religious or ethnic background, whether male or female, want to live in a world characterized by peace and non-violence, economic opportunity and job security, environmental sustainability and the rule of law, where rules will apply to all, regardless of social status or nearness to the centers of power. Ideally, ambitious politicians eager to persuade voters to allow them to gain office should find it much better to promise security, improved living standards, social justice and human rights, environmental responsibility and public accountability, rather than to appeal to deep-seated nationalisms and baser instincts, which disproportionately attracts those who have been left behind in current conditions. And this, in turn, reflects the emergence of a truly global civil society, with broadly shared values that – while honoring diversity – transcends ethnicity, nationality, religious preference and social status.

Second, "sovereignty" is no longer the sacred principle that it once was. Numerous constitutions have been amended to enable participation in supranational bodies, such as the European Union, or in other bodies the aim of which is to establish peace and security. Article 24.2 of the Constitution of the Federal Republic of Germany states that "For the maintenance of peace, the Federation may enter a system of mutual collective security, in doing so, it will consent to such limitations upon its rights of sovereignty as will bring about and secure peaceful and lasting order in Europe and among the nations of the world."[12] Italy's 1948 constitution is no less clear: "Italy renounces war as an instrument of offense to the liberty of other peoples or as a means of settlement of international disputes, and, on conditions of equality with other states, agrees to the limitations of her sovereignty necessary to an organization which will ensure peace and justice among nations, and promotes and encourages international organizations constituted for this purpose." Even the United States imposed limitations on its own sovereignty on core national defense issues by signing the 1949 North Atlantic Treaty, whose Article 5 spells out that:

> The Parties agree that an armed attack against one or more of them in Europe or North America shall be considered an attack against them all and consequently they agree that, if such an armed attack occurs, each of them, in exercise of the right of individual or collective self-defence recognised by Article 51 of the Charter of the United Nations, will assist the Party or Parties so attacked by taking forthwith, individually and in concert with the other Parties, such action as it deems necessary, including the use of armed force, to restore and maintain the security of the North Atlantic area.

And, of course, the United Nations Charter itself imposes certain limited restrictions on the sovereignty of its members in a range of provisions. For example, in relation to the (intended) evolution of the organization, its Article 108 imposes a two-thirds majority for votes in the General Assembly – other than for permanent members of the Security Council – on amendments to the Charter; this majority, in theory, was to prevent any one member or small group of members from blocking the evolution of the organization.

For those of us who argue that in 1945 we missed a great chance, maybe one can say that coming out of the war the world was not sufficiently stabilized; the reconstruction of the entire European continent remained ahead. Maybe the idea of a global community of nations in what was still the colonial era was premature; there were only 51 signatories of the UN Charter in San Francisco. By the late 1970s, membership in the United Nations had risen to 152 countries. Clark and other fellow thinkers arguing for a stronger UN in the 1940s can perhaps be critiqued for overestimating the readiness of world leaders and communities to take the medicine of a stronger UN, but they cannot be faulted for correctly diagnosing the flaws of

---

[12] Constitution of 1949, as amended in Unification Treaty of August 31, 1990.

basing an international order on inflated notions of national sovereignty or for trying to address anarchies inherent in the current system, which has proved unable to address our host of global problems: the dangers of nuclear weapons, the huge economic and social costs associated with the absence of effective collective security mechanisms, violent extremism, repression by autocratic regimes, as well as the emergence of a range of new problems (e.g., climate change). These have largely gone unattended either because we do not have the institutions to confront them in a meaningful way or because they simply have exceeded the political and operational capacities of existing institutions. Ideals of robust and functional international governance did not die altogether in the 1940s; they were partially resurrected in 1957 with the creation of the European Economic Community, the precursor of today's European Union. The EU has helped build up a strong regional political identity and has shifted "legitimacy and political balance away from reliance on the state as supreme international actor."[13] It remains the most important experiment to date in supranational economic and political integration and may be an early model for more ambitious political arrangements in the future.

CONCLUDING REMARKS

In this book we have taken the view that the more sensible approach in developing the foundations of an enhanced global constitutional order is to build on the existing institutional infrastructure associated with the United Nations. The UN Charter, despite the many extraordinary aims, legal principles and values it enshrines (which should, of course, be retained and strengthened), is today a too-weak form of global constitutionalism. As we have argued, it is heavily constrained by the commitments it makes to uphold outdated and unclear notions of state sovereignty, it is saddled by the veto, it is inadequately resourced, it has not succeeded in establishing a genuine international system of rule by law, it has consistently proved incapable of controlling or preventing internationally relevant abuses of power and other forms of deviant state behavior. One might even concede Falk's statement that "The United Nations never has had the sort of role or created the kinds of expectations that one could identify with even a minimalist constitutional order."[14] But it is what we have; it has universal membership, it has accumulated during the past 75 years a body of texts and practices that have precipitated important changes in specific areas (e.g., a remarkable strengthening in the legal underpinnings of our human rights framework), it has participated, however ineffectively, in most of the peace and security debates of the postwar period, and the Security Council has the power to enact binding international law. More importantly, as Clark and Sohn showed in their magisterial work, as with any founding document, the UN Charter can be amended,

---

[13] Falk, "The Pathways of Global Constitutionalism," p. 30.
[14] Ibid., p. 16.

modernized and adapted to the needs of the present. It is our view that we would be better served by improving upon this foundation rather than going back to the beginning and starting over again.

The scenarios developed in Chapter 21 show that the range of possible futures is multiform, and the only certainty is that there will be surprises. This book represents our reasonable efforts to shine some light on the possible ways ahead, to provide a vision of where we might need to go and to suggest workable mechanisms for the next steps in our evolving system of governance. It tries to strike a balance between what idealism says would be desirable, what the reality of our present situation says is necessary and what might seem feasible to a political realist. No one person or group of persons has all the answers. As we go forward, we will all need to adopt an attitude of constructive exchange, consultation and learning as we experiment with pathways for more effective governance at multiple levels, collecting and sharing best practices as experience accumulates. Systems science suggests that humanity will make it through this age of transition to achieve a new equilibrium at a global level of social organization, including in the realm of international governance. This will open opportunities for a new flourishing of human civilization and well-being around the world. We hope that the efforts we all undertake now will eventually be fruitful in contributing to the evolution of human society as it realizes that the Earth is – inevitably – one interdependent community, with all of humanity as its citizens.

ANNEX

Voting Shares in a Reformed General Assembly

TABLE 1. *Updated General Assembly voting shares under Schwartzberg proposal*

Country	Assessed share[1]	Population[2] in % : P	GDP share[3] in % : C	Membership share[4] in % : M	Scenario W share[5] in %
193 Member Countries					
Afghanistan	0.007	0.474	0.041	0.5181	0.344
Albania	0.008	0.038	0.023	0.5181	0.193
Algeria	0.138	0.552	0.358	0.5181	0.476
Andorra	0.005	0.001	0.003	0.5181	0.174
Angola	0.010	0.398	0.155	0.5181	0.357
Antigua & Barbuda	0.002	0.001	0.002	0.5181	0.174
Argentina	0.915	0.591	0.769	0.5181	0.626
Armenia	0.007	0.039	0.019	0.5181	0.192
Australia	2.210	0.329	1.331	0.5181	0.726
Austria	0.677	0.118	0.438	0.5181	0.358
Azerbaijan	0.049	0.132	0.094	0.5181	0.248
Bahamas	0.018	0.005	0.012	0.5181	0.179
Bahrain	0.050	0.020	0.051	0.5181	0.196
Bangladesh	0.010	2.199	0.432	0.5181	1.050
Barbados	0.007	0.004	0.005	0.5181	0.176
Belarus	0.049	0.127	0.106	0.5181	0.250
Belgium	0.821	0.152	0.521	0.5181	0.397
Belize	0.001	0.005	0.002	0.5181	0.175
Benin	0.003	0.149	0.016	0.5181	0.228
Bhutan	0.001	0.011	0.004	0.5181	0.178
Bolivia	0.016	0.148	0.057	0.5181	0.241
Bosnia & Herzegovina	0.012	0.047	0.029	0.5181	0.198
Botswana	0.014	0.031	0.026	0.5181	0.192
Brazil	2.948	2.795	2.588	0.5181	1.967
Brunei Darussalam	0.025	0.006	0.021	0.5181	0.182
Bulgaria	0.046	0.094	0.097	0.5181	0.236
Burkina Faso	0.003	0.256	0.022	0.5181	0.266
Burundi	0.001	0.145	0.005	0.5181	0.223
Cabo Verde	0.001	0.007	0.003	0.5181	0.176
Cambodia	0.006	0.214	0.040	0.5181	0.257
Cameroon	0.013	0.321	0.058	0.5181	0.299
Canada	2.734	0.490	1.748	0.5181	0.919
Central African Republic	0.001	0.062	0.003	0.5181	0.194
Chad	0.004	0.199	0.018	0.5181	0.245
Chile	0.407	0.241	0.355	0.5181	0.371

	Assessed share[1]	Population[2] in % : P	GDP share[3] in % : C	Membership share[4] in % : M	Scenario W share[5] in %
Country					
China	12.005	18.515	16.947	0.5181	11.993
Colombia	0.288	0.655	0.478	0.5181	0.550
Comoros	0.001	0.011	0.001	0.5181	0.177
Congo	0.006	0.070	0.017	0.5181	0.202
Costa Rica	0.062	0.066	0.069	0.5181	0.218
Côte d'Ivoire	0.013	0.324	0.064	0.5181	0.302
Croatia	0.077	0.055	0.075	0.5181	0.216
Cuba	0.080	0.153	0.096	0.5181	0.256
Cyprus	0.036	0.016	0.026	0.5181	0.187
Czech Republic	0.311	0.141	0.286	0.5181	0.315
DPRK (North Korea)	0.006	0.340	0.032	0.5181	0.297
Democratic Republic of the Congo	0.010	1.086	0.051	0.5181	0.552
Denmark	0.554	0.077	0.319	0.5181	0.305
Djibouti	0.001	0.013	0.003	0.5181	0.178
Dominica	0.001	0.001	0.001	0.5181	0.173
Dominican Republic	0.053	0.144	0.117	0.5181	0.260
Ecuador	0.080	0.222	0.142	0.5181	0.294
Egypt	0.186	1.303	0.627	0.5181	0.816
El Salvador	0.012	0.085	0.036	0.5181	0.213
Equatorial Guinea	0.016	0.017	0.020	0.5181	0.185
Eritrea	0.001	0.079	0.007	0.5181	0.202
Estonia	0.039	0.018	0.033	0.5181	0.190
Ethiopia	0.010	1.402	0.131	0.5181	0.683
Fiji	0.003	0.012	0.007	0.5181	0.179
Finland	0.421	0.074	0.256	0.5181	0.283
France	4.427	0.896	2.765	0.5181	1.393
Gabon	0.015	0.027	0.024	0.5181	0.190
Gambia	0.001	0.028	0.003	0.5181	0.183
Georgia	0.008	0.050	0.025	0.5181	0.198
Germany	6.090	1.104	3.990	0.5181	1.871
Ghana	0.015	0.385	0.083	0.5181	0.329
Greece	0.366	0.144	0.245	0.5181	0.302
Grenada	0.001	0.001	0.001	0.5181	0.174
Guatemala	0.036	0.226	0.103	0.5181	0.282
Guinea	0.003	0.170	0.018	0.5181	0.235
Guinea Bissau	0.001	0.025	0.002	0.5181	0.182

(continued)

TABLE 1. (*continued*)

Country	Assessed share[1]	Population[2] in % : P	GDP share[3] in % : C	Membership share[4] in % : M	Scenario W share[5] in %
Guyana	0.002	0.010	0.005	0.5181	0.178
Haiti	0.003	0.147	0.013	0.5181	0.226
Honduras	0.009	0.124	0.033	0.5181	0.225
Hungary	0.206	0.131	0.203	0.5181	0.284
Iceland	0.028	0.005	0.022	0.5181	0.182
India	0.834	17.885	5.404	0.5181	7.936
Indonesia	0.543	3.526	1.932	0.5181	1.992
Iran (Islamic Republic of)	0.398	1.084	0.929	0.5181	0.844
Iraq	0.129	0.511	0.383	0.5181	0.471
Ireland	0.371	0.064	0.351	0.5181	0.311
Israel	0.490	0.116	0.347	0.5181	0.327
Italy	3.307	0.809	2.142	0.5181	1.156
Jamaica	0.008	0.039	0.020	0.5181	0.192
Japan	8.564	1.693	5.238	0.5181	2.483
Jordan	0.021	0.130	0.061	0.5181	0.236
Kazakstan	0.178	0.241	0.291	0.5181	0.350
Kenya	0.024	0.664	0.112	0.5181	0.431
Kiribati	0.001	0.002	0.000	0.5181	0.173
Kuwait	0.252	0.055	0.191	0.5181	0.255
Kyrgyzstan	0.002	0.083	0.014	0.5181	0.205
Lao's People Democratic Republic	0.005	0.092	0.030	0.5181	0.213
Latvia	0.047	0.026	0.041	0.5181	0.195
Lebanon	0.047	0.081	0.068	0.5181	0.222
Lesotho	0.001	0.030	0.004	0.5181	0.184
Liberia	0.001	0.063	0.004	0.5181	0.195
Libya	0.030	0.085	0.057	0.5181	0.220
Liechtenstein	0.009	0.001	0.007	0.5181	0.175
Lithuania	0.071	0.038	0.066	0.5181	0.207
Luxembourg	0.067	0.008	0.064	0.5181	0.197
Madagascar	0.004	0.341	0.023	0.5181	0.294
Malawi	0.002	0.249	0.013	0.5181	0.260
Malaysia	0.341	0.422	0.569	0.5181	0.503
Maldives	0.004	0.006	0.006	0.5181	0.177
Mali	0.004	0.248	0.026	0.5181	0.264
Malta	0.017	0.006	0.016	0.5181	0.180
Marshall Islands	0.001	0.001	0.000	0.5181	0.173
Mauritania	0.002	0.059	0.010	0.5181	0.196
Mauritius	0.011	0.017	0.020	0.5181	0.185
Mexico	1.292	1.725	1.704	0.5181	1.316

Country	Assessed share[1]	Population[2] in % : P	GDP share[3] in % : C	Membership share[4] in % : M	Scenario W share[5] in %
Micronesia (Federated States of)	0.001	0.001	0.000	0.5181	0.173
Monaco	0.011	0.001	0.007	0.5181	0.175
Mongolia	0.005	0.041	0.023	0.5181	0.194
Montenegro	0.004	0.008	0.007	0.5181	0.178
Morocco	0.055	0.477	0.188	0.5181	0.394
Mozambique	0.004	0.396	0.023	0.5181	0.312
Myanmar	0.010	0.713	0.175	0.5181	0.469
Namibia	0.009	0.034	0.019	0.5181	0.190
Nauru	0.001	0.000	0.000	0.5181	0.173
Nepal	0.007	0.391	0.047	0.5181	0.319
Netherlands	1.356	0.229	0.889	0.5181	0.545
New Zealand	0.291	0.064	0.205	0.5181	0.262
Nicaragua	0.005	0.083	0.023	0.5181	0.208
Niger	0.002	0.287	0.014	0.5181	0.273
Nigeria	0.250	2.549	0.683	0.5181	1.250
Norway	0.754	0.071	0.403	0.5181	0.331
Oman	0.115	0.062	0.121	0.5181	0.234
Pakistan	0.115	2.631	0.614	0.5181	1.254
Palau	0.001	0.000	0.000	0.5181	0.173
Panama	0.045	0.055	0.080	0.5181	0.218
Papua New Guinea	0.010	0.110	0.025	0.5181	0.218
Paraguay	0.016	0.091	0.054	0.5181	0.221
Peru	0.152	0.430	0.304	0.5181	0.417
Philippines	0.205	1.401	0.547	0.5181	0.822
Poland	0.802	0.507	0.778	0.5181	0.601
Portugal	0.350	0.137	0.262	0.5181	0.306
Qatar	0.282	0.035	0.241	0.5181	0.265
Republic of Korea (South Korea)	2.267	0.687	1.775	0.5181	0.993
Republic of Moldova	0.003	0.047	0.015	0.5181	0.193
Romania	0.198	0.262	0.326	0.5181	0.368
Russian Federation	2.405	1.930	2.592	0.5181	1.680
Rwanda	0.003	0.163	0.016	0.5181	0.232
Saint Kitts and Nevis	0.001	0.001	0.001	0.5181	0.173
Saint Lucia	0.001	0.002	0.002	0.5181	0.174

(*continued*)

TABLE 1. (*continued*)

Country	Assessed share[1]	Population[2] in % : P	GDP share[3] in % : C	Membership share[4] in % : M	Scenario W share[5] in %
Saint Vincent and the Grenadines	0.001	0.001	0.001	0.5181	0.174
Samoa	0.001	0.003	0.001	0.5181	0.174
San Marino	0.002	0.000	0.002	0.5181	0.173
Sao Tome and Principe	0.001	0.003	0.001	0.5181	0.174
Saudi Arabia	1.172	0.440	1.137	0.5181	0.698
Senegal	0.007	0.212	0.032	0.5181	0.254
Serbia	0.028	0.094	0.068	0.5181	0.227
Seychelles	0.002	0.001	0.002	0.5181	0.174
Sierra Leone	0.001	0.101	0.007	0.5181	0.209
Singapore	0.485	0.075	0.414	0.5181	0.336
Slovakia	0.153	0.073	0.132	0.5181	0.241
Slovenia	0.076	0.028	0.059	0.5181	0.202
Solomon Islands	0.001	0.008	0.001	0.5181	0.176
Somalia	0.001	0.197	0.013	0.5181	0.243
South Africa	0.272	0.757	0.525	0.5181	0.600
South Sudan	0.006	0.168	0.010	0.5181	0.232
Spain	2.146	0.622	1.534	0.5181	0.891
Sri Lanka	0.044	0.286	0.165	0.5181	0.323
Sudan	0.010	0.541	0.145	0.5181	0.401
Suriname	0.005	0.008	0.006	0.5181	0.177
Swaziland	0.002	0.018	0.007	0.5181	0.181
Sweden	0.906	0.134	0.545	0.5181	0.399
Switzerland	1.151	0.113	0.636	0.5181	0.423
Syrian Arab Republic	0.011	0.244	0.046	0.5181	0.269
Tajikistan	0.004	0.119	0.016	0.5181	0.218
Thailand	0.307	0.922	0.779	0.5181	0.740
The FYR of Macedonia	0.007	0.028	0.019	0.5181	0.188
Timor-Leste	0.002	0.017	0.005	0.5181	0.180
Togo	0.002	0.104	0.008	0.5181	0.210
Tonga	0.001	0.001	0.001	0.5181	0.173
Trinidad and Tobago	0.040	0.018	0.031	0.5181	0.189
Tunisia	0.025	0.154	0.080	0.5181	0.251
Turkey	1.371	1.078	1.406	0.5181	1.001
Turkmenistan	0.033	0.077	0.068	0.5181	0.221
Tuvalu	0.001	0.000	0.000	0.5181	0.173
Uganda	0.008	0.572	0.052	0.5181	0.381
Ukraine	0.057	0.599	0.218	0.5181	0.445

Country	Assessed share[1]	Population[2] in % : P	GDP share[3] in % : C	Membership share[4] in % : M	Scenario W share[5] in %
United Arab Emirates	0.616	0.126	0.518	0.5181	0.387
United Kingdom	4.567	0.882	2.817	0.5181	1.406
United Republic of Tanzania	0.010	0.765	0.097	0.5181	0.460
United States of America	22.000	4.350	19.981	0.5181	8.283
Uruguay	0.087	0.046	0.067	0.5181	0.210
Uzbekistan	0.032	0.433	0.119	0.5181	0.357
Vanuatu	0.001	0.004	0.001	0.5181	0.174
Venezuela	0.728	0.427	0.284	0.5181	0.410
Vietnam	0.077	1.276	0.399	0.5181	0.731
Yemen	0.010	0.377	0.049	0.5181	0.315
Zambia	0.009	0.228	0.044	0.5181	0.263
Zimbabwe	0.005	0.221	0.025	0.5181	0.255

1. For the budget period 2019–21 as determined by the General Assembly.
2. P is each country's population share in the total population of all 193 UN members, 2017.
3. C is calculated as the weighted average of a country's GDP share at market prices and GDP at PPP, for all 193 UN members, using 2017 numbers.
4. M is current voting power in the General Assembly (1/193), in percent.
5. W = (P+C+M)/3

References

Abashidze, Aslan. 2016. "The Process of Strengthening the Human Rights Treaty Body System." *Journal of Eurasian Law* 9(1): 1–13.

Acemoglu, Daron, and James A. Robinson. 2013. *Why Nations Fail: The Origins of Power, Prosperity, and Poverty*. London: Profile Books.

Adams, Simon. 2014. "Regulating the Veto in the Event of Mass Atrocities." Remarks at Ministerial Side-Event: United Nations Headquarters, New York, September 25. www .globalr2p.org/publications/337.

Adler, Mortimer, and John J. Logue. 1994. *How to Think about War and Peace*. New York: Fordham University Press.

Aghion, Philippe, U. Akcigit, J. Cagé, and W. R. Kerr. 2016. "Taxation, Corruption, and Growth." *European Economic Review* 86: 24–51.

Akhavan, Payam. 2017. *In Search of a Better World: A Human Rights Odyssey*. Toronto: House of Anansi Press.

Alesina, Alberto, and David Dollar. 1998. "Who Gives Foreign Aid to Whom and Why?" Cambridge, MA: NBER Working Paper No. W66, June 12.

Alesina, Alberto, and Beatrice Weder. 2002. "Do Corrupt Governments Receive Less Foreign Aid?" *American Economic Review* 92(4): 1126–1137.

Alexander, Titus, and Robert Whitfield. 2018. *Creating a Global Consciousness*. Blog on One World Trust, November 5, 2018. www.oneworldtrust.org/blogs.

Al Hussein, Zeid Ra'ad. 2018. "Open Voices Grassroots Leaders Provide the Best Hope to a Troubled World." *The Economist*, August 30.

Alighieri, Dante. 2008. *On World Government*, translation by Herbert W. Schneider. New York: Griffon House.

Allen, K.E., S.P. Stelzner, and R.M. Wielkiewicz. 1998. "The Ecology of Leadership: Adapting to the Challenges of a Changing World." *Journal of Leadership & Organizational Studies* 5(2): 62–82.

Allison, Graham. 2017. *Destined for War: Can America and China Escape Thucydides's Trap?* New York: Houghton Mifflin Harcourt.

2017. "The Thucydides Trap: When One Great Power Threatens to Displace Another, War Is Almost Always the Result – But It Doesn't Have to Be." *Foreign Policy*, June 9.

Alston, Philip. 1994. "Economic and Social Rights." In Louis Henkin and John Lawrence Hargrove (eds.), *Human Rights: An Agenda for the Next Century*. Studies in

Transnational Legal Policy, No. 26, pp. 137–166. Washington, DC: American Society of International Law.

2014. "Against a World Court for Human Rights." *Ethics & International Affairs* 28(2): 197–212.

Altinay, Hakan (ed.). 2011. *Global Civics: Responsibilities and Rights in an Interdependent World*. Washington, DC: Brookings Institution Press.

Ambraseys, Nicholas, and R. Bilham. 2011. "Corruption Kills." *Nature* 469(7239): 153–155.

Ambrosius, Lloyd E. 2002. "Wilson's League of Nations: Collective Security and National Independence." In *Wilsonianism: Woodrow Wilson and His Legacy in American Foreign Relations*. New York and Basingstoke: Palgrave Macmillan, pp. 51–64.

Andersen, Thomas B., J. Bentzen, C.-J. Dalgaard, and P. Selaya. 2011. "Does the Internet Reduce Corruption? Evidence from US States and Across Countries." *World Bank Economic Review* 25(3): 387–417.

Anello, Eloy. 1997. "Distance Education and Rural Development: An Experiment in Training Teachers as Community Development Agents." Doctoral dissertation, University of Massachusetts, Amherst. Doctoral dissertations available from Proquest. AAI9721427. https://scholarworks.umass.edu/dissertations/AAI9721427.

2008. *A Framework for Good Governance in the Public Pharmaceutical Sector. Working Draft for Field Testing and Revision*. Geneva: World Health Organization, pp. 1–45. www.who.int/medicines/areas/policy/goodgovernance/GGMFramework2008-04-18.pdf.

Anello, Eloy, and J.B. Hernández. 1996. *Moral Leadership*. Santa Cruz, Bolivia: Núr University. Unpublished translation from the Spanish.

Angier, Natalie. 2000. "DNA Research Shows Race Is Only Skin Deep." *The International Herald Tribune*, August 24.

Annan, Kofi. 2004. *The Rule of Law and Transitional Justice in Conflict and Post-Conflict Societies*. UN Security Council Report of the Secretary-General, August 23. UN Doc. S/2004/616.

2006. Progress Report of Armed Conflict, A/60/891, UN General Assembly. New York: United Nations.

Applebaum, Anne. 2018. "A Warning from Europe." *The Atlantic*, October, 53–63.

Arias, Oscar. 2006. *Fundación Arias para la Paz y el Progreso Humano*. www.un-ngls.org/spip.php?page=amdg10&id_article=2592.

Arms Control Association. 2018. *Nuclear Weapons: Who Has What at a Glance*. June. www.armscontrol.org/factsheets/Nuclearweaponswhohaswhat.

Atkinson, A.B. 2015. *Inequality: What Can Be Done?* Cambridge, MA: Harvard University Press.

Autesserre, Severine. 2019. "The Crisis of Peacekeeping: Why the UN Can't End Wars." *Foreign Affairs* 98(1), January/February: 101–116.

Bahá'í International Community. 1998. *Valuing Spirituality in Development: Initial Considerations Regarding the Creation of Spiritually Based Indicators for Development*. A Concept Paper Written for the World Faiths and Development Dialogue, Lambeth Palace, London, February 18–19.

2008. *Eradicating Poverty: Moving Forward as One*. New York: Bahá'í International Community, 16 pages, booklet and online statement. http://bic.org/statements-and-reports/bic-statements/08-0214.htm.

2010. *Rethinking Prosperity: Forging Alternatives to a Culture of Consumerism*. Bahá'í International Community's Contribution to the 18th Session of the United Nations Commission on Sustainable Development, May 3. www.bic.org/statements/rethinking-prosperity-forging-alternatives-culture-consumerism.

2012. *Beyond Balancing the Scales: The Roots of Equity, Justice and Prosperity for All.* Baha'i International Community's Contribution to the UN Global Thematic Consultation on "Addressing Inequalities." New York, October 12. www.bic.org/statements/beyond-balan cing-scales-roots-equity-justice-and-prosperity-all.

2018. *Migration: A Chance to Reflect on Global Well-Being.* Statement for the Sixth Intergovernmental Negotiations on the Global Compact for Migration, Geneva, July 12. www.bic.org/statements/migration-chance-reflect-global-well-being.

Bahá'u'lláh. 1990. *Gleanings from the Writings of Bahá'u'lláh.* Wilmette, IL: US Bahá'í Publishing Trust.

Banerjee, Ritwik. 2016. "Corruption, Norm Violation and Decay in Social Capital." *Journal of Public Economics* 137(C): 14–27.

Baratta, Preston, Joseph. 2004. The Politics of World Federation, *Vol. 1*: United Nations, UN Reform, Atomic Control. Westport, CT: Praeger.

2004. The Politics of World Federation, *Vol. 2*: From World Federalism to Global Governance. Westport, CT: Praeger.

Barrett, Scott. 2007. *Why Cooperate? The Incentive to Supply Global Public Goods.* Oxford: Oxford University Press.

Bassiouni, M. 2013. "Islamic International Law and International Humanitarian Law." In *The Shari'a and Islamic Criminal Justice in Time of War and Peace.* Cambridge: Cambridge University Press, pp. 150–248.

Bassiouni, M., and William A. Schabas (eds.). 2011. *New Challenges for the UN Human Rights Machinery: What Future for the UN Treaty Body System and the Human Rights Council Procedures?* Cambridge, Antwerp, and Portland, OR: Intersentia.

BBC News. 2002. "Del Ponte Calls for Snatch Squad." March 21. http://news.bbc.co.uk/2/hi/ europe/1884953.stm.

Beinhocker, Eric D. 2006. *The Origin of Wealth: Evolution, Complexity, and the Radical Remaking of Economics.* Cambridge, MA: Harvard Business School Press, and London: Random House Business Books.

Bentham, Jeremy. 1789. *The Principles of International Law,* Essays 3 and 4: Of War, Considered in Respect of Its Causes and Consequences and a Plan for Universal and Perpetual Peace. London: Sweet and Maxwell (reprinted 1927).

Bentzen, Jeanet S. 2012. "How Bad Is Corruption? Cross-Country Evidence of the Impact of Corruption on Economic Prosperity." *Review of Development Economics* 16(1): 167–184.

Berne Declaration/EcoNexus. 2013. *Agropoly – A Handful of Corporations Control World Food Production.* Zurich: Berne Declaration.

Besson, Samantha. 2004. "Sovereignty in Conflict." *European Integration Online Papers (EIoP)* 8(15), np.

Bilder, Richard B. 1994. "Possibilities for Development of New International Judicial Mechanisms." In Louis Henkin and John Lawrence Hargrove (eds.), *Human Rights: An Agenda for the Next Century.* Studies in Transnational Legal Policy, No. 26. Washington, DC: The American Society of International Law, chapter 12, pp. 317–346.

Birdsall, Nancy, Liliana Rojas-Suarez, and Anna Diofasi. 2017. "Expanding Global Liquidity Insurance through Precautionary Lending: What the IMF Can Do." Center for Global Development Briefs, March 8. www.cgdev.org/publication/expanding-global-liquidity-insurance-imf.

Blackwell, David. 1995. *Renewing the United Nations System – A Summary.* A Review of Renewing the United Nations System by Erskine Childers with Brian Urquhart, Dag Hammarskjold Foundation, Uppsala, Sweden, 1994. Global Policy Forum. www.global policy.org/component/content/article/225/32382.html

Blum, Steven D. 1984. *Walter Lippmann, Cosmopolitanism in the Century of Total War.* Ithaca, NY: Cornell University Press.

Bobonis, Gustavo J, Luis R. C. Fuertes, and R. Schwabe. 2016. "Monitoring Corruptible Politicians." *American Economic Review* 106(8): 2371–2405.

Boorman, Jack, and Andre Icard. 2011. *Reform of the International Monetary System: The Palais Royal Initiative.* Ebook.

Borchardt, Klaus-Dieter. 1995. *European Integration: The Origins and Growth of the European Union.* Luxembourg: Office of Official Publications of the European Communities.

Borger, Julian. 2019. "US Nuclear Weapons: First Low-Yield Warheads Roll off the Production Line." *The Guardian*, January 29.

Bosco, David. 2014. *Rough Justice: The International Criminal Court in a World of Power Politics.* Oxford: Oxford University Press.

Bourguignon, Francois, and Christian Morrisson. 2002. "Inequality among World Citizens." *American Economic Review* 92(4): 727–744.

Bourdieu, P. 1987. "The Force of Law: Toward a Sociology of the Juridical Field." *The Hastings Law Journal* 38(5): 818–853.

Boutros-Ghali, Boutros. 1992. *An Agenda for Peace: Preventive Diplomacy, Peacemaking and Peace-Keeping,* Report of the Secretary-General Pursuant to the Statement Adopted by the Summit Meeting of the Security Council, New York, January 31.

1997. *An Agenda for Peace 1995.* New York: United Nations Publications.

Boyle, Kevin. 2009. "The United Nations Human Rights Council: Origins, Antecedents, and Prospects." In Kevin Boyle (ed.), *New Institutions for Human Rights Protection.* Oxford and New York: Oxford University Press, pp. 11–47.

Bregman, Rutger. 2018. *Utopia for Realists: And How We Can Get There.* London: Bloomsbury Paperbacks.

Bricker, Darrell, and John Ibbitson. 2019. *Empty Planet: The Shock of Global Population Decline.* New York: Penguin Random House.

Broecker, Christen. 2014. "The Reform of the United Nations' Human Rights Treaty Bodies." *American Society of International Law* 18(16), www.asil.org/insights/volume/18/issue/16/reform-united-nations%E2%80%99-human-rights-treaty-bodies.

Brown, Peter G., and Geoffrey Garver. 2009. *Right Relationship: Building a Whole Earth Economy.* San Francisco: Berrett-Koehler Publishers.

Browning, Christopher S. 2013. *International Security: A Very Short Introduction.* Oxford: Oxford University Press.

Bummel, Andreas. 2019. *The Case for a UN Parliamentary Assembly and the Inter-Parliamentary Union.* Berlin: Democracy Without Borders.

Burgers, Jan Herman. 1992. "The Road to San Francisco: The Revival of the Human Rights Idea in the Twentieth Century." *Human Rights Quarterly* 14(4): 447–477.

Brzezinski, Zbigniew. 1993. *Out of Control: Global Turmoil on the Eve of the 21st Century.* New York: Macmillan.

Buitelaar, Tom, and Richard Ponzio. 2018. "Mobilizing Smart Coalitions and Negotiating Global Governance Reform." In William Durch, Joris Larik and Richard Ponzio (eds.), *Just Security in an Ungoverned World.* Oxford: Oxford University Press, pp. 463–487.

Cabrera, Luis. 2017. *Global Government Revisited: From Utopian Dream to Political Imperative.* Great Transition Initiative, October. www.greattransition.org/publication/global-government-revisited.

Camdessus, Michel. 2008. "International Financial Institutions: Dealing with New Global Challenges." Washington, DC: Per Jacobsen Foundation.

Carney, Mark. 2015. Quoted in Paul Brown, *Climate Change Threatens Global Financial Crash*. *Climate News Network*, October 2. http://climatenewsnetwork.net/climate-change-threatens-global-financial-crash/?utm_source=Climate+News+Network&utm_campaign=1bd3656d6b-Carney_s_crash_warning10_2_2015&utm_medium=email&utm_term=0_1198ea8936–1bd3656d6b-38775505.

Carson, Rachel. 1962. *Silent Spring*. Boston: New York: Houghton Mifflin.

Cassese, Antonio. 2005. *International Law* (2nd ed.). Oxford: Oxford University Press.

———. 2012. *Realizing Utopia: The Future of International Law*. New York: Oxford University Press.

Castaneda, Jorge, and Augusto López-Claros. 2009. "Nominate Nine Wise Men and Women to Restore IMF's Credibility." *Financial Times*, May 4.

Ceballos, Gerardo, Paul R. Ehrlich, and Rodolfo Dirzo. 2017. "Biological Annihilation via the Ongoing Sixth Mass Extinction Signaled by Vertebrate Population Losses and Declines." *PNAS* 114(30): E6089–E6096.

Center for Global Development. 2015. *Commitment to Development Index 2015*. www.cgdev.org.

Chayes, Sarah. 2015. *Thieves of State: Why Corruption Threatens Global Security*. New York and London: W.W. Norton & Company.

Chen, Wen-Hao, Michael Förster, and Ana Llena-Nozal. 2013. "Demographic or Labour Market Trends: What Determines the Distribution of Household Earnings in OECD Countries?" *OECD Journal: Economic Studies* 1: 179–207.

Childers, Erskine B., and Sir Brian Urquhart. 1992. *Toward a More Effective United Nations, Reorganization of the United Nations Secretariat: A Suggested Outline of Needed Reforms, Strengthening International Response to Humanitarian Emergencies*. New York: The Ford Foundation.

Childers, Erskine, with Brian Urquhart. 1994. *Renewing the United Nations System*. Uppsala, Sweden: Dag Hammarskjold Foundation. www.daghammarskjold.se/wp-content/uploads/1994/08/94_1.pdf.

China Institute of International Affairs. 1959. *China and the United Nations*. New York: Manhattan Publishing Group.

Churchill, Winston. 1946. Speech delivered at the University of Zurich, September 19. https://rm.coe.int/16806981f3

Clark, Christopher. 2012. *The Sleepwalkers: How Europe Went to War in 1914*. New York: HarperCollins.

Clark, Grenville. 1944. "Dumbarton Oaks Plans Held in Need of Modification: Viewed as Repeating Essential Errors of League of Nations and Offering No Assurance of International Security – Some Remedies Suggested." *New York Times*, October 15: ProQuest Historical News Papers; The New York Times, p. E8.

———. 1944. "A New World Order: The American Lawyer's Role." *Indiana Law Journal* 19(July): 289–300.

———. 1950. *A Plan for Peace*. New York: Harper & Brothers Publishers.

Clark, Grenville, and Louis B Sohn. 1966. *World Peace through World Law: Two Alternative Plans*. Cambridge, MA: Harvard University Press.

Classens, Stijn, Giovanni Dell'Ariccia, Denis Igan, and Luc Laeven. 2010 "Lessons and Policy Implications from the Global Financial Crisis." IMF Working Paper, WP/10/44/. Washington, DC: International Monetary Fund.

Claude, Jr. Inis. L. 1962. *Power and International Relations*. New York: Random House.

Claude, 1971. *Swords into Plowshares: The Problems and Progress of International Organization* (4th ed.). New York: Random House.

Clausen, Bianca, A. Kraay, and Z. Nyiri. 2011. "Corruption and Confidence in Public Institutions: Evidence from a Global Survey." *The World Bank Economic Review* 25(2): 212–249.

Coady, David, I. Parry, L. Sears, and B. Shang. 2015. *"How Large Are Global Energy Subsidies?" IMF Working Paper WP/15/105*. Washington, DC: International Monetary Fund.

Collier, Paul. 2007. *The Bottom Billion: Why the Poorest Countries Are Falling and What Can be Done about It*. New York: Oxford University Press.

Collins, Jim. 2011. "Level 5 Leadership: The Triumph of Humility and Fierce Resolve." In Peter F. Drucker, Daniel Goleman and William W. George (eds.), *HBR's 10 Must Reads on Leadership*. Boston, MA: Harvard Business Review Press, pp. 115–136.

Commission on Global Governance. 1995. *Our Global Neighborhood: Report of the Commission on Global Governance*. Oxford: Oxford University Press.

2015. *Confronting the Crisis of Global Governance*. Report of the Commission on Global Security, Justice & Governance, June 2015. The Hague: The Hague Institute for Global Justice and Washington, DC: The Stimson Center.

Cooke, David, and William R. Torbert. 2005. "Seven Transformations of Leadership." In *HBR's 10 Must Reads on Leadership*. Boston, MA: Harvard Business Review Press, 2011, pp. 137–161.

Cooper, Richard N. 1984. "A Monetary System for the Future." *Foreign Affairs* 63(1): 166–184.

1988. "International Cooperation: Is It Desirable? Is It Likely?" Address, International Monetary Fund Visitors' Center, Washington DC.

Council on Foreign Relations. 2018. *The UN Security Council*. www.cfr.org/backgrounder/un-security-council

Crimmins, James E., 2018. "Jeremy Bentham." *The Stanford Encyclopedia of Philosophy* (summer ed.), Edward N. Zalta (ed.), https://plato.stanford.edu/archives/sum2018/entries/bentham/

Cruickshank, Emlyn W, Kirsty Schneeberger, and Nadine Smith (eds.). 2012. *A Pocket Guide to Sustainable Development Governance* (2nd ed.). Commonwealth Secretariat/Stakeholder Forum. www.stakeholderforum.org/fileadmin/files/PocketGuidetoSDGEdition2webfinal.pdf

Daalder, Ivo H., and James M. Lindsay. 2018. "The Committee to Save the World Order: America's Allies Must Step Up as America Steps Down." *Foreign Affairs* 97(3): 72–83, November/December. www.foreignaffairs.com/articles/2018-09-30/committee-save-world-order.

Dafoe, Allan, and Anders Sandberg. 2018. "Why Care Now?" *Global Challenges Foundation Annual Report 2018*. https://globalchallenges.org/en/our-work/annual-report/annual-report-2018/why-care-now.

Dahl, Arthur Lyon. 1996. *The Eco Principle: Ecology and Economics in Symbiosis*. London: Zed Books and Oxford: George Ronald.

2004. "The Competitive Edge in Environmental Responsibility." In Michael E. Porter, Klaus Schwab, Xavier Sala-i-Martin, and Augusto López-Claros (eds.), *The Global Competitiveness Report 2004–2005*. World Economic Forum. Basingstoke and New York: Palgrave Macmillan, pp. 103–110.

2016. *Corruption, Morality and Religion*. International Environment Forum blog. http://iefworld.org/ddahl16l, November 18.

2018a. *Information: Private Property of Public Good?* International Environment Forum blog. https://iefworld.org/node/921, April 12.

2018b. "Contributions to the Evolving Theory and Practice of Indicators of Sustainability." In Simon Bell and Stephen Morse (eds.), *Routledge Handbook of Sustainability Indicators and Indices*. London and New York: Routledge, pp. 42–58

2018c. "UNEP and the CSD Process for Sustainable Development Indicators." In Simon Bell and Stephen Morse (eds.), *Routledge Handbook of Sustainability Indicators and Indices*. London and New York: Routledge, pp. 347–363.

Davies, J.B., and A.F. Shorrocks. 2000. "The Distribution of Wealth." In A.B. Atkinson and F. Bourguignon (eds.), *Handbook of Income Distribution*. Vol. 1. Amsterdam: North Holland, pp. 605–675.

Del Ponte, Carla (in collaboration with Chuck Sudetic). 2009. *Madame Prosecutor: Confrontation with Humanity's Worst Criminals and the Culture of Impunity*. New York: Other Press.

de Zayas, Alfred-Maurice. 2014. *Report of the Independent Expert on the Promotion of a Democratic and Equitable International Order*, July 17, p. 3. https://wilpf.org/wp-content/uploads/2014/09/report-De-Zayas.pdf.

Diamond, Jared. 1997. *Guns, Germs, and Steel: The Fates of Human Societies*. New York and London: W. W. Norton.

Dixit, Avinash. K. 2015. "How Business Community Institutions Can Help Fight Corruption." *The World Bank Economic Review* 29 (suppl 1): S25–S47.

Doyle, Michael. W., and Nicholas Sambanis. 2007. "Peacekeeping Operations." In Thomas G. Weiss and Sam Daws (eds.), *The Oxford Handbook on the United Nations*. New York: Oxford University Press, 323–349.

Dreher, Axel, and M. Gassebner. 2013. "Greasing the Wheels? The Impact of Regulations and Corruption on Firm Entry." *Public Choice* 155(3/4): 413–432.

Dumitriu, Petru. 2016. *Knowledge Management in the United Nations System*. Geneva: UN Joint Inspection Unit. www.unjiu.org/sites/www.unjiu.org/files/jiu_document_files/products/en/reports-notes/JIU%20Products/JIU_REP_2016_10_English.pdf.

Dyble, M., G.D. Salali, N. Chaudhary, A. Page, D. Smith, J. Thompson, L. Vinicius, R. Mace, and A.B. Migliano. 2015. "Sex Equality Can Explain the Unique Social Structure of Hunter-Gatherer Bands." *Science* 348(6236): 796–798.

Easterly, William. 2006. *The White Man's Burden: Why the West's Efforts to Aid the Rest Have Done So Much Ill and So Little Good*. New York: The Penguin Press.

Economic Intelligence Unit. 2018. *Democracy Index 2018* www.eiu.com/topic/democracy-index.

Eichengreen, Barry. 1996. "The Tobin Tax: What Have We Learned?" In Inge Kaul Mahbub ul Haq and Isabelle Grunberd (eds.), *The Tobin Tax – Coping with Financial Volatility*. New York: Oxford University Press, pp. 273–287.

Einstein, Albert. 1947. "To the General Assembly of the United Nations," para. 10. http://lotoisdumonde.fr/initiatives/FSMAN/Einstein-UN-letter-1947-oct.pdf.

1956. *Out of My Later Years*. New York: Philosophical Library.

1990. *The World as I See It*. New York: Quality Paperback Books.

Elliott, Lorraine. 2002. "Expanding the Mandate of the UN Security Council to Account for Environmental Issues." UN University Position Paper. http://archive.unu.edu/inter-linkages/docs/IEG/Elliot.pdf

Esty, Daniel C., and Maria H. Ivanova (eds.). 2002. *Global Environmental Governance: Options & Opportunities*. New Haven, CT: Yale School of Forestry and Environmental Studies.

European Parliament. 2018. *Eurobarometer Survey Shows Highest Support for the EU in 35 Years*. EU Affairs, May 23. www.europarl.europa.eu/news/en/headlines/eu-affairs/20180522STO04020/eurobarometer-survey-highest-support-for-the-eu-in-35-years).

Evarts, Eric C. 2018. *Report: Global CO2 Emissions at Record Levels in 2018*. Green Car Reports, December 7. www.greencarreports.com/news/1120348_report-global-co2-emissions-at-record-levels-in-2018

Eyffinger, Arthur. 2011. *T.M.C. Asser [1838–1913]: Founder of The Hague Tradition*. The Hague: T.M.C. Asser Press.

Falk, Richard. 1993. "The Pathways of Global Constitutionalism." In Richard Falk, Robert Johansen and Samuel Kim (eds.), *The Constitutional Foundations of World Peace*. New York: State University of New York Press, pp. 13–38.

2001. *Religion and Humane Global Governance*. New York: Palgrave Macmillan.

2014. "New Constitutionalism and Geopolitics: Notes on Legality and Legitimacy and Prospects for a Just New Constitutionalism." In S. Gill and A.C. Cutler (eds.), *New Constitutionalism and World Order*. Cambridge and New York: Cambridge University Press, pp. 295–312.

2014. *(Re)Imagining Humane Global Governance*. Abingdon and New York: Routledge.

Falk, Richard, Samuel S. Kim, and Saul H. Mendlovitz. 1982. *Toward a Just World Order*. Studies on a Just World Order, Vol. 1. Boulder, CO: Westview Press.

Falk, Richard, A., Samuel S. Kim., Donald McNemar, and Saul H. Mendlovitz. 1991. *The United Nations and a Just World Order*. Vol. 3. Boulder, CO: Westview Press.

Falk, Richard, Friedrich V. Kratchowil, and Saul H. Mendlovitz. 1985. *International Law and a Just World Order*. Studies on a Just World Order, Vol. 2. Boulder, CO: Westview Press.

Falk, Richard, Robert C. Johansen, and Samuel S. Kim. 1993a. "Global Constitutionalism and World Order." In Richard Falk, Robert Johansen and Samuel Kim (eds.), *The Constitutional Foundations of World Peace*. New York: State University of New York Press, pp. 3–12.

Falk, Richard, and Andrew Strauss. 2001. "Toward Global Parliament." *Foreign Affairs* 80(1): 212–220.

2011. *A Global Parliament Essays and Articles*. Berlin: Committee for a Democratic U.N.

Financial Times. 2011. "Watchdog Says IMF Missed Crisis Risks." February 10.

Fihn, Beatrice. 2017. Nobel Lecture Given by the Nobel Peace Prize Laureate 2017, International Campaign to Abolish Nuclear Weapons (ICAN), Delivered by Beatrice Fihn and Setsuko Thurlow, Oslo, December 10, 2017. www.nobelprize.org/prizes/peace/2017/ican/26041-international-campaign-to-abolish-nuclear-weapons-ican-nobel-lecture-2017/

Finnemore, Martha, and Kathryn Sikkink. 1998. "International Norm Dynamics and Political Change." *International Organization* 52(4): 887–917.

Fontaine, Pascal. 1988. *Jean Monnet: A Grand Design for Europe*, Periodical 5, Luxembourg: Office for Official Publications of the European Communities, pp. 30–31.

Franck, Thomas. 1990. *The Power and Legitimacy among Nations*. New York: Oxford University Press.

1994. "Democracy as a Human Right." In Louis Henkin and John Lawrence Hargrove (eds.), *Human Rights: An Agenda for the Next Century*. Studies in Transnational Legal Policy, No. 26. Washington, DC: American Society of International Law, pp. 73–102.

2001. "Are Human Rights Universal?" *Foreign Affairs* 80(1): 191–204.

Franda, Marcus. 2006. *The United Nations in the Twenty-first Century, Management and Reform Processes in a Troubled Organization*. New York: Rowman & Littlefield.

Freedman, Rosa, and Ruth Houghton. 2017. "Two Steps Forward, One Step Back: Politicisation of the Human Rights Council." *Human Rights Law Review* 17(4): 753–769.

Freedom House. 2018. *Freedom in the World Index 2018.* https://freedomhouse.org/report/freedom-world/freedom-world-2018

Friedman, Benjamin M. 2005. *The Moral Consequences of Economic Growth.* New York: Alfred A. Knopf.

Friedman, Thomas L. 1999. *The Lexus and the Olive Tree: Understanding Globalization.* New York: Farrar, Straus and Giroux.

Frowein, J.A. 1998. "Are there Limits to the Amendment Procedures in Treaties Constituting International Organisations?" In G. Hafner et al. (eds.), *Liber Amicorum Prof. Seidl-Hohenveldern, in Honour of His 80th Birthday.* Boston, MA: Brill, pp. 201–218.

Fry, Douglas P. 2012. "Life without War." *Science* 336(6083): 879–884.

Frye, William R. 1957. *A United Nations Peace Force.* New York: Oceana Publishers.

G20 Leaders' declaration. 2018. *Building Consensus for Fair and Sustainable Development,* Buenos Aires, Argentina, November 30–December. www.g20.utoronto.ca/2018/buenos_aires_leaders_declaration.pdf.

Gat, Azar. 2017. *The Causes of War and the Spread of Peace: But Will War Rebound?* Oxford: Oxford University Press.

Gilens, M., and B. Page. 2014. "Testing Theories of American Politics: Elites, Interest Groups, and Average Citizens." *Perspectives on Politics* 12(3): 564–581.

Giles, Sunnie. 2016. "The Most Important Leadership Competencies, According to Leaders around the World." *Harvard Business Review,* March 15. https://hbr.org/2016/03/the-most-important-leadership-competencies-according-to-leaders-around-the-world

Gillis, Melissa. 2017. *Disarmament: A Basic Guide.* (4th ed.). New York: United Nations Office for Disarmament Affairs.

Global Centre for the Responsibility to Protect. 2018. *UN Security Council Resolutions and Presidential Statements Referencing R2P,* 22 January: www.globalr2p.org/resources/335.

Global Challenges Foundation. 2018. New Shape Prize, https://globalchallenges.org/en/our-work/the-new-shape-prize. Awardees: https://globalchallenges.org/en/our-work/the-new-shape-prize/awardees.

Global Justice Monitor. 2014. Interview with Navi Pillay: "Africa Has Benefited Most from the ICC." *Journal of the Coalition for the International Criminal Court* 46: 18–19.

Goertz, Gary, Paul F. Diehl, and Alexandru Balas. 2016. *The Puzzle of Peace: The Evolution of Peace in the International System.* Oxford: Oxford University Press.

Gonzales, C., S. Jain-Chandra, K. Kochhar, and M. Newiak. 2015. "Fair Play: More Equal Laws Boost Female Labor Force Participation." International Monetary Fund Staff Discussion Note SDN/15/02. www.imf.org/external/pubs/ft/sdn/2015/sdn1502.pdf.

Gorbachev, Mikhail. 2018. "A New Nuclear Arms Race Has Begun." *New York Times,* October 25.

Gosovic, Branislav. 1992. *The Quest for World Environmental Cooperation: The Case of the UN Global Environment Monitoring System.* London and New York: Routledge.

Governance Matters: Worldwide Governance Indicators. http://info.worldbank.org/governance/wgi/index.aspx#home

Groff, Maja, and Sylvia Karlsson-Vinkhuyzen. 2019. "The Rule of Law and Accountability: Exploring Trajectories for Democratizing Governance of Global Public Goods and Global Commons." In Samuel Cogolati and Jan Wouters (eds.), *The Commons and a New Global Governance.* Cheltenham: Edward Elgar, pp. 130–159.

Grayling, A.C. 2017. *War: An Enquiry.* New Haven, CT, and London: Yale University Press.

Guinote, Ana. 2017. "How Power Affects People: Activating, Wanting, and Goal Seeking." *Annual Review of Psychology* 68: 353–381. https://doi.org/10.1146/annurev-psych-010416-044153.

Gupta, Sanjeev, H. Davoodi, and R. Alonso-Terme. 2002. "Does Corruption Affect Income Inequality and Poverty?" *Economics of Governance* 3(1): 23–45.

Habermas, Jürgen. 2012. "The Crisis of the European Union in the Light of a Constitutionalization of International Law." *The European Journal of International Law* 23(2): 335–348.

Haji, Iqbal. 1997. "The 'Problem' of Voluntary Funding." *UN Chronicle* 34(4): 75.

Hallward-Driemeier, M., T. Hasan, and A. Rusu. 2013. "Women's Legal Rights over 50 Years: Progress, Stagnation or Regression?" Policy Research Working Paper No. 6616, Washington, DC: World Bank.

Hamel-Green, Michael. 2018. "The Nuclear Ban Treaty and 2018 Disarmament Forums: An Initial Impact Assessment." *Journal for Peace and Nuclear Disarmament*, DOI: 10.1080/25751654.2018.1516493.

Hanley, Paul. 2014. *Eleven*. Victoria, BC: Friesen Press.

Harari, Yuval Noah. 2018. "Why Technology Favors Tyranny." *The Atlantic*, October. www.theatlantic.com/magazine/archive/2018/10/yuval-noah-harari-technology-tyranny/568330/.

Hathaway, Oona Anne, and Scott Shapiro. 2017. *The Internationalists: How a Radical Plan to Outlaw War Remade the World*. New York: Simon & Schuster.

Havel, Vaclav. 2000. President of the Czech Republic, Statement at Millennium Summit, General Assembly Plenary – 3 – Press Release GA/9758 8th Meeting (PM) September 8. www.un.org/press/en/2000/20000908.ga9758.doc.html

Heineman, Ben W., and F. Heimann. 2006. "The Long War against Corruption." *Foreign Affairs* 85(May/June): 75–86.

Heinrich, Dieter. 2003. "Extension of Democracy to the Global Level." In Saul H. Medlovitz and Barbara Walker (eds.), *A Reader on Second Assembly & Parliamentary Proposals*, Wayne, NJ: Center for UN Reform Education, pp. 68–73.

——— 2010. *The Case for a United Nations Parliamentary Assembly*, Berlin: Committee for a Democratic U.N.

Henkin, Louis. 1991. "Law and War after the Cold War." *Journal of International Law* 15(2), http://digitalcommons.law.umaryland.edu/mjil/vol15/iss2/2.

——— 1994. 'Preface." In Louis Henkin and John Lawrence Hargrove (eds.), *Human Rights: An Agenda for the Next Century*. Studies in Transnational Legal Policy, No. 26. Washington, DC: American Society of International Law, pp. vii–xx.

——— 2005. "Symposium, War and Terrorism: Law or Metaphor." Santa Clara Law 45, p. 817, 819. http://digitalcommons.law.scu.edu/lawreview/vol45/iss4/2.

Henkin, Louis, and John Lawrence Hargrove. 1994. *Human Rights: An Agenda for the Next Century*. Studies in Transnational Legal Policy, No. 26. Washington, DC: American Society of International Law.

Higgins, R. 2007. "The Rule of Law: Some Skeptical Thoughts." Lecture at the British Institute for International and Comparative Law. Annual Grotius Lecture, London, October 16.

——— 2008. *The Role of the International Court of Justice in the Contemporary World*, Abu Dhabi: Emirates Center for Strategic Studies and Research.

Holcombe, Randall. G., and C. J. Boudreaux. 2015. "Regulation and Corruption." *Public Choice* 164(1–2): 75–85.

Homer-Dixon, Thomas. 2006. *The Upside of Down: Catastrophe, Creativity, and the Renewal of Civilization*. Toronto: Vintage Canada.

Hoopes, Townsend, and Douglas Brinkley. 1997. *FDR and the Creation of the U.N.* New Haven, CT: Yale University Press.

Howard, Lise M. 2019. "Five Myths about Peacekeeping." *Washington Post*, July 14, p. B2.

Human Rights Watch. 2018. *Human Rights Watch Statement for the General Debate of the International Criminal Court's Seventeenth Assembly of States Parties*, December 8, www.hrw.org/news/2018/12/08/human-rights-watch-statement-general-debate-international-criminal-courts.

Humphrey, John P. 1984. *Human Rights and the United Nations: A Great Adventure*. Dobbs Ferry, NY: Transnational Publishers.

Hutchins, Robert et al. 1947. *Preliminary Draft of a World Constitution*. Chicago, Illinois: University of Chicago Press.

ICSC (International Civil Service Commission). n.d. The Noblemaire Principle, in Compendium, International Civil Service Commission. https://icsc.un.org/compendium/display.asp?type=22.12.1.10.

Ignatieff, Michael. 2017. *The Ordinary Virtues: Moral Order in a Divided World*. Cambridge, MA, and London: Harvard University Press.

ICSU (International Council for Science). 2017. *A Guide to SDG Interactions: From Science to Implementation*, ed. D.J. Griggs, M. Nilsson, A. Stevance, and D. McCollum. Paris: International Council for Science. www.icsu.org/cms/2017/05/SDGs-Guide-to-Interactions.pdf.

International Court of Justice. 1996. Legality of the Threat or Use of Nuclear Weapons, Advisory Opinion of July 8. ICJ Reports 1996. The Hague: International Court of Justice, pp. 226–267. www.icj-cij.org/files/case-related/95/095-19960708-ADV-01-00-EN.pdf.

International Energy Agency. 2018. *World Energy Outlook 2018*. www.iea.org/.

International Environment Forum. 2010. *Climate Change and Human Rights*, https://iefworld.org/node/249.

International Herald Tribune. 2000. "DNA Research Shows Race Is Only Skin Deep." August 24.

IMF (International Monetary Fund). 2009. *World Economic Outlook*.

IMF (International Monetary Fund). 2006. *Global Financial Stability Report*, Washington, DC.

IMF (International Monetary Fund). 2014. "Quota Formula – Data Update and Further Considerations." IMF Policy Paper. Washington, DC, August.

IMF (International Monetary Fund). 2008. *Independent Evaluation Office Report: Governance of the IMF: An Evaluation*. Washington, DC.

IMF (International Monetary Fund). 2018. *Governance and the IMF – Evaluation Update 2018*, Independent Evaluation Office of the International Monetary Fund, Washington, DC.

IPBES (Intergovernmental Science-Policy Platform on Biodiversity and Ecosystem Services). 2018. *Summary for Policymakers of the Thematic Assessment Report on Land Degradation and Restoration of the Intergovernmental Science-Policy Platform on Biodiversity and Ecosystem Services*, ed. R. Scholes, L. Montanarella, A. Brainich, N. Barger, B. ten Brink, M. Cantele, B. Erasmus, J. Fisher, T. Gardner, T. G. Holland, F. Kohler, J. S. Kotiaho, G. Von Maltitz, G. Nangendo, R. Pandit, J. Parrotta, M. D. Potts, S. Prince, M. Sankaran, and L. Willemen. Bonn: IPBES secretariat.

IPCC (Intergovernmental Panel on Climate Change). 2014. *Climate Change 2014: Synthesis Report. Contribution of Working Groups I, II and III to the Fifth Assessment Report of the Intergovernmental Panel on Climate Change* [Core Writing Team, R.K. Pachauri and L.A. Meyer]. Geneva: IPCC.

IPCC (Intergovernmental Panel on Climate Change). 2018. *Global Warming of 1.5°C* (SR15), Special Report. Summary for Policy Makers. Geneva: Intergovernmental Panel on Climate Change, October 6. www.ipcc.ch/report/sr15/.

Jackson, Tim. 2017. *Prosperity without Growth: Foundations for the Economy of Tomorrow.* 2nd ed. London: Routledge.

Jäger, J., Kok, M.T.J., Mohammed-Katerere, J., Karlsson, S.I., Lüdeke, M.B., Dalbelko, G.D., Thomalla, F., Soysa, Id, Chenje, M., Filcak, R., Koshy, L., Martello, M.L., Mathur, V., Moreno, A.R., Narain, V., and Sietz, D., 2007. "Vulnerability of People and the Environment: Challenges and Opportunities." In UNEP (ed.), *Global Environmental Outlook-4. Environment for Development.* Nairobi: United Nations Environment Programme, pp. 301–394.

Jenks, B., J. Topping, and H. Keijers. 2018. *Financing the UN Development System: Opening Doors.* Uppsala: The UN MPTF Office and the Dag Hammarskjold Foundation.

Johnson, Robert. 1982. "Toward a Dependable Peace: A Proposal for an Appropriate Security System." In Richard Falk, Samuel S. Kim and Saul H. Mendlovitz (eds.), *Toward a Just World Order*, Vol. 1. Boulder, CO, Westview Press, pp. 271–283.

Joyce, James. 1961. *Ulysses.* New York: Random House.

Kant, Immanuel (trans. and with Introduction and Notes by M. Campbell Smith). 1795. *Perpetual Peace: A Philosophical Essay.* London: George Allen & Unwin Ltd.

Karlberg, M. 2004. *Beyond the Culture of Contest.* Oxford: George Ronald.

Karlsson-Vinkhuyzen, Sylvia. 2017. "Contribution to 'Roundtable on Global Government.'" *Great Transition Initiative*, October. www.greattransition.org/roundtable/global-gov-sylvia-karlsson

Karlsson-Vinkhuyzen, Sylvia, Maja Groff, Peter A. Tamás, Arthur L. Dahl, Marie K. Harder, and Graham Hassall. 2017. "Entry into Force and Then? The Paris Agreement and State Accountability." *Climate Policy.* Doi:10.1080/14693062.2017.1331904

Karlsson-Vinkhuyzen, Sylvia, Arthur Lyon Dahl, and Åsa Persson. 2018. "The Emerging Accountability Regimes for the Sustainable Development Goals and Policy Integration: Friend or Foe?" *Environment and Planning C: Politics and Space* 36(8): 1371–1390, special issue on Integrative Governance. https://doi.org/10.1177/2399654418779995.

Katirai, Foad. 2001. *Global Governance and the Lesser Peace.* Oxford: George Ronald.

Kaufmann, D. 2003. "Governance Redux: The Empirical Challenges." *The Global Competitiveness Report 2003–2004.* World Economic Forum. Oxford: Oxford University Press.

2004. "Corruption, Governance and Security: Challenges for the Rich Countries of the World." *The Global Competitiveness Report 2005–2006.* World Economic Forum. Oxford: Oxford University Press.

Kaufmann, D., and Aart Kraay. 2002. "Growth without Governance." *Economia* 3(1): 169–229.

Kaufmann, Daniel, Aart Kraay, and Massimo Mastruzzi. 2007. *Governance Matters VI: Governance Indicators for 1996–2006* (July). World Bank Policy Research Working Paper No. 4280. https://ssrn.com/abstract=999979

2010. *The Worldwide Governance Indicators: Methodology and Analytical Issues.* Draft Policy Research Working Paper, World Bank, September. http://info.worldbank.org/governance/wgi/pdf/WGI.pdf.

Kaul, I., I. Grunberg, and M. A. Stern. 1999. *Global Public Goods: International Cooperation in the 21st Century.* New York: Oxford University Press.

Kaul, I., P. Conceição, K. Le Goulven, and R.U. Mendoza (eds.). 2003. *Providing Global Public Goods. Managing Globalization.* Oxford: Oxford University Press.

Keeley, Lawrence H. 1996. *War before Civilization: The Myth of the Peaceful Savage.* Oxford: Oxford University Press.

Kelly, E., Elizabeth W. Morrison, Naomi B. Rothman, and Jack B. Soll. 2011. "The Detrimental Effects of Power on Confidence, Advice Taking, and Accuracy." *Organizational*

Behavior and Human Decision Processes 116(2): 272–285. https://doi.org/10.1016/j.obhdp.2011.07.006

Kelsen, Hans. 1935. *The Legal Process and International Order.* London: Constable & Co. Ltd.

Kelsen, Hans. 1942. *Law and Peace in International Relations.* Cambridge, MA: Harvard University Press.

    1944. *Peace through Law.* Chapel Hill: University of North Carolina Press.

Kennan, George F. 1984. *American Diplomacy.* 60th Anniversary Expanded Edition. Chicago: University of Chicago Press.

Kerry, John. 2016. *Remarks at the World Economic Forum,* U.S. Department of State, January 22. https://2009-2017.state.gov/secretary/remarks/2016/01/251663.htm.

Keynes, John Maynard. 1973. The Collected Writings of John Maynard Keynes, *Volume 7:* The General Theory of Employment, Interest and Money. London: The Macmillan Press.

Ke-young Chu, Sanjeev Gupta, Benedict Clements, Daniel Hewitt, Sergio Lugaresi, Jerald Schiff, Ludger Schuknecht, and Gerd Schwartz. 1995. *Unproductive Public Expenditures: A Pragmatic Approach to Policy Analysis.* Pamphlet Series, No. 48. Washington, DC: Fiscal Affairs Department, IMF. www.imf.org/external/pubs/ft/pam/pam48/pam4801.htm

Kirsch, Nico. 2012. "Chapter VII Action with Respect to Threats to the Peace, Breaches of the Peace, and Acts of Aggression, Article 43." In Bruno Simma, Daniel-Erasmus Khan, Georg Nolte, Andreas Paulus, and Nikolai Wessendorf (eds.), *The Charter of the United Nations: A Commentary.* Oxford Commentaries on International Law series (3rd ed.), 2 vols. Oxford: Oxford University Press, pp. 1351–1356.

Kissinger, Henry. 2014. *World Order.* New York: Penguin Press.

Klitgaard, Robert. 1988. *Controlling Corruption.* Berkeley and Los Angeles: University of California Press.

Klug, F. 2015. A *Magna Carta for All Humanity: Homing in on Human Rights.* London: Routledge.

Koh, Harold Hongju. 1997. "Why Do Nations Obey International Law?" *Faculty Scholarship Series.* Yale Law Journal 106: 2599–2659. https://digitalcommons.law.yale.edu/fss_papers/2101.

Koskenniemi, M. 1990. "The Politics of International Law." *European Journal of International Law* 1(1): 4–32.

Krause, Eleanor, and Isabel V. Sawhill. 2018. "Seven Reasons to Worry about the American Middle Class." Washington, DC: Brookings Institution, Social Mobility Memos, June 5. www.brookings.edu/blog/social-mobility-memos/2018/06/05/seven-reasons-to-worry-about-the-american-middle-class/.

Krause, Keith. 2007. "Disarmament." In Thomas G. Weiss and Sam Daws (eds.), *The Oxford Handbook on the United Nations.* Oxford: Oxford University Press, pp. 287–300.

Krugman, Paul. 2002. "Argentina's Crisis Is a U.S. Failure." *International Herald Tribune,* January 21.

    2019. "Elizabeth Warren Does Teddy Roosevelt: Taxing the Superrich Is an Idea Whose Time Has Come – Again." *The New York Times,* January 28.

Kuehl, Warren F. 1969. *Seeking World Order, the United States and International Organization to 1920.* Nashville, TN: Vanderbilt University Press.

Landell-Mills, P., and I. Serageldin. 1991. "Governance and the External Factor." *The World Bank Economic Review* 5(1): 303–320.

Lapowsky, Issie. "Free Money: The Surprising Effects of a Basic Income Supplied by Government." www.wired.com/story/free-money-the-surprising-effects-of-a-basic-income-supplied-by-government/.

Larson, Arthur. 1968. *Eisenhower: The President Nobody Knew*. New York: Charles Scribners.

Laurenti, Jeffrey. 2003. "An Idea Whose Time Has Not Come." In Saul H. Medlovitz and Barbara Walker (eds.), *A Reader on Second Assembly & Parliamentary Proposals*. Wayne, NJ: Center for UN Reform Education, pp. 119–129.

　2007. "Financing." In Thomas G. Weiss and Sam Daws (eds.), *The Oxford Handbook on the United Nations*. New York: Oxford University Press, pp. 675–701.

Lawton, Graham. 2018. "The Scandal of Scholarship (Review of the Film 'Paywall: The Business of Scholarship.' Directed by Jason Schmitt)." *New Scientist*, 240(3201): 46. October 27.

Laybourn-Langton, Laurie, Leslie Rankin, and Darren Baxter. 2019. *This Is a Crisis: Facing up to the Age of Environmental Breakdown*. London: IPPR – Institute for Public Policy Research. www.ippr.org/research/publications/age-of-environmental-breakdown.

Leff, Nathaniel. 1964. "Economic Development through Bureaucratic Corruption." *American Behavioural Scientist* 8(3): 8–14.

Leinen, J., and Andreas Bummel. 2018. *A World Parliament: Governance and Democracy in the 21st Century*. Berlin: Democracy Without Borders.

Leitenberg, Milton. 1977. "Disarmament and Arms Control since 1945." *CrossCurrents* 27(2): 130–139. www.jstor.org/stable/24458313.

Leitenberg, Michael. 2006. "Deaths and Wars in Conflicts in the 20th Century." Cornell University, Peace Studies Program, Occasional Paper 29.

Lewis, Michael. 2018. *The Fifth Risk*. New York: W.W. Norton & Company.

Lhotsky, Jan. 2016. "The UN Mechanisms for Human Rights Protection: Strengthening Treaty Bodies in Light of a Proposal to Create a World Court of Human Rights." *Journal of Eurasian Law* 9(1): 109–122.

Lincoln, Abraham. 1848. Abraham Lincoln to William H. Herndon, February 15, 1848. *Collected Works of Abraham Lincoln*, Vol. 1. http://quod.lib.umich.edu/l/lincoln/lincoln1/1:458.1?rgn=div2;view=fulltext.

Lindert, Peter H., and Jeffrey G. Williamson. 2001. "Does Globalization Make the World More Unequal?" Cambridge, MA: National Bureau of Economic Research, NBER Working Paper No. 8228, April. www.nber.org/papers/w8228.

Lipson, Charles. 1984. "International Cooperation in Economic and Security Affairs." *World Politics* 37(1): 1–23, www.jstor.org/stable/2010304.

López-Claros, Augusto. 1987. "The Search for Efficiency in the Adjustment Process: Spain in the 1980s." Occasional Paper 57, Washington DC: International Monetary Fund.

　2003. "Drowning in a Sea of Debt." *The New Times*, Moscow, May.

　2004. *Sixty Years after Bretton Woods: Developing a Vision for the Future*. http://augustolopezclaros.com/wp-content/uploads/2018/06/BrettonWoods_RomeSummary_Jul2004_A4.pdf?x28456.

　2015. "Removing Impediments to Sustainable Economic Development: The Case of Corruption." *Journal of International Commerce, Economics and Policy* 6(1): 1–35. DOI: 10.1142/S1793993315500027.

　2018. "Is There a Spiritual Dimension to Economic Development?" http://augustolopez-claros.blogspot.com/2018/04/is-there-spiritual-dimension-to.html.

López-Claros, Augusto, and Bahiyyih Nakhjavani. 2018. *Equality for Women = Prosperity for All: The Disastrous Global Crisis of Gender Inequality*. New York: St. Martin's Press.

López-Claros, Augusto, and Danielle Pletka 2005. "Without Reforms, the Middle East Risks Revolution." *International Herald Tribune*, April 8.

Lucas, Robert E.B (ed.). 2014. *International Handbook on Migration and Economic Development*. Northampton, MA: Edward Elgar.

MacKenzie, Debora. 2008. "The Collapse of Civilization: It's More Precarious than We Realized," "The End of Civilization." 28–31; "Are We Doomed? The Very Nature of Civilization may Make Its Demise Inevitable." 32–35. *New Scientist* 2560. Cover story, April 5.

2012. "Doomsday Book." *New Scientist* 2846: 38–41.

Mandelbaum, Michael. 1999. "Is Major War Obsolete?" *Survival* 20(4): 20–38.

Mandelson, Peter. 2008. "In Defence of Globalization." *The Guardian*, October 3.

Mani, Rama. 2007. "Peaceful Settlement of Disputes and Conflict Prevention." In Thomas G. Weiss and Sam Daws (eds.), *The Oxford Handbook on the United Nations*. New York: Oxford University Press, pp. 300–322.

Manning, Patrick. 2017. "Inequality: Historical and Disciplinary Approaches." AHA Presidential Address. *American Historical Review* 113(1): 1–23.

Marin-Bosch, Miguel. 1998. *Votes in the UN General Assembly*. The Hague: Kluwer Law International.

Marshall, George. 2014. *Don't Even Think about It: Why Our Brains Are Wired to Ignore Climate Change*. London: Bloomsbury.

Mathews, Jessica T. 1997. "Power Shift." *Foreign Affairs* 76(1): 50–66.

2019. "America's Indefensible Defense Budget." *The New York Review of Books*, July 18, pp. 23–24.

Mauro, Paulo. 1995. "Corruption and Growth." *Quarterly Journal of Economics* 110(3): 681–712.

Maxwell, Nan. 1990. "Changing Female Labor Force Participation: Influences on Income Inequality and Distribution." *Social Forces* 68(4): 1251–1266.

May, C. 2014. "The Rule of Law as the Grundnorm of the New Constitutionalism." In S. Gill and A.C. Cutler (eds.), *New Constitutionalism and World Order*. Cambridge: Cambridge University Press, pp. 63–75.

McKibben, Bill. 2012. "Global Warming's Terrifying New Math." *Rolling Stone*, August 2.

2018. "Life on a Shrinking Planet." *The New Yorker*, November 26.

Meadows, Donella H., Dennis L. Meadows, Jorgen Randers, and William W. Behrens III. 1972. *The Limits to Growth*. A Report for the Club of Rome's Project on the Predicament of Mankind. New York: Universe Books.

Meadows, Donella H., Dennis L. Meadows, and Jorgen Randers. 1992. *Beyond the Limits: Confronting Global Collapse, Envisioning a Sustainable Future*. White River Junction, VT: Chelsea Green.

Meadows, Donella, Jorgen Randers, and Dennis Meadows. 2004. *Limits to Growth: The 30 - Year Update*. White River Junction, VT: Chelsea Green.

Melecky, Martin, and Sue Rutledge. 2011. "Financial Consumer Protection and the Global Financial Crisis." Munich Personal RePEc Archive Paper 28201, University Library of Munich.

Mendlovitz, Saul H., and Barbara Walker (eds.). 2003. *A Reader on Second Assembly & Parliamentary Proposals*. Wayne, NJ: Center for UN Reform Education.

Mertus, Julie A. 2005. *The United Nations and Human Rights – A Guide for a New Era*. Global Institutions Series. New York: Routledge.

Meyer Jr., Cord. 1945. "A Serviceman Looks at The Peace." *The Atlantic Monthly* 176(3): 43–48.

Milanovic, B. 2005. *Worlds Apart: Measuring International and Global Inequality*. Princeton, NJ: Princeton University Press.

2011. *The Haves and the Have-Nots: A Brief and Idiosyncratic History of Global Inequality*. New York: Basic Books.

2013. "Global Income Inequality: Historical Trends and Policy Implications for the Future." Powerpoint presentation at the World Bank.

2016. *Global Inequality: A New Approach for the Age of Globalization*. Cambridge, MA: The Belknap Press of Harvard University Press.

Monkelbaan, Joachim. 2018. *Governance for the Sustainable Development Goals: Exploring an Integrative Framework of Theories, Tools and Competencies*. Springer Sustainable Development Goals Series. Singapore: Springer. https://doi.org/10.1007/978-981-13-0475-0.

Montgomery, David R. 2007. *Dirt: The Erosion of Civilizations*. Berkeley: University of California Press.

Murdock, G.P. 1965. *Culture and Society*. Pittsburgh, PA: University of Pittsburgh Press.

Myrdal, Gunnar. 1968. *Asian Drama: An Inquiry into the Poverty of Nations*. New York: Pantheon.

Nathan, Otto, and Heinz Norden. 1981. *Einstein on Peace*. Avenel Edition, New York: Schocken Books.

National Academy of Sciences. 1972. *Institutional Arrangements for International Environmental Cooperation*. A Report to the Department of State by the Committee for International Environmental Programs, Environmental Studies Board. Washington, DC: National Academy of Sciences.

Nevicka, Barbara, Femke S. Ten Velden, Annebel H.B. De Hoogh, and Annelies E.M. Van Vianen. 2011. "Reality at Odds with Perceptions: Narcissistic Leaders and Group Performance." *Psychological Science* 22(10): 1259–1264. Originally published online September 19. DOI: 10.1177/0956797611417259.

Nevicka, Barbara, Annebel H.B. De Hoogh, Deanne N. Den Hartog, and Frank D. Belschak. 2018. "Narcissistic Leaders and Their Victims: Followers Low on Self-Esteem and Low on Core Self-Evaluations Suffer Most." *Frontiers in Psychology* 9: 422. doi: 10.3389/fpsyg.2018.00422.

Nilsson, Måns, Dave Griggs, Martin Visbeck, and Claudia Ringler. 2016a. "A Draft Framework for Understanding SDG Interactions." ICSU Working Paper. Paris, International Council for Science. www.icsu.org/publications/reports-and-reviews/working-paper-framework-for-understanding-sdg-interactions-2016/SDG-interactions-working-paper.pdf.

Nilsson, Mans, Dave Griggs, and Martin Visbeck. 2016b. "Policy: Map the Interactions between Sustainable Development Goals." *Nature* 534: 320–322 doi:10.1038/534320a

Noonan, John T. 1984. *Bribes*. New York: Macmillan.

Nouwen, S. 2012. "Justifying Justice." In J. Crawford and M. Koskenniemi (eds.), *The Cambridge Companion to International Law*. Cambridge: Cambridge University Press, pp. 327–351.

Nuclear Threat Initiative. 2013. *U.S. Nuclear Weapons Spending Compared to Other Government Programs*, October. www.nti.org/media/pdfs/US_nuclear_weapons_spending.pdf?_=1380927217.

Nye, Joseph. 1967. "Corruption and Political Development: A Cost-Benefit Analysis." *American Political Science Review* 61(2):417–427.

OECD (Organisation for Economic Co-operation and Development). 2018. *Beyond GDP: Measuring What Counts for Economic and Social Performance*, www.oecd.org/social/beyond-gdp-9789264307292-en.htm.

Okada, Keisuke, and S. Samreth. 2017. "Corruption and Natural Resource Rents: Evidence from Quantile Regression." *Applied Economics Letters* 24(20): 1–4.

O'Neill, Daniel W., Andrew L. Fanning, William F. Lamb, and Julia K. Steinberger. 2018. "A Good Life for all within Planetary Boundaries." *Nature Sustainability* 1(2): 88–95. https://doi.org/10.1038/s41893-018-0021-4.

Oxfam International, 2018. "Richest 1 Percent Bagged 82 Percent of Wealth Created Last Year – Poorest Half of Humanity Got Nothing." Press Release January 22, www.oxfam .org/en/pressroom/pressreleases/2018-01-22/richest-1-percent-bagged-82-percent-wealth-created-last-year.

Palmer, Geoffrey. 1998. "International Law and the Reform of the International Court of Justice." In A. Anghie and G. Sturgess (eds.), *Legal Visions of the 21st Century: Essays in Honour of Judge Christopher Weeramantry*. The Hague: Kluwer Law International, pp. 579–600.

Pappa, Evi, R. Sajedi, and E. Vella. 2015. "Fiscal Consolidation with Tax Evasion and Corruption." *Journal of International Economics* 96: S56–S75.

Parliament of the World's Religions. 1993. *Towards a Global Ethic: An Initial Declaration.* www.parliamentofreligions.org/sites/default/files/Global%20Ethic%20booklet-update-web_0.pdf.

Pattison, James. 2008. "Humanitarian Intervention and a Cosmopolitan UN Force." *Journal of International Political Theory* 4(1): 126–145.

Paupp, Terrence E. 2014. *Redefining Human Rights in the Struggle for Peace and Development,* New York: Cambridge University Press.

Payne, Kenneth. 2018. "AI, Warbot." *New Scientist* 239(3195): 41–43.

Pencavel, John. 2006. "A Life Cycle Perspective on Changes in Earnings Inequality among Married Men and Women." *Review of Economics and Statistics* 88(2): 232–242.

Penn, William. 1915. *The Peace of Europe: The Fruits of Solitude and Other Writings.* New York: Dent.

Penn, Michael, Maja Groff, and Naseem Koroush. 2020 (forthcoming). "Cultivating Our Common Humanity: Reflections on Freedom of Thought, Conscience, and Religion." In *The Cambridge Handbook of Psychology and Human Rights.* Cambridge: Cambridge University Press.

Peterson, M. J. 2007. "General Assembly." In Thomas G. Weiss and Sam Daws (eds.), *The Oxford Handbook on the United Nations,* New York: Oxford University Press, pp. 97–117.

Peterson Hill, Nancy. 2014. *A Very Private Public Citizen: The Life of Grenville Clark.* Columbia: University of Missouri Press.

Pew Research Center: Pew Forum on Religion and Public Life. 2012 (September). *Rising Tide of Restrictions on Religion.* http://assets.pewresearch.org/wp-content/uploads/sites/11/2012/09/RisingTideofRestrictions-fullreport.pdf).

  2016 (February 26). *Latest Trends in Religious Restrictions and Hostilities.* http://assets .pewresearch.org/wp-content/uploads/sites/11/2015/02/Restrictions2015_fullReport.pdf.

Pillay, N. 2012. *Strengthening the United Nations Human Rights Treaty Body System.* A Report by the United Nations High Commissioner for Human Rights. United Nations Human Rights Office of the High Commissioner, www2.ohchr.org/english/bodies/HRTD/docs/HCReportTBStrengthening.pdf.

  2013. "The Negative Impact of Corruption on Human Rights." Opening Statement to the Office of the United Nations High Commissioner on Human Rights, Geneva, March 13.

Pinker, Steven. 2011. *The Better Angels of Our Nature: Why Violence Has Declined.* New York: Viking.

2018. *Enlightenment Now: The Case for Reason, Science, Humanism, and Progress.* New York: Viking.

Pope Francis. 2015. *Laudato Si': On Care for Our Common Home.* http://w2.vatican.va/content/francesco/en/encyclicals/documents/papa-francesco_20150524_enciclica-laudato-si.html.

Posner, Eric A., and Miguel. de Figueiredo. 2005. "Is the International Court of Justice Biased?" *Journal of Legal Studies* 34: 599–630. www.ericposner.com/Is%20the%20International%20Court%20of%20Justice%20Biased.pdf.

Puchala, Donald. 2003. *Theory and History in International Relations.* New York: Routledge.

Pugh, Michael. 2007. *"Peace Enforcement."* In Thomas G. Weiss and Sam Daws (eds.), *The Oxford Handbook on the United Nations.* New York: Oxford University Press, pp. 370–387.

Putnam, R.D. 2000. *Bowling Alone: The Collapse and Revival of American Community.* New York: Touchstone Books/Simon & Schuster.

Rajan, Raghuram. 2010. *Fault Lines: How Hidden Fractures Still Threaten the Global Economy.* Princeton, NJ: Princeton University Press.

Randers, Jorgen. 2012. *2052: A Global Forecast for the Next Forty Years.* A Report to the Club of Rome. Commemorating the 40th Anniversary of The Limits to Growth. White River Junction, VT: Chelsea Green.

Rauschning Dietrich, Katja Wiesbrock, and Martin Lailach. 1997. *Key Resolutions of the United Nations General Assembly 1946–1996.* Cambridge: Cambridge University Press.

Reinhart, Carmen M., and K. Rogoff 2009. *This Time Is Different: Eight Centuries of Financial Folly.* Princeton, NJ: Princeton University Press.

Report of the Commission on Global Governance. 1995. *Our Global Neighborhood.* New York: Oxford University Press.

Report of the Commission on Global Security, Justice and Governance. 2015. *Confronting the Crisis of Global Governance.* The Hague: The Hague Institute for Global Justice and The Stimson Center.

Reves Emery. 1946. *The Anatomy of Peace.* New York and London: Harper and Brothers Publishers.

Reynaud, Paul. 1951. *Unite or Perish: A Dynamic Program for a United Europe.* Mazal Holocaust Collection. New York: Simon and Schuster.

Ripple, William J., Christopher Wolf, Thomas M. Newsome, Mauro Galetti, Mohammed Alamgir, Eileen Crist, Mahmoud I. Mahmoud, and William F. Laurance, and 15,364 scientist signatories from 184 countries. 2017. "World Scientists' Warning to Humanity: A Second Notice." *BioScience* 67(12): 1026–1028. https://doi.org/10.1093/biosci/bix125.

Rischard, J. F. 2002. *High Noon: 20 Global Problems and 20 Years to Solve Them.* New York: Basic Books.

Ritchie, Nick, and Kjølv Egeland. 2018. "The Diplomacy of Resistance: Power, Hegemony and Nuclear Disarmament." *Global Change, Peace & Security* 30(2): 121–141.

Roberts, Adam. 2008. "Proposals for UN Standing Forces: A Critical History." In Vaughan Lowe, Adam Roberts, Jennifer Welsh, and Dominik Zaum (eds.), *The United Nations Security Council and War: The Evolution of Thought and Practice since 1945.* New York: Oxford University Press, pp. 99–130.

Rockström, Johan, et al. 2009. "A Safe Operating Space for Humanity." *Nature* 461(7263): 472–475 doi:10.1038/461472a

2017. "A Roadmap for Rapid Decarbonization." *Science* 355(6331): 1269–1271.

Rodrik, D., A. Subramanian, and F. Trebbi. 2004. "Institutions Rule: The Primacy of Institutions over Geography and Integration in Economic Development." *Journal of Economic Growth* 9(2): 131–165.

Rose-Ackerman, Susan. 1997. "Corruption, Inefficiency and Economic Growth." *Nordic Journal of Political Economy* 24: 3–20.

1998. "Corruption and Development." In Joseph Stiglitz and Boris Pleskovic (eds.), Annual World Bank Conference on Development Economics. Washington DC.

Rose-Ackerman, Susan and Bonnie J. Palifka. 2016. *Corruption and Government, Causes, Consequences, and Reform.* (2nd ed.). New York: Cambridge University Press.

Roth, Kenneth. 2004. "Defending Economic, Social and Cultural Rights: Practical Issues Faced by an International Human Rights Organization." *Human Rights Quarterly* 26(1): 63–73.

Rousseau, Jean-Jacques. 1767. *A Project for Perpetual Peace: By J.J. Rousseau, Citizen of Geneva.* Translated from the French, with a Preface by the Translator. London: J. Johnson and T. Davenport in Paternoster Row. [Eighteenth century collections online] and Castel de Saint-Pierre, Charles Irénée, and Jean-Jacques Rousseau, Trans. Edith M Nuttall. 1927. A project of perpetual peace, Rousseau's essay, London: R. Cobden-Sanderson.

Rubin, Robert. 2019. "Why the World Needs America and China to Get Along." *The New York Times*, January 2.

Russell, Bertrand. 1943. "The Future of Pacifism." *The American Scholar* 13(1): 7–13. www .jstor.org/stable/41204635.

1961. *Has Man a Future?* London: Penguin.

1978. *The Autobiography of Bertrand Russell.* London: Unwind Paperbacks.

Russell, Ruth B. 1958. *A History of the United Nations Charter: The Role of the United States, 1940–1945.* Washington DC: Brookings.

Sachs, Jeffrey. 2010. Quoted in Eric Nee, *Stanford Social Innovation Review*, Summer 2010, Interview with Jeffrey Sachs (Environment). https://ssir.org/articles/entry/qa_jeffrey_sachs

Sagan, Scott D., and Kenneth N. Waltz. 2003. *The Spread of Nuclear Weapons: A Debate Renewed.* New York: W.W. Norton.

Sano, Hans-Otto. 2007. "Is Governance a Global Public Good?" In Erik André Andersen and Birgit Lindsnaes (eds.), *Towards New Global Strategies.* Leiden and Boston, MA: Martinus Nijhoff, pp. 217–235. DOI: 10.1163/ej.9789004155077.i-520.17.

Scheidel, W. 2017. *The Great Leveler: Violence and the History of Inequality from the Stone Age to the Twenty-First Century.* Princeton, NJ: Princeton University Press.

Schell, Jonathan. 1982. *The Fate of the Earth.* London: Jonathan Cape.

1984. *The Abolition.* (5th ed.). New York: Alfred A. Knopf Inc.

2003. *The Unconquerable World, Power, Nonviolence, and the Will of the People.* Metropolitan Books.

Schumacher, E.F. 1973. *Small Is Beautiful: A Study of Economics as If People Mattered.* London: Blond & Briggs.

Schwartz, S. H. 2012. "An Overview of the Schwartz Theory of Basic Values." *Online Readings in Psychology and Culture* 2(1): 1–20. https://doi.org/10.9707/2307-0919.1116.

Schwartzberg, Joseph E. 2013. "A Credible Human Rights System." In Joseph E. Schwartzberg (ed.), *Transforming the United Nations System: Designs for a Workable World.* Tokyo and New York: United Nations University Press, pp. 110–128.

2013. *Transforming the United Nations System: Designs for a Workable World*. Tokyo and New York: United Nations University Press. www.brookings.edu/book/transforming-the-united-nations-system/.

Scott, Shirley. 2005. "The Failure of the UN to Hold a Charter Review Conference in the 1950s: The Future in the Past?" *ANZLH E-Journal*, 76: 70–79.

Sen, Amartya. 1997. *Human Rights and Asian Values*, Sixteenth Annual Morgenthau Memorial Lecture on Ethics and Foreign Policy, 25 May, Carnegie Council. www.carnegie council.org/publications/archive/morgenthau/254.

1999. *Development as Freedom*. Oxford: Oxford University Press.

2009. "Adam Smith's Market Never Stood Alone." *Financial Times*, March 11.

Sewall, May Wright. 1900. "Telegram Sent to Lenore Selena in Support of the International Demonstration of Women for the Peace Conference." In Lenore Selena (ed.), *The International Demonstration of Women for the Peace Conference of May 15th 1899*. Munich: August Schupp, p. 70.

Shaxson, Nicholas. 2016. *Treasure Islands: Tax Havens and the Men Who Stole the World*. London: Vintage.

Sheiman, Bruce. 2009. *An Atheist Defends Religion: Why Humanity Is Better Off with Religion Than without It*. New York: Alpha (Penguin Group).

Shiller, Robert. 2009. "A Failure to Control the Animal Spirits." *Financial Times*, March 9.

Shlaim, Avi. 1974. "Prelude to Downfall: The British Offer of Union to France, June 1940." *Journal of Contemporary History* 9(3): 27–63.

Shultz, George P., William J. Perry, Henry A. Kissinger, and Sam Nunn. 2007. "A World Free of Nuclear Weapons." *Wall Street Journal*, January 4.

Sieff, Michelle. 2017. "Violence against Women and International Security: Why Assault by Intimate Partners Deserves Greater Focus." *Foreign Affairs*, November 28.

Siegle, Joseph. T., Michael W. Weinstein, and Morton Halperin. 2004. "Why Democracies Excel." *Foreign Affairs* 83(5): 57–71.

Simoni, Arnold. 1972. *Beyond Repair, the Urgent Need for a New World Body*, Donn Mills, ON: Collier-Macmillan, Canada, Ltd.

Sinclair, Guy Fiti. 2017. *To Reform the World: The Legal Powers of International Organizations and the Making of Modern States*. Oxford: Oxford University Press.

Sky, Jasper. 2018. *Repurpose the Military Initiative (RMI): A Call to Re-allocate 15% of Military Troops and Spending to Building Civilian Infrastructure Where It's Needed Most*. November 12. https://medium.com/@jaspersky/repurpose-the-military-initiative-rmi-a-call-to-re-allocate-15-of-military-troops-and-spending-7cb0bf846ea9.

Slaughter, Anne-Marie. 2004. *A New World Order*. Princeton, NJ: Princeton University Press.

Smith, Adam. 1937. *The Wealth of Nations*. New York: The Modern Library.

Smith, Dan. 2017. "Introduction." In SIPRI, *Armaments, Disarmament and International Security*. Oxford: SIPRI/Oxford University Press, p. 1.

Soros, George. 2002. *George Soros on Globalization*. Oxford: Public Affairs Ltd.

Spijkers, Otto. 2011. *The United Nations: The Evolution of Global Values and International Law*. Cambridge: Intersentia.

Srivastava, Leena. 2018. Governance of Catastrophic Climate Change. *Global Challenges Foundation Annual Report 2018*. https://globalchallenges.org/en/our-work/annual-report/annual-report-2018/governance-of-catastrophic-climate-change

Starmans, Christina, Mark Sheskin, and Paul Bloom. 2017. "Inequality Isn't the Real Issue." *The Wall Street Journal*, April 29–30, p. C3.

Stassen, Harold. 1994. *United Nations, A Working Paper for Restructuring*, Minneapolis, MN: Lerner.

Steffen, Will, et al. 2015. "Planetary Boundaries: Guiding Human Development on a Changing Planet." *Science* 347(6223): 736–746. February 13. DOI: 10.1126/science.1259855.

Steffen, Will, Johan Rockström, Katherine Richardson, Timothy M. Lenton, Carl Folke, Diana Liverman, Colin P. Summerhayes, Anthony D. Barnosky, Sarah E. Cornell, Michel Crucifix, Jonathan F. Donges, Ingo Fetzer, Steven J. Lade, Marten Scheffer, Ricarda Winkelmann, and Hans Joachim Schellnhuber. 2018. "Trajectories of the Earth System in the Anthropocene." *PNAS* 115 (33): 8252–8259. August 14, 2018 https://doi.org/10.1073/pnas.1810141115

Stern, Nicholas, and Samuel Fankhauser. 2016. "Climate Change, Development, Poverty and Economics." London: Grantham Research Institute on Climate Change and the Environment.

Stiglitz, Joseph E. 2012. *The Price of Inequality: How Today's Divided Society Endangers Our Future*. New York: W. W. Norton.

Stiglitz, Joseph E., Amartya Sen, and Jean-Paul Fitoussi. 2009. *Report by the Commission on the Measurement of Economic Performance and Social Progress*. www.stiglitz-sen-fitoussi.fr.

(SIPRI) Stockholm International Peace Research Institute. 2016. *SIPRI Yearbook 2016*. Stockholm. www.sipri.org/yearbook/2016.

2017. *Armaments, Disarmament and International Security*. Oxford: SIPRI/Oxford University Press.

2017. Military Expenditure Database. www.sipri.org/databases/milex.

2018. *SIPRI Yearbook 2018*. Stockholm. www.sipri.org/.

Stoddart, Hannah (ed.). 2011. *A Pocket Guide to Sustainable Development Governance*. London: Stakeholder Forum/Commonwealth Secretariat. www.stakeholderforum.org/fileadmin/files/sdgpocketguideFINAL-no%20crop%20marks.pdf.

Streit, Clarence K. 1940. *Union Now, the Proposal for Inter-democracy Federal Union*. New York and London: Harper & Brothers Publishers.

Subedi, Surya P. 2017. *The Effectiveness of the UN Human Rights System: Reform and the Judicialisation of Human Rights*. London and New York: Taylor & Francis.

Suber, Peter. 2012. *Open Access*. Cambridge, MA: MIT Press. bit.ly/oa-book.

Surowiecki, James. 2014. "The Mobility Myth." *The New Yorker*, March 3. www.newyorker.com/magazine/2014/03/03/the-mobility-myth.

Swart, Lydia, and Jonas von Freiesleben J. 2013. *Security Council Reform from 1945 to September 2013. Center for UN Reform Education*. New York: UN. http://centerforunreform.org/?q=node/604.

Szombatfalvy, Laszlo. 2010. *The Greatest Challenges of Our Time*. Stockholm: Ekerlids.

Tangermann, Stefan, and Augusto López-Claros. 2004. *Agricultural Policy in OECD Countries Due for Reform*, Op-Ed, November. http://augustolopezclaros.com/wp-content/uploads/2018/06/OpEdNov2004_IntlPub_A4.pdf?x28456.

Tanzi, Vito. 1998. "Corruption around the World: Causes, Consequences, Scope, and Cures." *IMF Staff Papers* 45(4): 559–594.

Tanzi, Vito, and H. Davoodi. 1997. "Corruption, Public Investment, and Growth." IMF Working Paper 97/139. Washington, DC: International Monetary Fund.

Tanzi, Vito, and L. Schuknecht. 1997. "Reconsidering the Fiscal Role of Government: The International Perspective." *American Economic Review Papers and Proceedings* 87:164–168.

Teilhard de Chardin, Pierre. 1969. *Human Energy*. London: Collins.

The Daily Telegraph. 2009. "Queen Told How Economists Missed the Financial Crisis." July 26.

The Economist. 2018. "The World Has Not Learned the Lessons of the Financial Crisis." September 8.

The Economist. 2018. "Same Old Scam: The UN Human Rights Council's Lousy Election." October 17.

The Economic Value of Peace. 2018. *Measuring the Global Economic Impact of Violence and Conflict,* Institute for Economics and Peace. http://economicsandpeace.org/wp-content/uploads/2018/11/Economic-Value-of-Peace-2018.pdf.

The Washington Post. 2019. "Wealth Concentration Returning to Levels Unseen since '20s." February 9.

Tobin, James. 1978. "A Proposal for International Monetary Reform." *Eastern Economic Journal* 4(3): 153–159. www.jstor.org/stable/20642317.

——— 1996. "Prologue." In Mahbub Ul Haq, Inge Kaul, and Isabelle Grunberg (eds.), *The Tobin Tax, Coping with Financial Volatility.* New York and Oxford: Oxford University Press, pp. ix–xviii.

Tomuschat, Christian. 2012. "Ch. VI Pacific Settlement of Disputes, Article 33." In Bruno Simma, Daniel-Erasmus Khan, Georg Nolte, Andreas Paulus, and Nikolai Wessendorf (eds.), *The Charter of the United Nations: A Commentary,* Oxford Commentaries on International Law series (3rd ed.), 2 vols. Oxford: Oxford University Press. Vol. I, pp. 1069–1085.

Trebilcock, Michael J., and Ronald J. Daniels. 2008. *Rule of Law Reform and Development: Charting the Fragile Path to Progress.* Cheltenham: Edward Elgar.

Trechsel, Stefan. 2004. "A World Court for Human Rights?" *Northwestern Journal of International Human Rights* 1(1): 1–18.

Truman, Edwin. 2001. "Perspectives on External Financial Crises." Institute for International Economics, Washington DC, December 10. www.piie.com/commentary/speeches-papers/perspectives-external-financial-crises.

Tulliu, Steve, and Thomas Schmalerger. 2003. *Coming to Terms with Security: A Lexicon for Arms Control, Disarmament and Confidence-Building.* UNIDIR/2003/22. Geneva: United Nations.

Turchin, Peter. 2006. *War and Peace and War: The Rise and Fall of Empires.* New York: Plume Books (Penguin).

——— 2010. "Political Instability May Be a Contributor in the Coming Decade." *Nature* 463 (7281): 608. doi:10.1038/463608a.

——— 2016. *Ultrasociety: How 10,000 Years of War Made Humans the Greatest Cooperators on Earth.* Chaplin, CT: Beresta Books.

Tutu, Desmond. 1999. *No Future without Forgiveness.* London/Sydney/ Auckland/Johannesburg: Rider.

Ul Haq, Mahbub, Inge Kaul, and Isabelle Grunberg. 1996. *The Tobin Tax, Coping with Financial Volatility.* New York and Oxford: Oxford University Press.

UNCTAD/FAO. 2017. "Commodities and Development 2017." New York and Geneva: United Nations. https://unctad.org/en/PublicationsLibrary/suc2017d1_en.pdf.

UNDP. 1994. *Human Development Report 1994.* New York: Oxford University Press.

UNESCO. 2017. *Education for Sustainable Development Goals – Learning Objectives.* Paris: UNESCO. https://unesdoc.unesco.org/ark:/48223/pf0000247444.

——— 2017. *Reading the Past, Writing the Future: Fifty Years of Promoting Literacy.* Paris: UNESCO.

Ungerer, H., J. Hauvonen, A. López-Claros, and T. Mayer. 1990. "The European Monetary System: Developments and Perspectives." Occasional Paper No 73. Washington, DC: International Monetary Fund.

UN (United Nations). 1945. *Charter of the United Nations and Statute of the International Court of Justice.* New York: Office of Public Information, United Nations.

——. 1948. *Universal Declaration of Human Rights.* www.un.org/en/universal-declaration-human-rights/index.html www.ohchr.org/EN/UDHR/Documents/UDHR_Translations/eng.pdf.

——. 1972. *Report of the United Nations Conference on the Human Environment* held at Stockholm, June 5–16, 1972. A/CONF.48/14. New York: United Nations.

——. 1992a. *Agenda 21: Programme of Action for Sustainable Development.* United Nations Conference on Environment & Development, Rio de Janeiro, Brazil, June 3–14, 1992. New York: United Nations. https://sustainabledevelopment.un.org/content/documents/Agenda21.pdf.

——. 1992b. *United Nations Framework Convention on Climate Change.* New York: United Nations. https://unfccc.int/sites/default/files/conveng.pdf.

——. 1993. *World Plan of Action for Education on Human Rights and Democracy,* United Nations. http://un-documents.net/wpa-ehrd.htm.

——. 1998. *Secretary-General Says Establishment of International Criminal Court Is Gift of Hope to Future Generations,* Press Release SG/SM/6643 L/2891, July 20. www.un.org/press/en/1998/19980720.sgsm6643.html.

——. 1999. *Report of the Independent Inquiry into the Actions of the United Nations during the 1994 Genocide in Rwanda,* UN document S/1999/1257, December 16.

——. 2016. *The Rule of Law in the UN's Intergovernmental Work.* www.un.org/ruleoflaw/what-is-the-rule-of-law/the-rule-of-law-in-un-work/.

——. 2018. UNFCCC (United Nations Framework Convention on Climate Change) (*Talanoa Dialogue Platform.* https://unfccc.int/topics/2018-talanoa-dialogue-platform.

United Nations General Assembly, Convention Relating to the Status of Refugees, July 28, 1951, United Nations, Treaty Series, vol. 189, p. 137, www.refworld.org/docid/3be01b964.html.

United Nations General Assembly. 1989. "Enhancing the Effectiveness of the Principle of Periodic and Genuine Elections." Resolution 44/146. New York: United Nations. www.un.org/documents/ga/res/44/a44r146.htm.

——. 1997. "Renewing the United Nations: A Programme for Reform." A/51/950, July 14. New York: United Nations. https://undocs.org/A/51/950.

——. 2000. "United Nations Millennium Declaration." General Assembly Resolution 55/2. New York: United Nations. www.un.org/millennium/declaration/ares552e.htm.

——. 2002. *Strengthening the Rule of Law,* February 27, 2003, UN Doc. A/RES/57/221.

——. 2005. *2005 World Summit Outcome,* October 24, 2005, UN Doc. A/RES/60/1.

——. 2009. Department of Economic and Social Affairs, Division for the Advancement of Women and United Nations Economic Commission for Africa, *Good Practices in Legislation on "Harmful Practices" against Women-Report of the Expert Group Meeting,* May 26–29.

——. 2012. *Declaration of the High-Level Meeting of the General Assembly on the Rule of Law at the National and International Levels: Resolution/Adopted by the General Assembly,* November 30, A/RES/67/1, p. 2: www.refworld.org/docid/50c5e6e02.html.

——. 2012. *Report of the United Nations Conference on Sustainable Development,* Rio de Janeiro, Brazil, June 20–22. A/CONF.216/16. New York: United Nations. www.un.org/ga/search/view_doc.asp?symbol=A/CONF.216/16&Lang=E.

——. 2014a. *The Road to Dignity by 2030: Ending Poverty, Transforming All Lives and Protecting the Planet,* Synthesis Report of the Secretary-General on the Post-2015 Agenda.

Document A/69/700, December 4. New York: United Nations. www.un.org/ga/search/view_doc.asp?symbol=A/69/700&Lang=E.

2014b. *Strengthening and Coordinating United Nations Rule of Law Activities*. Report of the Secretary-General, July 24, UN Doc. A/69/181.

2015a. *Transforming Our World: The 2030 Agenda for Sustainable Development*. Outcome Document of the Summit for the Adoption of the Post-2015 Development Agenda, New York, September 25–27. A/70/L.1. New York: United Nations. www.un.org/ga/search/view_doc.asp?symbol=A/70/L.1&Lang=E.

2015b. *Human Rights, Democracy and the Rule of Law*. Resolution Adopted by the Human Rights Council, March 23, UN Doc. A/HRC/28/L.24, p. 2; Citing the UN Secretary-General in: United Nations General Assembly. 2014. *Strengthening and Coordinating United Nations Rule of Law Activities*. Report of the Secretary-General, July 24, 2014, UN Doc. A/69/181.

2018. Resolution 73/271: Scale of Assessments for the Apportionment of the Expenses of the United Nations, December 22.

United Nations Office for Disarmament Affairs. 2018. *Securing Our Common Future: An Agenda for Disarmament*. New York: United Nations.

UN Office of the High Commissioner for Human Rights. 2013. *The Human Rights Case against Corruption*. Geneva: Office of the High Commissioner, United Nations Human Rights. www.ohchr.org/Documents/Issues/Development/GoodGovernance/Corruption/HRCaseAgainstCorruption.pdf.

UNRISD. 2016. *Policy Innovations for Transformative Change: Implementing the 2030 Agenda for Sustainable Development*. UNRISD Flagship Report 2016. Geneva: United Nations Research Institute for Social Development. www.unrisd.org/flagship2016.

United Nations Security Council. 2004. "The Rule of Law and Transitional Justice in Conflict and Post-Conflict Societies." *Report of the Secretary-General*, August 23, UN Doc. S/2004/616.

United Nations Treaty Collection, Chapter IV: Human Rights: https://treaties.un.org/pages/Treaties.aspx?id=4&subid=A&lang=en (accessed 3 July 2018).

UN Secretary-General's High-level Panel on Digital Cooperation. 2019. "The Age of Digital Interdependence." Report presented June 10. New York: United Nations. www.un.org/en/pdfs/DigitalCooperation-report-for%20web.pdf.

Urquhart, Brian. 1973. *Hammarskjold*, London, Sydney, and Toronto: The Bodley Head.

1991. "Sovereignty vs. Suffering." *The New York Times*, April 17.

1993. "For a UN Volunteer Military Force." *New York Review of Books*, June 10.

Van Rijckeghem, Caroline, and B. Weder. 1997. "Corruption and the Rate of Temptation: Do Low Wages in the Civil Service Cause Corruption?" IMF Working Paper 97/73. Washington, DC: International Monetary Fund.

Vinkhuyzen, Onno M., and Sylvia I. Karlsson-Vinkhuyzen. 2014. "The Role of Moral Leadership for Sustainable Production and Consumption." *Journal of Cleaner Production*. 63: 102–113. http://dx.doi.org/10.1016/j.jclepro.2013.06.045.

Viola, Eduardo, Matias Franchini, and Thais Lemos Ribeiro. 2012. "Climate Governance in an International System under Conservative Hegemony: The Role of Major Powers." *Revista Brasileira de Política Internacional* 55 (special edition): 9–29.

von Weizsacker, Richard, and Moeen Qureshi (co-chairs), Independent Working Group on the Future of the United Nations. 1995. *The United Nations in Its Second Half-Century*. New York: Ford Foundation.

Walter, Barbara F., Lise M. Howard, and V. Page Fortna. 2019. "The Extraordinary Relationship between Peacekeeping and Peace." Unpublished manuscript.

Walters, F.P. 1965. *A History of the League of Nations*. London, New York, and Toronto: Oxford University Press.

Waltz, Kenneth. 2001. *Man, the State and War: A Theoretical Analysis*, New York: Columbia University Press.

Watts, Jonathan. 2018. "Domino-Effect of Climate Events Could Move Earth into a 'Hothouse' State." *The Guardian*, August 7. www.theguardian.com/environment/2018/aug/06/domino-effect-of-climate-events-could-push-earth-into-a-hothouse-state.

Wei, Shang-Jin. 2000. "How Taxing Is Corruption on International Investors?" *Review of Economics and Statistics* 82(1): 1–11.

West, Darrell M., and Jack Karsten. 2017. "Solutions for Global Science Issues Require New Forms of Governance." *Brookings Institution Blog*, May 4.

White, E.B. 1946. *The Wild Flag, Editorials from New Yorker on Federal World Government and Other Matters*. Boston, MA: Houghton Mifflin Company.

White, J. ,and K. Young. 2008. "Nothing about Us without Us: Securing the Disability Rights Convention." In J. Williams, S.D. Goose, and M. Wareham (eds.), *Banning Landmines: Disarmament, Citizen Diplomacy, and Human Security*. Lanham, MD: Rowman and Littlefield, pp. 241–262.

Wilkinson, R., and K. Pickett. 2009. *The Spirit Level: Why More Equal Societies Almost Always Do Better*. London: Allen Lane.

Williams, Jody. 2008. "New Approaches in a Changing World: The Human Security Agenda." In Jody Williams, Stephen D. Goose, and Mary Wareham (eds.), *Banning Landmines: Disarmament, Diplomacy, and Human Security*. Lanham, MD: Rowman & Littlefield, pp. 281–297.

Williams, J., and S.D. Goose. 2008. "Citizen Diplomacy and the Ottawa Process: A Lasting Model?" In J. Williams, S.D. Goose, and M. Wareham (eds.), *Banning Landmines: Disarmament, Citizen Diplomacy, and Human Security*. Lanham, MD: Rowman and Littlefield, pp. 181–196.

Witschel, Georg. 2012. "Ch.XVIII Amendments, Article 108." In Bruno Simma, Daniel-Erasmus Khan, Georg Nolte, Andreas Paulus, and Nikolai Wessendorf (eds.), *The Charter of the United Nations: A Commentary*, Oxford Commentaries on International Law Series (3rd ed.), 2 vols. Oxford: Oxford University Press, Vol. 2, pp. 2232–2242.

Wolf, Mark L. 2018. "The World Needs an International Anti-Corruption Court." *Daedalus, the Journal of the American Academy of Arts & Sciences* 147(3): 144–156.

World Bank. 2007. *World Development Report: Development and the Next Generation*. Washington, DC: World Bank Group.

2016a. *Migration and Development: A Role for the World Bank Group*. Washington, DC: World Bank Group.

2016b. *Women, Business and the Law 2016: Getting to Equal*. Washington, DC: World Bank Group.

2017. *The Global Findex Database 2017*: https://globalfindex.worldbank.org/.

2017. *Doing Business 2018: Reforming to Create Jobs*. Washington, DC: World Bank Group.

2018. *Migration and Remittances: Recent Development and Outlook*, December.

World Commission on Environment and Development. 1987. *Our Common Future*. Oxford: Oxford University Press.

Wouters, J., Bart De Meester, and C. Ryngaert. 2004. *Democracy and International Law*. Leuven: Leuven Interdisciplinary Research Group on International Agreements and Development (LIRGIAD).

Wouters, Jan, and Tom Ruys. 2005. *Security Council Reform: A Veto for a New Century.* Working paper No. 78, June 2005. Leuven: Institute for International Law. www.law .kuleuven.be/iir/nl/onderzoek/working-papers/WP78e.pdf.

WWF (World Wildlife Fund). 2018. *Living Planet Report 2018: Aiming Higher.* Gland: WWF International. http://wwf.panda.org/knowledge_hub/all_publications/living_planet_report_2018/.

Yee, Sienho. 2009. "Notes on the International Court of Justice (Part 2): Reform Proposals Regarding the International Court of Justice – A Preliminary Report for the International Law Association Study Group on United Nations Reform." *Chinese Journal of International Law* 8(1): 181–189.

Index